T0330102

LITERARY CONJUGATIONS

Edited by Richard T. Gray

Money Matters

ECONOMICS AND THE GERMAN
CULTURAL IMAGINATION,
1770–1850

RICHARD T. GRAY

UNIVERSITY OF WASHINGTON PRESS
Seattle & London

Support for this book was received from the Graduate School Fund
for Excellence and Innovation (GSFEI) of the University of Washington Graduate School.

UNIVERSITY OF WASHINGTON PRESS
PO Box 50096, Seattle, WA 98145
www.washington.edu/uwpress

LIBRARY OF CONGRESS CATALOGING-IN-PUBLICATION DATA

Gray, Richard T.
    Money matters : economics and the German cultural imagina-
tion, 1770–1850 / Richard T. Gray.
        p.   cm. — (Literary conjugations)
    Includes bibliographical references and index.
    ISBN 978-0-295-98836-8 (hbk. : alk. paper) —
ISBN 978-0-295-98837-5 (pbk. : alk. paper)
    1. Economics—German—History—To 1800.   2. Economics—
Germany—History—19th century.   3. Economics—Germany—
Sociological aspects—History.   4. Economics and literature—
Germany—History.   I. Title.
    HB107.A2G73   2008
    330.0943'09034—dc22   2008020065

CONTENTS

Money Matters

INTRODUCTION

It is more easy to write on money than to obtain it; and those who gain it jest much at those who only know how to write about it.

—Voltaire ("Money" 13)

Whether Power to command the Industry of others be not real Wealth? And whether Money be not in Truth, Tickets or Tokens for conveying and recording such Power, and whether it be of great Consequence what Materials the Tickets are made of?

—George Berkeley (*Querist* 4)

NE OF THE MOST PERSISTENT INTELLECTUAL-HISTORICAL constellations of Enlightenment and post-Enlightenment culture is the belief in a fundamental antinomy between economic practices and cultural interests. Writing on the distinctions between third-world literature and the literary artifacts of the "first" world, Fredric Jameson has made the global observation that the culture of Western capitalism, as opposed to that of the third world, betrays "a radical split between the private and the public, between the poetic and the political, between what we have come to think of as the domain of sexuality and the unconscious and that of the public world of classes, of the economic, and of secular power" (69). When he summarizes this opposition as marked by two names central to modern German intellectual history, "Freud versus Marx"

(69), Jameson is apparently using a rhetorical strategy to allude to the—from his perspective—ludicrous nature of this juxtaposition. After all, Freud himself liked to conceive of the dynamic qualities of the human psyche in terms of an "economy," a closed system of circulation and exchange among the distinct agencies he identified as the principal players in human psychology, the ego, id, and superego, and whose currency was human desire or libido. Moreover, certain strains of contemporary theory have tended to emphasize nothing if not the extraordinary coherence between Marxian political economy and Freudian psychology.[1] Be that as it may, Jameson's point is that on the level of cultural self-understanding, the private sphere of the psychologically constituted individual is commonly viewed as wholly segregated from the public domain of the politically and economically determined citizen of civil society. Indeed, as Jameson insists, for centuries we in the West "have been trained in a deep cultural conviction that the lived experience of our private existences is somehow incommensurable with the abstractions of economic science and political dynamics," and that as a result any hint of economic themes or content in serious cultural endeavors like literature or philosophy strike us not merely as out of place, but as downright disruptive (69).

The purpose of this book is to challenge this ideological presumption. Its aim is to investigate the extent to which in those formative years of German cultural, political, and economic history from the mid-eighteenth to the mid-nineteenth century—in which not only capitalist economic models and industrial modernism took hold, but in which, not coincidentally, the idealist aesthetics of autonomy were also formulated and solidified—economic thought has a seldom recognized influence on the cultural regime. The object of the chapters that follow is to demonstrate the extent to which economics does not simply "infect" the high-cultural domains of German-speaking Europe, but also the degree to which the landmark documents of this high German culture—in particular literature and philosophy—are complicit with and participate in the establishment and solidification of modern economic paradigms.

Immanuel Kant helped lay the foundation for the isolation of aesthetic and economic interests in his *Kritik der Urteilskraft* (Critique of judgment, 1790), when he stigmatized economic issues as entirely "mercenary" and hence as strictly irrelevant for considerations of aesthetic value or for the production of the artifacts of intellectual culture. In paragraph 43 of this treatise, which is dedicated to the very definition of art, Kant moves through a series of principal distinctions, first juxtaposing art to nature, then contrasting it to science (*Wissenschaft*), and finally distinguishing it from products of skilled labor, or the economic commodity.

> *Art* is also distinguished from *craft*; the first we call *free*, the second can also be called *art for payment* [*Lohnkunst*]. We look upon the first as if it were only play, that is, an occupation that is pleasing in and of itself, and only achieves its purpose under these conditions; we look upon the second as a form of labor, that is, as an occupation that is in and of itself unpleasant (burdensome), and that is only made attractive by its effect (for example, payment), and which hence can be forced upon us. (238)[2]

True works of "art," according to Kant, can be segregated from mere "handicrafts" or products of skilled labor by the attitude that stimulates their creation. Art serves its own purpose, it represents an end in itself that is generated autonomously by the individual and that satisfies no need other than the pleasure one takes in its successful creation. When viewed in terms of its *production*, in short, the work of art is decidedly not an economic fact—although it may subsequently be subjected to economic contingencies. This autonomy of purpose is what Kant has in mind when he calls art "free" and asserts that it is created out of the nonserious attitude of "play." Human-made products that may require just as much technical skill as a work of art, however, if they are produced for some ancillary purpose other than the pleasure of their own creation, do not qualify for Kant as works of art: they are derived from more mercenary motivations, enforced upon the creator by external factors such as need or duress, and as a result have the status of burdensome labor. As we know, Kant will apply the term "genius" to those autonomous artists who create out of their own independence and the self-reliance on their own imaginations.[3]

Of the many manifestations of adherence to this ideology of an aesthetics of autonomy and the strict separation of (literary) art from economic production and practice, let me cite just one example drawn from no lesser a "genius" than Johann Wolfgang von Goethe. Looking back in his autobiography *Dichtung und Wahrheit* (Poetry and truth, 1811–33) on the formative years of his literary development and the aesthetic attitudes that informed his writings, as well as those of his contemporaries, Goethe remarked,

> But the production of literary works was viewed as something holy, and one considered it almost simony to accept an honorarium or ask that it be increased. Authors and publishers stood in the most marvelous reciprocal relationship. Both appeared, depending on how one looked at it, as patrons and as clients. (*Goethes Werke* 9: 517)

No doubt, the picture Goethe paints here is overly idealized, and in his subsequent reflections on the literary life of the time he comments on the debilitating impact of literary piracy and the general poverty of freelance writers (9: 517–18). Yet his assertion that writing was conceived as a "holy" enterprise, one that could only be tainted by any proximity with mundane issues such as money and economics, surely summarizes the attitude by which many creative writers justified their own poverty. About a hundred years later, the Prague-German writer Franz Kafka (1883–1924) will call upon a metaphor from a similar religious register, referring in one of his notebooks to literary writing as a "form of prayer" (354). Perhaps this suffices as an indication of the perseverance with which, through to the avant-garde movements of the early twentieth century, artistic production was idealized as an activity whose sanctity could only be besmirched by its association with the pragmatic concerns of quotidian economic praxis.

The influence and tenacity of this ideology of aesthetic autonomy still dominates scholarship on German literary and cultural studies. As a result, there is a pronounced tendency among critics to ignore or set aside economic issues in the analysis of literary, philosophical, and cultural documents, as well as in the study of developments in intellectual culture in general. This is still the case, despite the poststructuralist intervention that called the viability of this ideology of (economic) autonomy into question— one thinks of Jacques Derrida's seminal essay "Economimesis," which laid out in especially provocative fashion the ways in which idealist aesthetic theory, despite its attempt to deny the role of economics in intellectual culture, itself relied at strategic moments on borrowings from economic discourse. Curiously, even those few critics who insist on the role economic and monetary issues play in cultural production tend to subscribe to Kant's basic opposition between artistic or literary culture and economics. For Jochen Hörisch, for example, one of the leading German literary scholars concerned with the economics of culture and a primary representative of what has come to be called the New Economic Criticism,[4] literary texts assume a privileged critical stance vis-à-vis economic questions precisely *because of* their self-defined autonomy from monetary interests. According to Hörisch, literary language and monetary relations, as discrete and largely inimical semiotic systems, are locked in a quasimythic struggle. Literature, for Hörisch, remains, despite the dominance of money and its reliance on what is merely quantifiable, "anachronistically loyal to the superfluous alphabet" and "observes the triumphant advance of money and numbers with ever increasing irritation" (*Heads or Tails* 12). In other words, literary language, precisely because of its independence from economics as "communicative system,"[5] can establish itself as a *competing* discourse that enjoys the privileged potential for undermining and critiquing the numerical "language" of economics. Hörisch thus maintains: "[N]othing has less cover [i.e., collateral] than poetic speech. Yet for this very reason literature is in a position to pursue a line of questioning normally shunned, the question of the validity [*Geltung*] and cover [or collateral: *Deckung*] of other codes" (*Heads or Tails* 16). Literature, in other words, takes on the status of a kind of supercode, or metacode, that is capable of critically interrogating the dominant quantifying codes of modern economic life. To be sure, this is indeed *one* of the roles modern literature can assume with regard to the monetary economy, and Hörisch deserves considerable credit for exploring this critical function of poetic discourse. But that is not the whole story.

In contrast to this, my investigations seek to call into question Kant's overriding assumption—representative, as it is, of the Enlightenment and post-Enlightenment ideology of an aesthetics of autonomy—and attempt to interrogate the very *complicity* of literary and intellectual production with parallel developments in the economic and monetary spheres. My hypothesis is that from the Enlightenment through to the period of realism and beyond, German literary and intellectual culture exhibits what I call an economic unconscious. Conceived in theoretical coherence with the

Freudian notion of the unconscious as a subphenomenal determinant that structures the phenomenal and epiphenomenal manifestations of an individual's psychic life, I understand the economic unconscious of German intellectual culture to be a matrix of subliminal structuration in which economic issues influence the aesthetic, formal, conceptual, discursive, and thematic dimensions of literary and philosophical texts. Some of the authors and artifacts examined here are more open about their engagement with economic and monetary issues; others attempt explicitly to disguise or repress the seminal impact of economic issues on their makeup, and this tension leaves its indelible imprimatur on these works. The title of my book, "money matters," is intended to indicate not only my interest in the thematic and structural manifestations of economic and monetary issues in the works and theories under investigation, but also to highlight that in these texts money does, in fact, *matter*—that economic issues prove to be of central importance in the very structure and conception of some of the principal works of German intellectual culture in the period under investigation.

Friedrich Nietzsche was one of the first thinkers to critically diagnose the inherent interconnections between economic practices and rational thought in general. In his *Genealogie der Moral* (Genealogy of morals, 1887) he noted, "Setting prices, measuring values, gauging equivalents, exchanging—these activities preoccupied the primitive thought of human beings to such an extent that in a certain sense they can be conceived as *the very basis* of thought itself" (*Kritische Studienausgabe* 5: 306). Just a few years later, in his monumental *Philosophie des Geldes* (Philosophy of money, 1900), the German sociologist Georg Simmel picked up this theme and rigorously explored the parallels between historical developments in the monetary economy and the evolution of modern culture and rational thought. Anthropologists such as Marcel Mauss and Karl Polanyi have confirmed this intimate interconnection between economic practices and the structures of human reason and social relations. My study investigates on the basis of selected documents the curious dialectic between the simultaneous denial and affirmation of the connections between economic practice and intellectual culture from the emergence of German civil society in the 1770s through the mid-nineteenth century. This is a period of European history characterized not merely by tremendous social upheaval, marked by the revolutions of 1789, 1830, and 1848, but also by great technological and industrial transformation. In addition, this book spans the period that can justifiably be called the generative phase of modern economic science, beginning with the theories of the French physiocrats, moving through the publication and wide-ranging impact of Adam Smith's *Wealth of Nations*, and leading up to the critique of capitalist economic practices in the theories of Karl Marx and Friedrich Engels. In its intellectual-historical dimension, my research is marked off by Kant, on the one side, who helps institute the segregation of economics and intellectual culture discussed above, and Marx, Nietzsche, and Simmel, on the other, as the primary thinkers who sought to refute the relevance of this distinction.

There are several reasons why German-speaking Europe from the 1770s through the mid-nineteenth century comprises a particularly fruitful test case for an analysis of these wider interactions between economic, philosophical, and literary discourses. One is the tardiness of German economic developments by comparison with other parts of western Europe, in particular England and France. One consequence of this, for example, is that French physiocratic principles and Smithian market theories, which represent distinct phases of European economic history, are received and debated in Germany at the same time and in concentrated form. The years in question likewise encompass the formative years of capitalism and industrialization in German-speaking Europe. This is also the period that paves the way for German sociopolitical and economic unification under a Prussian state led by Otto von Bismarck. "Germany" during the period under consideration is really nothing but an abstract notion that brings together under one name a set of politically, economically, culturally, and even religiously distinct principalities. In the case of German-speaking Europe, then—viewed from the perspective of the unified, centralized nation-states of western Europe—economic and political retardation converge in such a way that each complicates the other. To be sure, this "backwardness" symptomatic of German economic and political conditions had, viewed from a different perspective, certain theoretical advantages: because its political fragmentation and economic disarray essentially prohibited Germans from sharing in the fruits of world exploration and colonialist expansionism, they were more inclined to view these developments with the critical eye of the outsider. As we will see, this backdrop of emergent colonialism—the beginnings of what today we term the global economy—forms a touchstone to which the texts under consideration here frequently allude, although they rarely address it directly. German-speaking Europe in this period, however, was undergoing the central transformation from a locally organized, subsistence-based economy to a commercialized economic mode grounded on increased exploitation of natural resources, international trade, colonialist enterprises, and the lure of money as a universal symbol for the satisfaction of all wants and desires. Although the Germans were largely excluded from participating in colonial discovery and expropriation, they nevertheless enjoyed and profited from the internationalization of trade and the introduction of colonial commodities. By the same token, the other side of the Germans' exclusion from colonialist enterprises was a heightened mystique and valorization of the homeland—what the Germans call *Heimat*—among German-speaking peoples. In this sense the Romantic glorification of nature forms a fundamental backdrop for a critical assessment of the ecological price one pays for the rise of the modern industrial economy. But what especially sets Germany apart from the rest of Europe in the years from 1770 to 1850 is the fact that relative economic and political retardation coincide with a period of phenomenal intellectual, cultural, and literary blossoming. My study rests largely on this historical parallelism among economic, sociopolitical, philosophical, and literary-historical developments in German-speaking Europe. As should become clear in the chapters that follow, life in Germany during this period was characterized by a unique configuration in which economics, politics, and diverse branches of culture—above all philosophy and literature—asserted competing claims as the organizing center around which German unity might emerge.

The period from 1770 to 1850 in Germany is ideally suited to an analysis of this imbrication between politics, economics, and intellectual culture. In the economic domain, this time span marks the transition from substantialist to functionalist conceptions of the monetary economy, characterized above all by the modulation from specie, as the material indicator of economic value, to purely semiotic monetary instruments, such as bills of exchange and paper money. Of course, one of the ramifications of German political fragmentation was also a concomitant monetary chaos, in which myriad currencies competed against one another. In the sociopolitical sphere, these years delineate the development of civil society in

German-speaking Europe, from the emergence of German national consciousness to Romantic theories about the confluence of economics and political nationalism. In terms of economic development, this is the period in which the German states move from a fragmented agrarian economy through the process of industrialization and emerge with a commercial economy that will eventually harbor colonialist pretensions. In the realm of cultural history, finally, this epoch encompasses the origins and the maturation of a German national literature with genuine claims to the status of a paradigm-shaping world literature, as well as the development of German idealist philosophy from Kant through the Romantics to Nietzsche. While cultural sociology has given ample study to the parallel development of German civic society and bourgeois literary and philosophical models, little attention has been paid to possible intersections between economic and literary-philosophical developments in this period. My study will hopefully help fill this void.

This book is structured around a series of case studies, drawn from distinct historical periods and based on readings of a mixture of philosophical, political, economic, and literary texts. Taken together, these inquiries attempt to demonstrate how, during these formative years, the economic and sociopolitical consolidation of Germany goes hand in hand with, and is ideologically buttressed by, arguments developed in the economic unconscious of mainstream cultural artifacts. Although the chapters are linked by a web of coherent arguments, they also stand alone and can be read individually as independent studies. The book is organized into two parts, defined largely by focus and by the principal objects under analysis. The first four chapters (part 1) are the most general in scope, addressing larger historical and cultural issues and the role economic questions played in their formulation and resolution. The remaining chapters (part 2) highlight specific economic themes that emerge from detailed readings of selected literary works. Part 1 deals more broadly with general issues of intellectual, philosophical, and economic culture during the years in question. Although still historical "postholes" in the sense that they investigate closely circumscribed time periods and cut across diverse intellectual spheres, these chapters tend to have a more historical, diachronic orientation. Part 2 shifts more specifically to a set of synchronic studies predicated on close interpretive readings of specific literary texts. These literary case studies revisit and refine issues sketched more broadly in part 1, indicating both the breadth and the depth with which economic questions permeate German intellectual culture of this period.

Throughout the book, the chapters are organized roughly chronologically, based on the primary authors and materials with which they deal, so that when read from beginning to end the book charts an implicit historical trajectory. The only exception to this is the conclusion, dealing with part 2 of Johann Wolfgang von Goethe's *Faust*, which antedates Adalbert Stifter's *Bergkristall* by approximately two decades. There are good reasons for this exception. First, *Faust II* treats so many of the economic themes— and their sociocultural consequences—covered in the works examined in previous chapters that it functions well as a kind of coda for the book as a whole. But second—and most importantly—Goethe's *Faust II* marks that crucial juncture at which the economic *unconscious* of German intellectual culture emerges into a state of literary-cultural consciousness. *Faust II* does not merely reflect critically and historically upon the complicity of intellectual culture in economic developments, it *performs*, in its own textual constitution, the apparent inescapability of this complicity of intellect and economics.

The first chapter introduces the complex interrelations of money and culture by examining the role monetary metaphors play in the formulation of German language theory in the eighteenth century. Concentrating on the conceptions promulgated by people like Johann Caspar Lavater, Gottfried Wilhelm Leibniz, Johann Gottfried Herder, and Johann Georg Hamann, this chapter demonstrates how a new theory that views language as the *generator* of ideas, rather than merely as a vehicle for representing already existing thoughts, is consistently underwritten by images drawn from the monetary sphere. This chapter highlights the historical parallelism between the shift from a substantialist to a functionalist paradigm in the development of monetary instruments and the formulation of a theory of language that stresses the meaning-*productive* capacities of linguistic signs.

Chapter 2 addresses once more the connection between monetary and linguistic theory, but shifts this discussion to a new historical era, this time concentrating on the linguistic and economic thought of the early German Romantics. Investigating the interrelationships between the semiotic theory of Novalis and the economic and monetary program of his friend and intellectual associate Adam Müller, this investigation demonstrates how the traffic between economic and linguistic spheres moves in both directions. If Novalis conceives communication along the lines of a mercantile contract, his semiotic theory in turn powerfully influences Müller's conception of money as the glue that binds a nation into a contractual community. Müller emerges as one of the first economic theoreticians to valorize fiduciary currency precisely because of its purely semiotic constitution, insisting in particular on the communal faith on which it relies for its successful functioning.

Chapter 3 extends this analysis by comparing Müller's theory of money with that defended by Johann Gottlieb Fichte in his political-economic treatise *Der geschlossene Handelsstaat* (The closed commercial state). For these two Romantic thinkers it is money—not a common language, national or racial heritage, or a shared culture—that constitutes the central symbol or "mythology" around which a coherent and autonomous German nation can emerge. Müller and Fichte both oppose the use of universally accepted currencies such as gold and silver as monetary instruments for their national state. Instead, they argue for the establishment of an entirely arbitrary and substantively worthless national currency—like paper money—whose value is established by the credence the national community invests in it. Especially in Fichte's case, this economic theory can be seen as coherent with certain systematic principles of Romantic transcendental philosophy. Additionally, with Fichte one can chart a historical shift among the Romantic thinkers from a conception of the nation-state grounded in economic principles to one anchored in shared language or racial attributes. This chapter also looks ahead to the post-World War II reconstitution of German nationalism on an economic rather than a linguistic, racial, or cultural basis.

If the first three chapters set the stage for the investigation as a whole by mapping out crosscurrents between economics and philosophical discourses from the late eighteenth century through the early decades of the nineteenth, the fourth chapter concentrates more closely on the intersection of economic and aesthetic theory in this same period. It takes as its jumping-off place the widespread and heated debate over physiocratic economic principles that raged in Germany in the 1770s and 1780s, reading these documents as deep-seated reflections on changing notions of value in both economic and intellectual culture. The contributions to this controversy by Johann Georg Schlosser, in particular, lay out a shift from a theory of value based in material substance to one grounded in human psychological and conceptual patterns. Schlosser is one of the first to defend a theory of *imaginary* value, explicitly tied to human libidinal interests and fantasies. I follow this theme of the role of libidinal and imaginary investments through to Karl Marx's theory of commodity fetishism, and then turn to parallels in aesthetic theory and literary practice at the end of the eighteenth century. On the example of Ludwig Tieck's artist novel *Franz Sternbalds Wanderungen* (The travels of Franz Sternbald), I locate the transition in aesthetic theory from a concentration on mimetic representation to a valorization of the imaginative products of the creative genius as historically and conceptually parallel to the transformation in value theory that is occurring in the domain of economics. This chapter closes with an interpretation of Eduard Mörike's novella *Maler Nolten* (The painter Nolten), which I read as a critique of the unfettered imagination propagated by Tieck and his fellow Romantics. With its turn from general cultural analysis to the reading of two exemplary literary works, this chapter forms the transition between parts 1 and 2 of the book.

Chapter 5 presents the first in the series of more concentrated literary analyses, exploring the autobiography (*Lebensgeschichte*) of Johann Heinrich Jung-Stilling, a work that contributed in major ways to the establishment of the autobiography as a preeminent literary genre in Germany during the waning decades of the eighteenth century. Jung-Stilling presents an especially interesting case study because, aside from being a popular writer and one of the most visible advocates of the religious movement known as Pietism, he was also one of the first recognized German political economists, and in this capacity he contributed in major ways to the founding of economics in Germany as a serious academic discipline. Not only did Jung-Stilling teach at the first German economic academy in Kaiserslautern, but he went on to hold a university professorship in economics at the University of Marburg and wrote many foundational books on the rudiments of economic theory and practice. My reading of his *Lebensgeschichte*, which appeared in installments over the course of several decades, attempts to demonstrate how even for the devout Pietist Jung-Stilling, economic thought begins to displace religious faith. My argument is that the providentialism Jung-Stilling advocates is no longer grounded in religious doctrine, but instead has assumed a monetary nature, so that God becomes a kind of central banker who makes monetary gifts to his chosen clients. I also try to expose how the transformative events of Jung-Stilling's life, which he attributes to divine grace, are in fact functions of his own strategic plans and evidence of his economic opportunism.

Chapter 6 supplements my earlier examinations of the role of economics and money in German Romanticism by turning to the popular late-Romantic tale *Peter Schlemihl* by the French-born German author Adelbert von Chamisso. Chamisso's prototypical story of mysterious enrichment represents a merger of the *Fortunatus* and *Faust* legends, relating how its eponymous hero trades his shadow for a magic purse that produces infinite quantities of gold. The paradox of this novella is, of course, that Schlemihl, due to the absence of a shadow, can never truly capitalize—at least in any social respects—on his limitless monetary resources. My interpretation reads Schlemihl's predicament as an aftereffect of the very excess he enjoys. Using Georges Bataille's theory of loss and expenditure as a critical backdrop, this reading argues that under the conditions of a self-replenishing supply of money, loss itself becomes the one thing Schlemihl cannot possibly experience. This, I assert, is the meaning of Schlemihl's lost shadow, and the need for limitation and scarcity as constitutive moments in any definition of (economic or cultural) value drives Schlemihl's decision to jettison his magic purse and turn to the life of an ascetic botanist. In his scientific endeavors, Schlemihl learns to embrace the limitations he has come to recognize as a founding moment of the economic value system.

The next two chapters modulate to a new literary-historical epoch, the period that in German cultural and literary studies is often referred to as the age of "poetic" realism. Chapter 7 compares the young Karl Marx's critique of laws against wood poaching with the wood-poaching incident in Annette von Droste-Hülshoff's *Die Judenbuche* (The Jews' beech). My hypothesis here is that the anti-Semitic elements in this text, which stigmatize the Jews as outsiders who disrupt the formation of an "indigenous" community, function as a disguise for, and displacement of, critical questions about the Germans' own industrial exploitation of nature. I thus read the murder of the Jew Aaron as a displacement for the murder of the forest ranger Brandis by the notorious band of wood poachers, whose activities represent the primary economic backdrop for Droste-Hülshoff's novella. Here my investigations take an ecocritical turn, exploring how the economic pressures of the burgeoning industrial and colonial economy—in particular the demand for wood to be used in shipbuilding—spell ecological disaster for the forests on which the characters in this novella depend.

Chapter 8 continues with this theme of industrialization, increased commercialism, and their consequences, but it examines a text whose perspective on this problem, instead of being implicitly critical, as in Droste-Hülshoff's *Judenbuche*, subtly valorizes the shift from a natural to a commercial economy. Adalbert Stifter's famous Christmas story *Bergkristall* (Rock crystal), to whose interpretation this chapter is devoted, is traditionally viewed as a last-ditch defense of an idyllic, preindustrial central European culture; but my reading emphasizes the travels of the children between their native village and the industrializing city on the other side of the mountain pass as a fundamental act of commerce. If the mythology of this crossing of the pass was previously dominated by the story of the baker who died in a snowstorm trying to carry his wares across this divide, the children's rescue from a similar predicament introduces a new narrative into the village. This new mythology touts the successes of commercial enterprise and the transgression of natural boundaries for the purpose of economic progress. The children's father, the shoemaker Sebastian, becomes the representative of this new paradigm that valorizes economic rationalization, industrial production, and an expansion of commercial exchange.

My conclusion, as noted, focuses on Goethe's *Faust II* as a literary text that brings together the entire panoply of economic and theoretical issues treated in the chapters that precede it. The infamous paper-money episode of Goethe's drama recapitulates the themes introduced in the opening chapters: the semiotic nature of money, the impact of economic transformation on sociopolitical and cultural life, the devilish magic that seems to underpin economic advancements. But the course of Faust's personal evolution into a colonial entrepreneur, an industrialist commanding an army of laborers, and a large scale real-estate developer parallels in many respects the general economic transformations examined in earlier chapters and representative of the period in question. In this regard *Faust II* is indeed, to allude to the title of Heinz Schlaffer's book on this work, an allegory of the nineteenth century—at least of its economic and industrial development. As in Droste-Hülshoff's *Judenbuche*, moreover, *Faust II* paints a picture of mass ecological destruction bought at the price of short-term economic windfalls. It is no coincidence that at the end of his life Faust mistakes the sound of the lemurs digging his grave for the completion of the dikes and canals that would signal the establishment of his envisioned utopian colony. However, *Faust II* also addresses several other overriding themes pursued in this study, among them the problematic nature of economic and aesthetic mediation, the convergence of aesthetic and economic conceptions of value (in the Helen episodes), critical questions about the redemptive capacity of economic progress, and a critique of an economics and poetics of excess.

Methodologically and theoretically my research emerges out of a little acknowledged direction in American literary and cultural studies that has come to be known as the New Economic Criticism. Broadly speaking, this critical direction is founded on two recent theoretical impulses. The first is the identification of money as a fundamental semiotic system that is structurally related to other primary forms of symbolizing practiced by a given culture—a theory represented above all by the work of Jean-Joseph Goux. The second impulse is a new materialist-historicist turn, represented primarily in the works of Michel Foucault, but manifest as well in the American New Historicism, which concentrates its attention on linkages between transformations in intellectual culture and changes that occur in what Marx called the material base. The Marxian doctrine that the intellectual and cultural "superstructure" and the economic "base" are inherently connected clearly figures prominently in this conception. However, it is crucial to insist that this relationship always be grasped as an inherently dialectical and reciprocal one, with intellectual and material culture mutually influencing each other in unpredictable ways. Finally, my investigations are informed theoretically by Niklas Luhmann's systems theory, which identifies cultural and economic practices as closely interrelated communicative codes. Methodologically my examinations and interpretations operate—this constitutes, I believe, their principal virtue—by attempting to establish a productive dialectic that allows me to move back and forth between detailed readings of literary, philosophical, and economic texts, on the one hand, and overriding speculative historical hypotheses, on the other. In the best-case scenario, these broad hypotheses shape but do not overdetermine the individual readings, while these readings in turn enrich and problematize the general hypotheses.

• • •

Scholarly research in the humanities enjoys the great benefit of being able to profit (paradoxically) from nonprofit institutions. This has decidedly been the case for my work on this book, which received the generous support of several organizations. The American Council of Learned Societies awarded me a senior research fellowship, which allowed me to make substantial progress toward completion of the middle sections of the manuscript. The Alexander von Humboldt Foundation honored me with a Senior Research Prize (*Forschungspreis*) that provided me with the luxury of working and writing while in residence at the University of Tübingen for a year. I want to express my special gratitude to the Humboldt Foundation for its generosity, but in particular to my German sponsor, Professor Georg Braungart, a long-time collaborator and friend, whose nomination made the research prize possible. While in Tübingen I profited greatly from the outstanding collection of eighteenth-century materials in the university library, and I want to thank the staff of special collections in particular for their assistance, patience, and consistently friendly demeanor. The College of Arts and Sciences at the University of Washington also deserves thanks for recognizing my research by naming me Byron W. and Alice L. Lockwood Professor in the Humanities. I extend my gratitude in particular to the Lockwood Foundation, which has shown a deep commitment to the humanities by endowing these professorships. The Lockwood funds made it possible for me to enlist the services of an outstanding research assistant, Tim Coombs, whose thoughtful reflections and conscientious work supported me especially during the finals stages of the project and the completion of the manuscript. I also want to express particular thanks to my collaborators at the University of Washington Press, who have shown great care and consideration in shepherding the book through the editorial and publishing process: Jacqueline Ettinger, acquisitions editor for the Literary Conjugations series, for her unfailing advocacy of this project; Mary Ribesky, assistant managing editor, for moving the book smoothly through the final stages; and Julie Van Pelt, whose painstaking and conscientious copyediting made for a much tighter and more consistent manuscript. Every author should be so fortunate as to have such a fine and cooperative editorial team working on his or her behalf.

Some parts of this book have previously appeared in print. An early version of chapter 1 was published in *The German Quarterly*, volume 69 (1996), and was reprinted in the collection *The New Economic Criticism*, edited by Martha Woodmansee and Mark Osteen and published by Routledge (1998). Chapter 2 appeared in abbreviated form in a special edition of *New Literary History*, volume 31, number 2 (2000), devoted to economic criticism. Chapter 3 was published in preliminary form in volume 36 (2003) of *Eighteenth-Century Studies*. A rudimentary version of the chapter on Stifter was printed in a Festschrift honoring my former teacher Frank Ryder, *Politics and Literature*, edited by Mark Cory and Beth Bjorklund (Camden House, 1998). My interpretation of Droste-Hülshoff's *Judenbuche* appeared in streamlined form in the October 2003 issue of the *German Studies Review* and was awarded the DAAD prize for the best literary essay in that journal from 2003 to 2004. Let me take this opportunity to thank the German Studies Association awards committee, chaired by Professor Todd Kontje, for their recognition of this piece and their generous laudation. Finally, a segment of chapter 4 was published in a Festschrift for John McCarthy, *Practicing Progress: The Promise and Limits of Enlightenment*, edited by Richard E. Schade and Dieter Sevin (Rodopi, 2007). My gratitude goes to these journals and publishers for permission to reprint these essays here in revised and updated form.

Aside from those already named, many individuals have supported my research on this project in diverse ways. I want to thank in particular the colleagues and students in the Department of Germanics at the University of Washington for helping to create a stimulating and interactive intellectual environment: this provides a culture in which research can thrive. Among these friends and collaborators I want to single out Jane Brown, who has supported my research for longer than either of us would care to admit; Eric Ames, Richard Block, and Brigitte Prutti for injecting their energy, wit, and insights into the intellectual mix of the department; the many undergraduate and graduate students who have helped me work through the ideas and interpretations for this project in numerous classes over the past several years; and finally my colleague and wife, Sabine Wilke, who undoubtedly has made the largest emotional and intellectual investment into this project—and received the most meager payout. Last—surely not least—I want to thank my daughter Cora for her patience and for the many hours of enjoyable diversion on the tennis court, without which I surely would never have developed an effective backhand or found the physical and intellectual stamina to complete this book.

Part One

ECONOMICS AND
INTELLECTUAL
CULTURE

1 / Buying into Signs

Money and Semiosis in Eighteenth-Century German Language Theory

Monetary culture means that life is caught up . . . in its means.

—Georg Simmel (*Philosophie des Geldes* 336–37)

Exchanging Words for Money and Money for Words

THE METAPHORICAL FIELD CIRCUMSCRIBING ANALOGIES between language and money is undoubtedly one of the most productive in all of Western culture. Quintilian's admonition in the *Institutio Oratorio* that one expend words as carefully as one spends money (2: 1.6.1), Ovid's remark in the *Ars Amatoria* that words, like coins, are minted by public authority (3.479f), Nietzsche's famous comparison of current words to coins that have lost their impression due to overcirculation ("Über Wahrheit und Lüge" 881), and Saussure's identification of linguistic significance with monetary value (*Course in General Linguistics* 115): what all these metaphors have in common is that they draw on issues of monetary practice to elucidate the operation and use of language. The historical extension of this metaphorical field is matched by its broad cultural dispersion throughout the European languages: comparisons between money and language are just as likely to be found among English or French as they are among German writers.[1] The unusual vitality of this analogy between money and language is further reflected in the expansive semantic territory it encompasses. Aside from the common identification of words with coins, many other elements drawn from the sphere of finance, such as the notions of circulation, exchange, credit, banking, counterfeiting, investment, and so on, are frequently applied as metaphorical vehicles for the illumination of linguistic practices. But the metaphorical exchange between the realms of economics and linguistics runs in both directions, so that issues such as truth and falsehood, rhetorical embellishment, and reasonability, which are central to the discourse on language, are often transferred by means of metaphor to the domain of economics. The vitality and diversity of this metaphorical field gives the best indication that the analogy between money and language in particular, and between the realms of economics and linguistics in general, is underwritten by a wealth of substantive capital. Indeed, as Jean-Joseph Goux has argued (110), the coherence and organic nature of this relation indicates that what is at work here is not a mere analogy, but rather a deep-seated isomorphism between the domains of money and language.

In the revolutionary year 1789, Friedrich Gedike (1754–1803), the editor of the *Berlinische Monatsschrift*, one of the leading periodicals promoting Enlightenment culture in Germany, published an article titled "Verba valent sicut numi, oder von der Wortmünze" (Words have value as do coins, or On verbal coins). Gedike's primary purpose in writing this essay was the rehabilitation of the word "Enlightenment," which, according to his assessment, had taken on negative connotations over the course of its use and abuse (260–61). But what makes Gedike's essay a revealing historical document is that to salvage the concept of Enlightenment he persistently relies on the analogy between monetary and linguistic economies. In fact, Gedike's essay can be viewed as a metaphorical treasury that stores a more or less complete inventory of the analogical connections between money and language that were current in German language theory during the final decades of the eighteenth century: as coins serve to ease material commerce, so do words facilitate intellectual commerce (253–54); as money condenses wealth into a more portable and useful form, so do words make knowledge more flexible and manageable (254); words have values, as do coins, but like the latter their face values are often inconsistent with their actual material worth, their *Schrot und Korn*, or their weight and alloy (254–55); the meanings of words can shift with each usage, just as the value of coins can vary at different times of their circulation (255); much like the "clippers and pickers" profit from conscious manipulations of the value of coins, linguistic counterfeiters lend the stamp of credibility to words of meager intrinsic worth in order to deceive their interlocutors (256); moreover, just as the seigniorage, the cost of minting, is deducted from the metal content of a coin, so that the intrinsic value even of legitimate currency never completely measures up to its face value, the meaning of words that have just been freshly minted can also never be established with total accuracy and precision (255); finally, just as there are wardens of the mint whose charge it is to guarantee the weight of the coinage and to draw light coins out of circulation, so there must be wardens of language who oversee the coining of phrases and police their usage (256–57). Clearly, Gedike sees himself as just such a warden over the mint of language, and he hopes that his essay will help his contemporaries distinguish between "true and false enlightenment" as between "true and false ducats" (270).

Gedike's essay bears testimony to the obsession of the late eighteenth century with exploring the isomorphism between the function and value of monetary currencies in the protocapitalist economy and the function and value of words in the Enlightenment economy of linguistic truth. Gedike's inflated use of the money-language conceit is grounded in an awareness of its prevalence in the language theory of the eighteenth century. Indeed, this image is veritably omnipresent in theoretical discourses on language in this period, occurring not only in the linguistic reflections of Johann Caspar Lavater (1741–1801), Gottfried Wilhelm Leibniz (1646–1716), John Locke (1632–1704), David Hume (1711–76), Johann Gottfried Herder (1744–1803), Johann Georg Hamann (1697–1733), Johann Wolfgang von Goethe (1749–1832), and A. R. J. Turgot (1727–81), but arising in the linguistic theories of many lesser-known figures as well. What is more, Gedike's essay is representative of the way in which eighteenth-century authors explored the richness of this metaphorical field, mining not only the mother lode, but also exploiting its many associative veins.

The depth to which this homology penetrated the thought of bourgeois intellectuals in this period is probably best demonstrated by the fact that the metaphorical exchange between the realms of economics and linguistics ran in both directions, so that just as monetary images were employed to describe the functioning of language, examples from the realm of language were used in economic treatises to elucidate the operation and essence of money. Turgot, one of the leading French physiocrats, remarked already in 1769 on the underlying systematic, formal affinities between money and language. "Money has in common with measures in general," he argued in his essay "Value and Money," "that it is a type of language, differing among different peoples and in everything that is arbitrary and conventional, but of which the forms are brought closer and made identical, in some respects, by their relation to a common term or standard" (133). Language, like money, Turgot had already recognized, is governed by the logic of the general equivalent.[2] Similarly, the eighteenth-century German economist Johann Georg Büsch (1728–1800) identified the semiotic nature of money and language as the basis of their inherent relationship. In his *Abhandlung von dem Geldsumlauf* (Treatise on the circulation of money) of 1780 he noted: "We have languages as signs of concepts. We have money as signs of the value of things" (1: 151). Moreover, in order to justify the wholly arbitrary relationship between monetary units and the commodities for which they can substitute, Büsch relies on a theory of language that defines both its articulated sounds and its written signs as instituted by arbitrary human convention (1: 150). Thus, already for Büsch the monetary and linguistic economies appear as systems whose operation depends on the circulation of signs. Indeed, as we will see, this semiotic affinity forms the principal *tertium comparationis* that underwrites the analogy between money and language for eighteenth-century thinkers.[3]

Succumbing at this juncture to an urge for historical speculation, let me sketch briefly some of the sociological and intellectual-historical factors that help to account for this rampant appropriation and exploitation of the money-language conceit in eighteenth-century letters. It can scarcely go unnoticed, first of all, that this century was one of far-reaching economic and monetary transformation. As a counter to the increasing dominance of mercantilist economic and monetary policies, which laid stress on a positive trade balance and defined wealth in terms of surplus metallic coin,[4] physiocratic doctrine, which emphasized agricultural production and championed the virtues of unregulated trade, emerged late in the century and became one of the most hotly debated economic issues of the day.[5] Of primary importance in drawing general attention to the operation of monetary systems was certainly the infamous instability of the major

European currencies during this period, due largely to the corrupt inter-vention of political authorities into the practices of coinage and currency. In this regard Adam Smith noted in *The Wealth of Nations,*

> For in every country of the world, I believe, the avarice and injustice of princes and sovereign states, abusing the confidence of their subjects, have by degrees diminished the real quantity of metal, which had been originally contained in their coins. The Roman As, in the latter ages of the Republick, was reduced to the twenty-fourth part of its original value, and, instead of weighing a pound, came to weigh only half an ounce. The English pound and penny contain at present about a third only; the Scots pound and penny about a thirty-sixth; and the French pound and penny about a sixty-sixth part of their original value. (1: 43)

This general tendency toward a devaluation of currency seemed to reach its culmination with the substitution of paper for metallic coin. Indeed, the introduction of paper currencies in the form of bank notes was an event for many no less earth-shattering than the Lisbon earthquake of 1755, since it called into question the traditional definition of money as a commodity with intrinsic value.[6] The effects of John Law's monetary reform in France between 1716 and 1720, which included the introduction of paper money, are well known and scarcely need mention.[7] Less well known are the manip-ulations of the value of the Prussian taler undertaken by Frederick the Great during the Seven Years' War in order to finance his war debt. The result of these governmental interventions into the Prussian monetary system was a steep decline in the value of the taler, leading not only to a widespread mistrust in this coin and the state whose stamp guaranteed its value, but opening the door to general misgivings about the institution of money itself.[8] Finally, due to the discovery of large quantities of silver and gold in the New World and their influx into Europe, the value of these metals under-went substantial fluctuations, and this led to a radical destabilization of the value of gold and silver coins.[9] Between 1500 and 1800, the mines of the Americas accounted for no less than seventy percent of the world's out-put of gold and eighty-five percent of its production of silver. This radical influx of specie into the European economies caused the prices of the pre-cious metals to fall by about one-third of their former value, and this, in turn, resulted in a concomitant inflation in the prices of consumer goods, which by one estimate reached as much as four hundred percent in Spain by 1800 (Weatherford 99–101). This variation in the value of metallic coin demonstrated above all the fact that money was but one commodity among others, subject to the oscillations in price dictated by the logic of the market, especially the parameters of supply and demand. The upshot of these diverse events for the general European populace was an intense psychological uncertainty concerning matters of money and value, predicated on the unsettling recognition of the fundamentally *abstract* nature of money, a substance whose materiality had hitherto scarcely been called into question. What was beginning to make itself felt, in short, was the paradigm shift from a substantialist to a functionalist conception of money. Consistent with this transformation was the emerging theory of monetary circulation, which played down money's significance as a commodity and began to see it as a mere expedient of commerce and exchange, an "oil which renders the motion of the wheels [of trade] more smooth and easy," in the words of David Hume (309).

At the same time, and parallel to this concern with the transformation of monetary instruments, the eighteenth century was a time of intense deliberation on the origin, nature, and function of language. Central here is the emergence of the discipline of semiotics as fundamental to the science of knowledge, a proposition first advanced by Locke in his *Essay Concerning Human Understanding* (1689) and subsequently carried over into German philosophy by Johann Heinrich Lambert (1728–77) in his *Neues Organon* (1764), one of whose four parts dealt explicitly with the nature of signs and their role in the discovery of truth.[10] As Ulrich Ricken has argued (10–17), language theory of the eighteenth century was marked by a transition from the rationalist Cartesian paradigm to the sensualist, sign-oriented model advanced by Locke and Etienne de Condillac (1714–80). This shift was significant because it led to a reconceptualization of language, previously viewed as a mere communicative vehicle, to a theory that recognized it as a cognitive, creative, knowledge-producing medium. But the insight into the semiotic nature of language was both a boon and a bane for eighteenth-century philosophy: a boon because it made possible this knowledge-productive conception of an *ars characteristica* or an *ars combinatoria*, a calculative sign-language on the basis of whose manipulation previously unknown truths could be discovered;[11] a bane because, to quote Locke, words "interpose themselves so much between our understandings, and the truth which it [sic] would contemplate and apprehend, that, like the medium through which visible objects pass, the obscurity and disorder do not seldom cast a mist before our eyes, and impose upon our understandings" (274).

The same was true for the eighteenth-century conception of money, which, as the above-cited passage from Büsch's *Abhandlung von dem Geldsumlauf* indicates, was also beginning to be conceived as a semiotic system. In fact, one of the major economic debates of the eighteenth century turned on the semiotic character of money: whereas progressive economists such as Adam Smith had recognized that as pure sign, that is, in the form of paper currencies, money could function as a stimulator of trade and a catalyst to the increase of wealth (1: 291–302), more conservative economists like Turgot (and the physiocrats in general) asserted that this "sign-money," as it was already called, was but a mere deceptive sleight of hand, an economic edifice built without a foundation. Thus in his "Letter on Paper Money" Turgot unequivocally maintained that "[i]t would be ridiculous to imagine that money is only token wealth, the repute of which is based on the stamp of a prince" (4). Similarly, in his "Reflections on the Formation and Distribution of Wealth" Turgot defended gold and silver as natural money with inherent value: "[G]old and silver [are] constituted money, and universal money, and that without any arbitrary agreement among men, without the intervention of any law, but only by the nature of things. They are not, as people imagine, signs of value; they have a value themselves" (62–63).

This, then, is the most significant point of convergence between the eighteenth century's philosophy of language and its theory of money: both were conceived principally as *semiotic* intermediaries whose interposition in their respective domains of exchange had the potential to be either immensely productive or immeasurably destructive. Indeed, the recognition of the semiotic nature of words and money extended deep into the theories of each discipline. For just as the philosophers of the eighteenth century came to realize that words are signs twice removed—signs of concepts that in turn are signs of things—economists came to understand "sign-money," defined as any currency whose symbolic value stamped upon it does not coincide with its real value as commodity or as precious material, explicitly as a sign of a sign, specie being understood generally as an immediate sign of value.[12] In an essay published in Gedike's *Berlinische Monatsschrift* in 1796, the economist Moses Wessely (1737–92) can thus propose the following definition: "*Symbolic money*, the symbolic sign of a bill of exchange drawn on society (*paper money*), is only the representative of a representative" ("Geld und Zirkulazion" 308). This understanding of verbal expression and emergent "symbolic money" as second-order systems of signification is perhaps the fundamental homology that underpins the comparison of money and language in the eighteenth century.

Well before the French Revolution, German intellectuals were aware that they were living in a time of profound intellectual and social transformation. The economic and monetary revolutions of the eighteenth century, marked by the shift from a substantialist to a functionalist paradigm, were perhaps the most concrete, tangible forms in which these changes were experienced. In monetary theory these transformations were expressed in the recognition that, with the introduction of paper currency, two of the functions traditionally served by money as specie, to be a store of value as well as a medium of exchange, had been disassociated. Wessely articulated this split by asserting that paper money only has value when used in exchange for something, that is, when being spent, whereas specie has value independent of its role in the circulation of goods (311). Wessely's attitude toward "symbolic money" was characteristically ambivalent: although he recognized its beneficial effects as a stimulant to circulation, useful especially during economic declines (308), he also attacked the *Spekulationsgeist*, the "spirit of speculation" it introduced and warned that the use of paper money amounted to nothing other than a mortgaging of the energies of future generations in order to satisfy the needs of the present (310).

It was a friend of Wessely's, the dramatist, essayist, and aesthetician Gotthold Ephraim Lessing (1729–81), who articulated this paradigm shift most poignantly, while simultaneously associating this transformation in the monetary realm with parallel changes in the spheres of thought and linguistic expression. In his late drama *Nathan der Weise* (Nathan the wise, 1779), Lessing portrayed his protagonist facing the recognition that in the modern world two systems of understanding and expression, each of which articulates its own "truth," contest one another. In his audience with Sul-

tan Saladin, the Jew Nathan is taken unawares when, expecting to be peti-
tioned for a loan of money, he is asked instead to make a statement of
absolute truth. Before responding with the famous parable of the three rings,
Nathan deliberates on this request in a trenchant monologue.

> I thought of money;
> And he wants—truth. Yes, truth! And wants it so—
> So bare and blank—as if the truth were coin!—
> And were it coin, which anciently was weighed!—
> That might be done! But coin from modern mints,
> Which but the stamp creates, which you but count
> Upon the counter—truth is not like that!
> As one puts money in his purse, just so
> One puts truth in his head? Who is the Jew here? (402)

Challenged to a statement of truth in a situation with potentially men-
acing personal and political ramifications, Nathan recognizes that he must
choose between two distinct forms of truth, the "ancient" and the "modern." The sultan, who functions as the representative of the modernist
paradigm, treats truth as though it were mere symbolic money, a token
that could stand in to assist in counting up a debt. Thus the Jew Nathan,
the usurer in economic matters, accuses Saladin of being a usurer in matters of truth and language, and he hence justifiably asks who the real
"Jew" is. For Lessing's Nathan the conflict of truths can be reduced to an
essential antithesis between contrary systems of value. In ancient times
the currency used to measure value had its own inherent worth, established intrinsically by the preciousness of the material that represented
it. In the modern age, by contrast, value becomes extrinsic and systematic; it no longer resides in the material through which it is expressed,
but has become instead purely symbolic, lent "currency" by the arbitrary
stamp imposed by political authority. Specie, as a manifestation of eternal, intrinsic value, stands in for ancient "truth" as the reconfirmation
of the known.

Michel Foucault has described this mode of thought, which he associates with what he calls the Renaissance episteme, as a form of knowledge
that "condemned itself to never knowing anything but the same thing"

(*Order of Things* 30). Opposed to this epistemic pattern, in Foucault's model, stands the classical mode of thought. Its purpose is not, as in the Renaissance episteme, "to attempt to rediscover beneath [signs] the primitive text of a discourse sustained, and retained, forever," but rather "to discover the arbitrary language that will authorize the deployment of nature within its space, ... to fabricate a language, and to fabricate it well—so that, as an instrument of analysis and combination, it will really be the language of calculation" (62–63). One of the intellectual constants in eighteenth-century language theory, as the passage from Lessing's *Nathan* makes clear, is the assumption of a homology, on the one hand, between specie as a manifestation of intrinsic value and "ancient" truth as the reiteration of the already known or believed, and, on the other hand, between symbolic money as a mere placeholder of absent value in the calculus of economic circulation and "modern" truth as a speculative form of knowledge that employs arbitrary signs to generate new "truths" ex nihilo.

Ambivalent Economics in Eighteenth-Century German Theories of Language

The disquiet about the incipient paradigm shifts in the economies of money, knowledge, and truth that were transpiring during the eighteenth century manifests itself in exemplary fashion, as the passage from Lessing's *Nathan* demonstrates, in analogies between money and language. This is especially true of eighteenth-century German language theory. In what follows I will concentrate on the use of money metaphors in reflections on language by four German thinkers: Gottfried Wilhelm Leibniz, Johann Caspar Lavater, Johann Gottfried Herder, and Johann Georg Hamann. These textual examples not only document the persistence of this homology between money and language in the linguistic theory of the time, but also help us assess how the historical shakedown occurring in the realm of monetary policy unconsciously influenced the way people thought about language. My hypothesis is that the move from a substantivist to a functionalist (or from what Ricken terms a Cartesian to a sensualist) conception of language cannot simply be understood as an intraphilosophical development, as historians of language and philosophers have generally tended to assume, but that it was profoundly affected by a cross-fertilization with ideas that emerged in economics, particularly with regard to advances in monetary policy and the sign-character of monetary instruments.

In paragraph five of his *Unvorgreifliche Gedanken, betreffend die Ausübung und Verbesserung der teutschen Sprache* (Unpresuming thoughts concerning the use and improvement of the German language), first published in 1719, Leibniz attempts to elucidate the character of words as signs by enlisting an analogy with money. The specific metaphorical vehicle he selects, token money, gives evidence that the historical shift from a substantivist to a functionalist monetary system had begun to remap the metaphorical relationship between money and language already quite early in the eighteenth century.

> However, where the use of language is concerned, it is the case . . . that words are not only the signs of concepts, but also of things, and that we need signs not only to express our opinion to others, but even to assist our thoughts themselves. For just as in large trading centers, as in games and in other places, one does not always pay money, but in its place makes use of notes or tokens [*Zeddel oder Marken*] until the final settlement of accounts or payment is made, so, too, reason makes use of the representations of things, especially when a great deal of thinking must be done, namely by replacing them with signs, so that it is not necessary repeatedly to call to mind the thing every time it occurs. (520)

Leibniz gives the money-language metaphor a peculiarly modern twist insofar as the traditional analogy between words and specie is replaced by the comparison between words and symbolic counters. While the issuance of such paper notes, or bank notes, had its inception as early as 1407 at the bank of Genoa, these paper currencies were a relatively uncommon phenomenon in Germany at the time Leibniz published this treatise, and this fact underscores the radical nature of Leibniz's modification of the traditional metaphor. But as the quotation makes apparent, this transmogrification is by no means wanton; indeed, it serves to elucidate some of the fundamental aspects of words when conceived explicitly *as signs*.

It is important to note, first of all, that at about the same time as Locke, Leibniz too arrived at the conclusion that words are second-order signs insofar as they do not immediately signify things themselves, but rather represent our mental conceptions of these things. The comparison with bank notes as second-order signs of first-order monetary signs is eminently adequate to the illumination of this semiotic reduplication. Second, Leibniz stresses the centrality of verbal signs not only as mediators in the act of communicative exchange, but also in the very process of thought itself. Here, too, symbolic money supplies an appropriate analogy for the elucidation of this inter-active and intra-active function; for this sign-money not only passes as currency in commercial exchange, but also serves as a token, a counter, by which people can take stock of their bank assets. Finally, Leibniz refers to the fundamental role signs play in the economy of thought and expression, a doctrine that was central to Enlightenment semiotics (Wellbery 229–30): signs perform an abbreviating function for reason, since they can be manipulated more easily and efficiently than either the things themselves or their concepts. It was precisely this argument of efficiency and increased productivity, of course, that was touted as one of the primary virtues of bank notes by their eighteenth-century advocates. The economist Johann Georg Büsch, for example, refers to the ability of symbolic money to produce wealth and drive economic growth as the "magical power [*Zauberkraft*] of money" (1: 78). It is no coincidence that in his treatise on language, Leibniz uses a strikingly similar metaphor to elucidate the productivity of language when understood as a system of signs, calling it a "Kabbalah" (*Unvorgreifliche Gedanken* 521).

Leibniz's exploitation of the conception of ersatz money as a means for concretizing the operation of signs in the economies of thought and language does not end here. In paragraph seven of this same treatise he turns to the images of the "counter" (*Rechen-Pfennig*) and the "promissory note" (*Wechsel-Zeddel*) in order to explain how thought is made more efficient and productive by the implementation of signs.

> For this reason one often uses words as ciphers [*Ziffern*] or as counters [*Rechen-Pfennige*], in the place of representations and things, until one moves step by step to the final sum, and with the reasoned conclusion arrives at the thing itself. From this it becomes evident how important it

is that words, as models and, as it were, the promissory notes [*Wechsel-Zeddel*] of reason, be properly conceived, properly distinguished, adequate, abundant, free-flowing, and appropriate. (521)[13]

This "art of signs" (*Zeichen-Kunst*), which Leibniz compares with algebra, forms the basis for the theory of productive—rather than merely *re*productive—knowledge that represents one of the central accomplishments of Enlightenment epistemology. "By means of this art of signs," Leibniz maintains, "we are able today to discover things at which the ancients were not able to arrive; and yet the entire art consists in nothing but in the use of properly employed signs" (521). Leibniz's exploitation of metaphors from the realm of nascent capitalist economics thus helps him formulate and explain the theory of productive knowledge that is characteristic of the functionalist conception of language. Symbolic money, Leibniz realizes, as a sign of value that, stripped completely of its materiality, stimulates the circulation of commodities is intimately related to an instrumental knowledge that deploys arbitrary signs for the purpose of calculation and discovery. Some of the attributes Leibniz associates with this conception of a knowledge-productive language of calculation seem to be borrowed directly from notions of monetary circulation. In particular his assertion that the signs of such a language must be "abundant" and "free-flowing" suggests that monetary circulation is the model he has in mind and that it has imposed itself upon his linguistic theory.

Leibniz goes to great pains to stress that this epistemological calculus depends on the adequacy of signs: they must be "properly conceived" (*wohl gefasset*), "properly employed" (*wol angebracht*), "adequate" (*zulänglich*), and "appropriate" (*angenehm*) if this mental magic is to arrive at truth. However, he is generally at a loss when it comes to defining precisely what makes any particular sign "proper," "adequate," or "appropriate." Clearly, the entire palette of metaphors he has exploited to explain these signs has emphasized nothing if not their ultimately arbitrary character, their role as conventionalized tokens that by definition have no intrinsic connection with the concepts or things they represent. Adequacy can no longer be defined in terms of referentiality between signs and concepts, but can be gauged only by the efficient functioning of the epistemological equation: productivity becomes the sole measure of adequate signs and their proper use, just as the adequacy of monetary instruments is measured by their ability to stimulate economic growth. Viewed in this manner, language no longer merely represents a stable and finite body of knowledge, but instead serves as a generative mechanism that actually increases the stock of human knowledge.

Leibniz himself, however, was never wholly satisfied with this conclusion. Despite his consistent application of metaphors that would seem to indicate that he was a convinced nominalist, both in monetary and linguistic matters, he turns out to be a closet metallist, at least where his theory of language is concerned. For later in this same treatise, when he attempts to explain the referential connection between verbal signs and the concepts or things they signify, he explicitly asserts "that words do not evolve as arbitrarily or accidentally as many people believe" (536). He goes on to theorize that words originally evolved out of the imitation in sound of the concepts they signified. The German word *Welt* (world), Leibniz proposes, is etymologically related to the German words *Wirren*, *Wirbel*, and *Wogen* ("whirl," "whirlpool," "wave"), as well as to the English word "wheel," and he identifies the common phoneme "w" in these words with the gyrating motion each of them describes. In pronouncing this phoneme, he suggests, the articulatory organs imitate this circular movement (535–36). This hypothesis, which Hans Aarsleff has dubbed the "affective theory of the sound-thing connection" (65), obviously stands in egregious contradiction with the metaphors of the "note," the "counter," and the "promissory note" that Leibniz employs to explain the thought-economy and calculative productivity made possible by explicitly *arbitrary* linguistic signs.

For the moment I want simply to make a note of this contradiction in the critical balance sheet, without yet calculating the bottom line. Before doing that it is necessary to determine whether this equivocation is unique to Leibniz or if it is present in the works of other German writers as well. Only once we have seen that it also occurs in modified form in Lavater's, Herder's, and Hamann's writings on language will we have accumulated enough evidentiary capital to risk a speculative historical conclusion.[14]

It is perhaps not insignificant that Lavater, Herder, and Hamann have in common a coherent intellectual and spiritual background: all three of them were trained as Protestant preachers, inspired in part by the Pietistic teachings so prevalent in the Protestant areas of the German-speaking world in the late eighteenth century. Given this background we would sponta-neously expect them to argue for a substantivist theory of language as the nonmediated word of God, and, indeed, this is generally the case. But even when they make substantivist arguments about the nature of language as semiotic system, their rhetoric often betrays elements that run counter to this position. This is nowhere so true as when they turn to metaphors drawn from the realm of monetary practice to elucidate the operations of language.

In the 1770s Lavater achieved European fame—some might say, with some justification, European infamy—for his theory of physiognomics. The motivating impulse behind Lavater's physiognomic theories was a crusade against arbitrariness in all its forms, in particular against the doctrine of arbitrary signs.[15] Physiognomics for Lavater was the worldly incarnation—literally—of a natural semiosis that closely approximated the cognitive immediacy he held to be the principal characteristic of divine consciousness. In his *Aussichten in die Ewigkeit* (Views on eternity), a set of essays published between 1768 and 1778 in the form of a collection of letters, Lavater recorded the principles that informed his religious philos-ophy, and here he first set down his belief in the language of physiognomy as an approximation of divine language (3: 108–17). But what is especially curious about Lavater's views is the manner in which they integrate cen-tral recognitions of Enlightenment epistemology with the transcendental-ism of the religious fanatic. In the thirteenth letter of this collection, for example, Lavater gives a capsule summary of Enlightenment cognitive the-ory when he distinguishes "intuitive cognition" from "symbolic cognition" on the basis of the types of signs each employs.

> If an object has an immediate effect on our senses, the impression we are conscious of as a result of this effect is called *sensual, intuitive* cognition, *perception*, experience.
>
> If an object does not have an immediate effect but instead is repre-sented to us by means of *arbitrary* signs, then our cognition is *nonsen-sual, logical, symbolic*. (3: 2–3)

The crucial distinguishing feature between these two types of knowledge, according to Lavater, is their degree of mediacy or immediacy. Intuitive cognition requires either no mediation at all, or mediation by means of

37

natural signs that are intrinsically related to the objects they signify. Symbolic cognition, by contrast, depends on the intervention of arbitrary signs. For Lavater, as for Enlightenment epistemology in general, the relationship between these types of cognition is conditioned by a specific telos: the aim of human cultural development is the progressive elimination of arbitrary signs, their elevation to the status of natural signs, so that ultimately symbolic, mediated knowledge would be completely replaced by intuitive, immediate knowledge (Wellbery 7). For Lavater, the Protestant preacher, this telos takes the form of a projection into the afterlife, where human cognition merges with the perfect knowledge of the Christian divinity (see *Aussichten* 3: 21–22).

When in the sixteenth letter from this collection Lavater sets about distinguishing this heavenly language from worldly language, he draws on an analogy from the realm of economic exchange:

> We would have just as little need of money if we possessed everything
> we wish to possess; or if we could exchange thoughts for thoughts, sen-
> sations for sensations with the very same ease with which we exchange
> compendious money for voluminous things. Money is not wealth, it is
> only a sign of wealth; the sign loses all its value when the signified thing
> is available in large enough quantities. All words, signs of thoughts, seem
> to lose their value, and will presumably disappear, when we will become
> capable of communicating our thoughts *immediately* to one another. (3:
> 104–05)

Much could be said about the implied economic theory that underwrites Lavater's transcendental utopia. While money is absent in most utopian social projections, what is curious about Lavater's vision is the *reason* why it becomes superfluous: his afterlife is one so suffused with immediate gratification of every imaginable sort that all signs, as the tokens of unfulfilled or delayed gratification, have become unnecessary. In other words, Lavater conceives heaven in terms of absolute immediacy and plenitude; it is a world of total excess, and where such fullness holds sway, signs, both monetary and linguistic, as the representations of absent things, simply disappear, because they no longer have any function. In other words, Lavater's paradise is a world without desire simply because it is one of absolute plenitude, one in which lack is unknown and every wish is immediately fulfilled.

Under such utopian conditions—marked by the absolute and immediate presence of all things—money and words, as signs of *absent* things, or as representations of what is lacking, would become wholly incidental. But what interests us here is not so much Lavater's transcendental perspective, with its implied economics of plenitude, excess, and universal gratification, as the principles underlying his notion of money that allow it to serve as a metaphor for human language, understood as counter to the pure, immediate language of heaven.

Clearly, Lavater is working with a peculiarly modern conception of money as a wholly symbolic mediator: money has no intrinsic value, is not specie, but has been reduced completely to a sign of value, to symbolic money as a representation of commodities. But what is especially curious—and especially telling—about Lavater's argument is the way he absolutizes symbolic money as money per se. He does not, as one might expect, juxtapose paper money and solid coin in order to distinguish between the artificial language of worldly existence and the genuine expression of the transcendental realm, but focuses instead on the notion of money in general as a medium of exchange. Money becomes the focal counterexample for an elucidation of divine language precisely because of its mediating and representational nature, which Lavater obviously accepts as its primary function. The reduction of money to its role as mediator, of course, is one of the central principles of modern economics, and Lavater's metaphor is capitalized by a rich investment from this economic philosophy. This metaphor, in fact, forms the locus of an ideological dialectic that invades Lavater's discourse. For in order to project the divine world as the transcendence of a worldly mediacy whose paradigmatic representatives are money and the arbitrary sign, Lavater must first acknowledge that these principles dominate economic and communicative exchange in the bourgeois world. In other words, Lavater already assumes an empirical reality whose economic and linguistic systems are so dependent on mediation, arbitrariness, and nominalism that the only world he can imagine as free of these principles is the transcendental realm of divine immediacy and superabundance. The demonization of arbitrary monetary and linguistic signs in the quotidian world of bourgeois exchange thereby merely serves Lavater as an ideological foil for the valorization of heaven as a domain that has no need for such artificial intermediaries.

If Lavater accepts the nominalism characteristic of the world of economic and communicative reality only in order to ideologically overcome it in a substantialist vision of the transcendental, Herder's theory of language develops as a bald attempt to deny that human language itself originates as a nominalist structure. In his *Abhandlung über den Ursprung der Sprache* (Treatise on the origin of language, 1772), Herder rejects the very conception of arbitrary signs, and he argues that all languages have as their source the same set of natural signs (500). He is especially emphatic in his repudiation of the idea that human language evolves by means of arbitrary societal convention: "Primitive man, the recluse in the woods," he maintains, "would have had to invent language for himself. . . . It was the understanding of his soul with itself, an understanding that was just as necessary as it was necessary that the human being was a human being" (*Abhandlung* 428). Language emerges, according to this theory, in a process of Adamic naming in which human beings stamp the "signature of the soul on a thing" (486). At the point when he seeks to lend this argument the most rhetorical force, Herder radically switches metaphorical registers and turns to a money metaphor: "And wouldn't for the first human being such a signature of the soul on a thing, by recognition, by characteristic feature, by language, not be just as much the mark of ownership as a stamp on a coin?" (486). Unfortunately, the metaphor Herder chooses, that of the stamp on a coin, is inconsistent with the substantialist theory he seeks to defend. What he apparently wants to say is that just as the stamp on a coin signifies the authenticity of its minting, the word, as a signature of the soul on a thing, is a brand that signifies universal ownership and guarantees verbal validity. The difficulty Herder apparently seeks to finesse with this image of the stamp on the coin seems to be the paradox of a universal individuality, for the mint is what assures the universal validity and value of the coin. According to his theory, each and every human "soul" would have to somehow be preprogrammed to identify everything it names by means of a unique, individual, and yet somehow *universal* "signature." Lacking some such form of universality, communication among human beings could never occur. Thus what Herder is attempting to broach with the metaphor of the imprint on a coin is precisely the universal acceptability of arbitrary linguistic denominations.

However, the stamp on a coin is not a sign of possession for those who use it, but merely the authorizing mark of the political entity that issues it. This imprint functions solely because it is instituted and underwritten by political authority, and it seems unlikely that Herder wanted to suggest such an authoritarian origin for language and meaning—unless he is relying here on an implicit theory of divine legislation. Moreover, the stamp, as the mark of that political authority that stands behind the coin, serves merely to guarantee the weight and purity of the metal of which it is made. Thus, according to Adam Smith, the practice of affixing "a publick stamp upon certain quantities of such particular metals" arose in order "to prevent . . . abuses, to facilitate exchanges, and thereby to encourage all sorts of industry and commerce" (1: 40). Viewed from this perspective, the stamp on the coin is nothing if not the embodiment of convention: it is, quite literally, the coin's nominalist aspect, and as such far removed from anything like a "signature of the soul." We recall that for Lessing's Nathan it is precisely coin "which but the stamp creates" that marks the paradigm shift from ancient, intrinsic money to the valueless symbolic currency of the modern world. What is noteworthy about Herder's metaphor, then, is that it actually undercuts the position he wants to defend. The fact that he turns to a money metaphor at all to buttress his conception of language's origin testifies to the fact that during this period the appeal to this metaphorical field was nothing if not obligatory for theoreticians of language. What Herder's metaphor betrays is that, even when he was still consciously attempting to support a substantivist view of language, he—like Leibniz and Lavater—had unconsciously come to accept the abstract, symbolic nature of money "which but the stamp creates."

Herder explicitly acknowledges the conventionality of minted coins in the first collection of his fragments *Über die neuere deutsche Literatur* (On recent German literature, 1767). Here he also employs the analogy of words and coins, but this time instead of applying it positively to underwrite the inherent significance of words, he uses it negatively to emphasize their abstract, arbitrary character: "Allow me to compare words that refer to abstract ideas [with coins]. Both are arbitrarily coined and become current by means of an arbitrarily established value; the most solid ones among both are hoarded as treasures, while the smaller ones are used to make change" (42). In this comparison, modern, abstract languages are likened to monetary economies in which value and significance are arbitrarily ordained and attain currency based solely on conventionalized usage. Some of these abstract words are "solid" coins whose nominal value closely approximates their inherent worth; others are inferior coins, token money, in which denomination and substance are greatly divergent. Herder's analogy is implicitly based on a linguistic version of Gresham's Law, which asserts that bad money will drive good money out of circulation because people will tend to hoard the latter. When applied to philosophical abstractions and notions of truth, this law has especially ironic consequences: it suggests—as Herder himself actually claims—that valuable concepts will be drawn out of circulation and that only faulty notions will be current in popular debate. The concession that certain abstract words can represent treasures worthy of hoarding hardly compensates for the debilitating consequence that they will thus tend to lose philosophical currency, and Herder's proposition here also stands apart from the otherwise austere critique of abstraction in language that he expresses both throughout this series of essays and in his *Abhandlung über den Ursprung der Sprache*. But what is especially significant is Herder's ability to exploit the comparison between money and language to defend both a traditional substantialist and a modern nominalist theory of language. That the nominalist interpretation of money and of language has already noticeably infiltrated and occupied Herder's thought is indicated by the fact that even when used to support a substantialist interpretation of language, the image of money he invokes is ineluctably, if subliminally, nominalist in character. Thus, while Herder is vociferous in his attack on the "spirit of commerce" (*Handelsgeist*), whose increasing dominance in the bourgeois world he laments, and warns his contemporaries that this commercial spirit threatens to supplant the spirit of wisdom (*Journal meiner Reise* 383, 410), his own theory of language is unwittingly informed and infected by this very spirit of commerce. As we will see in the next chapter, it was not until several decades later, in the thought of the German Romantics, that the commercialism of bourgeois monetary and philosophical exchange could be openly embraced as a mechanism harboring enormous creative—and value-creative—potential.

Although German bourgeois intellectuals of the eighteenth century could apparently not escape the contagion of capitalist commercialism, few confronted the realities of the emerging international market and its nominalist monetary economy as directly as did Johann Georg Hamann. To be sure, like Leibniz, Lavater, and Herder, Hamann also hypostatized an ideal mode of thought believed to exist outside the abstraction of money and arbitrary signs. However, he identified this realm of immediacy not as an originary, affective natural language, as did Leibniz and Herder, nor as divine cognition, as did Lavater, but rather as the domain of religious belief. In a letter to Friedrich Jacobi (1743–1819) dated 30 April 1787, Hamann states apodictically, "Belief is not for everyone, and also not communicable like a commodity" (*Briefwechsel* 7: 156). In a bourgeois world increasingly dominated by the principle of exchange, belief becomes for Hamann the only mode of human thought and expression that escapes the logic of commodification. To be free of this logic, however, is to be noncommunicable in a double sense: neither transferable as a commodity, nor communicable through language, so that belief takes on—coherent with Pietistic views—a wholly personal and monadic character. Striking also is Hamann's antiegalitarian posture: if the free market is the great democratizer that makes—in theory, at least—all things available to all people (we are reminded of Lavater's utopia of heavenly abundance), then religious belief is the only value not subject to this universal marketability. However, as we will see in chapter 5, devoted to an analysis of Johann Heinrich Jung-Stilling's *Lebensgeschichte*, Hamann's attempts to insulate the terrain of religious belief from the encroachments of economic discourse must ultimately be regarded, even in the narrower context of German Pietism, as largely unsuccessful.

If Hamann can rescue belief from the abstraction of exchange only by denying that it is a language, then this bespeaks an acceptance of language as a fundamentally arbitrary system. And indeed, Hamann is one of the first German intellectuals to come to terms in a significant way with the arbitrary nature of the linguistic sign. In this sense he is an important precursor to the Jena Romantics, people like Novalis and Adam Müller, who will ardently defend the arbitrary character of both the linguistic and the monetary sign. In his "Metakritik über den Purismum der Vernunft" (Metacritique of the purism of reason, 1784), Hamann admits that the meaning of words derives from the "connection of an a priori arbitrary and indifferent . . . verbal sign with the intuition of the object itself" (226). At the same time, he cannot give himself over absolutely to this doctrine, so he restricts it with the qualification that the connection between verbal sign and object, though a priori arbitrary, is a posteriori necessary (226). Arbitrariness is thereby sublated into the pragmatic principle of the consistent and accurate use of any particular verbal sign. It is in keeping with Hamann's qualified acceptance of the arbitrary nature of the linguistic sign that the applications of monetary metaphors in his discussions of language underscore language's functional, systematic aspects. In a passage from his *Sokratische Denkwürdigkeiten* (Socratic memoirs, 1759), for example, Hamann stresses precisely the relativity and context-bounded quality of meaning: "Words have their value, like numbers, based on the place in which they stand, and the determination and relations of their concepts are, like coins, variable according to time and place" (75). Of significance here is not only Hamann's historicizing thesis, which opens up linguistic signs to variable interpretation over time, but also his assertion that the meanings of words cannot be separated from the relationships they enter into when used in certain contexts. Hamann obviously assumes that coins do not possess any absolute, intrinsic value, and he uses this understanding of money to deny that words have any specific a priori meanings. What makes Hamann's appropriation of the coin-word comparison so radical is the way it breaks with the traditional use of this analogy. For if the comparison of coins and words is generally employed to elucidate the referential function of language, Hamann's emphasis on the context-bound nature of coins and words evokes its systematic, syntagmatic function. He thus reveals himself to be a proto-structuralist who anticipates the Saussurean insight that the value of verbal signs is determined by their relational structure with other signs.

The metaphor with which Hamann opens his essay "Vermischte Anmerkungen über die Wortstellung in der französischen Sprache" (Mixed remarks on word order in the French language, 1761) likewise relies on an analogy between money and language that highlights their structural and systematic isomorphism.

> Money and language are two objects whose examination is as profound and abstract as their use is universal. Both stand in a closer relationship than one would otherwise suppose. The theory of one explains the the-

ory of the other; for this reason, they appear to derive from common grounds. The richness of all human knowledge is based on the exchange of words. . . . All the goods . . . of commercial and social life relate to money as their general measure. (97)

Hamann appears in this passage as a precursor of Karl Marx insofar as he not only acknowledges money as the general equivalent in bourgeois commerce, but also recognizes that under the conditions of the capitalist marketplace all human interactions are mediated by money as the absolute measure of all things. Marx radicalizes this view in his "Ökonomisch-philosophische Manuskripte" (Economic-philosophical manuscripts, 1842) when he writes, "Since money, as the existing and active concept of value, confuses [*verwechselt*], exchanges [*vertauscht*] all things, it is hence the universal *confusion* [*Verwechslung*] and *exchange* [*Vertauschung*] of all things" (566). The same insight that underwrites Marx's critique of money as the embodiment of human alienation in capitalist societies informs Hamann's variation on the comparison of words and coins: this is the awareness that money concretizes a basic form of representation and symbolization that extends into myriad realms of human intersubjective behavior. Hamann's metaphors indicate that he perceives the intimate interrelationship between the linguistic and financial domains as structured systems, an insight that Niklas Luhmann would later formalize in his systems-theory approach to economics, which defines economic exchange as a form of communication (*Wirtschaft* 14). The common element that determines their isomorphism is their character as processes of exchange based on the circulation of arbitrary signs. With this we return to the protocapitalist theory of symbolic money's productive power that informed Leibniz's use of the money-language metaphor.

Economics and the Paradigm Shift in Linguistic Theory

We are justified, I believe, in taking Hamann's statement about the close relationship between money and language at face value: for eighteenth-century philosophers of language, economic theory appeared to be intimately related to linguistic theory. But what the examples from Leibniz, Lavater, Herder, and Hamann demonstrate is an incipient equivocation and transformation in the conception of the money-language analogy. If this metaphor traditionally endorsed a substantivist theory of referential meaning by comparing truthful words with full-weight coins whose constant value is guaranteed by their intrinsic worth, in the eighteenth century this version of the metaphor is increasingly supplanted by one that underscores the nominalist view that the truth of words, like the value of symbolic money, is established extrinsically and syntagmatically by their systematic function in the circulation of language. This has far-reaching implications especially where eighteenth-century semiotics is concerned; for if semiotic thought of this period is constantly rent by an ambivalence toward the arbitrary character of linguistic signs, which it views simultaneously as the instrument of productive thinking and the source of delusion and error (Wellbery 5), then this conflicted assessment reflects the eighteenth century's ambivalence toward token money as the arbitrary representation of economic value as well.

The fact that the four thinkers discussed here attempt to hold on to a substantialist view of linguistic truth while simultaneously employing metaphors that tend rather to valorize the functionalist, nominalist conception of linguistic signs betrays the degree to which they were ultimately attracted by the possibilities of a semiotic system that, like the token money of emergent capitalist theory, would be capable of producing and increasing knowledge based simply on the deployment of "well-made" signs. Leibniz, Lavater, and Herder, at least, were linguistic and epistemological "metallists" who nonetheless unconsciously transferred the virtues of paper currency to their theories of language and knowledge. They accepted the abstract, arbitrary nature of money before accepting the nominalist, conventional, and systematic interpretation of language. However, they unwittingly read the abstract character of money into their theories of language by way of their use of money metaphors. Hamann is the first openly to embrace this modern, structuralist conception of language and to apply metaphors of money that are coherent with this view. His implicit critique of these economic and linguistic realities, however, is reflected in the attempt to cordon off religious belief, as the sole remaining realm of authentic and unmediated knowledge and expression, from the acknowledged semiotic mediation and nominalism of bourgeois economic and linguistic commerce. What we witness in the intellectual trajectory from Leibniz to Hamann, then, is the gradual jettisoning of substantivist conceptions of language through the analogy with an increasingly functionalist monetary system. This is a process by which these bourgeois intellectuals literally buy into signs. Experiencing in the concrete economic realm of capitalistic monetary practice the productive potential of "properly employed signs," they begin to accept a vision of language as an artificial construct, a relational system of arbitrary tokens with the potential vastly to increase the stores of human knowledge. The vision they share, to a greater or lesser degree, is a conception of language as a money of the mind, and they imagine themselves as the *nouveaux riches* of bourgeois thought.

If we extend the line of the trajectory sketched here, it leads us to the early German Romantics, in particular to Novalis and Adam Müller, each of whom embraced and valorized the arbitrary nature of linguistic and monetary signs. If for Novalis the use of words in speculative philosophy is reminiscent of the concept of money ("Das allgemeine Brouillon" 378–79), Müller's economic theory turns on a celebration of paper money as the principal monetary form because it is pure stamp, pure sign of the credit and credibility of the state (*Versuche einer neuen Theorie des Geldes* 139–40). These are deliberations, however, that go beyond the subject of the present chapter; thus until they can be redeemed by the arguments of subsequent analysis, they will, for the time being, have to be bought on credit.

2 / HYPERSIGN, HYPERMONEY, HYPERMARKET

Adam Müller's Theory of Money and Romantic Semiotics

Money is not merely the absolutely fungible object . . . , rather it is the fungibility of things personified.

—Georg Simmel (*Philosophie des Geldes* 128)

Thoroughly Contrary Müller

IN A LETTER TO HIS FRIEND FRIEDRICH VON GENTZ (1764–1832) dated 13 September 1802, Adam Müller (1779–1829) emphatically states, "My entire existence turns, as you know, around the notion of contrariety [*Gegensatz*]" (*Lebenszeugnisse* 1: 37). In the most concrete sense, this reference to the role of *Gegensatz*, of contrariety, opposition, and antithesis in Müller's life, refers simply to his first intellectual project, his *Die Lehre vom Gegensatz* (The doctrine of contrariety, 1804), on which he was working at the time he composed this letter. In a more profound sense, however, Müller's statement points to the central position of the idea of opposition, of interactive contraries, for the entirety of his thought and his philosophy of life. This deeper meaning is confirmed in a letter to Karl Gustav von Brinkmann (1764–1847) written almost two years later, on 10 April 1804, just prior to the publication of Müller's *Lehre vom Gegensatz*. In this letter Müller unequivocally asserts, "Never distinguish . . . my life from the matter of contrariety [*Gegensatzes*]. All the phenomena of my life, the smallest and the largest alike, are directed toward it, no single thought or action strays from this sphere, all of them have their stable and eternal place in it" (*Lebenszeugnisse* 1: 128–29). Here Müller clearly identifies the concept of contrariety as the anchoring principle of his entire existence, the sun in the solar system of his diverse intellectual pursuits.

The idea of contrariety, defined as a kind of equilibrium of opposites, does indeed run like a constant leitmotif throughout Müller's works. In his anthropological thought, this concept describes the interrelation between the sexes; in his political doctrine, it defines the relationship between the aristocratic and bourgeois classes; in his theory of eloquence it is codified in the dialogic structure that, according to Müller, informs all effective speech;[1] in his economic theory, finally, it takes the form of a fundamental reciprocity among people and between people and commodities. In Müller's economics, *Gegensatz* is transmogrified into *Wechselwirkung*, reciprocity or mutual interchange, the dynamic give-and-take that forms the basis of all economic exchange. Money, both as matter and as concept, takes center stage in Müller's economic thinking because it is the epitome, the highest manifestation, of this reciprocal relationship. Contrariety, reciprocity, dialogue, dialectic: these are the various names with which Müller designates the primary figure of his thought, the productive interaction of opposing principles or forces.[2]

Beyond identifying the fundamental structure of Müller's thought, the term *Gegensatz* also fittingly describes the critical reception that Müller and his writings have undergone. Indeed, Müller's statement that contrariety informs his entire existence can be read as an ironically prophetic commentary on his intellectual legacy, which is marked by radically opposing views, especially where his political stance is concerned. Even in the closely circumscribed field of German studies, Adam Müller is scarcely a household name. Where he is known, he is often recognized only through his association with some of the major poets and thinkers of the first half of the nineteenth century, not for his own writings. Müller was deeply influenced by his friend Friedrich von Hardenberg (1772–1801), more commonly known by the pen name Novalis.[3] His respect and admiration for this leading figure of the so-called Jena Romantic Circle was so great that Müller planned, but never realized, an edition of Novalis's posthumous papers.[4] Müller was also lifelong friends with two other prominent members of the Jena Circle, the brothers August Wilhelm (1767–1845) and Friedrich Schlegel (1772–1829).[5] But he is perhaps best known as the discoverer of, and collaborator with, the late-Romantic writer Heinrich von Kleist (1777–1811), with whom Müller jointly edited the short-lived literary journal *Phöbus*. Kleist and Müller also later collaborated on the publication of the *Berliner Abendblatt*; in fact, Müller's role in the financial insolvency of this journal put tremendous strain on the otherwise close relationship between the two partners and friends and perhaps played a role in Kleist's untimely suicide.[6]

Born into solid bourgeois conditions as the son of a Prussian finance official in 1779, Müller eschewed his Protestant upbringing, his Prussian roots, and his bourgeois social background. In 1805, on a visit to Vienna, he converted to Catholicism, joining the wave of Romantics who were becoming born-again Catholics. From this time on his political allegiances lay with Catholic Austria, a state that, in Müller's mind, came closer to approximating the feudal political order he, like so many German Romantics, thoroughly idealized. In 1826, on the recommendation of Prince Clemens von Metternich (1773–1859), the autocrat of the post-Napoleonic Restoration in central Europe, Müller was elevated to the social status of a noble, and he henceforth carried the aristocratic title Ritter von Nitterdorf. Müller's venomous attacks on the principles of the French Revolution—in which he closely followed the arguments outlined by Edmund Burke (1729–97) in his *Reflections on the Revolution in France*, a work that was translated into German by Müller's friend and mentor Friedrich von Gentz[7]—and his close political collaboration with Prince Metternich and the forces of the post-1815 Restoration have earned him the reputation as a profoundly conservative political thinker. Moreover, Müller's indictment of individualism, his belief that the citizens of a state should sacrifice themselves totally for the well-being of the political order, and his glorification of war as the necessary and productive form of political conflict have caused some critics to view him as a thinker who helped pave the way for some of the more pernicious sociopolitical principles of German fascism.

By the same token, Müller is often cited as an uncommonly pragmatic and progressive thinker where his economic theories are concerned, and in the period between the world wars Othmar Spann's (1878–1950) Universalist school sparked a veritable Müller renaissance in the discipline of economics. To be sure, Müller's economic doctrines draw much of their energy from his opposition to the economic liberalism of Adam Smith (1723–90). Indeed, many of Müller's economic policies are formulated in direct contradistinction to Smith's principles. For example, where Smith defends the division of labor, Müller opposes it; while Smith argues for the autonomy of the market and defends laissez-faire economic practices, Müller takes an interventionist stance, giving absolute authority over economic matters to the state; Smith valorizes competition as productive and cost-effective, whereas Müller vilifies it as the cause of human strife and disunity; Smith views private property as the holy shrine of sound economic theory and sees the protection of property rights as the primary purpose of the state, while Müller sees private property as a demonic institution that fuels human egoism and undermines the communitarianism necessary for any well-functioning state; finally, Smith is a confirmed metallist who argues the importance of specie as the primary monetary form, whereas Müller is a monetary nominalist, a staunch advocate of paper currencies.

The radicality of Müller's critique of classical liberal economic doctrine is best evidenced by a sample quotation. In the essay "Von der Notwendigkeit einer theologischen Grundlage der gesamten Staatswissenschaften und der Staatswirtschaft insbesondere" (On the necessity of a theological foundation for all the sciences of state and of political economy in particular, 1820), Müller seems to be testing the discursive registers that will shape the vitriolic rhetoric of two later critics of economic liberalism, Karl Marx and Friedrich Engels.

> Slavery to money, the form of slavery that is dominant today, is the worst form of slavery because it is tied to a false sense of apparent freedom. It makes no difference whether one sells me off once and for all or resells me anew each day; instead of taking responsibility for my body and therefore placing it in one's care, one only extracts from it its essential element, its energy, and sardonically leaves me the rest of the carcass to dispose of freely. (*Schriften zur Staatsphilosophie* 232)

Slavery to money, a slavery that masquerades as personal freedom, drains the individual of all its energy and vitality and leaves behind nothing but an empty shell, a powerless and worthless body. Müller invests just as much vehemence and rhetorical capital in his attack on the division of labor, which induces him to introduce the notion of *Entfremdung*, of alienation, into the political-economic vocabulary decades before the term is used in this way by Marx and Engels.[8] Müller thus holds the dubious distinction of being one of the few nineteenth-century German intellectuals who has come to be interpreted both as a protofascist political thinker and as a proto-Marxist economic theoretician. Faced by such apparent contradictions, it is tempting to claim that Müller's thought was simply fractured by irresolvable inconsistencies. This is, in fact, what many of Müller's contemporaries believed, and they openly accused him of intellectual malleability, lack of firm principles, even mendacity and opportunism.[9] But Müller himself supplies the foundation that helps make sense of these apparent contradictions: they are nothing other than those productive *Gegensätze*, those contrarieties, oppositions, and antitheses, which Müller claimed were the very substance of his intellectual existence.

Fiduciary Money and the Hypermarket of Incessant Circulation

Müller's unabashed advocacy of fiat money, of paper currencies as pure signs of value, is undoubtedly both his most controversial and his most forward-looking economic idea. While Müller already formulated a rudimentary form of this principle in his *Elemente der Staatskunst* (Elements of statecraft), first published in 1810,[10] his full-blown theory of money only appeared in 1816 under the title *Versuche einer neuen Theorie des Geldes* (Attempts at a new theory of money). The manuscript for this work, according to Müller, was completed already in the years 1810 and 1811, in response to the furious debate that raged in economic circles in Europe about the precarious depreciation of the London bank notes.[11] In this treatise, Müller comes down squarely on the side of credit money, of paper currencies. He explicitly argues, for example, against the notion, common at this time, that paper money is a mere second-order representation of metallic money; in fact, he reverses this relationship, giving priority to the "word," to the stamp that makes metal into minted coin: "[T]he principal thing is what by means of a stamp, by means of a kind of credit, first elevates metal to the status of money, and which in the further development of civil society is represented in bank notes" (*Versuche* 140). Legal tender, in other words, is constituted not by any intrinsic value, by the worth of the precious metals from which it is made, but by the "credit"—that is, the faith, belief, and confidence—placed in it and in the state that secures its value. We should recall here that the very term "fiduciary money," commonly used to designate purely symbolic currencies, derives from the Latin word *fides*, or "trust," and stresses precisely the element of confidence, faith, and credit—in the sense of credibility—that lends such monetary symbols their economic power. For Müller this credence constitutes the essence of money, and hence he views paper currencies as the logical extension and natural culmination of the monetary form, the pure expression, as legal tender, of this faith and confidence in the state that issues the currency and in the community that uses it. "The true essence of paper money," he writes in *Versuche*, "namely an ideal money, is already present to the extent that there are coins, and it is the indispensable condition of possibility for a coin as such" (196). Using the terminology of German critical philosophy, Müller calls "ideal money," the word or stamp that certifies a coin's authenticity, the "condition of possibility" of money as such: there is no monetary instrument if one strips away this ideal element, this symbol or sign that expresses a communal accord, a mutual promise or obligation.

This belief in the fundamentally intangible nature of money leads Müller to a radical hypothesis about the history of the monetary form. He opposes the claim that the history of human commerce can be broken down into a period of barter, prior to the introduction of monetary instruments, and exchange proper, where money or some other supercommodity functions as a general equivalent that facilitates the transfer of goods. Even in the simple barter economy, according to Müller, a third term, a form of ideal money, is present: this is the intangible trust, the interrelationship and interdependence of the bartering partners, which must underwrite even the most primitive act of exchange (*Versuche* 180–82). Thus money, for Müller, is nothing other than the representative, the symbol, of this natural sociability, this solicitous codependence among human beings.[12] As such, his theory of money is "idealistic" in the twofold sense of that word: it is based on a somewhat naive idealization of the human instincts for community, on the one hand, and on the other hand it relies on an idealization, a desubstantialization of money in the philosophical sense. In this regard, Müller's monetary theory clearly upholds the thesis, defended most vigorously by Jean-Joseph Goux, that the common cause uniting philosophical idealism and the modern monetary economy resides in their deprivileging of matter and coin in favor of intangible abstractions about the pure idea of value (Goux 96–97).

The astonishingly progressive and radical nature of Müller's monetary theory cannot be fully appreciated when divorced from its historical context. Skepticism toward paper currency was widespread in Europe at this time. David Hume, for example, referred in his essay "On Money" to paper currency as "counterfeit money" (311), and Adam Smith, Müller's self-chosen economic adversary, believed that paper currencies threatened to undermine "the commercial and moral fabric of European civilization" (qtd. in Hirst 26). It is well known that in part 2 of *Faust*, Goethe associated paper money with the work of the devil, and he thereby expressed the common belief of the period that fiat currency represented a kind of diabolical alchemy that produced value out of nothing (*Faust* lines 6037–71).[13] Even on the level of practical experience there was little at this time that spoke in favor of an economic theory that defended fiduciary money. John Law's unsuccessful experiment in France had not been forgotten, and during the French Revolution, of course, the Jacobins had introduced the notoriously unstable assignats. Given Müller's opposition to everything else even remotely connected with the French Revolution, it would seem that this association alone would be enough to turn him into an opponent of paper money. Closer to home, the state of Prussia introduced bank notes in 1806; but the Prussian defeats at Jena and Auerstedt soon led to the steep depreciation and ultimate collapse of this currency. This is the economic context in which Müller's advocacy of fiat money must be viewed if we are to appreciate the truly controversial nature of his monetary and economic policies. The question then becomes, On what basis and by means of what principles did Müller ground and defend his theory of money as an essentially ideal and nonmaterial phenomenon? My hypothesis is that Müller's valorization of sign-money is based on the semiotic theory and linguistic philosophy of his fellow Romantics, especially on the thought of

Novalis. Müller himself was quite open about the influence of Novalis's thought on his economic theories, and he acknowledged this in a footnote to his treatise (*Versuche* 126). Yet if it has become a veritable commonplace to interpret Müller's political theories as a transposition of Romantic aesthetic positions into the sociopolitical realm,[14] scholars have completely ignored the close proximity of Müller's economic doctrines to Romantic poetic principles, in particular his reliance on their sophisticated semiotic theories.

In order to address this issue we must begin by placing Müller's theory of money within the context of his overall economic principles, above all the function he ascribes to money in the workings of the political economy. The first point to be made here is that Müller is a fanatical circulationist who believes that the significance of money lies in its ability to advance and intensify commercial exchange. This stress on money as the medium of circulation follows directly from Müller's belief that monetary ties symbolize the interpersonal bonds joining human beings together into a community. Early in his *Versuche einer neuen Theorie des Geldes* he thus claims,

> In money, in a universally valid commodity that is accepted by everyone, the entire personality, the most personal bond that ties together laborers and consumers, makes itself manifest. . . . The bond of manufacturing and of the market is actually a personal bond, just as money, which can only be conceived in circulation, moving from one person to another and mediating between two people, can never be conceived as an object of absolute private property. (29)

Müller opposes the idea, common in the eighteenth century, that monetary economies are wholly impersonal and hence disrupt and alienate intersubjective bonds among individuals. The German economist Johann Georg Büsch (1728–1800), for example, wrote in his *Abhandlung von dem Geldsumlauf* (Treatise on the circulation of money, 1780), "Wherever money is employed, no one is tied any longer to particular individuals in order to satisfy his needs from those individuals" (1: 156). For Müller, by contrast, money manifests precisely that interpersonal bond that links two individuals in exchange, the mutual obligation that they enter into by making a commitment of compensation with equal value. This explains why in both his economic and his political theories Müller idealizes the feudal relationship between lord and serf, since for him this relationship is marked by fealty, by mutual interdependence and obligation. As the serf commits his labor and energy to the lord, the lord offers protection and social security to the serf (see *Versuche* 145). To be sure, if money were symbolized by pure matter, by the market value of the precious metals that constitute it, for example, then it would represent a merely reified, purely economic connection. But according to Müller's theory, the essence of money is the word-sign, as oath or promise, that passes between two individuals, and as such it is the symbol of a wholly personal, communitarian bond that joins together laborer and consumer, seller and buyer. The idealized money Müller defends thus has no value in itself, nor need it have any intrinsic value, since its worth derives from its mediating function, the bond it forges between two or more individuals or between people and commodities. We see here how Müller anticipates by almost one hundred years the central thesis of Georg Simmel's *Philosophie des Geldes* (Philosophy of money, 1900), which similarly reduces the significance of money purely to its functional role in exchange and circulation (see 128).

The quoted passage also indicates the strategic position Müller's non-material conception of money has in his crusade against the principles of Smithian liberal economics: if money only has value when circulating, when mediating between distinct objects and different individuals, then it can never be the basis of private property. With this, Müller rejects the entire idea of monetary capital as a value in and of itself. But Müller's doctrine also opposes Adam Smith's liberal economic policies on a much more profound, human-psychological level. For if Smith was convinced that economic human beings pursue first and foremost their own self-interest, and only unwittingly, as a by-product of self-interest, further the common good— this is the argument supported by his famous metaphor of the "invisible hand" (1: 456)—Müller completely reverses these priorities. For him, economic human beings do not exist prior to acts of exchange, quasi as monadic, self-interested subjects, but are produced qua economic beings by this primordial act of exchange, which already constitutes the most rudimentary form of community. Exchange, by very definition, both generates and presupposes that trust and communitarianism that for Müller defines the very essence of symbolic money. This is the sense in which for him—as we will see in more detail in the next chapter—symbolic currency can assume the properties of an identifying mark, similar to a banner or a flag, that unites a community of users as a distinct and recognizable group.

Incessant consumption, never-ending exchange—not the hoarding of monetary tokens—is thus the iron law that underpins Müller's economics. The analogy to language, to which Müller frequently turns to elucidate the function of money, is germane here: words only have value when used in communication, when placed into a relation of exchange with others; words never have any worth when "hoarded" or left unstated. Just as there can be no verbal capital, for Müller there can also be no monetary capital, since its worth is constituted in the dynamic of exchange, in the interrelationship of things, in the *Wechselwirkung*, the reciprocity of circulation itself.[15] Thus Müller openly criticizes the very idea of profit, what he calls the "insane notion [*Wahn*] of an absolutely tangible surplus of production over consumption, of return over expenditure," because every surplus, all profit, must be reinvested, must remain part of the great "interchange [*Wechselwirkung*] of production and consumption," in order to have any economic significance whatsoever (*Versuche* 76). Müller's view of the economic and monetary system is quite simply a *perpetuum mobile*, an absolutely dynamic process of consumption and production, of economic "death" and economic "life," to use his own metaphors (76), in which nothing ever attains a position of absolute stasis. That is precisely what Müller objects to in private property and hoarded capital: it is productive potential that has been withdrawn from the dynamic system of never-ending circulation and hence becomes "dead," that is, unproductive capital.

In this regard, at least, the French physiocrats might be viewed as significant precursors of Müller's economic program; for the physiocrats also defended the significance of reinvesting profit into production and promoted the dynamics of circulation. Indeed, François Quesnay's (1694–1774) remarkable and innovative *tableau économique* was ingenious precisely because it portrayed in relatively simple graphic form the flow of economic energy—of money and value—from production to consumption and back again to production.[16] In short, the *tableau* demonstrates precisely the economic give-and-take of economic forces that Müller would later defend as the essence of economic activity as such, namely its interactive nature as dynamic *Wechselwirkung* (fig. 1). What Müller advocates might be termed

TABLEAU ÉCONOMIQUE.

Objets à considérer, 1.º Trois sortes de dépenses ; 2.º leur source ; 3.º leurs avances ; 4.º leur distribution ; 5.º leurs effets ; 6.º leur reproduction ; 7.º leurs rapports entr'elles ; 8.º leurs rapports avec la population ; 9.º avec l'Agriculture ; 10.º avec l'industrie ; 11.º avec le commerce ; 12.º avec la masse des richesses d'une Nation.

DÉPENSES PRODUCTIVES *relatives à l'Agriculture, &c*	DÉPENSES DU REVENU, *l'Impôt prélevé, se partage aux Dépenses productives et aux Dépenses stériles.*	DÉPENSES STERILES *relatives à l'industrie, &c*

Avances annuelles *pour produire un revenu de 600.ᵗᵗ sont 600.ᵗᵗ*
600. *produisent net* 600.ᵗᵗ

Revenu annuel de

Avances annuelles *pour les Ouvrages des Dépenses stériles, sont* 300.ᵗᵗ

Productions .... *moitié* .... *moitié passe ici Ouvrages, &c.*

300.ᵗᵗ *reproduisent net* .... 300.ᵗᵗ *moitié* .... *moitié* 300.ᵗᵗ
passe ici

150. *reproduisent net* .... 150. ... *moitié &c* ... *moitié* .... 150.

75. *reproduisent net* .... 75. .... 75.

37.10. *reproduisent net* ...... 37.10. .... 37..10

18..15. *reproduisent net* .... 18..15. .... 18..15

9....7....6. *reproduisent net* ...... 9....7....6. .... 9....7....6.

4..13....9. *reproduisent net* ...... 4..13....9. .... 4..13....9

2..6..10. *reproduisent net* ...... 2..6..10. .... 2..6..10

1....3....5. *reproduisent net* .... 1....3....5. .... 1..3..5

0....11....8. *reproduisent net* .... 0..11..8. .... 0..11..8

0...5..10. *reproduisent net* .... 0...5..10. .... 0..5..10

0....2..11. *reproduisent net* .... 0....2..11. .... 0..2..11

0....1....5. *reproduisent net* .... 0....1..5 .... 0..1..5

&c.

REPRODUIT TOTAL .... 600.ᵗᵗ *de revenu ; de plus, les frais annuels de 600.ᵗᵗ et les interêts des avances primitives du Laboureur, de 300.ᵗᵗ que la terre restitue. Ainsi la reproduction est de 1500.ᵗᵗ compris le revenu de 600.ᵗᵗ qui est la base du calcul, abstraction faite de l'impôt prélevé, et des avances qu'exige sa reproduction annuelle, &c. Voyez l'Explication à la page suivante.*

1 / François Quesnay's *tableau économique* of 1759. The first attempt at a graphic illustration of the economy as a closed system of dynamic interactions among mutually interdependent elements.

consumerism with a vengeance. I have chosen to give it the somewhat more neutral designation of a "hypermarket," a nexus of furious and incessant exchange: economics as a giant juggling act in which an infinite number of commodities or monetary signs are constantly in circulation, without any of them ever coming to a standstill or being withdrawn from the game of exchange. In this regard Müller once again anticipates the position of Simmel almost a hundred years later, who writes in his *Philosophie des Geldes*, "There is certainly no clearer symbol for the absolutely dynamic character of the world than money. The meaning of money resides in the act of its expenditure; as soon as it is at rest it no longer has the specific value and meaning of money per se. . . . [Money] is nothing but the vehicle of a dynamic process in which everything that is not itself dynamic is completely eradicated" (714).

The Differential Nature of Monetary Signs and Economic Values

Müller's definition of money as pure sign, as an entity lacking any material, inherent value of its own, is strategically calculated to support this system of perpetual circulation. "In and of itself money," he maintains, "the most marketable commodity, has no value, and it is absolutely nothing without the traffic between people and things . . . ; but conversely there is also no traffic between people and things without this higher mediating entity, without money" (*Versuche* 181–82). As the "higher" third term, money is nothing but the most tangible manifestation of this reciprocal process itself: it is mediation embodied—embodied not in precious metals or in paper, but in the *word*, in a sign, in the stamp of authority. The monetary sign, as sign, points to the interactive process of communication and stands in for that "credit" or "credibility," that interpersonal obligation, which Müller sees as the condition of possibility for all exchange. As such, dematerialized money, money as pure sign, as "fiat" or fiduciary currency, becomes a kind of hypermoney that fuels the hypermarket Müller imagines as an infinite process of circulation. Indeed, as the above quotation indicates, for Müller there are no economic "objects," no commodities with any value in and of themselves. They too, like money, have been dematerialized, or at least their economic value has been displaced from the things themselves to their relations with other things or with human beings as potential consumers. In other words, in Müllerian economics there are no positive terms, no objects that have inherent value; rather, all economic value is the product of a differential system, of reciprocal relationships among objects, on the one side, and consumers, on the other. I have formulated this statement in conscious analogy to Ferdinand de Saussure's famous dictum about language from his *Course in General Linguistics*: "[I]n language there are only differences *without positive terms*" (120). Müller's economic and monetary doctrines, with their emphasis on synergetic interrelations and reciprocal interactions, function much like the structural system of language theorized by Saussure.

If Müller's dialectical thought figure of contrariety and reciprocity is driven by any philosophical agenda, then this is his fundamentally antiessentialist worldview. In a central passage from his treatise on money, he claims that "the goods of life [are] nothing in and of themselves, . . . they only [become] something by means of a certain symbolic usage" (*Versuche* 78). This statement applies *mutatis mutandis* for Müller's theory of money as well, since for him money has no significance as substance in and of itself, but only by means of its symbolic—today we would say its semiotic— implementation. It is no coincidence, then, that in his first and most philosophical treatise, *Die Lehre vom Gegensatz*, Müller explicitly indicts the Kantian notion of the thing-in-itself (203).[17] This displacement of self-identify and a priori givenness into value constitution by means of differential or structural relations is one of the constants of Müller's thought, concretized in the leitmotif of *Gegensatz* and reciprocal relations. It should be clear, then, that in Müller's view there are no economic things-in-themselves, no economic values-in-themselves, but only relations among commodities, on the one hand, and consumers, on the other. This is precisely what makes his economic theory "structuralist" in the Saussurean sense. Thus already at the end of the first chapter of his *Versuche einer neuen Theorie des Geldes*, Müller asserts that anyone who deals with the issue of political economy must recognize first and foremost "*that everywhere he is dealing with relationships [Verhältnissen] and reciprocal interchanges [Wechselwirkungen]*" (13).

One of Müller's primary objections to traditional liberal economic doctrine, especially to Smithian economics, is its overemphasis of substance, of economic "facts," of quantification, to the detriment of relations, dynamic interdependencies, and reciprocal interactions. This is concretized for Müller in Smith's preference for specie, in his defense of private property, and in his emphasis on the role of surplus and capital as economic stimulants. Near the conclusion of his *Versuche*, Müller expresses the belief that he has unequivocally proven "the extent to which the neglect of economic *relations* [*Verhältnisse*] has distorted all economic points of view as such" (274). In order to stress once more the significance of relationships as the primary phenomena of political economy, Müller turns to an extended analogy with language.

> Just as language, in its proper and perfect usage—as one can witness in the works of the great writers of all time—contains both a signifying [*bezeichnendes*] and a representational [*abbildendes*], an arithmetic and a geometric element, the barbarism of our age, like that of all other Alexandrian times, has established the essence of science to consist in the exclusive cultivation of the signifying or arithmetic element of language. People have come to believe that the absolutely essential, indeed, holy element that literature expresses by means of rhythm, through metaphors, and in the differences of its distinct forms, is not only unnecessary in science, but should be banished from it. Science is whatever can be expressed in signs, in numbers, in symbols [*Chiffren*]. (275)

This passage reveals a great deal about how Müller understood his economic project. On the most obvious level, he lays claim to having eschewed economics as a strict science dependent on mere numbers and calculations and to having introduced a poetic element into its study. This distinction between "scientific" and "poetic" approaches to one and the same object is concretized in two distinct functions of language, which Müller designates with two complementary sets of oppositions. On the one hand, he contrasts the "denotative" (*bezeichnendes*) structure of scientific discourse with the "representational" (*abbildendes*) function of poetic language; on the other hand, he circumscribes or elucidates this first opposition by supplementing it with that between "arithmetic" structures, associated with science, and "geometrical" patterns, associated with poetry. We can best decipher precisely what Müller means by these terms if we deal with them in reverse order. The opposition between the arithmetic and the geometrical modes of understanding is central to Müller's entire tract on money, and it is likely that he derived this opposition from his friend, the poet Novalis.[18] Müller gives a highly illuminating example of what he means by "arithmetic" and "geometric" functions earlier in this work (see *Versuche* 204). Arithmetic refers to things that are purely quantifiable and measurable, and Müller cites the length of a straight line as an example of something that can be arrived at by arithmetic means. To this he contrasts the measure of the angle created by the intersection of any two lines. This angle, in this respect exemplary for what Müller calls geometric functions, can only be arrived at and expressed through its relationship to the other angle produced by this junction and by its measure relative to the 360 degrees of a full circle. Thus, what Müller understands under "geometric" measures is nothing other than values that are not given in themselves, but that can only be derived from their relationship to something else or to a differential structure. In other words, arithmetic sums are absolute and self-identical, whereas geometric sums are relative and reciprocal, measured in contradistinction and in relationship to something else.

If we now transfer this recognition to Müller's first opposition, drawn from the domain of language rather than from that of mathematics, we can more clearly understand exactly what he means by the terms *bezeichnend* (literally, "signifying") and *abbildend* (representational). *Bezeichnend* refers to nothing other than the "denotative" aspect of language, to the semantic reflex by which any word or sign is identified or associated with a specific meaning. Müller rejects this process of denotation, of positive linkage between signifier and signified, as too limiting and mechanical, and he associates the reliance on this *adaequatio* relationship, this one-to-one correspondence between signifier and signified thing or concept, to what he derogatorily calls "science." What he terms the "representational" or "geometric" element of language is nothing other than the structural or contextual circumscription of a sign and its meaning based on its relationship to other signs. The *Abbild*, or "picture," is a representation that specifically replicates, by means of a kind of geometrical congruence, the structural relationship among a series of elements. Applying the terminology of Roman Jakobson from his essay "The Metaphoric and Metonymic Poles," the function of *bezeichnen*, or denotation, is metaphorical, based on the vertical axis of semantic attribution, whereas the principle of *abbilden*, or representation, is metonymical, based on the horizontal axis of syntactical relation and contextual interconnection (Jakobson 76–82). The model of linguistic signification that Müller valorizes and identifies with poetic diction, in other words, is one that is based on *Gegensatz* and *Wechselwirkung*— in structuralist terminology, *difference*—to determine the value and significance of any individual term. The linguistic model he has in mind, then, is explicitly protostructuralist, defining the value of any particular sign on the basis of its systematic position within a given utterance or within the entire system of a language itself. Transferred to the domain of economics, this linguistic model underwrites a system in which commodities do not possess any substantial value, but only acquire value when placed in relation to other commodities and to people's needs: only its relative position in the structural nexus of the entire economic system, composed as a series of reciprocal exchanges, can establish a commodity's value. This means, of course, that this value is historically variable, not absolute, because the structural relationships are in a constant state of flux.

Müller's Economic Theory and Romantic Semiotics

I want to turn now to a passage from Novalis's "Fichte-Studien" (Fichte studies, composed 1795–96), his notes in response to his reading of Johann Gottlieb Fichte's (1762–1814) *Wissenschaftslehre* (Doctrine of science, 1794), in order to indicate the proximity of Müller's conception of language, and the hypermoney it produces when transferred to the economic realm, to the semiotic theory of language—in particular of *poetic* language—articulated by the early Romantics.

The eleventh entry in Novalis's "Fichte-Studien" contains a longer deliberation about the relationship of signifiers to their signifieds. It is likely that this meditation on the functioning of linguistic signification is not only a general response to problems articulated in Fichte's *Wissenschaftslehre*, in particular Fichte's exposition of the proposition of identity, but also represents a critical reaction to the thoughts on the origin of language and the nature of speech Fichte had formulated in the essay "Von der Sprachfähigkeit und dem Ursprunge der Sprache" (On the linguistic faculty and origin of language). This essay was published in 1795, just a few months before Novalis began recording his reflections on Fichte's philosophy in

63

November of that same year. Fichte's essay introduces no radical new insights into the ongoing eighteenth-century debate about the faculty of language and its origin. His semiotic theory follows more or less the Enlightenment pattern, affirming the arbitrary nature of linguistic signs, especially the signs for abstract thought, and repeating the accepted wisdom that the signified concept must exist prior to its signification by means of any sign.[19] Fichte's theory of signification, in other words, like that of most of his contemporaries, is based on a metaphorical or vertical relation (to use Jakobson's terminology once more), a defined, if yet arbitrarily chosen, one-to-one correspondence between the signifier and its signified. In his ruminations on the process of signification, Novalis will radically depart from this model. Part of the reason for Novalis's departure can be attributed to his different attitude regarding the relationship of language and thought. If for Fichte, thought, or the mental concept, always precedes language or word, the latter only arising as a tool or medium to express the preexistent thought, for Novalis thought and language are inseparable from the outset. For example, in an entry from "Das allgemeine Brouillon" (Sketches for a general compendium), Novalis's notes for an encyclopedic work, he remarks simply, "Thought is speech" (*Schriften* 3: 297). A second note from this same collection is even more explicit in its fusion of thought and language: "A *thought* is nec[essarily] *verbal* [*wörtlich*]" (3: 463). Given this belief in the inescapable imbrication of language and thought, Novalis would find it necessary to formulate a semiotic theory that accounts for the inseparable reciprocity of the intellectual, that is, the creative element of language, and its expressive or representational dimension. This is precisely what he attempts to accomplish in the response to Fichte that is recorded as the eleventh entry of the "Fichte-Studien."

After giving a brief outline of the issues he wishes to address in this note, including a "theory of the sign" and the nature of thought, speech, and writing, Novalis contemplates specifically the connection between the signifier and its signified.

> Relation of the sign [*Zeichen*] to the signified [*Bezeichneten*].
>   Both are in different spheres, which can reciprocally determine each other.

The signified is a free effect, the sign likewise.

They are therefore similar in the signifying agent [*Bezeichnenden*]— otherwise utterly different—but this, too, only for the signifying agent— both exist in relation to one another only in the signifying agent. (2: 108)

It is helpful to interrupt the quotation at this point so we can take stock of Novalis's main points before proceeding. His first assertion is that signifier and signified are wholly independent of one another; they exist, as he writes, in different "spheres." This is simply another, although more radical, way of designating the fundamentally arbitrary nature of the relation between signifier and signified: they are incommensurable with one another, belonging to absolutely discrete realms. At the same time, they are capable of mutually determining each another, of having an influence on one another. Word and concept, language and thought, thus belong to distinct spheres, but these domains stand in a *potential* relationship of reciprocity with one another. I have emphasized the word "potential" here because the dimension of the signifier and that of the signified cannot be mediated without the intervention of a third element: this is what Novalis calls *der Bezeichnende*, or the signifying agent, the human being or the mind that employs the sign for the purposes of communication.

Novalis stresses that the union of the signifier and the signified can only take place in and through this signifying agent; this agent establishes their relationship and, what is more, this relationship exists only for the single agent who creates it. Now this is an important point on two accounts. First of all, it is significant to realize that Novalis has gone well beyond a purely automatic, structural system in which differential relations distinguish and identify the meanings of signifiers;[20] a human consciousness has entered the picture, a consciousness that mediates between the mutually exclusive domains of signifier and signified and for whom alone they exist in an arbitrarily established relationship. Second, if this is so, then meaning is constituted for this signifying agent, this individual consciousness alone: it is difficult to see how Novalis will be able to move from this hypothesis to the fact of successful linguistic communication, without appealing to a totalitarian notion of meaning imposed from above on the basis of greater authority and power. Has Novalis painted himself into a semiotic corner? Let us return to his note to see if, and if so how, he can resolve this conundrum.

Insofar as the signifying agent is *wholly free* either in the effect of the signified or in the choice of the sign, not at all dependent on his or her nature as determined in itself—so both [sign and signified] are in a reciprocal relation only for him, and neither of them stands in a necessary relation to the other for a second signifying agent.

They are utterly separate for a second signifying agent.

Thinking, like everything else, can be communicated to a second signifying agent only *from outside*, only through space, by means of an intuition [*Anschauung*], or a feeling. . . .

Consequently, only through a sign. But if, as noted above, sign and signified are utterly separate, if their relation exists merely in the first signifying agent, it can only be an accident or a miracle if the signified comes across to a second signifying agent through such a sign.

Objectively and subjectively necessary signs—which are fundamentally one and the same thing—are thus the only means by which something thought [*Gedachtes*] can be communicated. (2: 108–9)

Novalis goes on to stress the absolute independence of the signified and the signifier from any grounding in the nature of the signifying agent itself: both of them are wholly arbitrary and individual, as is their established relationship. This leads him to the conclusion that for a second signifying agent this relationship would not obtain, and signifier and signified would again be banished to their independent spheres: they would be without any relation, and hence no communicable meaning would be constituted. At this point Novalis finds it necessary to introduce a new notion to explain the possibility of mediation as the prerequisite for communication: he refers to this conception alternatively as *Anschauung* (intuition) or *Gefühl* (feeling). But even after hypothesizing this new metaphysics of an emotional or intuitive element, he returns to a restatement of the original dilemma: only pure accident or a miracle could account for the coincidence of the signifier-signified relationship in two independent signifying agents. This leads him to the hypothesis that signifiers used for the purpose of communication must be objectively and subjectively necessary signifiers. But this simply adds a new level of complexity to the dilemma, because Novalis has presupposed all along that the signifier and the signified are established and connected in a purely subjective and arbitrary manner. There seems to be no place in this theory for anything that can be called objectively necessary—nor, for that matter, even for something that might only be subjectively necessary. Necessity, in fact, has never entered the picture until now. Let us return to Novalis's note once more to see how he resolves this problem.

> In order to communicate, therefore, the first signifying agent needs only to choose signs whose necessary relation to the signified is grounded in the homogeneous disposition of the second signifying agent. He will therefore have to study the homogeneity of this foreign disposition with his own while communicating. . . .
>
> Every *comprehensible* sign must therefore stand in a *schematic* relation to the signified.
>
> To clarify this, we need to investigate the original schema more closely.
>
> The schema acts reciprocally [*in Wechselwirkung*] with itself. Each part attains its function only through that of the others. The first signifying agent has thus found an original schema in the second signifying agent—and he chooses the signs for communication in accordance with this. . . . The first signifying agent stands in a reciprocal relation [*in Wechselwirkung*] with the second. He accommodates himself to the second in the sign, the second to the first in the signified—*Free contract* [*Freyer Vertrag*] *quasi.* (2: 109–10)

Novalis now hypothesizes a certain a priori affinity between the two signifying agents, a "homogeneous being" that somehow forms the basis for an affective, unifying relationship. The task of the first signifying agent, hence, is to study the second agent with whom he or she wishes to communicate in order to discover the basis of this homogeneity and craft his or her sign-use accordingly. What we need to take note of here is that Novalis is essentially interpolating a hermeneutical speculation into the act of communication: the first signifying agent must interpretively consider the agent with which it seeks to communicate in order to discover a specific common ground, a shared "schematism," that will make this communication possible. The first agent must then choose a signifier with a relationship to the signified that can be legitimated and understood on the basis of the homogeneity between the two human agents. Communication becomes unthinkable without this complex process of hermeneutical nego-

67

tiation that approximates a kind of *Einfühlung*, a sympathetic interpretive identification on the part of the first agent with the second. Implicit in Novalis's argument is the notion that communication is only possible where this common ground exists; where it is absent, no mutual understanding can ever be achieved. The precondition for interpersonal understanding, in short, is an already present and inherently discoverable homogeneity or "sympathy" between the two communicating agents. We need to take special note of the term Novalis employs here for this interactive sympathy: *Wechselwirkung*, "reciprocity," the same concept Müller will use to designate the interactive nature of his economic and monetary community. This is the point at which we perceive perhaps most concretely the close affinity between Novalis's semiotic and Müller's economic theories.

In this context it is useful to reevaluate another statement by Novalis regarding the relationship of signifier to signified. Under an entry titled "*Magic*: Mystical doctrine of language" in "Das allgemeine Brouillon," Novalis remarks, "*Sympathy* of the *sign* with the signified (One of the fundamental ideas of Cabbalistic thought)" (*Schriften* 3: 266). In Cabbalistic conceptions, of course, this sympathy is inherent in the relation of the signifier to the signified itself, hence the magical nature of this connection, which allows the signified to be invoked as soon as the signifier is mentioned. But in a certain sense what Novalis has done in the fragment on the theory of semiotics from the "Fichte-Studien" is simply to transfer this sympathetic relationship between signifier and signified, which is characteristic of "magical" semiosis, to the relationship between the two signifying agents: sympathy between signifier and signified has been personalized as a hermeneutical act that gauges or fathoms an inherent homogeneity, a shared term, between the communicative partners and strategically structures sign-use according to this common element.

In order to designate this common ground or this shared term that forms the necessary precondition for imparting meaning from one sign-using agent to another, Novalis turns to the concept of the schema or the schematism, which Immanuel Kant (1724–1804) had first introduced into critical philosophy. In his *Kritik der reinen Vernunft* (Critique of pure reason, 1781), Kant employed this concept to solve the dilemma of how purely intellectual or abstract ideas might be applied to empirical matters. The issue, in other words, is one of finding a way to mediate between the intellectual or supersensible realm, and the experiential or sensible domain, which for Kant are wholly incommensurable with one another. The schema, Kant hypothesizes, is a structure shared by all human beings that, because it partakes of both the sensible and the supersensible domains, makes their synthesis possible (*Kritik der reinen Vernunft* 187–94). Following Kant's lead, German idealist philosophy applied the notion of the schematism as a shorthand designation for a form of mediation or synthesis, based on a common structure or shared element, that could function as a bridge between two otherwise mutually exclusive spheres. Fichte resorted to this concept in his essay "Von der Sprachfähigkeit und dem Ursprunge der Sprache" in order to explain how signifiers derived from the sensible realm could be applied for supersensible or abstract concepts and still be comprehensible in acts of communication. Fichte's concern is essentially with the very possibility of metaphorical transference from the concrete to the abstract and the communicative viability of such a process. His solution to this problem is that such metaphorical transferences or translations must rely on shared human schematisms, to which other human beings can refer as a kind of *tertium comparationis* in order to make these fundamentally creative and imaginative metaphors comprehensible ("Von der Sprachfähigkeit" 322). It is likely that Novalis adopted his use of the schematism from Fichte's essay;[21] but Novalis radicalizes and generalizes the dilemma of communication and communicability much more than Fichte had, since in his semiotic theory the concept of the schematism must be called upon to explain the possibility of shared meaning as such, whereas for Fichte it only served to explain how abstract concepts can be made comprehensible to others. Moreover, it is not clear from Novalis's exposition of this semiotic problematic whether the schematism on which the first signifying agent would rely for communication constitutes a universal human faculty, as it clearly does for Kant and Fichte, or if it is merely a common feature limited to these two agents or to some smaller, more narrowly circumscribed group.

Novalis's insistence on the necessity of a hermeneutical speculation on the part of the first signifying agent seems to presume that the common schematism would not need to be a universal phenomenon; for if it were universal, any act of interpretation, especially one based on "sympathy" or "empathy" with the second agent, would be unnecessary—the existence of the requisite schematism could simply be assumed. In such an instance, anthropological identity would constitute the basis of a universal human understanding. But this is clearly not what Novalis had in mind, for if that were the case no conscious negotiation of meaning would have to take place between the two agents. His conception of communication and shared understanding thus suggests that this schematism, this shared third term or this common ground that makes reciprocal understanding possible, could have its basis in, say, cultural affinity, local character, ethnicity, national resemblance, or even in the faith that underwrites acts of economic exchange. The commonality that defines the schematism is for Novalis not a universal given, but rather something that is negotiated on a case by case basis: thus he writes of a *Freyer Vertrag*, a free compact or an independent contract as the basis of interhuman comprehension. What Novalis presupposes, then, as the necessary condition for communication is the evolution and/or existence of an *interpretive community*, a collective that "sympathizes" with a certain manner of sign-use and hence has negotiated the validity of these signs. The Romantics expended a great deal of energy theorizing about just such interpretive or, if you will, semiotic communities. One need only think of their notions of "symphilosophizing" or "sympoeticizing," of collective intellectual effort and production, or of their demand for the development of a new mythology. This dream of a new mythology was, in fact, nothing other than the vision of a coherent semiotic and interpretive community. Adam Müller's theory of money is but one more manifestation of this drive for interpretive community. For Müller, money is the symbol of an economic mythology, that is, an economic discourse that provides community and coherence for all the members of a state. Money marks the shared interpretive or semiotic community of a particular political economy.

For Novalis, the semiotic act is already structured as an act of exchange, understood as a complex negotiation of meaning between two independent, sign-using individuals. Thus he describes the reciprocal interaction between the two communicative partners in terms of the search for common ground, for a shared value system: "The first signifying agent stands in a reciprocal relation with the second. He accommodates himself to the second in the sign, the second to the first in the signified—*Free contract quasi*" (*Schriften* 2: 110). The first agent adjusts his *signifier* to the requirements of the second agent; the second agent adjusts the *signified* to the needs of the first agent. Through this process of concessions to the other, shared meaning evolves as a kind of transaction, or barter, by which the parties involved arrive at signifying agreement. What Novalis describes here, in short, is an act of economic exchange projected onto the dimension of human communicative intercourse: meaning evolves as though it were a commodity whose value must be negotiated between two partners so that they can find a common basis for exchange. The schematism that makes this exchange possible in the realm of economics is, of course, money. Money is the universal third term, the shared structure or common ground that facilitates the exchange of commodities by translating them into a "currency," a commonly accepted measure of value. The presence of this implicit economic paradigm in Novalis's semiotic theory is underscored by the frequency with which, throughout his writings, he draws on the analogy between language and money, between semiotic relations and economic circulation (see, e.g., *Schriften* 2: 258, 462, 3: 244, 378–79, 464).

The semiotic theory of the early Romantics, especially as concretized in the thought of Novalis, already implies a kind of symbiotic relationship between linguistic signs and money, human communicative interaction via signs and economic circulation by means of money. This is precisely the symbiosis examined in the first chapter of this book on the example of German language theory of the eighteenth century, and Novalis's deliberations on the relationships between monetary and linguistic signs constitute a further extension of this critical homology. In the case of Müller we might say that the metaphor by which words and money have traditionally been conjoined has been literalized, so that money becomes the marker of a concrete and primordial act of economic-communicative interchange. In this process, however, something very interesting has occurred. Although, as we saw in chapter 1, the historical trajectory of the money-language metaphor moves generally, in German linguistic theory, toward the identity of words and concepts with symbolic money, this phenomenon was not always greeted sanguinely. Lavater and Hamann, in particular, sought to set aside a mode of more authentic communication that transcended the economy of arbitrary signs—for Lavater manifest in the discourse of heaven, for Hamann in the language of religious faith. For the latter, as we recall, faith is not simply "communicable like a commodity" (*Briefwechsel* 7: 156). For Müller, by contrast, quite the opposite is the case: faith is not merely communicable like a commodity, it is constituted in the very act of commodity exchange, as the credit, credibility, and creditability established or negotiated by the trading partners. If belief is the founding principle of any religious community, it is also the underlying principle of any economic union. And based on this credit, faith, and trust, economic exchanges become for Müller the very basis of secular community building.

Economics and the Poetic Imagination

After this excursus on Novalis's theory of the sign, the hermeneutical component of semiotic communicability, and the negotiated transaction that makes human understanding possible, we can return to Adam Müller's theory of money and examine the points of confluence between their ideas. My primary concern is not to demonstrate the magnitude of Müller's intellectual debt to Novalis, but rather to indicate the ways in which Müller's monetary theory and Novalis's semiology are mutually illuminating. Indeed, I believe that we not only better understand Müller's monetary theory— especially his insistence on the purely semiotic character of money and on credit, credibility, and the state as the shared elements that make economic exchange possible—when we view it in the context of Novalis's semiotic theory, but that we also have a greater insight into certain aspects of Novalis's conception of human communicative interchange, especially the hermeneutical component inherent in his semiology, when we examine it against the backdrop of Müller's theory of money.

In his miscellaneous fragments for diverse collections of philosophical aphorisms, Novalis cryptically notes, "Essay on money. / Poeticization of the financial sciences" (*Schriften* 2: 647). Müller's own *Versuche einer neuen Theorie des Geldes* can be seen as an elaboration of this undeveloped statement by Novalis, an attempt to articulate a poetic theory of economics. We recall that Müller associated the "geometric" or struc-

tural aspect of his theory with the poetic function of language, juxtaposing it to the simple denotative function of "arithmetic" or scientific
language. Müller thus conceives the productivity of the economic sphere
in analogy to the imaginative creativity of the poetic domain: both of
these are structured according to the principle of nonidentity, the notion
that only a dynamic reciprocity can generate meaning and value. Novalis
expresses this problematic most clearly in a fragment that expounds upon
the notion of *das Schweben*, constant oscillation between two opposing
poles.

> All being, being as such is nothing but being-free—*oscillating* [*Schweben*]
> between extremes that must necessarily be both joined and separated.
> All reality flows from this light-source of oscillation [*Schwebens*]—
> everything is contained in it—object and subject are created by it, not
> it by them.
>
> I-ness or the productive power of the imagination, *oscillation*
> [*Schweben*]—determines, produces the extremes between which oscilla-
> tion takes place [*geschwebt wird*]—This is a deception, but only in the
> realm of common reason. Otherwise it is something thoroughly real, for
> oscillation [*Schweben*], its cause, is the source, the *mater* of all reality, is
> reality itself. (*Schriften* 2: 266)

Novalis here elevates the doctrine of reciprocity—now rechristened "oscillation," *das Schweben*—to a metaphysics of existence as such. All being
is defined as being-free, that is, as the perpetual oscillation between two
fixed points. But these fixed polar opposites do not predate or precede the
dynamics of oscillation itself; on the contrary, oscillation is the primordial
force that generates its own polar oppositions as its limits. Novalis even
goes so far as to claim that this oscillating force creates all the substance
of reality. Exploiting a play on words, Novalis calls this dynamic system
the *mater*—the mother, but also the matter, the substantive material—
of all reality: it is creative energy par excellence. This explains why Novalis
identifies this oscillating motion with the productive power of the imagination and with illusion: it is the illusion, the semblance of art that he has
in mind here.

This notion of oscillation is closely allied to a central term of German

73

idealist aesthetic theory: the notion of *Spiel*, or "play," first introduced in Friedrich von Schiller's (1759–1805) *Über die ästhetische Erziehung des Menschen in einer Reihe von Briefen* (On the aesthetic education of human-kind in a series of letters, 1795). For Schiller, the notion of *Spiel* refers not solely to "play" in the sense of game, but also in the sense of latitude, room to move, or back-and-forth motion.[22] In Schiller's aesthetic theory, this connotation of the word "play" is crucial, since the *Spieltrieb*, the play-drive associated with aesthetics, has the function of mediating between and synthesizing two other opposing drives, the drive for sub-stance (*Stofftrieb*) and the drive for form (*Formtrieb*) (*Über die ästheti-sche Erziehung* 612–14). Thus in Schiller's aesthetic theory we already find in rudimentary form a conception of the productive power of the aes-thetic imagination as a dynamic oscillation, a mediating reciprocity that conciliates two extremes. What is more, Schiller's aesthetic treatise cul-minates in a political argument, a theory about the application of this aes-thetic principle to the political state (667–69). Müller's political-economic theory, which postulates economic reciprocity as the very essence of the political state, can be viewed as a logical extension of Schiller's aestheti-cally based political state. For Müller, the state, like commodities and money, is not a positive fact or a concrete institution: it is a dynamic rela-tionship of mutual obligation, of promise, credit, credence, and trust, a relationship that manifests itself most clearly in the monetary instrument as guarantor and expression of this trust. In his opposition to self-identity and a priori substance in favor of reciprocal or systematic relation, a struc-ture by which identity is constructed only on the basis of difference, we can locate the theoretical coherence between German idealist aesthetic the-ory, the semiology of the early Romantics, and Müller's conception of money and his system of economics. The creative imagination plays the same role in Novalis's metaphysical epistemology as money, defined as pure sign, plays in Müller's metaphysical economics. As opposed to Karl Marx, who views *logic* as the money of the mind ("*Logic*—the *money* of the mind," as he noted in "Ökonomisch-philosophische Manuskripte" [571]), Müller and the early Romantics see the *poetic* or *creative imagi-nation* as the money of the mind, the productive force underlying all human activity and the bond that forges every form of human community. Just as Novalis theorizes the human imagination as an originary dynamic system of interactive reciprocities or *Gegensätze* that, like a mother, gives birth to reality, Müller conceives money in terms of the perpetual motion of economic circulation and the infinite productivity it generates. Relations, not stable things, are the pillars of the poetic, the semiotic, and the economic domains.

The Romantics often associated this dynamic productivity of the creative imagination with the spirit of commerce. One of Novalis's fragments from "Das allgemeine Brouillon," for example, is titled "On the *mercantile* spirit" and reads,

> The spirit of commerce [*Handelsgeist*] is the *spirit of the world*. It is the *sublime* spirit as such. It places everything in motion and connects everything. It awakens countries and cities—nations and works of art. It is the spirit of culture—the spirit of the perfection of the human race. The *historical* spirit of commerce—which slavishly accommodates itself to *given needs*, to the conditions of time and place—is merely a bastard of the genuine, *creative* spirit of commerce. (*Schriften* 3: 464)

The spirit of commerce that manifests itself in mercantile exchange as a historically circumscribed phenomenon, according to Novalis, is just an epiphenomenon of a larger commercial spirit that is the essence of all creativity. This larger spirit of commerce is related to what the Romantics refer to as *Geselligkeit*, "sociability," in the interpersonal domain, and to what they valorize as *Witz*, "wit," or creative intellect, in the realm of thought. This "commerce," this dynamic interaction between things and ideas, is the motor that drives all cultural constructs and all human community. Indeed, it represents, as Novalis maintains, the culmination of the human race. Müller makes a similar claim for the nature of money when he asserts that it represents nothing other than "the quality of sociability [*Geselligkeit*], which is inherent in all things to a greater or lesser degree" (*Versuche* 139). For Novalis as for Müller, the model of such a culture of reciprocity, of obligation and fealty, is the Catholic Middle Ages.

The most interesting point of contact between Novalis's semiology and Müller's theory of money certainly lies in the subtle hermeneutics each of them implies. If Novalis sees the hermeneutical negotiation between two subjects who communicate via signs fundamentally as an economic transaction, Müller sees economic transactions as hermeneutical acts in which two partners try to discover a common ground and reach an economic agreement on the basis of some shared value. The rapprochement of economic agents engaged in the process of exchange is propelled by a hermeneutical energy that negotiates, on a case by case basis, the common value for exchangeable commodities. The condition of possibility for this hermeneutical act is what Müller calls credit, or the reciprocal obligation and spirit of common trust in which both parties participate. What Müller makes clear to us even today is the fundamentally *interpretive* nature of every act of economic exchange, the complex and subtle hermeneutical transactions that are involved in every process of arriving at a mutually agreed upon value. This is the level on which Novalis's theory of semiotics and language, on the one hand, and Müller's monetary theory, on the other, reciprocally elucidate each other in the most penetrating way. Through an examination of Novalis's deliberations on semiology we can better understand Müller's valorization of idealized money, or sign-money, as the energy behind the incessant economic circulation he envisions. At the same time, Müller's appeal to credit and the common basis of shared community as the necessary condition for successful economic exchange and prosperity sheds light on the hermeneutical dimension that enters into Novalis's otherwise strictly structuralist semiology.

It should not come as a surprise that Novalis and Müller would incorporate hermeneutical positions into their theories; one of the focal points of the intellectual debates among the early Romantics, after all, was hermeneutics as a science of interpretation. This culminated in Friedrich Daniel Schleiermacher's (1768–1834) foundation of a philosophical hermeneutics. Recognition of the implied hermeneutics in Novalis's semiology, at any rate, is especially important in a scholarly climate in which structuralist and poststructuralist appropriations of Novalis's thought have become the norm. By pointing to the hermeneutical interventions that enter into all communicative acts, according to Novalis's theory, my intent is not to question the insights that structuralist and poststructualist scholarly positions have brought to an understanding of Novalis's semiotic theory, but only to demonstrate that Novalis's conception of the differential system of sign-creation and sign-use cannot be properly understood without supplementing it with an understanding of the hermeneutical barter that must also be present in the communicative act as Novalis conceives it. Reading Novalis's semiotics against the backdrop of Müller's theory of money produces an interpretation that corroborates Manfred Frank's general theoretical position that structural systems do not, in and of themselves, produce meaning. On the contrary, they require the interventions of interpretive beings who expend hermeneutical energy and provide "hypothetical judgments" so as to *create* meaning.[23] The power of the human imagination, as *Schweben* or "oscillation," is, according to Novalis's theory, essentially a power for the negotiation of difference. It is this process of creative negotiation, for both Novalis and Müller, that creates not merely shared conceptual and linguistic meaning, but also shared economic *value*. We will see in chapter 4, which deals with the German debate over physiocracy, how already prior to the Romantics the creative imagination came to be viewed in the domain of economics as the fundamental value producing force.

What is perhaps most fascinating about Novalis's and Müller's intellectual positions is the curious marriage of conservative politics and progressive ideas. That Novalis, the author of the retrograde and nostalgic political doctrines defended in *Glauben und Liebe* (Faith and love, 1798) or *Die Christenheit oder Europa* (Christianity or Europe, 1799) could also espouse a radically protostructuralist semiotic theory appears to be an intellectual incongruity. It seems similarly incongruous that Müller, the defender of the absolutist state and the feudal social order, could advocate an economic program built upon the modern notions of fiduciary money and the hyperactive consumer market. In Müller's case, these progressive notions paradoxically serve an economic theory that seeks to invoke the status of archaic gift economies as described by Marcel Mauss. In *The Gift*, Mauss argues that the morality and organization of the gift, as modeled in primitive societies, form the generative underpinning for modern market economies. The most important feature of the archaic economy, according to Mauss, is the manner in which the collective imposes obligations of exchange and contract upon individuals. The force of this obligation and its power to engender a virtually limitless economics of exchange is concretized in the potlatch. By representing an abundance of giving beyond all reasonable expectations, the potlatch also imposes upon its benefactors the obligation of reciprocation (Mauss 3–7). The qualities of Mauss's archaic economy—obligation, reciprocity, and an incessant dynamic of exchange—read like a summary of the features Müller highlights in his theory of economics.[24] One way of explaining Müller's economic theory would be to say that it simply translates the underlying principles of the archaic economy into the abstract discourse of German idealist philosophy. One might even claim of the German Romantics in general that their proclivity for applying a modern critical vocabulary and complex intellectual structures to defend the nostalgic ideal of an archaic society forms the crux of their progressively tinged conservatism. In Müller's case, the emphasis on the semiotic character of money ultimately underscores the highly symbolic nature of even the most advanced economic exchange. Perhaps it was the early Romantics' fascination with symbolic economies of all sorts that fueled Müller's theory of economics as a fundamentally symbolic system founded on the hypersigns of money. What is certain, at least, is that the *fides*, the trust and confidence, that underpins paper currencies as fiduciary money also underwrote Müller's insistence on the importance of fiat currencies, since as pure signs such monetary instruments symbolize nothing other than the reciprocal relations of those who use them. We will see in the next chapter how, not only for Müller but also for Fichte, fiduciary money—precisely because it was founded on notions of credit, reciprocity, faith, and shared values—came to be theorized as the potential basis for establishing a German national state as an autonomous economic and monetary community held together by the "credit" invested in a shared, nationally unique, and arbitrary monetary currency.

3 / Economic Romanticism

Monetary Nationalism in Johann Gottlieb Fichte and Adam Müller

That money "circulates" simply means that it is possible to reproduce the capacity for payment on the basis of payments. Circulation is autopoiesis: reproduction of the elements of the system by means of the elements of the system.

—Niklas Luhmann (*Wirtschaft* 131)

German Economic Nationalism

WHEN THE PHRASE "MONETARY NATIONALISM" IS USED today in the context of German history, it is usually taken to refer to the relatively recent past: to the close identification of the Federal Republic of Germany after the currency reform in 1948 with the emerging power of the D-mark, or to the economic incentives that helped shape German reunification four decades later. Who would deny that the introduction of the D-mark into the Western zones of occupied Germany was the fundamental founding act of the Federal Republic—even more so than the ratification of the *Grundgesetz*, the German federal constitution, in 1949—just as the agreement on the currency union was the principal step on the path to reunification in 1989? Reflecting on the economic pressures that guided German reunification, the historian Wolfgang Mommsen has claimed that in the Federal Republic, the self-confidence of proven economic success functioned as a substitute for German national pride, forming the core political self-understanding of West German citizens (62). Similarly, in a widely publicized article first printed in the weekly newspaper *Die Zeit* in March 1990, Jürgen Habermas coined the phrase "D-mark nationalism" and warned of the dangers of predicating German reunification on the colonialist extension of the D-mark to the territory of the former German Democratic Republic ("Yet Again German Identity" 89–90). As an alternative, Habermas argued for a renegotiation of the West German constitution as the basis for a *political*, and not merely an economic, unification of the two postwar German states. Only such an act, according to Habermas, would have been able to ground the political self-identity of the newly unified Germany in the statutes of a commonly instituted civil society. When Helmut Kohl and his economic minister, Theo Waigel, raised the flag of a new economic nationalism above the ruins of the Reichstag, as Habermas pointedly remarks (100), they also preempted the possibility of creating the basis for a new German nationalism founded on a uniformly ratified constitution and on mutually established political institutions.

Today references to D-mark nationalism might seem historically passé, since the D-mark, along with most other currencies of western Europe, has been supplanted by the Euro. But we only need recall the deep-seated trepidation of the German populace in anticipation of this monetary makeover to realize that for the Germans there was more at stake in embracing this new European currency than just the threat of potential economic instability and of a softer currency: with the abandonment of the D-mark, the Germans essentially abandoned the primary basis of their postwar—and post-unification—national identity. Will D-mark nationalism ultimately be replaced by a new German Euro-internationalism? That, at least, was the promise embedded in the rhetoric of West German politicians during the process of unification: "United Germany as the center of a united Europe" was the catchphrase with which German politicians sought to waylay European fears of a united Germany as a new nationalistic powerhouse. It is clearly too early today to answer the question about the direction in which German nationalism will move with the disappearance of the D-mark. Worthy of note is that the growing European Union is itself predicated primarily on acts of economic unity: Article 9 of the Maastricht Treaty, after all, defines the basis of European cooperation as a customs and monetary union (Habermas, *Staatsbürgerschaft* 19). However, perhaps now, after the de facto institutional end of D-mark nationalism, is the proper time to reflect more generally on the history of German monetary nationalism. In this spirit I want to examine what might be considered the root theories of German monetary nationhood as they were articulated in two works by German Romantic thinkers, in Johann Gottlieb Fichte's (1762–1814) *Der geschlossene Handelsstaat* (The closed commercial state, 1800) and Adam Müller's (1779–1829) *Versuche einer neuen Theorie des Geldes* (Attempts at a new theory of money, 1816). Since Romanticism is often identified as the cradle of German ethnolinguistic nationalism, it seems especially important to acknowledge that other models for German nationalism were generated in this period as well, and that monetary nationalism, or a unified state organized around a unique symbolic currency, represented one of the most prominent alternatives that competed with a nationalist state founded on ethnolinguistic distinction.[1]

One might claim that it is anachronistic to apply the term "monetary nationalism" to ideas developed in the opening decades of the nineteenth century, since this concept itself is of much more recent coinage, first appearing in 1937 in the title of F. A. Hayek's book *Monetary Nationalism and International Stability*.[2] Yet already the second phrase in Hayek's title, "international stability," overlaps with one of the primary motivations behind Fichte's defense, in *Der geschlossene Handelsstaat*, of the national state as a wholly autonomous and isolated economic entity. For Fichte, this economic autonomy is a prerequisite for the end of European colonial exploitation of the world and it hence forms the necessary basis for a future world peace (*Geschlossene Handelsstaat* 373). In order to understand how radically Fichte's view departs from the generally accepted position of his time, we only need recall that just five years prior to the publication of *Der geschlossene Handelsstaat*, in 1795, Immanuel Kant (1724–1804) had published his utopian political pamphlet *Zum ewigen Frieden* (Toward eternal peace), in which he argued, among other things, that the necessities of international economic trade and exchange are the principal driving force behind human peaceful coexistence, mutual understanding, and world community (221).[3] In this regard, Kant appears as a precursor of those who today advocate the beneficence of a "global economy."

Similarly, one of the most influential political thinkers among the German Romantics, the poet Novalis (Friedrich von Hardenberg, 1772–1801), echoes Kant's valorization of economic exchange as the ground for cooperative community. In an entry from his notebooks "Das allgemeine Brouillon" (Sketches for a general compendium), we find under the heading "Vom *merkantilischen* Geiste" (On the *mercantile* spirit) a soaring panegyric on the spirit of trade as the essence of culture.

> The spirit of commerce is the *spirit of the world*. It is the *sublime* spirit as such. It places everything in motion and connects everything. It awakens countries and cities—nations and works of art. It is the spirit of culture—the spirit of the perfection of the human race. The *historical* spirit of commerce—which slavishly accommodates itself to *given needs*, to the conditions of time and place—is merely a bastard of the genuine, *creative* spirit of commerce. (*Schriften* 3: 464)

Since we have already examined this remark in the preceding chapter, we need not analyze it in detail here. It is important to note in the present context, however, that Novalis's description of the spirit of economic trade anticipates the idealized, creative, phenomenologizing qualities of Hegel's dialectic of spirit: commerce is lionized as the motor behind all human cultural innovation. The specific properties he attributes to this commercial spirit, moreover, are significant for the present context, since they recur in both Fichte's and Müller's theories of the nation held together by economic relations and monetary symbols: the powers of infinite movement—circulation, in economic parlance—and of interconnection—what Fichte and Müller view as social integration. Furthermore, Novalis refers here to the power of commerce to found nations, and Fichte's and Müller's monetary theories will concentrate primarily on this theme. But unlike them, Novalis understands this production of nationhood as a single precipitate of a more broadly conceived spirit of exchange that gives rise to all the monuments of human culture. Fichte and Müller will circumscribe this idea more narrowly by defining commercial interactions, driven by a specific inconvertible national currency, as the cornerstone of national identity.

Monetary Nationhood in Fichte's Der geschlossene Handelsstaat

When writing *Der geschlossene Handelsstaat*, Fichte was not nearly as sanguine as Kant or Novalis about this universalized human spirit of exchange. In fact, as early as 1796, in a review of Kant's *Zum ewigen Frieden*, Fichte openly attacked the reality of international commerce as a form of selfishness that legitimates theft from others in the interests of self-enrichment. Here Fichte sarcastically and sardonically notes,

> The goods in our states have by no means all been used up and distributed, and there remains so much that can yet be desired and appropriated; and ultimately if everything at home should come to be consumed, the commercial exploitation [*Unterdrückung*] of foreign peoples and territories will provide a constantly flowing, bountiful resource. (Rev. of Kant's *Zum ewigen Frieden* 435)

Fichte not only alludes to the motives of mastery over and enslavement of others, as part and parcel of international trade and as a reflex of Europe's burgeoning colonialist enterprise, but even diagnoses the mechanism behind *internal* trade as a ravenous consumerism concerned only with selfish advantage and the satisfaction of personal desire. Fichte is clearly much more pessimistic than either Kant or Novalis with regard to the psychological mechanisms that motivate human acquisitiveness and the desire for economic gain. Moreover, unlike Adam Smith, who believed that economic human beings worked toward the common good *in spite of* being motivated by self-interest, Fichte tended to believe that humans had to be cajoled by governmental regulation and oversight into acting for the benefit of communal interests. From this perspective it is relatively easy to understand why just four years later he would argue in *Der geschlossene Handelsstaat* for an interventionist stance in which the state monitors and controls not only all internal production, consumption, and trade, but forbids and actively prevents its citizens from participating in any international commerce whatsoever (419–20, 428, 435).

In his theory, Fichte anticipates down to specific details the principles of twentieth-century socialist planned economies: state establishment of prices and wages; exclusive state control over international commodity items, especially luxuries; absolute closure and autonomy from the world of international commerce; regulation of consumption; state control over property; state oversight over the type and number of occupational choices. Not surprisingly, this fact was not lost on scholars of Romantic political theory in former East Germany.[4] Indeed, in general Fichte's treatise has been recognized as one of the pioneering documents of a utopian socialism in the German tradition.[5] In *Der geschlossene Handelsstaat* Fichte broadens his critique of international commerce as the root of colonial expansionism and excess into a full-fledged attack on the principles of mercantilism, which advocated the advancement of national wealth by implementing policies that attracted the precious metals into a nation and limited their outflow, and which guaranteed and expanded this wealth by integrating the goods and products of that state's colonial empire into the "domestic" economy. Fichte inveighs against these mercantilist practices, asserting that they increase the prosperity of a few privileged nations while bringing about the total impoverishment of the rest of the world (462; see also 393). In this sense Fichte is one of the first to offer a critical analysis of what today we call the north-south divide in global political economics, and if he were alive today we might imagine him joining the ranks of those who protest against the hegemonic economic policies of the World Trade Organization.

In *Der geschlossene Handelsstaat* Fichte is fighting a war on two fronts: against the traditions and realities of mercantilism, on the one hand, and against Adam Smith's laissez-faire economic principles, on the other (Batscha 176). If he maligns mercantilism as a self-centered will to mastery over others for the ends of amassing national wealth, he decries the "invisible hand" of supply and demand that provides equilibrium in Smith's market as "anarchy of trade" (*Geschlossene Handelsstaat* 453) and baldly identifies profit as nothing but *Raub*, or blatant theft (447). The primary strategic weapon he brings to this economic battlefield is a theory of money that, for its time, is wildly heretical. Fichte argues for nothing less than the abolition of all international currencies and the institution of a *Landesgeld* (392), a limited national currency, which would by definition restrict all commerce to the internal domain of the nation that issues this restrictively negotiable currency. Of course, the Holy Roman Empire of

German Nations possessed a nominally unifying currency: the reichstaler, or imperial taler, whose silver content was first established in 1566 (fig. 2). But the reichstaler competed with innumerable local currencies and, due to unstable valuations, never asserted territorial dominance. Moreover, since it was a silver-based coinage, the reichstaler circulated on the basis of its silver content, and it thus failed to satisfy the primary criterion for the national currency Fichte had in mind. For the "closure" of Fichte's commercial state is predicated entirely on the introduction of a national currency that makes no claim to transnational validity or acceptance, and on the complementary banishment of all universal "world" currencies—above all minted gold and silver. Let us set aside the impracticality and inherent absurdity of what we can call, following Ernst Bloch (644), Fichte's Chinese Wall theory of economic autonomy, especially given the historical context of blossoming colonialism and emergent capitalism, by pointing to Fichte's awareness that his suggestions will be brushed aside or ignored as impossible to implement (*Geschlossene Handelsstaat* 390, 393, 511). He excuses himself and justifies his treatise, despite this awareness, by pointing to the discrepancy between theory and practice, and he ultimately insists that *in theory* his position represents the most rational conception of the national state. Fichte resigns himself, in other words, to the recognition that in matters of political economy, rational theory will bow to the contingencies and convenience of irrational but really existing practices (398).

Or does he? After all, he dedicates this treatise to the Prussian minister of finance Karl August von Struensee (1735–1804) (see *Geschlossene Handelsstaat* 389), and Fichte personally sent a copy of this work to the Prussian king (Verzar 95). Is this just an expression of political opportunism, as one critic has suggested (Streisand 81–82)? It is true, of course, that Fichte completed the manuscript of *Der geschlossene Handelsstaat* immediately after taking up residence in Berlin, subsequent to losing his professorial chair in Jena in the aftermath of the so-called *Atheismusstreit*, the dispute over atheism in which he took the unpopular side of tolerance. Hence he was strongly motivated to win recognition by the Prussian state and its representatives. But surely Fichte must have been aware that the peculiar ideas presented in this economic program were unlikely to put him in the good graces of the king and his finance minister, or secure him a professional

2 / Reichstaler, or imperial taler. First issued in 1566, it represented an initial attempt to establish a unified currency for German-speaking Europe during the Holy Roman Empire of German Nations.

future as a civil servant in the Prussian state! Thus it seems that Fichte must not merely have believed firmly in the inherent rationality of his economic proposals, but simultaneously subscribed to an optimistic faith in the ultimate victory of a rational theory over a set of irrational practices. Moreover, the very structure and argument of this work indicates that Fichte viewed it as an attempt to mediate between existing economic reality and the rational ideal manifest in his theory of the closed state: the tripartite structure of this text operates according to a logic of thesis, antithesis, and synthesis, with Fichte presenting his theory in part one, describing the realities and consequences of economic mercantilism in part two, and in part three, which he calls the "political" program of his treatise, offering practical measures for adjudicating between current economic conditions and the ideal practices of the wholly "rational" autonomous state he valorizes. Given Fichte's persistent concern with the practical applicability of theoretical philosophy, perhaps it was this pragmatic political dimension that caused him to consider *Der geschlossene Handelsstaat* one of his best and most rigorously conceived philosophical tracts (Vaughan 118).

In order for Fichte's national currency to circulate freely and effectively within the nation that institutes it, but be rejected as legal tender beyond the borders of this state itself, it must have specific properties. According to economic historians, the introduction of money into the economic process represents a revolutionary advance because as general equivalent, money concentrates several economic functions into one single entity. Money is, above all, a medium and facilitator of exchange; but it also serves as a sign and measure of value, as well as providing a manner of setting aside and storing wealth for potential later uses. This third function of money forms the link between economic circulation and the libidinal economy, insofar as it makes provision for the mechanism of delayed gratification.[6] But the capacity of money as a vehicle for hoarding wealth is also what invites the abuses of "capital" that Karl Marx would diagnose a half century after Fichte. Anticipating certain aspects of the critique of money articulated by Marx, Fichte seeks to truncate money's multiple functions by eliminating its capacity to store wealth, insisting only on its exchange function and its role as a general equivalent or sign of value (*Geschlossene Handelsstaat* 492). This entails an absolute rejection of specie, of gold and silver as the substances that constitute international currency and whose accumulation was the aim of mercantilist economic policy. This is where Fichte brings forward his most radical idea—an idea that closely links his monetary theory with that of Adam Müller: he denies the intrinsic value of gold and silver as monetary instruments and claims that the essence of money resides solely in its semiotic or symbolic function. Indeed, he goes so far as to claim that it is precisely the *least* valuable available material that should be employed as the stuff of monetary currency.

> Everything useful found at the surface of the state will constantly be applied for the use of the people. . . . It is hence necessary that a lasting, never diminishing and never increasing representation of its [the state's] value, a sign of this value, constantly be present. The less useful this sign is in and of itself, the less innate value it has, the more appropriate it is as a *mere sign* [*blossen Zeichen*]; for everything that is useful belongs to the internal wealth of the nation and should be enjoyed by it, not employed for any other purposes. (*Geschlossene Handelsstaat* 432–33, emphasis added)

Fichte intertwines two very different arguments here, one economic, one semiotic. In simple economic terms what he demands is that his national currency have absolutely no use value, but that its worth instead be made manifest entirely in exchange value. The economic logic for this is simple enough: nothing of any usefulness or inherent value should be diverted from the productive capacity or the natural resources of the state to be used merely for the functional purpose of circulation. Fichte is arguing, in short, for the sole use of so-called fiat currencies, a monetary instrument made of some substance like paper that merely represents, but does not embody, any concrete value. Fichte might have called upon philosophical authority in support of this view. He was surely aware that Plato, in *Laws*, had similarly suggested that his ideal republic would banish gold and silver as monetary instruments and replace them by mere tokens or scripts used primarily for the ends of bookkeeping. For his ideal city-state Plato thus stipulates,

> No one is to be allowed to possess any gold or silver in any private capacity. There is a need for currency in daily exchange—the money that can scarcely be avoided when dealing with craftsmen, and that is required by all who pay hired help—slaves and foreigners—their wages. For these purposes, we assert that they should possess a kind of coin that carries value among themselves but is useless among other human beings. (*Laws* 5.742a)

Like Fichte, Plato stresses that such base coinage would serve the purpose solely of domestic trade; gold and silver should be reserved exclusively for the ends of international exchange (5.742a–b), and in this sense we might view Fichte's closed commercial state as an eighteenth-century rendition of the Platonic city-state.[7] Moreover, Plato, like Fichte, insists that these regulations must be imposed in order to ensure the most beneficial community relations among the populace of his city-state: "The hypothesis that underlies our laws aims at making the people as happy and as friendly to one another as possible" (5.743c). In this sense, then, already for Plato the establishment of a fiat currency, and the subsequent limitations it places on wealth, contribute to the solidarity and hence the stability of the state. This is a doctrine to which Fichte—and Müller—will give precedence in the formulation of their own theories of a national state founded upon the institution of an inconvertible fiduciary currency.

When viewed in semiotic terms, Fichte's defense of fiat currency is based on the desire to strip money of any substantial worth and attribute to it instead a purely symbolic function. "Money," he asserts, "is in and of itself absolutely nothing; it only *represents* something due to the will of the state" (*Geschlossene Handelsstaat* 434). Money, in other words, is nothing but an arbitrary sign that is invested with the authority of the state. How does the state imbue this sign with its authority? By making it the sole legal tender accepted for all state-certified transactions, such as the payment of taxes, fees, and so on (433).[8]

To Fichte's contemporaries this monetary theory was heretical in both its economic and its semiotic dimensions. On the economic front, skepticism toward "fiat" or "ideal" currencies such as paper money was widespread in Europe, and I cited some of its most prominent skeptics in the previous chapter. Furthermore, the practical experience Europeans generally associated with paper money, namely John Law's unsuccessful experiment in France and the notoriously unstable assignats issued during the French Revolution, bore concrete testimony against the introduction of any currency not secured by reserves of gold or silver. Moreover, shortly after the publication of *Der geschlossene Handelsstaat* and following the defeats at Jena and Auerstedt, Prussia itself would suffer the turmoil of the collapse of a paper currency introduced in 1806 to finance the war against Napoleon. What people of the time commonly associated with paper currencies, especially with those issued by the state (rather than by a bank of issue or by a merchant), was the cynical manipulation of the monetary system for the selfish profit of the government (Glasner 21). In this regard, then, despite the fact that Fichte could appeal to the philosophical authority of Plato in support of his own theory, his proposals were not likely to win many advocates for their immediate practical implementation. To be sure, as Michel Foucault has shown,[9] the shift from substantialist to functionalist theories of money was representative of a larger transformation in the economic sphere that marks the discontinuity between the "Renaissance" and the "Classical" epistemes (see chapter 1). But opposition to this revolutionary development in monetary theory was pronounced both among the general populace and in intellectual circles, and in the early 1800s its representatives, such as Fichte, were regarded as theoretical outsiders.

In terms of its semiotic aspect, Fichte's hypothesis was also destined to meet stiff resistance. According to accepted doctrine of the time, propounded in Germany above all in the semiotic theories of the Enlightenment philosophers Gottfried Wilhelm Leibniz (1646–1716), Christian Wolff (1679–

1754), and Johann Heinrich Lambert (1728–77), natural signification, where a firm, empirically comprehensible relationship exists between the signifier and the signified, is more reliable than arbitrary signification, where the signifier-signified connection is grounded solely in convention. Gold and silver coins were taken as veritable prototypes for the authenticity and immediate "truth" of natural signification. The value the metallic coin "represents" in its numerical stamp is underwritten by the value of the precious metal out of which it is minted. In an economy based on specie, monetary value is grounded in an iconic relationship between the symbolic value of the coin and the substance value of its metallic content. Indeed, substance is supposed to vouchsafe the nominal value of the coin, countering symbolic fluctuations with the stable content of the gold or silver itself. Fichte undercuts the very logic of this relationship, reminding us "that the value of these metals ultimately comes down to the universal agreement about their value" (*Geschlossene Handelsstaat* 455). In other words, for Fichte gold and silver are no less arbitrary signs of value than are paper, leather, wood, or any other substance: the general agreement about their value is itself nothing but a universally accepted convention. Viewed from this perspective, the introduction of a new national currency in Fichte's rational state demands nothing more—but also nothing less—than a simple alteration of conventions and the implementation of legislative measures to assure the acceptance of the new monetary standard.

In real, pragmatic terms, although it flies in the face of common economic and semiotic assumptions, Fichte's proposal contains a potentially alluring amelioration of the monetary chaos that ruled throughout the German states at this time. It seems unimaginable to us today that at the time Fichte composed *Der geschlossene Handelsstaat* in 1800, there were no less than seventy currencies accepted and in circulation in the state of Prussia alone (Krause 237). In fact, according to the estimate of one historian of money, there were as many as five hundred different mints in the German territories of Europe (Trapp 67–68), and as late as 1833 one numismatic catalog listed over three hundred silver coins minted in Germany that were accepted as legal tender (95). Moreover, this general chaos of circulating coins in the German territories was further complicated by the fact that older coins were rarely withdrawn from circulation and reminted, and hence continued to be available, and that certain "hard" foreign currencies, such as the French louis d'or, were also universally accepted, sometimes even coveted. By 1870 the number of circulating currencies had been reduced throughout the German territories to a mere seven; this nonetheless meant that there were still seven competing currencies, which were distributed, moreover, by thirty-three different banks of issue (Hamerow 253). During the phase-in period of the euro, European citizens of today complained about the confusion caused by the short-term simultaneous circulation of just two currencies, the euro and their displaced national money. By comparison, how much greater and more persistent must have been the confusion of currencies in Fichte's Prussia. One can easily understand how the everyday act of simple monetary transactions brought home to citizens of the German principalities in the most concrete way the burdens of political fragmentation.

This points to a further motivation, beyond the demand of greater rationalization and simplicity, that drives Fichte's appeal for the introduction of a single unified national currency in his autonomous state: it guarantees the internal cohesion and community orientation of the citizens of that state itself. Let us recall the two expedients Novalis associated with the spirit of commerce: it infuses the world with dynamism and it fosters integration. These are exactly the two attributes Fichte hopes to secure for his closed commercial state based on the introduction of an inconvertible national currency: a stimulation of economic circulation within this strictly bounded commercial domain, and the integration of its citizens into a unified populace that identifies, via the monetary instrument arbitrarily instituted by state authority, both with this state itself and with the cohesive and autonomous community it constitutes. This is monetary nationalism pure and simple: the ex nihilo creation of a national community based on the privileged and exclusive use of a single inconvertible national currency.

Toward the end of his treatise, Fichte explicitly lays out the nationalist aims of this monetary instrument and the autonomous commercial state it engenders.

> It is clear that in such an autonomous nation, whose citizens live only among themselves and have extremely little contact with foreigners, who preserve their peculiar lifestyle, institutions, and customs by means of these regulations, who love with devotion their fatherland and everything

related to their fatherland, a high degree of national pride and a keenly distinctive national character will soon emerge. It will become another, thoroughly different nation. This introduction of a national currency is its true creation. (*Geschlossene Handelsstaat* 509)

We could hardly find a more lucid expression of the monetary nationalism Fichte pursues in this work: by ensuring the autonomy of the nation and forcing its citizens to interact as a nationally segregated group, the introduction of an arbitrary national currency has the potential not merely to transform the nation, but actually to *institute* it qua nation. In 1800 when composing *Der geschlossene Handelsstaat*, Fichte does not (yet) identify any trait *inherent* to the Germans that could serve as the basis for their integration into a national unity. In the absence of such an inherent national feature, nationalism must be procured by *inventing* a unifying symbol around which all Germans could rally: this symbol was a national currency.

More recently the German sociologist Niklas Luhmann has emphasized precisely this integrative property of money, arguing for an understanding of the monetary medium that stresses its symbolic, rather than its purely semiotic function. Accordingly, Luhmann conceives the system of monetary exchange in analogy to systems of communicative interchange.

Symbols thus are not signs. Money is also not a sign for something else, say, for some intrinsic value. Symbols are meaningful forms [*Sinnformen*] that make possible the unity of what is different. They *are* this unity, their external form is a representation of this unity, but not a sign for something else.

In communicative interrelationships symbols function as media that make it possible for the sender (alter) and the receiver (ego) to strive for unity while still retaining their differences. (*Wirtschaft* 257)

It is hard to imagine a better description of what Fichte sought to accomplish with the conception of a fiat national currency he presented in *Der geschlossene Handelsstaat*. The utopian aim of German politics in 1800 was nothing other than the achievement of a form of national unity that would respect the differences among those "German" territories and peoples who would amalgamate into the unified German national state. It is certainly no coincidence that before it is conceived in terms of ethno-linguistic identity, German nationalism is theorized along the lines of the commercial transaction. Acts of commercial exchange constitute the veritable prototype for structural interactions in which difference—distinct goods or products—is dissolved into equality—the abstractly, even subjectively conceived "equal value" between two different commodities that makes their exchange possible.

For Fichte, money becomes the symbol for this process by which one accomplishes unity in—and in spite of—difference. His fiat national currency is intended to function precisely as a symbol of this national identity, an identity instituted by semiotic convention and state authority, not grounded in any intrinsic connection among the citizens of the state, such as race, language, ethnicity, or shared cultural traditions. Seven years prior to his *Reden an die deutsche Nation* (Speeches to the German nation, 1807)—speeches that have become infamous as documents that defend a linguistically and culturally oriented theory of German nationhood based on the self-aggrandizing proposition that Germans belong together in a national community because they constitute an originary, self-identical, and authentic *Urvolk* (see 313–15, 460)—Fichte formulates a very different theory of German nationhood based on economic and monetary principles.[10] There is, let me stress, nothing at all substantial, intrinsic, or "authentic" in the theory of monetary nationalism Fichte outlines in *Der geschlossene Handelsstaat*. On the contrary, its logic is inherently simple: money by fiat produces national community by fiat; and this fiat money, along with the circulation and symbolic exchanges it generates, forms the only necessary bond that joins the national populace into an integral commonwealth. This is a principally nondiscriminatory theory that includes in the national community all those who participate in its economic exchanges, regardless of race, religious creed, class, and so on. From this central hypothesis follow all the other propositions Fichte articulates in this treatise. Above all, it explains his belief that this newly established monetary state would have to, and would have the absolute right to, assume the "natural" borders dictated to it by geography (*Geschlossene Handelsstaat* 482, 502). For Fichte's contemporaries, this was certainly an unmistakable call for German national consolidation along geographically defined natural borders, with national identity established according to economic and monetary union.

Let us return to Luhmann briefly in order to try to understand the cohesive, integrative character of the monetary symbol, since this will be significant for our discussion of Müller's theory of money as well. Luhmann is careful to insist on the original meaning and function of the *symbolon* (*Wirtschaft* 257). A symbol is a unified substance or form that is divided or broken into separate pieces; these fragments are distributed among a group of people who form a community or a secret society, and fitting the pieces of the *symbolon* back together at its unique fractures makes it possible to ascertain that its bearers are legitimate members of this community. The symbol, in short, serves as a purely conventional and arbitrary means of identification that represents the communal bond among a diverse group of individuals who, lacking such a sign, would not recognize each other as members of the same group. Symbols, in short, must stand in when no intrinsic criterion such as language, ethnicity, religion, or the like guarantees identity and shared community. The symbol not only represents the integrity of the group, but also serves as the concrete medium that fuses these individuals into a community identifiable as such, despite other differences. Similarly, those not in possession of the symbol are *excluded* from participation in this community and rendered recognizable as Others. These integrative and segregative functions are precisely the attributes Fichte associates with the national currency around which he structures his closed commercial state. Indeed, fiat currency is the "rational" principle upon which this state, this inherently *national*—but decidedly not *ethnic*—state, is erected.[11]

What remains constant in the nationalist theories Fichte propounds throughout his life is that they are conceived in terms of structures of mediation. What changes in the first decade of the nineteenth century, in response in part to pressing political exigencies, is the *currency* on which he predicates the integration of the Germans into a seamless national community. If in *Der geschlossene Handelsstaat* it is money that assumes this integrative function, in *Reden an die deutsche Nation* national education, or *Bildung*, plays an analogous role, operating as the general equivalent of a German national community. Whereas in the earlier treatise money serves as the glue that binds the German people, as consumers and symbol users, into an autonomous and self-identical community, in the later work *Bildung* is charged with creating the common basis of German national identity.[12] However, according to Fichte's argument, the condition of possibility of this *Bildung* is the authenticity of the Germans' shared language; for this, he claims, is what makes them more receptive to *Bildung* than any other people (*Reden* 311). Thus Fichte's conception of *Bildung* already bears an ethnolinguistic tinge that fundamentally redefines his earlier conception of German monetary nationalism.

We can throw this transformation into relief by contrasting the ethnologically nationalistic conception of *Bildung* in *Reden an die deutsche Nation* with the much more international and general theory of knowledge Fichte advocates in *Der geschlossene Handelsstaat*. In both instances knowledge functions as a kind of currency; however, in the earlier text it is knowledge in general that plays this role, and as a *universal* currency it underwrites a curious countereconomy that resists and undercuts the autocratic demand for the absolute economic closure of the nation-state. Not only are scholars and artists the only citizens of Fichte's autonomous state allowed to travel outside its boundaries, and who hence require access to international monetary instruments (*Geschlossene Handelsstaat* 506), but this nation itself must seek to attract and naturalize as citizens as many foreign scientists, engineers, industrialists, and artists of international repute as possible (500). What Fichte articulates here might be called a mercantilist theory of knowledge or scholarship: instead of amassing gold and silver as the measure of state wealth, Fichte's autonomous commercial state would attempt to colonize the domains of thought, knowledge, and information to ensure its political and economic hegemony. For the Fichte of the *Der geschlossene Handelsstaat*, at least, the balloon of the closed national economy is constantly punctured by the value of practical and theoretical knowledge, which operates as the single valid international currency. Fichte writes,

> There is nothing except knowledge [*Wissenschaft*] that so clearly
> dissolves all the differences of environment and of nations, and that
> purely and simply belongs to the human being as such, and not to the
> citizen. By means of knowledge human beings are, and should be, con-
> stantly interconnected, even after their segregation into distinct nations
> is completed in all other respects. (512)

Only knowledge is not a strictly national possession, but instead a universal human attribute that, once the world is divided up into commercially monadic nation states, will transcend these national boundaries and join human beings together *as* human beings, rather than as autonomous national citizens. What transpires in Fichte's thinking between *Der geschlossene Handelsstaat* and *Reden an die deutsche Nation* is that the initially *international* character of knowledge articulated in *Handelsstaat* is lent a more narrow ethnic-nationalist cast in *Reden* when it undergoes chrysalis into the specifically German notion of *Bildung*.

Monetary Nationalism and German Transcendental Idealism

In order to understand how deeply Fichte's monetary nationalism is rooted in mainstream Romantic thought, it is important to recognize that its theoretical makeup is entirely consistent with the transcendental idealism of Fichte's philosophical position. On the most general level, by insisting that all money is a *blosses Zeichen*, a "pure sign," or a mere conventional symbol of value (*Geschlossene Handelsstaat* 432, 487), Fichte fundamentally desubstantializes and idealizes it. But beyond this, the relationship between money and commodities mirrors the dialectical dynamic of the *Ich* and the *Nicht-Ich*, the I and the non-I, in Fichte's transcendental system: money, as a pure ideality, interacts with commodities as the objectively real, and in this interaction money itself is "realized." Thus Fichte writes of his national currency,

> It [*Das Landesgeld*, the national currency] relates immediately to commodities and it is realized in them; it is hence true, immediate, exclusive money. The mere expression: "something is realized in money" already contains the entire false system. Nothing can be realized in money, for money itself is not something real. The commodity is the true reality, and money is realized in it. (492)

Only in his artificial and inherently valueless national currency does money finally arrive at its essence as a priori ideality; this ideal money takes on reality in its dialectical interface with commodities as the objectively real. Indeed, we might go so far as to assert that money constitutes commodities qua commodities by *acting* upon them in such a way that causes them to enter into circulation; and commodities, *mutatis mutandis*, constitute money by functioning as the "body," the material substance or phenom-enological residue in which its ideality is made empirically manifest. To be sure, Fichte's national currency, as *symbolon*, does require represen-tation in some material form; but he demands that it be constituted of a *unique* substance that sets it apart from all other commodities (485–86). Although he claims to know exactly what substance is ideally suited to function as the monetary medium, Fichte refuses to divulge what it is, claiming that this must remain a state secret and hence cannot be revealed in print (437, 487).

Perhaps we can best understand the coherence of Fichte's transcendental system of knowledge in the *Wissenschaftslehre* (Doctrine of science, 1794) and the autonomous economic system proposed in *Der geschlossene Han-delsstaat* by viewing them through the lens of Luhmann's systems theory.[13] Both Fichte's transcendental and economic programs qualify, above all, as closed, self-maintaining, self-producing autopoietic systems in Luhmann's sense. In *Über den Begriff der Wissenschaftslehre* (On the concept of the science of knowledge), the summary of his transcendental system written in 1794, Fichte maintains that the entirety of his science of knowledge must be based on a single grounding principle whose absolute certainty cannot be questioned. All the other propositions of this "science" are linked to this founding principle and draw their validity from it. Of this anchoring principle he writes,

> Hence at least one proposition would have to be true, a proposition that would bestow its truthfulness on all the others; so that if, and to the extent that, this one proposition is true, a second one would be true as well, and if, and to the extent that, this second proposition is true, a third would also have to be true, etc. Thereby several propositions, which perhaps would even be quite distinct, would have one truth [*Gewissheit*] in common and would constitute one and the same science by the very fact that they *all* share this truth [*Gewissheit*]—and that it is *the same* truth [*Gewissheit*]. (*Über den Begriff der Wissenschaftslehre* 40–41)

We know, of course, what constitutes the fundamental principle of the *Wissenschaftslehre*: it is the proposition I = I, or I am I (*Über den Begriff der Wissenschaftslehre* 61). Fichte claims that the transcendental ego posits itself and hence that this principle of identity has absolute validity in and of itself. What this means is that there is no "origin" or ground beyond this ego that might serve as the basis of its constitution; for if this were the case, what grounds the ego from without, not the ego itself, could lay claim to being the absolute transcendental principle. The self-grounding or a priori nature of the ego is thus fundamental to the structure of Fichte's system: it generates the transcendental system of knowledge as a *closed* but *stable* conglomerate of valid interrelationships among the logical propositions of knowledge.[14] This structural constitution is exactly replicated in the closed economic system of Fichte's *Der geschlossene Handelsstaat*; however, here the grounding transcendental principle is not I = I, but instead, money = money, or money is money. Or, to put it another way, money is valid because it is money. And *because* this monetary principle is valid, all the economic exchanges within this system are valid and constitute a closed, internally coherent system.

Novalis, one of the most powerful and reflective readers of Fichte, recognized the relevance of this analogy. In his notebooks Novalis recorded under the heading "Philosophy" the following entry:

> The S[cience of] K[nowledge] or pure phil[osophy] is the relational schema of the s[ciences] as such. It is produced from the *idea* of using, instead of actual, identifiable, individ[ual] things, universal things that can be substituted for every thing (vid. conc[ept] o[f] *money*), or of using such words and of attempting to carry out the usual operations by means of them, as simple, isolated, *unadulterated signs* [*unvermischbaren Zeichen*] and materials—which thereby appear purely in all their consequence and interconnection . . . [as] gener[ally] *valid* [*Geltende*] propositions. (*Schriften* 3: 378–79)[15]

If, according to Novalis, the very system of the *Wissenschaftslehre* is predicated on an abstraction from real things and a reliance on a universal general equivalent—a kind of "money of the mind," to allude to Marx's famous phrase ("Ökonomisch-philosophische Manuskripte" 571–72)—then the same is true for the valid transactions mediated by the purely idealized currency of Fichte's autonomous commercial state.[16] Novalis recognized, in short, that *Geld*, or money, becomes *geltend*, or valid and valuable, precisely on the basis of its institution as the founding proposition of a closed economic system.

Gold and silver coins could never perform the function of a grounding principle in Fichte's sense because they refer beyond themselves to a system of value dependent on the market in precious metals. Fichte's fiat money, by contrast, posits itself, much in the same way as does his transcendental ego: its validity as money resides solely in the arbitrary declaration that it will function as such, as well as in the mediating role it plays within the closed economic system itself. In fact, this fiat money as founding principle produces and guarantees the autonomy of the closed commercial state in the first place. Fichte thus is one of the first to theorize in detail an idea of money in its modern systems-theory conception as a form of self-reference. "Money is instituted self-reference," Luhmann writes in *Die Wirtschaft der Gesellschaft*. "Money has no 'innate value,' it exhausts its meaning in its reference to the system that makes possible and conditions the use of money" (16). We observe, then, a curious homology between the system of transcendental knowledge propounded in the *Wissenschaftslehre* and the economic system Fichte outlines in *Der geschlossene Handelsstaat*. Indeed, given Fichte's insistence on the practical implementation of his theoretical philosophy, we are justified in interpreting this economic program as nothing other than the pragmatic, political extension of his transcendental system of knowledge.[17]

Adam Müller, "Credit," and the Monetarized Nation

If Fichte were the only thinker among the German Romantics to formulate a substantive theory of monetary nationalism, this might strike us as an anomaly or as a mere curiosity. But the fact that Adam Müller developed a conception that in many respects resembles Fichte's ideas indicates that monetary nationalism represents a theoretical direction more persistently pursued by the Romantics than has generally been acknowledged. Indeed, Müller will turn the screw of Fichte's idealized, transcendentalist money one turn further, pointing ahead to the purely ethereal money of modern electronic funds transfers, by insisting that the essence of money resides solely in its symbolic function and that it hence requires no concrete substance whatsoever. We may be surprised to discover that Fichte and Müller express such compatible economic theories, for with regard to their political points of departure they represent diametrically opposite poles of German Romantic thought, Fichte beginning as a radical republican who defended the principles of the French Revolution,[18] Müller as the "political Romantic," to apply Carl Schmitt's phrase,[19] who advocated a return to the medieval feudal order.

The intellectual distance between Fichte and Müller seems to be confirmed by the irony that Müller composed a scathing critique of Fichte's *Der geschlossene Handelsstaat*, which he published in the 1801 issue of the *Neue Berlinische Monatsschrift*. In this review Müller attacks Fichte as a hopeless amateur in matters of political economy and the science of the state, maintaining that this treatise could only be written by someone whose ignorance is compounded by the arrogance with which he asserts that his ideas represent the only rational state theory ("Über einen philosophischen Entwurf von Hrn Fichte" 436–38). Following Kant and Novalis in identifying commerce and exchange as the pathway to peaceful coexistence among human beings (456–57), Müller protests in particular against the severe limitations Fichte places on trade, the starkly interventionist nature of his state, and against the coercive and authoritarian element in Fichte's theory. For those familiar with the rabidly anti-Smithian character of Müller's later economic theories—as outlined in the previous chapter—it will come as a shock to recognize that in this early review he takes sides with Smith against Fichte, going so far as to celebrate Smith as "the great founder of political economy" (458). A decade later, when writing his *Versuche einer neuen Theorie des Geldes*, Müller would sing an entirely different tune, jettisoning in toto the principles of Smith's laissez-faire market and his capital-oriented economic policies. In fact, Müller's later economic doctrines draw much of their energy from their opposition to the economic liberalism of Smith, to the extent that many of Müller's economic policies are formulated in direct contradistinction to Smith's principles. As we saw in the previous chapter, however, Müller was also a staunch advocate of fiduciary money, and it is this position, above all, that constitutes the primary link between the monetary theory he developed in the *Versuche einer neuen Theorie des Geldes* and the conception of a national currency formulated by Fichte. Moreover, for Müller as well, the invention of a fiat currency ultimately serves the end of creating a closed, integral community or a unified German national state.

Since the foregoing chapter investigated in detail Müller's unabashed advocacy of fiat money and its relationship to the semiotics of language propagated by the German Romantics, the main points of his more general economic program only need to be summarized in brief here. In the *Versuche* Müller comes down squarely on the side of credit money, arguing, as did Fichte, against the notion that paper money is a mere second-order representation of metallic money; indeed, he reverses this relationship, giving priority to the "word," to the stamp that makes metal into minted coin, defining this nominalist aspect of the coin as its principal feature (see *Versuche* 140). Legal tender, for Müller, is constituted not by any intrinsic value, but rather by the "credit" placed in it and in the state that issues it and secures its value. Thus for Müller money is nothing other than the symbol of a primordial human sociability, a solicitous codependence among human beings. In addition to defending money in its purely symbolic form, we also saw that Müller firmly believed in the strictly circulationist function of money and in the idea that value is created through the differential interaction of structural components, as a *Wechselwirkung*, or dynamic reciprocity, rather than being defined by some inherent substance. Moreover, Müller opposes the idea that monetary economies are wholly impersonal and hence disrupt and alienate the intersubjective bonds among individuals. Whereas Karl Marx, for example, would subsequently attack money as "the fraternization of impossibilities" and as a power that "forces contradictions to embrace each other" ("Ökonomisch-philosophische Manuskripte" 567), Müller praises money for precisely these same integrative and binding powers.[20] For him, money manifests precisely the interpersonal bond that joins two individuals in any act of exchange, the mutual obligation they share whenever they enter into a commercial transaction. Müller's definition of money as pure sign is strategically calculated to support a system of perpetual interhuman circulation.

> [I]n and of itself money, the most marketable commodity as such, has
> no value and it is absolutely nothing without the traffic between people

and things; . . . but conversely there is also no traffic between people and things without this third, higher mediating entity, without money. (*Versuche* 181–82)

As the "higher third term," money is the most tangible manifestation of this reciprocal process: it is mediation, as an absolutely immaterial process, embodied in the materiality of the sign or symbol. The monetary sign, as sign, points to the interactive process of communication and stands in for the "credit" or "credibility," the interpersonal obligation, that Müller views as the condition of possibility for all exchange and all community integrity.

Let us turn now to the nationalist aspect of this monetary theory. We should note, first of all, that the very notion of financial credit, with its orientation toward payment in a distant future, merges the dimension of a future temporality with the interhuman dimension of trust, confidence, and mutual faith. Financial credit and personal credibility (or creditworthiness) are always two sides of the same coin, so to speak. This intertwining of a perspective toward the future with communitarian bonds lends the concept of credit a potentially powerful role in any project for establishing national identity or shared communitarian sentiment. J. G. A. Pocock has argued more generally for the eighteenth century that the emergent institution of credit contributed to a radical transformation of political behavior. In his words, credit "is based upon opinion concerning a future rather than memory of a past" (*Machiavellian Moment* 440), and as such it helps bring about a significant temporal reorientation in political thinking. It should be obvious that such a reorientation away from the past and toward a future, rife with yet unrealized potential, was nowhere so much the order of the day at the turn to the nineteenth century in Europe as it was in the German territories. When the Germans looked back to a national past, the best political institution they could discover there was the Holy Roman Empire, which the Romantics often enough idealized and mystified as a unified Catholic Middle Ages. Of course, by the time Müller began writing his political and economic treatises, the last remnants of the Holy Roman Empire had been—mercifully—snuffed out by Napoleon. There was no better time than the period in which Müller was writing to attempt to establish an orientation toward a new German national future.

What better way to try to accomplish this than by deploying the ideology of credit, which already entailed a temporal orientation toward the future and implied an unspoken bond of trust, faith, and credibility? And what better way to institutionalize these intangible bonds of a shared community and a common future than in the concrete symbol of a fiduciary currency? In this sense, Müller's program for a German symbolic currency always had as one of its implicit principles the organization of a German nation, understood as a community that shared a certain symbology representative of their immaterial personal bonds, and based on the introduction of a common inconvertible fiat currency.

This nationalist orientation of Müller's economic program, however, is much more than merely implicit in his monetary theory. He articulates it explicitly as early as 1810, in a telling passage from his *Elemente der Staatskunst* (Elements of statecraft) in which he identifies individuals with the money of the national state.

> That all individuals in the state should assume the character of money, or increasingly become true money; that their true value should be elevated in exchange, in commercial intercourse, in social life; that their . . . *civic character* should be enhanced: all this should be the great and inherently national aim of every state economist.—The more every single individual in the state, be it person or thing, enters into relationships with all others—the more it makes itself, in short, into money—the more concentrated and vital the state will become, the more fluidly it will move, the greater the energy it will be able to generate, the more it will be able to produce. (1: 355)

What we call circulation in the economic realm manifests itself as sociability in the interpersonal domain of the community. The circulatory power of monetary signs proves to be the very model and basis of this social interaction: it defines, it *creates* the national state as a solidarity inaugurated by the "credit" and obligation of monetary exchange.

As the institution that founds confidence and faith in the monetary instrument by assigning it its stamp, the state forms the nucleus of this dynamic system of never-ending interaction, exchange, and mutual obligation. For this reason, Müller, similar to Fichte, objected to external trade or exchanges that extend beyond the confines of the individual state precisely because he believed such international commercial interactions threatened to undermine the alliance that constitutes the national community (Briefs 295). Much like Fichte, Müller blamed metallic money as a universal, international currency for the breaching of national bonds in favor of abstract and more distant connections. In an essay on paper money, "Vom Papiergelde," published in 1812, Müller voiced this critique in the most uncompromising terms.

> Since those who possessed metals, precisely because of the universal validity [*Allgemeingültigkeit*] of their possession, acquired the same position and power throughout all of Europe, the preference for what is nearer, for the neighborly [*Nachbarliche*], for the fatherland, and for all that is national increasingly disappeared, which allowed the superficial notions of the universal state, of humanity, cosmopolitanism, philanthropy to take hold everywhere. (31)

Metallic coin is not merely the symptom of an alienation from the more proximate ties of immediate community and nationhood, it is held up as the *cause* of this alienation, paving the way for abstract notions such as "humanity" and "cosmopolitanism." According to this view, it is precisely the *universality* of specie that makes it a threat to the more localized national state. Inconvertible paper money, by contrast, forces buyers and sellers to think in local terms, and hence it appears as an antidote to the mercantile economy that focuses on the accumulation of precious metals, an antidote, moreover, that will return human beings to the more immediate ties of national community. In the very same essay Müller thus can maintain,

> All neighborly [*nachbarlichen*], national transactions must be settled with the representative of personal services, with paper money. The power of this paper resides solely in the intimacy of this neighborly [*nachbarlichen*] and national union and in the credit [*Glauben*] placed in it. (33–34)

Paper money, as pure symbolic abstraction, represents nothing but the neighborly bonds of community, the faith and trust of immediate interpersonal obligation. As was true for Fichte, for Müller as well, paper money becomes the symbol of national unity and national identity.

We can now better understand what I meant when I said that Müller takes the desubstantialization of money even further than does Fichte. If for Fichte the national bonds created by money still rely on the designation of some arbitrary and self-identical substance as the monetary currency, the "symbol" by which the citizens of the closed commercial state identify their membership in this exclusive community, for Müller the sign of this identity is localized in the entirely intangible relationships spawned by the state-sponsored monetary sign. In short, money has become abstract *Wechselwirkung*, reciprocity or reciprocal interaction as such. In this sense the concept of money promulgated by Müller fuses into a single dialectical interchange the two characteristics Novalis associated with the spirit of commerce: circulation and integration. The circulation stimulated by the purely ideal monetary sign simultaneously and necessarily forges the links that bind the participants in exchange into an integral national community. The very act of exchange *presupposes* absolute "credit"—faith, trust, and confidence—among those who enter into a commercial contract; but it also creates and enhances this credit with each successful act of "commerce." The state underwrites this community grounded in mutual faith by supplying its own trustworthiness and authority as the grain of sand that will eventually produce the pearl of national reciprocity and community identity. What is more, the deferred future marked out by the institution of credit is nothing other than the future of the (national) state that issues the symbolic monetary instrument and thereby guarantees its value and validity.

By way of conclusion, let us explore two broader historical questions connected to the monetary nationalism of German Romanticism. The first relates to the almost uncanny historical constellation of Fichte's and Müller's nationalist theories themselves. If we expand our scope beyond the confines of their economic programs, we are struck by the fact that both undergo a parallel shift from an initial focus on monetary nationalism to a subsequent concentration on linguistic and ethnocultural nationalism. We have already briefly noted this transformation in Fichte from *Der geschlossene Handelsstaat* to *Reden an die deutsche Nation*. What is curious is that Müller passes through a similar transfiguration. I am thinking of the arguments he makes in his *Zwölf Reden über die Beredsamkeit und deren Verfall in Deutschland* (Twelve lectures on eloquence and its decline in Germany), which were presented in Vienna in 1812, a year or so after he had finished the manuscript of his *Versuche einer neuen Theorie des Geldes*. We should note at the outset that the fluidity with which both Fichte and Müller move from a nationalism based on money to one based on language confirms the hypothesis presented in the two previous chapters that, in German Romanticism, as in eighteenth-century German thought in general, a well-defined homology links the domains of economics and linguistics, money and language. In his lectures on eloquence, Müller attacks the German reliance on the written word, comparing it to the mercantilist dependence on a monetary unit based on specie (*Zwölf Reden über die Beredsamkeit* 327),[21] and he argues instead for a concept of eloquence located in the living exchange of verbal speech and active dialogue. Here verbal exchange embodies the same reciprocity that money represents in Müller's economic and political theory. Moreover, Müller's *Zwölf Reden über die Beredsamkeit* culminate in a glorification of the German language, which, in his view, is peculiarly suited to an eloquence more elevated than what can be achieved in French or English (444). Yet this is by no means the end point of his linguistic chauvinism: he goes on to assert that the German language is inhabited by an endemic *Geist*, a spirit or intellect unknown to other languages (448). As was true for Fichte, this greater authenticity of the German language reflects positively on the speakers of German, because, as Müller claims, "without independence, without the immediacy of intellectual energy, [it is impossible] . . . to speak this [the German] language well" (449). In this conception, German national identity is generated as a by-product of German linguistic identity, rather than being produced by the design and device of an idealized monetary instrument.

Finally, we can draw some conclusions about the implications of this parallel redefinition of national identity by Fichte and Müller for the broader history of German nationalism. We recognize, first of all, that for these two thinkers monetary nationalism presented itself as a possibility *prior to* their turn to a linguistically and ethnically based form of nationalism. One can even hypothesize that ethnolinguistic nationalism only came to the forefront among the Romantics *after* the theory of monetary nationalism proved impossible to put into practice. Whereas a unitary and nationally binding monetary instrument had first to be *invented*, *implemented*, and, above all, *accepted* by the wider German populace, ethnolinguistic identity—with a little bit of tweaking, given differences in dialect—could be asserted as given. To be sure, monetary and ethnolinguistic forms of nationalism are not mutually exclusive positions, neither for the Romantics nor for later generations. What we witness in Fichte and Müller can best be described as a dramatic shift in weight, against the historical backdrop of the war against Napoleon and the exaggerated nationalism it fostered, from a primarily economic to a linguistically and ethnologically defined theory of nationalism. It is also important to recognize that monetary and ethnolinguistic nationalism emerge as the two primary avenues of German nationalism at a time when *political* unification, given the realities of territorial, religious, and ideological fragmentation, seems to be the least likely alternative for German national identity.

If we step back even further and take into our purview more recent German history, we recognize a kind of elliptical trajectory in the evolution of modern German nationalism. Receiving one of its first elaborate theorizations as monetary nationalism in Romantic economic theory, it quickly shifts to an ethnolinguistic focus. Over the course of the nineteenth century this impulse builds into a full-blown culturally based conception of German nationalism, which ultimately gives way at the end of the nineteenth and beginning of the twentieth century to the notion of the racial state, the conception of German national identity along genetic-racial lines.[22] When German nationalism is reconfigured in the wake of the demonic form racial nationalism assumed in the Third Reich, it revives the monetary nationalism that was generated by economic Romanticism prior to the Romantics' emphasis on ethnolinguistic nationalistic theories: it emerges not as political nationalism, since Germany is once again territorially and ideologically divided, but rather as the monetary nationalism of the Federal Republic. Ironically, postwar D-mark nationalism represents a kind of modern realization of Fichte's and Müller's theories of monetary nationhood, which had existed only latently or "theoretically," and were effectively and practically displaced by ethnolinguistic nationalism throughout the nineteenth and early twentieth centuries.

In what direction will German national identity go now that postwar D-mark nationalism has been put to rest? Will the introduction of the euro foster a new international identity among the Germans? These are questions best answered by political prophets, not by literary and cultural historians. Instead of trying to deal with these knotty issues related to the Germans' political and economic future, we will return to our examination of cross-fertilizations between economic theory and intellectual developments in the later decades of the eighteenth century, turning this time to the German reception of French physiocratic doctrine and the fallout it had for larger issues of cultural value and modes of literary representation.

4 / Economics and the Imagination

Cultural Values and the Debate over Physiocracy in Germany, 1770–1789

Many things become clear once one has a firm determination of what value is.

> —Georg Friedrich Wilhelm Hegel (*Grundlinien der Philosophie des Rechts*, in *Theorie-Werkausgabe* 7: 136)

A [cynic is a] man who knows the price of everything and the value of nothing.

> —Oscar Wilde (*Lady Windermere's Fan* 67)

The German Debate over Physiocracy

OVER A PERIOD OF ABOUT TWENTY YEARS, FROM 1770 through 1789, a heated economic controversy raged in German-speaking Europe that focused on the principles of the economic system known as physiocracy, which had emerged in France about twenty years earlier out of the collaboration between François Quesnay (1694–1774) and the Marquis Victor de Mirabeau (1715–89).[1] Based on what it considered the "natural" or divinely ordained order of the world, physiocracy in many respects represented a transitional or even contradictory political-economic program.[2] Placing priority on agriculture and eschewing industrial forms of production such as manufacturing, it tended to view landed property owners as the economic, political, and moral backbone

of civil society, thereby lending support to the social and proprietary structures of the feudal order. In keeping with this, the French physiocrats championed hereditary monarchy as the ideal form of government, stressing the
role of a powerful political leader as the prerequisite for economic and
social stability. By contrast, however, the physiocrats also were vociferous
opponents of the feudal guild system, arguing explicitly for its suspension
and freedom of occupational choice for all, and they were staunch advocates of free-trade policies, believing fervently that production and consumption are best controlled by internal market factors rather than by
top-down economic regulations. In this regard they looked ahead to the
free-market economic system that was beginning to take hold in Europe
and whose theoretical foundations were laid with the publication of Adam
Smith's *Wealth of Nations* in 1776. If the physiocrats are commonly identified as the first school of modern economic thought, then this has to do above
all with Quesnay's attempt, laid out graphically in his famous *tableau économique* (economic table), first published in 1759, to conceive of economics as an interactive, if closed system, in which all elements work together
in mutual interdependence and harmony (see fig. 1).

In German-speaking Europe, physiocracy found two devoted principal
advocates: the Swiss civil servant Isaak Iselin (1728–82), whose *Versuch über
die gesellige Ordnung* (Essay on the civil order, 1772) is one of the first systematic expositions of physiocratic economic and political theories written
in German, and the economist Johannn August Schlettwein (1731–1802),
active first in Carlsruhe at the court of Margrave Karl Friedrich of Baden
(1728–1811)—himself an advocate of physiocratic economic policies—then
after 1777 as professor of political economy and public administration at
the University of Giessen. Schlettwein's *Die wichtigste Angelegenheit für
das ganze Publicum: Oder die natürliche Ordnung in der Politik überhaupt*
(The most important matter for the general public, or The natural order in
politics as such), published in two volumes in 1772 and 1773, represents,
alongside Iselin's *Versuch über die gesellige Ordnung*, the other founding
document of the German physiocratic movement. Both Iselin and Schlettwein committed their lives to the advocacy of physiocratic economic principles, as made manifest not only in their many publications on the subject,
but also in the creation of journals dedicated to the elucidation and dissemination of physiocratic ideas. In 1776 Iselin founded the *Ephemeri-*

den der Menschheit (Ephemerides of humanity), based on the model of the French periodical *Ephémérides du citoyen*, which was the ideological organ of the physiocratic school. Iselin edited this influential journal until his death in 1782, and it continued publication for several more years, through 1786. For his part, Schlettwein initiated the *Archiv für den Menschen und Bürger in allen Verhältnissen* (Archive for the human being and citizen in all circumstances), of which eight volumes appeared from 1780 to 1784 and which was followed in 1785 through 1788 by a five-volume sequel, the *Neues Archiv für den Menschen und Bürger in allen Verhältnissen.*

The year 1778 marks the beginning of the public controversy surrounding physiocratic economic thought that flared up among German intellectuals. It was in this year that Christian Wilhelm von Dohm (1751–1820) published an essay highly critical of physiocracy in one of the leading German cultural journals of the day, the *Deutsches Museum.* Somewhat innocuously titled "Über das physiokratische System" (On the physiocratic system), this essay appeared in the October 1778 issue of this journal and was republished in book form that same year under the title *Kurze Darstellung des physiokratischen Systems* (Brief portrayal of the physiocratic system). Dohm was not alone in his vocal opposition to all the central tenets of physiocratic economic policy. Approximately simultaneously with his essay an unsigned critique of physiocratic tax policy, "Etwas über das Steuerwesen und die physiokratischen Grundsätze, die Einrichtung desselben betreffend" (On taxation and the physiocratic principles concerning its implementation), appeared in 1778 in the *Hannoverisches Magazin,* and in 1779 another anonymously authored critique was published in the *Gelehrte Beyträge zu den Braunschweigischen Zeitungen.* This second essay was conceived as a response to an article by Jakob Mauvillon (1743–94), a military officer and teacher at the military academy in Cassel. Mauvillon's essay, titled "Von der öffentlichen und privat Üppigkeit (Luxe) und den wahren Mitteln ihr zu steuern" (On public and private luxury and the true means for controlling it), appeared in 1777 and used arguments drawn from physiocratic principles to indict luxury as economically unproductive. Mauvillon had already displayed his allegiance to French physiocracy several years earlier when he translated A. R. J. Turgot's (1727–81) *Investigation on the Nature and Origin of Wealth* into German.[3] Mauvillon even-

tually emerged as one of the most avid and intelligent defenders of physiocracy against its detractors, publishing in 1780 a rebuttal of the critiques
by Dohm and the two previously mentioned anonymous essayists in a book
titled *Physiokratische Briefe an den Herrn Professor Dohm, oder Vertheidigung und Erläuterung der wahren Staatswirthschaftlichen Gesetze die
unter dem Namen des Physiokratischen Systems bekannt sind* (Physiocratic
letters addressed to Professor Dohm, or Defense and explanation of the
true economic laws that have come to be known as the physiocratic system). Already in 1779, Karl Gottfried Fürstenau (1734–1803) rallied support for physiocratic economic policies in his *Versuch einer Apologie des
physiokratischen Systems* (Attempt at an apologia of the physiocratic system), and the publicist Wilhelm Ludwig Wekhrlin (1739–99) joined the
ranks of physiocracy's vocal supporters by championing the benefits of
this economic program in his journal *Chronologen*.[4] However, these
statements for the defense simply gave rise to more vicious rebuttals, and
in 1780 one of the foremost German political economists of the time,
Johann Friedrich von Pfeiffer (1718–87), published a strident attack on
physiocracy in a book that bore the provocative title *Der Antiphysiokrat,
oder umständliche Untersuchung des physiokratischen Systems* (The anti-
physiocrat, or Detailed examination of the physiocratic system). Contributions taking both sides of the debate subsequently appeared in journals
throughout German-speaking Europe, and political economists came to be
defined according to the position they assumed, pro or contra, with regard
to this highly visible controversy. Fürstenau went so far as to claim that
the term "physiocracy" itself had become so fashionable and vague that
it had lost its specific meaning (3), and in this sense his treatise represents
an attempt to lend physiocratic principles more definition and precision.
This dispute ultimately reached such a high pitch in German intellectual
circles of the final decades of the eighteenth century that it assumed the
status of a public event (Braunreuther 59), and Georg Andreas Will
(1727–98) confirmed the popular importance of this quarrel when in 1780
he began holding public lectures on physiocracy and the contentious discussions surrounding it. These lectures were published two years later in
book form as *Versuch über die Physiokratie, deren Geschichte, Literatur,
Inhalt und Werth* (Essay on physiocracy, its history, scholarship, substance,
and value).[5]

As this brief summary indicates, much more was at stake in this impassioned controversy over physiocratic theory than a simple squabble about economic principles. At the very least, this dispute helped catapult political-economic questions into the forefront of intellectual discussions in Germany at the time, and the issues it raised turned on pivotal themes that spilled over from the narrower field of economic theory into broader topics of cultural-political relevance. The heart of this conflict was constituted by divergent definitions of the human being as a creative and productive creature, discordant conceptions of the role of surplus and excess as motivators of human actions, differing views of the nature and meaning of productivity, and, above all, by a disagreement about the function of the human imagination in the generation of surplus value and of value as such in the more general domain of human cultural production. The aim of the deliberations that follow is to interrogate this controversy surrounding physiocracy as a kind of focal point at which these larger cultural and anthropological questions began to crystallize in the closing decades of the eighteenth century.

The Theory and Practice of Physiocracy
in German-Speaking Europe

When Johann Heinrich Jung-Stilling (1740–1817) delivered his inaugural lecture in 1778 upon his appointment as professor for public finance and administration (*Kameralwissenschaften*) at the Kameral-Hohe-Schule in Kaiserslautern—the first institution of higher education in the German territories that concentrated on questions of state economic policy and public administration[6]—he summarized in just a few brief sentences some of the most hotly contested issues in economic discussions of the day. Economic theory, Jung-Stilling maintains, is inherently bound up with one's understanding of the human being, the nature of his or her physical and psychological needs, and one's ability to satisfy these needs.

> The preservation and elevation of the human being is promoted by particular means. These means are (when limited to earthly life) nothing other than products of the earth. The preservation of existence is pro-

moted by fundamental drives anchored in human nature or by physical
desires. They cause the emergence of essential needs, which are occupied
with the struggle for their own satisfaction. However, the elevation of
the human being—be it false or genuine—stems from psychic sources,
from the imagination. These also summon up psychological desires,
which ultimately, due to the power of habit, have an influence on the
finest substance of the body itself, thereby producing coincidental and
luxurious needs, after whose satisfaction one strives with almost the
same hunger as for the means to satisfy one's essential needs.
("Öffentlicher Anschlag" 18–19)

What Jung-Stilling outlines here is a fundamentally dualistic economic
order: on the one hand, there are physical needs that are satisfied by the
products of the earth; on the other hand, humans experience psychological desires, produced not by existential needs, but generated instead in the
human imagination, and these likewise demand fulfillment. The dualistic
character of the human being as *physis* and *psyche* corresponds to two separate and distinct economic orders, a first order devoted to the requirements for sustaining the body, a second order dedicated to satisfying the
demands of the imagination or the psyche. This is a dichotomy that Karl
Marx (1818–83), writing nearly a century later in the opening pages of
Das Kapital (1867), would express in terms of the metaphors of the stom-
ach (*Magen*) and the imagination (*Phantasie*) as the sources of all the needs
satisfied by commodities (49). As purely physical beings, humans are concerned primarily with issues of self-preservation and subsistence: they seek
to discover and/or produce the means to satisfy their base bodily needs.
But as psychological creatures, an entirely new dimension enters into their
existence: a domain we might identify as pure desire or luxury, as the demand
for refinements or cultural amenities that eventually become so much a
part of our everyday existence that they attain the status of a second nature
whose fulfillment becomes equally or even more important than the satisfaction of elementary existential needs.

If for us, as citizens of the twenty-first century, the interpenetration of
desire, psychology, and economics proposed here by Jung-Stilling seems to
articulate a popular commonplace, this was by no means true for Germans
living in the final quarter of the eighteenth century. What stands out most

about Jung-Stilling's proposition is the idea that satisfaction of existential needs, while fundamentally necessary, represents but a steady-state economy, without essential development or progress, whereas the *elevation* of the human species requires the emergence of that mysterious second economy, tied to fabricated or "imaginary" desires, which evolve out of the human being's more complex psychological makeup. In other words, what Jung-Stilling articulates is a rudimentary description of an economic theory based on a notion of libidinally driven human nature. As we will see, conceptions of this libidinal economy were just beginning to gel in theoretical deliberations at the end of the eighteenth century, paving the way for a paradigm shift in economic thought that Joseph Vogl locates around the turn from the eighteenth to the nineteenth century in Germany (*Kalkül und Leidenschaft* 12–17). We might even speculate that it is nothing other than this psycholibidinal undercurrent in modern economic theory that expresses itself in such metaphors as Adam Smith's infamous "invisible hand," which bears testimony to the dawning sensibility that economic forces operate behind the back (or below the surface) of rational human subjects. What stands out in Jung-Stilling's proposal, at any rate, is the implicit assertion that human beings only enter into an advanced stage of cultivation with the emergence of this second-order economy of libidinal— as opposed to existential—needs. Of particular interest for the present investigation is the human faculty to which he attributes the power of generating these subsidiary economic drives and desires: the capacity for imagination. It is here, in the human fantasy—not in some deep-seated will or elementary psychological drive—that what Jung-Stilling calls "imaginary" needs are generated; and for him these imaginary needs become the motor driving cultural and economic progress. Since the subsistence needs of human beings are finite, growing only in proportion to the growth in population, they represent a static, closed economy; by contrast, those desires generated by the imagination are unlimited and hence constitute the potential for an infinite, open-ended economy of never-ending growth—the growth economy that has become the accepted standard for industrial and postindustrial nations.

For the late eighteenth century, prior to the advent of Romanticism, Jung-Stilling's valorization of the *imagination* as the force powering not merely the libidinal economy but cultural progress as such is a radical, even heretical view. To be sure, Jung-Stilling himself is not able to embrace without reservation this second-order economy of the imagination as a positive force—hence his aside that cultural elevation can follow either a "false" or a "genuine" path. Indeed, Jung-Stilling tends to view the production of "luxury" goods that satisfy libidinal desires with the skepticism of many of his contemporaries, in particular those who defended the physiocratic system.[7] But what is especially noteworthy about Jung-Stilling's arguments in the quoted passage is that the term "reason," one of the dominant discursive touchstones of the time, does not come into play at all. In this sense, Jung-Stilling's insistence on the imagination as the *productive* and creative human faculty par excellence bespeaks a profound break with the traditional values of Enlightenment culture—with rationality, calculated foresight, planning, and deliberate action. His economic human being, goaded on by desires produced in the imagination, is shot through with an element of irrationality and unpredictability that defies rational control and oversight. It is precisely this irrationally desiring human being, driven by sensuality and unfettered imagination, that is the bogeyman of many conservative economists of the period. The physiocrat Johann August Schlettwein, for example, denounces sensual pleasures and the fantasies of the imagination as diversions that direct productive energies away from the gratification of more basic human existential needs. He concludes by condemning individuals with such libidinal, luxury-oriented proclivities in no uncertain terms: "Hence the effect of those human beings whose purpose lies solely in enjoying the pleasures of the senses and of the imagination is to be a dam against the propagation of human life" (*Grundfeste der Staaten* 404–05). We should note the fundamental opposition between the metaphors employed by Jung-Stilling and Schlettwein: what for the former is a mechanism driving cultural refinement, the latter views as a dam that hinders precisely any such cultural progress or evolution. Of course, there is a certain amount of class antagonism underwriting Schlettwein's critique: his reproof is spoken by the bourgeois intellectual who condemns the wanton wastefulness of an aristocratic leisure class, warning against its epidemic spread to the rising middle classes, a phenomenon made most palpable in the incipient rise of fashion and the cultural debates surrounding this economic and cultural phenomenon.[8] However, this denunciation of the "superfluous" products of the luxury-goods economy became a much more general economic position in this period, and it represents one of the positions defended most stalwartly by the advocates of physiocracy.[9]

To the extent that he downplays the dominance of pure reason in economic life, Jung-Stilling assumes a role among German economic thinkers that is parallel to that of the Sturm und Drang writers in the domain of literature—people such as Jakob Michael Reinhold Lenz (1751–92), Friedrich Maximillian Klinger (1752–1831), the young Johann Wolfgang von Goethe (1749–1832), and Friedrich von Schiller (1759–1805).[10] His acknowledgement of the turbulence of the passions derives from the purported struggles he experienced taming his own insistent desires (if we believe his enormously popular *Lebensgeschichte*, the autobiography published episodically over the course of Jung-Stilling's life). In the retrospective summary of his life that he appends to the fifth volume of *Lebensgeschichte*, published in 1804 and bearing the title *Heinrich Stillings Lehr-Jahre* (Heinrich Stilling's years as pedagogue), he names as the inherent impulse dominating his "natural character" not the religious piety that came to be his lifelong mission, but rather a proclivity for sensual pleasures and enjoyments that stood in diametrical opposition to his religious education (*Lebensgeschichte* 602). From the vantage point of this personal self-appraisal it is easy to see why, in the essay "Leitlinien erfolgreicher Wohlstandsmehrung" (Rules for the successful accumulation of wealth, 1783), addressed to the German princes, Jung-Stilling insists, in words similar to those that Schlettwein used to attack the second-order economy of imaginary desires, that it is incumbent upon economic and political leaders to build barriers against the addiction to luxury. In this context Jung-Stilling not only voices his skepticism about the penchant for commerce as something that reinforces the drive for luxury and excess, but even draws a parallel between free trade and a free-spirited sensibility that ignores the dictates of religion (44). In other words, luxury, as the enjoyment of excess and the fulfillment of desires that go beyond existential needs, is not only economically problematic but also morally and religiously reprehensible. Ultimately, then, Jung-Stilling displays a profound ambivalence about the value of an economy based on the imagined needs of luxury and sensual gratification: whereas the economist in him grudgingly concedes its productivity as a stimulus to economic growth, the Pietistic religious fanatic condemns it for its tendency to give way to intemperance and imprudent self-gratification.

Jung-Stilling's ambivalence toward an economy of excess is representative of a greater intellectual-historical problematic, one that is reflected in the debate over physiocracy carried out in Germany at this time, and it is this controversy that forms the necessary context for Jung-Stilling's deliberations. As the first systematic economic theory, complete with a model of socioeconomic equilibrium, a set of firmly held economic principles, specific ideas for reforms, and an input-output scheme that anticipates in rudimentary fashion modern econometrics,[11] physiocratic doctrine took the relatively immature and underdeveloped discipline of political economy in Germany by storm.[12] To be sure, in a general cultural-political ambience in which French models, regardless of the field they represented, tended to be shunned simply because of their nation of origin, physiocratic theory constantly fought an uphill battle on the right side of the Rhine.[13] Its reception in Germany was further complicated by the fact that its rise among German economists as a theoretically viable program occurred simultaneously with its practical demise in France, which came with the failure of A. R. J. Turgot's physiocracy-schooled reforms, culminating in his dismissal as French minister of finance in 1776. Even one of the most ardent defenders of physiocracy, Jakob Mauvillon, thus found it necessary to address this issue at the very outset of his *Physiokratische Briefe*, seeking to dispel the widespread belief that any attempt to put physiocratic theory into practice was bound to end in disaster, as it had in France (7–8).[14] It is further significant that the fall of Turgot in 1776 coincided with the first publication of Adam Smith's *Wealth of Nations*, and physiocratic doctrine in Germany, although in many respects coherent with Smithian economics,[15] had to contend with the competition posed by this emergent economic theory.[16] Thus physiocracy sought to gain a foothold in Germany at precisely the time it was on the verge of being theoretically overtaken by Smith's more sophisticated political-economic system (Blaich 11).[17] However, the simultaneous reception of physiocracy and Smithian economics can also be seen as an indication that German-speaking Europe was at a significant crossroads in its economic development in the final decades of the eighteenth century, about to make that transition, for which nations like England and Holland had paved the way, from a subsistence to a full-blown market and monetary economy (see Luhmann, *Wirtschaft* 77).

The debate over physiocracy reflects, among other things, the turmoil that accompanied this transition from a feudally oriented economy, based on landed wealth and agricultural production, to an industrial economy grounded in monetary wealth and manufacturing. Karl Marx has persuasively demonstrated the extent to which this "process by which manufacturing and agriculture were segregated" went hand in hand with a displacement of peasant farmers from their traditional lands and from agriculturally oriented activities to the growing metropolitan centers and new jobs as part of the industrial proletariat serving the needs of manufacturing (*Kapital* 765, 776). Nor were eighteenth-century political economists themselves ignorant of this transformation. The German economist Johann Beckmann (1739–1811), for example, drew a telling distinction between *Landwirtschaft*, the term traditionally used to designate an agricultural economy, and what he called, based on the semantic opposition between *Land* and *Stadt* ("country" and "city"), the *Stadtwirtschaft*, or metropolitan economy of manufacturing and industry. In the preface to the inaugural volume of his *Physikalisch-ökonomische Bibliothek*, a journal dedicated to bringing extensive reviews of new scholarly literature in the field of economics, Beckmann employed this pair of opposing terms to designate the two major directions in economic theory his journal would cover ("Vorbericht" in Beckman, vol. 1).

If this emergent transformation was the preeminent fact of economic life in late eighteenth-century France and Germany, then the physiocrats tended to assume a decidedly conservative, perhaps even reactionary position in this debate, vociferously defending the values of feudal society and stressing the importance of the rural, agricultural economy. It should come as no surprise that the France of the mid-eighteenth century was the birthplace of physiocracy, given that it had remained, in contrast to England, a predominantly rural and agrarian society.[18] This was just as true for most of German-speaking Europe in the final decades of the eighteenth century, and it is certainly no coincidence that it was here that physiocracy received its most thorough and affirmative reception (Schumpeter 290). Margrave

Karl Friedrich of Baden, who assumed the throne in 1746, before he had even turned eighteen years old, was one of the most visible aristocratic advocates of physiocracy throughout Europe.[19] He was among the first Germans to embrace the writings of the French physiocrats, with which he had familiarized himself already in the 1760s, long before the mainstream debates about physiocratic policies assumed prominence in the German public sphere. When he decided in the summer of 1769 to implement physiocratic principles in selected areas of Baden, he initiated an epistolary correspondence with the Marquis de Mirabeau. Initially this correspondence turned on the question of how to impose the *impôt unique*, the single tax on agricultural products that formed one of the cornerstones of physiocratic theory, and although Karl Friedrich received no pragmatic answer to his question, the correspondence between him and Mirabeau continued for several years.[20] Karl Friedrich did indeed institute physiocratic reforms in three villages under his control, Dietlingen, Theningen, and Balingen, in 1770. These reforms were introduced under the administrative leadership of the physiocrat Johann August Schlettwein, who served Karl Friedrich from 1763 until 1773, when he was dismissed in part because of the failure of the physiocratic regulations he was responsible for implementing. As a result largely of citizen protests, these physiocratic reforms were annulled in the villages of Theningen and Balingen just a few years after their introduction, while Dietlingen was to suffer under them for over twenty years, until 1792 (Higgs 86).

Karl Friedrich emerged as one of the most competent interpreters of physiocratic theory, composing his own summary—written in French—of the physiocratic system, his *Abrégé des principes de l'économie politique* (Outline of the principles of political economy). This treatise appeared in print in 1772, lent the official stamp of ideological approval by the physiocratic movement due to its publication in the journal run by the French physiocrats, the *Ephémérides du citoyen*. Ten years later, in 1782, Schlettwein published a German translation under the title "Kurzer Abriß von den Grundsätzen der politischen Ökonomie" (Short summary of the principles of political economy) in his *Archiv für den Menschen und Bürger*. Karl Friedrich composed this piece with a specific pragmatic intention: it was to serve as a document for instilling in the future rulers of Baden the economic principles according to which he believed the duchy could best be governed (Roscher 484). The style in which it is composed is coherent with this pedagogical purpose, and it is no exaggeration that this work represents one of the best, most accurate, and succinct portrayals of the rudiments of physiocratic economic policy ever written (Schumpeter 292).[21]

Karl Friedrich's Baden was an area that, as the margrave insightfully perceived, presented ideal political-economic circumstances for an experiment with physiocratic principles. The duchy, which encompassed no major cities and was almost purely agrarian in character, was largely dependent on the production of agricultural goods, and in this agrarian context the priority the physiocrats gave to the investment of resources into agricultural production promised to bring economic progress and financial rewards. More important, however, is that Karl Friedrich corresponded perfectly with the image of the paternalistically inclined enlightened despot valorized in physiocratic dogma. The Swiss physiocrat Isaak Iselin, for example, wrote in his *Versuch über die gesellige Ordnung*, "Only those princes who seek both to make society as a whole more consummate and to raise the level of prosperity of all citizens can make human beings truly happy," and he concludes by claiming that rulers must be "instruments of divine providence in the service of the lower classes" (119). Finally, and most significantly, Karl Friedrich practiced what he preached, eschewing all displays of excessive luxury in dress and celebrations at his court, restricting consumption of alcohol, and discouraging dancing, card playing, and other activities that threatened to siphon off human and material resources that could be invested more profitably in agricultural production (Windelband 115). In this regard he subscribed with heart and soul to the condemnation of luxury as a diversion of precious resources into the promotion of individual vanity, a critique that was a central tenet of physiocratic philosophy. In fact, in his summary of the principles of political economy Karl Friedrich stigmatizes luxury goods by using the exact same term Jung-Stilling would apply a few years later, calling them *Arbeiten der Einbildung*, "works of the imagination," produced by *Arbeiter für die Einbildungskraft*, "workers serving the power of imagination" ("Kurzer Abriß" 258). He concludes by demeaning such workers as "the least secure of all, and those who consistently contribute the least to the lasting prosperity of the state" (258). Karl Friedrich thus draws the same distinction as Jung-Stilling between a first-order economy of existential needs and a second-order economy of "imaginary" products that fulfill less critical, even superfluous desires. In the emerging struggle between an economy defined by need and one centered around desire, Karl Friedrich, like the physiocrats in general, clearly fell on the side of the former.[22]

Karl Friedrich's position on the question of luxury and "imaginary" products best accords with that defended by the physiocrats in general. In this regard, the physiocrats were indeed realists—one might even call them materialists[23]—who took into account the pressing needs of the bulk of the population, especially the lower classes. According to Stephen Gudeman, as late as 1815 the purchase of bread alone constituted between forty and sixty percent of the total expenditures of the average worker (49), and given the reality of such a strongly need-based economy, the physiocrats' focus on laws intended to regulate and enhance the production of grains made good pragmatic and humanitarian sense. In this context we can also best understand the ignorance and haughtiness of Marie Antoinette's response, "Let them eat cake!," to the assertion that French citizens were suffering from a lack of bread: this exchange presents a condensed encapsulation of the conflict between a privileged class addicted to gratuitous satisfactions and a mass of lower-class citizens whose primary concern consisted of fulfilling the most rudimentary existential needs. In this respect, at least, the program of the French physiocrats truly anticipated the demands made by the French revolutionaries more than a decade after Turgot's fall.[24]

In its broad theoretical outlines physiocracy emerged above all as a countermovement against the mercantilist policies that dominated European economic thought from the sixteenth through the mid-eighteenth century. Quesnay and the French physiocrats thus conceived their own doctrines in part in opposition to those promulgated by Jean-Baptiste Colbert (1619–83), one of mercantilism's leading European theoreticians and advocates (Keller 4–6). Fundamentally intertwined with the European colonialist enterprise, mercantilism emphasized the importance of foreign trade, whereby a positive trade balance—that is, a larger proportion of exported than imported goods—was interpreted as the primary indication of a healthy and successful economy. In his *Theorien über den Mehrwert*

(Theories on surplus value), Karl Marx pointed out that for mercantilism, surplus value derived solely from such acts of foreign exchange, with trade or foreign commerce becoming the very mechanism by which wealth is accumulated (37). Thus commodity goods themselves were not seen as the basis of national wealth, but rather conceived solely as items to be traded on the international market in exchange for gold and silver currencies. For mercantilist nations, wealth came to be identified exclusively with monetary riches, and the accumulation and hoarding of gold and silver emerged as the ultimate aim of mercantilist economic policies. The political implications of these doctrines were far-reaching, since they implied, given a finite supply of minted gold and silver, a bitter antagonism among nations competing for these limited resources and the constant struggle to discover new markets (Beer 13). Finally, mercantilism tended to privilege manufacturing over agriculture, restricting manufacturing enterprises to the mother country and reducing colonies or trading partners to the suppliers of raw materials and the purchasers of its manufactured products.

Physiocracy took a stand against all of these foundational principles of mercantilism. Although the physiocrats were not opposed to trade as such—indeed, they were among the first to promote a strictly anti-interventionist, laissez-faire policy that glorified the benefits of free trade—they tended to downplay the importance of foreign trade, emphasizing instead the productive role of domestic commerce as a force that increased national productivity and wealth and that simultaneously forged bonds that tied citizens together into an interactive social organism. In this sense the physiocrats look ahead specifically to the economic theories promoted by the German Romantics, especially Johann Gottlieb Fichte and Adam Müller, who, as we saw in the previous chapter, insist on the community-constitutive and nation-building function of the domestic economy. In his *Physiokratische Briefe*, for example, Mauvillon explicitly maintained that national wealth is predominantly a function of internal trade (83). As opposed to the economics of national antagonism promulgated by mercantilism, then, physiocracy tended to focus on domestic matters (Ware 607; Irwin 67) and highlighted the constitutive function of economics in the building of cultural and political community.[25] This stress on the domestic economy was buttressed in particular by the physiocrats' insistence on agriculture as the chief domain in which economic production transpired. Aside from reflecting the primacy they placed on the satisfaction of immediate subsistence needs, this emphasis also bespoke the physiocratic belief that land, especially agriculturally productive land, formed the elemental basis of national identity (Fox-Genovese 218). Jung-Stilling offers a succinct explanation of this principle in his "Leitlinien erfolgreicher Wohlstandsmehrung," in which he unequivocally asserts,

> There is one wholly certain and incontrovertible basis for all national fortune. And what is it? Well, it is the native soil, which constitutes the state and which can never be stolen from it. Ravaging conquerors can drive the people from the land, but they can never destroy the land itself. It is thus the genuine, true source of all wealth. (45)

A trade, a factory, a manufacturing process can easily be moved to another location—a fact we are even more acutely aware of today—but agricultural land is fixed, and hence it constitutes the very substance of the state and its inherent wealth. According to Jung-Stilling, land is even free from expropriation by a foreign power and thus represents national wealth.

To the extent that Jung-Stilling's assertion stresses the significance of landed wealth, it is representative of the entire value theory defended by the physiocratic movement. Although in some regards clearly falling back into feudal economic standards, it is just as much an expression of the physiocratic protest against the moneyed interests codified in particular in mercantilist economic doctrine.[26] Physiocracy reacted especially vehemently against the mercantilists' glorification of money as the basis of wealth and their proclivity for hoarding monetary instruments. Indeed, Quesnay attacked money for its sterility, its inability to increase economic productivity (Beer 133), and he viewed the mercantilist drive to hoard money as an essentially unproductive act that withdrew resources from the process of circulation (Meek, *Economics of Physiocracy* 26). This critique of money was adopted and expanded by German advocates of physiocratic theory. In his *Versuch über die gesellige Ordnung*, for example, Isaak Iselin remarked,

As long as money is viewed solely with regard to this characteristic, merely as a sign and a means for representing the true wealth that is exchanged and not as wealth in and of itself, it will serve solely to promote economic circulation and hence be useful. But as soon as one begins to esteem it as true wealth as such, it must perforce produce desires and prejudices, and ultimately even laws and ordinances, that disrupt the economic order, impede circulation, and cause innumerable misfortunes. (57–58)

For the physiocrats, money is not wealth; rather it serves solely as a *sign* of wealth, whose function is reduced to this act of representation and the circulation of goods it thereby promotes. To treat money as inherently valuable is to open the door to previously unknown and detrimental desires and prejudices; these must then be institutionalized and protected, Iselin asserts with a clear swipe at mercantilist policy, by artificial laws and regulations that have the sole effect of interfering with the natural flow of economic circulation. The physiocrats were thus among the first to make the critique of money as intrinsic value into a cornerstone of their economic theory. In this respect they can be regarded as precursors not only of Müller and Fichte, but also of Marx, who in the *Grundrisse* defined money as *bloße Einbildung*, "pure imagination" (144), and in *Das Kapital* insisted that, when viewed exclusively as a medium of circulation, money expresses the commodity value or exchange value of goods and as such need only be "imaginary [*vorgestelltes*] or ideal money" (111). This brings us back to one of the primary themes we have been following: the definition of a second-order economy of consumer goods, whose value is represented solely in monetary terms rather than with regard to their use value in satisfying existential, subsistence needs, and its association with desire and the phantasms of the creative imagination.[27]

There are several principles fundamental to physiocratic economic philosophy that implicitly inform Iselin's critique of money when conceived as a form of wealth. One of these is the vehemently anti-interventionist policy and the belief in absolute free trade that is a leading article of the physiocratic faith. Iselin succinctly outlined the logic underpinning this unfaltering dedication to unhindered competition and free trade in *Versuch über die gesellige Ordnung*.

> However, providence has wisely arranged things in such a way that this
> struggle for their separate advantages works toward the general welfare;
> and that by means of this competition everyone is compensated on one
> side for what they have lost on the other. . . . The opposite necessarily
> occurs when one dissolves this competition. A few individuals make
> gains without those over whom they have won an advantage ever being
> justly compensated.—In such instances all of society suffers, the natural
> process of human industry is interrupted, the order established by God is
> disrupted, and the laws of nature transgressed. (63)

We note, first of all, that the "struggle" of competition, in which each individual pursues his or her own self-interests, is teleologically preprogrammed
to culminate in the furtherance of the general welfare.[28] The physiocrats
were among the first to rigorously propose and defend the idea of an "invisible hand" that acts behind the scene of economic interaction and actually
choreographs the actions that transpire on the economic stage, a notion
associated with Adam Smith's *Wealth of Nations*, where it received its most
thorough articulation (1: 456). Quesnay gave paradigmatic expression to
this principle when he wrote, "The whole magic of a well-ordered society
is that each man works for others, while believing that he is working for
himself" ("Miscellaneous Extracts" 70). To be sure, there is a profound difference between Smith's conception of the invisible hand and the physiocratic belief that the economic process is directed behind the scenes to lead
to the common good. For Smith, this guiding "hand" emerges from the
structure of the economic process itself, from market forces and the laws
of exchange, whereas for the physiocrats divine intervention is at work.
That is why Iselin praises the "wisdom" of divine providence, for the physiocrats believed that the laws regulating economics are embedded in the natural world and hence are part and parcel of a divinely ordained blueprint
that has programmed the worldly order in such a way that, left on its own,
it will provide for the systematic improvement of the human lot.[29] It is easy
to understand, then, based on this axiom, why the physiocrats valorized
free trade and shunned all forms of human intervention into the economic
process: such intervention bespoke a contemptible arrogance that wrenched
control over the natural economic process out of God's hands and substituted for divine guidance the bungling machinations of mere mortals.

Productivity, Nature, Surplus Value

In his historically oriented examination of the development of theories of surplus value, Karl Marx praises the physiocrats as the first to make the significant conceptual move of transferring the basis of surplus value from the domain of circulation and exchange, where it was located for the mercantilists, to the realm of production. For Marx this is an important modification because it paves the way for capitalist market theories that will likewise locate the mechanism for generating surplus value in the domain of production (*Theorien über den Mehrwert* 14). By the same token, Marx criticizes the physiocrats for restricting the creation of surplus value to what he facetiously calls the domain of *Urproduktion*, "primordial production," namely to the reproductive biogenesis of agricultural products (14). With this he points to what can be viewed as the central tenet of physiocratic economics: the belief that genuine productivity, defined as an excess of output over input, transpires solely in nature, that is, in the realm of biological propagation, which in economic terms is identified with the domain of agriculture. At root this is an essentialist position, formulated in part in reaction to the mercantilist view that value is concretized in the artificial medium of money.

As opposed to the mercantilist faith in monetary wealth, the physiocrats insisted that all value was made manifest in the substance of the natural world and produced by the regenerative cycle of nature. They tended to express this belief in terms of the sole productivity of the soil, and one of the catchphrases to which they frequently appealed was the claim that the fruits of the land were a "gift of nature."[30] In defense of this principle, which the most prominent German critic of physiocracy, Christian Wilhelm von Dohm, had called into question ("Über das physiokratische System" 312–14), Mauvillon asks the pointed and ultimately (for him) rhetorical question: "Out of what can one claim that anything is produced?" To which he gives the simple reply: "Out of the bosom of the earth alone" (*Physiokratische Briefe* 25). Economic value is thereby simplistically equated with the natural substance, indeed, with the subsistence value of agricultural products, and any other conceptions about the manner in which economic value accrues to products are simply rejected. Thus, instead of interpreting human labor as a value-adding operation, quantified in labor hours, the physiocrats measure the value added to a commodity by human work according to the amount of food consumed to generate the energy necessary to accomplish that work. Value never goes beyond the mere physical facts of consumption and, in the case of human labor, consumption and production are conceived as a zero-sum game. The physiocrats are still bound up, in short, with what Fernand Braudel has termed "material life," the economic formation prior to industrialization and the market economy, which concentrated almost exclusively on the material means of human subsistence (40).

This insistence on the satisfaction of material needs has certain consequences for the physiocrats' definition of production and, in particular, of human productivity. Earlier in his *Physiokratische Briefe*, in an attempt to address the role accorded to human beings in this process of natural production, Mauvillon insists on a definition of human "productivity" that is restricted to the agricultural stewardship of the earth.

> If one takes the meaning of the word "production" in its literal sense—
> to designate, namely, the generation of a thing, a concrete body, a material, a substance, that previously did not exist—then it is completely
> obvious that only the labor of someone who works the land produces
> something. (*Physiokratische Briefe* 13–14)

According to physiocratic doctrine, the only avenue by means of which the human being can play a truly productive role is by working the land: only here, in the cooperative union of reproductive nature and the laboring hand and mind of the human being, can one speak of a creation ex nihilo. And these are precisely the extremely narrow parameters within which physiocratic theory conceptualizes the notion of production: it refers only to the generation of new substance, along the lines of natural reproduction. Thus when the farmer plants ten seeds of corn that grow to be ten corn plants, each producing, say, ten thousand kernels of corn, this act is "productive" in the physiocratic sense. In this process, human productive activity is reduced to that of a midwife who assists nature, or the soil, in its biogenetic, its inherently *re*productive operation of organic regeneration. In other words, nature alone is capable of fundamental creativity, of producing something that, in Mauvillon's words, "previously did not exist," and human beings themselves are not inherently creative or productive creatures. Schlettwein is most direct and forthcoming about this denial of human productivity or creativity: the third "fundamental truth" he lists among the basic principles of physiocratic economic policy states that no humans can ever produce anything on their own, but rather are restricted to the cultivation and modification of materials generated by nature (*Evidente und unverletzliche . . . Grundwahrheiten* 6). For the physiocrats, in short, the realm of absolute creativity is reserved for nature, that is, for God, as the author of the natural world.[31]

The flip side of this is the extremely controversial and easily repudiated physiocratic position that manufacturing, which gives form to natural products, must be seen as a principally unproductive activity. This is one of the points that, in the German controversy over physiocracy, its detractors most often cited and maligned. The anonymous author of the acerbically critical essay "Etwas über das Steuerwesen und die physiokratischen Grundsätze, die Einrichtung desselben betreffend" (On taxation and the physiocratic principles concerning its implementation) attacks this idea and, relying instead on Smithian economic principles while simultaneously looking ahead to Marx's theories of value and surplus value, maintains that the sole productive power is human labor. He poignantly remarks, "We would have very little if we had nothing but what nature produces either on its own, or through the labor of the farmer. At least little that is of much use" (227). And after bringing several examples of non-agricultural processes that transform the fruits of nature into useful commodities, including the instance of the miller who grinds the grains the baker will turn into bread, he emphatically concludes, in direct opposition to physiocratic dogma, "The earth is not really the sole font from which human beings nourish themselves, rather this stems primarily from their labor and industry" (227). Adam Smith was even more absolutistic in his claim: "Labour . . . is the only universal," he noted in *Wealth of Nations*, "as well as the only accurate measure of value, or the only standard by which we can compare the values of different commodities at all times, and at all places" (1: 139–40). But what is especially clever about the formulation wrought by the anonymous author of "Etwas über das Steuerwesen" is that it turns the physiocrats' own insistence on the usefulness of commodities for human sustenance against the physiocrats themselves, simply by pointing out that few "gifts of nature" are enjoyable in the raw form in which they naturally occur, and that it is human labor and creativity that transform nature's products into useful commodities. He thereby focuses on a conception of value based on use, defined in terms of existential needs and their satisfaction, rather than on a theory of value predicated solely on human labor, and he insists on the role of human creativity in shaping natural products into functional utilitarian items.

Over the course of this debate about the nature of productivity and the notion of value, a rudimentary distinction between use value and exchange value begins to emerge. The author of this essay on physiocratic taxation, for example, explicitly refers to the scholastic notion of value as a function of form, not of substance: "Forma dat esse rei" ("Form gives things their being") is the formula he cites ("Etwas über das Steuerwesen" 227). He thereby implicitly splits the commodity into two separate value aspects, one defined by its "content" or substance, the other by its "form." Similarly, the anonymous respondent to Christian Wilhelm von Dohm's "Über das physiokratische System," writing in the *Deutsches Museum*, draws a distinction between *natürlicher Werth*, the "worth" or value of a product based on its naturally given characteristics, and the increased *price* this natural product can command once it has become the object of human labor and been transformed into a more useful commodity. This second level of value, the price the humanly transformed commodity will fetch on the open market, is determined by factors other than its natural constitution, namely by competition, supply and demand, and so on ("Anmerkungen zu des Herrn Prof. Dohms Abhandlung" 437). In short, the "value" of the humanly transformed commodity (its "market price") is established by purely economic considerations that are independent of its use value, namely by the process of exchange itself, and this "value" is discrete from the value of the raw materials that make up the commodity's substance.[32] In his *Grundfeste der Staaten* of 1779, Schlettwein formulated an essentially identical distinction, juxtaposing the "natural value" of products—which he identifies not with their inherent worth as raw materials, but instead with the cost of their production—to their "selling value," the price paid for them on the open market, governed by need and competition (327).

The Dual Character of Value and the Commodity

The debate over physiocracy articulates, among other things, a struggle in the larger field of economics to come to terms with the nature of human productivity and the manner in which it is concretized in (economic) value. Imagination and ingenuity, on the one hand, compete with labor, on the other, as the distinctly human contributions that add value to natural objects in the process of transforming them into useful commodities. As we have seen, the physiocrats downplayed both of these human investments, emphasizing instead the value-producing power of nature. Yet the debate over the nature of the commodity and the surplus value that accrued to natural objects based on human creativity was not put to rest by the physiocratic intervention. Indeed, to the extent that this economic controversy ultimately crystallized around the juxtaposition of natural content and form-giving, creative human transformations of this content, this economic debate impinged closely on wider questions of *aesthetics* and definitions of *cultural* productivity in general. Since the aim of this chapter is to outline precisely this confluence, it is important to pursue, as a kind of excursus, vacillations in the economic theory of value and surplus value that emerge at the end of the eighteenth and the early decades of the nineteenth century.

It is but a small—yet revolutionary—step from the conception of the dichotomous value forms of the commodity articulated in the dispute over physiocracy to Karl Marx's definition, in the opening section of *Das Kapital*, of the commodity as a mysteriously double-sided entity, indeed, as a self-contradictory—Marx will call it fetishized—conglomerate, a *sinnlich übersinnliches Ding*, or "sensual supersensual thing" (85). What precisely is it about the commodity that lends it this two-sided, paradoxical character as, on the one hand, a concrete, tangible, and empirical object, and, on the other, an intangible, mysterious, and supersensual construct? Marx traces this complexity of the commodity form back to the conditions of production themselves, in particular to the role of human creativity and labor in the refinement of products derived from the natural world.

In the introduction to *Grundrisse der Kritik der politischen Ökonomie* (Outlines of a critique of political economy), the notes Marx compiled in 1857–58 as a first attempt to summarize his views on the history and development of modern economic theory and practice, he sketches the rudiments of a notion of production that does not merely satisfy already existent needs, but anticipates, and hence creates, new ones. Reflecting on the changing nature of needs themselves as a function of developments in production, Marx writes,

> Hunger is hunger, but hunger that is satisfied by cooked meat, eaten with forks and knives, is a fundamentally different hunger than one that devours meat with the help only of hand, nails, and teeth. Thus production does not merely produce the object of consumption, but the mode of consumption as well, not just objectively, but also subjectively. Production hence creates the consumer. . . . Production does not merely supply a material to satisfy a need, but also supplies a need for this material. . . . Production thereby not only produces an object for the subject, but also a subject for the object. (13–14)

What Marx alludes to in this passage, without directly addressing it, is the process of cultural refinement and its connection to the modes and techniques of economic production, an issue already addressed, as we have seen, by Jung-Stilling in his reflections on the distinction between essential and "imaginary" needs. Although hunger seems to be a universal need, tied to the drive for sustenance and survival, Marx suggests that the nature of hunger as drive is actually distinct at different historical and cultural stages in the civilizing process. The hunger of the primitive human being that is satisfied by raw meat cannot be identified with the hunger for a charbroiled sirloin steak. Nor can, we might add, the hunger for a burger and fries be compared with that for a fine gourmet meal. In other words, production does not merely produce consumable commodities, but it also simultaneously produces the *manner* of consumption, the conditions under which these commodities can and will be consumed.

There is, then, as Marx suggests, not only an objective side to the process of production and consumption, but also a subjective side, and the latter is largely responsible for historical developments in the evolution of civilization. Somewhat reluctantly, perhaps, Marx has smuggled the actions of human agents into the economic process: they appear as a creative force that not only transforms the natural world by means of their productive labor, but also modifies, through this act of transformative production, the very character of human needs, wants, and desires. If production, as Marx aphoristically phrases it, supplies material to satisfy a human need, then it also generates a human need for a material refined and transformed by human labor in a particular way. According to Marx, production does not only produce objects for consumption, it also produces the *subjects* who consume these commodities. One of Marx's fundamental insights is that all commodities are bound up in this dynamic, principally dialectical process of fulfilling natural, existential needs, while at the same time creating new cultural necessities. Production, in short, is also the production of new *desires*, and this supercession of the basic fulfillment of subsistence needs by the generation of hitherto undiscovered desires marks the fundamental transformation from a feudal to a capitalist economy.[33]

The physiocrats were intent on disentangling these two dialectically intertwined moments in the process of production: for them, existential wants and the natural products that satisfied them should be clearly segregated from "imaginary" needs, generated by human agency and satisfied by "luxury" items, defined simply as all consumption that exceeds the requirements of basic sustenance. It was above all this obsession with subsistence that accounted for the physiocrats' overly restrictive definition of economic value: only to the extent that commodities satisfy natural needs do they have "value"; all refinements that merely alter the *form* of the commodity's natural substance are of a purely aesthetic character, and as such do not add value to the item, even if they enhance its usefulness. Clearly, then, the physiocrats purchased their theory of value, which aligned economic production with the sole creativity of nature, at the price of a radical impoverishment of human agents as producers. Essentially, all forms of human creativity, all generators of substantial economic value that had a human origin, were written out of the process of production and consumption. This amounts to a radical reduction of economic value to an "objective" standard, indeed, to a measure that considers solely the givenness of the commodity in nature and its capacity to satisfy the dire necessities of human sustenance. By contrast, Marx recognized that all commodities are essentially both natural and "imaginary," substance and refined form, satisfying both the existential requirements of the human being as physical creature, and his or her psychological needs as cultivated consumer. For Marx, human creative agency contributes in principal ways to the process of commodity production: not only is the commodity, in its raw form, acted upon and transformed by human agency, but in a process of reciprocal, dialectical exchange the commodity acts in turn upon the agents who consume it, thereby transforming them and their needs. The interactive process of production and consumption thereby entails a spiraling development of the human agents who participate in it.

The penetrating and exhaustive analysis of the commodity form that Marx presents in the opening section of volume 1 of *Das Kapital* is informed by this theory of production and consumption as mutually determining phases of a complex economic process in which human agency is inherently implicated.[34] To be sure, Marx had anticipated this analysis of the dichotomous nature of the commodity in *Grundrisse*, where he noted how the commodity assumes "a double-life, next to its natural [life] a purely economic one, in which it is a mere sign [*Zeichen*], a cipher [*Buchstabe*] for a relationship of production, a mere sign [*Zeichen*] of its own value" (60). In its "natural" existence, the commodity is an empirical substance with certain definable physical qualities, whereas in its "economic" being it is reduced to the status of a pure *sign*, a mark that signifies something fundamentally transcendental: economic value. In *Das Kapital* Marx elaborates on this dichotomy between what we might call substantive and signifying value by alluding to the conceptual dyad that opposes use value to exchange value, commenting that the use value of things is realized in the immediate human relationship with those things themselves, "that is, in the immediate relationship between human being and thing," whereas their economic value is generated by a more circuitous process that passes through the detour of exchange (98). If the first is, so to speak, a "natural process," or an immediate relationship between humans and nature, the second results from a decidedly *social* process, the interactive exchange into which humans enter as producers and consumers. As a remark from his *Theorien über den Mehrwert* indicates, Marx was well aware that the aim of the physiocrats was to strip away this social dimension from the domain of economics, reducing it solely to the interaction between humans and nature. The physiocrats, Marx maintains here, sought to restrict the notion of exchange to that between human and nature, ignoring, or denying the value of, exchanges that transpire between two or more human beings (19). Thus for the physiocrats economics as such is a *natural* process, one that is divinely ordained and eternally stable, whereas for Marx it reflects a *social* interaction and is hence historically conditioned and variable according to human social relations. Moreover, for Marx the physiocratic interpretation of value as constituted in the relationship between humans and nature represents an alienated conception of the true essence of value as a human social product: physiocracy encourages us to interpret as a "gift of nature" what is in fact the product of human social exchange (*Theorien über den Mehrwert* 20–21).

In *Das Kapital* Marx more closely relates this opposition between natural and social value to the distinction between use value and exchange value. He apodictically states that "[t]he usefulness of a thing constitutes its use value," and he goes on to align these useful qualities with the physical attributes of the object. "But this usefulness," he remarks, "does not hover in the air. Conditioned by the characteristics of the physical commodity, it cannot exist independently of the latter" (50). Use value, in short, is intrinsic to the material substance of commodities themselves. By contrast, however, exchange value has no such intrinsic, material, or concrete determination: we might say that it does indeed "hover in the air," something like a good fairy, or an aura, accompanying every material commodity. Exchange value is a purely quantitative attribution, derived systematically from the relationship of one commodity to all others.

> Exchange value appears, first of all, as the quantitative relation, the proportion, in which use values of one sort can be exchanged for use values of another. . . . Exchange value hence appears to be something contingent and purely relative; an intrinsic, immanent exchange value (*valeur intrinsèque*) thus [is] a *contradictio in adjecto*. (50–51)

Marx continues by stressing that exchange value is nothing but an "expression," the "manifest form" (*Erscheinungsform*) of its substantive content (51). This shift from use value to exchange value, from intrinsic substance to formal, quantitative expression, entails a process of abstraction in which, according to Marx, the sensual, physical characteristics of the commodity are extinguished (51). Given this, we can better understand why Marx conceives of the commodity as a paradoxical, "sensual supersensual thing" (85): as an amalgamation of use value and exchange value, matter and form, thing and sign, it is always the site at which a struggle between conflicting principles of evaluation takes place, one based on its physical nature (use value), and one grounded in a transcendental process of pure abstraction from its physicality (exchange value).

One way to interpret the physiocrats' insistence on nature as the sole generator of wealth and economic value is to see it as the reflex of a more general transformation in eighteenth-century economics regarding the conception of value. Feudal society recognized solely a theory of value anchored in nature, and this value theory was reflected in the social sphere by the personal dependencies, the feod, that structured the relationships between rulers and ruled (Marx, *Kapital* 91). Civil society, by contrast, tends, at least since Adam Smith, to view value exclusively as the product of human labor. For the most part, the science of economics—which was inaugurated, not coincidentally, by the physiocrats[35]—recognizes only these two possible forms of value, one given in nature and the other produced by human labor.[36] As we have seen, in the controversy over physiocracy that was carried out in German-speaking Europe in the final decades of the eighteenth century, questions surrounding the definition and formation of value assumed center stage. In their value theory, at least, the physiocrats defended an antiquated conception that aligned wealth with the "gifts of nature" and emphatically denied the value-constitutive capacity of human labor and industry. This was in the final analysis the issue around which their valorization of agriculture and their demeaning of manufacturing turned. The critics of physiocracy, as a rule, appealed to a labor theory of value in their critiques of physiocratic doctrine. Even Marx, in *Das Kapital*, names the earth and the human laborer as the sole "fonts of all wealth" (530). Indeed, the basis of Marx's theoretical breakthrough is his recognition that human labor is itself a commodity in the capitalist marketplace, and that, moreover, it represents a kind of supercommodity insofar as it is the only one that generates surplus value (169). If for the physiocrats it is nature that, by means of its reproductive capacity, provides humans with a "gift" of added value, for Marx it is labor as commodity that, as he expresses it, has the capacity to "bear living offspring" or to "lay golden eggs" (169).

Marx's metaphors are significant here; they enact the transposition of the "sole" productivity, the *re*productivity of nature, as defended by the physiocrats, into the netherworld of the fairy tale. All value production, in the sense of generating surplus value, is modeled not on nature, but rather on the entirely imaginary and unnatural process of a goose laying golden eggs. In this central point, Marx concurs fully with capitalistic market-oriented theories of value as produced exclusively by human labor. The reason why he subscribes so fully to this notion is relatively simple to understand: aside from the fact that it is crucial for his conception of the relationship between capitalism and surplus value, or the production of capital itself, it offers a measurable and hence purportedly objective standard for the circumscription of economic value. Value for Marx can be measured in human labor hours, and as a quantifiable sum it can serve as the empirical basis for a materialist economics that seeks to define itself as an exact science. *Surplus* value, however, remains a mysterious, in Marx's words, "occult quality," related fundamentally to the fetishistic, "supersensual" nature of the commodity as exchange value.

Despite his reliance on labor as the basis of an objective economic value theory, when Marx discusses the value form of the commodity, the issues of price and monetary, or exchange value, and in particular the fetish character of the commodity, he often slips—perhaps unwittingly?—into a conception of value that explodes the nature-labor dichotomy generally accepted in the modern science of economics. At these times he gives voice to what we can term, with some caution, a subjectivist theory of value. This subjective value is still created by human agents, to be sure, as is labor value; but it is not generated as a by-product of the workings of the human physical organism, but instead is begotten in the mind, as a kind of ideal projection onto the empirical world of substances. The operative terms here for Marx are commonly the words *Vorstellung* (representation or imagination) or *Phantasie* (fantasy), and as such his deliberations on this subjective form of value invoke one of the themes that emerged in the critical debate over physiocracy more than half a century earlier: the role of the human creative imagination in a second-order economy driven by manufactured desires for refinement instead of by existential needs.

Let us begin by examining a passage from *Das Kapital* in which Marx suggests that even the physical labor enacted by the worker presupposes a prior ideational act that, as it were, anticipates and mentally projects the result (or product) in which this labor will culminate.

> At the end of the labor process a result is produced that at the beginning of this process was already present in the imagination [*Vorstellung*] of the worker, that is, ideally. It is not true that he merely effects a change in the form of a natural substance: he simultaneously realizes in this natural substance his purpose, of which he is aware, which determines the manner of his activity as a law, and to which he must subordinate his will. (193)

Marx is clearly alluding to the position of the physiocrats that manufacturing only refashions an already existent matter, lending form to, or reshaping, a natural substance. However, like the opponents of the physiocratic doctrine of natural value, he denies that labor can be limited to this form-giving function. Unlike them, he stresses another human activity that accompanies, or precedes, the act of manual labor itself: the engagement of the creative imagination in the conceptualization of the labor process. Prior to the physical act of laboring, a kind of imaginary labor has already taken place, and this imaginary projection serves the worker as a blueprint to which he subordinates his will and according to which he organizes and completes the manual manipulations that will transform the natural object. According to this passage, every act of manual labor is always already preceded by the workings of the human imagination, by an ideational projection of the transformation that can and should be undertaken upon the given piece of natural matter. Human creative agency thus becomes a prerequisite for the successful completion of any planned and organized act of productive labor.

Theodor Adorno recognized the importance that this association of imagination—he called it fantasy—with productive labor had in general for the eighteenth century. "In the eighteenth century," he remarks, "in the case of Saint Simon as well as in d'Alembert's *Discours préliminaire*, it [fantasy] is counted, along with art in general, as part of productive labor, it participates in the idea of the unleashing of productive forces" (Einleitung 62). The productivity of imagination was also, as we will see, a position that emerged in the German debate over physiocracy. But this imaginative productivity has not always been viewed positively, and even Marx will later come to stigmatize the role of imagination in the modern world as a contributing factor in the fetishization of commodities. This same ambivalence about the potentials and/or dangers of the imagination, as the last segment of this chapter will document, also characterized German cultural and aesthetic theory in this period.

When discussing the exchange value of commodities in terms of their price, Marx stresses the leap from material substance to a represented idea of value.

> The price or monetary form of commodities is, like their value form as such, an ideal or imaginary [*vorgestellte*] form that is distinct from their concrete, real bodily existence. The value of iron, linen, wheat, etc. exists, although invisibly, in these things themselves; it is represented by means of their equality with gold, a relationship with gold that, so to speak, merely haunts their minds. (*Kapital* 110)

The "invisible" soul of intrinsic value, of use value, lives, as it were, in the body of the commodity itself. But its exchange value is less tangible even than this invisible soul: it is an ideational ghost that merely haunts the "mind" of the commodity, a ghost, moreover, that can only be exorcised by means of an act of exchange that expresses this commodity's value in a relationship to gold, that is, to money as the general equivalent.[37] In the same context, Marx stresses that the expression of commodity value, or exchange value, in monetary terms is nothing but an ideational procedure. Exchange value, it would seem, is created by the human agent in a mental process that consists in abstraction and imagination. In *Grundrisse* Marx explains this same transformation of exchange value into its monetary expression in slightly different terms: "Exchange values (commodities) are transformed in the imagination [*Vorstellung*] into certain weights of gold or silver, and ideationally set = to this imaginary [*vorgestelltem*] quantity of gold etc., as expressing it" (122). The exchange value of commodities is thus transmuted, in the imagination, into certain quantities of money (or the general equivalent) so that the value of the commodity can be *posited*—that is, mentally created, hypothetically established—on the basis of this relationship to the general equivalent. Value exists as nothing but an ideational, imaginary ghost until it is made into a concrete fact by a real act of exchange, which simply confirms this imaginary value in retrospect. This imaginary value is, of course, nothing but the subjective attribution of a human agent: it is what the French economist A. R. J. Turgot, in his 1769 essay "Value and Money," called "esteem value" (142).

In the section of *Das Kapital* in which Marx investigates the "fetish character" of the commodity (85–98), this role of ideational projection, of the imaginative activity of human beings in the process of constituting value, comes especially to the fore. In an attempt to explain the process by which human beings objectify the social products of their own labor and project them as objects with naturally given characteristics, he turns to an analogy from physics. When light strikes the optic nerve, a subjective stimulation of that nerve takes place; but this subjective stimulation is then projected outward as a concrete object. Marx claims that a similar process is at work in the constitution of the commodity form, except that, whereas in the act of visual perception a real object present in the natural world causes the stimulation of the optic nerve, in the case of the commodity form no underlying physical, causal relationship is in evidence.

> By contrast, the commodity form, and the value relationship of the products of labor in which it is portrayed, has absolutely nothing to do with their physical nature and the objective relationships that derive from it. It is only the specific social relationship of human beings themselves that here assumes for them the phantasmagorical form of a relationship among things. Thus in order to find an appropriate analogy, we must flee to the nebulous realm of the religious world. Here the products of the human mind appear as autonomous figures that have their own life and stand in a relationship among themselves and with human beings. The same is true in the commodity world of the products of the human hand. I call this the fetishism that adheres to the products of labor as soon as they are produced as commodities, and which hence is inseparable from commodity production. (86–87)

The analogy with the functioning of the optic nerve is apparently employed as a way to elucidate the noetic process that takes place between the moment when the optic nerve receives a specific physical stimulus and its translation of this physical input into a mental function: an image of the stimulating object as it is represented in the intellect. Marx's primary concern, in other words, is to find a way to clarify the process by which, in the act of perception, one extrapolates from the physical world of objects and translates the data drawn from these extrapolations into mental functions, so as then to project back into the empirical world a (visual) representation of the physical object. But he recognizes the inappropriateness of this analogy on at least two counts. First of all, he does not want to assume, as one does in the domain of optics, that in the commodity world the point of departure is an actual empirical object. If in the act of perception the stimulus emitted by the objective world is the originary act, which is then processed by the nerves and the intellect, in the world of commodities the direction is reversed: the mental act of projection is primary and the empirical world is shaped, as it were, by this ideational act. Second, since in the optical analogy the empirical object actually gives off light that is received by another object, the human eye, we are dealing here with a simple one-to-one connection between two physical substances. This is by no means the case, Marx insists, in the world of commodities. Here an analogy from physics is inappropriate, and one must, however reluctantly, "flee" to the "nebulous realm" of religion in order to find one that better suits the situation he wants to illustrate.

It is important to register that this turn to a model drawn from religious thought represents a significant *re*turn to the origins of Marx's own materialist critique: namely, to Ludwig Feuerbach's (1804–72) analysis, in *Das Wesen des Christentums* (The essence of Christianity), of the mechanism of alienation as human beings' projections of their own supreme capacities onto an imaginary entity—a deity—and the subsequent embracing of this deity as a transcendental fact (Feuerbach 80–81). The conceptual structure of what Feuerbach termed *Entzweiung*, or "self-estrangement," is especially prominent in Marx's early writings, those composed prior to the 1848 revolution, but it returns repeatedly at especially crucial moments in his later thought, as it does here in his analysis of the fetish character of commodities. Seen in this context, Marx's point about the mysterious quality of the commodity seems to be a relatively simple one: commodities are, first of all, "products of the human mind," that is, they are originally conceptions, ideas, and blueprints for the transformation of the objects of nature. In a second step, these creations are endowed with a life of their own, which means two distinct things: as "ideas" they take on an existence independent of their creators, on the one hand, and, on the other, they are realized as physical objects in the exertion of human manual labor and the processes of production. However, once realized, detached from the processes of both mental and manual production and turned loose in the world of commodities—that is, of exchange values—these objects appear as alien things that no longer have any connection whatsoever with their creators: they become, so to speak, rebellious teenagers who cut off all ties with their parents, their progenitors, and assert their independence to live in a (commodity) world all of their own. It is this projective process— the translation of human ideational creations into physical objects that take on a life of their own and the ultimate subjugation of humans themselves to these self-created objects—that Marx is trying to illuminate with his appeal to the notion of the fetish.

We should note that the word "fetish" itself is of contested origin, having two possible and distinct etymological sources. One derivation sees the word emerging from the Latin *factitio*, meaning "man-made" as opposed to natural, via its Portuguese form *feitiço*. An alternative etymological root, propagated above all by Charles de Brosses in his 1760 book on religious fetishism, *Du culte des dieux fétiches*, with which Marx was likely familiar, sees the word stemming from the Portuguese *fetisso*, which means "magic" (McLaughlin, *Writing in Parts* 6–7). It is not necessary to decide which of these derivations Marx was actually referring to or if he preferred one to the other, since both are eminently relevant for an application to the commodity form. Commodities are, as Marx emphatically states, man-made; moreover, as he stresses in this passage, they also take on a kind of magical life of their own. Indeed, we might go so far as to identify the commodity world, as Marx views it, precisely in terms of the occult quality that man-made things assume. What is it that gives these products of human (mental and physical) labor the aura of the magical? It is, above all, what we might call a double investment of the human imagination into these objects. The first investment takes place, as we have already seen, prior to the creation of the commodity as object: its creation, as a kind of Platonic idea, in the mind of its creator. But in a second step, after it is produced as tangible object and conceived as a commodity, that is, as an object available for exchange, it is invested a further time with the energy of the imagination: it is endowed with *value*, with "esteem value" and, ultimately, when it becomes a tradable commodity, with *exchange* value, and thereby is transmogrified into an object that *appears* to have an existence independent of human beings.[38]

Marx's point is that in this process of value investment into the commodity, the human social relations responsible for producing this object in the first place become reified and oppose their human creators as an autonomous, alien domain. The world of commodities "reflects" the world of human social relations, but only in distorted, alienated form. Human beings essentially suppress the immediate, interpersonal, social relations that give birth to human-made objects and embrace instead the impersonal interrelationship between commodity and commodity, and between commodity and human beings as their exchangers, as the fetishized, imaginary version of their originary social relation. Instead of living in an intimate world of their own making, human beings enter into the alien world of the commodity, where objects are no longer their own products, but instead become objects of *desire*. The world of commodity fetishism is nothing other than a world in which the products of the human imagination and of human labor have become libidinal objects that, split off from their creators, provoke the drive for their *re*possession, their *re*appropriation (Apter 2).

We must understand that in their subjugation to the world of commodities, according to Marx, human beings are by no means passive victims; indeed, they themselves are ultimately culpable for their self-subjugation. Ironically, it is the creative, imaginative, even fantastic energy of the human mind that breeds this alienation: for Marx, it would seem, the human agent under the conditions of capitalist production is always already an *ideological* entity in the Althusserian sense that it creates an *imaginary* relationship that disguises its *real* social conditions (Althusser 153). But what is it, we might ask, that makes human agency under the conditions of commodity production into a self-alienating ideological prism? It is, above all, the narrow focusing of intellectual energy into determinations of *value*. This is the sense in which Jack Amariglio and Antonio Callari are perfectly correct in their assertion that in his conception of commodity fetishism Marx conjoins his theory of value and his treatment of subjectivity (192). It is precisely in its reduction to value consciousness, to the general projection and assessment of abstract exchange value, that human agency perverts its own labor products into mysterious fetishes: the fetish is nothing other than the concretization of this value consciousness (Apter 3), and under the conditions of capitalist commodity production, such value consciousness is the dominant—yet alienated—form of human subjectivity.

Physiocratic doctrine, as the very first systematic economic theory to identify economics as the shaping force behind human social, political, and cultural relations (Hensmann 110),[39] emerges at a historical cusp that can be designated in many ways. Whether conceived as the move from feudal to bourgeois modes of production, or as a transformation from a predominantly agrarian to a largely industrial society, or as a paradigm shift from a subsistence economy to a market or surplus economy (Luhmann, *Wirtschaft* 97), physiocracy, and the heated debate over its principles, marks not merely the historical site of this transition, but the terms in which it was conceived and intellectually digested. In this sense, physiocracy truly was a transitional philosophy (Priddat 8), and the internal contradictions inherent in its economic policies and practices can be explained in terms of its position as a kind of bridge between two conflicting worldviews. The reconceptualization of value from a product of nature with inherent, God-given worth to a creation of the human being, invested with imaginative, emotional, and psychic energy, is one of the primary issues in this historical transformation. Parallel to this runs the development of a new moral-economic sensibility, one that replaces an ethic of abstention with one of increased production and consumption.[40]

What stands out in the debate over physiocracy is the emerging recognition that value assessments have no objective validity whatsoever, but instead are fantasies of the human imagination that somehow take on the guise of objective facts. In the German controversy over physiocracy at the end of the eighteenth century, the argument over the objective or subjective nature of value becomes one of the key issues in an economic dispute that has far-reaching cultural implications. This controversy about the nature of value is, in a sense, the economic equivalent of the quarrel between the ancients and the moderns. The proponents and defenders of physiocracy appealed to a form of objective value that derived solely from nature, rejecting even the more modern objective value norm of human labor. To be sure, physiocracy's detractors pointed to the productivity of human labor as a significant factor in the creation of value. But an important strain of the criticism directed against the physiocratic theory of value also high-lighted the subjective, indeed, the *imaginary* quality of the value associ-ated with commodity items. We have already begun to see the important role the notion of the imaginary played in the discussion surrounding the physiocratic notion of value, especially in the so-called second-order econ-omy of luxury goods. We can now develop the substance of this prob-lematic more fully on the basis of works composed by a central figure in the physiocracy debate, Johann Georg Schlosser.

Johann Georg Schlosser: The Imaginary Value of Imaginary Things

One of the clearest assertions of the subjective and imaginary nature of value was expressed by Johann Christian Schmohl (1756–83), a partici-pant in the controversy over physiocracy who emerged as one of the most vehement opponents of this economic school. In an essay titled "Ver-mischte land- und staatswirtschaftliche Ideen" (Miscellaneous ideas on agri-culture and national economy), published in the January 1781 issue of the *Deutsches Museum*, Schmohl launched an all-out attack on the phys-iocratic doctrine of wealth and value, and he went so far as to accuse the antagonists of physiocracy of not having criticized it thoroughly enough at this, its weakest point: "The physiocrats erred in their conceptions of wealth, value, production, and taxes; this is where one should have refuted them!" (49). He then goes on to indict the physiocratic notion of intrin-sic value, insisting above all that value is a culturally relative concept: for the peoples of South America or Africa, he claims, gold is of much less significance than it is for Europeans. He punctuates this argument with the apodictic assertion that all value is conventionally derived and as such ultimately a creation of the imagination: "All value is conventional, or imaginary [*imaginär*], even genuine and real value. Nothing is a real value for one person that is not an imaginary value for someone else. Thus what-ever we pay money for is ultimately what has value" (50). Schmohl antici-pates Marx insofar as he already analyzes the commodity as a fundamentally dualistic, contradictory entity: material, on the one hand, but "imaginary" on the other. Marx, of course, would call this imaginary aspect the "supersensual" dimension of the commodity. But Schmohl goes even further than Marx in some respects: he takes the radical step of abstracting completely from the "sensual" side of the commodity, thereby essentially reducing all value to esteem value—there is no natural, "real" product that is not invested with "imaginary" energy to ascertain its value. Moreover, he explicitly identifies this imaginary worth with the expression of value in monetary terms. Schmohl is already operating, in short, in an absolute world of the commodity and of commodity value.

The only other contributor to the German debate over physiocracy who embraced as completely as did Schmohl the reality of the modern monetary economy and its influence in both economic and cultural life was Johann Georg Schlosser (1739–99). Born into a family that exerted considerable influence in his native Frankfurt am Main, Schlosser is largely known through his association with perhaps the most famous denizen of that city, Johann Wolfgang von Goethe, whose sister Cornelia became Schlosser's wife. A friend of Isaak Iselin, one of the most vocal and influential advocates of physiocracy in German-speaking Europe, Schlosser initially felt a strong attraction for the agricultural orientation of physiocratic economic theory. His *Katechismus der Sittenlehre für das Landvolk* (Catechism of morality for the rural populace), which was published anonymously in 1771, was one of his best known and most widely read works, marking him as a significant advocate of the "back to nature" philosophy following the model of Jean-Jacques Rousseau (1712–78). Schlosser thereby helped to nourish the veritable "agromania" that flourished at this time, a fascination for the landed, agricultural peasantry that touched the imagination of middle-class citizens and aristocrats alike.[41] Although this sympathy with the agrarian lifestyle—the alienated sympathy of the city dweller, to be sure—tied him with Iselin and other intellectuals with physiocratic leanings, Schlosser did not buy fully into the worldview of Enlightenment rationalism, represented especially strongly by Iselin, which underpinned much of physiocratic thought.

François Quesnay was associated with the French *philosophes* and contributed articles on economic subjects to the *Encyclopedia*. Among the physiocrats of German-speaking Europe, Iselin was especially indebted to Enlightenment paradigms.[42] In his position as founder and editor of the *Ephemeriden der Menschheit*, Iselin was certainly the most influential and respected among the German physiocrats. His stature was further enhanced by the fact that he was far less dogmatic and arrogant than Schlettwein, whose narrow-minded, shamelessly proselytizing promotion of physiocratic principles tended more to discourage than to win supporters for his cause. Iselin, by contrast, closely identified with the educational and culturally progressive principles of the Enlightenment, and he subscribed above all to its optimistic view of the human species as endowed with the capacity for reason and hence as eminently perfectible. He made this Enlightenment stance absolutely clear in his introductory remarks to the first two issues of the *Ephemeriden der Menschheit,* in which he stressed, relying completely on the metaphorical registers of Enlightenment discourse, that the journal's aim was to "spread light" and "elevate" the economic, political, and moral standards of its public ("Entwurf der *Ephemeriden der Menschheit"* 5, 11). Reason, he unequivocally asserted, is the highest human faculty, and he explicitly described the ideological program of his journal as an attempt to help lead humanity away from the immediacy of the senses and tyranny of an unfettered imagination to a life guided solely by "pure, bright reason" ("Fortsetzung des Entwurfs der *Ephemeriden der Menschheit"* 12–13).

Schlosser, by contrast, far from denigrating the human power of imagination and seeking to subject it to the disciplined control of reason, affirmed the creativity and productivity of the human fantasy, in the realm of poetic creation as well as in the domain of economics.[43] It was this principal disagreement that brought about a significant ideological parting of the ways between Iselin and Schlosser, although they remained on good personal terms until Iselin's death in 1782. When he delivered a eulogy for Iselin before the Helvetian Society in Olten, Switzerland, in June 1783, Schlosser made a point of referring to these ideological differences, praising Iselin as an idealist and optimist who trusted completely in human goodness, while designating himself as a realist who viewed human beings more pessimistically as driven by passions and habits ("Rede auf Isaak Iselin" 420–21). Schlosser's turn away from Iselin and physiocratic economic principles was thus largely motivated by this gulf that separated their discordant interpretations of humanity and human destiny.

In the section dedicated to statecraft in the desultory notes and aphorisms published in 1777 under the title *Politische Fragmente* (Political fragments), Schlosser describes two competing economic models: one he calls the *Ackerbaustaat*, the agricultural state, and the other he designates as the *Handelstaat*, the commercial or trading state, which he identifies closely with the emergence of monetary wealth—with what Marx would later call capital. Schlosser notes in particular that a historical political-economic transition has transpired in the Europe of his day, from a form of prosperity grounded in land and agriculture to one based principally in money. "Before monetary wealth emerged," he remarks, "the agricultural state was the most prosperous; today it seems to be true of the commercial state, and it is indeed the most prosperous—at least according to what we now call prosperity" (*Politische Fragmente* 34). The addendum Schlosser appends to this statement, almost as an afterthought, is actually of crucial importance; it indicates that the metamorphosis he is portraying takes place not merely on the level of the economic system, but also in the conceptual framework of human beings themselves, who, based on the changing economy, have completely altered their definition of what prosperity means. In the very next fragment, Schlosser elucidates this distinction further.

> Before monetary wealth emerged, that state was considered prosperous in which as many people as possible could appease their hunger. Agricultural products are exhaustible [*erschöpflich*]; if the price is exhaustible, so is the commodity. Everything given by nature is exhaustible.—The creations of the imagination [*Einbildungskraft*] are not exhaustible. Monetary wealth is a product of the imagination [*Einbildung*]. It made prices inexhaustible [*unerschöpflich*]; and now the commodity as well. (34–35)

Although stated in an outwardly simple, concise, and matter-of-fact way, the implications of Schlosser's comments are profound and far-reaching. The agricultural state, which Schlosser's contemporaries were certain to identify with the economic program of the physiocrats, is associated with the products of nature, and it defines prosperity solely in terms of human subsistence and the satisfaction of existential needs. Such an economic system is radically finite and closed—"exhaustible" is Schlosser's preferred term—in the sense that the needs of basic human sustenance are limited and eminently capable of being satisfied: agricultural production has achieved such a level of sophistication, in Schlosser's view, that all demands for the sustenance of human life can be fulfilled. However, independent of and parallel to this agricultural subsistence economy exists a "new" monetary economy that knows no bounds and no limits, that is "inexhaustible," to use Schlosser's term, and is grounded neither in nature nor in manual labor, but in the human power of the imagination, in *Einbildungskraft*. Schlosser's chain of logic is relatively straightforward: nature is exhaustible, as are its products, the price those products can command, and the needs they satisfy; the imagination is inexhaustible, so too the products it can create, the needs it can generate, and, in economic terms, the prices that can be charged for the commodities it helps produce.

The distinction Schlosser draws is actually quite an ancient one, going back as far as Aristotle, who in sections 8 and 9 in book 1 of his *Politics* juxtaposed economics, which he referred specifically to natural production, and chrematistics, which he identified with monetary accumulation (1256a1–10). If for Aristotle the former represents a restricted, closed economic sphere, the latter is open-ended and unlimited. But Aristotle, unlike Schlosser, explicitly criticizes the phenomenon of monetary accumulation as "artificial" or "unnatural" (1257b23–31, 1258a14–18), just as he accuses merchants of being unproductive in the narrow sense because they do not increase wealth, but only manage the process by which it changes hands (1257a16–25). The position of the physiocrats was thus closely aligned with that defended by Aristotle, promoting an economy based on subsistence needs and their satisfaction by the products of nature, while criticizing as artificial and inherently dangerous an economy founded on nonessential commodities, on luxury items available simply for money.[44] Although Schlosser seems to embrace this Aristotelian distinction, he by no means accepts the negative evaluation of the monetary economy (Binswanger, "J. G. Schlossers Theorie" 27–28). Quite the opposite: because it is infinite and born of the creative power of the human imagination, this secondary economy has the potential of being endlessly productive and hence a generator of constant economic growth.[45] This is true, above all, because, as Schlosser indicates, the needs produced by the imagination are complex and infinite, whereas those generated by nature are simple and finite: "The needs of the imagination are manifold; those of nature are only monofold. Who among us does not purchase five-sixths more things over the course of a year than nature, at the height of its prosperity, would require?" (*Politische Fragmente* 36–37). Schlosser obviously recognizes the economy of his own age—at least for citizens of his class and with comparable economic means—as one driven primarily by the demand for, and the supplying of, luxury items, commodities that exceed the simple needs of mere survival. For Schlosser, the economy of the real world—as opposed to the ideal one envisioned by the physiocrats—is already governed by *excess*. And, one might add, for him the human organ of excess is the imagination. Thus Schlosser maintains that superfluity and the imagination work hand in hand, with imagination constantly creating new commodities and the demand for new commodities, thereby fueling excess.[46]

But it is far from Schlosser's intention, in his *Politische Fragmente* at least, to play these two economies, that of subsistence and that of excess, off against one another, giving one priority over the other. On the contrary, he ultimately treats them as complementary, as serving two fundamentally different types of human wants: those produced by nature and those generated by the human imagination. Thus his advice to rulers who seek to increase the prosperity of their own territory is relatively simple. If the native soil is not especially fruitful, then concentrate your energies on the production of goods to satisfy the imaginary needs of your neighbors. Conversely, those states that enjoy the benefit of a rich and fertile soil should focus their productive efforts on the enhancement of this natural resource, and woe to them if they are seduced away from exploiting this fertility for agriculture and turn instead to commercial activities. A sensible economy, in short, is one that best accords with the resources of each geographical and political locality: if it is rich in agricultural potential, it must capitalize on this; if its wealth lies in human creativity and imaginativeness, and it is poor in agricultural land, then it should serve the second economy of luxury needs and focus its energies on manufacturing and exchange (38). The ideal state, we can presume from Schlosser's arguments, would have a balanced economy based on both agriculture and commerce, and hence be able to satisfy all the needs of its citizens. Seen from this perspective, then, the primary error of physiocratic theory would be the absolutism and exclusivity with which it focuses on the production of agricultural goods and asserts this to be the *only* sensible and rational aim for any economic system. One size, according to Schlosser, does not fit all.

ECONOMICS AND THE IMAGINATION

Schlosser's insights into the limitations of physiocratic economic policies stem in part from the practical experiences he garnered as a regional
governor in Margrave Karl Friedrich's duchy of Baden. He entered into
the services of Karl Friedrich in 1773 and remained in his employ for over
twenty years, until 1794, or just five years prior to his death. His tenure
as civil servant in Baden thus began at about the time Schlettwein's ended.
Schlosser and Schlettwein were by no means friends, but what separated
them above all were their divergent economic philosophies. Schlettwein,
the physiocratic ideologue, was responsible for overseeing the implementation of physiocratic principles in the towns of Balingen, Theningen, and
Dietlingen. Schlosser, who in 1774 inherited the governorship of the region
that encompassed Balingen and Theningen, had to contend with the repercussions of the economic system Schlettwein had helped institute. By 1776
the number of complaints and negative reports had reached such critical
mass that in March of that year Schlosser addressed a report to the margrave outlining the dire economic conditions that were stifling productivity in those towns subjected to the physiocratic system. On the basis of
Schlosser's report, the physiocratic experiments in Balingen and Theningen were—mercifully, so it seems—put to an end.[47] But Schlosser's final
settling of accounts with physiocracy, already evident in the *Politische Fragmente* of 1777, is presented in a treatise, published in 1784 and dedicated
to his brother-in-law Goethe, entitled *Xenocrates oder Über die Abgaben*
(Xenocrates, or On taxation).

Xenocrates is set in ancient Athens and written as a dialogue between
two friends, Demosthenes, who advocates physiocratic principles, in particular the single tax on agricultural production, and Xenocrates, who represents Schlosser's views about the new monetary economy that emerges
from the creativity of the human imagination. Because of its discursive and
systematic nature, this text gives a more complete picture of Schlosser's
economic philosophy than do the piecemeal aphorisms of the *Politische
Fragmente*. Moreover, written at a time when all the other major contributions to the dispute over physiocracy had already appeared, it can be read
as a kind of capstone to this entire controversy. One of the primary focuses
of the fictional dialogue is the physiocratic position regarding the sole
productivity of nature, defended by Demosthenes, and the position represented by the opponents of physiocracy—championed by Xenocrates—

that the shaping and form-giving processes must also be considered productive. In this discussion the central question of value is finally condensed into the juxtaposition of the natural, subsistence economy with an economy of excess, with Xenocrates claiming that each must be seen to have its own distinct and characteristic definition of value. Just as the items we consume can be broken down into material substance and formal properties, each of these must be aligned with their own measure of value: matter, Xenocrates asserts, stands over against the form-producing energies of human beings (*Xenocrates* 97–98). But even the products of nature are conceived as the fruits of human energy: "Both the material that is supposed to be produced as well as the forms into which it is shaped must be produced by the application of human energies" (99). There are, in short, no such things as "gifts of nature," as the physiocrats would have it, but only products generated by the productive energies of human beings. However, the human capacities that contribute to this doubly creative process must themselves be divided into two categories: matter-producing and form-giving powers.

As in the *Politische Fragmente*, Schlosser/Xenocrates gives priority to the form-giving powers, which, once again, are linked to the human imagination, since experience shows that for any single material need a given individual will have a hundred formal needs (104–05). Moreover, the imagination, because it awakens new needs, also stimulates new human energies and thereby makes human beings more productive. Imagination, according to Schlosser, drives needs; increased needs, in turn, stimulate human production; and human production ultimately fosters the development of an increasingly refined and sophisticated culture.

Just consider . . . how the power of the imagination [*Einbildungskraft*]. . . , once set in motion. . . , acquired more latitude and created new needs upon needs. . . . [Just consider] how [the human being] was no longer satisfied with living in caves, but instead shaped Paris's marble into Ionic columns; [just consider] how he was no longer satisfied with viewing the human figure in its common stature and posture, and instead sculpted human figures according to his own ideals of symmetry and grace. In short, just consider the many thousands of needs . . . that even the humble wise man, . . . as long as he does not sacrifice the better part of himself to them, is unwilling to renounce; and then just calculate what an amazing amount of human energy is set in motion every day . . . just in order to satisfy this type of need, and how it compares with the amount of matter that . . . is consumed. (101–02)

The imagination, as the form-giving force of the human intellect, is the veritable motor driving economic development and increased prosperity. The needs created by the imagination, although addressed largely to considerations of comfort and aesthetics, contribute in significant ways to the human civilizing process and become indispensable imperatives that demand satisfaction. The spiral of economic progress and increased human industry is driven not by existential demands, which are finite, but rather by the limitless aesthetic demands and improvements in the *quality* of life that Schlosser identifies with the products of the imagination. To give form and refinement to the commodities human beings make use of in their everyday existence is to give form and refinement to human existence itself: the aesthetic education of the human race is achieved not through human interaction with works of art, but through constant contact with the aesthetics of the commodity, the economic concretization of the creative power of the human imagination. Moreover, human beings themselves, according to a note from Schlosser's *Politische Fragmente*, tend to give priority to imaginary needs over requirements of subsistence, as evidenced by their willingness to eat less in order to save money to acquire, say, a new vest (37). Schlosser is thus one of the first to articulate in rudimentary form an idea of commodity aesthetics, to acknowledge its role in the human psychic economy, and to valorize it as a principal tool in a luxury economy based on infinite growth, as well as its role in the civilizing process in general.

Schlosser subscribes to a theory of economics that champions constant innovation, the generation of ever-increasing, limitless needs, over the simple satisfaction of the requirements for bare subsistence. The ever-expanding economy powered by the creativity of human imagination is the primary instrument of human progress and development, measured precisely in terms of the amount of "refinement" and cultural distinction human beings achieve. Luxury is no longer a kind of excess, an ornament that enhances but does not alter the basic conditions of existence, but rather something just as indispensable as the means for one's sustenance. As opposed to the truly Spartan worldview of physiocracy, which concentrates solely on the bare-bones necessities of human existence,[48] Schlosser envisions a veritably modern, commodity- and luxury-oriented economy that alters the very character of human existence, gradually elevating the *material* conditions of human life by ratcheting up human beings' imaginary expectations and demands for comfort and everyday amenities. To the Spartanism of physiocracy he juxtaposes, in short, the Epicureanism of pleasure and satisfaction promoted by an economic prosperity that is driven by the imaginative creativity of human beings.

To be sure, Schlosser's economics still manifests the Enlightenment project of human perfectibility; but it draws a significant link between improvement in the material conditions of human life and the moral improvement of the individual human being. But whereas physiocracy, by concentrating on the satisfaction of finite needs, projected a state of human indolence as its utopian aim, Schlosser insists on the constant stimulation of human industry as the paramount moral virtue, and indolence, or satisfaction with just making do, as the supreme vice (*Xenocrates* 125). In this economy of constant advancement, expansion, and innovation, aesthetics, the form-giving capacity of the human imagination, takes center stage; indeed, economics and aesthetics are defined as the forces that join together to propel the material and intellectual advancement of the human species. The cornerstone of this progressive economic-aesthetic program is a conception of the imagination as the impulse behind the generation of surplus value (Blaich 20): to add value to the materials given in nature is to transform them through the work of the imagination, to give them form, and to realize this form-giving vision though appropriate acts of human labor.

For Schlosser, aesthetics is the principal mode by which humans add value to nature, and exchange value, as the excess that transcends the simple usefulness of commodities, is measured solely by the degree and success of aesthetic enhancement.

> Just as needs are no longer satisfied by the simple products themselves—
> that is, no longer are restricted simply to their mere usefulness, but
> rather also to their form, color, beauty, etc.—so must there be something

else that satisfies this new need. This is the formal fashioning [*Formge-bung*] of these products. And since the raw product is no longer of suffi-cient value to pay for this, a new price must be set that incites the fashioners [*Formgeber*] to form the material according to the demands of the new need; and this is nothing but another type of fashioning [*Formgebung*]. (*Xenocrates* 112–13)

In Schlosser's modern commercial state, *das Nutzbare* (what is useful), as he formulates it succinctly in his *Politische Fragmente*, must always be "sub-ordinate to the beautiful" (39). And this very difference between the use-ful qualities of a commodity and its *aesthetic* attributes, those lent it by the human power of imagination and the capacity to shape and give form, define the difference between its use value and its exchange value. The hours of human labor it takes to realize the aestheticized commodity, as well as the cost of subsistence for the laborer who actually performs the work, barely merit consideration for Schlosser (*Xenocrates* 102–03); for it is solely the *subjective* value superadded to the material substance when lending it form and refinement that enhances its exchange value, and as a result its price. Aesthetics, or the imaginative input of the human being, is the ulti-mate value-creating, value-assigning force: far from being structured accord-ing to the laws of reason or those of nature, economics is governed by the incalculable and unforeseeable creativity of the imagination. The human aesthetic sensibility and the drive for distinction prove to be the "invisible hand" at work behind the scenes of economic progress, propelling a pros-perity that, like the imagination, knows no bounds.

From Mimesis to Imagination

If the controversy over physiocracy marks a transition in economic think-ing from the predominance of the products of nature and their usefulness in satisfying human existential needs to a valorization of the human imag-ination as the limitless force that creates and fulfills an ever-expanding set of aesthetic or cultural needs, then it betokens a much more deep-seated intellectual-historical transformation that was occurring in this period. We have seen that this debate centered on questions of value creation and the human role in the production of surplus value. Whereas for the physiocrats

nature is the sole productive force, capable, due to its reproductive energies, of creating something out of nothing, or yielding an output that sur-
passes material input, for the opponents of physiocracy, whose views reach
paradigmatic expression in the economics of Schlosser, this productive
capacity has been transferred from nature to the human power of the imagination. If for the physiocrats human beings are restricted to the role of
midwives who assist in nature's reproduction, for Schlosser and his fellow
advocates of the modern "imaginary" economy it is the human mind itself
that is the sole font of economic productivity and surplus value. Moreover, it is explicitly not those qualities of the human intellect that foster
rationality, logic, or systematic reasoning to which these antiphysiocratic
economists turn, but rather to the unsystematic, lawless, unpredictable
forces of the human fantasy, the potency of ideation, imagination, and creativity. This shift in economic thinking is perfectly coherent with a fundamental transformation that occurs simultaneously in the realm of aesthetics:
it is the move from mimesis to imaginative creativity as the principal motivation behind artistic creativity—in particular, poetic creation—a shift that
Meyer H. Abrams felicitously designated in terms of the metaphorical move
away from the image of the mirror to that of the lamp as the privileged
figure for rendering the act of aesthetic production.[49] Abrams located this
shift in the domain of poetics approximately at the turn from the eighteenth to the nineteenth century (22); but the foregoing analysis of the controversy over physiocracy in Germany reveals that a similar transformation
was taking place just two decades earlier in the realm of economic thought.
This suggests the possibility that this aesthetic transformation is intimately
tied to changes in the conceptualization of economic theory and practice
during the closing decades of the eighteenth century. In what follows I will
attempt to document some of the significant moments in this shift from
mimesis to imagination using the example of two literary works, Ludwig
Tieck's *Franz Sternbalds Wanderungen* (Franz Sternbald's travels, 1798)
and Eduard Mörike's *Maler Nolten* (The painter Nolten, 1832).[50]

Already in 1790, when his *Kritik der Urteilskraft* (Critique of judgment) was first published, Immanuel Kant (1724–1804) thought it possible to assume that his readers subscribed to an absolute dichotomy between
the creative genius and the spirit of imitation. In this foundational work
of modern aesthetic theory he blithely maintains, "Everyone is in agree-

ment that genius is to be opposed absolutely to the *spirit of imitation*" (243). The three qualities Kant identifies with artistic genius are originality, that is, independence from any and all preordained rules; exemplariness, which establishes the products of the genius, themselves not derived from imitation, as imitable in their own right; and the mysterious, analytically or scientifically inscrutable origin of the genius's ideas—in a word, "inspiration" (242–43). When discussing the nature of aesthetic ideas, Kant also highlights the limitlessness and hence infinite productivity of the power of imagination.

> If we associate with a concept an idea drawn from the imaginative power [*Einbildungskraft*] that is intended to represent this concept, but which on its own instigates so much thought that it could never be compressed into a definite concept, and which hence aesthetically expands this concept in a limitless way; then in this process the imaginative power is creative and it brings movement into the capacity for intellectual ideas (reason). (251)

When coupled with a specific concept for the purpose of its aesthetic portrayal, an imaginative idea *exceeds* the bounds of the concept in a limitless manner; much as for Schlosser the form-giving imagination supplies the matter of nature with economic surplus value, for Kant the application of the aesthetic imagination to a concept expands the significance of the concept itself. In both instances, imagination is conceived as a fundamentally creative, indeed, *value*-creative force. Moreover, Kant's assertion that creative imagination injects a certain dynamism into the human capacity to generate intellectual ideas resonates with the language of economic circulation. And as with Schlosser, in the economy of the mind as Kant envisions it, imagination propels an infinite, limitless production. With Kant, however, it is not economic prosperity that is promoted by the imagination, but rather the riches of the intellect: imagination is a mind-expanding force that increases the wealth of ideas and stimulates intellectual circulation.

This association of the work of the imaginative genius with productivity and growth can be traced back at least as far as Edward Young's (1683–1765) *Conjectures on Original Composition*, first published in

1759, a work that exerted tremendous influence on German aesthetic thought in the second half of the eighteenth century (Abrams 201–03). Young juxtaposes—in language strikingly reminiscent of the German debate over physiocratic economic principles regarding the nature of productivity and surplus value—the organic growth indicative of the aesthetic original to the artificiality of artistic imitation: "An *Original* may be said to be of a *vegetable* nature; it rises spontaneously from the vital root of genius; it *grows*, it is not *made. Imitations* are often a sort of *manufacture* wrought by those *mechanics, art* and *labor*, out of pre-existent materials not their own" (*Conjectures* 7). If we contrast this statement with the definition of art given by Denis Diderot (1713–84) in the *Encyclopedia*, we can grasp the depth of this transformation in aesthetic ideology as well as its relationship to the economic revolution marked by the controversy over physiocracy. Diderot writes, "The purpose of all *art* in general, or of all systems of instruments and of rules leading to a similar end, is to imprint certain determined forms on a base given in nature" (qtd. in Gudeman 86). If for the physiocrats manufacturing was a principally *sterile* process, which simply enhanced a pregiven material substance without itself producing anything substantially new, then this is also how Diderot, giving voice to the aesthetic ideology of the Enlightenment in general, views the productivity of art: it reshapes nature, but it does not produce something new, something that had not previously existed. Young identifies the mechanical, rule-bound character of this aesthetic program with the doctrine of mimesis. As was true for the physiocrats, even the labor invested in this nonproductive transformation of nature is of negligible significance, since it does not, strictly speaking, add value. In contrast to this, Young, like the opponents of physiocracy, emphasizes the immediate creativity of the aesthetic original, the *organic* generative power of its productive potential and the growth it makes possible.

This notion of the productive capacity of the original genius, powered by the creativity of the imagination, becomes a constant in Romantic thought throughout Europe toward the end of the eighteenth and the beginning of the nineteenth century. For Samuel Taylor Coleridge (1772–1834), for example, the imagination "generates and produces a form of its own" due to the fact that it is nourished by "the very powers of growth and production" (qtd. in Abrams 169). In the German philosophical tradition it is the Romantic philosopher Friedrich Wilhelm Joseph von Schelling (1775–1854) who is most closely associated with a theory of artistic creativity in which the human creator reproduces the productive energies of organic nature. In the 1807 essay "Über das Verhältnis der bildenden Künste zu der Natur" (On the relationship of the visual arts to nature), for example, Schelling makes a programmatic statement about the manner in which the arts mediate between nature and the human soul by stressing that they possess "a productive power similar to that of [nature]" (392), and he takes this point as an occasion to criticize the influential art historian Johann Joachim Winckelmann (1717–68) for not invoking in his theory of the arts the idea of a living, creative power of nature (395–96). Art for Schelling exhibits a procreative power that is identical to the reproductive capacity of nature, and he describes the endowment of this productive force in human beings in words that harbor a clear allusion to the physiocrats' notion of the surplus value of organic reproduction in the domain of agriculture as a "gift of nature": "This intellectual power of propagation cannot create a doctrine or set of instructions. It is a pure gift of nature, which here comes full circle for a second time, realizing itself absolutely by transposing its creative power into its own creation" (424). Here it is not the productivity of the organic world itself, and its ability to satisfy the subsistence needs of human beings, that is mystified as a gift of nature, as was true for the physiocrats; rather, for Schelling nature's "gift" is the transference of its own productive potential to one of its own creations, namely, to select human beings, that is, to *artists*. Nature thus reproduces itself in a higher sense, regenerating not so much its own products as *reproducing its own reproductive capacity* in the creative, imaginative power of the artistic human being.

In the influential essay "Economimesis," Jacques Derrida analyzed this theory of aesthetic production in terms of what we might call an enhanced mimesis, the imitation not of the products of nature themselves, but instead of nature's own productivity, which he calls "anthropo-theological mimesis" (9–10). To be sure, this is an insight articulated by Abrams nearly fifty years earlier when he summarized the Romantic view of the poetic imagination by saying, "The imagination, in creating poetry, echoes the creative principle underlying the universe" (119). My point here is that the rapprochement between economics and aesthetics that Derrida attempts to accomplish in "Economimesis" can also be approached from an intellectual-historical perspective. Indeed, when viewed in the context of the terms in which the dispute over physiocracy was carried out, the postulate of an "anthropo-theological mimesis" becomes superfluous, since, as we will see, the operative terms in which this transformation must be comprehended are better encompassed by the juxtaposition of mimesis, as imitation of nature, and imagination, as production out of pure fancy and fantasy.

If we turn briefly now to Ludwig Tieck's (1773–1853) novel *Franz Sternbalds Wanderungen*, we can trace the ways in which the initial stages of this transformation from mimesis to imagination were conceptualized in the context of theories of art. As we will see, there is a close resemblance between the terms in which this aesthetic transformation is articulated and notions of productivity and value as they are formulated in the economic debate over physiocracy. Set in the fifteenth century, or during the waning of the Middle Ages, *Franz Sternbalds Wanderungen* relates the story of a painter and the gradual transformation of his aesthetic sensibilities. As both a *Bildungsroman*, a novel of development, and a *Künstlerroman*, a novel specifically about the maturation of an artist's sensibilities, this work is particularly well suited for an examination of how the late eighteenth century understood the process of aesthetic change it was undergoing. The artist Lukas von Leyden, who at the beginning of the novel is one of the chief mentors of Tieck's protagonist, Franz Sternbald, articulates the doctrine of artistic mimesis, to which he and his young disciple adhere, in terms that recall the discourse of the sole productivity of nature as propounded by the physiocrats. Responding to a remark about the rarity of pure creative invention, made by a fictionalized Albrecht Dürer, who is Sternbald's other primary mentor, Lukas von Leyden comments,

"You are absolutely right," Lukas said, "to pull something out of the air, in the most literal sense, would truly be one of the most peculiar things that could ever happen to any human being. It would be a totally new type of derangement, for even the madman does not invent his fever dreams. Thus nature is the only innovator, she makes loans to all artists out of her great treasure-house; we always only imitate nature; our inspiration, our inventions, our search for what is new and exceptional is simply comparable to the attention an infant directs at its mother, never letting a single movement she makes escape its eyes." (115)

It is hard to imagine a more programmatic—or, for that matter, more pellucid—defense of the principle of mimesis in artistic creation than the one Tieck places in the mouth of Lukas von Leyden. As was true for the physiocrats, nature is represented here as the sole productive principle in the world, and human "creativity" cannot be equated with production in this strict sense, but must instead be viewed as a mere copying of what nature has already produced. Mimesis as artistic principle is one that, in the language of economics, does not produce surplus value. By contrast, however, human invention, the generation of imaginative visions and fantasies, represents such a radical departure from the norm that it borders on insanity. And besides, in the final analysis, even these fantasies, like fever dreams, ultimately retain their connection to the empirical realm of nature. Imitation of the works of nature thus remains the sole occupation of the artist, and what is thought of as new, original, or remarkable can be attributed to a sharpening of the perceptual faculties for the nuances of nature itself. This is what Lukas wants to say with his analogy that compares the relationship of the artist to nature with that of an infant to its mother: because the infant never takes its eyes off its mother, but instead constantly observes her every move, it discovers ever new details in her habitus and actions. Art in this understanding is but a variety of natural science that places nature under its mimetic microscope, thereby turning out aspects of the natural world that otherwise pass unnoticed.

At the outset of his artistic career, Franz Sternbald subscribes completely to this mimetic doctrine that views nature as the sole font of creative productivity and that hence limits art to the status of a flawed re-creation of nature's more perfect creation. To the young blacksmith he meets at the beginning of his travels, Sternbald thus expresses the aim of his art as the ever truer representation of the natural world, in this instance of the human face (24). And in a seminal scene in the first book of part 1 of the novel, Franz experiences the frustrating limitations of the mimetic ability of his own art when compared with nature's own mimetic capacities: as he sits attempting to draw a landscape that lies before him, he recognizes in dismay that the world he seeks to portray mimetically in his painting is imitated much more successfully in the reflection he sees in a neighboring pond.

> Franz pulled out his drawing paper and wanted to begin to sketch the landscape; but real nature appeared to him dry in comparison with the image reflected in the water, and he was even less satisfied with the lines he had put down on paper, which in no way imitated what he saw laid out before himself. (51)

Nature is not only the sole productive force in the universe, but it is also the most accurate *mimetic* artist, providing a copy so engaging that it even overshadows the original it imitates. Compared even to this second-order reproduction found in nature, the mimesis practiced by the human artist is fundamentally flawed and insufficient. This recognition becomes a watershed experience in Sternbald's artistic development: if, on the one hand, it brings home to him the idea that nature is the sole productive force in the universe, it also hints, in nature's reproduction of nature itself, that only a *reflexive* art can hope to approximate the generative power of nature. Indeed, nature's self-reflexivity as it imitates itself in the waters of the pond represents an *enhanced* reproduction that outshines even nature's own original. For the *real* landscape appears to him "dry" (*trocken*), a hint at its static and unproductive qualities, whereas only the reflected imitation is liquid, fluid, and potentially productive. This scene thus looks ahead to a new artistic conception that stresses the self-reflexivity of the human artist as an aesthetic paradigm that transcends the impossible limitations attendant upon the mimetic reproduction of nature.

In the first book of part 2 of the novel, in a discussion that focuses on the artistic imitation of a landscape and hence alludes to this earlier failure to depict a natural scene and the artistic disillusionment this experience entails, Sternbald gives voice to a new aesthetic program defined by artistic self-reflexivity.

> Sternbald said . . . : "I believe I understand how you think about landscapes, and it seems to me that you are right. For what shall I do with all those branches and leaves, with this exact copy of the grasses and

the flowers? It is not this plant, not the mountains that I want to tran-
scribe [*abschreiben*], but rather my disposition [*Gemüt*], my mood
[*Stimmung*], which has control over me in this precise moment. This
is what I want to take hold of for myself and communicate with others
of a like mind." (258)

The philosophy of aesthetic mimesis is derogated here as a simple transcription of nature, indeed, as an act of *plagiarism* (*abschreiben*), and in
this sense not creative in the least. If the program of mimesis dictates that
artists direct their gaze outward, following the details of nature as an infant
does the movements of its mother, Sternbald's new aesthetic program
testifies to an inward turn in which the visionary *reflection* of nature in
the human subject itself becomes the artistic aim.

We recognize the parallelism to the self-reflexive, but enhanced reproduction of nature by nature as described in the reflection of the landscape
in the pond from the earlier scene. Now, however, it is the subjective character of the artist that functions as the refracting tain of an internal mirror, recording not so much the essence of nature itself as the *impression* it
leaves in the subjectivity of the aesthetically sensitive perceiver. Sternbald
has, in effect, assumed the place of the reflective pond in the earlier scene:
as a self-reflexive artist, he is nature re-creating nature, and his creativity,
conforming with Schelling's aesthetic theory, reenacts the creative productivity of nature itself. Art's objective is now to project the transitory,
fleeting disposition that the experience of nature evokes in the artistic subject, to hold that moment fast in the artistic work and thereby communicate
this inward, subjective mood to other receptive human beings. Nature, to
be sure, is not removed from the picture; but it is now incorporated into
a complex dialectic that includes the individual, creative response of the
artistic subject. Artistic creation is no longer an essentially unproductive
act that merely produces a diminished copy of the original creation of
nature; instead it enhances and adds value to the natural world by trans-
figuring it through its coupling with the disposition, attitudes, and emotional sensibilities of the artist him- or herself. William Wordsworth gave
voice to this new artistic attitude in a letter to Francis Wrangham dated
18 January 1816 when he wrote, "Objects . . . derive their influence not
from the properties inherent in them, not from what they are actually in

themselves, but from such as are bestowed upon them by the minds of those who are conversant with or affected by those objects" (qtd. in Burwick 46). Art creates by adding value, by producing something that did not previously exist; and it accomplishes this by explicitly activating the subjective elements of the artistic personality, which are projected onto the objects of the world. The attribution of aesthetic value, the value-adding process of aesthetic production, can only be measured in these purely subjective terms, as the supplementary investment of emotion and imagination by the artistic mind into its chosen object.

There is an almost uncanny similarity between this Romantic notion of art as a subjective enhancement of a natural object and Marx's conception of the fetishism of the commodity, which is mystified and alienated from the subjects whose labor created it by their own imaginary investment in its value as a commodity. The aesthetic process, in this understanding, transforms the mere object of nature into—to use the words Marx applied to the fetishism of the commodity—a *sinnlich übersinnliches Ding*, a "sensual supersensual thing" (*Kapital* 85). The major difference between the Romantic theory of subjective creativity and Marx's notion of the commodity is the gulf that separates the value placed on each: the same process viewed in an overwhelmingly positive manner in the realm of aesthetics receives a negative assessment in the sphere of economics. But even among the Romantics themselves the aesthetic conception of art as emotional excess was not always seen so sanguinely.[51] If for Tieck, composing *Franz Sternbald* in the 1790s, at the very inception of the Romantic movement in Germany, this theory can be presented as fresh, and as a revolutionary break with the dogma of mimesis, by the time Eduard Mörike (1804–75) began writing *Maler Nolten* thirty years later, in the late 1820s, the very aesthetic subjectivity Tieck praises has become a wanton and threatening—because uncontrolled and uncontrollable—phantasm. In Mörike's novella the aesthetic product of the imagination attains the dangerous, alienating, occult quality of Marx's fetishistic commodity.

Like *Franz Sternbalds Wanderungen, Maler Nolten* is about the life of a painter, Theobald Nolten, and the development of his artistic sensibilities. The work begins with the visit of a certain elderly Baron Jaßfeld at the home of the painter Tillsen to remark on the new and unusual artistic style the former discovered on the previous day when attending an exhibition of Tillsen's latest works. Jaßfeld is bewildered and somewhat upset by the nature and content of these paintings, whose surprising originality he characterizes as "an audaciousness and greatness in the composition of figures, a freedom in all respects," and he expresses his skepticism about "the conspicuous divergence in the poetic sensibility, in the choice of objects" (Mörike, *Maler Nolten* 10). What especially stands out for Jaßfeld, the conservative art patron, however, is the fantastic nature of these paintings, an imaginative creativity that borders on the bizarre: "Here one finds a thoroughly exceptional direction of the human fantasy [*Phantasie*]; wondrous, fantastic, in part rash and bizarre in a pleasant sense" (10). If these paintings are boldly imaginative, even fantastic, they yet remain "pleasantly" bizarre, and hence do not completely offend the aesthetic taste of Jaßfeld. But as it turns out, it is precisely this pleasantness that constitutes their foreign element, not the strangely bizarre figures and compositions that make up the paintings' subject matter. The painter Tillsen goes on to explain that these works, although strictly speaking the creation of his "hand" (15), are by no means the product of his own imagination. A year previously he purchased some sketches from a man whose speech and actions left the impression that he was insane, and these became the compositional models for the paintings. As it turns out, the sketches Tillsen purchased from this bedraggled stranger were actually the work of the story's protagonist, Theobald Nolten, stolen from him by a servant, who passed them off as his own work and sold them to Tillsen. As chance would have it, Nolten, who is studying art in the same town, visits Tillsen's exhibition and sees his own fantasies exhibited in oil under Tillsen's name. This motivates him to seek out this older colleague and tell of his surprise to find his own dream visions depicted in his works of art (21–23). Thus the "pleasantly bizarre" works that so amaze Baron Jaßfeld actually emerge, as Tillsen himself admits, from a "double source": their content and compositional structure (what makes them "bizarre") is the work of Nolten, while their execution and their clarity of style (what makes them "pleasant") stem from Tillsen.

Curiously, each artist sees the work of the other as the ultimate complement to his own, as the potential fulfillment of his artistic mission. Tillsen recognizes in Nolten's vivid imagination "precisely all those things . . . that I am lacking, that I will always lack, and prevent me from ever becoming a true painter!" (16), while Nolten expresses his undying gratitude to Tillsen for lending the chaos of his visions such stylistic refinement and compositional order.

> You have revealed me to myself by lifting me high above myself and carrying me onward. You awakened me with a friendly hand from a state of dark impotence, you pulled me up to the sunlit heights of art at the very moment when I was beginning to have doubts in my own powers. A rogue had to rob me so that you, with your clear mirror, would have the opportunity to reveal my future stature. . . . Let me kiss the tranquil hand that has forever given order to the confused threads of my being— my master, my savior! (22)

The friendship that ensues between Nolten and Tillsen is an allegory for the fusion of content and form in artistic production, for the marriage of dark and light, brooding fantasy and clarifying order, emotional outburst and stayed composition. However, if in its opening scenes Mörike's novella holds out hope for the merging of these two distinct aesthetic enterprises, its narrative development portrays their gradual unraveling, to the point that its protagonist is ultimately said to perish from the excesses of his own imagination. Thus upon his death the narrator comments, "Since, however, some violent terror must have been the cause of death, the assumption was inescapable . . . that in this instance the imagination [*Einbildung*], as we know from many other examples, dealt the fatal blow" (449). Death from unbridled imagination: that is the story related in *Maler Nolten*, and it voices a concrete warning against the demonic aspects of imagination unbound. Indeed, Nolten's fantasies become so real, are projected so totally into the world of empirical reality, that they take control of him and lend him the guise of someone who is utterly insane (449). Like the human agents who populate Marx's world of commodity fetishism, Nolten becomes captivated by his own subjective, imaginary visions that he projects out into the empirical world. The discipline and formal control Nolten hoped to gain from Tillsen have obviously been lost, and the work of art, or the artistic imagination itself, has become so absolute as to be fetishized in exactly the same way as Marx's commodity.

Nolten's father is given the role of identifying the dangerous temperament of his son and criticizing his artistic fantasies as a divergence from the law of mimesis. Nolten's refusal to paint "an ordinary tree, a house and other such things based on a worthy original" and his proclivity instead for depicting solely "his own whimsies, witchlike caricatures" (230), call forth nothing but the father's condemnation. He views his son as succumbing to the temptations of the devil, of departing from the "path of healthy order" and of displaying a peculiar fascination for all that is "exaggerated" and "unnatural" (229). Toward the end of this novella Nolten's tendency to get lost in the maze of his own imaginations is scenically depicted as he wanders through a garden labyrinth, reading poems composed by his alter ego, the poet Larkin, and giving himself over completely to, as the narrator poignantly remarks, the *Wundergärten der Einbildung* (398), the "fantastic gardens"—that is, the *labyrinth*—of the imagination. That very power of the creative fantasy that had been the watchword of the early Romantics, which had distinguished and rescued their artistic endeavor from sterile mimesis as the mere imitation of nature, and whose productivity they valorized, has now become a threatening, even deadly monster. An overinvestment of imagination sends the world of the artist into a fatal tailspin; without the control, refinement, and order associated at the beginning of the novella with the work of the painter Tillsen, imagination, far from being a productive force, becomes a power of destruction.

Economics and Aesthetics of the Imagination

Death by imagination: that is not merely the fate that befalls the protagonist of Mörike's late-Romantic novella, but also the fear that most dogged the defenders of physiocratic economic policy when they envisioned the phantasmagorical economy of luxury goods and the infinite field of new desires and wants this emerging industrialized economy could engender. This same critical evaluation of the role of the imagination in the world of economic commodities resurfaces in the mid-nineteenth century with Marx's analysis of commodity fetishism, and on this score Mörike's novella and Marx's *Das Kapital* share a significant central theme, articulated in the one instance in the domain of aesthetics, and in the other in that of

modern economics. But between the condemnation of the imagination proffered by the physiocrats and the attack voiced by Marx and Mörike, there
is a brief interlude—marked in economics by the critics of physiocracy and
in aesthetics by literary Romanticism—in which the imagination is valorized
as the pinnacle of human productivity, as the mark of nature's originary
creative power, transposed into one of its own creations: imagination as
nature redoubled.

My point in presenting this brief sketch of the vicissitudes the evaluation of subjectivity and the imagination undergoes from the last third of
the eighteenth century to the mid-nineteenth century has been to indicate
a certain historical parallelism between the domains of economics and aesthetics with regard to the assessment of the role imagination plays in their
theories of value. We have witnessed how in the controversy over physiocratic economic policy, subjective imagination emerges as the creative force
that stimulates a hitherto unheard-of productivity, an economic expansion
associated by thinkers such as Schlosser with the modern commercial and
manufacturing economy. In this conception, it is the human imaginative
power, not the reproductive force of nature nor the labor of manual workers, which is responsible for the creation of surplus value. This represents
a radically new and modern economic theory, one that looks ahead to the
role of human psychology in the realm of economic production and that
identifies the world of values with the intangibilities of human *desires*.[52]
However, the fear of fantasy as a dangerous departure from the solid
ground—the fertile soil—of nature always lurks behind valorizations of
its productivity. What makes the imagination seductive both as economic
and as aesthetic force is precisely its potential for infinite productivity, for
limitless growth and development. At the same time, this very productivity
generates as its evil twin an anxiety over the lack of any restraint, control
mechanism, or brake shoe that might retard the seemingly self-propelling
movement of limitless economic and aesthetic creativity. Pure potential is
seen to have the underside of radical ungovernability. It thus contains not
only the seeds of infinite perfectibility, but also those of infinite decline,
the possibility that human beings will succumb to their own worst instincts,
drives, and desires: to greed, self-absorption, solipsism, alienation. Without an "invisible hand," a conception of divine providence or some such
overriding guiding mechanism, it seems impossible to steer the ship of

human economic and aesthetic culture on a course that could guarantee the future welfare of all.

The valorization of the fundamental productivity of subjective, imaginative investments in the object as commodity remains but a relatively brief intermezzo in the early history of economic thought. The insight into the fundamentally *subjective* nature of value, which is defended most forcefully by the German critics of physiocracy, is repressed in the history of economics, replaced by the domineering conception of objective value as measured in terms of human labor.[53] Via Adam Smith and eventually David Ricardo (1772–1823) and Karl Marx, among others, economic theory returns to an objective conception that measures surplus value in terms of human labor. Marx's attack on the fetishism of the commodity, viewed as a subjective investment that deceives human beings into misrecognizing the social nature of their own economic products, sounds the death knell of subjective value theories in the realm of economics. Only in such mysteriously metaphorical and analogical instances as Marx's discussion of commodity fetishism does this repressed issue of subjective value rise, temporarily and in metaphorically distorted form, to the surface of mainstream economic debate. Similarly, in the sphere of aesthetics the Romantic glorification of the imagination as the font of all artistic creation, and the concomitant rejection of mimesis as a valid aesthetic practice, is eventually demonized even by the Romantics themselves, questioned as an unnatural and exaggerated program that requires the mollifying control of reason, order, and objective composure. Just as objective value theories reassume dominance in the field of economics, mimesis returns in the domain of aesthetics in the guise of the rejuvenated and programmatic realism of the nineteenth century. Our examination of the controversy over physiocracy in German letters at the end of the eighteenth century thus helps shed light on certain homologies in the evolution of aesthetic and economic theory in this period, demonstrating how, when considering their assessment of the productivity and perils of the imagination, as well as their theories of value, economic and aesthetic history can be read together as mutually illuminating disciplines.

Part Two

LITERARY ECONOMIES

5 / COUNTING ON GOD

Economic Providentialism in Johann Heinrich Jung-Stilling's *Lebensgeschichte*

*At least six times I was asked the question: "Henri, what's the word
for 'belief' [Glaube] in French?' And six times, each more tearfully, I
answered: "It is 'le credit.' And the seventh time, cherry red in the face,
the enraged examiner shouted: "It is 'la religion'"—and blows rained
down upon me, while all my classmates laughed.*

—Heinrich Heine (*Ideen: Das Buch le Grand* 270)

Social Climbing: The Metamorphoses
of Johann Heinrich Jung-Stilling

HE ANECDOTE FROM HEINRICH HEINE'S TRAVELOGUE *IDEEN:
Das Buch le Grand (Ideas: The book Le Grand) that serves as the
epigraph to this chapter alludes with considerable humor to a problem that is treated with deadly seriousness in Johann Heinrich Jung-Stilling's
(1740–1817) *Lebensgeschichte,* his episodic autobiography published in
five volumes over the course of nearly three decades (1777–1804): semantic crossovers between the realms of economics and religion. The irony of
Heine's anecdote resides, of course, in the fact that his translation of the
German word *Glaube* ("belief," or "faith") into French as *crédit* is perfectly correct; and yet the fictitious examiner purportedly testing Heine's
knowledge of the French language takes umbrage at this word, rife with
economic associations, and insists instead that "belief" be translated as

"religion." Behind this questionable rendering stands a complex but powerful ideology: on the one hand, the denial of any connection whatsoever
between language and the real world of economics—as stand-in for the
affairs of the secular world—and belief in God and the otherworldly; on
the other hand, the notion of faith in a transcendental being confined strictly
to the framework of organized religion and the church. The examiner
implies, in fact, that true belief is only possible within the context of religious institutions, and he underwrites this implication with the most persuasive rhetoric possible: a hail of blows that punish the body for the offences
of the spirit. All of these elements, from the slippage between religious and
economic thought, to the ideologically blinded insistence on an identity
between true faith and Christian religious doctrine, through finally to an
asceticism that views physical abuse as an appropriate pedagogical tool
for enforcing a "proper" religious lifestyle, are operative in Jung-Stilling's
Lebensgeschichte. The major difference is that in Jung-Stilling's autobiography Heine's biting sarcasm is completely absent.

Johann Heinrich Jung-Stilling is certainly one of the most fascinating,
multitalented, and protean individuals of the eighteenth century, not only
in Germany but in Europe in general. Born into extremely humble circumstances as the son of a tailor and occasional schoolteacher, and the
grandson of a charcoal burner, he advanced to become one of the most
prominent statesmen of the German Pietistic Revival movement at the end
of the eighteenth and the beginning of the nineteenth centuries, ultimately
ending his vocational life as a professional religious proselyte under the
patronage of one of Germany's more powerful territorial princes, the *Kurfürst* (electoral prince) and subsequently (after 1806) grand duke of Baden,
Karl Friedrich (1728–1811).[1] The author of numerous religious-didactic
novels, the most noteworthy and influential being *Das Heimweh* (Home-
sickness, 1794–96),[2] Jung-Stilling also single-handedly wrote and published several religious journals addressed to the common people, the most
successful being *Der graue Mann* (The gray man), which was printed for
over twenty years, from 1795 until 1816, with the last issue appearing
shortly before his death. It was above all on the basis of these widely
read, extremely popular, and, indeed, populist religious works that Jung-
Stilling came generally to be known as the "patriarch" of German Pietistic Revivalism.[3]

More dizzying even than this phenomenal ascent up the ladder of German civil society, which brought Jung-Stilling into personal contact with some of the ruling elite of Europe, including Czar Alexander I of Russia,[4] was the veritable odyssey of the professional course he followed on his way to attaining this final post as *Hofrat*, spiritual advisor at the court of the grand duke of Baden. Due to his innate intelligence, his demanding education, and his autodidacticism, Jung-Stilling served variously as village schoolteacher and private tutor, but his inherent unsuitability for the role of pedagogue caused him to fall back repeatedly into the lowly position of a tailor's apprentice. His climb into the higher social echelons did not actually begin until he followed the suggestion of one of his employers that he study medicine and become a physician. After a mere three semesters at the University of Strasbourg, where he came into close personal contact with the young Johann Wolfgang von Goethe (1749–1832) and other representatives of the budding German *Sturm und Drang* movement, including Jakob Michael Reinhold Lenz (1751–92) and Johann Gottfried Herder (1744–1803), Jung-Stilling received his medical degree and began a practice as a physician. Despite his highly regarded and well-recognized success as an oculist, in particular as a cataract surgeon,[5] Jung-Stilling failed to establish an economically successful medical practice, and when in 1778 he received an offer to assume a professorial chair—not in medicine, the field he had studied, but rather in political economy—he jumped at the opportunity.

Jung-Stilling owed this truly marvelous turn in his professional development and, as we will see, in his financial fortunes, to the publication of a scant number of political-economic essays, which drew largely on his pragmatic experiences as a youth who had grown up in a rural, agrarian environment and on the training he received as the apprentice to a wealthy merchant and factory owner. These essays appeared in the journal of the Kaiserslautern Physikalisch-Ökonomische Gesellschaft (Physical-Economic Society), organized by Friedrich Casimir Medicus (1736–1808) for the purpose of promoting economic development. When this society gave birth to the first institution of higher learning in Germany dedicated to matters of political economy, the so-called Kameral-Hohe-Schule, founded in 1774 and initially situated in Kaiserslautern but subsequently (1784) integrated into Heidelberg University, Jung-Stilling was hired as the third of three full-time professors.⁶ It was only then, at the age of thirty-eight, that Jung-Stilling received his first stable salary, the relatively modest sum of six hundred guldens per year, so that his entry into the life of the professional economist coincided with the inception of a secure economic existence based on a regular and dependable income. Jung-Stilling flourished as a professor of political economy for twenty-five years, first in Kaiserslautern and Heidelberg, and eventually at the University of Marburg (from 1787 to 1803), where he held the very first professorial post in the discipline of economics. In this period he published no less than eleven textbooks in different areas of political economy, from a basic outline of this emerging discipline—at this time still called *Kameralistik* (cameralism) in Germany, due to its association with the princely *Kammer*, the state treasury—to specialized studies dedicated to such topics as agriculture, forestry, trade, and bookkeeping.⁷

Because of the encyclopedic breadth he displayed in the coverage of this nascent field and the large number of rudimentary texts (usually based on university lecture courses) he published over a relatively short time span, Jung-Stilling developed into one of the founding fathers of political economics as academic discipline in Germany. However, by 1803 he became disillusioned with teaching, both because of his students' declining interest in economics courses and also because he objected ideologically to the revolutionary spirit, in the wake of the French Revolution, then sweeping the Marburg student body. As a result, Jung-Stilling resigned his professorship to assume the position of religious advisor to Kurfürst Karl Friedrich of Baden. The degree to which his duties as professor of economics had turned to painful drudgery can be gauged by the fact that, despite his perennial economic woes, Jung-Stilling was even willing to accept a lower salary in return for the greater freedom of this new position at court and the ability to devote himself solely to what he now saw as his "true calling" (*Lebensgeschichte* 478, 569, 613),⁸ a life dedicated to being a popularizer and proselyte for Pietistic religious views.

If this vertiginous social and economic ascent was exceptional in its multifariousness, speed, and degree, it was also symptomatic in many ways of the demands and expectations placed by a new generation of middle-class intellectuals on the structures of civil society. One of the reasons for the tremendous popularity of Jung-Stilling's *Lebensgeschichte*, especially its early episodes, published under the separate titles *Henrich Stillings Jugend* (Stilling's childhood, 1777), *Henrich Stillings Jünglings-Jahre* (Stilling's youth, 1778), and *Henrich Stillings Wanderschaft* (Stilling's apprenticeship, 1778), was the heroic story they told about the struggles of an individual against social and economic disadvantage and the successful realization of upward social mobility on the basis of education, ambition, and the tireless investment of personal energy. Only in the last two episodes of Jung-Stilling's autobiography, *Henrich Stillings häusliches Leben* (Stilling's domestic life, 1789) and *Heinrich* [sic] *Stillings Lehr-Jahre* (Stilling's years as pedagogue, 1804), do these phenomenal quantum leaps to ever higher positions in German civil society come to be interpreted as symptoms of divine grace, rather than as the result of an intense personal drive and the fruits of individual achievement. What is unique about Jung-Stilling's *Lebensgeschichte* as historical document, however, is not simply the function it served in representing these new potentials for social and economic advancement, but even more so the role its publication played as an instrument in the development of Jung-Stilling's life itself: in this instance autobiography does not serve merely as a record of past events; rather, its promulgation as text, its entrance into the public sphere as (fictionalized) life document, intervenes in and helps shape the future development of the life it purports merely to describe.[9]

Henrich Stillings Jugend took the German literary scene by storm, becoming one of the most noteworthy literary-cultural events of 1777 and paving the way for the fame and fortune of its as yet anonymous author (Panthel 582) (fig. 3). Curiously enough, Jung-Stilling himself had little to do with initiating the publication of this text; it was none other than his friend Goethe who requested the manuscript of Jung-Stilling's childhood experiences, subjected it to emendations and revisions, and then submitted it for publication without its author's knowledge. Jung-Stilling only became aware that *Henrich Stillings Jugend* would appear in print when out of the blue he received in the mail an honorarium of 115 reichstalers,[10] forwarded to him by Goethe. In a later volume of his *Lebensgeschichte* this event is interpreted as one of the primary examples of divine intervention into Jung-Stilling's life, whereby the initiative of his friend Goethe is wholly elided (*Lebensgeschichte* 343–44). This displacement of human initiative by blind faith in divine guidance is one of the most curious and

Henrich Stillings
Jugend.

Eine

wahrhafte Geschichte.

Berlin und Leipzig,
bey George Jacob Decker.
1777

3 / Title page and vignette from the first edition of *Henrich Stillings Jugend*.

characteristic ideological reflexes in Jung-Stilling's interpretation of his life, and it promotes a perverse kind of self-glorification that, while overtly playing down the value of the self and its contribution to its own successes, covertly valorizes this same self as the chosen instrument of divine guidance and revelation.[11]

No doubt, the monetary windfall that accompanied the publication of *Henrich Stillings Jugend* must have seemed like a gift from heaven, coming as it did at a time when Jung-Stilling's medical practice was on the verge of collapse, the debts he had accrued to pay for his university studies were steadily increasing, and economic and existential ruin seemed inevitable. Moreover, due to his miserable economic prospects, Jung-Stilling was unable to secure any additional credit to help feed himself and his family (see *Lebensgeschichte* 333–34).[12] The unexpected receipt of this honorarium, of course, opened Jung-Stilling's eyes to the possibility of earning money as a freelance writer, and it is no coincidence that the second two volumes of his autobiography were written in quick succession, hard on the heals of this surprising windfall and the shockwaves the reception of *Henrich Stillings Jugend* sent through the German literary scene. By December 1777 the second volume, *Stillings Jünglings-Jahre*, was complete and ready to send to the publisher, George Jacob Decker (1732–99) in Berlin (Jung-Stilling, *Briefe* 85), and just two months later, by the beginning of February 1778, the third volume was finished and ready for printing (*Briefe* 86–87). That Jung-Stilling's motivation in publishing these further volumes was largely monetary in nature can be seen from the very first letter he sent to Decker. Here he pleaded, in a painfully obsequious tone,

> Dear Mr. Decker! Setting aside your businessman's heart and placing in its stead that of the upright German: is one louis d'or too much per broadsheet for Stilling's autobiography? I truly require that amount, I'm not wealthy, and I even have debts to friends who have helped me out. Please do everything you can and grant me one louis d'or [per sheet]. (*Briefe* 83)

Pointing to his dire financial circumstances, with mounting debts and severe existential need, Jung-Stilling begs for an honorarium of one louis

4 / Louis d'or, or "golden Louis." This coin circulated throughout Europe as an internationally recognized currency and was especially coveted.

d'or—one of the most precious, stable, and hence sought-after gold coins of the period—for each broadsheet of printed text (fig. 4).[13] Moreover, Jung-Stilling is clever enough to appeal to his publisher's patriotism and human compassion, rather than to his business sensibilities, and in the context of the resounding success of the first volume of his autobiography his demand for relatively high payment has considerable weight.

Jung-Stilling would quickly learn that the publication of fictional texts was no El Dorado that would suddenly bestow upon him large quantities of much needed cash (see *Lebensgeschichte* 386). Nonetheless, the appearance of the first volumes of his autobiography and their surprising literary success—a success that still endures today, making this one of the standard works of eighteenth-century German literary history—mark Jung-Stilling's coming-out as a significant figure in German public life. In this sense this work also prefigures and paves the way for his later success as a religious writer, as Jung-Stilling himself clearly recognized (*Lebensgeschichte* 613; see Hirzel 25).[14] Fortunately, however, Jung-Stilling would never have to live from his writing alone, and soon after the publication of the second and third volumes of his autobiography he received his appointment as professor of political economy at the Kameral-Hohe-Schule in Kaiserslautern, a post that provided him with a regular salary sufficient to cover his most immediate existential needs (*Lebensgeschichte* 353–54).

"Forgive Us Our Debts": Providentialism as Ideological
Mask for Personal Ambition

Because it was composed and published in individual installments over the course of several decades, Jung-Stilling's *Lebensgeschichte* displays, not surprisingly, a somewhat desultory character. Moreover, as a consequence of the temporal disparities that inform the individual volumes of this work, its perspective, style, and tone constantly shift (Günther 69). Yet in spite of this, Jung-Stilling's autobiography as a whole displays a surprising amount of thematic coherence. This is predicated neither solely on the unifying thread of a single life story, nor on the artificially imposed structure presented by the leitmotif of divine providence as the guiding force in Jung-Stilling's life,[15] but develops largely as a reflex of the common social, psychological, and economic parameters within which the author/narrator views his own development. Symptomatic of this is the fact that the very first paragraph of *Henrich Stillings Jugend* introduces, on a subtle but persistent subtextual level, most of the themes that will dominate the entire story of his rise to social and cultural prominence.

In Westphalia there lies a diocese in a very mountainous region, from whose peaks one can look out over numerous dukedoms and principalities. The main village containing the church of this diocese is called Florenburg. For ages its inhabitants have felt revulsion at being called a village [*Dorf*], and that is why—despite the fact that they are forced to live from agriculture and livestock-farming—they have continually sought to place themselves above their neighbors from the surrounding communities, who are mere farmers; in turn the latter have always accused the citizens of this village of suppressing its true name Floren-*dorf* and replacing it with Floren*burg*.[16] Be that as it may, this town is, in fact, the seat of the local government, whose head in my day was Johannes Henrikus Scultetus. Uncouth, unknowing people called him Master Hanns outside the town hall, but well-to-do citizens [*hübsche Bürger*] were in the habit of saying Master Schulde. (*Lebensgeschichte* 1)

On the most superficial level, this paragraph invokes the natural and sociological environment into which its protagonist was born, thereby establishing the setting in which a large portion of Jung-Stilling's autobiography takes place. On his trips from village to village, and especially during his years of travel, he will often climb the hillsides mentioned in the first sentence and take in the panorama that extends over the valleys with their dispersed villages. At the same time, the fictional name he ascribes to his native town of Hilchenbach, "Florenburg," alludes in subtle ways to a— real or merely projected?—prosperity that sets this town apart from neighboring communities. The semantic stem -*burg* indicates that we are dealing with a municipality, most likely with a market town, perhaps adorned with a fortress or aristocratic residence, as in fact was true for Jung-Stilling's native Hilchenbach. The opening syllables of this name, *Floren*, hint in German as in English at the peculiarly "flourishing" character of this community, so that the word *Florenburg* might be translated quite literally as "flourishing town." Supporting its economic importance is its role as the center of a religious diocese, marked by the existence of the church.

The anecdote Jung-Stilling invents to justify the portentous, if somewhat pretentious name of this village suggests that its inhabitants are bound together by the shared sense of their relative economic and social superiority: they feel demeaned by the thought that their town might be designated as a mere *Dorf*, a "village," with all the associations of rural backwardness and economic dependence this word brings into play. Like their neighbors in adjacent communities, they also live, as Jung-Stilling is careful to note, from agriculture and livestock; but they nevertheless insist that they are not mere farmers. Citizens from the neighboring villages take offense at this presumptuous ostentation, viewing it as evidence of an overweening haughtiness, and their revenge assumes the form of a tale in which the highfalutin name Floren*burg* is generated as a substitutive displacement for the village's true name, Floren*dorf*. Thus this opening paragraph, far from simply portraying the natural and social environment out of which its protagonist emerges, subtly invokes the themes of striving, ambition, and upward socioeconomic mobility that are prominent motifs in Jung-Stilling's own life. By the logic of association, the text suggests that Jung-Stilling is a genuine product of Floren*burg*, whose indigenous citizenry encapsulates the social-psychological drive for self-betterment that is characteristic of Jung-Stilling's own life of striving. Florenburg and its citizens become the avatars of a drive toward self-improvement that expresses itself above all in a break with a strictly rural lifestyle and the transition to an emerging market economy, one in which trade, money, and manufacturing are beginning to replace subsistence farming, barter, and a primary concentration on agriculture. Jung-Stilling, the fledgling economist, was well aware of the transformation the very concept of economics was undergoing during his lifetime, from a focus on household management in a rural setting to the rationalization and complexity of managing assets in a market economy.[17] Florenburg and its citizens, as described in the opening paragraph of Jung-Stilling's text, are emblematic of this transition, insofar as they seek to suppress and transcend their rural, agricultural past. We will then not be surprised to discover that Henrich Stilling, as a product of this socioeconomic environment, is touched by this personal drive for ambitious self-betterment, economic improvement, and the pretentious self-approbation that accompanies the awareness of one's own socioeconomic advancement.

If the fictional name of Henrich Stilling's native town is rife with implications about the character of its inhabitants, the same is true for the name of its civil magistrate, the official whose very office underwrites the elevated status of this community as the center of the local regional government. In a rhetorical gesture that mimics the inflated boastfulness of Florenburg's citizens, this magistrate's name is given in Latin, the language of the educated classes, rather than in quotidian German: Johannes Henrikus Scultetus. The magistrate's family name actually refers directly to the position he holds: *scultetus* is the Middle Latin rendering of the indigenous German word *Schultheiß*, which means simply "village mayor." But the term *Schultheiß*, which is displaced here by its Latin equivalent— much as in Freudian dream texts a meaningful element of the latent dream content will be elided by a similar but more obscure and innocent term— conjures up a series of significant associations. The first component of this compound noun, *Schult*, is etymologically related to the common German word *Schuld*, meaning "guilt," "debt," or "obligation." The word *Schultheiß*, then, refers to someone whose task is to remind others of their civic duties and responsibilities. The person who holds this post is, as it were, the local representative of higher authority, an on-site civil designee of the ruling prince, and his job is to enforce adherence to the civil order. Jung-Stilling highlights the etymological root of this word when he asserts that the well-to-do citizens of Florenburg—*hübsche Bürger* is the peculiar phrase he uses to describe them—call the magistrate "Master Schulde." This designation likewise invokes an extremely complex chain of semantic associations. On the simplest level, *Schulde* is nothing but a shortened form of *Schultheiß*, and as such a nickname akin in its formation to the name "Master Hanns," with Hanns representing an abbreviated form of Johannes. This is, we are told, how the "uncouth" and "unknowing" members of the community designate their mayor. But the phrase "Master Schulde"—the shift from the old-German "t" to the new-German "d" is certainly significant here—has other, more far-reaching implications. Read as a reference to moral and civic issues, it could be translated as "Master Guilt," thereby alluding to the institutional role of the magistrate in reminding people of their transgressions against the civil order. This is, of course, wholly in keeping with the actual role of the *Schultheiß*, who might be conceived as a kind of superego, a local father figure who stands in for the political authority of the prince-father. However, "Master Schulde" can also be rendered as "Master Debt" or "Master Debtor," and in this version it could be taken as a cipher for the economic instrument that distinguishes the "well-to-do citizens" of Florenburg from all the "uncouth" and "unknowing" farmers upon whom they—and the narrator!—look down: mastery over the arcane knowledge of credit and debt as a method for fueling social and economic advancement.

The citizens of Henrich Stilling's native town not only understand how to strategically employ inflated rhetoric by manipulating the very name of their village, but also comprehend the virtues of implementing certain financial tools for their economic rise. We should hence not be surprised to learn that Henrich Stilling, as the fictional guise for the autobiographer Johann Heinrich Jung-Stilling and the product of Florenburg's socioeconomic and psychological environment, has mastered this same art of social climbing on the installment plan. "Master Debt" is a nickname that applies perfectly to Jung-Stilling himself, who spent a major portion of his life laboring under the financial obligations he acquired in order to study medicine and thereby rise up into the ranks of the professionally trained German middle class.[18] Living beyond his means became a successful formula for Jung-Stilling, who seems to have been constitutionally incapable of renouncing unaffordable pleasures.[19] Even after he managed to pay off his debilitating debts in 1801, and despite the substantial salary he received as a professor in Marburg and later as advisor to Karl Friedrich of Baden, by 1814 Jung-Stilling was again two thousand guldens in arrears (Vinke 59). We will see in what follows how Jung-Stilling interprets financial relief from his indebtedness—from his *Schulden*, his debts, "guilt," or "trespasses" (in the Biblical sense)—as the primary manifestation by which divine providence intervenes in his existence.

The pathos of the early volumes of Jung-Stilling's *Lebensgeschichte* stems largely from the struggle of its protagonist against the conditions of an objective reality that is projected almost exclusively as an inhibiting, inimical antagonist (see Lauterwasser 92). But the confounding, hostile force of this environment expresses itself largely, although certainly not exclusively, in terms of material and monetary want. Upon the marriage of his parents Jung-Stilling can thus claim, as a prefiguration of his own fate, that only the "existential needs of life" prevented his elders from attaining true "bliss on earth" (*Lebensgeschichte* 14). In this context we can also well understand why Jung-Stilling would naturally gravitate toward and embrace a calling as professor of economics, since for him the sole purpose of economic practice was to alleviate the material wants of human beings (see his *Versuch einer Grundlehre sämmtlicher Kameralwissenschaften* 178–79). In this sense economics in the eighteenth century was often conceived eudae-monistically, pursuing the pseudoreligious, utopian aim of creating conditions for the greatest prosperity and happiness of all.[20] At any rate, already in his early youth Jung-Stilling experienced the squelching of one of his most profound desires, due to a lack of economic means: his dream of studying theology was stymied because he lacked the financial resources required to pursue a university education. In the retrospective section he appended to the fifth volume of his autobiography, he highlighted this event as a life-shaping experience: "I wanted to study theology, and that would also have pleased my father. However, this was entirely impossible, his entire fortune would not have sufficed to support me for even just two years at an institution of higher learning. I was hence forced to remain a school-teacher and a tailor" (*Lebensgeschichte* 605). If his employment as an educator at least allowed Jung-Stilling to quench his inherent thirst for knowledge (see *Lebensgeschichte* 142), it nevertheless remained an occupation to which he saw himself damned by want of sufficient monetary resources to purchase a better, more fitting professional existence. Money thereby took on the ominous guise of an absolute limiting condition that threatened to stifle all of Jung-Stilling's worldly ambitions.

Viewing matters psychologically, one might argue that this failure to pursue theological studies due to lack of money steeled Jung-Stilling's resolve not to bow to financial duress when the question of his university studies in medicine arose some years later. Indeed, it seems almost ironic that at this juncture he blithely went ahead and committed himself to this precarious course, knowing full well that he had no source whatsoever from which to derive the necessary funds for his higher education. In *Henrich Stillings Wanderschaft*, he portrays this decision to spite his financial limitations and act on his dream of becoming a physician as a crucial turning point in his life.

> His entire future happiness was now completely dependent on the possibility of becoming an upstanding physician. However, for that to happen he was in need of at least a thousand reichstalers, whereby all his worldly possessions taken together amounted to scarcely a hundred. As a consequence, things looked pretty dismal for him in this regard; if he was lacking on this account, then he was lacking in everything.
>
> And yet, although Stilling could picture all of this quite vividly, he still firmly placed his faith in God and drew this conclusion:
>
> "God does not initiate anything that he does not intend to finish in the most marvelous way. Now it is true unto eternity that He and He alone completely ordained my current situation, without any complicity on my part."
>
> "Hence, it is also eternally true that he will accomplish everything with me in the most marvelous way."
>
> At times this conclusion lent him so much courage that he told his friends in Rasenheim, with a smile on his face: "No matter what needs may arise, my Father in heaven will always provide money for me!" (*Lebensgeschichte* 258–59)

We see here the extent to which Jung-Stilling, when he places his fate in divine hands, is literally counting on God: depending on him not only for direction, but anticipating that this will manifest itself in the form of monetary windfalls. It is particularly telling that at the very moment when Jung-

Stilling takes his most fundamental leap of faith, embracing the firm belief that divine providence will supply the means to help him realize his medical education, his discourse is structured by the rational rigor of syllogistic logic. Working from the—highly questionable—hypothesis that the decision to study medicine is not a product of individual choice, but instead is imposed upon him by divine prescription, Jung-Stilling draws the "logical" conclusion that God will also provide the means to realize these plans, for God does not begin anything he does not intend to finish. Why God did not provide Jung-Stilling with adequate financial means several years earlier, when he wished to study theology, is a question the autobiography neither poses nor answers; and this seems to be an especially egregious oversight, given that Jung-Stilling will later recognize his dedication to religious proselytism, not to medicine, as his true calling. Wouldn't theological studies have presented a more direct and effective path toward the realization of this goal? But of course, one cannot ask such questions of this text, since—despite the logical form in which it is often couched—this trust in divine providence is and remains inherently irrational. This irrationality is underscored by the fact that the interventions of providence manifest themselves in Jung-Stilling's life almost exclusively in the form of monetary transactions. This fundamental interweaving of God and money is the central tenet of the passage cited above. All Jung-Stilling lacks for the realization of his plans to study medicine is money, and, as the text so forcefully states, in wanting this he is wanting everything. In short, Jung-Stilling already acknowledges money, in the words of Karl Marx, as that "pure potentiality [*das wahre Vermögen*]" ("Ökonomisch-philosophische Manuskripte" 549) that makes all things possible; and in this sense, money has already become the worldly manifestation of the divine. It is certainly no coincidence that, logically speaking, money takes priority here over the will of God, and that it is hence only after Jung-Stilling's monetary needs are divulged that God is introduced—almost as an afterthought. Lacking any *worldly* means for acquiring the necessary cash, the only alternative available, barring criminal activity, is reliance on divine providence as a heavenly cash machine.

On the basis of the maxim that to lack money is to lack everything, we can understand the veritable obsession Jung-Stilling displays throughout his autobiography with lucre and its possession. Jung-Stilling seems to con-

ceive his very existence as structured around the ebbs and flows of his financial liquidity. Even the notebook he kept with a record of significant events
in his life is dominated more by references to finances than to any other
single topic.[21] The mystique money holds for him can also be seen in the
way he consistently mentions exact amounts of cash, often even convert-
ing one form of currency into another, louis d'or into guldens (*Lebensgeschichte* 595), or talers into guldens (635), for example. Jung-Stilling is
extremely aware of the relative value of individual coins and currency types,
recognizing that in an economy still dominated by specie, it is not number and quantity that count, but rather the weight and fineness of coins
(fig. 5).[22] On a more general level, his recognition that the limitations of
his life are defined by the limitations of his money supply simply reiterates
in negative terms the more positive general maxim that money represents
pure potentiality, the ability to acquire anything and everything and hence
to satisfy all desires.[23] In other words, Jung-Stilling's virtual mania for
money reflects a kind of devotion, to allude to a famous remark by Karl
Marx, to money as the god among commodities (*Grundrisse* 132–33), as
the supercommodity that controls the possession and nonpossession of all
things and that hence regulates human happiness and unhappiness.

For Jung-Stilling there is nothing inconsistent in confounding the need
for money with the need for divine intervention: he takes the phrase from
Genesis 22:8, "The Lord will provide" (*Lebensgeschichte* 255, 260), in a
wholly literal and material sense: God is envisioned as a kind of divine
banker who will supply the financial means to satisfy not only Jung-Stilling's
immediate needs, but also to fulfill his long-term ambitions.[24] This, after
all, is exactly the image of God Jung-Stilling has in mind when he writes,
with overblown pathos, of the "cash-box of providence [*Casse der Vorse-
hung*]" (551): heaven as a giant transcendental counting house with God
as the dispenser of funds, an omniscient and omnipotent moneylender. If,
as Joseph Vogl has claimed (*Kalkül und Leidenschaft* 183), the monetary
code always implies a providential steering of events, then Jung-Stilling relies
entirely on this monetary providentialism. However, he consistently disguises
this economic motive behind the appeal to divine guidance.

From the moment he decides to transcend the limits of his socioeconomic station and study medicine, despite his overriding financial limita-

5 / One-third taler coin, issued in Prussia in 1774 under Frederick the Great.

tions, Jung-Stilling will spend his life counting on God in a double sense: relying on him, on the one hand, for guidance in his life decisions; but expecting, on the other hand, this intervention to manifest itself in monetary form, as cold cash that can be counted up and counted on. Thus throughout the remainder of his autobiography there is hardly an example of divine intercession in which money is not involved in one way or another. We recall that the honorarium Jung-Stilling received from Goethe for the publication of *Henrich Stillings Jugend* was interpreted as a gesture of divine intervention (*Lebensgeschichte* 344). Money also plays a pivotal role when Jung-Stilling receives the offer to come to Kaiserslautern as professor of economics. The firm salary of six hundred guldens, with an additional three hundred in instructional fees, is certainly one of the decisive factors motivating this move (see 353). And yet in this case money also potentially stands in the way of his accepting the new position as professor of political economy, and hence of further ascending the ladder of social advancement: Jung-Stilling has amassed such a huge debt in order to finance his medical training and during his years as a practicing physician that his creditors can prevent him from leaving Elberfeld to assume his new post (356). Once again it is divine providence—one is tempted to see it as economic coincidence—that rescues Jung-Stilling and makes it possible for him to embark upon this new episode in his life. A host of well-intentioned benefactors make contributions that amount to eight hundred guldens, not enough by any means to pay his debts in full, but at least sufficient for demonstrating Jung-Stilling's creditworthiness and thereby assuaging the doubts of his creditors, making it possible for him to leave town. As in the episode with the honorarium for *Henrich Stillings Jugend*, here too Jung-Stilling's human benefactors are completely elided, interpreted away so that he can more convincingly glorify the mysteries of divine providence.[25] When acknowledged at all, the human beings who actually supply him with money are reduced to instruments of divine will and thereby stripped of any charitable or humanizing motivations of their own.[26]

Jung-Stilling is no less motivated by money when his next major life change offers itself, the move to a professorial chair at the University of Marburg (*Lebensgeschichte* 430). In a letter to Israel Hartmann dated 6 March 1787, he praises the Lord for the substantial salary increase this new position will bring and envisions the possibility of finally being able to pay off his long-standing debts (*Briefe* 130–31).[27] However, the single most significant monetary windfall attributed to divine intercession occurs in 1801, when, on a trip to Switzerland to cure cataract patients, Jung-Stilling unexpectedly receives, from diverse sources, not only the amount of money required to retire all his debts, but also enough to cover his travel costs to Switzerland and back (see *Lebensgeschichte* 548–50). Jung-Stilling's reflections on what he views as a monetary miracle draw an explicit connection between his faith in the Lord and a reliance on emergency payments from the heavenly counting house.

> That was a blessed trip for the discharging of debts! A significant knot burdening Stilling's life had now been marvelously untied: having amassed a debt of 5½ thousand guldens, he now succeeded in paying back every red cent, sincerely and honestly, including all the accumulated interest, and he accomplished this without possessing any wealth of his own, simply on the basis of faith. Hallelujah! (*Lebensgeschichte* 552–53)

The 5½ thousand guldens mentioned here constitute the amount of money Jung-Stilling borrowed in order to finance his medical studies in Strasbourg, the additional credit he took on while living in Elberfeld, and the accumulated interest on this sum. The "coincidence" that the amount of money he acquires on the trip to Switzerland exactly covers his long-standing debt and his travel expenses confirms for him its divine origin. This passage thereby draws a direct connection to the leap of faith Jung-Stilling took when he decided to pursue his university education despite his poverty, counting only on God as a heavenly benefactor who would somehow cover the necessary expenses. We have to imagine Jung-Stilling transferring the notion of Christ's redemption of human sins over to the mundane sphere of finance: in the same miraculous way that Christ "pays" for people's sins through the sacrifice of his own life, he will also pay off their financial obligations. It is the semantic slippage in the German word *Schuld* for guilt and debt that underwrites this exchange between the realms of Christian morality and of money. The "discharging of debts" (*Schulden-tilgung*) mentioned in this passage operates on both of these semantic levels: it points most concretely to the alleviation of Jung-Stilling's financial debts, but it also alludes to the redemption of human guilt. Jung-Stilling conflates the figure of a Christ who forgives us our sins with the conception of a Christian deity as a charitable banker who also pays off our monetary debts.

It comes as no surprise that when Jung-Stilling attempts explicitly to defend the role of providential intervention in his life, the example he chooses is again one that involves money (see *Lebensgeschichte* 307–08). In this incident Jung-Stilling and his wife receive their regular delivery of charcoal for cooking and heating, but for the first time lack the ready cash to pay for these sorely needed briquettes. However, instead of refusing delivery, Jung-Stilling and his wife beseech God for deliverance, and—of course—their prayers are answered. In the very moment the coal merchant approaches to receive his payment, a patient who owes Jung-Stilling money for an overdue fee appears at the door and places ten reichstalers in his hand. Jung-Stilling can then pass on this money to the coal merchant, without having to face the humiliation of appearing to be financially insolvent. Such coincidences constitute the very substance of Jung-Stilling's reliance on providence and become a cardinal factor in his religious faith. Thus in his commentary on this event he remarks, "Stilling experienced very many such incidents, and they served to strengthen his faith and encourage him to persevere" (308). But if the miraculous appearance of money in the nick of time strengthens Jung-Stilling's belief in God, then the opposite is also the case: periods in which he lacks the means to meet his existential needs, fulfill his wishes, or pay his debts come to be seen as "tests of his faith" (261, 269–70, 297, 519). Thus if one were to graph Jung-Stilling's financial fortunes and the oscillations in the strength of his Christian faith, they would follow absolutely parallel courses: his faith diminishes as his wealth dwindles and increases as his financial solvency grows.

In retrospect Jung-Stilling comes to recognize the contradiction between his long-held belief that studying medicine was God's will and his relative lack of success as a medical professional, admitting that, ultimately, he lacks the talent and the commitment to be able to make an adequate living as a physician.

> As is well known, Stilling and his spouse did not possess even the most meager fortune, and hence they could not acquire even the most meager real credit.—Apart from his medical practice he had no other occupation, no means for making a living, . . . he knew of no other means of subsistence; yet at the same time, providence had led him to take up this profession—what a contrast—what a contradiction—what a challenge to the steadfastness of his faith and his trust in God! (350–51)

Unable to comprehend how God could guide him toward a profession from which he reaps no financial rewards, toward which he has no personal inclination, and which provides little professional success or satisfaction, Jung-Stilling is forced to question the very cogency of divine wisdom. Indeed, his years spent in Schönenthal (the fictionalized name for Elberfeld in his autobiography) were marked by constant poverty, pressing debts, frustrated ambitions, and growing doubts about himself and his divine "calling." In the end he was only able to come to terms with the fact that divine guidance forced him into such miserable circumstances by justifying his poverty and the burden of his lifelong debts as a disciplinary measure, strategically employed by his divine taskmaster as a way to cure him of his natural inclination to enjoy frivolous sensual pleasures. Thus in the retrospective summary that concludes the fifth volume of his autobiography, Jung-Stilling begrudgingly valorizes his burdensome debts as "a veritable medicine against sensuality and imprudence" and praises the Lord for adopting measures suitable to eradicating these evil inclinations at their very roots (612).

Jung-Stilling's perennial oscillation between poverty and financial windfalls thus becomes the material manifestation of a religious ideology that sees human beings pendulating between their inherent sinfulness and their divine salvation. Poverty and indigence are interpreted as the weapons necessary to enforce a life of ascetic renunciation, consistent with the teachings of Pietism; but the obverse of this punishment by forced denial is the miraculous appearance of material rewards in the form of monetary godsends. In this sense the generally upward course of Jung-Stilling's autobiography provides evidence in support of Max Weber's thesis that the ascetic ethos of Pietism and other forms of doctrinal Protestantism, such as Calvinism, ultimately served to nourish and reinforce a regimentation and rationalization of living conditions that promoted professionalization, economic progress, and capital accumulation (Max Weber 20, 198–203). Jung-Stilling's life might be seen as paradigmatic for this dialectic of ascetic renunciation and socioeconomic advancement, with the reality of capital accumulation appearing as the mystifying miracle of monetary reward from on high.

For Jung-Stilling's contemporaries, it was less easy to resolve the apparent contradiction between his proselytic religiosity and his insistence that divine guidance tended to manifest itself in terms of monetary magic. In his *Geschichte der poetischen Literatur Deutschlands* (History of German literary writing), the Romantic writer Joseph von Eichendorff (1788–1857), for example, contrasted Jung-Stilling negatively with another famous advocate of Pietistic principles, the Swiss pastor Johann Caspar Lavater (1741–1801), remarking that Jung-Stilling's insistence on the mundanely material character of divine revelation twists it into caricature: "The very thing that makes Lavater significant, his heroic faith and the notion of uninterrupted divine revelation, we see revert almost to caricature in the instance of *Jung-Stilling*'s extreme one-sidedness" (Eichendorff 221). Eichendorff goes on to assert that whenever God's hand becomes as "visible" and "dictatorial" in secular matters as it does in Jung-Stilling's autobiography, it takes on an inevitability and fatalism that threatens the very notion of human virtue (222). Goethe's comments in his own autobiography, *Dichtung und Wahrheit* (Poetry and truth), turn out with even greater sarcasm the paradox inherent in Jung-Stilling's association of divine guidance with monetary rewards. Even though he attributes these remarks to a third party who remains unnamed, there can be little doubt that they reflect Goethe's own opinion: "No!, in truth, if I were in as good standing with God as Jung[-Stilling], then I would not petition the Lord on high for money, but rather for enough wisdom and good counsel to prevent me from pursuing so many silly escapades that cost money and result in so many miserable years of indebtedness" (*Goethes Werke* 10: 90). Implicit in this critique is the idea that Jung-Stilling himself lacks the discipline and the good sense to avoid situations that will cost him money and send him into debt. But in fact it was primarily Jung-Stilling's personal drive for social advancement and self-improvement, not the submission to sensual frivolities, that caused his financial difficulties. When he made the decision to forge ahead with his medical studies, knowing full well that he lacked the economic means to finance them, he opted for a future bought on credit. The logic that supports this decision is that of delayed gratification: sacrifices or "investments" made today to increase one's "marketability" will pay off in the future in the form of increased earning potential. However, Jung-Stilling constantly seeks to hide this logic of personal ambition and socioeconomic advancement behind the ideological guise of a divine "calling," made manifest as godly intervention into the mundane functions of economic life.

Jung-Stilling's autobiography can be read as a massive attempt to repress the socioeconomic motivations that informed his life decisions by disguising them as adherence to divine will, imposed upon the individual from above. His seemingly irrational attachment to his first wife, Christine Heyder, a young woman characterized above all by weakness and chronic illness, is a prime example of just such an event, pursued with shrewd strategy as an indispensable stepping stone for Jung-Stilling's self-betterment, but mystified as a match made in heaven. Their engagement to wed is described as a kind of spontaneous, near-mystical union, in which Jung-Stilling initially believes himself to be guided by the will of God (*Lebensgeschichte* 250). Only subsequent to Christine's early death, after ten years of marriage and mutual poverty, does he come to question the role of divine providence in this fateful decision.

Thus he asked himself how it could have come about that God led him down such difficult paths, since his marriage had been ordained completely by divine providence.—But is this really true?, he asked himself. Isn't it possible that human weakness, that impure motivations also played a role? Now it suddenly dawned on him: he recognized in the pure light of truth that his father-in-law, his late wife, and he himself had acted neither according to religious prescriptions, nor according to the laws of healthy reason. (397)

It is interesting to note precisely how Jung-Stilling defines the nature of this misalliance: he stylizes himself primarily as a scholar, unable to earn a sufficient income and, moreover, incapable of budgeting his resources in a rational manner. Christine, by contrast, as the daughter of a merchant, was raised in a household in which the man assumes responsibility for economic planning and the management of money. Neither of them, in short, was capable of taking over the rational organization of their household affairs, so that the sparse funds Jung-Stilling's profession brought in easily slipped through their fingers, without any consideration for the repayment of their debts. Christine, Jung-Stilling concludes, would have made a wonderful, devoted wife for a rational merchant—someone like her father—but her marriage to an impractical scholar, devoid of financial management skills, could only end in disaster (397–98).

It is not difficult to read a self-exculpatory demeanor out of these deliberations. We note, first of all, the irony that Jung-Stilling, the professional economist, who in his scholarly textbooks would preach the methods of rational business management,[28] claims here that he himself was incapable of practicing what he preached. Moreover, as we have seen, if anyone was obsessed with money and its management, it was Jung-Stilling. But by abdicating his own responsibility for financial oversight of his affairs, he is able to place the blame for ten years of misery, relative poverty, and increasing debt on Christine and their infelicitous marriage. If in this moment of "enlightenment"—the word is Jung-Stilling's (397)—he is ultimately forced to doubt the role of God's hand in the making of this unholy—because uneconomic—alliance, then one is left to look for other, more personal designs. Jung-Stilling suggests a couple of possibilities: simple human weakness or impure motivations. Of these two, the latter seems the most likely candidate, and there is considerable evidence that points to strategic maneuvering on Jung-Stilling's part as the impulse behind this marriage. To be sure, Christine could not bring into the union the one thing Jung-Stilling most fervently desired: substantial amounts of money (254). This, we presume, is why not even "healthy reason" can account for this marriage. But the affiliation with Christine promises something that is almost as good as cold, hard cash: namely, the credit, credibility, and creditworthiness of her father, the merchant Peter Heyder. It is this borrowed "credit"—both real and personal—upon which Jung-Stilling will build his future.[29]

Before turning to the covert economic motive that underwrites the marriage to Christine, we must examine the overt ideological reflex with which Jung-Stilling himself ultimately legitimates this misalliance as part of God's divine scheme. We have already witnessed the mechanics of this strategy in Jung-Stilling's justification of his debts as God's way of weaning him of his sinful addiction to sensual pleasures. Ultimately he will interpret his miserable and impoverished ten-year marriage to Christine as but one more disciplinary weapon in God's holy arsenal. As Jung-Stilling explains it, "God had used his [Stilling's] own impurity as a soap for the purpose of purifying him all the more" (398). God, in other words, is an especially shrewd pedagogue, one who exploits the impurities of his pupils as the very means to accomplish their purification. This notion of moral edification, of *Läuterung*, progressive refinement and removal of impurities, becomes one of the overriding themes of Jung-Stilling's autobiography, especially in its later volumes (see 171, 351, 369, 373, 398, 483). In this text the process of purification functions as the religious counterpart to the secular notion of *Bildung*, the educational motive that shapes the developmental progress of the protagonists of other autobiographies (Lauterwasser 90). One thinks here of works such as Karl Phillip Moritz's (1756–93) *Anton Reiser* (1785– 94),[30] or even of Goethe's semiautobiographical novel *Wilhelm Meisters Lehrjahre* (Wilhelm Meister's apprenticeship, 1796). But even Jung-Stilling's choice of metaphors, *Läuterung*, betrays his underlying obsession with issues of money and value. This word refers, among other things, to the refinement of the precious metals gold and silver and their segregation, especially in the minting of coins, from the base metals such as copper with which they were commonly alloyed. Jung-Stilling makes it perfectly clear that this is the context he has in mind when he employs this metaphor; thus in its very first occurrence in *Lebensgeschichte*, he refers to God as a great *Schmelzer*, a smelter who refines human beings "like gold in a fire" (171). This very same metaphor, God as a purifying smelter, occurs two further times, applied specifically to the developmental process of Jung-Stilling's life (373, 483). In a letter to Johann Caspar Lavater dated 17 February 1800, Jung-Stilling turns to this same image of purification in God's holy fire to describe the process by which human beings—in this instance applied to Lavater himself—attain what he refers to as the "moment [*Blick*] of perfection" (*Briefe* 238). In a note appended to the margin of this letter, Jung-Stilling the economist goes on to explicate the nature of this technical metaphor. *Blick*, he notes, refers in metallurgy to that moment in the process of refining silver when it achieves its absolute purity (238). Clearly, Jung-Stilling is nearly incapable of conceiving the workings of God outside the framework of questions of money, value, and the precious metals in which monetary worth was concretized at this time. The discourse in which economists of his day discussed the problematic of money, the nature of specie, and the mechanisms of debt and credit consistently invade his conceptions of the divine being who guides his personal fortunes and misfortunes.

If we return now to the motivations that impel Jung-Stilling to marry Christine Heyder, we can examine in more detail the precise nature of the "impurity" in his personality that drives him to take this fateful step. We have already noted that his covert desire is to appropriate the credit and credibility of Christine's father, the merchant Peter Heyder, and the reflex of this desire emerges the very first time Jung-Stilling enters the Heyder household. Jung-Stilling relates this episode, not coincidentally, immediately after he has described his resolve to study medicine, and the structural logic of Jung-Stilling's narrative is compelling: the visit to the Heyders must somehow resolve the dilemma of how he will finance his university education. The moment he lays eyes on the Heyder family and the surroundings in which they live, Jung-Stilling is overcome by a profound sense of admiration and awe, triggered by their simple elegance and the cheerful sincerity of their interpersonal relations.

> As soon as Stilling entered the house and perceived in everything an element of order, cleanliness, and luxury without ostentation, he was overjoyed and sensed that he would be able to live here. And when he

entered the living room and saw how Herr Friedenberg [the fictional Peter Heyder] himself, his wife, and their nine beautiful, well-bred children interacted, he noticed how all of them were dressed neatly and elegantly, but without pretension, and how all their faces radiated truthfulness, honesty, and cheerfulness; at that moment he was completely enraptured, and he genuinely wished to be able to live forever among these people. There was no commotion, no turbulent emotion, but instead only effective activity based on harmony and good will. (*Lebensgeschichte* 246)

What Jung-Stilling experiences in the Heyder household is something like a phantasmagoric homecoming: he steps out of his banal reality into the idealized vision of the life and lifestyle he would ultimately like to lead. Truth, integrity, the modest but never ostentatious wealth of the merchant, effectiveness, harmony: the Heyders embody—at least in Jung-Stilling's imagination—the perfect bourgeois family, paragons of a lifestyle marked by comfort but also by moderation. In his economic theory, Jung-Stilling was an advocate of just such modest comfort and a vicious opponent of ostentatious luxury and wasteful splendor.[31] The fact that he twice mentions the lack of ostentation in the Heyder household points precisely to this ideal of economic moderation. It is obviously nothing other than his unexpressed wish "to live forever with these people" that triggers his mysterious love for Christine, Heyder's eldest daughter. On the broadest psychological level, then, Christine represents the pathway by which he can indeed join this household and this family and concretely enter the scene that represents his socioeconomic ideal. The well-ordered, stable, and modestly affluent environment embodied by the Heyder family takes on a kind of symbolic luminescence for Jung-Stilling, holding out the promise of a future marked by the same level of social reputability and economic comfort. The fact that the marriage to Christine culminates instead in a demeaning existence of material need, large-scale indebtedness, and utter misery, simply exposes all the more crassly the dimension of wish fulfillment that Jung-Stilling projects onto the middle-class idyll of the Heyder household. In this regard, when he resolves to marry Christine, Jung-Stilling falls victim to his own illusions.

In *Lebensgeschichte* it is incumbent upon Judge Goldmann, the son of

Pastor Goldmann (the fictional Johann Eberhard Goebel), to diagnose Jung-Stilling's penchant to succumb to fantasies that awaken unrealistic desires. In his analysis, this is a function of Jung-Stilling's having read too many novels: "I think that by reading too many novels, you put impossible ideas into your own head. The episodes of good fortune that poetic fantasy creates for its heroes take up residence in one's head and heart and awaken a hunger for similar miraculous transformations" (154). In his relationship with Christine and the Heyder household, Jung-Stilling has truly succumbed to the fictional fantasies of the novel, imagining himself as a protagonist whose life is governed by happy circumstances and chance occurrences. Indeed, one might view the entire discourse of divine providence, which forms one thematic thread of this autobiography, as a transmogrification into religious terminology of the contingencies that structure utopian novels. This would also offer another way of explaining why God's intercession manifests itself in the guise of monetary windfalls: a novelistic convention is lent reality and credibility by being read as the plan not of an omniscient narrator, but of an all-powerful God as the author of individual human lives.[32]

That Jung-Stilling's union with Christine is motivated less by love than by the wish to become a part of this idealized family is corroborated by the language he uses when he tells father Heyder of their marriage plans. Instead of asking for Christine's hand, he requests the honor of being counted among Heyder's children: "Are you with all your heart willing to accept me as one of your children?" (254). Jung-Stilling is careful to add that, although he is prepared to embrace all the duties of the child, he does not expect to receive any assistance or financial support for his planned studies. In fact, he insists almost overemphatically that his only wish is to possess the sickly Christine: "My sole desire is to possess your daughter; indeed, as God is my witness, the thought that you might believe I have base intentions in seeking this union is the most horrible one imaginable to me" (254). Heyder responds as one might expect: he reassures Jung-Stilling that he believes him to be too honest and too Christian to harbor any devious intentions, and he reminds him that, since he must look out for the future of all his nine children, he does not have the means to pay for his future son-in-law's education (254). One cannot help but suspect that Jung-Stilling's desire to join this family, despite his avid protestations to the contrary, is motivated by just such presumptions of financial support. What other reason might there be for wanting to marry someone as frail and sickly as Christine? What else could explain the suddenness, even rashness of this decision to wed? And Jung-Stilling's preemptive assurances that he has no ulterior motives in entering this marriage have the ring of disingenuousness. Is he not rather trying to assuage his own pangs of bad conscience? Moreover, it is surely no coincidence that at this moment of extreme bad faith he appeals to God as his witness. It seems likely that this deception—perhaps it is a self-deception?—that forms the crux of his union with Christine is the "impurity" he will later identify as the "soap" with which God hopes to effect his purification.

It is, ultimately, none other than his father-in-law Peter Heyder who provides Jung-Stilling with the necessary start-up capital to travel to Strasbourg and begin his medical studies (257). Once he arrives in Strasbourg, Jung-Stilling manages to survive financially by learning the virtues of credit, borrowing money from various sources (see 261, 265, 267–68), without, as yet, knowing the misery of nagging debt. When his Strasbourg obligations become too diverse and unmanageable, it is once again his father-in-law who comes to the rescue and who teaches Jung-Stilling a new economic strategy: the consolidation of debt. Pooling resources with Herr Liebmann (presumably a fictional cover for a certain Herr Lausberg), Heyder takes out credit in his own name and sends a promissory note in the amount of three hundred talers to Jung-Stilling, who can therewith pay off all his Strasbourg creditors. When the note arrives, Jung-Stilling responds in characteristic manner: "He [Stilling] laughed out loud, walked up to the window, looked with a joyous gaze toward heaven, and said: 'Only you could have accomplished this, almighty Father!'" (270). The elation with which he receives this money disguises the diabolical logic of the manner in which debt begets further debt; Jung-Stilling seems unaware that this note is not a gift with no strings attached, but merely represents the postponement of an inevitable—and incrementally increasing—payback. The gesture with which he gazes up toward heaven makes clear that the almighty father at whom Jung-Stilling directs his gratitude is the Lord above; but his language is, in fact, ambiguous, and the father referred to could just as well—in fact, more appropriately—be father-in-law Heyder, to whose account and to whose credit this money must actually be reckoned. We have already seen how typical it is of Jung-Stilling to suppress the human agents of his monetary fortunes, attributing their work to God alone. Here the word "father" operates as the semantic switch box for the discursive exchange that allows the secular mediator to be displaced by God, the great mediator in the sky. Increasingly, Jung-Stilling is beholden to one major creditor, his father-in-law Peter Heyder; but this "father" is consistently overshadowed by God the Father, a process by which economic indebtedness (*Schulden*) is metamorphosed into Christian obligation (*Schuld*)—and in the process erroneously rendered financially inconsequential.

When Christine suddenly falls seriously ill and Jung-Stilling feels obliged to return home to visit her and help her recover, father-in-law Heyder promises to pay the travel expenses (273). And after Christine's recovery, when Jung-Stilling plans to return to Strasbourg to complete his studies, it is again Heyder's mediation that provides a financial resource from which Jung-Stilling can draw the necessary credit (284). Finally, when in Strasbourg he finds himself yet again in a financial bind, to whom else should he turn other than father-in-law Heyder.

> Here once again a great deal of money was needed, and he [Stilling] wrote home about this. Mr. Friedenberg [Heyder] was aghast at this news. During lunch that day he decided to test his children. All of them were at the table, large and small. Their father began: Children, your brother-in-law is in need of a substantial sum of money; how do you feel, would you send it to him if you had it? They answered unanimously: "Yes, and even if we had to pawn our own clothes!" With this the parents were moved to tears, and Stilling swore them eternal love and loyalty as soon as he heard this story. In a word, a promissory note in sufficient amount arrived in Strasbourg. (286)

Both the events of this scene and the language in which it is related confirm that Jung-Stilling has, indeed, become an integral member of this family: he writes "home" and lays out his needs, and the family decides as a unit to make whatever sacrifice is necessary to provide him with the required funds. Jung-Stilling's vision of becoming one of Heyder's children has been realized and his purpose fulfilled: he completes his studies in Strasbourg and returns "home" as a doctor of medicine, prepared to begin his profession as a physician. But along the way he has amassed a considerable debt, both moral and financial, to the family he joined by means of his marriage to Christine.

Jung-Stilling is well aware that credit and creditworthiness are closely allied with socioeconomic standing and that his total lack of financial resources, as he sets out upon his new career, is a hurdle that will be difficult to vault: "Stilling and his spouse did not possess even the most meager fortune, and hence they could not acquire even the most meager real credit" (350). Prominently missing in this accounting, of course, is the fact that Jung-Stilling not only lacks all economic liquidity, but that he is in fact hopelessly in arrears. In such a circumstance, there is no possibility of attaining "real" credit. Yet his marriage with Christine has allowed him to acquire, as a kind of substitute for this real credit, the *personal* credit that accrues to his higher social standing as an educated professional. However, even this is borrowed credit, since it derives ultimately from the personal and real credit of his father-in-law. Jung-Stilling the economist was well aware of this fundamental distinction between real and personal credit. In his *Grundlehre der Staatswirthschaft* of 1792, for example, he explains that whereas real credit is based on the tangible goods or the monetary holdings in a person's possession, personal credit is founded upon the character and integrity of that individual: that is, on intangibles (609).[33] Jung-Stilling's own line of "credit" draws solely on the real and personal resources of Peter Heyder's creditworthiness: the reputation of his father-in-law as a trustworthy and successful merchant becomes his own calling card as he compiles debts to increase his own personal credit (his position as a physician). As Jung-Stilling freely admits, "Mr. Friedenberg [Heyder] was the underwriter of the capital that had made it possible for him to attend the university" (302; see also 338). In other words, without being sponsored by his father-in-law, Jung-Stilling would never have gained the "credit" with which to acquire his education. Thus when he writes in the self-justifying "Retrospective" of his autobiography that he married Christine, despite knowing "that her father was unable to support me in any manner whatsoever" (611), he is—purposefully or unwittingly?—ignoring the obvious facts: namely, that the true motor behind his socioeconomic advancement was *not* the grace of God, but was instead the initiative and generosity of his father-in-law. Is it any wonder that his debts, the *Schulden* he collects based on his father-in-law's collateral, would assume for Jung-Stilling that peculiar double quality of financial debts and moral indebtedness? This is all the more true given that Jung-Stilling's failure to pay off his economic obligations ultimately threatens to bring about Heyder's financial ruin. When the creditors from whom Heyder borrowed in order to extend secondary credit to Jung-Stilling decide, after several years of nonpayment, to call in their debts, it is Heyder, not Jung-Stilling, who faces the prospect of bankruptcy (386). The tables have turned in a precarious way, for if it was Jung-Stilling who first profited from the credit and credibility of his father-in-law, now it is Heyder himself whose creditworthiness is threatened by his financial and personal association with his insolvent son-in-law. The momentum of social advancement on the installment plan, purchased through the credibility of his father-in-law as financial backer, is on the verge of reverting into social and economic collapse for both parties. Not surprisingly, this leads to strained relations, indeed, to profound alienation between Jung-Stilling and Christine's father, culminating at the moment when Jung-Stilling decides to abandon the medical profession Heyder helped finance and move to Kaiserslautern as a professor of economics.

The ironies of this situation could hardly be more pronounced: Heyder attributes Jung-Stilling's inability to pay off his debts to bad economic management (367), and now it is precisely this financial bungler who has been called to the university to teach others how to manage finances and generate wealth! We recall here the popular saying, "Those who can, do; those who can't, teach." This maxim seems to apply aptly to Jung-Stilling in his role as economist. Ultimately Heyder even blames Jung-Stilling for the poverty and misfortune in which his daughter has been forced to live for the ten years of their marriage, conditions to which he attributes her early death in 1781 (389). His bitterness toward Jung-Stilling certainly increased when, following Christine's death, his son-in-law wrote to him that the marriage to Christine had been a serious error (398). And yet the real error of the years in Strasbourg and Elberfeld was more likely attributable to Jung-Stilling's transgression of a law that he would articulate, in his *Versuch einer Grundlehre sämmtlicher Kameralwissenschaften* (Attempt at a foundational doctrine of all cameralistic sciences, 1779), as the cardinal rule of every successful businessperson: never borrow more money than you can possibly hope to repay (162). Jung-Stilling fell victim to a major miscalculation: he wrongly assumed that the personal credit he acquired through his professional advancement to a doctor of medicine would translate directly into financial gain. The correction of this assumption was the lesson of the wretched years in Elberfeld.

Ultimately Jung-Stilling was, like the magistrate of Florenburg, a *Meister Schulde*, a master of debt and credit, who, lacking any and all real and personal creditworthiness of his own, managed to sap the credit of his father-in-law to purchase his own social and economic advancement. In the marriage to Christine, Jung-Stilling thus pursued a strategy of rational calculation, exploiting the familial connection to her father as the collateral to finance his university studies. It is more than just simple denial when Jung-Stilling insists throughout his autobiography that God intervenes in and controls not merely the general course of the world, but the lives of specific individuals (see *Lebensgeschichte* 344). This logic of providential determination not only frees him of his *Schulden*, his guilt feelings with regard to his marriage, but also allows him to assume strategic *Schulden*, the economic debts that will ultimately help propel him into the higher echelons of civil society. This is a profitable exchange, in which the word *Schuld*, with its ambivalences and ambiguities, functions as a kind of mediator, a monetary instrument, through which both psychological transferences and the transfer of financial resources can move. In this sense, André Amar's analysis of the psychoanalytic significance of money has relevance for the thematic of money as it manifests itself in Jung-Stilling's *Lebensgeschichte*. Amar declares, "Money is not a thing, rather it is a symbol for debts and demands. Money is marked by the sign of guilt/debt [*Schuld*]" (395). Wherever questions of money occur in Jung-Stilling's autobiography, they impinge upon issues of *Schuld*, of financial debt and religious guilt or sin. Indeed, we might conclude, applying to this particular text an argument pursued in more general terms by Amar (398), that transference of the moral weight of religious *Schuld* to the material domain of monetary *Schulden* is a significant moment in the historical process of secularization. This transformation is concretized especially well in the peculiarly persistent association of divine intercession with monetary transactions in Jung-Stilling's *Lebensgeschichte*: these financial interventions do not simply allow Jung-Stilling to pay off his economic debts; they also relieve him of any nagging guilt he might harbor about the ways and means of his eventual rise to fame and fortune.

Friedrich Nietzsche was one of the first to articulate this semantic back-sliding between religious and moral notions of guilt, on the one hand, and the interpersonal and economic implications of debt, on the other: concepts designated in German by the very same word, *Schuld*. In the second essay of *Zur Genealogie der Moral* (On the genealogy of morals, 1887), in which he attempted a kind of historical archaeology of the very idea of guilt, Nietzsche asserted,

> The feeling of guilt/indebtedness [*Schuld*], of personal obligation . . . had its origin, as we have seen, in the oldest and most primordial personal relationship that exists, in the relationship between buyer and seller, creditor and debtor [*Schuldner*]. This is where one person first confronted another; this is where one person was first *measured by* another. No level of civilization has ever been discovered, even the very lowest, in which at least some aspects of this relationship would not make themselves noticeable. (*Kritische Studienausgabe* 5: 305–06)

According to Nietzsche, the primitive basis of *all* human interactions is mercenary in character, based on the exchange of goods or services, monetary transactions, and the inequality that always places one individual in the debt of another. *Schuld*, understood as indebtedness, personal obligation, or ethical guilt, all have their origin, if we follow Nietzsche's logic, in economic relationships: debt and credit, buying and selling, giving and taking. Nietzsche's point, of course, is that human beings' inflated sense of moral culpability or transcendental guilt is actually reducible to mundane economic interactions. Human beings, Nietzsche implies, generate the feeling of sinfulness by extrapolating and abstracting from common situations predicated on economic indebtedness.

This is precisely the process we see at work in Jung-Stilling's autobiography, portrayed most graphically on the example of his relationship with his father-in-law Peter Heyder. We witness here above all the extent to which, coherent with Nietzsche's claim, seemingly lofty human social and moral interchanges are grounded in more fundamental acts of economic exchange. Over the course of his existence with Christine Heyder, Jung-Stilling's economic indebtedness to her father is progressively transmogrified into forms of ethical and religious guilt. His relationship with Peter Heyder begins precisely as one based on financial obligation, debt, and credit. However, once it is mystified as an instance of divine intervention promoting the meaningful advancement of Jung-Stilling's life, this purely financial relationship is inflated into a transcendental matter of guilt. Moreover, Heyder's daughter Christine proves to be but a pawn that helps to broker the financial relationship between these two men and elevate its status through an association with the divine institution of marriage. In short, the decision to enter into a union of Christian wedlock with Christine represents nothing but a displacement of the blatantly financial relationship that underlies the ties between Heyder and Jung-Stilling. His marriage to the sickly Christine, who is unlikely to find any other suitor, represents a form of compensation, a kind of personal leveraging of the financial credit he expects to receive from her father. But the *guilt* Jung-Stilling ultimately bears due to this marriage stems in fact from his subliminal awareness that Christine is little more than a tool to be applied for *his own* advancement. This is the psychological moment at which the economic *Schuld* to Heyder becomes yoked to moral *Schuld* as well. Jung-Stilling's strategy for divesting himself of both of these "debts" is as simple as it is effective: he abdicates responsibility for both by reinterpreting *his own* instrumentalization of Christine as a pawn in the service of his social advancement as an act of divine will. Christ stands in for all of Jung-Stilling's obligations.

My analysis of the financial and personal motivations underlying the marriage to Christine Heyder contradict one of the primary precepts Jung-Stilling attempts to promulgate about his life and its progression: the thesis that the various transformations he went through are not functions of *self*-determination, of personal drive, active decision making, or an intrinsic will to power, but rather are enforced upon him from outside as the reflexes of divine guidance that steer him through every turn on the road of life—God as a kind of metaphysical global-positioning system. In the retrospective survey that concludes the fifth volume of his autobiography, Jung-Stilling makes his most concerted effort to defend the predominance of providence and divine intercession in the development of his life (599–628). His argument runs like this: He admits the existence of great, self-determining individuals who are motivated by a single life impulse and who shape their own lives completely, for good or for evil. This is true for the majority of famous, influential persons, for those whom Georg Wilhelm Friedrich Hegel (1770–1831), in his *Vorlesungen über die Philosophie der Geschichte* (Lectures on the philosophy of history, 1822–23), would call world-historical individuals (*Theorie-Werkausgabe* 12: 45). Jung-Stilling then proceeds, following a logic of self-effacement, to deny that he is one of these strong-willed, self-determining geniuses. To be sure, he admits that his religious piety and his activities as a proselyte for Pietistic principles manifest the impulses of a fundamental drive, but he denies that this drive is an inherent, integral component of his natural character. Confirming his status as a "tool" placed in the service of divine wisdom, he contends that his religious zeal is an artificial implant, forced upon him by God, that runs completely counter to his spontaneous, natural inclinations.

> To be sure!—Yes! I had one [such powerful fundamental drive], and I still have it today: it is an extensive engagement, penetrating all aspects of my being, for Jesus Christ, his religion, and his Kingdom.—However, it is important to note that this drive was by no means anchored in my natural character—for this latter, by contrast, is dominated by an especially irresponsible enjoyment of sensual pleasures, both physical and intellectual, a drive that likewise penetrates all aspects of my being; I beg you not to ignore this foundation of my character. That first, good, fundamental drive was implanted in me entirely from without. (*Lebensgeschichte* 602)

Jung-Stilling goes on to explain how the beatings he suffered during his childhood at the hands of his father were part and parcel of God's strategy for squelching his natural proclivity for the enjoyment of sensual pleasures, and thereby for fashioning him into a salutary religious tool (604).

We have already seen how Jung-Stilling interpreted his years of poverty and the suffering that resulted from his massive debts as another reflex in this divine plan to stamp out those lascivious drives that he saw as the spontaneous impulses of his natural character (612). His arguments culminate in the following assertion, directed immediately at his readers:

> Now all of my readers will probably be convinced that I am not a great
> man, great mind, or great genius—for I have contributed nothing at all
> to my life's development; even my natural inclinations first had to be
> carefully prepared and trained by means of great exertion over the
> course of my protracted life of suffering [*Leidenswege*]. I was nothing
> but passive material in the shaping hand of the artist; clay in the hand
> of the potter. (616)

In his role as a prominent religious figure, Jung-Stilling faces a peculiar
double bind: on the one hand, his autobiography demonstrates nothing if
not the astonishing *secular* rise of an extraordinarily driven individual, born
into a lowly, agrarian environment, who would advance—by hook or by
crook—to the very pinnacles of German civil society; on the other hand,
his religious ideology, which demands individual modesty, moderation, and
contentment with one's lot in life, seems to stand in opposition to the facts
of his social advancement. This contradiction can only be resolved by the
appeal to divine guidance as a force that determines the destiny of the individual. The very uniqueness of Jung-Stilling's phenomenal rise to prominence testifies, according to his interpretation, to the fact that his existence
follows a preordained plan (600), inscribed before the fact into the book
of life by the Christian God. In this sense his autobiography represents for
him nothing other than a transcription, after the fact, of this initial divine
inscription. Jung-Stilling stresses this theory of divine predestination by highlighting, even exaggerating, his own baseness and unsuitability for becoming
such an instrument of divine wisdom. Self-deprecation thus goes hand-in-
hand, paradoxically, with the self-glorification of himself as a chosen tool
of the Lord. But if Jung-Stilling truly has no inherent qualities that qualify him as an especially useful and appropriate substance for divine shaping, then his selection as God's instrument can only be based on pure chance,
on the luck of the draw. To be sure, this is a logical consequence that Jung-
Stilling seeks to avoid at all costs. This explains his diatribe against theories that project human fate as a function either of blind coincidence or
of a mechanical, machinelike determinism (600–01). The logic he applies
to justify his own chosenness is as simple as it is eloquent: God privileges
precisely the *least* suitable, the most inferior material as his matter of choice
because the discrepancy between this baseness and the lofty results high-

light the greatness and power of the Lord himself. To remain within Jung-
Stilling's metaphor of God as sculptor: only the supreme artist can make
a sublime work of art out of the most common and resistant clay. In short,
if Jung-Stilling's social and economic ascent seems miraculous, this is
merely proof that it truly is predicated on miracles. He is living testimony
to God's ability to work wonders.

In the 1803 issue of his populist religious journal *Der graue Mann*, Jung-
Stilling explicitly addresses the accusation that his belief in the providential nature of his life is an expression of uninhibited pride and shameless
self-aggrandizement. To refute this imputation, he asserts that those who
are familiar with the workings of the Christian divinity will know

> that the most exemplary fate says nothing about a person's superior
> qualities, but simply that the Lord constructs his greatest and most awe-
> inspiring instruments precisely out of the worst, most common material,
> so that He can be all the more exalted through them. But let's not waste
> another word on this, so as not to leave the impression that I am boast-
> ing about excessive modesty. (*Sämmtliche Schriften* 7: 517)

Boasting about one's modesty: this paradoxical formulation could stand
as the general formula for Jung-Stilling's approach to the narration of his
life story. We recall Nietzsche's famous parodistic revision of Luke 18:14
from the first volume of *Menschliches Allzumenschliches* (Human, all too
human): "Whoever lowers himself wants to be elevated" (*Kritische Studienausgabe* 2: 87). This perverse dialectic between self-degradation and
swaggering self-glorification is characteristic of the relationship between
the narrating and the narrated self throughout Jung-Stilling's autobiography, in particular its later volumes, in which the assertion that he has not
contributed actively to his own social advancement, but instead has simply followed divine signposts, becomes the overriding theme (see *Lebensgeschichte* 222, 236, 314–15, 344, 474, 488, 608, 616).

Jung-Stilling attributes to his father his own indoctrination into what
we might term the masochistic impulse of Pietism: the belief that human
beings must violently discipline and repress all their personal inclinations
and desires and submit passively to the dispensations of divine providence.
In the report about his own development into a professor of political eco-

nomics, which he inserts as an introduction to his *Lehrbuch der Staats-Polizey-Wissenschaft* (Textbook on the science of state policy, 1788), he ascribes to his father the adherence to one cardinal pedagogical principle: "[T]he human being must be kept docile from the cradle onward, so that subsequently he can come to terms with all the contingencies that life presents" (vii). He then goes on to claim that in his daily existence his father practiced this principle, systematically extinguishing every passion, desire, and wish his son expressed by submitting him to severe physical abuse (vii).[34] And yet contrary to this self-assessment as a docile, passive token manipulated by the hand of God, we have seen on the example of his marriage to Christine Heyder the degree to which the evolution of Jung-Stilling's life must be interpreted as a function of rational planning and calculation in the pursuit of his own social ambitions. The appeal to divine guidance serves merely as an ideological smokescreen that hides the more mundane, personal, and, indeed, ethically questionable motivations that fuel his meteoric rise to a position of tremendous social distinction.

If the later volumes of *Lebensgeschichte* are structured around this theme of passive submission to the will of God, the earlier volumes are marked by a kind of counterdiscourse that emphasizes Jung-Stilling's ambition, personal aspirations, and quest for honor and esteem. The idea that Jung-Stilling could evolve to be a fine gentleman, a *Herr*, is first promulgated by his much-loved and admired grandfather, who views instruction in Latin as the necessary first step along this path. It is left to Pastor Stollbein to voice a warning against such fantasies of upward mobility: "You farmers think that there is nothing to becoming a gentleman. You plant this ambition, which actually comes from the devil, in your children's hearts" (62; see also 126). The message is clear: ambition and the desire to rise up in life are the work of the devil and must be extinguished, rather than nourished. And yet Jung-Stilling continues to be haunted by the impossible dream of becoming a prince or even a king. On one of his journeys through the indigenous landscape he loves so dearly he imagines where he will build his future castle—to be called the "Henrichsburg," Henrich's castle, in honor of himself, of course—and envisions the city that will lie at its feet (92). To be sure, these are the typically self-aggrandizing fantasies of the child, fed in this case, as Jung-Stilling admits, by the literature he has read. But this nagging desire for celebrity and distinction remains a prominent

feature of Jung-Stilling's personality, a trait on which other individuals frequently comment. Judge Goldmann, who, as we recall, criticized Jung-Stilling
for believing in the incredible flukes of fortune that are related in fictional
literature, also indicts his drive for knowledge and academic accomplishment as a secret wish for fame and esteem (154). This same Judge Goldmann will eventually force Jung-Stilling to recognize the "devilish
arrogance" that lurks behind his limitless drive for social advancement.
"Whence will I derive the strength to withstand my devilish arrogance,"
Jung-Stilling ultimately asks himself, and he goes on to confess that his charitable impulses are mere covers for the personal desire to become a prominent individual.

> My heart is the most deceitful creature on God's earth; I never cease
> to believe it is my intention to serve God and my fellow human beings
> with my pursuit of science—but in fact, this is not true! I would really
> only like to become a great man, to ascend to great heights so that I
> can fall all the farther.—Oh! Whence will I derive the strength to over-
> come myself? (160)

One could read this passage as Jung-Stilling's ultimate insight into the
secret workings of his own heart, revealing his covert desire to mask his
true ambitions for fame and fortune by parading them as service to God
and humanity and as passive submission to the demands of divine providence. This duality has its complement in the extreme contrary reactions
people have toward his personality, either loving his goodness and simplicity or hating his aspirations for celebrity.

> Stilling was one of those human beings to whom no one responded
> with indifference; one could only either love or despise him. Those
> who responded in the former manner where struck by his good heart
> and gladly forgave him his faults; the latter viewed his good heart as
> inane naïveté, his actions as ingratiating, and his talents as pretensions.
> (134–35)

There is a certain tone of self-defensiveness in this passage, marked above
all by the implication that those who hate Jung-Stilling simply misconstrue

his "good heart" as naïveté, his actions as obsequious, and his skills as affectations. However, one could just as easily turn this evaluation around and claim that those who love Jung-Stilling mistake his outward simplicity for a good heart, his obsequiousness for genuine sentiment, and his pretense to distinction for distinction itself. Regardless of how one falls down on this issue, it is significant to recognize precisely the way in which, in Jung-Stilling's self-assessment, modesty and haughtiness appear as two aspects of a single phenomenon. Just as important, Jung-Stilling never seems to act on the occasional critical insight into his own motivations by moving to quell his aspirations for high regard, prominence, and boundless social and economic "credit." When his repeated attempts to become a schoolteacher ultimately fail and he resigns himself to the life of a tailor, he confidently asserts that his "inclination to rise up in the world" has been "stamped out at the root" (214). However, as we have seen, the marriage to Christine is just as much an expression of this inherent need to ascend the ladder of social and economic esteem as is his assumption of the position of schoolmaster.

If Jung-Stilling is correct in his own analysis—modeled, as we might expect, on Biblical rhetoric—that haughtiness is merely the prelude to one's fall, then one might be inclined to interpret the episodic quality of this text—and of Jung-Stilling's life in general—as a demonstration of this rhythm. Certainly the indigence and poverty in which the marriage to Christine and his medical studies culminate seem to be reflexes of this dynamic of supercilious rise and abject fall. However, the general momentum of Jung-Stilling's autobiography is marked by an upward spiral toward moderate wealth, social respectability, and public prestige—despite periodic setbacks. In the end this is perhaps testimony not so much to divine intervention and guidance, as to the persistence and tireless compulsion with which Jung-Stilling invested in the construction of his self to the ends of his own social advancement.

Conflated Fathers: Pater Familias, Pater Politicus, Pater Divinus

Nowhere is Jung-Stilling's own initiative as the motor behind a fundamental change in his professional existence more in evidence than in the assumption of his position as religious advisor to Karl Friedrich of Baden. Jung-Stilling's acquaintance and frequent religious correspondent, Johann Caspar Lavater, who maintained a vital epistolary exchange with Karl Friedrich, had previously served in this function. But Lavater's death in 1801 created a vacancy Jung-Stilling was only too happy to fill.[35] The first contact between Karl Friedrich and Jung-Stilling occurred in 1796, when the then margrave of Baden read the religious allegory *Das Heimweh* and wrote to its author to inquire about its figurative allusions. This marked the beginning of a correspondence centering on religious matters that would culminate in April 1801—just a few months after Lavater's death and during Jung-Stilling's return from the trip to Switzerland that resolved his financial problems—in Jung-Stilling's first audience with Karl Friedrich in Carlsruhe, where the seat of his government was located. This was followed by a second audience a year and a half later, in September 1802, in which Jung-Stilling requested that the margrave find a position at court for his eldest son Jakob, who was trained as a jurist. It was also at this audience that Jung-Stilling most likely broached for the first time the question of his own possible employment by the margrave as a religious proselyte and cataract surgeon (Schwarzmaier 145). We do not know what actually transpired during this second audience; but the correspondence between Jung-Stilling and Karl Friedrich that ensued gives a clear indication that the idea of Jung-Stilling laying down his Marburg professorship, which had become so odious to him, and assuming duties as a religious writer attached to Karl Friedrich's court has its source in an initiative on Jung-Stilling's part. This stands in crass contradiction to the portrayal of these events Jung-Stilling provides in his *Lebensgeschichte*, where the initiative is depicted as coming from Karl Friedrich (592). This interpretation, which construes the margrave as the instrument in the final realization of the divine course Jung-Stilling's life is intended to follow (594), is coherent with Jung-Stilling's tendency to stylize his own ambitions and strategic initiatives as the reflexes of divine will.

The seed for his eventual patronage by Karl Friedrich is planted in a letter of Jung-Stilling's dated 1 December 1802, written just a few weeks after the second audience with the margrave. Here Jung-Stilling reports on rumors he claims to have heard from contacts in Heidelberg about Karl Friedrich's intention to bring him to Carlsruhe as his religious advisor, and he coyly insists that he is not the source of these rumors: "For if His Majesty were to hear [these rumors], he might easily stumble upon the idea that I was their source, which is certainly not the case" (*Briefe* 309). Jung-Stilling's strategy seems as clear as it is effective: under the pretense of writing to Karl Friedrich to dispel any impression that he has unleashed certain rumors, he subtly reminds the margrave of their discussions a few weeks earlier in Carlsruhe and, almost as an aside, presses the case of the benefits that will accrue to both parties if Jung-Stilling enters Karl Friedrich's services. Jung-Stilling thereby exploits this opportunity to communicate to the margrave his firm belief that God will free him of his academic position so that he can devote himself solely, and with renewed vigor, to his religious writings; and he even is so unabashed as to assert that when this occurs, his intention is to take up residence in Karl Friedrich's duchy of Baden. This constitutes much more than a subtle hint; it is a clear signal that Jung-Stilling is fishing for an invitation to join the Carlsruhe court.

This letter, for whatever reason, failed to evoke the desired response, and so Jung-Stilling wrote to Karl Friedrich again three months later, on 20 March 1803, complaining once again of the horrible predicament in which he was languishing in Marburg, wishing to dedicate himself solely to his work for the Lord but bound by contract and ethical duress to carry out his professorial duties (*Briefe* 313–14). Since this indirect appeal again elicited no response from Karl Friedrich, Jung-Stilling took a more direct course a few weeks later in a letter dated 11 May 1803. Reiterating his request that Karl Friedrich, who by now has become *Kurfürst*, find a suitable position for his son Jakob, Jung-Stilling concludes by expressing his confidence that divine wisdom will find a solution for his own predicament as well: "In view of my own difficult situation, which is becoming more troublesome by the day, I merely wait for my divine guide to decide the further development. He will either show Your Majesty a way to make it easier for me to have a greater impact, or He will decide matters in another manner. *His will be done!*" (*Briefe* 316).

We can scarcely imagine a clearer example demonstrating how an event that, in his autobiography, Jung-Stilling portrays as a miracle of divine intervention derives in reality from the persistence with which he bombards Karl Friedrich with surreptitious pleas for a resolution of his personal predicament. The cleverness and guile that underwrite this personal mission is evident in the subtle innuendo with which he suggests that if Karl Friedrich does not submit to becoming the vehicle of divine grace, God will find some other resolution. But even more telling, perhaps, is that the Biblical phrase that concludes this plea contains an ambivalence about the Lord whose will should be done. Behind this apparent reference to the Lord God lurks an allusion to Karl Friedrich as the secular lord, so that this phrase can be read as a subliminal goad to Karl Friedrich to take concrete action in conformity with his own will. A similar semantic ambiguity relating to the word "father" occurred in *Lebensgeschichte* when Jung-Stilling received the promissory note Peter Heyder sent to relieve his debts in Strasbourg: standing at the window, Jung-Stilling gazes toward heaven and thanks his "almighty Father" for the financial relief he arranged (*Lebensgeschichte* 270). As noted in the above analysis of this passage, Jung-Stilling elides the human assistance of the civic and juridical father-in-law, Peter Heyder, by reducing him to a mere instrument of divine will. In his negotiations with Karl Friedrich a similar displacement takes place. In this instance, however, it is not the *pater familias*, the head of Jung-Stilling's ideal (and idealized) family who is confused with the divine Father, but rather the *pater politicus*: the secular head of the ideal (and idealized) state. Jung-Stilling is absolutely clear in the latter case about his motivations: he strategically employs the rhetoric of divine providence in order to manipulate Karl Friedrich into making a decision in line with Jung-Stilling's wishes. The ploy used covertly throughout *Lebensgeschichte* as a tactic for legitimizing Jung-Stilling's engineering of his own professional and social advancement is wielded openly here as a way to exert pressure. Not even the soon-to-be Grand Duke Karl Friedrich could withstand this religious browbeating: by the end of May he has taken the bait, not only engaging Jung-Stilling's son at the judicial court in Mannheim, but also encouraging Jung-Stilling to resign his professorship and concentrate his energies on religious proselytism in his new occupation as *Hofrat* at the court of Baden (*Briefe* 318).

Lest we think that happy endings are so easy to induce, one major problem remains, *the* problem that characterizes the entirety of Jung-Stilling's life, at least as he portrays it in *Lebensgeschichte*: money. Due to the devastation and the expense of the Napoleonic Wars, Karl Friedrich is severely limited in his means, and he can provisionally only offer Jung-Stilling a modest salary of twelve hundred guldens. This sum is dwarfed by the twelve hundred talers Jung-Stilling receives in Marburg. At a taler for gulden exchange rate of about two to one, the salary offered by Karl Friedrich represents only half of what Jung-Stilling's Marburg professorship pays, not including its other substantial subsidiary benefits. In his autobiography Jung-Stilling depicts the dilemma presented by the discrepancy as a struggle between reason and faith: reason—that is, *economic* reason—dictates that he reject the low-paying offer made by the *Kurfürst* and retain his considerable professorial salary; faith demands that he accept the new position as confirmation of his religious calling, despite the lower pay (592). Faced with this tormenting decision between what makes good economic sense and what would fulfill his own most profound desire, Jung-Stilling opts for— neither, that is, both! He pursues a carefully calculated strategy in which he negotiates, in several successive stages, financial remuneration from the *Kurfürst* that is approximately equivalent to what he enjoys in Marburg.

When Jung-Stilling responds to Karl Friedrich's initial offer in a letter dated 5 June 1803, financial questions assume center stage.[36] Not content with contrasting the 1,200 guldens Karl Friedrich has offered with the 1,200 talers he receives in Marburg—Jung-Stilling calculates the exact equivalent to be 2,160 guldens—he also points out that his professorial post guarantees insurance benefits for his wife and twelve dependents in the event of his death. As a compromise, Jung-Stilling suggests that Karl Friedrich provide him with free living quarters and an adequate supply of foodstuffs for his subsistence, and he asks in addition for assurances that his family will be provided for after his death. These requests notwithstanding, he concludes with a final plea for greater monetary remuneration, noting that his activities as an eye surgeon would justify a higher compensation (*Briefe* 319–20). Jung-Stilling proves himself to be a skilled salesman, someone who refuses to leave untried any argument that might convince the *Kurfürst* to increase his salary and subsidiary benefits. Essentially, he asks to be made a kept man, someone who enjoys free housing, free food, and a respectable salary to boot. Apparently even Jung-Stilling was embarrassed by the audacious yet groveling tone of this epistle and its financial requests; in a letter written ten days later, on 26 June 1803, he apologizes for making such demands and finally agrees to accept the position in Baden (*Briefe* 320).

But his importunate solicitations were not without effect: the stipulations he set eventually became, in all fundamental points, the ultimate conditions of his employment in Baden. As a result, Jung-Stilling could report in letters to several acquaintances the news of his new calling, explicitly citing the "handsome salary" granted him by the generosity of the *Kurfürst* and, of course, by divine dispensation (see *Briefe* 323, 325, 327).[37] But it is clear that without Jung-Stilling's active agitation and wily negotiations, this position, with sufficient remuneration, might never have materialized.

In his bargaining with Karl Friedrich, Jung-Stilling assumes the role of an active mercenary for his own economic cause. As was true of his marriage to Christine and his medical studies in Strasbourg, his final position as religious writer under the patronage of a prominent German prince is the product of his own desires and machinations. The portrayal of this final turn in his life as confirmation of his divine calling and proof of the truth of the Christian religion (*Briefe* 325–26) is nothing but an ideological cover-up that disguises his own moneygrubbing behind the mysterious circumstance of divine intercession. What constantly lurks behind Jung-Stilling's praise of God, in other words, is an almost craven hunger for money and the existential comfort and security it can purchase. His virtual obsession with the material and financial conditions of his existence can be seen in the fact that, upon the death of Karl Friedrich in 1811 and the subsequent loss of his free housing and his place at the *Kurfürst*'s table, Jung-Stilling was bold enough to submit a legal claim to the Baden authorities, demanding restitution of these privileges or comparable compensation in monetary form (see *Briefe* 487; Schwarzmaier 159).

Earning or Learning: Jung-Stilling's Critique of the Monetary Economy

If the contingencies of the monetary economy take on a propitious air in Jung-Stilling's *Lebensgeschichte* due to their consistent characterization as windfalls granted by divine providence, there is an alternative, much more ominous depiction of the monetary interests underpinning the modern capitalist economy that runs as a kind of leitmotif throughout this text. Any number of episodes might serve as emblematic of this relatively overt critique of an emergent obsession with money and wealth and the deleterious effects it has on human social relations and moral values. One especially memorable example is the anecdote related by Conrad Brauer, a man Jung-Stilling meets in a tavern on his first trip to Schönenthal/Elberfeld, who tells how unbridled competition instigated by one of his own brothers caused his financial ruin, as well as that of a third brother (*Lebensgeschichte* 190–91). A onetime developer and owner of a flourishing wool-weaving business, Brauer now languishes in financial squalor due to the machinations of this sibling, who is never mentioned by name. As opposed to the honest wealth acquired by Conrad Brauer through the legitimate business of his woolens factory, his brother obtains his fortune by marrying an extremely rich but exceptionally ugly woman and assuming control of her wealth. When she dies of mortification as a result of his treachery, he takes a beautiful young bride in her stead and uses his substantial financial means to squeeze the profits of his elder brother's business and force him into financial collapse. Conrad Brauer relates his brother's tactic in the following way:

> He then began to pursue tactics of profiteering, and this to my own disadvantage; for he traded in woolen cloth, and he won away all my trading partners by selling his goods at a lower price than I could offer. With this my business began to decline, and my situation got worse by the day. He took note of this, and for that reason started to be more accommodating toward me, even promising to lend me as much money as I needed. I was foolish enough to believe him. Ultimately, when the time seemed right to him, he took possession of everything in the world I owned. My wife died of mortification, and I live today in misery, poverty, and affliction. (191)

Money and credit play the central roles in this drama of guile and duplicity, for it is solely on the basis of his undeserved wealth that the middle brother in this family can undersell his elder brother's woolen wares, even if that means taking an initial loss in order to force his brother to capitulate. Once he has sent his brother reeling by winning away his customers, he deals the knockout blow by lending him money, thereby paving the way for the hostile takeover of his business. This allows the middle brother to establish a monopoly with which, we are led to presume, he can assert his dominance in the woolens trade and proceed to fleece other potential competitors. This anecdote could stand as a general morality tale about the negative economic impact of concentrated capital. Insofar as it portrays the evils of greed that stem from financial superabundance, it stands as a negative counter to Jung-Stilling's own life story about the struggle to find the means to finance his social rise. Money and credit are neutral instruments, we might conclude; in the hands of evil individuals they effect evil, whereas in the hands of divine providence they foster good. But it is, in fact, difficult to find examples in this text of money working toward positive ends *except* when it falls into the hands of Jung-Stilling himself.

In *Lebensgeschichte* the hunger for cash is one of the most characteristic symptoms of the impending shift from a rural, subsistence economy to one increasingly dominated by money, trade, and competition. We have already examined the undercurrents of this economic transformation in the description of the town of Florenburg, which opens this autobiography. The death of his grandfather introduces this metamorphosis into Jung-Stilling's very family. When Uncle Simon, who has married into the Stilling family, takes over the grandfather's homestead, the winds of change manifest themselves both in the physical rearrangement and spiritual transformation of the old domicile. Walls are removed to create more space, and "the trusty old table," a kind of placeholder for the grandfather, who is characterized as "full of blessings and hospitality" (82), is displaced by a table that is "full of locked drawers" (82). If openness and hospitality are being replaced by the secretiveness of locked drawers, the placid aura of the household is driven off by a new restlessness: "[T]he gentle breeze of the Stilling spirit was transformed into the storminess of an anxious lust for money and possessions" (82). Hot on the heels of this description comes the narrator's commentary that, with the death of the grandfather, the focus of his tale will now turn exclusively to the grandson, Jung-Stilling himself. There are two ways to read this remark in the context of the economic mutations that have just been described as a consequence of the grandfather's death. The more optimistic one, and in all likelihood the one Jung-Stilling had in mind, is that the grandson will pick up where the life of the grandfather left off, hence embodying a resistance to the new reigning sensibility that lusts for money and material possessions. But a second reading of this passage is also possible, one in which Jung-Stilling's life is not a continuation of the attitudes and lifestyle of his grandfather, but instead reflects the modern drive for worldly possessions and the restive desire for social and economic refinement that his Uncle Simon introduces into the family. And in fact, as we have seen, this implication is confirmed by Jung-Stilling's own transformation from a rural bumpkin into "a distinguished, influential [weltförmiger] man" (291). His individual development is clearly marked by the very same desire for money, worldly possessions, and social distinction, the only difference being that in his case wealth and ambition are legitimated as the signs of divine guidance, whereas in the instance of Uncle Simon they are lambasted as indicators of personal greed and moral degeneracy.

At almost every station along his path in life Jung-Stilling is confronted by the insatiable appetite for money that marks the new economic paradigm. In Leindorf (the fictional Kredenbach) he feels oppressed by the "vain and frosty mentality" of the town's inhabitants and by "the constant drive of their hunger for money," which dominate all social and economic interactions (140). As evidence of the evil spawned by this financial greed we are introduced to the story of the counterfeiter Graser, whose fascination with alchemy and the philosopher's stone eventually leads him to a far more practical and effective, if highly illegal, means of conjuring up wealth: the minting of bogus coins (141–44). Jung-Stilling sees himself as a positive countermodel to those whose desires are directed solely at money, and he contrasts his own "insatiable hunger for knowledge" with the seemingly omnipresent lust for wealth (142). What the narrating I purposely overlooks in this juxtaposition is that knowledge is just one more currency with which social advancement and personal prestige can be purchased. The problem, however, is that in Schönenthal/Elberfeld, where Jung-Stilling settles to pursue his profession as a physician, only the currency of cold, hard cash, not that of knowledge and learning, is honored.

> He now suddenly found himself displaced into the large, glittering, metropolitan, money-grubbing world of the merchant [Kaufmannswelt], with which he had absolutely nothing in common, and in which scholars were valued only according to the measure of their monetary assets, in which

sensitivity, reading, and learnedness were laughable, and in which the only people who enjoyed honor were those with substantial earnings. (292)

This new environment is shot through with all the indications of the new economic order, in which honor, reputation, and distinction are tied solely to material possessions, in particular to money and influence. His many years in this merchant town, moreover, will confirm for Jung-Stilling the basic opposition between learning and earning that he already senses at the outset: his life in Schönenthal/Elberfeld will be one of persistent poverty, nagging debt, and perennial lack of "credit," both financial and personal (297), since in this environment personal credit is solely a function of one's financial creditworthiness. In such an economic climate, the bestowal of money, such as the windfalls Jung-Stilling receives through the grace of divine intervention, are tantamount to the granting of respectability. But are these godsends qualitatively different from the illegitimate profit taking of the counterfeiter Graser or of the deceptions practiced by Conrad Brauer's brother? Certainly not if money, in order to be legitimate, must be honestly earned. The sole difference seems to be that Graser and Brauer's brother rely on their own—admittedly, perfidious—initiative, whereas Jung-Stilling purportedly waits, as a passive vessel, for the new investments that will—inevitably, it seems—be made by the Lord above.

The incongruence between Jung-Stilling's commitment to knowledge and learning and the surrounding world of wealth, economic productivity, and trade is exposed most crassly when he enters the Steifmann (Stahlschmidt in real life) household in Dorlingen (the fictional Himmelmert) as tutor.[38] Herr Steifmann—the name attributed to this figure in the autobiography suggests the "stiffness" of his character—stands out as a prototypical profiteer who has managed to take advantage of the opportunities provided by the new economic paradigm. He is the owner not merely of a large agricultural estate, replete with oxen, cattle, sheep, goats, and pigs, but also manages a steel factory and directs a trading company that markets the commodities his factory produces. He is, in short, the model of the multifaceted businessman who particularly flourished in this protoindustrial phase of economic development, prior to the strict division of labor that would accompany the industrialization of the nineteenth century. His economic practices, in particular the founding of an industrial factory in a predominantly rural environment, are consistent with those the economist Jung-Stilling himself promulgated.[39] And yet the relationship between Steifmann and Stilling, between the "haves" and the "have-nots," is marked by such a profound incompatibility that even their capacity to carry on everyday communication is disturbed and disrupted: "He [Herr Steifmann] did not understand a single word of all the things Stilling was accustomed to talk about, and Stilling understood just as little about the things of which his patron spoke. As a result, they both remained silent whenever they were together" (106). The silence that separates these two figures is the very sign of their disparity. The soulless anti-intellectualism of the Steifmann family is concretized in the fact that, among their many possessions, there are scant books, and the ones they do own show few signs of use (107). But the disharmony between Jung-Stilling and the atmosphere in this family expresses itself above all as a conflict of antithetical discourses, with the bawdy, double-tongued irony of the merchant and his family running roughshod over the purported sincerity of the simple, if well-educated and intelligent, provincial.

> He [Stilling] had no particular fondness for anyone in this household. Everyone saw in him a simple-minded, stupid boy; for he did not understand their vile, ironically ribald, and ambiguous statements. He always answered with sincerity, according to the sense of the words as he understood them, and sought to win everyone over with his lovingness. And precisely this was the perfect way to become everyone's lackey. (107–08)

The vileness of this family, marked economically by their monetary wealth, expresses itself discursively as ribald irony and profound ambiguity. The kindheartedness and sincerity with which Jung-Stilling responds to their equivocations are taken as signs of naïveté and stupidity. Thus once again material wealth, in all its supposed obscenity, proves itself superior to learnedness, honesty, and unsophisticated candor.

But there is a certain irony that infects even this description of the disparity between sincerity and irony, for the duplicitousness of irony is also characteristic of the style in which Jung-Stilling writes his own *Lebensgeschichte*. To be sure, the doublespeak of Jung-Stilling's autobiographical style, grounded in the discrepancy between narrating and narrated self, has none of the baseness and bawdiness that he lambastes in the language of the Steifmann household; but the *Prahlsucht*, the "boastfulness" (135) that accompanies all of Jung-Stilling's protestations of his own sincerity corrupts his own narrative discourse and condemns it to irony. Moreover, the irony of this more subtle form of irony is that it becomes all the more duplicitous the more fervently it insists on its own sincerity; as *Lebensgeschichte* gradually jettisons the ornaments and fictional embroidering of the early volumes and makes pretenses to the straightforward, if dogmatic, didacticism characteristic of the style of its later episodes, its discursive irony actually increases rather than diminishes.[40] Indeed, the more Jung-Stilling, as narrator of his own life story, cultivates a rhetoric of authenticity that appeals to divine guidance, the more he falls victim to an ideological self-deception that hides the extent to which he himself has bought into the new dominant economic paradigm of debt and credit. It is no coincidence, then, that the diatribes against the lust for money and wealth, which are especially prominent in the first three volumes of his autobiography, disappear by degrees as his life story progresses, to be replaced by the money of divine providence, which purchases education, respect, social distinction—and which ultimately brings Jung-Stilling the honorable title of *Hofrat*, as court advisor to the grand duke of Baden. When viewed from the perspective of economics, what thus stands out in Jung-Stilling's *Lebensgeschichte* is the manner in which the critique of a modern society whose interactions are grounded in the inherent immorality of acquisitiveness gives way to a glorification of monetary gains that are attributed to the "invisible hand" of the divine banker. Ultimately, Jung-Stilling legitimizes capital accumulation as the mark of divine chosenness and the expression of transcendental will and insight.

Religious Conversion: Faith in God into Faith in Money

The overriding tendency of literary criticism that addresses the economic thematic of the literature produced in Germany during the final decades of the eighteenth century, in which a new socioeconomic paradigm begins to transform every aspect of human life, has been to take the critique of capitalist economic practices that structures the superficial veneer of such

texts at face value. Thus even Jochen Hörisch, in one of the most insightful and theoretically complex investigations of this economic problematic
as concretized in German literature in particular, claims with absolute indu-
bitability, "German literature, as is generally known, resisted the conversion from God to money [characteristic of the modern age since about 1750]
particularly stubbornly" (*Heads or Tails* 26). Hörisch alludes to an especially important theme here, namely, to the widely held belief that the
process of secularization in the European eighteenth century is characterized above all by a shift from faith in God to faith in monetary instruments. It is in this sense that Niklas Luhmann makes the general observation
that "[b]ourgeois society is the first to replace the omnipresence of God
with the omnipresence of money" ("Knappheit" 191).

Jung-Stilling's *Lebensgeschichte* marks precisely the historical moment
in which this substitution of God by money occurs, and it is surely significant that it is the work of a self-defined *religious* writer in which this
"conversion" manifests itself most concretely. Hörisch's belief that literature and literary discourse resist this transformation is especially compelling
for those who seek reassurances about the fundamental otherness of literary discourse and who pin their hopes of a radical revolt against economic
modernism on the seditious force of the literary text. One need only think
in this regard of the seminal arguments made by Julia Kristeva in her book
Revolution in Poetic Language,[41] or of the transformative power ascribed
to literary language, by virtue of its "negativity," its resistance to standard-
ized discourse, in the theories of the Russian formalists.[42] And while it may
be true that the German Romantics develop a theory and deploy a literary practice that critically deconstructs the discourse of capitalist economic
interests—a question I will address in subsequent chapters—there is no
reason to extrapolate from this model and apply it to *all* the literature of
the eighteenth and early nineteenth centuries. What Jung-Stilling's *Lebensgeschichte* demonstrates more persuasively than almost any other work of
German literature from this period is precisely the *complicity* of the literary text with the discourse of economics that was beginning to shape German social life in its entirety. Indeed, Jung-Stilling himself, as someone
who emerges as one of the founders of German political economy as academic discipline, is perfectly suited as an object of inquiry into the eco-

nomic transformations of this epoch and the nature of their fallout in its literary expressions.

Jung-Stilling's *Lebensgeschichte* can be read as a document that marks especially well the transition from an ideology grounded in the omnipresence and omnipotence of God, to allude to Luhmann's above-quoted statement, to one based instead in the omnipresence and omnipotence of money. Although it exhibits on a superficial level a searing critique of the social, moral, and discursive repercussions of the conversion to a worldview dominated by the almighty taler, on a more profound level this text itself succumbs to the principles of the new economic paradigm it ostensibly criticizes. The steep curve of upward mobility that distinguishes Jung-Stilling's life, and that helps account for the seminal place of this text in the development of such central eighteenth-century genres as the autobiography and the *Bildungsroman*, is unthinkable outside the context of this new economy. As we have seen, the very devices underwriting Jung-Stilling's advancement as scholar and professional intellectual are the instruments of this new economy: credit, debt, rationalization, ascetic self-abnegation. Although Jung-Stilling did not shy away from appropriating these economic tools for his own benefit—or even, when push came to shove, as in his negotiations with Karl Friedrich of Baden, of exploiting all the tricks of the shrewd wheeler-dealer—in his autobiography he consistently disguises submission to these new economic principles behind the religious rhetoric of an appeal to the wisdom and intercession of divine providence. There is perhaps no other single text in the German literary canon that evinces so compellingly the slippage between God and *Geld*, between the Christian divinity and the magic of money. In its veritable conflation of God and money, this work both demonstrates and historically marks the cusp of that transition from faith in God to faith in money that is the hallmark of the modern capitalist era. That this conflation expresses itself in a reliance on the belief in providentialism is certainly more than just a coincidence; this doctrine stood at the center of the secularizing transitions from a dependence on religious faith to a reliance on the systematic structures and rational mechanics of the human social and economic world. In this transformation, the trope of providential thinking as the external guidance of the divinity is transferred to the internally regulated system (Poovey 227–37).

Hegel's philosophy of history is perhaps the best example of this displacement of divine plan by a specific internal structure, in this instance the dynamic of reason as it develops in history. In his *Vorlesungen über die Philosophie der Geschichte* (Lectures on the philosophy of history), Hegel belittles the "trifling belief in divine providence" (*Theorie-Werkausgabe* 12: 26) and proposes instead that reason is the guiding principle of the world (12: 25). For Hegel, evidence of what he calls the *List der Vernunft*, the "cunning of reason" (12: 49), can be found in reason's exploitation of human passions not to effect the ends those humans themselves seek to achieve, but rather for the hidden purposes of world history itself. More germane to Jung-Stilling, of course, is certainly Adam Smith's theory of the "invisible hand" that directs human economic actions toward the common good by instrumentalizing their innate self-love. In a famous formulation from the *Wealth of Nations* (1776), he writes, "It is not from the benevolence of the butcher, the brewer, or the baker, that we expect our dinner, but from their regard to their own interest. We address ourselves, not to their humanity but to their self-love, and never talk to them of our own necessities but of their advantages" (1: 26–27). The sleight of hand by which self-interest is disguised as caritas or human charity, which for Smith has become the golden rule of economic success, perfectly describes the ironic discourse characteristic of Jung-Stilling's autobiography: here too, the self-serving economic interests and motivations of the narrated self are disguised behind the rhetoric of humanity, selflessness, and sacrifice with which the narrating self relates his own life story. For Smith as for Jung-Stilling, the altruistic appeal to human charity or to divine benevolence merely disguises the passionate force of human self-interest as the fuel powering personal economic and social advancement. This is a thought closely akin to Hegel's notion of the "cunning of reason," twisted in the case of Smith to fit the model of economic, rather than historical, progress.[43] Operating behind the backs of human beings, who themselves are fundamentally driven by self-interest, the quasitranscendental structure of the invisible hand intervenes to ensure the equity and stability of economic exchange.

Jung-Stilling himself gives voice to the basic precept of this theory when he writes in the first volume of his *Lebensgeschichte* that God, as divine lawgiver, recognizes self-interest as the basis of all human actions, but that he gives human beings the means to ennoble and refine this fundamental *amour-propre* (43). When in his *Grundlehre der Staatswirthschaft* (Basic doctrines of political economy, 1792) he remarks that the aim of political economy is nothing other than "the business of ensuring human happiness [*das Beglückungsgeschäfte*]" (37), he implicitly transfers to the domain of economics one of the primary tasks of the Christian divinity. And indeed, we can hardly imagine a more concrete manifestation of Smith's invisible hand than the divine banker of Jung-Stilling's *Lebensgeschichte*, who consistently showers his protégé with guldens from heaven whenever he seems about to succumb to the exigencies and brutalities of economic life under the competitive conditions of emerging capitalism. Jung-Stilling can count on God in the very same way that Smith's economic subjects can count on the stabilizing, mollifying effect of the invisible hand in the practices of economic exchange.

Yet Jung-Stilling's autobiography also demonstrates that if God is a banker, then life is a repayment plan. For, as my analysis has sought to show, the dynamic of secularization, in which money replaces God, also draws considerable energy from the semantic tensions and crossovers between economic and religious language, in particular from the ambivalences of the German word *Schuld*, meaning both debt and trespass (in the Biblical sense). Here we witness what can only be viewed as a peculiar reversal of the original exchange between humans and the transcendental world, a reversal that is at the very root of the concept of money. If in pagan rituals animals, as a form of money, are sacrificed to the divinity in return for the promise of future prosperity (Grün 55), in Jung-Stilling's *Lebensgeschichte* it is God who brings the monetary sacrifices, thereby "buying" the faith and devotion of his chosen subjects. However, God's investments in Jung-Stilling's life and development are anything but gifts; they are advance payments that increase the debt of the payee to the wisdom of divine providence. Jung-Stilling makes restitution for this debt to the Lord both by means of his religious proselytism and on the basis of his *Lebensgeschichte* itself, which exchanges the discursive currency of the capitalist market economy for that of doctrinaire Christian ideology. Jung-Stilling was able to make a considerable profit in this exchange, since he paid off his debts to the Lord in what was nothing other than an inconvertible paper currency, the very pages of his *Lebensgeschichte*.

One final aspect of the transformation sketched here, and its relevance for Jung-Stilling's econo-Christian ideology, must be mentioned: a marked shift in the terms in which the nature of determinism is conceived, a turn from the biological to the economic. The open attack on the theory of determinism that Jung-Stilling articulates in the retrospective that concludes the fifth volume of his *Lebensgeschichte* gives evidence that this problem haunted his autobiographical project as a whole. For him there are only two alternatives when considering the possibility that human destiny is shaped beyond human will itself: either we are materially and biologically determined by our physical nature, or our fates are guided by divine providence.

> This . . . horrible idea: namely, that the human being only appears to act freely, but in actuality functions much like a machine, is what one calls determinism. This is not the place to refute this abominable nonsense; but if it is requested of me, rest assured that—thanks be to God!—I can provide irrefutable proof of its falsehood.
>
> I am thus working from the assumption that God rules the world with infinite wisdom, but in such a way that defines human beings as free creatures who also contribute their part. (600)

Clearly, what Jung-Stilling has in mind when he thinks of determinism is the mechanistic materialism defended most openly by Julien Offray de La Mettrie (1709–51), whose *L'Homme machine* (Machine man, 1748) provided the prototype for mechanical explanations of the world. The paradox of Jung-Stilling's position, of course, is that at base his own Christian worldview is every bit as deterministic as is La Mettrie's, the difference being nothing but the governor conceived as the steering mechanism behind human destiny. In the case of La Mettrie it is material biology, and the Pietistic counterpart to this biological determinism can be found in this same period in the physiognomic theories of the Swiss pastor Johann Caspar Lavater (1741–1801), whose monumental *Physiognomische Fragmente* (Physiognomic fragments, 1775–78) sought to tie human character to the physical features of the face and body.[44] Jung-Stilling, by contrast, assigns guidance over human fate solely to divine wisdom, and his remark that human free will is part and parcel of this godly universe remains an afterthought. Indeed, the very fact that Jung-Stilling passes over any more detailed proof of the role of free will in the divine world makes his claim that he has irrefutable evidence ring hollow.

Careful readers of his autobiography can scarcely fail to notice that a form of fatalism governs the events of the life described in this text: not the mechanistic-biological determinism of La Mettrie, but rather the economic fatalism, the "invisible hand," of Adam Smith. In other words, in his religiously tinged struggle against biological determinism, Jung-Stilling simply replaces it with another form of fatalism: economic determinism. To be sure, the economic character of the destiny he describes in his *Lebens-geschichte* is consistently and strategically masked by the appeal to divine providence and the conception of God as an omniscient and benevolent moneylender. Yet, as I have sought to demonstrate, this is nothing but an ideological reflex. Indeed, it is *the* ideological reflex that structures Jung-Stilling's entire autobiography: the reinterpretation of economic determinism as the planned intervention of an all-knowing deity. This is the sense in which Jung-Stilling, in the portrayal of his life, encourages us to count on God: to submit our economic destiny to the whims of the omnipresent "invisible hand" that guides every aspect of our existence under the conditions of modern capitalism—money.

6 / Deep Pockets

The Economics and Poetics of Excess in Adelbert von Chamisso's *Peter Schlemihl*

Trade has separated the shadow from the body and made it possible to own each separately.

—Jean-Charles-Léonard Simonde des Sismondi (qtd. in Marx, *Grundrisse* 131)

For since their pleasure is in excess, men look for the art which produces the excess that brings the pleasure.

—Aristotle, *Politics* (1.9.1258a6–8)

Schlemihl's Shadow: Inflation, Excess, Scarcity

IF THE FRENCH-BORN GERMAN POET ADELBERT VON CHA-misso (1781–1838) had never written or published *Peter Schlemihls wundersame Geschichte* (Peter Schlemihl's fabulous story, composed 1813), his scintillating Romantic tale about a man who trades his shadow to the devil for a purse that produces infinite quantities of gold, it seems safe to assume that he would have been relegated to the status of a minor footnote in German literary history. As fate and the contingencies of literary reception would have it, Peter Schlemihl's "fabulous" story has been enshrined as a literary classic, one of the most characteristic and most frequently read pieces of prose fiction produced by the uniquely creative generation of German Romantic poets. For this work alone Chamisso's name figures prominently in the pantheon of German, indeed, of world literature. According to the estimates of one scholar, as early as 1919 *Schlemihl* had appeared in well over one hundred German editions, and a nearly equal number of translations had been published in almost every European language (Brockhagen 380). Among the translations of *Schlemihl*, there are thirty-three French renditions and nearly as many English-language editions (Lahnstein 95–96). Moreover, *Schlemihl* has provided the stimulus for uncountable further artistic renderings of its themes and motifs.[1] One of the most remarkable of these is the variation on the theme of the lost shadow developed by Chamisso's contemporary, the Romantic poet Ernst Theodor Amadeus Hoffmann (1776–1822), in the fourth chapter of his *Abenteuer der Sylvesternacht* (Adventures on New Year's Eve, 1815), which bears the title "Die Geschichte vom verlorenen Spiegelbild" (The story of the lost mirror image). Hoffmann's protagonist, Erasmus Spikher, trades away his mirror reflection, not his shadow, of course; but Hoffmann tips his hat to Chamisso by having Spikher meet the shadowless Peter Schlemihl at a pub.[2] Equally significant is the manner in which Schlemihl's story has stimulated the imagination of visual artists. Among these, the etchings by George Cruickshank (1792–1878) for the 1824 English translation (fig. 6), the woodcuts by Adolf von Menzel (1815–1905), and the colored woodcuts by the German Expressionist artist Ernst Ludwig Kirchner (1880–1938) provide ample testimony to the almost uncanny ability of this tale to pique and stimulate the artistic imagination (fig. 7). Add to this the fact that *Schlemihl* is one of the most frequently interpreted pieces of German fiction—competing in this regard with works such as Franz Kafka's *Die Verwandlung* (The metamorphosis, 1912)—and we have a good sense of the powerful sway this text has held over the modern Western imagination for almost two centuries. As I will attempt to demonstrate in this chapter, it is no coincidence that this novella, in which tropes of excess and of infinite productivity figure so prominently, would itself prove to be such an intellectually and imaginatively productive force in the life of the Western intellect.

Given the broad dissemination and highly animated reception this text has received, it is a poignant irony that the letters appended to Schlemihl's story as a kind of preface by the author and his two friends and editors, Julius Eduard Hitzig (1780–1849) and Friedrich Heinrich Karl de la Motte

6 / Removal of Schlemihl's shadow by the Gray Man. Frontispiece by George Cruickshank from Adelbert von Chamisso, *Peter Schlemihl*, trans. Sir John Bowring, illus. George Cruickshank (1824; 3rd ed., London: R. Hardwicke, 1861).

7 / *Verkauf des Schattens* (Selling of the shadow). Colored woodcut by Ernst Ludwig Kirchner from Adelbert von Chamisso, *Peter Schlemihls wundersame Geschichte: Mit Farbholzschnitten von Ernst Ludwig Kirchner*, ed. Werner Feudel (Leipzig: Reclam, 1980). © Ingeborg and Dr. Wolfgang Henze-Ketterer, Wittrach/Bern.

Fouqué (1777–1843), play with the possibility of suppressing the text completely, so as to keep it out of public circulation. In the letter that opens the exchange among these three regarding the manuscript of what is passed off as the real-life Peter Schlemihl's autobiographical account, Chamisso insists that this text is intended solely for the eyes of Hitzig and Fouqué, and he remarks on how "unpleasant" it would be for him if this "confession" were to appear in public as a work of fiction (*Schlemihl* 17–18).[3] Chamisso's remarks are tinged with a certain irony of their own, since Chamisso's letter is addressed to Hitzig, a book dealer and publisher. In short, word and deed seem to be curiously out of sync: Chamisso's admonition that Schlemihl's story be kept out of public circulation is expressed in a cover letter accompanying the manuscript when it is sent to a person whose very business is the publication and circulation of such literary accounts.

The series of ironic refractions contained in these prefatory letters does not end here; what is at issue in these epistles is above all the circulation of this story as commodity in the literary marketplace, and in this sense these deliberations anticipate the problematic of monetary and commodity circulation that lies at the heart of *Peter Schlemihls wundersame Geschichte*. Thus in the second letter, Fouqué completely turns around the logic of Chamisso's initial request. Writing to Hitzig, he maintains that the best way to "shade" Schlemihl's story—the German term *beschirmt* alludes playfully to the shadow theme developed so fully in the fictional account itself—from the eyes of unwanted readers is precisely to *print* it (*Schlemihl* 18). Fouqué goes on to argue, in a witty ironization of the role of literature in the bourgeois public sphere at the beginning of the nineteenth century in Germany, that an unnamed "genius" rules this public domain and infallibly places printed texts into the hands of their intended and most suitable readers (19). Fouqué's reference to "an invisible padlock" that protects "each and every work of the mind and the imagination" from being opened by inappropriate persons (19) should probably be read as a satirical comment on the fate of genuinely inspired literary artifacts in a public sphere rife with works of print: to wit, that they are doomed to become luxury items in the literal sense, read—and, above all, purchased—by few. *Schlemihl* would turn out, in fact, to be the exception that proves this rule; and it is to this that the third and final introductory letter, written by Hitzig to Fouqué, refers. Citing the worldwide circulation this tale has received just three years subsequent to its initial publication—not only throughout Europe, but even as far away as America—Hitzig expresses his gratitude to Fouqué for daring to break the vow of secrecy by submitting Schlemihl's story for publication (19–21). According to the logic of these prefatory letters, then, it is only due to a quirk of the public sphere—a failure of the receptive padlock that ostensibly shunts works of genius away into the protective shadowy realm of the unacknowledged and unread—that *Schlemihl* emerged as one of the most productive, most quickly circulating commodities in the literary market of the time.

Two years prior to the publication of *Schlemihl*, Chamisso himself diagnosed a kind of inflationary economy as a plague within the German bourgeois republic of letters. Writing to Fouqué in early 1812, he complained that everyone seemed to be writing, but that no one bothered to read anything except to use what one read to generate more writing (*Werke* 5: 352). He continues by apostrophizing the "writing populace," accusing them of composing without inspiration, without the guidance of true muses, and, for the most part, without any genuine readers. For his part, Chamisso claims that, in the absence of a profoundly moving experience as the motivating factor, he would prefer to deny himself the pleasure of writing at all (352). Chamisso himself, in short, was painfully aware that the excessive and extravagant writing of his time threatened to open the literary floodgates to such a degree that works of genuine inspiration and emotional affect would be drowned in the waves of pulp fiction. The epistolary prefaces to *Schlemihl* refer indirectly to this assessment. Chamisso was certainly taken by surprise when *Schlemihl*—to remain within my metaphorical conceit—rose above the inflationary flood of trivial literature. Looking back with a distance of five years on the fabulous reception of *Schlemihl*, Chamisso noted the exceptional status of this text by placing it outside the regular circulatory logic of commodity economics: in a letter to his friend Louis de la Foye from early 1819 he cites as the most telling symptom of *Schlemihl*'s popularity the fact that it is regularly *stolen* from lending libraries (*Werke* 6: 167). Nothing could confirm more forcefully the way in which this work of literary fiction, which focuses so centrally on questions about the circulation of commodities and money, in its own status as material commodity participates in, but simultaneously disrupts, the very logic of commodity economics.

Critical engagements with Chamisso's story have tended to concentrate on the problematic interpretation of Schlemihl's shadow and the meaning of its loss. In this regard there are almost as many interpretive answers as there are interpreters themselves. The shadow has been taken, for example, as a metonymy of the true self (Blamberger 111–12), as symptomatic of a split between semblance and essence (Fink 25), as a moral value, a virtue that must be earned (Berger 127), as the unconscious aspect of the psyche (Neumarkt 121–22), as representative of the pseudovalues of bourgeois society (Wilpert 40), and, of course, as the immortal soul itself (White and White 224–25). The fact that Schlemihl loses his shadow has alternately been interpreted as a symptom of a lack of substance (Block 97), as a sign of a divided self (Brockhagen 408), as the loss of the ideal bourgeois synthesis between money and morality (Freund, *Chamisso* 38), as loss of the ability to communicate (Gille 76), as the forfeiture of bourgeois respectability (Mann 55–56), as sacrifice of the social self (Wiese, "Adelbert von Chamisso" 109), simply as the general loss of personal identity (Loeb 405), or as an indelible mark of difference or nonbelonging (Block 97; Butler 8–9). A much smaller group of critics has sought to come to terms with this multiplicity of possible referents by insisting on the multivalency of the shadow itself as symbol. Thus Loeb associates the shadow with the symbol in the Goethean sense, and declares it, as a consequence, to be uninterpretable (398). Similarly, Martin Swales cites its ultimate ambiguity ("Mundane Magic" 250), and Neubauer subscribes to the thesis that the shadow escapes any definitive symbolic reference whatsoever (24). Kuzniar has drawn the most radical, and, in many respects, the most stimulating conclusion from this multivalency of the shadow, identifying it from a semiotic and Derridean perspective as a prototypical signifier that lacks any real signified (190), and she goes on to explain the diverse hermeneutical confrontations with this image as so many futile attempts to discover what by definition cannot be found (191). Kuzniar comes closest to the position with regard to Schlemihl's shadow that I will assume here, however, when she identifies it with the Freudian notion of displacement and hence as the placeholder of a desire for something lost in the process of exchange (190). This position has the virtue of highlighting the relational structure implied in the very notion of a shadow, for a shadow is the product of an interaction between light and a solid body.

Chamisso himself, in the preface to the 1838 French edition of *Schlemihl*, stressed the relational interdependence between a light source and a real object as the structural matrix that generates a shadow, citing the definition from a treatise on physics (see *Sämtliche Werke* 2: 703). The shadow thus must always be seen in a configuration with two other entities, a "source" of energy and an object that throws the shadow. When viewed in economic terms, this energy source in Chamisso's text is an economics of plenitude; and the object on which it sheds its light, and which produces a shadow, is the *Glücksseckel*, the inexhaustibly productive purse for which Schlemihl trades his shadow (*Schlemihl* 28–29).[4] But we also need to stress at the outset that this purse has a significant second analogue in the story: namely, the pocket from which the Gray Man, the incarnation of the devil, draws a seemingly endless supply of commodities. These two inexhaustible resources are the "deep pockets" referred to in my chapter title, and they represent what the sociologist Niklas Luhmann cites as the two dominant and interrelated spheres of circulation in the modern economy: the domains of commodities and of the monetary supply (*Wirtschaft* 64). To follow the analogy further: if Schlemihl's shadow is, in this economic context, the negative of the plenitude embodied in the magic purse and the Gray Man's deep pocket, then it must symbolize their opposite, namely scarcity, lack, or loss. Schlemihl's loss of his shadow, then, would represent—only somewhat redundantly—the loss of loss. This is not as complicated as it may sound; for when he gains the purse that fulfills any and every economic need, the one thing that Schlemihl loses is the ability to experience loss or lack as such. The irony, of course, is that the bottomless moneybag, the item that is supposed to satisfy all desires, actually generates a new and insatiable longing: Schlemihl's drive to retrieve and reaquire his lost "shadow," to experience once more the limitation of loss or lack.

What does it mean, in economic terms, for loss to be lost, absence to be absent, or lack to be lacked? Let us begin with a simple assertion by Georges Bataille from his 1933 essay "The Notion of Expenditure" that seeks to explain the linkage between wealth, expenditure, and the respect they engender: "Wealth appears as an acquisition to the extent that power is acquired by a rich man, but it is entirely directed toward loss in the sense that this power is characterized as power to lose. It is only through loss that glory and honor are linked to wealth" (122). The power of wealth, Bataille suggests, resides in the loss that accrues to the wealthy person in the expenditure of a portion of that wealth. It is only by dint of this loss, a negative sum in the balance book, that expenditure assumes an air of distinction at all, so that the spender, while sacrificing a piece of his or her wealth, in return gains fame and honor. The power of money is not in the having, but in the spending of a *limited* resource, and as such its mystique is generated by the dynamic of loss. In the terms of Luhmann, the law of commodity exchange is structured around the binary code payment/non-payment, in which payment for one item implies the inability to pay for another, based on the overriding principle of scarcity (*Wirtschaft* 249, 197). However, in the case of a wealth whose spent resources are constantly and immediately replenished, the very notions of scarcity, loss, and sacrifice are abrogated: loss as principle has, so to speak, been lost.

This is precisely the problem with which Peter Schlemihl is confronted in the first eight chapters of his autobiography, up to the point at which he throws his magic purse into the abyss (*Schlemihl* 67–68). When he opts to exchange his shadow for this bottomless purse, Schlemihl seems to be guided by the belief in a simple equation: wealth, power, and human respect are directly proportional to one another, so that one who possesses endless wealth will also wield infinite power and be regarded with infinite respect. Yet his experiences continually prove the contrary, and no matter how much money, jewels, or landed property he showers on those with whom he comes into contact, the anticipated linkage between this expenditure and the accrual of respect and power never materializes. In the fictional logic of Chamisso's novella, of course, the reason for this is Schlemihl's lack of a shadow. But in economic terms, Schlemihl's dilemma is grounded in a fundamental mis-calculation: his misprision that power and honor are aligned with the plus column in the business ledger, rather than being a function, as Bataille indi-cates, of the sacrifice manifest by the loss deducted in the minus column. In short, Schlemihl is a victim of the very *excess* that was intended to solve all his problems: the superfluity placed at his disposal by the magic purse. Only if his wealth were strictly limited, and if, as a result, expenditure resulted in loss and sacrifice, could Schlemihl expect his (spent) money to buy him social preeminence.

In certain archaic societies, the needless expenditure and loss marked by the potlatch win the giver both social honor and the obligation and subordination of others.[5] Schlemihl's world is one in which, due to his infinite resources, the extravagant loss and expenditure of the potlatch is impossible. In this sense, Schlemihl lives up to his name, as Chamisso described its meaning in a letter to his brother from March 1821: schlemiels, he explains, are "clumsy and unfortunate people who never succeed at anything. A schlemiel . . . falls on his back and breaks his nose, he always appears at the wrong time" (*Sämtliche Werke* 2: 695). In short, only a schlemiel/Schlemihl could acquire a source of infinite wealth, experience it as a curse, and end up longing to experience a significant financial loss. What titillation could there be in a stock market devoid of the possibility of loss or of a devastating crash?

Drawing on Brian Rotman's deliberations on the historical impact of the sign "zero" when it was imported into the European mathematical system during the Middle Ages, we can elucidate the structural function of Schlemihl's shadow as a kind of metasign that marks not absence itself, but the absence of absence. The replacement of Roman numerals by Hindu numerals, including the sign of zero, which was unknown to the Romans, had, as Rotman demonstrates, far-reaching repercussions for the modern development of mathematics and economics in the West (7–16). In the Hindu numerical system, the sign zero has a unique function; unlike the positive numerals one through nine, zero does not refer to a quantity of things, but rather to the absence of any such quantity. Indeed, zero is not a numerical sign of the same order as, for example, the sign "one," because what it refers to, in fact, is nothing other than the absence of the other numerical signs: "as a numeral, the mathematical sign zero points to the absence of certain other signs, and not to the non-presence of any real 'things'. . . . At any place within a Hindu numeral the presence of zero declares a specific absence: namely, the absence of the signs 1, 2, . . . 9 at that place. Zero is thus a sign about signs, a meta-sign" (Rotman 12).

A parallel claim could be advanced for the symbolic function of the shadow, or, perhaps more correctly, of its loss, in the textual and financial economy of *Schlemihl*. The lost shadow does not stand for the absence of any real thing, rather it functions as a metasign that points to the absence of other signs. Like the numeral zero, it signifies "nothing" in the literal sense: it is a placeholder for the absence of another sign. On a hermeneutical level, this explains the seemingly infinite substitution of possible referents for Schlemihl's lost shadow by interpreters: the lost shadow is a zero sign that invites its own displacement and replacement by some positive meaning (numeral). But in the economic framework of the novella, the shadow as metasign, like the numeral zero, also marks the empty place of loss and sacrifice in a system characterized by the infinite generation of commodities and wealth. In the economy of Schlemihl's magic moneybag, the shadow as zero sign hence plays the supplementary role of marking the endless inflation that occurs whenever zeros are randomly appended to any positive number. Germans living in the inflationary monetary upwind of the 1920s experienced in their everyday life the vertigo of this multiplication of pure numbers by the simple addition of zeros. The irony of such inflation, of course, is that as the number value increases through the supplementary zeros, the real commodity value—the buying power of the inflated bill—proportionately *decreases*.[6] Schlemihl's lost shadow, like the metasign zero, thus has a double reflex: it marks not only the absence of loss and sacrifice that arises under the conditions of infinite wealth, but also the inflationary dynamic of money and value that develops as a corollary to the infinite resources of Schlemihl's bottomless purse. The boundless wealth to which Schlemihl has access represents a surplus that threatens the social order of value predicated on scarcity, and no potlatch of extravagant sacrifice is capable of diminishing or destroying this surplus.[7]

Niklas Luhmann was one of the first social theoreticians to deliberate explicitly on the structural significance of scarcity for the modern economic system. In the essay "Knappheit, Geld und die bürgerliche Gesellschaft" (Scarcity, money, and civil society), he asserts that the invention of money as a supercommodity, defined above all by its scarcity, is the founding principle not merely of the modern economy, but of postfeudal civil society as such (192). In the context of this insight, Schlemihl's *Glücksseckel*, which eschews precisely the principle of scarcity, runs counter to the grounding theory of modern economics, to what Luhmann calls the paradox of scarcity: namely, that every use of a scarce item, while satisfying a need for that item, simultaneously *increases* its scarcity (*Wirtschaft* 98). This is precisely *not* the case for Schlemihl: he can use his gold wantonly because it is always replenished, and as a result the underlying economic paradox of scarcity is suspended. In this sense we can read Chamisso's *Schlemihl* as an attempt to vindicate the principle of scarcity by presenting a systematic critique of an economics of excess.

In order to comprehend the significance of scarcity—or, in more general terms, of strategic limitation and renunciation—for the operation of the modern economy, we must first turn to the historical context. As we saw in our analysis of the German debates about physiocratic theory in chapter 4, prior to the boom in industrialization that began around the turn to the nineteenth century, all productive forces were viewed as tied to, and hence limited by, nature. If the physiocrats restrictively limited productivity to the reproductive power of nature itself, then this was just one way of insisting, at a historical moment in which man-made industrial production was beginning to demonstrate its inherent creative potential, on the principle of strictly finite (re)productive capacities. Historically speaking, as long as monetary signs were tied to metals such as gold and silver, the monetary supply, like the productive forces of the physiocrats, was limited by the availability of these metals *in nature*. Prior to industrialization, in other words, nature is believed to place inevitable constraints both on the supply of money and on the forces of production. The breaching of any natural restriction of productive energies with the advent of industrialization is paralleled by the suspension of natural checks on the monetary supply with the shift from specie to various forms of symbolic money, such as bank notes or bills of exchange. A lifting of the natural curbs on commodity production hence corresponds to the potentially infinite opening of the money supply when fiduciary signs replace value forms tied to metallic coin. Only with the advent of industrialization, according to Luhmann, does the previously dominant belief that production is subject to natural limitations prove to be untenable (*Wirtschaft* 44). In the absence of such natural limitations, scarcity must be created artificially, and it is generally enforced by a strict circumscription of the money supply. But insofar as it explodes precisely any such monetary limitation, Schlemihl's magic purse disrupts the normal operation of the economic system. Luhmann is careful to point out that in the postindustrial economy both the supply of commodities and of money must be governed—no longer naturally, but rather, artificially—by the overriding principle of scarcity

(*Wirtschaft* 64). This historical moment of potentially infinite production and inflation, which marks the hinge between the premodern and the modern industrial economy, is registered in *Schlemihl* by the purse that generates an inexhaustible supply of gold, on the one hand, and the coat pocket of the Gray Man, on the other, which generates an endless supply of commodities. *Schlemihl* thus marks the very historical moment at which all "natural" inhibitions of the money supply and of the productive forces are suspended by the devilish "magic" of infinite production and the bottomless purse of the printed paper bill.[8] Chamisso thereby locates the story of Peter Schlemihl at the transitional point in economic history when natural limitation gives way to infinite production and the possibility of boundless excess.

The story of *Schlemihl* is structured according to a paradoxical logic that ties fortune to misfortune, a logic inherent in the perverse fate of the schlemiel as Chamisso defined it. But within the dynamics of Chamisso's story, the mechanism controlling this reversal of fortune into misfortune is desire. Luhmann remarks that just as in the modern industrial economy there is no *natural* limitation to the monetary supply, likewise there is no natural limitation to the human *desire* to acquire money (*Wirtschaft* 116). The potential for infinite wealth thus also opens onto the boundlessness of human desiring. This is the point Karl Marx makes in *Grundrisse* when he associates the modern monetary form with the drive for *abstract* enrichment—that is, not for specific acquisitions, but for the pure *capacity* to acquire as such—or when he calls money the philosopher's stone of the economic domain, able to procure any form of "knowledge"—that is, any commodity—whatsoever (133). This perfectly describes the precarious situation in which Chamisso's Peter Schlemihl finds himself: although he commands the infinite monetary resources to acquire any object he desires and hence to satisfy all desires *in theory*, in practice there is one desire that will always remain unfulfilled—the longing to recapture his "shadow." Thus, according to the logic of loss and sacrifice adumbrated here, the one desire that Schlemihl will never be able to fulfill under the conditions of economic superabundance provided by his magic purse is precisely the desire for exuberant loss; and this, according to Bataille, represents a desire that is psychologically and existentially *primary* and *superordinate* to the desire for acquisitions ("Notion of Expenditure" 121).

If, in Luhmann's systems-theory view of the modern economy, economic subjects are constantly confronted with the option either of making payment to acquire some good or service or of refusing payment and thereby renouncing the possibility of acquiring that good or service, then the binary code payment/nonpayment parallels on the psychic plane—in the libidinal economy—the binary code satisfaction/abstention. In every potential act of consumption, the consumer is confronted with the either/or choice of making payment, and hence of accepting the good or service as adequate compensation for the loss of diminished monetary resources, or of refusing payment and abstaining from acquisition. In the latter case, a need is left unsatisfied, but this lingering dissatisfaction is compensated by the money left unspent, which represents the potential to satisfy some other desire. According to Luhmann, this dialectic of profit and loss is the defining feature of all modern economic communication. As opposed to verbal communication, where "information" is shared by the sender and the receiver, in the domain of economics all exchanges—for Luhmann these are simply another type of communicative act (*Wirtschaft* 14)—are characterized by the differential between profit and loss: what the "sender" gives, the receiver "takes"; and what the payer "sends," the payee "receives" (247). In the communicative acts of economics, no parity among the parties is ever involved: one party must lose what the other gains and vice versa.

In the fictional world of Chamisso's *Schlemihl*, this most basic of all modern economic principles is undermined. Schlemihl as "payer" is never faced with the prospect of loss, and so the profit/loss dichotomy that structures all economic exchange is annulled. Seen from this perspective, this novella can be read as a searing critique of an economy of absolute excess, an economy that has banished the principle of scarcity, the dichotomy of profit and loss, and the binary code payment/nonpayment and has substituted for them the principles of limitless luxury, excess, and extravagant expenditure. To the extent that he longs for limitation under the conditions of excess, Peter Schlemihl does indeed represent a kind of anti-Faust (Brockhagen 401); and the trajectory of his life story moves in a direction opposite to that of the traditional Faust figure, from infinite desire and its immediate satisfaction to an insight into the need for strategic limitation, renunciation, and abstention. The novella thereby provides a critical commentary on the ideology of eternal striving and infinite economic bounty, or what has come today to be called the growth economy. However, it does not launch this critique from a utopian position *outside of* economics as such, but rather by appealing precisely to an economic system, much like the one theorized by Luhmann, that acknowledges the importance of scarcity and limitation. Far from celebrating extravagant expenditure, waste, loss, and the exuberant sacrifice of the potlatch, Chamisso's *Schlemihl* criticizes such an economy of excess from a solidly bourgeois economic perspective that lauds the virtues of limitation and self-denial.[9] The lesson of *Schlemihl* thus approximates the admonition expressed by the Good Spirit in Chamisso's "Faust: Ein Versuch" (Faust: A study, 1803), his poetic rendition of the Faust theme written ten years before the composition of *Schlemihl*: *lern entbehren*, "learn to do without" (*Sämtliche Werke* 1: 400). Whether in the realm of pure knowledge or in that of economics, the message Chamisso's Faust, like his Peter Schlemihl, must learn, is the renunciative asceticism that Max Weber, in "Die protestanische Ethik und der Geist des Kapitalismus" (Protestant ethics and the spirit of capitalism), would come to identify with the very spirit of capitalist economics.

Peter Schlemihl *and the Economics of Excess*

In a letter to Karl Bernhard von Trinius (1778–1844) dated 11 April 1829, in which Chamisso responded to an inquiry about the inspiration behind *Peter Schlemihl*, the by then famous author of this Romantic "fairy tale" recounted the underlying impeti that gave rise to its composition.

> While on a trip I had lost my hat, portmanteau, gloves, handkerchief, and all my portable possessions. Fouqué asked whether I had not also lost my shadow, and we went on to paint a mental picture of such a misfortune. Another time we were leafing ... through a book by Lafontaine,[10] in which an extremely obsequious man at a social gathering pulls from of his pocket whatever anyone demands. I opined that if one asked the fellow nicely, he would even pull horse and carriage out of his pocket. With this *Schlemihl* was essentially conceived, and subsequently when I was out in the country and had enough boredom and leisure, I began to write. (*Werke* 6: 118)

Although critics have tended to refer to this account as justification for focusing on the motif of the lost shadow, the infinitely deep pocket of the unnamed figure drawn from the work of Lafontaine has called forth scant critical attention, even though Chamisso clearly couples it with the shadow motif as his second primary impulse, the conditions of possibility, for the composition of *Schlemihl*. Moreover, there is an obvious linkage between these two cardinal elements in Chamisso's narrative. The figure drawn from Lafontaine appears, replete with the characteristic obsequiousness associated with him in the above-cited letter,[11] as the primary antagonist in Chamisso's novella, where he is reconfigured as the infamous *Grauer*, the Gray Man who, as shadelike embodiment of the devil himself, seduces Schlemihl into trading away his "invaluable" shadow (*Schlemihl* 28) for an equally invaluable—because infinitely productive—purse. But when Chamisso's protagonist first meets the Gray Man at the garden party of Herr Thomas John, it is a very different emblem of infinite productivity that grabs his attention: out of the pocket of his coat the Gray Man magically extracts any object desired, regardless of its size and its geographical origin. The deep pocket that captured Chamisso's attention in Lafontaine's tale thus appears in a double manifestation when it is integrated into his own novella: it is taken over quite literally as the fathomlessly deep pocket of the Gray Man, and it occurs in a second manifestation as the endlessly regenerative moneybag Schlemihl acquires in return for his shadow (*Schlemihl* 29). We should emphasize here that as early as 1806 Chamisso had tried his hand at reworking the story of Fortunatus from the fifteenth-century chapbook,[12] the tale from which the motif of the bottomless *Glücks-seckel* is drawn. But the magic pocket contained in the work of Lafontaine clearly reinforced Chamisso's long-extant interest in the economic and social problematic that emerges around the idea of boundless wealth or unlimited productive capacity. The very doubling of this deep-pocket in *Schlemihl* indicates the central role it plays for the thematic and structural texture of Chamisso's novella. One might even go so far as to claim that it ranks in importance above the motif of the lost shadow itself. This is true, at least, in the strictly logical sense that Schlemihl loses his shadow by dint of his fascination for the mysteriously omniproductive pocket of the Gray Man, and that, indeed, he trades his shadow for a replica of this deep pocket.

The sociohistorical and economic backdrop for *Schlemihl* is the burgeoning colonialist economy of the early nineteenth century. Schlemihl himself has just returned from a sea journey of his own, a fact that suggests his own possible involvement in colonialist trade (*Schlemihl* 23). In addition, the harbor in which he lands and seeks to set down economic roots contains loosely veiled allusions to the German city of Hamburg, with which Chamisso was familiar and which played a significant role in German colonial enterprises at the time.[13] The scene during Thomas John's garden party, in which the Gray Man pulls multiple objects from his pocket, alludes on numerous levels to this socioeconomic backdrop. At a decisive moment, Herr John sees a tiny speck on the horizon and calls for a telescope, which the Gray Man obediently produces from his marvelous deep pocket.

> A speck of light appeared on the horizon between the dark waters and the azure sky. "Give me a telescope!," Mr. John cried out, and even before the crowd of servants could appear in answer to his call, the Gray Man, bowing deferentially, put a hand in his pocket and extracted a beautiful Dolland, which he handed over to Mr. John. Raising it immediately to his eye, John informed the guests that the speck of light was the ship that had set sail yesterday, but which had been held back in the harbor by unfavorable winds. The telescope passed from hand to hand, never again returning to that of its owner. (25)

One might read it as a function of the Gray Man's excessive obsequiousness that he produces not just any old telescope, but a Dolland,[14] regarded especially among seafarers as the highest quality instrument available at the time. It is worthy of note, however, that throughout this first chapter of the novella an excess of commodities and of money is frequently associated with an excess of emotions, so that the exaggerated politeness and groveling attitude of the Gray Man is just one more indication that he is the very manifestation of excess. Schlemihl himself betrays his susceptibility to seduction by the allure of excess in his very first exchange with Herr John, the representative of social distinction based on superabundant wealth. When Herr John casually asserts to Schlemihl that anyone who does not have at least a million at his disposal must be regarded as a "scoundrel," Schlemihl jumps at the opportunity to defend this expression of exorbitant wealth, and he does so with an overdose of emotion: "'Oh, how true!' I exclaimed, with unchecked overflowing emotions [*über-strömenden Gefühl*]" (24). Schlemihl's overflowing emotions prefigure the overflowing moneybag he will soon have in his possession, hinting that in this text the problem of excess is not restricted solely to the economic domain.

The passage that introduces the telescope comments in more subtle ways on this problematic of excess and its connections to the capitalist and colonial economy. The very way in which the telescope travels from hand to hand among the visitors at Herr John's party—without, as the narrator explicitly states, ever returning to its proper owner (whoever that might be!)—suggests the manner in which commodities circulate in the modern capitalist marketplace, without ever coming full circle and returning to their place of production.[15] Moreover, what holds true for the commodities from the Gray Man's pocket also becomes an iron rule for Schlemihl's magic purse—the gold it generates can never be returned to the bag (31)—as well as for his shadow: none of these "commodities" ever returns to its place of origin, and their extraordinary value accrues precisely due to this structure of unlimited displacement. In *Schlemihl* Chamisso focuses on the uncanny power of a colonial economy dependent largely on trade to produce wealth out of commodity circulation. This is underscored not merely by the fact that the general setting for this entire chapter is a merchant city like Hamburg, but also by the allusions to colonial merchandise that abound in the descriptions of Herr John and his social milieu. Schlemihl is impressed at the outset by the "exotic fruit from all climatic zones," which John presents to his guests "in the most expensive of vessels" (25). Both this food and the bowls in which it is served allude to a worldwide colonial trade that knows no limits. But the products the Gray Man extracts from his pocket also hint at the infinite reach of the colonialist enterprise: a Turkish carpet, an English telescope, a magnificent garden tent, a letter case, horses, and so on (25–26). The Gray Man and his pocket thereby become the symbols of the excesses made possible by this far-reaching colonial economy, and Herr John the representative profiteer who mercilessly exploits the money-making opportunities of this boundless market.

Even the geographical situation of Herr John's garden suggests this notion of excess and infinity. From this garden he commands a vantage point that looks out not only over the "dark waters" of the ocean, but also into the endless azure of the sky. In short, two traditional symbols of the infinite, ocean and sky, merge within the field of vision permitted from his garden (Schwann 207), and these might be interpreted as allusions to the two infinitely deep pockets that form the motivic foci of this story. More important is that the point of light Herr John discovers at the intersection of these two infinite realms is a ship, which refers on the simplest level to the commerce of the colonial marketplace and the place of the merchant and his ships as mediators in this boundless commercial enterprise. However, there is a fly in the ointment: the ship Herr John espies is not blithely sailing away to some distant shore, but, quite to the contrary, has been held up for a full day by unfavorable winds. This merchant vessel hampered by the forces of nature is the first symptom of a critical counterdiscourse opposing this economics of plenitude and superabundance. In this regard, this seemingly insignificant detail will in fact prove to be of major import for the economic problematic explored by this novella, for it anticipates the theme of natural limitation that will become the centerpiece of the concluding chapters. Surely it is no coincidence that at the end of the second chapter, after Schlemihl has made his deal for the magic purse and embraced this limitless economy, the Gray Man disappears and the narrator reports that the ships—now plural—that had been stranded in the harbor can now sail off in all directions: "But on this very day many ships, which had been held back in the harbor by unfavorable winds, had set sail, all to different parts of the globe, all destined to arrive at different shores, and the Gray Man had vanished into thin air, like a shadow" (*Schlemihl* 34). The verbal irony that the man who acquired Schlemihl's shadow should himself disappear "like a shadow" is symptomatic of the narrator's playful stance throughout this text (see Martin Swales, "Mundane Magic" 251–52). However, in this instance it serves in particular to draw our attention to the close association between the Gray Man and the merchant ships that sail out to diverse and distant shores. Once more this figure is yoked to the excessive and—literally—exorbitant trade of commodities and the infinite flow and circulation of goods and capital in the colonial economy. With the exchange of his shadow for the magic purse, Schlemihl has literally bought into this shadowy economics of colonial expansionism and immoderation, in which the ostensible ability to satisfy all desires serves merely to generate a boundless and ultimately insatiable desire for more.

Georges Bataille defines the concept of "expenditure," of extravagant spending for the purpose of loss, as a drive toward wastefulness that stands in opposition to all forms of "rational" consumption, connected to productivity or to the satisfaction of existential needs.

> Now it is necessary to reserve the use of the word *expenditure* for the designation of these unproductive forms [of loss], and not for the designation of all the modes of consumption that serve as a means to the end of production. Even though it is always possible to set the various forms of expenditure in opposition to each other, they constitute a group characterized by the fact that in each case the accent is placed on a *loss* that must be as great as possible in order for that activity to take on its true meaning. ("Notion of Expenditure" 118)

The reflexes Bataille associates with irrational wastefulness—a productivity divorced from meaningful consumption and tied instead to lavish, irrational spending—accurately characterize Schlemihl's actions subsequent to the acquisition of the magic purse. Confronted with the realization that his shadowlessness condemns him to being cut off from social life (*Schlemihl* 34), Schlemihl responds by wantonly distributing copious sums of money to the people he encounters. Whereas the first woman who remarks upon his lack of a shadow is compensated for her advice with a single piece of gold (29), as such encounters increase so do the amounts of gold immoderately distributed among the populace. When a group of schoolboys launches a searing critique against Schlemihl and his shadowlessness, he responds simply by showering gold upon them: "In order to get them off my back, I threw handfuls of gold among them" (30) (fig. 8). Attack—especially in the form of extravagant gifts—is clearly the best defense. This scenario repeats itself over and over again whenever Schlemihl comes into contact with potential critics (see 29, 39, 40, 42, 43, 46).

Schlemihl's joy in excess is lucidly portrayed when he tests the powers of the magic purse just prior to concluding the deal with the Gray Man: "I reached in and pulled out ten pieces of gold, then ten more, and ten more, and ten more" (29). It is much more than the pleasure in satisfying

8 / Schlemihl showering gold among the children. Woodcut by Adolf von Menzel from Adelbert von Chamisso, *Peter Schlemihls wunderbare* [sic] *Geschichte*, illus. Adolf von Menzel (Berlin: Deutsche Buch-Gemeinschaft, n.d.).

this compulsion to repeat that convinces Schlemihl to trade his shadow for the magic purse; indeed, this episode is also structured according to a strict mathematical logic that finds its expression in the recurring multiple ten, an inflationary addition of zeros. This veritable obsession with repetition and surplus finds its culmination in the gold orgy Schlemihl later choreographs in the privacy of his hotel room.

> And what do you think I did after that?—Oh, my dear Chamisso, I blush with shame even to admit it to you. I took the unfortunate bag [*unglücklichen Seckel*] out of my breast pocket and, driven by a kind of fury that spread out within me like a flaring conflagration, I began pulling gold out of it, and gold, and gold, and ever more gold; and I spread it on the floor, trampled on it and let it tinkle, and feasting my impoverished heart on its aura [*Glanz*] and its ring, I continued to add metal to the pile of metal, until I collapsed with exhaustion on this bed of riches and rapturously grubbed around and wallowed in it. (30–31)

This is a crucial passage in Chamisso's text, for here the narrator weds the automatic mechanism with which the moneybag produces infinite quantities of gold to the self-generating reflex by which the "flaring conflagration" of Schlemihl's lust for acquisition reproduces itself in a kind of geometrical progression. The epigenesis by which the *Glücksseckel* produces gold has its counterpart in an epigenetically increasing sense of ecstasy tied to the limitless desire for material gain. The delirium and quasi-Dionysian rapture into which Schlemihl falls in this scene strongly suggest the degree to which all his libidinal energies have been channeled into this voracious greed for ever-greater quantities of gold (fig. 9). His fascination with the "aura" (*Glanz*) of his growing mountain of gold suggestively links him with the well-respected but debauched Thomas John, whom Schlemihl is able to recognize immediately by the "aura" (*Glanz*) of Herr John's self-satisfied corpulence (23). Ernest Borneman has termed this psychological precipitate of endless greed the "Midas complex," and he stresses that this syndrome can only arise with the institution of a monetary economy. But Aristotle was perhaps the first to point to the paradox of King Midas as someone who has infinite wealth in minted money, but for all that cannot satisfy his own basic needs or necessities (see *Politics* 1.9.1257b13—15). What is characteristic of money as an instrument for storing value is precisely that it can be acquired *beyond* the bounds of immediate need, because as the imperishable representative of all values it also represents the potential fulfillment of all future needs and wants (see Marx, *Grundrisse* 144). This, according to Borneman, is the motor behind this psychological reflex of excessive acquisition (447), a phenomenon for which Chamisso provides a brilliantly illustrative mise-en-scène in the episode cited here. When Schlemihl literally wallows in his mountain of gold, he plays out the perversity of this psychological state that fuses excessive libidinal energy with an intemperate drive for acquisition and material satisfaction.[16]

It speaks for Chamisso's stylistic genius that he is able to capture the breathless titillation of this supercharged greed and the monotonous hyperproductivity of Schlemihl's moneybag in the very rhetoric and structure of the language in which it is reported. The paratactic syntax with which Chamisso joins an almost never-ending series of clauses imitates on the level of linguistic structure the endlessly supplementary logic of economic excess dictated by the magic purse. Just as Schlemihl repeatedly delves into

9 / Schlemihl asleep on his pile of gold
after his revelry of gold production.
Woodcut by John Gincano from Adelbert
von Chamisso, *Peter Schlemihl*, trans.
Sir John Bowring, illus. John Gincano
(Philadelphia: D. McKay, 1929).

NIGHT FOUND ME STILL REPOSING ON THE GOLD.

his purse to pull out more and more gold, the narrator succumbs to the
same additive compulsion. We should note here, looking ahead to a problem that will concern us at the conclusion of this chapter, that the text of
Schlemihl contains an ironic explanation of its own linguistic artistry: the
increase in rhetorical skills that Schlemihl, with a certain degree of surprise, takes note of in himself near the beginning of the third chapter (37)
is an attribute he ostensibly acquires, as a kind of epiphenomenal attribute of the infinitely productive purse, from the Gray Man, to whose especially persuasive rhetorical eloquence the text explicitly refers (66). To this
extent, Chamisso implies that the language with which Schlemihl, as autobiographical narrator of his own history, relates his account is itself affected,
or perhaps *infected*, by the logic of *rhetorical* excess.

The temporal discrepancy between Schlemihl as narrator and Schlemihl
as character in his own life story, which is constitutive of autobiographical narratives of this sort,[17] has the additional consequence of imbuing
Chamisso's novella with an ironic subtext that expresses itself especially
clearly in the passage under consideration here. On the simplest level, the
very name by which Schlemihl's magic purse is designated, *Glücksseckel*—
literally, "lucky" or "fortune-bringing purse"—is ironically overturned and

displaced into its opposite when the narrator refers to it as an *"unglück-lichen Seckel"* (30; emphasis added), an unfortunate, or *mis*fortune-bringing purse. The discrepancy between the narrator's discourse of misfortune and the character's wallowing in the fortune of his gold is indicative of the ironic rupture that distances the Schlemihl narrating the tale from the one who as its protagonist succumbs to a hopeless addiction to gold. This rupture, and the superior position and knowledge of the narrating I over the narrated I, also comes to the fore in the shame Schlemihl feels when he has to relate to his friend Chamisso the wanton monetary excesses and rapturous debauchery into which the deep pocket of the magic purse seduced him. When recounting this event, in other words, the narrating Schlemihl views this binge of moneygrubbing as a humiliation and condemns it from the high ground of a retrospective moral superiority. The temporal breach between the narrating self and narrated self thus also signals a moral discrepancy that opens up the space in this text for a didactic message leveled against the sins of excess in a whole range of spheres, not the least of which, of course, is the realm of the modern economy. And yet, as we will see, the critique of exorbitant plenitude is by no means restricted to the realm of economics; it merely receives its most characteristic and paradigmatic manifestation in that sphere.

It is evidence of the careful and often compellingly logical structure of this novella that this delirious episode of excess is immediately followed by Schlemihl's retelling of his first dream (31). Looked at from a Nietzschean perspective and concentrating on form rather than on content, one might be tempted to interpret this dream as the Apollonian answer to the Dionysian rapture related in the immediately preceding textual sequence. But on the declarative level, this dream vision presents a direct antithesis to the preceding scenario of blissful surfeit. In his dream Schlemihl sees the addressee of his autobiographical tale, Chamisso himself, seated at his desk in the confinement of his tiny room. He is situated among the paraphernalia associated with his occupation as botanist and natural scientist, surrounded by a skeleton, dried botanical samples, and books by the major representatives of the natural sciences of the day, Albrecht von Haller (1708–77), Alexander von Humboldt (1769–1859), and Carl von Linné (1707–78), as well as by literary works of Goethe and Chamisso's friend Fouqué. In this vision, we can easily imagine Chamisso hard at work on his botanical studies—that is, we might imagine this to be the case if in Schlemihl's dream Chamisso did not turn out to be as dead as the skeleton and the withered botanical specimens that are his objects of study. This dream, then, provides a negative commentary on the scientific pursuits in which Schlemihl himself will later engage, as seen from the perspective of the Schlemihl persona who is still enraptured by the allure of extravagant plenitude. Before Schlemihl can see Chamisso's menial pursuits as a scientist and his confining surroundings in a more positive light, he will have to be cured of his own addiction to the intemperance of excess. This occurs symbolically, of course, when he finally casts off the magic purse and then devotes himself, in virtual *imitatio* of the Chamisso of his dream, to his botanical research. We will have to examine the text closely, however, to trace the signals of this impending reversal.

"So lernt ich traurig den verzicht . . .": Peter Schlemihl *and the Ethos of Temperance*

Extravagant waste, *Verschwendung* or, in Bataille's terminology, expenditure, is already one of the central themes of the *Fortunatus* chapbook from which Chamisso adopted the motif of the infinitely productive moneybag.[18] This is true, as well, in Chamisso's own dramatic rendition of the Fortunatus legend, in which the more adventurous of Fortunatus's two sons, Andolosia, learns that the abundance his magical purse brings him serves only to awaken the envy and hostility of others ("Fortunati" 622–26). Moreover, in Chamisso's dramatic fragment the lesson Fortunatus passes down to his sons along with his magic purse and magic hat, his *Wunschhütlein* that spirits him away to any place he wishes, is that if he were faced once more with the choice between infinite wisdom and boundless wealth he would select the former (604). This theme of retrospective contrition, already present in the chapbook, is also symptomatic of the transformation Peter Schlemihl undergoes in Chamisso's novella. Even the nature of his conversion, from wealth to scientific wisdom, remains constant. But a further crucial lesson is still lacking for the protagonist of Chamisso's novella: he must learn to embrace limitation and practice the virtues of temperance and moderation, and as a result he acquires not the *infinite* wisdom Fortuna offers Fortunatus in the legend, but only a "mere fragment [*bloßes Fragment*]" of a larger, unattainable whole (*Schlemihl* 73).

Following his orgy of monetary excess and his subsequent dream about the mortified botanist Chamisso, Schlemihl begins to view his golden superabundance as a disgusting supersatiety: "With anger and disgust [*Überdruß*] I pushed aside this gold, with which just a short time earlier I had satiated my foolish heart; and now, in my annoyance, I had no idea how to dispose of it" (31). The German term *Überdruß*, which the narrator uses here to describe his feelings regarding this abundance of gold, suggests both disgust and excess. Because in this exaggerated form his "satiety" has metamorphosed into dissatisfaction, Schlemihl attempts to undo the immoderate actions he committed in his state of intoxicating exuberance by stuffing some of the gold back into the magic purse. But this proves impossible, since the moneybag refuses to accept back what it once generated: "I tried to get the bag to devour it [the gold] once more—to no avail" (31). The gold Schlemihl amassed in his fit of greed is thereby transformed from a blessing to a curse: it has become a burden that can only be diminished by being wantonly spent. If in the orgiastic spawning of his mountain of gold Schlemihl succumbs to a fit of monetary propagation, the consequence is that he is now condemned to liberate himself from the burden of this gold in fits of lavish expenditure. He converts his endless supply of gold into an infinite number of valuable commodities: "I accommodated myself and purchased above all many expensive commodities and precious jewels, just in order to get rid of some of my stockpiled gold. But it didn't seem possible to make even the slightest dent in this pile" (31–32). The logic of his actions is as compelling as it is paradoxical: the excessive value of his stockpiled gold can most quickly be diminished by trading it away for luxury items like precious gems, which themselves are commodities that manifest excessive and, in pragmatic and existential terms, *useless* value. The wealth Schlemihl gains with such ease, he blithely expends in a gesture of grandiose magnanimity. The paradox here is that the very quality that makes gold such a valuable substance and such a practical monetary instrument, its ability to *preserve* and *store* value, becomes the very basis of its burdensomeness. The only way to counteract this preservationist aspect of gold is to *spend* it. Schlemihl thus turns to the systematic disbursement of his wealth. This drive reaches its peak when he falls in love with Mina, the daughter of a forester, after being mistaken for an aristocrat traveling incognito.

In his guise as the mysterious Count Peter, Schlemihl throws a grand garden party that is in many respects comparable to the one he had earlier attended at the house of Herr John, where he met the Gray Man. To be sure, in contrast to the bright daylight in which Herr John holds his party, Schlemihl must celebrate at night so as to conceal his shadowlessness (41). The purpose of this feast is to help him win over the hearts and minds of Mina and her parents, and after designating her as "queen" of the ball he choreographs a scene in which his superabundant wealth is distributed among the attending guests and the general populace.

> I myself was in a state of indescribable intoxication [*Rausch*]. I had all the jewels I had purchased, just so as to get rid of some of my burdensome gold, all the pearls, all the precious stones, placed into two covered bowls; and during dinner they were distributed in the name of the queen among her friends and the ladies present. Meanwhile, gold was incessantly thrown among the joyous populace in quantities that exceeded all accepted limits. (42)

Schlemihl has in effect enacted a modern version of the potlatch, the practice of excessively lavish giving practiced in certain archaic societies (Mauss 37–42). The intoxication (*Rausch*) with which he now expends his wealth is the perfect counterpart to the Dionysian orgy in which it was produced. Moreover, the explicit statement that he distributes his gold in quantities that transcend the socially and economically established bounds of normal expenditure reinforces the fact that this is a gesture of extravagant waste. We have already examined the reasons why Schlemihl's potlatch will not ultimately win him the respect and obligation he desires and with which, according to Marcel Mauss, the potlatch was traditionally associated (39–40): exuberant spending under the conditions of infinite wealth does *not* represent a sacrifice. It is, we might say, waste for waste's sake— since that is the only way Schlemihl can get rid of what he calls his "burdensome gold." But under these conditions, extravagant spending does not win the spender the obligation and social respect of those who are the recipients of his gifts.

Even this exorbitant spending spree is not enough to free Schlemihl from the curse of his profusion of gold. His faithful servant Bendel, who "had grown accustomed to considering my [Schlemihl's] wealth as inexhaustible" and who, as a result, "does not spy around to discover its source" (42), must be enlisted in helping Schlemihl think up ever new ways of disposing of his gold: "Accommodating himself to my intentions, he [Bendel] assisted me . . . in devising ways . . . to waste [*vergeuden*] my gold" (42). The narrator's language is extraordinarily clear here: it takes the creative imagination of at least *two* individuals to think up enough opportunities to *waste* (*vergeuden*) the ungodly sums of gold Schlemihl has at his disposal. To be sure, as long as his shadowlessness remains undiscovered, Schlemihl can exploit his ability to buy himself power and respect. Not surprisingly, at this point in his story when he is at the peak of his social distinction, Schlemihl can assure Bendel, upon giving him a treasury of jewels and gold to assist him on his mission of discovering the whereabouts of the Gray Man, that wealth "levels many paths and makes many things easier" (33). Only much later will he temper this statement with the claim that "gold can't accomplish everything" (50). As Count Peter, however, he has set his sights considerably higher than just a leveling of paths: he strategically employs his excessive wealth as a means for garnering social power and mastery over others. He admits, for example, that in the region in which he has taken up residence he can be credited with having created "many good-for-nothings and idlers" (43). Others, at least, seem to be able to profit without negative consequences from Schlemihl's wealth—unless, of course, we view good-for-nothings and idlers as incarnations of nonproductivity, and hence as inherently objectionable. But what is most significant is the manner in which Schlemihl becomes aware that his power over others is closely related to the extravagance of expenditure and waste that his magic purse makes possible: it is his "princely opulence and wastefulness [*Verschwendung*]" that permits him to "subjugate everyone and everything" (43). Opulence and wastefulness become the very symbols of his life in the disguise of the seemingly all-powerful Count Peter.

One of the most bitter ironies of this tale, which is so replete with ironic turns, is that this very need to find ever-new forms of expenditure and waste ultimately leads to Count Peter's downfall. Schlemihl is in the very midst of his desperate attempts to rid himself of his excessive gold when Bendel confronts him with the fact that his other servant, Rascal—*nomen est omen*—is embezzling gold by the bagful. Yet Schlemihl takes this news very lightly: "'Let us,' I replied, 'grant that scoundrel his meager booty; I contribute my wealth to everyone else, why not to him as well?'" (42). Schlemihl views Rascal's theft as especially opportune, since he chalks up these losses as additional relief from his burdensome oversupply of gold. But Rascal will live up to his name and use the considerable wealth he diverts from Schlemihl's infinite resources to work against and undermine the intentions of his master. Thus when Schlemihl gives Mina's father—in an attempt to distract him and keep him busy—enough gold to purchase real estate with the value of "about a million" (46), this project is hampered because someone else, who finally turns out to be none other than Rascal (58), has already bought up all the best properties. The irony of this entire episode is that where Schlemihl, due to his missing shadow, cannot win over Mina and her father, Rascal, despite his moral turpitude, succeeds; not only does he get the girl, but he becomes a "rich and respected man" (57).

How can we explain the fact that Rascal, the absolute villain, succeeds where Schlemihl, the dupe of "fortune," fails? The simplest answer, of course, is that Schlemihl has no shadow, whereas Rascal has "an unimpeachable [*untadlichen*] shadow" (58). To be sure, Rascal will eventually get his due: we learn much later that he lost both his life and most of his wealth as the result of a criminal trial (77). But his short-term success must have some justification beyond the simple ironic juxtaposition he provides to Schlemihl's case. It is Mina's father who articulates the exact formula of Rascal's success. In the dialogue with his wife in which he justifies having promised Mina to Rascal, he first enumerates the various facets of Rascal's tremendous—but decidedly finite—fortune: he owns properties valued at six million, free of all debt, and a promissory note from none other than Thomas John to the tune of 4½ million. But when his wife objects that Rascal obtained this wealth by illicit and illegal means, the forester vehemently contradicts her: "'What are you talking about! He [Rascal] merely saved where others were being wasteful [*verschwendet wurde*]'" (58). In the context of Schlemihl's immoderate wastefulness, Rascal's cautious thriftiness appears as a grand virtue that overshadows his many vices.[19] The very irrationality of Schlemihl's intemperate expenditures creates the conditions in which the prudent frugality manifest in Rascal's strategy can be viewed as the paragon of economic rationality. This represents a significant juncture in this text, then, one at which Schlemihl's shadowlessness, as the ostensible cause of his failure, is most closely aligned with an economic practice centered on excess and wastefulness as the *true* cause of his downfall. In spite of his moral degeneracy, Rascal actually comes away as the standard-bearer for a rational economics that holds up thrift, prudence, wise investment, and moderation as its cardinal virtues.

When his utopian dream, concretized in his plans to marry Mina, collapses, Schlemihl takes to the road again, now a broken man. All his attempts to set down roots and establish a life of respected wealth and stable social relations have failed due to the excessive productivity and the concomitant reflex of exorbitant expenditure represented by the magic purse.[20] As he begins his journey once more, Schlemihl encounters another traveler who accompanies him for part of his way and expounds his own personal worldview.

> He laid out for me his views of life and the world, and soon came to a discussion of metaphysics, whose task it was to discover the single word that would provide the solution for all riddles. He expounded upon the problem with great clarity and then moved on to its resolution. (63)

As we know, this well-spoken, inherently persuasive philosophical fellow traveler turns out to be none other than the Gray Man himself (64). Yet even if the narrator did not tell us this, we would be able to draw this conclusion simply on the basis of what this wayfarer says. For the theory of metaphysics he outlines here, in which a single word will provide the key that resolves all the riddles of the world, is obviously nothing other than the philosophical counterpart to the magic purse. If the *Glücksseckel* represents that single object capable of generating absolute monetary wealth and hence of providing unlimited access to all the commodities of the vast colonial marketplace, the metaphysical "word" serves a parallel function in the "economy" of philosophical problems.

Chamisso is clearly alluding here, as scholars have generally recognized (see, e.g., Blamberger 116; Pavlyshyn 54), to various metaphysical-philosophical projects pursued by the German Romantics. Because Schlemihl eventually turns to the empirical study of the natural world, this reference to transcendental metaphysics is most commonly read as a critique of Romantic *Naturphilosophie*, with its holistic, highly speculative, and total-izing approach to nature. Viewed in this context, the single word that would ground this overarching metaphysical system would be something like the *Weltseele*, the "world soul," propounded by the Romantic philosopher Friedrich Wilhelm Joseph von Schelling (1775–1854), the founder of German *Naturphilosophie*.[21] But one could refer just as well to the philosophical system developed by Johann Gottlieb Fichte (1762–1814) in his *Wissenschaftslehre* (Doctrine of science), which he developed in various versions between 1794 and 1810. In Fichte's scientific system it is the self-aware-ness of the "I" that becomes the founding principle upon which all other tenets of human knowledge are predicated. Chamisso's association of such hierarchical transcendental systems, based purely on speculative princi-ples, with the empty rhetoric of the devil, on the one hand, and with the perverse economy of excess and waste, on the other, must thus be read as a more general parody of German philosophical idealism itself.[22] Even more significant, however, is that Chamisso was one of the very first crit-ics of economic practice to link the role of money in the systematic econ-omy of the modern commodity to the function of the transcendental grounding principle in idealist philosophy. This is a line of thought that has been developed more fully in recent years, in the wake of Marx's eco-nomic and Freud's psychoanalytic theories, in the critical work of Jean-Joseph Goux.[23]

In one of the letters he wrote shortly before his death, dated 9 June 1838 and addressed to his friend de la Foye, Chamisso claims that his ulti-mate *Glaubensbekenntnis*, his "confession of faith," is contained in the opening passages of the eighth chapter in *Peter Schlemihls wundersame Geschichte* (*Werke* 6: 255). The reference is clearly to the paragraph imme-diately following the above-cited exposition of the devil's view of meta-physics, where Schlemihl interrupts his story to relate his own reflections on the inadequacy of the metaphysical perspective. It is worth quoting this paragraph at some length, since it sheds considerable light not only on what Chamisso claimed was his own set of beliefs, but on the transfor-mation that occurs in his fictional hero Peter Schlemihl when he abandons his magic purse and turns his attention to the empirical study of nature.

You know, my friend, that after having studied the philosophers I have
clearly recognized that I have no calling for philosophical speculation,
and I have renounced this field completely. Since that time I have let
many things pass, I have *abstained* [*Verzicht geleistet*] from trying to
know and comprehend everything; and trusting, as far as was in my
power, in my own honest sensibilities, in my own inner voice, just as you
advised me, I have followed my own path. Now this rhetorician seemed
to me to be constructing, with uncommon talent, a firmly built edifice
that rose up on its own foundation and stood as if through its own inner
necessity. Yet it entirely lacked precisely what I would have sought to
discover in such an edifice, and as a result it became for me a mere work
of artifice whose elegant closure and perfection served the titillation
of the eye alone. (63–64; emphasis added)

In this passage the narrator Peter Schlemihl, who has abandoned his
earlier life of excess and waste by jettisoning the moneybag, speaks from
the heart and with a retrospective gaze. His critique of the Gray Man's
philosophical system as a carefully fashioned structure ostensibly complete
unto itself, as a totality whose singular coherence resides in a principle of
inner necessity, eventually culminates in the recognition that such perfection is nothing but a piece of artifice, titillating in its surface design, but
devoid of any true substance. What Chamisso voices here is not simply a
critique of the sand castles of transcendental philosophy, but of the entire
edifice of idealist aesthetics, with its insistence on the harmony, organic
integrity, and perfection of the whole. We will see at the conclusion of the
current chapter what kind of aesthetic theory Schlemihl/Chamisso would
substitute for this aesthetic idealism. But it is just as important for an understanding of the economic substructure of this novella that we read this critique as applicable to the economy of excess and waste to which its
protagonist Peter Schlemihl succumbs in that part of his life recounted in
chapters 1 through 7. Indeed, Schlemihl's experiences in this phase of his
existence demonstrate precisely that an economy of boundless production
and endless consumption is nothing but a deceptively beautiful theoretical
edifice that is destined to collapse—as it does for Schlemihl—as soon as
one tries to put it into economic practice. The utopia of absolute bounty,
plenitude, and rapturous expenditure is precisely that: a utopia that has

no rational grounding in the natural world in which modern Europeans live. The lesson Schlemihl extrapolates from his earlier failures is expressed in relation to his newfound scientific studies, which replace his greedy pursuit of wealth and happiness: it is the lesson of *Verzicht leisten*, of self-denial, abstention, renunciation, and doing-without. Schlemihl learns, in his own words, to "let things pass," to "abstain from trying to know and comprehend everything," and to "trust" in his "own inner voice."

The devil never ceases to hanker after possession of Schlemihl's soul, clearly the most valuable commodity in his own hellish economics of excess.[24] Indeed, what ultimately joins Schlemihl and the Gray Man in an indissoluble union is not so much their initial act of exchange, but that the one "commodity" or value that neither can produce on his own is the one his heart most desires: for the devil this is Schlemihl's soul; for Schlemihl it is his ever-evanescent shadow. Thus the devil, too, will ultimately fail to attain what he most desires.[25] But before he concedes defeat, he makes one last attempt to take hold of Schlemihl's most precious possession.

> He [the Gray Man] painted for me, as he often did, *with lavishly wasteful imagination* [*mit verschwenderischer Einbildungskraft*] and with the tantalizing allure of *the most glowing colors* [*der glänzendsten Farben*], carefully executed images of what I could accomplish in the world, by dint of the power of my magic purse, if only I could gain possession of my shadow once more. (66; emphasis added)

The Gray Man's most effective weapons, his "lavishly wasteful imagination" and his powerfully evocative, if bombastic and grandiloquent rhetoric, continually fail to win over Schlemihl, who has gradually learned to listen more intently, as he says, to his own inner voice. The qualities associated in this passage with the devil's imagination—it is "lavishly wasteful"—and his language—it paints pictures in the "most glowing colors"—are none other than the attributes identified with the infinite productivity and extravagance of the *Glücksseckel* itself. The Gray Man is the embodiment of these various economies of excess: the economic, the philosophical, the rhetorical, the aesthetic. The *Glanz*, or glitter of Schlemihl's gold (30), like the aura (*Glanz*) of Herr Thomas John (23), is nothing other than a refraction of the "most glowing colors" (*glänzendsten Farben*) of the Gray Man's hollow metaphysical-aesthetic edifice. Economic, philosophical, and aesthetic "speculation"—we need to recall the visual metaphor from which this term derives—prove to be the real shadows in the life of the shadowless Schlemihl. However, as his story proves, it takes genuine will power to resist the seductive semblances conjured up by the devil himself; and only when he attends to the inner voice that speaks to him of the virtues of limitation, self-denial, and moderation is Schlemihl finally able to get the devil off his back. This new life guided by limitation and temperance is codified in Schlemihl's turn to the empirical study of nature.

In order to understand the divergence between Schlemihl's life of excess and extravagant waste under the spell of the magic purse, on the one hand, and his life of asceticism as a wandering botanist, on the other, we need to return briefly to the early scene in which the Gray Man catalogs the objects he can offer in trade for Schlemihl's shadow. After listing a series of magical objects known from fairy tales, he hits upon the two treasures the goddess Fortuna gave Fortunatus in the chapbook of that name: *Fortunati Wunschhütlein*, a hat that transports its wearer to any place he desires, and *Fortunati Glücksseckel*, the infamous magic purse that Schlemihl ultimately chooses (28–29). To the best of my knowledge, it has thus far escaped the attention of scholars that the *Wunschhütlein*, the magic hat, is actually an analogue of the seven-league boots that provide the condition of possibility for Schlemihl's later botanical studies. But when the magic hat, which permits *unlimited* travel, is replaced by the seven-league boots, an important transformation has occurred: these boots introduce the element of *limitation*, which is fundamental to Schlemihl's general worldview as well as to his scientific practice in his profession as botanist. As opposed to the magic hat, an *unrestricted* transporter, these boots enforce upon their bearer an ideology of *Verzicht leisten*, of cautious circumscription and renunciation.

The very manner in which Schlemihl acquires his seven-league boots underscores the central issue of self-denial and limitation that dominates the last several chapters of the novella, in which Schlemihl's life as a botanist is recounted. In desperate need of new shoes, Schlemihl seeks out a market fair in a small town where in one booth new and used boots are offered for sale.

> I was in need of a new pair of boots. The next morning I attended earnestly to this business in a small village where a fair was being held, and where in one booth old and new boots were offered for sale. I selected and bargained for a long time. I had to *deny myself* [*Verzicht leisten*] a pair of new boots I would have liked to own; I was deterred by the extravagant price. I thus had to make do with a pair of used ones that were yet good and solid. (70; emphasis added)

This is the first time in Schlemihl's account of his life where he admits to being "deterred by the extravagant price"; previously, price had been of no consequence whatsoever. The drawn-out process of negotiation with the merchant is also something foreign to Schlemihl's experience. The central element of this passage is the notion of *Verzicht leisten*, learning to do without, to deny oneself something, or to abstain. We recall that it was this very same phrase that Schlemihl used when describing what motivated him to reject excessive metaphysical speculation and accept limitations in his drive for knowledge (see above, and *Schlemihl* 63). This, then, is the primary lesson that separates Peter Schlemihl the botanist, who then narrates his life story, from the Peter Schlemihl of the first seven chapters of that autobiography, who is hopelessly addicted to the luxury, extravagance, and ostentation provided by the Gray Man. If this infinitely longing Peter Schlemihl is a Faust-like figure driven by the immoderate desire for the limitless, the later Peter Schlemihl is a kind of anti-Faust who has learned to accept and even appreciate limitation.[26] The positive *value* of such limitation is brought out by the fact that Schlemihl is richly rewarded for his painful decision to forgo the expensive new boots and opt instead for used, worn ones. The secondhand boots he acquires turn out unexpectedly to have magic properties of their own: they are seven-league boots that miraculously transport their bearer in giant leaps across *almost* any terrain.

This exchange for an object with magical powers, which marks the beginning of this second phase of Schlemihl's autobiography, stands in obvious contrast to the exchange for the magic purse that ushered in his period of addiction to excess. Careful deliberation and a process of rational choice, with an eye for limitation, characterize the second purchase, whereas the first is entered into spontaneously and without foresight and cautious reflection. In this sense the events of Schlemihl's life do not simply lambaste an economics of excess, but actually celebrate one that is tempered by rational moderation and insight into the necessity of limitation. Indeed, one of the overriding consequences of Schlemihl's shadowlessness is that, even as he is blessed by boundless monetary abundance, he must incessantly confront his own limitations. Ultimately, this is the contradictory state into which Chamisso throws his protagonist when he introduces the intermediary stage of shadowlessness into the traditional Faustian pact with the devil.[27] Throughout this phase Schlemihl is caught in the tension between absolute material satisfaction, on the one hand, and his debilitating social limitations, due to his lack of a shadow, on the other. Final resolution can only come when Schlemihl opts to devote his life to one or the other of these poles. The devil wagers, of course, on Schlemihl's willingness to sell out to excess and extravagant material luxury; but he loses this wager when Schlemihl instead learns to honor the virtues of limitation and self-denial, made manifest both when he rejects the magic purse and when he embraces the restrictions enforced upon him by his seven-league boots.

The magic boots Schlemihl acquires are the functional counterpart to the *Wunschhütlein* for which he did *not* trade his shadow; but in contrast to the magic hat, which transports its bearer to any place he desires, the boots have specific limitations. There are certain places to which Schlemihl cannot travel by virtue of his boots alone. As a result, he is hindered in his attempts to explore the entire globe and catalog all botanical species.

> From the Malacca peninsula my boots took me to Sumatra, Java, Bali, and Lamboc. I attempted, often even placing myself in grave danger, and yet always in vain, to find a northwest passage across the tiny islands and rock outcroppings, with which this ocean is studded, to Borneo and the other islands of this archipelago. I was forced to abandon any hope. . . . I was prevented from visiting New Holland [i.e., Australia], that extraordinary country so essential for an understanding of the earth, its sun-drenched cloak, and its plant and animal life; the same was true

for the South Sea with its Zoophyte islands. Thus from the very outset everything I hoped to collect and construct was condemned to remain a mere fragment. (73)

The same Peter Schlemihl who sought to make his mark in the social world by ever more extravagant modes of spending has now become a gatherer and collector of simple botanical samples. However, if he had any ambitions of achieving a *totalizing* catalog of all the plants found across the globe, then this hope is doomed to frustration by the restrictions placed upon him by his seven-league boots. His empirical studies are destined to remain fragmentary, which means that he will never be in the position to gain a theoretical overview over the entirety of the botanical world. This also means that he will be prevented from compiling a systematic, hierarchically ordered taxonomy of all extant plants. In other words, his scientific project will always be distinct from the totalizing metaphysical enterprise to which the Gray Man gives voice, and which, as we have seen, has its structural parallel in the economics of excess and extravagant expenditure made possible by the magic purse. In his scientific studies, Schlemihl must learn to accept limitation without, however, succumbing to debilitating resignation. The position he assumes is one of compromise and rational moderation.

The positive character of specific constraints or limitations is highlighted by the motif of the "brake shoes" Schlemihl must place over his boots in order to restrict the distance they carry him. Only once they have been outfitted so that they are more fully under their wearer's control do the seven-league boot become appropriate instruments in the service of empirical scientific exploration. When Schlemihl begins to assemble the paraphernalia and tools necessary for his botanical studies, the very first matter he addresses is the problem of brake shoes for his boots, "for I had experienced how uncomfortable it was not to be able to shorten my stride, in order to investigate near-by objects at leisure, except by taking off my boots. A pair of slippers [*Pantoffeln*], pulled over my boots, had just the effect I hoped for" (74). Restriction is no longer a foible one must seek to overcome; on the contrary, it has become a virtue to be sought out and cultivated. The image of the slippers pulled over Schlemihl's seven-league boots—this is, we should note, how he appears to the fictional Chamisso when he delivers to him the manuscript of *Peter Schlemihls wundersame Geschichte* (18)—encapsulates the message that one must consciously attempt to "shorten" one's stride. To be sure, the fact that this limiting effect is achieved by donning house slippers (*Pantoffeln*) adds an ironic tinge to this motif. House shoes had become for the Romantics the concrete symbol with which they satirized the bourgeois philistine who avoided all adventures of the spirit, preferring instead to remain in the safety and comfort of the bourgeois private sphere.[28] What Schlemihl achieves, however, is a kind of perfect compromise between the absolute limitation associated with the stayed mentality of the philistine and the adventuresomeness of the world explorer. Moderation and temperance are clearly the message intended by the motif of the slippers as brake shoes.

Even as a scientific hermit, Schlemihl is bound up with the social world through forms of exchange, in particular commercial exchange. The remnants of the "magical gold" (74) he finds in his pocket do not suffice to equip him with all the rudimentary scientific instruments he requires. As a substitute for gold, he turns to African ivory as his new method of payment: "When the remainder of my magical gold was exhausted, I brought along as payment African ivory, which was easy to find; to be sure, I had to choose the smallest tusks, those whose weight did not exceed my own strength" (74). Throughout *Schlemihl*, money occurs consistently in its elementary form as pure natural commodity: there is never any mention, for example, even of minted coins, let alone of paper currency.[29] In this regard, it is consistent that both before and after Schlemihl's conversion to the doctrine of temperance he relies on naturally occurring objects as his monetary vehicle. Moreover, the relative ease with which he can obtain African ivory brings this resource into proximity with the gold of the magic purse, which was always available in infinite supply. Yet the available quantities of African ivory are not unlimited—less so even today than in Chamisso's time. But ivory, as opposed to gold, is theoretically a renewable resource, since it is a biological product, not a mineral. More important, however, is that ivory does not represent as great a concentration of wealth as does gold, so that it is necessary to exchange it in larger quantities in order to achieve the same value as a small piece of this precious metal. In this sense, ivory is by nature a more limiting monetary material than gold, and this restrictive aspect is reflected in Schlemihl's comment that he was confined to using the smallest tusks, that is, those he had the strength to carry, for his monetary exchanges. Viewed in juxtaposition to ivory as monetary substance, what stands out about the gold of the magic purse is precisely the *unnaturalness* of its boundless productivity. It is, after all, the natural qualities of ivory, its bulk and weight, that restrict Schlemihl's use of it as a monetary commodity,[30] and natural limitation is also what places constraints on the usefulness of his seven-league boots.

Although Schlemihl's existence after he casts off the magic purse is marked above all by the ascetic lifestyle of the quasi-Christian hermit (72), small symbolic reminiscences of his previous life of lavish intemperance remain. These are his tobacco pipe and the black poodle that is his sole companion. "For lack of fortune [*Glück*]," Schlemihl remarks, "I had nicotine as a surrogate, and as a substitute for human compassion and company I had the love of my faithful poodle" (75). The "lack of fortune" (*Glück*) that Schlemihl laments contains a veiled reference to the *Glücksseckel* he tossed into the abyss. In his newfound life of abstinence, the only token reminder of his past days of "fortune" and orgiastic excess is his addiction to nicotine. It stands in here as the placeholder of his earlier delirious addiction to the aura of gold and the commodities and social respect it ostensibly could procure. Once again, it is not absolute renunciation, but a path of compromising moderation that Schlemihl now exemplifies. Similarly, the poodle represents his previous drive to enter into the intimacies of human community—symbolized in the plan to marry Mina—and enjoy the respect of his fellow human beings. Because, as Schlemihl himself admits, he "was banished from human society" due to his own "early fault [*Schuld*]" (72)—the German word *Schuld*, as we have seen, has the implications of guilt as well as of monetary indebtedness—he must now seek surrogate forms of satisfaction in nature. The poodle is just one of those substitute forms of satisfaction, as are his botanical studies. But what characterizes all of Schlemihl's pursuits after his rejection of the excesses of infinite wealth is moderation, temperance, limitation.

This is the *nützlichen Lehre*, the "useful maxim" (79), that can be drawn from Schlemihl's story: that excessive production and consumption are *unnatural*, and that as such they lead down the path to debauchery. This, after all, is the conclusion Schlemihl himself draws as he reflects in retrospect on the "precipitous moral lapsus" that called down upon him the "curse" of his shadowlessness (59).

> Dear friend, whoever carelessly places just one foot outside the path of the straight and narrow is unwittingly led down other paths that draw him ever further downward. In vain he sees the lodestars shining in the sky; he has no choice but to descend irrevocably into the abyss and sacrifice himself to the Nemesis. (59)

But Schlemihl manages to escape this downward spiral, not only by refusing to sell his soul to the devil, but by resisting the final sell out to material excess that would be represented by his possession of the magic purse *as well as* a shadow. This fate is sufficiently prefigured for him by Herr Thomas John, whose condemned shade the Gray Man produces as but one more commodity out of his deep pocket (68). By contrast, the road to happiness is paved by the awareness of the need for self-denial, renunciation, and abstention. To cite once more the words of the Good Spirit in Chamisso's fragmentary Faust drama: *lern entbehren,* "learn to do without" (*Sämtliche Werke* 1: 400). That is the lesson at which the character Peter Schlemihl arrives, and he passes it on to his friend Chamisso as the message of his autobiography, *Peter Schlemihls wundersame Geschichte.*

Peter Schlemihl *as Critique of a Poetics of Excess*

In his defense of the principle of loss and extravagant waste as fundamental psychological human needs, Georges Bataille refers to social revolution as "a bloody and in no way limited social expenditure" that ultimately has positive redemptive results for the social and political organism ("Notion of Expenditure" 121). Those who have experienced such brutal revolutions may disagree with Bataille's conclusion about the ultimate benefits of exorbitant social loss. It is worth recalling, however, that Chamisso wrote *Schlemihl* during the devastating wars unleashed by Napoleon that wracked the European continent for nearly two decades and that Chamisso himself, as an officer in the Prussian military, took part in the struggle against the French invaders. If Bataille is correct in his assessment that the bourgeoisie hates nothing more than excessive expenditure and waste, regardless of whether it occurs in the economic, sociopolitical, or intellectual domains (124), then Chamisso, despite his aristocratic birth, was a bourgeois par excellence.

A critique of luxury and waste runs like a red thread throughout Chamisso's life, reaching its culmination in the searing attack on excess and extravagant expenditure expressed in *Schlemihl*. As early as February 1806, in a letter addressed to his friend Karl August Varnhagen von Ense (1785–1858), Chamisso praises the modesty of his lifestyle in the military and contrasts it to the luxury he witnesses in his friend's way of living. "I have proven by experience that straw makes a good bed, and that one is nourished by bread alone; this is no cause for worry. But I have seen you in zealous pursuit of luxury, and at times even succumbing to wastefulness [*Verschwendung*]—and *that* gives me cause for worry" (*Werke* 5: 135). These are words that could issue from the mouth of Peter Schlemihl himself once he has accepted his ascetic life of limitation, existing as a hermit who has dedicated himself to the empirical study of nature. Austerity stands as a positive value that contrasts starkly with opulence and wastefulness. Similarly, in a letter to de la Foye dated June 1825, Chamisso denounces splendor (*Prunk*) as the "epidemic of our age" (*Werke* 6: 212). But Chamisso does not view waste and excess as narrowly restricted to the realm of economics. To de la Foye he writes in October 1824, for example, an excoriating denunciation of the Prussian government for its tendency to "be wasteful [*verschwenden*] to the point at which everything breaks down" (*Werke* 6: 207). Extravagant wastefulness thus appears to Chamisso to be a general characteristic of his age, one against which he feels the need to raise his voice.

Viewed against the backdrop of the history of economics, the composition of *Schlemihl* in 1813 represents that moment in which a critique of luxury and excess in the domain of economics, like that expressed most vociferously by the French and German physiocrats, explodes into a more universal and generalized denunciation of an "economics" of excess that touches all the dimensions of intellectual culture: philosophy, aesthetics, poetry, science. Schlemihl's condemnation of the Gray Man's devilish metaphysics, as we have seen, can be read inclusively as a debunking of transcendental philosophy, of Romantic *Naturphilosophie* as one of the most prominent trends in natural science of the day,[31] and of an idealist aesthetic theory that stresses the principles of harmony and organic totality. We should not be surprised, then, that when Schlemihl delineates the scientific methodology that guides his empirical research, and that stands as a positive countermodel to the speculative metaphysical theory propounded by the Gray Man, this reads more like an *artistic* program or an *aesthetic* theory than it does a scientific or philosophical procedure. Describing how he came to devote himself to his botanical studies, Schlemihl writes,

> It was not a decision that I consciously made. But what appeared then before my inner eye as a bright and perfect original image [*Urbild*], I have since sought to portray accurately with quiet, rigorous, unremitting diligence, and my satisfaction depends entirely on the convergence of this portrayal with that original mental image [*Urbild*]. (72)

If we take this as a serious expression of Schlemihl's—Chamisso's?—aesthetic program,[32] then we would be hard pressed to include him among the generation of Romantic poets with which he is commonly identified. What Schlemihl outlines here is more a strategic program for a poetics of realism than for Romantic self-reflexivity and exuberant imagination. This has led several critics to suggest that *Schlemihl* marks a transition in German literary history from Romanticism to the various forms of realism that followed.[33] To be sure, the consistent application of empirical methodologies similar to those Schlemihl advances for his botanical studies is the hallmark of realistic literature. Moreover, what Schlemihl defends in this metacommentary on his own method is nothing other than a rather traditional theory of exact artistic mimesis, the closest possible overlap between *Urbild*, or "original image," and artistic copy. Of course, in Schlemihl's description it is not *reality* that serves as the primordial image that must be imitated, but rather a picture generated by the mind or the imagination—the "inner eye." In this sense Schlemihl's theory might be regarded as a kind of compromise between the extravagant fantasies of the Romantics and the mimetic accuracy of realism: the artist applies realistic methodologies so as to portray the products of the imagination, a practice that brings Chamisso's novella into proximity with the works of Kafka (Weigand

211). This explains why Schlemihl places so much emphasis on the diligence (*Fleiß*) invested in his portrayals and makes his own satisfaction with the final product a function of an accurate representation. It is important to recall here that Schlemihl earlier criticized the Gray Man for the exuberant wastefulness of his imagination—his *verschwenderische Einbildungskraft* (66). This critique could be applied just as aptly to the authors of German Romanticism, and perhaps this is what Chamisso had in mind when, in a letter to Karl Bernhard von Trinius in August 1822, he reproached E. T. A. Hoffmann, as representative of German literature, for mixing water with his ink (*Werke* 6: 192). Spreading one's ink too thinly, making it go too far and flow too quickly, is just another form of inflationary excess. How can one best tame a wild imagination? Chamisso's answer seems to be: by subjecting it to the exacting principles of mimesis. Mimesis, in other words, constitutes the *Hemmschuh*, the "brake shoe," for an imagination that threatens to be excessively, extravagantly productive. In this regard, the artistic or poetic purpose of *Schlemihl* might be viewed as the task of proving that it *is*, in fact, possible to paint a shadow. We recall that one of Schlemihl's strategies for hiding his shadowlessness was to hire a painter to create a fake shadow for him, but that this project was condemned to failure (35). And yet Schlemihl's defense of a mimetic depiction of visions generated by the "inner eye" of the imagination seems to promote just such a realistic and dynamic representation of something that is inherently intangible. This would seem to be, in the final analysis, the aesthetic program Chamisso valorizes and puts into practice in *Peter Schlemihls wundersame Geschichte*.

Among the cultural products Bataille identifies with the human need for excess and extravagant waste are all forms of art, whereby he differentiates between two distinct types of expenditure, actual and symbolic. Architecture, music, and dance, for example, require *actual* expenditures, whereas other art forms, poetry and literature in particular, represent expenditure in its largely symbolic variant ("Notion of Expenditure" 119–20). Indeed, for Bataille, poetry is "in the most precise way, creation by means of loss," a characteristic that brings it into close proximity with the notion of sacrifice (120). No literary scholar has sought to apply more consistently Bataille's argument about a poetics of excess to the nuts and bolts of literary interpretation than Jochen Hörisch. In his brilliant examination

of the confluences between the economics of money and German literature, *Heads or Tails*, he attempts to demonstrate the many ways in which
literature takes sides with excess as a way of criticizing the institution of
money (147). The primary spokesperson for this linkage between poetics
and extravagant expenditure is the figure of *Knabe Lenker*, the boy charioteer, from part 2 of Goethe's *Faust*: "I am that spendthrift [*Verschwendung*], poetry; / as poet I augment my worth / by squandering [*verschwendet*]
my very substance" (lines 5573–75).[34] This may be a maxim that applies
very well to a work of literature as extravagant and excessive as part 2 of
Faust, but it is by no means clear that it holds for every poetic work that
treats the problematic of money.

Schlemihl, it seems to me, provides an example of a major poetic work
that deals with an economic thematic but does *not* criticize the limiting
power of scarcity from the perspective of excess and wasteful expenditure.
Indeed, as I have sought to demonstrate throughout the chapters of this
book, literary and cultural responses to economic theory and practice are
as varied as these theories themselves and cannot be reduced to any single
common denominator. Chamisso's *Schlemihl* thus represents a historically
specific critical engagement with the economics of commodity capitalism
at the moment when it was being fueled from two major sources: emerging
industrialization, on the one hand, and the burgeoning market of colonial
goods, on the other. Against this backdrop Chamisso plays out the inherent paradoxes of an economics of excessive production and exorbitant
consumption. Moreover, he demonstrates the ways in which the perverse
proclivity for excess carries over from economics into diverse spheres of
intellectual and cultural production. If Romanticism did in fact represent
a poetics of excess, then Chamisso diagnoses the principles underlying the
overproductive Romantic imagination as reflecting a debauched economics of excess, to which he opposes an economics and a *poetics* of scarcity,
limitation, abstention, cautious mimetic control, and self-denial. In other
words, *Schlemihl* is not merely a vehicle for satirizing and debunking an
economics of excess, but is also one for criticizing the cultural and intellectual epiphenomena it spawns. In this sense it does not present a critique
of money and value from the perspective of an extravagant poetics; quite
the opposite, it lambastes a poetics of plenitude that proves to be *in league
with* an economics of excess and exuberant wastefulness. What is more,

this novella does not stop at voicing this critique on a thematic level; it seeks to pursue a literary practice of its own that is consistent with Schlemihl's philosophy of limitation and moderation. In this sense, *Peter Schlemihl* is indeed a classic work of bourgeois fiction, trumpeting the virtues of economic moderation, while practicing in its own discursive and aesthetic constitution a poetics that valorizes mimetic temperance as a governor for the creative imagination.

7 / RED HERRINGS AND BLUE SMOCKS

Commercialism, Ecological Destruction, and Anti-Semitism in Annette von Droste-Hülshoff's *Die Judenbuche*

[N]othing is more terrible than the logic of self-interest.

—Karl Marx ("Debatten über das Holzdiebstahlsgesetz" 130)

From the beginning it was wholly convenient to be able to find a scape-goat for the invasion of capitalism into the rural economy by appealing to the cliché of the "Jewish usurer."

—Jacob Toury (*Soziale und politische Geschichte der Juden in Deutschland* 381)

Structural and Narrative Dichotomies in Die Judenbuche

IN A LETTER TO RICHARD SCHÖNE DATED 30 OCTOBER 1890, the prominent realist prose writer Theodor Fontane (1819–98) voices a critique of Annette von Droste-Hülshoff's (1797–1848) novella *Die Judenbuche* (The Jews' beech, 1842) that perspicaciously lays out a problematic that has become a red thread for much of the subsequent criticism of this text:

Everything specifically Westphalian in this text, the portrayal of the countryside and its populace, is already better and more vividly represented in the essay "Bei uns zu Lande" and in her "Bilder aus Wesphalen";[1] and as far as her pure artistry in the genre of the novella is

concerned, I cannot rate that very highly. Of course, everything about
this work is atmospherically evocative and emotionally powerful; that
kind of plot *cannot help but* make a strong impression. But the amount
of artistry or technical skill is not outstanding. *Die Judenbuche* actually
contains two stories, and that is not an advantage for a text of a mere
fifty or sixty pages. In my opinion, the story about the uncle deserves
to be the chief story line, and then the story about the Jews would have
to be dropped. But if Annette was really concerned with bringing the
latter tale, then the preliminary events with the uncle could only be
a very short episode, not a full plot competing with the other one.
(Fontane, qtd. in Huge, *Erläuterungen und Dokumente* 63–64)

Fontane suggests that the success of Droste-Hülshoff's novella derives primarily from a felicitous choice of engaging plot lines, not from the evoca-
tiveness of its ethnographic depiction, which he sees accomplished better
in Droste-Hülshoff's more essayistic prose on Westphalia. Nor does he find
anything to praise in its technical or aesthetic composition. He implies, in
short, that *Die Judenbuche* ranks merely as an engaging piece of pulp fiction,
a good "read," as it were, and not as a first-rate work of literature. But the
substance of his critique is significant, since he attacks precisely those aspects
of the text that are often held up as exemplary: its descriptive power as
Sittengemälde, a milieu description, or as *Dorfgeschichte*, a story of rural
life, and its status as a canonical novella, one anthologized in 1876 by Paul
Heyse and Wilhelm Kurz in their influential collection *Deutscher Novel-
lenschatz* (Treasury of German novellas). Indeed, with regard to formal
issues, Fontane goes so far as to suggest that Droste-Hülshoff flagrantly
explodes the generic limitations of the novella as prose form by artificially
laminating two distinct and essentially unrelated narratives in a genre that
demands unity and concision.

Droste-Hülshoff herself seems to have pursued two distinct intentions
in creating *Die Judenbuche*. On the one hand, she tends to define this text
primarily as a *Sittengemälde*, an accurate portrayal of the mentality, customs, and lifestyle of the rural populace in the Paderborn province of Westphalia. This is underscored by the fact that she conceived this text as an
integral part of her larger ethnographic study of the Westphalian landscape
and its people, "Bei uns zu Lande auf dem Lande" (Life with us in the

Westphalian countryside), which remained unfinished upon her death. On the other hand, already in some of her earliest comments on *Die Juden-buche* Droste-Hülshoff refers to it as a crime story, a *Criminalgeschichte*, which bears the title of its central character, Friedrich Mergel.[2] To be sure, this crime story is based loosely on factual events, on the tale of a certain Hermann Winkelhannes who fled Westphalia after murdering a Jew, spent seventeen years as a slave in Algeria, and returned to Westphalia only to hang himself. Droste-Hülshoff was familiar with this story both from child-hood tales and from the written narrative recorded by her maternal uncle, Baron August von Haxthausen (1792–1866), in 1818 (Moritz 9–10; Rölleke, *Annette von Droste-Hülshoff* 111–13). But the immediate impulse behind the composition of *Die Judenbuche* stems from elsewhere, since the first notes Droste-Hülshoff composed for this text, "A forest ranger is mur-dered" (*HKA* 5.2: 256), allude not to the report about the Algerian slave, but to the narrative about wood poaching that constitutes the opening sec-tion of the novella. This gives a first indication that the events surround-ing the wood poachers is much more than a mere narrative lead-in to the story about the murder of the Jew and its consequences.

Fontane's critique of the structural and artistic constitution of *Die Juden-buche* speaks directly to this issue. His primary point is that the first half of the novella, leading up to the murder of the forest ranger Brandis, has little or no connection to the second half, the story about the murder of the Jew Aaron, Friedrich Mergel's flight, and his death by hanging in the Jews' beech. The most fundamental link between these two narratives is, of course, the identity of their shared main character, Friedrich Mergel. But "identity" is not a descriptor that is well suited to Droste-Hülshoff's protagonist, who undergoes a radical character transformation over the course of the novella. Moreover, this transformation is marked textually— one of Droste-Hülshoff's most important fictional elaborations—by sym-bolic nonidentity, codified in the introduction of Friedrich's mysterious doppelgänger, the alter ego Johannes Niemand. This occurs, significantly, at that critical moment in which Friedrich comes under the questionable tutelage of his uncle Simon Semmler (*Judenbuche* 10–11). Thus the dou-ble track of the novella's plot structure has its counterpart in the doubling of the text's main character; and the confusion about whether it is Friedrich or Johannes who eventually returns home reflects on the characterological level the structural confusion about the interrelationship between the two plots.

The lion's share of critical energy expended on *Die Judenbuche* revolves around resolving questions about the split personality of its protagonist and/or bringing the divergent threads of the bifurcated narrative into developmental relation with one another. For the most part, scholars have tended to view the second half of the text—the story surrounding the murder of the Jew Aaron, the consecration of the Jews' beech, and the flight, ultimate return, and eventual suicide of Friedrich in the branches of this consecrated beech tree—as the dominant plot. The prioritization of this segment of the novella is codified in the title *Die Judenbuche*, with which its first editor, Hermann Hauff (1800–65), baptized it. The introductory section—dealing primarily with establishing the local setting, recounting Friedrich's familial background, a description of the activities of the *Blaukittel* (Blue Smocks), a band of audacious wood thieves, and the eventual murder of the head forester Brandis by these wood poachers—is commonly relegated to the secondary status of a socially critical milieu study that merely preludes the "real" events of the religious-moral example story charted in the novella's second half.[3] But what happens if, in a text that generously deploys the technique of the red herring, constantly throwing out clues that distract the reader from pursuing a straight and easy interpretive path,[4] we read the shift away from the first narrative sequence to the second as a kind of red herring in its own right, as a diversionary tactic? The short answer is that the economically motivated murder of the forester Brandis, which symbolically parallels the murder of the Jew Aaron, now assumes a more central position. Shifting critical weight to the first part of the text has the consequence of moving the interpretive focus away from questions of guilt and innocence, crime and retribution, sin and religious grace, and concentrating instead on the marriage of economic transformation and ecological destruction that dominates the initial episodes of the story.

Recent scholarship on *Die Judenbuche* has greatly expanded our critical horizon, especially on the second plot line in the novella, by highlighting its relationship to the registers of anti-Semitic discourse prominent in nineteenth-century Germany (Chase; Doerr; Donahue; Helfer; Palmieri). At the same time, these interpretations have tended to relegate the economic issues addressed in the first half of the text to minor incidents. My reading will attempt to tie the economic, sociological, and ecological concerns of the first half of the novella with the ethical issues of the second by outlining how they are linked precisely by one of the most fundamental assumptions of anti-Semitism: the association of the Jews with the disruptive and destructive economic practices of industrial modernism.[5] Viewed from this perspective the murder of the Jew Aaron carries a double valence: it expresses, on the one hand, a protest against economic transformation, and, on the other, hides and distorts this protest behind an act of anti-Semitic aggression. This fundamental event in Droste-Hülshoff's novella thus manifests the allusion/illusion dialectic the Marxist theoretician Louis Althusser diagnoses as the principal structure of ideology (Althusser 153): as critical *allusion* to the need to overcome the destructive practices of economic modernism, the murder of Aaron itself is founded on the *illusion* that the Jews *alone* are responsible for this economic and ecological disaster. The murder of Aaron must be viewed as a substitutive displacement that shifts the blame for the evils of economic modernism from the indigenous Westphalian populace—represented above all by the *Blaukittel*—to the Jews. Just as Friedrich displaces blame for his own economic dependencies onto the moneylending Jew who helps him feed his habit for symbols of wealth and luxury (Chase 134), a critique of the modern profitmongering that fuels ecological devastation is displaced into an implicit critique of Jews as the proverbial representatives of the modern capitalist economy and its destructive principles.[6] This does not necessarily suggest that Droste-Hülshoff and her text are fundamentally anti-Semitic. On the contrary, I will argue that she didactically exploits a well-established tenet of popular anti-Semitism as a way not only of elucidating her own critique of modern economic practices (see Chase 129), but of exposing the self-exculpatory character of an anti-Semitic discourse that falsely lays the blame for this transformation at the feet of the Jews.

Wood Poaching and the Nineteenth-Century Discourse on Private Property

The wood-poaching episode in Droste-Hülshoff's *Judenbuche* invokes a larger discursive context that gained prominence throughout Germany in the first half of the nineteenth century. As the sociologist Josef Mooser has demonstrated, wood theft was by far the most widespread criminal act in Germany during this period. In Prussia in the year 1850, for example, whereas a total of 35,000 acts of common theft were reported, 265,000 cases of wood poaching—more than seven times as many incidents—were registered (Mooser 43). Droste-Hülshoff's Westphalia, with its extensive forests, became one of the focal points of this wave of mass criminality and the controversy it evoked, as she acknowledges in the opening pages of *Die Judenbuche*: "However, since extensive and profitable woodlands constituted this region's primary source of wealth, the forests were, of course, closely guarded" (4). The struggles that arise around wood poaching center not merely on differing conceptions of the law, but on divergent understandings of the relationship between nature and private property rights. At issue in the battle between the propertyless citizens, on the one side, and the landed aristocracy, along with their emissaries, the foresters, on the other side, is the question of control over this natural wealth. Friedrich Mergel's mother Margreth becomes the spokesperson for the propertyless villagers who reject aristocratic privilege over the forests when she says to her son, "Listen, Fritz, our Lord above lets the woods grow freely, and the animals move from one person's land into another's; they cannot belong to anyone" (*Judenbuche* 8)—a view Droste-Hülshoff attributes to her fellow Westphalians in general in an almost identical passage from her "Westphälische Schilderungen aus einer westphälischen Feder" (Westphalian portraits from a Westphalian pen, 1845; see *HKA* 5.1: 55). Droste-Hülshoff's description thereby confirms the general conviction of wood poachers at this time, as documented by Josef Mooser (44), that their acts were justified and should not be seen as criminally reprehensible.

Droste-Hülshoff's experience of this rampant poaching had a strongly personal dimension. During a stay in Abbenburg in August 1839—that is, at the time she began to work on *Die Judenbuche* in earnest—she was astonished and dismayed by the prevalence of such acts of thieving. In a letter to Christoph Schlüter dated 24 August 1839 she wrote,

> The poaching of animals and the pilfering of wood are still proceeding along their common course; more serious is the transporting of the con-

traband goods across the borders into the territories of Lipp and Braunschweig. One can no longer go walking after sunset without running
face-to-face into bandits with sacks, who look at one skittishly and then
run off as fast as their legs can carry them. Two nights ago we heard
shouting and shots right at our own gate, and the next morning we
found paths beaten through the grain fields where the smugglers had
fled. (*HKA* 9.1: 58)

Important about this report is the implication that the poaching of animals and trees represents a minor offence that ultimately leads to much
more serious criminal infractions, in this case the transport of these contraband articles across the border. In a dynamic that one might call the
addiction to crime, wood pilfering for personal use, as a widely accepted
transgression that evokes no pangs of conscience, opens the door to more
severe legal infractions that are aimed at monetary gain. It is no coincidence that immediately after reporting this incident in her letter to Schlüter,
Droste-Hülshoff remarks, "This reminds me of my story [*Die Judenbuche*]" (*HKA* 9.1: 58), implicitly suggesting that this progression from
petty misdemeanors to felonious acts is relevant for her novella as well.

As aristocratic landowners, Droste-Hülshoff's family had vested interests in the protection of landed property rights over the forests. They
opposed the veritably universal belief of the lower classes that they had a
natural privilege to collect and cut wood to satisfy their personal needs.
The heads of the Haxthausen family, on Droste-Hülshoff's maternal side,
had long asserted exclusive rights over most of the forests they owned.[7]
However, in 1828 the superior court in Paderborn handed down a ruling
that affirmed the rights of the peasants to cut and collect wood throughout the forests owned by the Haxthausen family. For over a decade this
"right based on public opinion and habit," as Droste-Hülshoff calls it
(*Judenbuche* 3), enjoyed the sanction of statutory law. In 1841, while
Droste-Hülshoff was finishing her work on *Die Judenbuche*, this situation
changed when the provincial diet in Paderborn rescinded the peasants' right
to cut wood and reinstated the exclusive property rights of the aristocratic
landowners over the forests (Wittkowski 192).

Droste-Hülshoff was not the only intellectual of this period who reacted to the controversy over wood poaching and to the questions surrounding the inviolability of private property this debate invoked. In 1842, the same year in which *Die Judenbuche* appeared, the young Karl Marx (1818–83) published a series of essays titled "Debatten über das Holzdiebstahlsgesetz" (Debates on the law regarding wood poaching) in the *Rheinische Zeitung*. At the same time as the Westphalian provincial diet in Paderborn adopted new laws regarding wood poaching on private land, the provincial diet of the Rhineland met in Düsseldorf from May to July 1841 and debated, among other things, a law that declared wood poaching to be an act of theft. Marx's deliberations on this issue—in this regard identical to those of Droste-Hülshoff—center on the conflict between statutory and common law. But a divergence emerges between Marx and Droste-Hülshoff around this juxtaposition of two forms of justice, one enshrined in the canonized laws of the land and the other acknowledged by tradition and habit, a discrepancy that turns on the question of which has historical priority and hence ultimate authority. When Droste-Hülshoff writes about the general sensibilities of the Westphalian populace toward the law that "alongside statutory law a second law had taken hold, one based on public opinion, habit, and obsolescence due to neglect" (*Judenbuche* 3), she accords to statutory law the place of historical priority, suggesting that the common-law notions of free public access to the forests emerge as an ancillary juridical sensibility based on disregard of canonical law. Droste-Hülshoff thus implicitly gives precedence to private property holdings over the traditional natural right to use the forest and its products for subsistence. Marx, not surprisingly, and with certain historical justification, reverses these priorities. In opposition to the Rhineland diet's assertion of the sanctity of private property, Marx asserts the priority of common-law practice: "The common-law right of habit, as a *domain set apart* from statutory law, is thus only reasonable in those instances in which this right exists *alongside* and *outside* the statutes, where habit *anticipates* a statutory law" ("Debatten" 116). While acknowledging that common and statutory law are in conflict, Marx claims that there are instances in which common law takes historical precedence and that, since it "anticipates" statutory law, the latter should be formulated in coherence with these common-law practices. But Marx goes even further: he valorizes common law as the exclusive right of the impoverished and underprivileged classes throughout the world.

We lay claim to the *common-law right of habit* for those who are impoverished; indeed, this is a common-law right that is not local, but rather is the common-law right of impoverished people in all countries. We go even further and assert that common-law right in general, by its very nature, can *only* be the right of these lowest, propertyless, and elementary masses. ("Debatten" 115)

The right to appropriate whatever they need for their sustenance, in other words, is an absolute right shared by all propertyless, poverty-stricken people the world over, and as such it enjoys priority over any statutes that contravene this natural right. Marx subsequently notes, moreover, that this common law is based on the "ambiguous nature [*schwankenden Charakter*]" of certain kinds of property, like the forests, their products, and the animals that live in and from them, which cannot be definitively declared to be either private or common property (118). The error of the Rhineland diet in defending the private property rights of the aristocratic landowners over the forests thus resides in its failure to recognize "that there are types of property that by their very nature can never assume the character of preordained private property," and that by their very elementary nature are subject only to what Marx terms the "occupational right based on class" (118). Marx's overriding criticism of the Rhineland diet's decision, then, is that it throws the weight of the state, manifest in its juridical statutes, behind the private interests of the landowners and hence *against* the traditional and primordial "right of occupation" held by the propertyless masses. The upshot of the diet's legal maneuver, which redefines the historically and existentially justified common-law practice of wood gathering as an act of *theft*, is that it effectively transforms law-abiding citizens into criminals ("Debatten" 110). In other words, it is not a mutation in attitudes, in psychology, or in the sense of right and wrong among the citizenry itself that accounts for the criminalization of wood poaching; rather, this change comes about as a kind of arbitrary edict through the intervention of the legal apparatus.

Droste-Hülshoff seems to subscribe to this same attitude when—exploiting the authoritative voice of the purportedly impartial narrator to provide gnomic commentary—she writes in the opening pages of *Die Judenbuche*, "For anyone who acts according to their own convictions, even if these are inadequate, can never completely founder; by contrast, nothing is more deadly to the soul than to side with external right and go against one's own internal sense of justice" (4). This statement seems to legitimate the view of the propertyless masses that their own *inner* sense of the rights of habit and tradition justifies wood poaching, and that they hence can ignore, with good conscience, those statutes promulgated by *external* legal authorities that contravene these inner rights. And yet, the course of Droste-Hülshoff's narrative, which suggests the progressive condemnation and criminalization of those lower-class citizens who act upon their common-law privileges, seems to run counter to this assertion. This discrepancy indicates that something other than this conflict between common law (or conscience) and statutory law lies at the heart of Droste-Hülshoff's text.

It would be incorrect to assume that Marx defends the absolute right of the propertyless classes to appropriate the woodlands and their natural products in any way they see fit. On the contrary, he is careful to draw strict distinctions between what citizens can claim as theirs to use freely, based on their common-law sensibilities, and those parts of the forest that are protected by the right of private property. In the instance of wood poaching he draws this line between fallen or dead wood, on the one hand, and green wood that still retains its organic connection to the land, on the other. About the latter Marx writes, in drastic language that evokes in suggestive ways the destructiveness associated with the wood-poaching episode in *Die Judenbuche*, "In order to take possession of green wood, one has to sever it from its organic connection. Just as this is a flagrant violation [*Attentat*] of the tree, it is likewise a flagrant violation of the owner of the tree" ("Debatten" 111–12). The word *Attentat*, which literally means "assassination," jumps out at the reader here and recalls the assassination of the forest ranger Brandis at the culmination of *Die Judenbuche*'s first narrative segment. Marx's inherently romantic but perhaps proto-ecological recognition that the unjustified felling of a healthy tree represents a brutal crime against nature could be taken by association to support the thesis in Droste-Hülshoff's novella that the wanton devastation of the forests by the *Blaukittel* has a direct parallel in the violent murders of the forest ranger Brandis and the Jew Aaron.[8]

A further affinity between Marx's diagnosis and Droste-Hülshoff's depiction of wood poaching is the reduction of the conflict between competing property claims to a struggle between the common citizens and the forest rangers who are delegated to protect the property rights of the landed aristocracy. Marx provides an extraordinarily sensitive analysis of the ambiguous and paradoxical position of these forest rangers, whose allegiances lie both with the property owners who employ them and with the common citizens from whose social ranks they are drawn.

> As an official charged with the protection of the woods, the forest ranger must defend the interests of the private property owners; but, by the same token, as tax assessor he must defend the wood poachers against the extravagant compensation claims of the owners. Whereas on the one hand he is perhaps supposed to work with his fists in the interest of the woods, he is also supposed to work with his head in the interest of the enemies of the woods. As embodied interest of the owners of the forests, he is simultaneously expected to represent a guarantee against these very same owners. ("Debatten" 123)

Marx's point is that the foresters hired by the landowners play two distinct roles: on the one hand, they are the guardians of the forest, charged with protecting it from unauthorized harvesting; on the other hand, they are the assessors of the forest's value, and in this guise they must defend the unauthorized harvesters against exorbitant claims for compensation on the part of the landowners.

Marx can only interpret the pursuit of these two roles as a conflict if he assumes that questions of value must be decided from the perspective of the common citizens, the poachers themselves. For what else prevents the foresters from simply affirming, in their roles as assessors, the outrageous claims of value asserted by the landowners? The only possible answer is that Marx assumes that the foresters, who themselves represent the propertyless class, will decide questions of value strictly in terms of *use*: the value that a specific tree has as firewood, as material for fence posts or houses, and so on. In other words, the foresters reject the *commercial* value, or the *exchange* value, of the forests. The paradoxical situation in which the foresters find themselves, then, is that although they view the forests as *agricultural* products and hence evaluate them in terms of *use*, they must protect the forests against exploitation by the poachers whose sole interest in the wood is its practical usefulness. Only for the landowners are the forests commercial rather than agricultural products, promising a surplus value based on their marketable exchange and reflected in their exorbitant claims for compensation. Marx thus draws the line between commercial and agricultural interests, use value and exchange value, strictly along the lines of class and the specific relationship to property: whether it serves the demands of immediate *subsistence*, or whether it serves the drive for abstract capitalized *profit*.

Peculiar to Marx's perspective is that it represents a highly romanticized, perhaps even naïve view of the propertyless classes, one that orients them solely within an agrarian context: issues of commercialism, surplus value, and profit have not yet entered the consciousness of the wood poachers envisioned in Marx's text. In this regard Droste-Hülshoff's novella presents—and this will perhaps come as a surprise to many—a more realistic and progressive picture: for the representatives of the agrarian world depicted in *Die Judenbuche*, the struggle for subsistence has already given way to profitmongering, the drive to acquire *surplus* value. As she makes clear in her initial description of the village B., the villagers uniformly and with apparent good conscience perpetrate acts of wood poaching strictly for *commercial* ends and monetary profit, not simply for their own personal use, as Marx presumes for his commoners.

The village B. had the reputation of being the most arrogant, wily, and fearless community in the entire principality. Its geographical location amid the deep and proud isolation of the forests [*Waldeinsamkeit*] nourished the inherent obstinacy of these villagers' disposition from an early age. The proximity of a river, which flowed to the sea and accommodated covered ships large enough to carry shipbuilding lumber easily and safely out of the region, contributed greatly toward enhancing the natural boldness of the wood poachers. . . . Thirty to forty wagons set off simultaneously in the beautiful nights of the full moon [*in den schönen Mondnächten*], with about twice the number of men of every age, from juvenile boys all the way up to the seventy-year-old village magistrate, who as an experienced ringleader led this procession with the same

proud self-assurance with which he assumed his place during legal proceedings. (*Judenbuche* 4)

The arrogance and cunning of the villagers could be read as symptomatic
of their insight into the emergence of commercial capitalism and their determination to exploit its potential by "capitalizing" on the exchange value
of the surrounding forests. Clearly the villagers no longer view their natural surroundings with the wonder and nostalgia of the Romantics, but
rather with an eye for its strategic exploitation. Droste-Hülshoff's references to *Waldeinsamkeit* and *schöne Mondnächte* invoke this discrepancy
by alluding to clichés of Romantic literature. But the proverbial *mond-
beglänzde Zaubernacht*, the night imbued with the magic glow of the full
moon, a standard trope of German Romantic literature, is now underwritten
solely by the black magic of commercial profit, by the ability to transform
an abundant natural resource into a scarce but all-important commodity:
money.[9]

By specifying that the river transports are large enough to carry wood
for shipbuilding, Droste-Hülshoff not only introduces the context of commercial enterprise into her story, but also points to the expansionist principles of nineteenth-century European colonialism with its ravenous appetite
for wood to build more commercial vehicles (Kreis 104). Indeed, wood
was the lifeblood of the protoindustrial economy, since it served, prior to
the use of coal, electricity, and petroleum products, as the primary raw
material used for the production of energy (Mooser 50). It is significant,
moreover, that the subtext of this passage describing the villagers' wood-
poaching activities seems to contradict the initial description of the village
Droste-Hülshoff provides in her opening paragraph: "The territory of
which the village B. was a part was at this time one of those completely
isolated corners of the world without factories and trade, without major
roads for the transport of troops, and where a strange face caused a sen-
sation" (*Judenbuche* 3). Yet, as the subsequent depiction of the brigades
of wood poachers will reveal, the village B. is far from being isolated; indeed,
it is connected to the surrounding world of commerce by a large and nav-
igable river. And contrary to the narrator's assertion, it has already succumbed to the temptations of trade. Moreover, in the figure of the village
magistrate, who feels just as comfortable as the ringleader of the illegal

wood poachers as he does as the representative of statutory law, Droste-Hülshoff gives a concrete example of the conflicting sense of justice characteristic of these villagers. The fact that wood poaching has become a universally practiced enterprise indicates the extent to which the indigenous population is infected by a fever akin to the gold rush: they are furiously staking their claims on the green trees that, through the magic of commercial capitalism, will be alchemically transformed into gold. The discrepancy between the narrator's initial description of the village and the facts of its illegal commercial activity thus point to the central transformation at the heart of Droste-Hülshoff's text: the shift from a locally organized subsistence economy to a commercial economy based on the exploitation of natural resources, international trade, colonial enterprise, and the lure of money as the abstract symbol of a newfound wealth.

Clearly, the common-law right to appropriate from nature what is necessary for one's subsistence has undergone a radical transformation here; although the condition of the village, which is "poorly built and smoky" (3), does not manifest in obvious fashion the villagers' newly discovered source of prosperity, it is clear that the purpose of their moonlit enterprises is the production of surplus value that will accrue directly to them instead of to the landowners. The fact that this new wealth is not reflected in an improved infrastructure in the village itself constitutes a central aspect of Droste-Hülshoff's critique: the shift among the villagers from considerations of use value to those of exchange value is not reflected in an improvement of their basic living conditions, but merely fuels wasteful expenditures on superfluous items that fulfill their *desires*, but not their *needs*.[10] Droste-Hülshoff portrays this problematic most concretely on the example of Friedrich Mergel, whose obsession with useless objects that ostentatiously reflect monetary wealth unleashes the narrative events of the second half of the novella.

The notorious band of wood poachers called the *Blaukittel* represents an egregious intensification of the practices already commonly employed by the villagers in B. Although the citizens of B. are initially suspected of providing the manpower for this troop of bandits, they are unexpectedly exonerated when one of the *Blaukittel*'s largest exploits occurs when all the villagers of B. were known to be carousing at an all-night wedding celebration (*Judenbuche* 17). The village of B. thus clearly is not the only one bitten by the bug for commercial profit; indeed, given the rampant dev-astation of the forests that Droste-Hülshoff's text evocatively chronicles—by the end of the story the Jews' beech stands alone, surrounded only by thick undergrowth, in what at the outset was a healthy, dense forest (*Juden-buche* 41)—commercial exploitation of the forests has become a dominant enterprise. Nonetheless, it is with the example of the *Blaukittel* that Droste-Hülshoff demonstrates the manner in which wanton destruction accom-panies the progressive commercialization of the forests. Here's how the court clerk Kapp describes the senseless ravaging of the forests practiced by the *Blaukittel*: "Those scoundrels . . . destroy everything; if they would at least show some regard for the young trees, but instead they even take oak trees as thin as my arm, not even big enough to turn out an oar pole! It's as though inflicting losses on others is just as important to them as their own profit!" (21). The activities of the *Blaukittel* thus seem to be doubly motivated: by the profit motive, on the one hand, but also by wanton despoliation of the forests, on the other. Josef Mooser provides an explanation for this impulse for rash destruction: it represents a form of social protest that manifests the spirit of opposition harbored by the lower, propertyless classes against the propertied landowners and the feu-dal system in general (Mooser 45–46, 81–82). But Droste-Hülshoff's wood poachers already represent a thoroughly rationalized and organized industrial operation (Kreis 102), and in this configuration the destruction they perpetrate appears less as a form of social protest than as the neces-sary collateral damage that accompanies the quick profit-taking strategy of industrialization itself. The speed at which their illicit operations must take place motivates them to practice a rudimentary form of clear-cutting.

The description of the *Blaukittel* and their particular modus operandi indicates that they were the first to refine the art of wood poaching into an industrial enterprise on a grand scale.

> Around this time the slumbering laws were awakened to a certain extent
> by a band of wood poachers known by the name of the *Blaukittel* who
> exceeded all their predecessors in cunning and audacity, to such a degree,
> that even the most patient person had to be stirred to action. Contrary
> to the normal state of affairs, in which one could point a finger at the

bocks who stood out from the rest of the herd, in this instance, in spite of extreme vigilance, it had proven impossible to discover the name of even one single individual. This band received its name from the uniform [blue] clothing it wore, and by which it made recognition of individuals more difficult, even when, for example, a forest ranger witnessed individual stragglers disappearing into the thicket. They laid waste to everything like a migratory caterpillar; entire expanses of forest were felled in a single night and the lumber carried off, so that the next morning one found nothing but wood chips and chaotic heaps of slash. Moreover, the fact that wagon tracks never led back to a village, but always only came from the river and returned to it, indicated that they were acting under the protection and perhaps with the assistance of the shipowners. (*Judenbuche* 17)

There is an element of verisimilitude in Droste-Hülshoff's choice of the blue smock as the identifying trait of this band of thieves: this was a common piece of work clothing worn at this time in the province of Paderborn, where Droste-Hülshoff's tale takes place (Rölleke, *Annette von Droste-Hülshoff* 150–51). At the same time, the blue smock is the mark of a certain class, namely of the industrial proletariat (Kraft 85), and the association of this band of wood pilferers with this type of clothing underscores the industrial nature of their enterprise.[11] But Droste-Hülshoff herself stresses another dimension of this article of clothing: its anonymity, which gives it the positive function of making the individual members of the band wholly indecipherable. Droste-Hülshoff specifically selects a metaphor from the domain of agriculture and animal husbandry to describe how the *Blaukittel*, as entrepreneurs, differ from run-of-the-mill wood poachers. In the latter instance, the "bocks" can be easily separated from the "herd"; in the former instance, every individual melds into a solid blue mass. Even at the level of metaphor, then, Droste-Hülshoff is at pains to segregate the protoindustrial, commercial character of this group of bandits from the agrarian poacher of Marx's analysis, who is motivated solely by immediate existential needs. These pirates have broken completely with "the normal state of affairs" in this region to the extent that they transmute the immoveable property of the aristocratically owned forests into *moveable* property that acquires a new value through its commercial marketability.

The fact that they operate in conjunction with the shipowners not only helps reinforce their anonymity (no wagon tracks lead away from the villages where they operate), but also supports the idea that they represent the interests of commercial enterprise in the service of a super-regional, colonial economy. But most important, perhaps, is that in the mindlessly destructive character of this band's practices Droste-Hülshoff attacks a dialectic between destruction and the profit motive that inheres in unbridled commercialism. The identification and exploration of this dialectic, as exemplified in the character of Friedrich Mergel, is one of the major accomplishments of Droste-Hülshoff's novella.

The Economic Subtext of Die Judenbuche

The metaphorical significance of Friedrich Mergel's family name has often drawn the attention of critics.[12] *Mergel* is a kind of soil mixed with dolomite lime and used specifically for the purposes of fertilization. Heinz Rölleke has pointed out, however, that the term *mergeln* is associated with a method of fertilization that gives the soil a short-term energy boost, but that ultimately leads to its fast-paced and progressive deterioration ("Kann man" 411). While Rölleke is correct to interpret this problematic in terms of economic questions, his limited application of this dynamic of rapid growth and subsequent depletion to the economic history of the Mergel family is too restrictive. In fact, this dialectic is indicative of the economic problematic at the core of Droste-Hülshoff's text, and the wood poachers' merciless exploitation and ultimate devastation of the forests for commercial profit constitutes its most obvious manifestation. The name Mergel itself thus connects Droste-Hülshoff's character to the dialectical intertwining of short-term profit with destruction of the natural world that is emblematized in the commercial exploitation of the forests. The ultimate link between the two seemingly disparate plots in Droste-Hülshoff's novella is forged by the dialectic inscribed in this economic problematic.

Die Judenbuche concerns itself centrally with the question of economic transformation, the shift among the populace of Droste-Hülshoff's native Westphalia from an agrarian economy based primarily on the use value of the surrounding natural world to a protocapitalist, industrially managed economy in which the natural world is assessed solely in terms of its exchange value on the worldwide, colonial market. Droste-Hülshoff indicts this transformation by exposing its effects on the character of her protagonist, Friedrich Mergel. What the *Blaukittel* episode shows is that Friedrich stands in a synechdochal relationship—part for the whole—with his fellow citizens of Paderborn province; his fate, his *seduction* (through his uncle Simon) by the allure of profit, can be taken as representative of more general changes occurring in Westphalia, and his story read as a more universal indictment of the dangers of the exchange-value economy.[13] Furthermore, this notion of representativity and universality is underscored by the motif of the blue smocks: in essence, the commoners of Paderborn have become indistinguishable, and Friedrich Mergel's fate can hence take on an allegorical dimension that relates it to the fate of his fellow Paderbornians in general.[14] The picture Droste-Hülshoff paints is not a pretty one. Indeed, she exposes a devastating deforestation of the Westphalian woodlands that will ultimately undermine the livelihood of the very people responsible for this destruction. In this sense she presciently diagnoses deforestation as the potential basis for a kind of ecological collapse similar to those Jared Diamond has recently investigated as the cause for the demise of the primordial civilizations on the Easter Islands and elsewhere.[15]

The overriding problematic of historical, socioeconomic transformation that lies at the root of Droste-Hülshoff's novella is projected on the text's figurative level in terms of a subtle displacement of its central symbols. The unusual texture of Droste-Hülshoff's narrative stems largely from the fact that it is structured by a symbolic economy that operates around displacements and disjunctions rather than coherence and consistency.[16] This is emblematized above all by subtle displacements in the tree and forest imagery so central to the novella. In the early segments of the text—up to the discussion between Friedrich and Simon that occurs in the Brederholz immediately after the latter "adopts" his nephew—this section of forest, which constitutes the primary locus for seminal events in the story,[17] is symbolized by a broad oak tree, the *breite Eiche* (*Judenbuche* 9; 12). According to Simon, the death of Friedrich's father, Hermann Mergel, occurred under this tree. When Friedrich accompanies Simon to his home in Brede, their path takes them—surely not coincidentally—through the Brederholz and past the spot at which Friedrich's father perished.

Now at some distance the darkness appeared to dissolve, and soon the two of them entered a relatively large clearing. The moon shone down brightly and revealed that just a short time ago axes had mercilessly ravaged the forest here. Everywhere tree stumps protruded, many of them several feet above the ground, because this was where they could most easily be cut down in a hurry. . . . In the middle of the clearing stood an old oak tree, more broad than tall; a pale beam of light that fell through its branches and illuminated its trunk revealed that it was hollow, a circumstance that had probably rescued it from the universal destruction. Here Simon suddenly grabbed the boy's [Friedrich's] arm.

"Friedrich, do you recognize this tree? It's the broad oak."— Friedrich gave a start and latched onto his uncle with his cold hands.— "Look," Simon continued, "this is where Uncle Franz and Hülsmeyer found your father, when in his drunken state he went to the devil, without atonement and final unction." (12)

Before even introducing the activities of the *Blaukittel* (17), Droste-Hülshoff positions her readers as witnesses of the seemingly senseless destruction they perpetrate. The light of the full moon is a recurring motif that connects this scene with the general description of poaching activities cited earlier (4), and subsequently with the description of the night in which the confrontation between Friedrich and the forester Brandis occurs (18). The scene analyzed here thereby serves symbolically to link Simon—and ultimately Friedrich as well—with the *Blaukittel* and their wanton, if economically motivated, destruction of the forest. The broad oak tree becomes a kind of representative of the threatened status of the Brederholz, portrayed as one of the densest, darkest, most primeval sections of forest in the Paderborn area (12). A landmark recognizable to all who live in the region, this oak is clearly one of the oldest, most individually remarkable trees in the forest. At the same time, its future existence seems questionable since its trunk is hollow. However, the narrator suggests that precisely this deficiency, which threatens the tree's long-term health, may in fact be responsible for its short-term survival: its hollow trunk makes it economically insignificant and hence protects it from the poachers' axes. But there is a more ominous implication in this suggestion that only its lack of economic exchange value rescues the broad oak: its *symbolic* value as an exceptional representative of its species, and hence as an object of renown and pride to the community, has become negligible, as has its *pragmatic* value as a landmark that provides the general populace with orientation in an otherwise disorientingly dense forest.

The broad oak is not the only remarkable tree that distinguishes the landscape of the Brederholz: standing at the entrance to the ravine that marks the geography of this section of forest is a wide beech tree. It is under the canopy of this beech, cast in this scene in a kind of supporting role to the broad oak, that Simon interrogates his nephew about his use of alcohol and—the all-important *Gretchenfrage*, the question Gretchen poses to Faust in the first part of Goethe's eponymous tragedy—about his sincerity with regard to religion: "These last words were spoken under the canopy of a broad beech tree, which vaulted over the entrance to the ravine" (12). Alcohol was the fatal weakness of Friedrich's father, and to bring this point home Simon has brought Friedrich to the very place of his father's death. Religion is the perceived weakness of Friedrich's mother. Only once he is assured that Friedrich has resisted both these potential susceptibilities is Simon satisfied that Friedrich can be initiated into the secrets of the *Blaukittel*, for whom Simon serves as a ringleader, and put to work as a lookout. Friedrich is ideally suited for this important task, since his shepherding duties regularly bring him into the forest and provide him with a legitimate cover for his spying. But what is especially significant about the cited scene is the manner in which the beech tree is juxtaposed to the broad oak, on the one hand, and, on the other hand, implicitly associated with Simon and the irresponsible exploitation of the native forests for short-term economic gain. The broad oak and the beech tree appear in this scene almost as competitors for symbolic dominance in the narrative. After this point, however, the broad oak effectively disappears from the text, to be systematically supplanted by the beech tree, which gradually assumes the status of the sole bearer of symbolic significance. Implicit in this successful displacement is the victory of those self-serving economic principles represented by Simon and the *Blaukittel* over tradition and the communitarian interests represented by the oak. What is important here is that well *before* the beech tree is associated with the Jews and with the murder of the Jew Aaron in the second half of the narrative, it has been identified with Simon

Semmler, the *Blaukittel*, and the wanton devastation of the forest for private financial gain.

The symbolic replacement of the broad oak by the beech tree is not fully concretized until the final pages of the novella, when the beech tree is depicted, in obvious parallel to the portrayal of the broad oak in the scene just examined, standing by itself in the middle of a large clearing: "In the surrounding area there was no tree other than the Jews' beech" (41), the text laconically reads.[18] Here we are not dealing simply with the beech tree mentioned in the earlier scene that marks the entrance to the ravine in the Brederholz, but rather explicitly with the *Jews'* beech, that is, with the beech tree at which the Jew Aaron was murdered. This beech tree is subsequently *acculturated*—and in this sense denaturalized—when it is purchased by the Jewish community, commodified, and transformed into the vehicle of religious-cultural significance by dint of the Hebrew inscription it bears. The displacement of the broad oak by the Jews' beech thus can be read as symptomatic of a set of further displacements: of nature by culture, of communitarian tradition by economic self-interest, of Germanic solidity and rootedness by "Jewish" opportunism. This final, ethnological dimension is suggested not merely by the term *Judenbuche* itself,[19] but also by the conventional association of the Germanic spirit with the oak tree. The Indo-Germanic peoples celebrated the oak as holy, and later cultural periods came to associate it with the strength and freedom of the Germanic spirit. In the juxtaposition of oak and beech the problematic of ethnological conflict between Germans and Jews is thus already suggested, and the displacement of the oak by the beech implies a kind of ominous displacement of a "Germanic" spirit by something Other that is designated as "Jewish."[20] It is important to stress, however, that on the figurative level all of these potential significations are inextricably intertwined: in the symbolic economy of the text, the displacement of the broad oak by the Jews' beech represents the displacement of Germanic traditionalism, of an immediate, vital, and sensitive communion with the natural world, and of an economy based on existential need and use value, by a foreign Other, a (self-)destructive alienation from nature, and a commercialized, modern economy based on exchange value.

The stages of this symbolic displacement are much more complicated than an ethnographic narrative pitting Germans against Jews suggests. Long before it marks the place at which the Jew Aaron is murdered, the beech tree plays a fundamental role in another primary event in the narrative: it is closely associated with Friedrich's treacherous deception of the forester Brandis, which results in the latter's murder at the hands of the *Blaukittel*.[21] At the conclusion of the venomous exchange between Friedrich and Brandis, the latter turns and moves off in pursuit of the other forest rangers he has sent on ahead. But Friedrich intervenes and sends him down a false path.

> Brandis turned away brusquely and walked toward the thicket.—"No, sir," Friedrich called out, "if you want to meet up with the other foresters, they went up that way past the beech tree."—"Past the beech tree?" Brandis asked with skepticism, "no, they went over there, toward the Mastergrund [another section of the forest]."—"I'm telling you, they went past the beech tree; the strap of tall Heinrich's rifle got caught in that twisted branch there; I saw it with my own eyes!"
>
> The forester followed the designated path. (20)

The geographical description that introduces this entire scene, placing Friedrich on a moonlit night at the "entrance to a narrow ravine" (18), indicates that he is at precisely the same location at which the interrogation by Simon occurred, "under the canopy of a broad beech tree, which vaulted over the entrance to the ravine" (12). The beech tree, mentioned no less than three times in the exchange between Brandis and Friedrich,[22] is the same tree under which Friedrich was first tested by Simon for his appropriateness as an accomplice. There can be little doubt, then, that in this scene the beech tree functions as the symbolic mark, thrice invoked, of Friedrich's guilt and his complicity in the commercially motivated destruction of the forests by the *Blaukittel* and ultimately in the murder of Brandis. Thus before it is ever tied to the murder of Aaron and consecrated by the Jewish community for vengeance against his murderer, the beech tree is connected to the dialectic of ecological destruction and economic exploitation that dominates the first half of Droste-Hülshoff's text, as well as to the murder of the forest ranger who attempts to put a stop to this illegal deforestation.

We can reinforce this association of the beech tree with Friedrich's "sin"—his capitulation to the seductions of exchange-value economics with its promise of instant wealth—by following up another set of intratextually linked scenes. The first of these occurs immediately following Friedrich's deception of Brandis and documents the boy's oscillation between the impulse of conscientious contrition that urges him to alert Brandis to the deception and the stubborn affirmation and justification of this act of treachery. The narrator meticulously describes the slow disappearance of the forester into the thicket and then focuses the reader's attention on Friedrich's ambiguous reaction.

> Here one branch dropped down behind him [Brandis], there another; the outline of his figure disappeared gradually. Then a flash penetrated the undergrowth. It was one of the steel buttons of his hunting jacket; then he was gone. During the process of this gradual disappearance Friedrich's face had lost its indifference and his features ultimately seemed to be uneasily agitated. Did he perhaps regret not having asked the forester to keep silent about what he had divulged? He took a few steps forward, then stood still. "It's too late," he said to himself and grabbed his hat. A faint rasping in the underbrush, not twenty paces away from him. It was the forester sharpening his flint stone. Friedrich listened.—"No!" he then exclaimed in a decisive tone of voice, gathered up his things and drove the livestock along the ravine. (20)

This is perhaps the most masterfully narrated, dramatically choreographed scene in the entire novella, brilliantly exploiting a ritardando like that of a slow-motion camera to chart Brandis's gradual disappearance and strategically interspersing it with clues—sometimes with red herrings—to Friedrich's complex and conflicted psychological state. Friedrich artificially calms his own disquiet about sending the forester into a trap by simply asserting that it is too late to call Brandis back. But this is revealed as a conscious self-deception when Friedrich hears the forester sharpen his flint stone but twenty paces away; and once again he resists the inclination to act mercifully and warn Brandis, this time expressing this resistance with a forceful "No!" Most critics who have examined this scene agree that the narrator's speculation about Friedrich's motivation for wanting to call Brandis back—namely, to insure that the forester doesn't reveal to the *Blaukittel* that Friedrich betrayed them by indicating their whereabouts—is quite simply a red herring.[23] Friedrich, after all, has really divulged nothing that the forest rangers didn't already know; and since he succeeded in warning the bandits by whistling loudly (18), he has in fact fulfilled his primary responsibility as a lookout. It is more likely that Friedrich's oscillation and uncertainty are emblematic of a struggle between allegiance to the traditional values of community solidarity and human sympathy,[24] on the one hand, and the seduction of the wealth he stands to gain through his complicity with the *Blaukittel*, on the other. In the end he opts here, as elsewhere, for the self-serving choice of personal wealth that will help him sustain his new role as village dandy, even though this means he must send Brandis into imminent danger.

Two other scenes in the novella are structured around a similar vacillation surrounding a choice between a noble and ignoble action. One of these is Friedrich's admission, following the murder of Brandis, of his complicity and shared guilt in this crime, culminating in his stated intention to unburden himself at confession (25–26). This act of contrition is hindered, however, by Simon's intervention, when he admonishes his nephew that good Christians do not betray their relatives. Friedrich is well aware that it was Simon's ax, whose handle is identified by a peculiar missing splinter, that was used to murder Brandis. In this instance, Droste-Hülshoff does not make us privy to Friedrich's deliberations as he chooses between conscience and crime; we are only told that Friedrich ultimately does not go to confession. Once again, Friedrich turns against his own best instincts, betraying his conscience in favor of his own economic self-interest—for to betray Simon would be to betray the source of his prosperity.

The only other structurally and psychologically parallel scene involves not Friedrich, but his mother Margreth. It occurs, not coincidentally, when Friedrich returns home for the first time after going to work for his uncle Simon. Margreth has just seen Friedrich's double Johannes Niemand and is lost in deliberations about Simon's possible paternity of this illegitimate child when Friedrich interrupts her.

> She [Margreth] sat this way for a while, immobile and with pursed lips,
> as in complete absent-mindedness. Friedrich stood before her and had

already addressed her twice. "What is it, what do you want?" she snapped
with a start.—"I have brought you some money," he replied, more astonished than alarmed.—"Money? Where?" She moved and the small coin
fell with a tinkle to the floor. Friedrich picked it up. "Money from Uncle
Simon, because I helped him with his work. Now I can earn something
on my own."—"Money from Simon? Throw it away, away!—No, give it
to the poor. No, no, keep it," she whispered almost imperceptibly, "we
ourselves are poor. Who knows if we won't be reduced to begging!"—
"On Monday I'm supposed to go to Uncle Simon again and help him
sow the fields."—"You're supposed to go to him again? No, no, never
again!"—She hugged her child with intense emotion.—"Alright," she
added, and a stream of tears suddenly ran down her sunken cheeks, "go
on, he's my only brother." (15)

Margreth obviously recognizes the tainted character of this money. Yet it
was she who agreed to Simon's "adoption" of Friedrich in the first place
(10–11), just as it is she who ultimately succumbs—as did Friedrich before
her—to the seduction of Simon's hard currency. Similar to the scene depicting Friedrich's vacillation about sending Brandis into a trap, Margreth deliberates back and forth not only about accepting the money, but also about
letting Friedrich return to Simon's services to earn even more, in both cases
finally giving in to the pressures of material need.

One could certainly read this scene as a justification of the moral failings of figures like Friedrich and Margreth on the basis of their compelling
poverty. Indeed, the very next piece of information Droste-Hülshoff gives
us is that Margreth is in such dire financial straits that she has had to transfer the use of her last piece of arable land to a creditor as payment on a
debt (15). Moreover, Margreth's fear that she will be reduced to begging
anticipates the slur voiced by the forester Brandis in his confrontation with
Friedrich: "You pack of scoundrels, who don't even have a roof shingle
they can call their own! As God is my witness, soon you will be reduced
to begging" (19). Brandis's comment is no exaggeration, for when the squire
searches Margreth's house after the murder of Aaron, among the things
he discovers there are papers connecting Friedrich with an unnamed person suspected of complicity with the *Blaukittel* (32) and an unusually large
number of outstanding payment demands from creditors, above all from

usurers (33). This gives rise to the telling commentary on the part of the squire, "I would never have thought that the Mergels were so deeply in debt" (33). To be sure, since the murder of Brandis the financial situation of the family has taken a turn for the worse: scared off by the scandal and fearful of the authorities' reaction to this crime, the *Blaukittel* cease their operations and Friedrich's source of monetary wealth disappears as quickly as it had appeared. But he has by now become so addicted to money and the superficial signs of wealth, authority, and power it provides—the silver watch, the fancy clothes, the silver vest buttons—that Friedrich must turn to Aaron, who trades on credit, in order to satisfy his unquenchable need (Chase 134; Kreis 114). In the final analysis, then, what links the purportedly disparate narratives about wood poaching and the murder of the forester, on the one hand, and Friedrich's need to live beyond his means, resulting in the murder of the Jew Aaron, on the other, is, viewed symbolically, the beech tree (Huszai 488), but likewise, on the motivic level, the seduction of the easy wealth provided by the modern commercial economy. The "magic" that allows the *Blaukittel* to exchange poached trees for money is the same "magic" that permits Friedrich to acquire goods from Aaron by merely signing his name to a piece of paper. William Donahue has provided an important insight that underscores this linkage: the recognition of a fundamental structural affinity between the manner in which the wood poachers mortgage the future of the forest for their own short-term economic gain and the way usury depletes the capital resource of the debtor on whom the usurer depends (51).

If this structural homology forms the bridge that joins the two disparate narratives in Droste-Hülshoff's novella, it is also the bridge across which the traffic of psychological displacement moves. It permits responsibility for the profit-oriented destruction of the forest, manifest in exaggerated form in the *Blaukittel*, to be shifted from the actual perpetrators, the natives of Paderborn themselves, to those proverbially profiteering Others, the usurious Jews. This, moreover, is the same strategy followed by the squire when, on the basis of a report from the president of the provincial court, he declares Friedrich, the native Paderbornian, innocent of the murder of Aaron and transfers guilt to the Jew Lumpenmoises (Whitinger 269). And indeed, it is the solidarity of the native villagers against the universally disdained Jewish Other that motivates them in the peasant wedding scene to divert their anger and mockery of Friedrich into anti-Semitic abuse of the Jew Aaron as soon as the latter arrives on the scene (*Judenbuche* 29). Anti-Semitism thereby serves as a convenient way for the Paderborn populace— who, after all, covertly support the activities of the *Blaukittel* and themselves participate freely in profitmongering acts of wood poaching—to ignore their complicity with the destructive dialectic of exchange-value economics and transfer guilt to a convenient Other. What Other could be a more convenient scapegoat than the Jews, whom Christian tradition has persistently indicted as unscrupulous profitmongers? Here it is significant to register the connection between this problematic of self-exculpation through the displacement of guilt and the concluding line of the poem with which Droste-Hülshoff prefaces her novella: "Drop that stone [you would throw at another]—it will strike your own head!" (3). In the context outlined here the poem reverberates with the admonition that we should scrutinize critically the recriminations we make against others so as to ensure that they are not displaced self-accusations: the stones we intend to throw at others might better be cast at us, the throwers. Perhaps it is the reverse of this dialectic, recrimination of others transformed back into self-incrimination, that motivates Friedrich Mergel's eventual suicide.

My point is that the same problematic of economic transformation from a subsistence-based, use-value economy to a profit-based, exchange-value economy, which structures the narrative about the wood poachers in the first half of *Die Judenbuche*, continues to shape the second half of the narrative, but on a more subliminal level, in the mode of Freudian repression, as it were. In this sense the displacement of this theme from its focal position in the first segment of the text to its subordinate role in the second reflects in the dimension of textual structure the psychological displacement by which the Paderborn natives—in particular Simon Semmler and Friedrich Mergel—exculpate themselves from complicity with the commercially motivated destruction of the forests by shifting guilt and responsibility to the Jews. If this is true, then *Die Judenbuche* is not so much a manifestation of anti-Semitism as it is a *critical representation* of one of the particularly insidious strategies of anti-Semitic discourse. This constitutes the didactic message of Droste-Hülshoff's novella: by representing this displacement of self-culpability onto a convenient Other, it exposes the mechanism by which the process of abjection operates and thereby opens the door to its critical analysis.

A detailed examination of Friedrich Mergel's transformation from an agrarian swineherd into a dandy who flaunts the wealth he acquires from the wanton destruction of nature will help us support the theory that Droste-Hülshoff's text operates around a structure of displacement. Critics have never questioned the seminal role of Simon Semmler in Friedrich's metamorphosis; if anything, they have mystified it by playing up Simon as a devil figure, an evil Mephistotelian seducer who lures Friedrich away from the path of the straight and narrow.[25] But even if we acknowledge Simon's role as seducer, we still need to ask precisely what it is he seduces Friedrich into. The standard answer, in keeping with the Judeo-Christian image of the devil and Droste-Hülshoff's adherence to Catholic doctrine, is that Simon leads Friedrich down the path of moral sin: more specifically, to the sin of *superbia*. But Friedrich's arrogance, his sense of superiority and power over his fellow villagers, is based exclusively on the superficial trappings of wealth that he derives, first, from the criminal activities of his uncle and the wood poachers, and second, from the uncollateralized credit he acquires from the Jew Aaron. In short, his haughtiness is fueled completely by the (false) promise of wealth made available by the destructive commercial practices of the wood poachers and the dependence on usurious credit. The figure of Simon forms a kind of lynchpin that joins together these two strands of unproductive—indeed, ultimately ruinous—economic enterprise: he stands, as Ronald Schneider has correctly claimed (*Realismus und Restauration* 287), as a kind of prototype for the petit bourgeois entrepreneur, an entrepreneur, one might add, whose economic demise is tied to his own shady dealings.

From the outset Simon is associated with the spirit of commercialism. If the people of the village view him as "a disagreeable, quarrelsome/wheeler-dealer [*Händel suchenden*] sort of fellow" (9), then the phrase *Händel suchend* indicates not merely, in its common understanding, his cantankerous nature, but alludes simultaneously to Simon's entrepreneurial spirit: he is a *Händler*, a wheeler-dealer always looking for ways to turn a quick profit. In this sense he is representative of the populace of Paderborn in general, whom Droste-Hülshoff describes at the beginning of the novella as "a breed of people who are more restless [*unruhiger*] and enterprising [*unternehmender*] than all their neighbors" (4), qualities she then directly links to their activities as wood poachers. It is surely no coincidence that both of these traits, "restless" and "enterprising," are later associated explicitly with Simon. The narrator paints anything but a complimentary picture of Friedrich's uncle when he is first introduced: "Simon Semmler was a small, restless [*unruhiger*], gaunt man with fish-like, bulging eyes and in general a face like a pike, an uncanny fellow" (9). And somewhat later he is described as someone "who simply could not live without having projects, who at times undertook [*unternahm*] important public tasks, for example, the building of roads" (16). The one cited example of Simon's important public projects, the building of roads, has significant implications; it ties him, on the more general level, to the construction of the infrastructure required for commercial progress, and more specifically to the roads and paths the wood poachers need in order to bring their booty to the ships waiting at the river. If, as Droste-Hülshoff's narrator claims, this province had previously been "without factories and trade, without major roads for the transport of troops" (3), then the "entrepreneurial" Simon (9), as the builder of roads and paths, is the very incarnation of industrial transformation.

The name Simon has often presented a bit of a puzzle to critics. Due to its Biblical origin, it stands apart from the names of all the other Paderborn natives in Droste-Hülshoff's novella. Martha Helfer suggests that this name is a sign of Simon's Jewish ancestry (237), to which I would simply add the caveat that "ancestry" must be understood in symbolic rather than in genealogical terms. Heinz Rölleke, alternatively, argues that the name Simon alludes to Simon Iscariot, the Biblical father of Judas, and that if we see Friedrich as Simon Semmler's metaphorical son, then this allusion implicitly identifies him with Judas ("Kann man" 413–14; see also Fricke 313). I would like to suggest the possible relevance of a further Biblical reference, to Simon Magus of Acts 8:9–24. This passage tells the story of a man named Simon from the city of Samaria who is known for his magical powers. When he witnesses how the apostles Peter and John bestow the Holy Spirit upon people simply by touching them, Simon expresses his desire to acquire this same power: "Now when Simon saw that the Spirit was given through the laying on of the apostles' hands, he offered them money, saying, 'Give me also this power, that any one on whom I lay my hands may receive the Holy Spirit.' But Peter said to him, 'Your silver perish with you, because you thought you could obtain the gift of God with money!'" (Acts 8:18–20). This Biblical Simon and Simon Semmler are joined by their worship of money and by their belief that money can be used as the vehicle of exchange for any commodity whatsoever, even for the power to dispense the Holy Spirit. But there are other traits that align these two Simons: one is a smug self-confidence in their own greatness (see Acts 18:9); another is their desire to have magical powers over others. Indeed, Simon Semmler might be viewed as a perverted parody of Simon the magician, who, when he lays his hands on people like his nephew Friedrich, bestows not the Holy Spirit, but instills instead the evil spirit of his own pride, greed, and shady commercialism.

Droste-Hülshoff makes no secret of the fact that Simon's adoption of his nephew is the direct cause of the radical transformations in Friedrich's character. Summarizing developments after Friedrich leaves home to work for his uncle, the narrator remarks, "From that time on the boy [Friedrich] was as if transformed; his dreamy nature completely disappeared, he behaved with confidence, began to pay attention to his appearance, and soon gained the reputation of an elegant, clever fellow" (16). This transmogrification from a withdrawn, dreamy shepherd into an outgoing pretty boy who exudes self-confidence is triggered solely by his newfound capacity to earn money, a pursuit that entirely consumes Friedrich's time and energy: "[A]ll his energies [were] directed toward outside earnings" (16). It is consistent with this that Friedrich, basking in the glow of his own magnanimity, gives his handmade violin to Johannes Niemand with the words, "My time for playing is past; now I have to earn money" (14).

Friedrich's transformation is framed by two occurrences of the metaphor of reflecting mirrors. When he first goes off with Simon, the latter is called a *Zauberspiegel* (11), a "magical mirror" that projects an image of Friedrich's future development: the unscrupulous character of Simon thereby appears as Friedrich's inescapable fate. The "great family resemblance" (11) that exists between these two figures consists in Friedrich's sudden, and economically motivated, appropriation of his uncle's character traits. Friedrich eventually even assumes the same pike face as his uncle (9, 27), so that their identification becomes complete. The appearance of Johannes

Niemand, Friedrich's mysterious doppelgänger, which is completely unmotivated by any contingencies of plot or aesthetic structure, is the primary technique Droste-Hülshoff implements to represent the radical transformation Friedrich undergoes. Here again the metaphor of the magically reflecting mirror is employed, with a new twist. Instead of reflecting Friedrich's future, as Simon does, Johannes, as Friedrich's *verkümmertes Spiegelbild*, his "stunted mirror reflection" (14), represents his past: he is the pale image of Friedrich's former self, the shy, withdrawn, fearful shepherd boy, the placeholder for the Friedrich who has become the arrogant, pretentious, and money-oriented dandy. This is reinforced by Johannes's surname, Niemand, which literally means "no one": he stands in for the "nothing" Friedrich used to be. The wedding scene, in which Johannes is caught stealing butter to tide him over for the winter, serves to highlight not only the consistency of this act of thievery with the criminal inclinations of Friedrich's character, but also underscores a significant difference. Whereas Friedrich, especially in his role as spy for the wood poachers, turns to theft as a way of acquiring surplus value, symbolized by his dependence on money (16), Johannes is motivated by the more immediate, existential need to sustain and feed himself: the object of his thievery is *butter*. The split in Friedrich's character that the doppelgänger motif invokes, in other words, mirrors the economic divide between an agrarian mentality founded on use value (Johannes) and a commercial, protocapitalistic sensibility focused on exchange value and profit (Friedrich).

Let us now attempt to chart Friedrich's psychological development by tracing the history of those artifacts, especially the silver buttons, that become the symbolic representatives of his obsession with external semblance. We should note, first of all, that after Friedrich sends Brandis down the wrong path, one of the last visible signs of the forest ranger is the glint of the steel buttons on his suit as they are illuminated by the rising sun (20). The shiny metal button and his hunting jacket represent both Brandis's greater wealth and his superior social authority. Friedrich's desire to deck himself out with silver buttons as the symbols of a similar wealth and authority imply that his treacherous deception of the forester is perpetrated not so much to protect the *Blaukittel*, or even to get revenge for Brandis's rancorous remarks, but more as an expression of Friedrich's wish to appropriate the social and economic status Brandis represents. Here again the acquisition of these symbolic values is dialectically tied to destruction. Just as the wood poachers thoughtlessly lay waste to the forest for the sake of monetary gain, Friedrich recklessly endangers a human being out of the desire to appropriate his symbolic capital. In the case of the wood poachers it is easier to understand that their destruction of nature is ultimately self-destructive: they eradicate the natural basis for their own subsistence by destroying the forests that constitute the distinguishing natural characteristic of their homeland. In Friedrich's case this connection is harder to see, but it is nonetheless present, concretized most vividly in the suicide that ends his life. This is the thrust of the economic message inscribed in *Die Judenbuche*: that the lure of profit and the seduction of semblance and superficial wealth made possible by capitalist commercialism ultimately harbor an inescapably self-destructive dialectic.

Friedrich certainly does his best to escape the fate of self-destruction: he runs away, but only to be exploited and misused as a slave laborer. In a sense this is an all too fitting fate, for if as the sorcerer's apprentice Friedrich had hoped to assume and wield the powers derived from colonial capitalism, ultimately he becomes the victim of the very powers he would control. When, twenty-seven years after his initial flight, the squire searches Friedrich's room—which he mistakenly believes to be the room of Johannes Niemand—the inventory he takes is telling: "[O]n the table [were] a basin, six new wooden spoons, and a box. The squire opened it; it contained five groschen [small coins], cleanly wrapped in paper, and four silver vest buttons. The squire looked at them attentively. 'A memento from Mergel,' he muttered, and left the room" (41). The whittled wooden spoons conclusively identify their owner for the reader as Friedrich Mergel, who is shown whittling just prior to the confrontation with Brandis (18). This further indicates that the coins and silver buttons are much more than mere "mementos" of Friedrich, as the squire presumes: they are incontrovertible signs that identify as Friedrich Mergel this character whom the villagers take to be Johannes Niemand. The scar by which the squire later identifies the hanging corpse as that of Friedrich is indeed nothing but a red herring. First of all, there has been no mention anywhere in the text of such a scar as an identifying trait of Friedrich; but more important, after discovering the artifacts of wealth in "Johannes's" room, the squire has all the evidence necessary to recognize that "Johannes" is none other than

Friedrich himself. His failure to do so represents just one more act of misprision in a text rife with such errors in judgment. Even more significantly, the squire's failed identification replicates and reinforces the dialectic of failed self-recognition that underpins the didactic core of Droste-Hülshoff's text.

In this interpretive context the Hebrew charm carved into the Jews' beech takes on a new meaning. "When you near this place, the same thing will happen to you as you did to me" (42), reads the inscription. Earlier versions of the charm, as recorded in Droste-Hülshoff's notes and manuscripts, were much more specific; in the draft immediately prior to the final version of the text, for example, the incantation reads, "When you near this place, you shall die a horrible death on this spot within three days" (*HKA* 5.2: 433). By contrast, in its final form the charm assumes a discursive generality that almost entirely defies specification: the precise nature of the retribution remains unnamed, and as a result even the act for which retribution is sought remains unidentifiable. What "sin" is being atoned for here? Is it the murder of the Jew Aaron, as we are led to believe by the connection of the Hebrew charm to the protest of the Jewish community against Aaron's death? Or is the crime that demands retribution the murder of the forest ranger Brandis (Huszai 491), in which the beech tree also plays a prominent role? The fact that it is Brandis's son who discovers Friedrich's corpse hanging in the tree would seem to support this latter hypothesis (*Judenbuche* 41). Or perhaps the beech tree represents the brutalized forests themselves, which take symbolic revenge on Friedrich for their devastation at the hands of the *Blaukittel* (Allerdissen 212–13)?[26]

The discursive generality of the charm in its final form suggests that it should be read inclusively rather than exclusively, subsuming all these possible references. And indeed, it is the symbol of the beech tree itself that ultimately associates these three events. The relationship of the beech to the murders of Brandis and Aaron is self-evident. But it is important to recall that one of the most concrete descriptions of the brutal ravaging of the forests by the wood poachers culminates in the image of a lone beech, felled when it is full of healthy foliage, but left to rot because the activities of the poachers were interrupted: "[A] beech tree lay across the path, felled in full foliage, its branches extended high above it and its fresh leaves quivering in the night wind" (*Judenbuche* 12). The beech tree is personified in this passage, its limbs stretched out as though pleading for mercy or demanding revenge for its untimely death. The senselessly destroyed beech thus stands as a representative for all the victims in this text, human or vegetable. In the final analysis, then, the Hebrew inscription boils down to a general maxim along the lines of you will reap what you sow.[27] Only in this respect is this incantation related to the Old Testament logic of eye for an eye, tooth for a tooth; for this charm is only superficially about retribution and revenge. On a more profound and suggestive level it encapsulates that dialectic of destruction perpetrated for the sake of personal gain that is characteristic of all the pernicious acts in this text and that is represented by the beech into which the incantation is inscribed. It is only fitting, then, that the beech tree should become the vehicle for the self-destruction of Friedrich Mergel, whose deeds and whose very name—the overproductive fertilizer that ultimately depletes the soil—signal the destructive dialectic between commercial profiteering and ecological demise. Friedrich stands as a concrete warning about the self-destructive proclivities of an overfertile capitalist economy and the psychological and characterological monsters it breeds.

The Ethnological Displacement of Economic Self-Critique

Before concluding I would like to point out the coherence of this reading of *Die Judenbuche*, which stresses economic (self-)critique, with the general tenor of Droste-Hülshoff's historical observations of her native Westphalia. A tendency toward aligning ethnographic analysis with a pseudo-Hegelian, pessimistically tinged philosophy of history is already apparent in Droste-Hülshoff's "Westphälische Schilderungen," which in this regard is prototypical for all her critical reflections on her contemporary Westphalia. In this text Droste-Hülshoff cites her motivation for depicting her native land as the desire to record for posterity a lifestyle that is threatened by encroaching modernization: "[L]et us therefore grasp one last time what is present today in all its peculiarity," she remarks in self-justification, "before the slippery/vulgar [*schlüpfrige*] stratum that is gradually overflowing all of Europe has also buried this tranquil corner of the earth" (*HKA* 5.1: 48). The metaphor of the "slippery/vulgar stratum" slowly covering all of Europe clearly evokes Droste-Hülshoff's nostalgic protest against the progress of enlightenment, the great equalizer that, like death, eradicates all differences and distinctions.

Ronald Schneider has shown how the three primary evils Droste-Hülshoff identifies with Paderborn province in this ethnographic study—cunning, the inclination to evil, and arrogance—are embodied in the character of Friedrich Mergel (*Realismus und Restauration* 241). He fails to note, however, that the complementary evils she attributes to the province of Sauerland also find their way into *Die Judenbuche* in the activities of the wood poachers in general, but above all in the character of Simon Semmler. Droste-Hülshoff portrays the Sauerland as the most industrial, commercialized province of Westphalia and as a region in which the people are most alienated from their natural environment. She offers a simple explanation: "The reason for this is obvious: it resides in the commercial relationships of the latter [the people of the Sauerland], which open up their homeland to foreigners and drive them into foreign lands, where, influenced by the culture of merchants, they water down their customs, and by marrying outsiders water down the blood of their line with each passing day" (*HKA* 5.1: 52). The openness to, indeed, the affinity of the populace of the Sauerland for trade and commerce effects a watering down of local customs as well as of the native bloodlines. In what follows, however, Droste-Hülshoff intensifies this criticism to a shrill lament: under the influence of their emergent industrial economy, replete with paper mills, iron works, salt mines, and a horde of merchants, the people of the Sauerland have lost their sensibility for religion, preferring "the sound of the money they import" to the music of the Catholic litany (*HKA* 5.1: 53). The relevance of this description for the economic transformation depicted in *Die Judenbuche*, and promoted above all by Simon Semmler, is obvious. All the corresponding elements are present here: money, commercialism, loss of religious faith, lack of identity. In "Westphälische Schilderungen" Droste-Hülshoff portrays her own native province of Münster as the heartland region of Westphalia that has most successfully resisted the march of enlightened rationality, commercial capitalism, and industrial modernization. Paderborn and Sauerland, by contrast, have already succumbed; and *Die Judenbuche* can be read as a kind of moralizing example story that presents to the populace of Münsterland a deterrent image of the fate that awaits them if they fail to resist the corrosive influence of modern commercialization.

In "Westphälische Schilderungen" Droste-Hülshoff voices this admonition, significantly, in the form of a Westphalian self-critique: Sauerland and Paderborn have already embraced what, in a letter to Melchior von Diepenbrock from May 1845, she terms the "universal *demoralization*" of the modern era (*HKA* 10.1: 287). In the same letter she calls for the construction of a dam "against immorality and perverted nature" (10.1: 287), and she may have viewed *Die Judenbuche* as just one preliminary step in this antimodernist, profoundly traditionalist, and conservative project. But what we discover from her critical examination of Westphalia in "Westphälische Schilderungen" is that Droste-Hülshoff explicitly conceived the decline and degeneration wrought by capitalist modernism in ethnological terms, identifying specific ethnically derived characteristics in the populaces of the Sauerland and Paderborn as the germ bearers of the modernist virus. In *Die Judenbuche* the self-critical aspects of this admonishing critique have largely been effaced—transported not merely into concrete characters whose fictionality makes this critique palatable to her Westphalian compatriots, as Droste-Hülshoff claims,[28] but displaced as well into a criticism of the corrupting impact of an ethnic group nonnative to Westphalia: the Jews. As Monika Richarz has shown (19), the temporal parallel of Jewish emancipation and the emergence of industrial society in Germany led to the conflation of these two phenomena, so that the Jews were often mistakenly identified as the motor behind this transformation. Similarly, in *Die Judenbuche* it is the Jew Aaron, depicted as exploiting the character faults of people like Friedrich for the sake of his own economic profit, who becomes the displaced target of Friedrich's vendetta. In this sense the Jewish characters in *Die Judenbuche*—not only Aaron, but Lumpenmoises, Wucherjoel, and the Jewish community in general—become the overcharged representatives of the economic and moral ills that plague Westphalian society.[29]

In many respects this ethnological displacement crystallizes around the figure of Simon Semmler, who partakes symbolically in the ethnic worlds both of the Westphalians and of the Jews. The embodied spirit of the modernist commercial economy commonly associated with Jewish entrepreneurs, he is additionally marked by his Biblical name as a liminal figure.

But more important is the role Simon plays in Friedrich's psychological economy and the manner in which in this domain Friedrich's anger and frustration with Simon are displaced into the murder of the Jew Aaron. It is Simon, after all, who assumes the function of Friedrich's father figure and authoritarian superego and who prevents Friedrich from going to confession and thereby venting his own sense of guilt. It is Simon, as well, who serves as the tempter who calls forth and nourishes Friedrich's greed, arrogance, and will to power. But instead of directing his reproaches at the person who is ultimately responsible, Friedrich displaces his anger and his abjection onto the only characters who stand lower in the social hierarchy: onto Johannes, whom Friedrich publicly beats and humiliates, and onto Aaron, whom he (allegedly) murders.

This displacement in Friedrich's psyche is mirrored in the text by the displacement of the narrative energy from the economic concerns central to the first half of the novella to the issues surrounding Aaron and his murder in the second half. My thesis has been that the second narrative sequence, which critics almost universally take to be the core of the novella, is actually subordinate to the first,[30] representing an ethnologically distorted displacement of the economic critique presented in the first narrative sequence, the story of the historical transformation from a feudal, agrarian economy based on use value to a modern, commercial, capitalist economy grounded in exchange value and profit. The tracks along which this ethnological displacement travels in Droste-Hülshoff's text are the well-worn associations of the Jews with the modern commercial economy, made available in plentiful supply in the general discourse of anti-Semitism omnipresent throughout the nineteenth century in Germany (Landes 19).

This image of the Jews as the disrupters of traditional values is codified more than a half century after the publication of Droste-Hülshoff's novella in Werner Sombart's vociferous attack on the Jews, in *Die Juden und das Wirtschaftsleben* (The Jews and economic life, 1911), as the transmitters of commercial capitalism. Defending a conservative traditionalism similar to that valorized by Droste-Hülshoff, Sombart writes with distinct nostalgia about the precapitalist socioeconomic configuration.

> Its principal characteristic was still stability, traditionalism. The individual human being, even when he was active in commercial enterprises,

had not yet lost himself in the noise and hubbub of these commercial activities. He was still his own master. Moreover, he also continued to preserve the dignity of the autonomous man, who does not betray himself simply to earn a profit. (150)

For Sombart it is the Jews who interfere with and transform this traditionalist idyll: "And it was the Jews who stormed this firmly established world. We see them violate this economic order and this economic sensibility in everything they do" (151).

Sombart's formula for capitalist (Jewish) modernism is self-betrayal for the sake of profit. Is there any better way to describe the mechanism at work in characters like Simon Semmler and Friedrich Mergel or in the destructive practices of the *Blaukittel*? And yet, in Droste-Hülshoff's novella, contrary to Sombart's allegation, it is clearly not the Jews who introduce and disseminate this new economic immorality into Westphalian society, but rather representatives of the indigenous Westphalian populace. Consistent with her depiction in "Westphälische Schilderungen," these socially disintegrative traits spring directly from the native soil—from the *Mergel*—of Westphalia itself. Only in a secondary move is this penetrating self-critique displaced from the Blue Smocks, the industrialized Westphalians, to the Jews via associations between capitalist economic practices and the Jews that are part and parcel of the discourse of anti-Semitism in nineteenth-century Germany. But this displacement from the Blue Smocks to the Jews is more than just a red herring that sends Droste-Hülshoff's readers down a false interpretive path; it mimics precisely the psychological mechanism of the novella's protagonist Friedrich Mergel, who displaces self-critique and indictment of the profitmongering sensibilities of his uncle Simon into an attack on the Jew Aaron, as representative of the Jews in general.

Droste-Hülshoff's representation of this displacement onto the ethnological Other constitutes the kernel of this text's didactic message: it exposes this ethnological self-exculpation—a flight into the excuses conveniently made available by popular anti-Semitic discourse—as the crucial psychological mechanism legitimating practices that contribute to economic and ecological self-destruction. Viewed in this way, the disintegration of Droste-Hülshoff's novella into two seemingly independent narratives actually makes strategic sense. The first plot depicts the participation of the Westphalians themselves in the economic exploitation of their natural environment, while the second story demonstrates how they deny their responsibility for this ecological disaster by passing it off on an ethnologically defined Other. The primary critical thrust of Droste-Hülshoff's novella remains an indictment of the exploitation of the natural world for profit and commercial self-interest; but it also exposes the act of human self-deceit by which responsibility for the resulting destruction is shunted off onto others. Ultimately, then, *Die Judenbuche* can be read as a perceptive and insightful analysis of the dialectical entanglement of the capitalist economy with the ecological (self-)destruction of the human life-world and the complex psychological self-justifications by which humans legitimate this destructive impulse.

8 / THE (MIS)FORTUNE OF COMMERCE

Economic Transformation in Adalbert Stifter's *Bergkristall*

Showing what is truly great in the miniscule, showing the way into the invisible, and, moreover, by penetrating all that is obvious, all that is ordinary, to let all that is unspoken in the spoken be heard—this kind of speaking is what is most effective about the language of the poet Adalbert Stifter.

—Martin Heidegger ("Adalbert Stifters 'Eisgeschichte'" 37)

Children do not make revolutions, and neither do mothers.

—Adalbert Stifter (*Sämmtliche Werke* 17: 324)

The Ideological Veneer of Stifter's Bucolic Idylls

NE OF THE MOST CHARACTERISTIC TRAITS OF ADALBERT Stifter's (1805–68) fictional world is its evocation of a premodernist historical period with an aura of invariability and permanence. Although he spent over twenty years of his formative life in Vienna, an international metropolis destined to become the intellectual crucible of modernism, few elements of the industrial world, with its hustle and bustle, its impersonality, its emphasis on competition, monetary gain, and proprietary relations, find their way into his fiction.[1] This is perhaps nowhere so true as for the novella *Bergkristall* (Rock crystal, 1845/1852), which tells of the inhabitants of Gschaid, a small village all but cut off from the rest of the world by mountainous terrain. Josef Scharl captures this character of Gschaid as a rural idyll in the illustration he created as a frontispiece for the 1945 English translation *Rock Crystal* (fig. 10). Indeed, this story explicitly thematizes the constancy and invariance of this village and its inhabitants, of whom it is said,

> They are very steadfast and things always remain the same. If a stone falls out of a wall, the same one is put back in, new houses are built in the same style as the old, damaged roofs are repaired with identical shingles, and if a household has dappled cows, they always raise such calves, and the house always stays the same color. (*Bergkristall* 187)

Just as the inanimate objects of the village always remain self-identical, the fallen stone placed back into the wall at its proper place, the roof repaired with the same kind of shingle, and even the house paint never changing color, the animate world of the village—the cows, and presumably the people as well—continually draw on the same gene pool, so that identical characteristics recur from generation to generation. Yet despite this assertion of the nearly absolute isolation of the village—no major roads pass through it, and the inhabitants form "a world of their own" and possess "a language that is distinct from that of the flatlands beyond" (186)—on the level of plot *Bergkristall* is concerned with fundamental transgressions of this law of constancy and autonomy. If, as Jens Tismar has maintained, the literary idyll of the nineteenth century (and beyond) in Germany is characterized by this status as idyll being both endangered and inherently dangerous (10), then this is decidedly true of Stifter's ostensibly bucolic novella *Bergkristall*. In the case of this text, the danger that threatens to undermine this idyll of a rural lifestyle not yet invaded by the modern commercial economy and its concomitant vices is a domestic product, harbored and bred within its very midst: the local shoemaker Sebastian, who disrupts the most honored economic and moral conventions of this autonomous village. Above all, he has imported a foreign element into the gene pool by marrying the daughter of the wealthy dyer from Millsdorf, a commercial center in an adjacent valley. The shoemaker himself, moreover, has a somewhat checkered past: he left the village in his youth and returned with a habitus and with habits out of keeping with the norms of Gschaid (195).

10 / Idyllic atmosphere of the isolated village of Gschaid. Frontispiece by Josef Scharl from Adalbert Stifter, *Rock Crystal: A Christmas Tale*, trans. Elizabeth Mayer and Marianne Moore, illus. Josef Scharl (New York: Pantheon, 1945).

And the offspring of his marriage, the children Konrad and Sanna, become by village standards veritable world travelers by constantly making the trip across the mountain pass to the town of Millsdorf in order to visit their grandparents. The entire life of this family, which stands in the center of the narrated events, is marked by transgressions of the isolation and apparent constancy of life in the village. In this sense, *Bergkristall* is anything but a simple *Dorfgeschichte*, a tale of rural life that portrays the opposition between life in the city and existence in the idyllic countryside, as Jürgen Hein has asserted (25, 29); rather, it depicts the incipient invasion of the commercial metropolis into the once pastoral life of the village. One of the principal questions raised by the text thus becomes whether these deviations from the law of invariance are ultimately reigned in and drawn into the circle of historical sameness, or whether they disrupt the closed circle of Gschaid by introducing change and expanding the horizon of the village. Critics have tended to defend the first line of argumentation, interpreting *Bergkristall* as a story about the integration of the foreign, the acceptance of the dyer's daughter and her children into the community of Gschaid, and the shoemaker's embracing of the interpersonal values of the village.[2] My interpretation will follow the second line, arguing that the shoemaker and his family represent a major transformation in the living and working conditions of Gschaid, a change that is essentially of an economic and commercial nature.

If Stifter's texts in general invoke bucolic idylls apparently untainted by modern commercialism, they also contain—by its very absence—an implicit critique of the economic reality in which Stifter and his contemporaries lived. This reality was one of burgeoning industrialization, expansion of the market economy, the rise of the moneyed bourgeoisie, and a parallel decline of the petite bourgeoisie and the independent craftsperson. Stifter's own family was adversely affected by this economic development. His father, Johann Stifter, was forced to abandon his trade as a linen weaver, turning instead to the flax trade and agriculture to win his livelihood, when cheap imports from English factories displaced higher-priced handmade linen throughout Europe (Naumann 1).

Stifter scholarship has traditionally been dominated by critics whose attitudes are those of the antiquarian historian as described by Friedrich

Nietzsche in the second of his "Unfashionable Observations," *Vom Nutzen und Nachtheil der Historie für das Leben* (On the utility and liability of history for life). The antiquarian outlook, according to Nietzsche, is one marked by unquestioning veneration of the past, by a sense of piety toward its symbols, and by the desire to preserve and possess them (1: 265–70). In this sense Stifter's critics have tended to emulate his antiquarian views. But to treat Stifter and his utopias in such an uncritical manner, as Horst Albert Glaser has argued (viii), is to take his utopianism at its word, without recognizing that it is created *ex negativo*, in explicit opposition to the prevailing reality of Stifter's day. For Glaser, as for other left-oriented critics, the industrial world is conspicuous in Stifter's fiction by its very absence: it is the missing, unidentified center that structures Stifter's pastoral vision.[3] Theodor Adorno, for example, formulates this discrepancy in Stifter's narratives in terms of an ideologically motivated denial of capitalist society that is so exaggerated as to point unwittingly to the nonideological truth that underpins its own flight into ideological disguise.

> What occurs against the will of this [Stifter's] prose, by means of the discrepancy between its form and an already capitalistic society, accrues to its expressiveness. Ideological exaggeration indirectly lends the work its nonideological truth content, its superiority over all literary texts that exhort the comfort of consolation and valorize the provincial refuge, and this earns it the authentic quality that Nietzsche admired. (*Ästhetische Theorie* 346)

What rescues Stifter's works from the curse of being merely conciliatory, according to Adorno, is that their structural center is marked by a discrepancy between literary form and the economic status of the world out of which it emerged. By definition, such structural centers can never remain completely unarticulated: they find their way secretly and inconspicuously into the narratives they create. As this chapter will attempt to demonstrate, nascent commercialism and the economics of exchange function as the unacknowledged ghostwriter of Stifter's *Bergkristall*—a ghostwriter whose signature can yet be detected in the palimpsest of the text.

Like all but one of the stories collected in the novella collection *Bunte Steine* (Medley of gemstones), *Bergkristall* has a compositional history that encompasses Stifter's experience of the 1848 revolution. First published in 1845 under the title *Der heilige Abend* (Christmas Eve), this story was revised in the wake of the revolution for inclusion in *Bunte Steine*, which appeared in 1852. It is well known that the revolution was far and away the most cataclysmic event Stifter ever experienced, initiating several major transitions in his life and thought (Requadt 147–48). One of these was his move from Vienna to Linz immediately afterward. Another was his new-found pedagogical mission, his sense that the role of intellectuals must be one of positive intervention in the general education of the masses, teaching them to rely on reason for the control of their otherwise unrestrained instincts. The conception of *Bunte Steine* as a book for young people provides evidence for this pedagogical purpose, as do Stifter's collaboration on a humanistic reader for use in the public schools and his assumption of the duties of school superintendent in Linz.[4] But the most concrete testimony to the fluctuation Stifter's thought underwent at this time can be found in the profusion of cultural-political essays he wrote in the months subsequent to the revolution. Ultimately, witnessing the chaos and violence of the events of 1848 transformed Stifter from a radical democrat who advanced the issues of political change into an archconservative who, skeptical about the ability of human beings to liberate themselves from their own egotistical drives, argued for the necessity of a repressive social and political order much like that represented in the antiquated Habsburg monarchy.[5] Thus in the essay "Die oktroyierte Verfassung" (The imposed constitution), written in March 1849, he explicitly turns against the idea of grassroots democracy and justifies acceptance of the constitution handed down from above by the Habsburg emperor. His primary argument against democracy by the people is that the commoners are not yet mature enough for self-rule, that they are far too driven by affects and egoistic desires to be entrusted with the freedom to decide their own political fate (40–41). Even more significant, perhaps, is that Stifter condemns the disorder and uncertainty caused by the revolutionary events almost solely on economic grounds. In this same essay he writes,

> The country is in a state of transition, in their business dealings all
> people hold back as much as they can, until they arrive at a state of
> security; trade, industry, the arts are stagnating, poverty is increasing

at a horrifying rate. This situation must be changed and replaced by one that elicits trust and establishes definite laws. (40)

This appeal to a stable order and the trust it engenders as the sine qua non for economic prosperity is one of the most prominent leitmotifs of the essays of this period. It is articulated most forcefully in a central passage from the essay "Der Staat" (The state), Stifter's defense of the political state as the guarantor of security.

> A well-founded political order provides every individual with a feeling of security, and on the basis of this feeling of security he enters into exchanges with others, so that by means of these transactions each might acquire what he needs. . . . The more orderly the political relations, the more things people need, since they also have an income; the craftsperson can create all the more, and he can provide work for all the more laborers. Experiencing a feeling of security, the merchant places more orders in distant lands, he imports products from these lands and exports our products to them. (23–24)

The entire system of trade, from the most rudimentary exchange between two individuals to the circulation of goods in the worldwide market, relies, according to Stifter, on the political stability afforded by the well-founded state. The needs of human beings are tied directly to their incomes, and an increase in the latter, brought on by expanding commerce, in turn stimulates production and raises income levels. Stifter's description reads like a textbook example of the codependence between overriding market forces and individual needs and actions, and he recognizes that this entire spiral, with its concomitant prosperity, is founded on the psychological qualities of confidence and faith. In that regard, at least, his views are related to the conservative views of the state formulated by Adam Müller, whose economic and political theories we examined in previous chapters. Stifter stresses this psychological factor in economic affairs when he turns his example around and enumerates the debilitating consequences of political insecurity: the withholding of agricultural products and manufactured goods from the market, a shortage of money in circulation, the eventual collapse of many businesses, and the impoverishment and suffering of the masses.

All of this leads Stifter to the assertion that the most sacred duty of every citizen—again reminiscent of Müller—is the preservation of the political order ("Der Staat" 24).

If we compare the orderliness and inherent rationality of this postrevolutionary portrayal of the market economy with Stifter's prerevolutionary view, articulated in the essay "Waarenauslagen und Ankündigungen" (Showcases and advertisements) from the 1844 essay collection *Wien und die Wiener in Bildern aus dem Leben* (Vienna and the Viennese in pictures from their lives), we get a sense of how dramatically the experience of the revolution altered Stifter's economic thinking. In this earlier work it is an irrational *Kauflust*, the obsessive desire to buy experienced by every individual, that drives the expanding consumer market. Stifter sets about explaining the sudden proliferation of showcases for the display and advertisement of commodities on the streets of Vienna. His reaction manifests a degree of critical insight into the subtle mechanisms of the consumer mentality that began to develop at the end of the eighteenth century—as we saw in our investigation of the theory of a value-creating imagination that emerged from the German debates over physiocratic doctrine—but that only attained the shrill and pointed tenor characteristic of Stifter's remarks considerably later, in particular with the criticisms of the Frankfurt School philosophers in the early decades of the twentieth century.[6] Stifter begins his examination with the simple remark that these display cases have the obvious purpose of advertising—and hence of selling—specific commodities. But he immediately recognizes "that these displays and advertisements not only have the purpose of convincing the *willing* purchaser to buy, but much rather and ultimately the purpose of convincing the *unwilling* one to buy" ("Waarenauslagen und Ankündigungen" 167; emphasis added). Stifter elucidates this with a comparison drawn from the Bible: the first skilled salesperson to seduce an unwilling consumer into buying something they did not want was the snake in paradise, and Eve was his first victim. This comparison is significant because it implies that the semblance and deceit of such salesmanship is the root of all evil, the underlying reason for the banishment of human beings from paradise. But the snake does not bear sole responsibility for this situation: it is able to prey on the instinctual *Kauflust*, the "lust to buy," that is "an ancient hereditary evil of the human race" (168). Thus the seductive salesperson, the modern snake, recognizes that the sale of his or her goods ultimately depends solely on the superficialities of external packaging, not on the usefulness or even the quality of the item itself. Indeed, the buying public, according to Stifter, has bought so completely into the conventions of commodity aesthetics that it refuses to buy whenever these conventions are not upheld (175). Clearly, it is a long way from these critical, even cynical remarks on nascent consumerism to the valorization of the market economy as the ultimate good elicited by a stable political apparatus, the position Stifter upholds in his postrevolution essays. This shift from the condemnation of commerce in the guise of consumerism and its glorification as the basis of all economic advancement and prosperity is inscribed into the novella *Bergkristall*, itself a product of this transitional period of Stifter's life.

Possessive Individualism: Sebastian the Shoemaker as Representative of Capitalist Innovation

The claim that *Bergkristall* thematizes economic and commercial issues can scarcely help but call forth resistance, if not indignation. Isn't this novella nothing but, in the words of Martin Swales, a "harmless tale" ("Litanei und Leerstelle" 76), just a simple story about two children who, surprised by a sudden snowstorm as they traverse a mountain pass on Christmas Eve on their way home from visiting their grandparents, are kept from falling asleep and freezing to death by the grandeur and mercy of nature (Egon Schwarz 266)? Isn't this tale the veritable prototype of Stifter's *sanftes Gesetz*, the "gentle law" articulated in his theoretical preface to *Bunte Steine*, which claims that even the most insignificant natural phenomena are the manifestations of higher laws, and that these laws of nature—the merciful rescue of two children, for example—have their parallels in the moral world of human nature (Doppler 13; Hankamer 85; Mason 79)? Where could this narrative of childish innocence, natural disaster, and grand rescue possibly be tainted by questions of commerce, consumerism, and economic exchange? This is the question I will attempt to answer.[7]

Etymologically, the name of the isolated village that serves as locale for *Bergkristall*, *Gschaid*, derives from a German word meaning "divergence," with the specific significance of "watershed." Geographically, the village of Gschaid lies on one side of a watershed, the ridge that separates it from the town of Millsdorf in the next valley, and this is certainly one of the relevant meanings of the name. But in historical terms the village of Gschaid also passes through a watershed transition in the course of the events Stifter's novella relates: it undergoes an economic paradigm shift from a self-sufficient, predominantly land-based, agricultural economy to one increasingly dependent on the production of man-made commodities, the influx and circulation of money, and trade with other commercial centers. In his "Die deutsche Ideologie" (The German ideology), written in 1845–46, at approximately the same time Stifter wrote the first version of *Bergkristall*, Karl Marx describes this transformation, which he ties to the emergence of the bourgeoisie as the ruling economic class, in terms of the shift from natural to man-made instruments of production.

> This is where the distinction between natural [*naturwüchsigen*] instruments of production and those created by civilization comes into prominence. *Arable land* (water, etc.) can be viewed as a natural [*naturwüchsigen*] instrument of production. In the first instance, that of natural [*naturwüchsigen*] instruments of production, individuals are subsumed under nature, in the second instance under a product of labor. Thus in the first instance property (landed property) also appears as immediate, natural domination, in the second as the domination of labor, in particular of accumulated labor, of capital. The first instance presupposes that individuals are bound together by some bond, be it family, clan, the land itself, etc. etc.; the second instance that they are independent of one another and only bound together by exchange. . . . In the first instance the dominance of property owners over the nonpropertied can be based on personal relations, on a kind of community; in the second instance it must have assumed a reified form in a third element, in money. ("Die deutsche Ideologie" 378–79)

In general, the villagers of Gschaid conform to what Marx terms the *naturwüchsige*, the "natural," or immediate economy. They view themselves primarily as the subordinates of nature, which they venerate almost to the point of deification. Similarly, nature appears to them to be the source and basis of all their personal wealth. This reliance on nature is concretized in their relationship to the "Gars," the snow-capped mountain that looms far above the village. Stifter's narrator explicitly cites the mountain as the basis of the villagers' livelihoods: it is the source of water that drives their mills, waters their fields, and quenches their thirst; it provides the wood to build and heat their homes (*Bergkristall* 189). But beyond these practical necessities, the Gars also serves as a source of infinite pride, and the villagers identify so closely with it that they often feel "as if they had produced it themselves" (187). The mountain is, as Marx says of the natural economy, the foundation of the villagers' conception of personal property. Moreover, as the distinguishing trait of the village, the mountain also symbolizes the villagers' communal bond. "As the most striking thing in their surroundings, the mountain is an object of the villagers' gaze, and it has become the focus of many stories" (187). Community in *Bergkristall*, as so often in Stifter's works, is explicitly defined in terms of narrative interchange.[8] As the primary subject of narrative for the people of Gschaid, the Gars represents their tacit communal bond. Manifest in their relationship to the mountain, then, is the natural economy that provides the villagers with their subsistence. Of course, the tale related in *Bergkristall* is but one more—the latest—in the series of stories surrounding this mountain. As we will see, however, this new narrative no longer stresses the natural economy of the mountain, but instead focuses on its transgression by the artificial economy of man-made goods, labor, and human commerce.

Given the symbolic significance of the Gars for the natural economy of Gschaid, it is especially telling that it also becomes a commercial resource for the villagers, and this is the first indication in the story of an impending transformation from a natural to a commercialized economy. For among its utilitarian aspects, mention is also made of its value in terms of attracting commercial tourism.

> Aside from providing the inhabitants with their peculiarity, the mountain also has genuine utility [*wirklichen Nuzen*] for them. For when a group of hikers comes into the valley in order to climb the mountain from that side, the inhabitants of the village serve as guides, and to have been a guide once, to have experienced this and that, to be familiar with this or that place, is a distinction to which everyone is proud to lay claim. (*Bergkristall* 187)

What Stifter describes here is a rudimentary form of something that takes place today on a much grander scale: ecotourism, the commercialization of those final outposts of untrammeled nature, a nature not yet touched by commercial exploitation, industrialization, and metropolitanization. Although the villagers venerate their mountain for its natural qualities, it is these same qualities, ironically, that make it exploitable for commercial tourism, a phenomenon that will ultimately strip it of its natural mystique.[9] Prerequisite for this exploitation of the Gars for the purposes of commercial tourism, of course, is a strict delineation between "nature" and the rural communities it supports, on the one hand, and the industrialized city, on the other; and this same segregation, according to Marx, signals the split between the natural and the commercial economies ("Die deutsche Ideologie" 379). This division is thematized in *Bergkristall* as the juxtaposition between Millsdorf, the *Marktflecken* or "commercial center" (192), and Gschaid, the rural, predominantly agricultural community. The possibility of exploiting the Gars for the purposes of tourism gives a first indication that the "Millsdorfization"—the commercialization and modernization— of Gschaid is already underway in the narrated time of Stifter's story. Ecotourism represents an important shift in the lifestyle of the villagers away from a reliance on nature for immediate sustenance to an indirect dependence based on its value to others. This is symbolized in the monetary compensation, the *Lohn* (187) they receive for their duties as tour guides. Moreover, Stifter's language hints at the priority of this monetary exploitation of the mountain over its more immediate, natural uses when he refers to the former as "genuine utility"—as opposed, we must presume, to merely apparent, or at least less valuable, utility. This touristic exploitation of the Gars thus provides an important interface between Gschaid and the external, commercial world. The Gars attracts well-to-do city slickers, for whom the experience of unblemished nature represents an uncommon adventure; but this ecotourism thereby breaches the autonomy and self-sufficiency of the village, importing not only the adventure-hungry tourists, but also their economic system.

In the person of Sebastian the shoemaker, the father of Stifter's children-protagonists, the representative of commerce and progressive economics has, in fact, already infiltrated the village of Gschaid and its economic attitudes. As the main producer of *Kunsterzeugnisse*, "man-made commodi-

ties" (*Bergkristall* 185), he conforms with those characteristics Marx identifies in the modern commercial economy: he is subordinate not to nature,
but to his own labor; he is an accumulator of landed possessions and capital;[10] his relationships with others are not communally based, but grounded
in business relations and exchange;[11] and he is explicitly associated with a
monetary economy. Beyond this, however, he is the only villager who cultivates business relations that extend beyond the perimeter of Gschaid itself,
and in this sense he is the incarnation of a commercialism that ruptures the
apparent autonomy and self-sufficiency of the village.

To be sure, the shoemaker is not the sole representative of modern commerce in this story; the model he emulates, the text suggests, is that of his
father-in-law, the dyer in Millsdorf.[12] In both versions of the story, Millsdorf, the more flourishing of the two towns, is expressly associated with
trade and commercial activity. In the earlier version, *Der heilige Abend*, it
is described as having "commerce" (*Verkehr*; 144) with outlying areas; and
in *Bergkristall* it is said to maintain citylike trades and livelihood (193).
Moreover, the dyer himself is one of the wealthiest, commercially most
successful citizens of Millsdorf, someone who owns large parcels of agricultural land and understands how to improve his economic situation, as
we read in the first version of the text, by employing trade and exchange
(*Der heilige Abend* 150). In the second version this connection to industrialization is drawn out even more: the dyer has "a sizeable business, with
many employees, and even—something that was otherwise unheard of in
the valley—operated with machines" (*Bergkristall* 195). More important
than his factory-like business and his commercial success, however, are the
personal characteristics he displays. His paramount virtues are productivity and profitability: "[T]he dyer was an active and enterprising man, who
was intent on making the most of all his business affairs and who could
not bear to see a minute wasted, whether by him or by others" (*Der heilige
Abend* 149). Indeed, his devotion to his business enterprise is so total that
he rarely has time for his grandchildren when they cross the pass to visit,
and he is so obsessively concerned with the accumulation of wealth that
he even refuses to give them the most meager present: "[F]or although he
only had the one daughter and everything would ultimately pass on to her
anyway, he refused to give away even the most trifling thing, because everything had to serve as the basis and work toward the advantage and man-

agement of his business, which was his pride and joy" (150). The dyer, in other words, is the paragon of what C. B. Macpherson has called "possessive individualism," a political and economic philosophy that stresses ownership, acquisition, and property as the foundation of personal worth and sociopolitical power (Macpherson 3).[13] He is not avaricious for the sake of avarice, but simply for the sake of good business sense, and his suppression of immediate pleasures for himself as well as for others represents nothing other than the typically bourgeois strategy of deferral, the rejection of *jouissance* in the present so that it can be "capitalized" to generate a greater wealth of pleasure in some unknown but titillating future. The dyer is, in short, a dyed-in-the-wool capitalist—dying wool in Millsdorf.

It is tempting to claim that Stifter is setting up the dyer as the fall guy, as a negative example who, by exerting nefarious pressure on his son-in-law, the shoemaker in Gschaid, can be held responsible for the latter's corruption, his exclusive commitment to his occupation, and his subsequent estrangement from family and community. But to make such a claim would be to overlook that in the years following the revolution of 1848, Stifter himself became an advocate of precisely that possessive individualism manifested in the characters of the dyer and the shoemaker. We have already examined the motive of economic prosperity as the tenor that dominates Stifter's sociopolitical thinking in the essays from the postrevolutionary period. But the radical imbrication of power and economic status in Stifter's political and social thought is perhaps most clearly expressed in the essay "Der Zensus" (The voter franchise), published in May 1849. At issue in this essay are the characteristics that qualify individuals for the right to vote in a democratic society and to stand for election as democratic representatives. Stifter's first impulse, true to the Enlightenment tradition, is to cite education. But, he then counters, education, especially practical experience, is difficult if not impossible to document. What trait, then, can be taken as an unmistakable sign of leadership abilities? Stifter's answer is as simple as it is astonishing: accumulated personal property, wealth. It is worth examining in some detail the logic and language with which he justifies this assertion.

> Anyone who has limited means is usually also limited in what he can
> learn, he interacts in a small circle of people, in a village, in a town, and

does not become familiar with other things that are of import for the state. How, for example, is the day laborer, the handyman and the like, someone who has never gotten beyond the limits of his own occupation, supposed to accomplish this? But someone who possesses greater means can acquire a better education, he has a larger business that leads him into many countries and areas, and he becomes acquainted with conditions on a grand scale and how they have an impact on the state. Moreover, he is tied by his personal property to the permanence of the state and its good fortune, so that he will scarcely enter into destructive experiments that could be harmful to the state. The propertyless, by contrast, are wont to do this, because they hope to profit from change. ("Der Zensus" 56–57)

The upshot of this argument is that the propertied elite, because they have everything to lose and little to gain from political change, will be the best managers of the state's affairs and the best defenders of the status quo. The propertyless or impoverished workers, by contrast, have everything to gain and little to lose from political change, and hence are more likely to wager on political upheaval and radical transformation. Most shocking, perhaps, is Stifter's claim that personal property and possessions are the precondition not for education, but for *educatability*, the ability or desire to learn as such. His assumption here seems to be that anyone who can manage great assets with success will by definition also have the managerial skills to oversee the functions of the state. If Stifter were alive today, he obviously would be an avid supporter of the moneyed elite—people like Ross Perot, Steve Forbes, George W. Bush, or, for that matter, perhaps even John Kerry. More to the point is his critique of the workers or villagers who can never extricate themselves from local issues and hence can acquire no broad perspective on matters of the state. This stands in crass opposition to the glorification of rural life so common in Stifter's fictional writings, including *Bergkristall*. What seems clear, at any rate, is that at the time in which he revised *Bergkristall* for inclusion in *Bunte Steine*, the possessive individualism manifest in the Millsdorf dyer and, by extension, in the Gschaid shoemaker, would scarcely have been an object of Stifter's unmitigated reprehension.

Ultimately it is the shoemaker who imports new commercial practices and the values of possessive individualism into the self-sufficient, natural economy of Gschaid. In fact, the shoemaker so resembles the dyer in his personal and business traits that he could be his clone. In the second version of the story, Stifter motivates this similarity by hinting that the shoemaker has entered into a veiled competition with the dyer to see if he can outdo the latter's economic success. The dyer himself, of course, incites this competition when he baldly asserts to his son-in-law that economic success is the sole measure of personal worth.

> A true man must carry on his business in such a manner that it flourishes and prospers, thus he must provide for his wife, his children, himself, and his servants, maintain house and home in a splendid fashion, and still have a considerable sum left over, for only the latter is capable of bestowing upon him prestige and honor. (*Bergkristall* 197–98)

It is not enough simply to run one's business so that it maintains a steady state; it must "flourish"—the same word, not coincidentally, that was used to describe the "flourishing" town of Millsdorf (192)—and grow. Furthermore, according to the philosophy of possessive individualism defended by the dyer, *superabundant* wealth—property holdings that exceed what is necessary for mere subsistence—extraneous capital, or money in the bank, are the only things that can provide one with dignity and prestige. Although it has been only forty years since the publication of Chamisso's *Peter Schlemihl* with its vehement critique of an economics of excess (see chapter 6), it seems that the Millsdorf dyer, at least, has not yet digested the lesson Chamisso's protagonist sought to promulgate.

With this statement of his economic philosophy, the dyer gives the shoemaker sufficient grounds on which to legitimate the drive for luxury and extravagance that are integral to his personality. Even before his unexpected self-reformation into a successful businessman, the shoemaker's distinguishing traits had been the unconventional exorbitance of his dress, his desire for pleasure, and his need for recognition, as expressed in his incomprehensible obsession with the winning of hunting trophies (*Bergkristall* 195). Stifter's text draws an implicit connection between the drive for recognition concretized in these hunting prizes and the shoemaker's subsequent economic pursuits: "The prize [awarded at these hunting competitions] usually consisted of coins set in mountings, and the shoemaker had to spend more of the same kind of coins than were contained in the prize in order to win it, especially since he was not very thrifty when it came to money" (195). Stifter makes a point of indicating that the basic weakness of the shoemaker prior to his reform is one of the cardinal sins against possessive individualism: the failure to budget his money wisely and subordinate his personal desires to his long-term economic well-being. Nonetheless, his prizes, the mounted coins he collects, contain an open reference to the commercial principles he will later uphold. Indeed, his error, this passage suggests, is that he displays an irrational preference for coins set in mountings, that is, for coins that do not circulate and whose value hence is purely symbolic. In fact, he is willing to spend many coins that are valid currency in order to acquire a single noncirculating coin that simply serves as a symbol of his prowess as a hunter. At this early station in his life, then, the shoemaker exhibits many of the same economic and moral vices that Annette von Droste-Hülshoff maligned in the character of Friedrich Mergel in *Die Judenbuche* (discussed in chapter 7). The major difference, of course, is that Friedrich's demise is predicated upon his excessive vanity and its expression in commodities intended to symbolize his economic breach with the rural community of Paderborn. As a result, Droste-Hülshoff's novella manifests a caustic critique of the new economic paradigm of commercialism and the unfettered monetary economy. Stifter, by contrast, tells the story of Sebastian's reform from an economy of waste and a morality of arrogant vanity into a paragon of capitalism; he is someone who *instrumentalizes* these very vices by making them into the basis of his economic and personal success. This turning point in Sebastian's character development thus also marks the shift from a critique of the modern commercial economy to its unquestioned valorization.

The lesson the shoemaker must assimilate is the fundamental lesson of capitalism: he must learn to defer gratification, to subordinate his immediate desires for prestige and accomplishment by diverting them into strategies for long-term economic planning and accumulation of wealth. Having always distinguished himself in school (*Bergkristall* 195), Sebastian turns out to be a model student in the school of (economic) life, as well, even outdoing his teacher, the Millsdorf dyer. By successfully channeling his previously unbridled desires completely into his occupational endeavors, the shoemaker establishes himself as one of the leading citizens of

Gschaid—second only to the preacher and the schoolteacher, whose shoes he makes (194)—and an entrepreneur whose recognition extends well beyond the village.

> Some time after the death of his parents, through which he inherited the family home, which he then lived in by himself, the shoemaker changed completely. Just as previously he had fooled around, now he sat in his workshop and hammered on his shoe-soles day in and day out. He boastfully wagered that he would award a prize to anyone who could make better shoes and footwear than he did. (196)

Significantly, instead of seeking to win prizes himself, as with his hunting trophies, the shoemaker now is in a position to award them—although he knows full well that no one can compete with the quality and value of his workmanship. The relationship with his father-in-law, then, reinforces his inclination toward ostentation, but helps harness and funnel it in more "productive" and economically profitable directions. The transformation of the shoemaker from an eccentric boaster to a model—if yet boastful—businessman thus represents a classic case of Freudian sublimation: his prior obsessions do not become any less obsessive, they are simply aim-inhibited and transferred to a new design, to the accumulation of wealth, a goal that, under the conditions of possessive individualism, now brings him precisely the kind of recognition he desired in the first place. What it does not bring him, of course, is acceptance among his fellow villagers: he remains the odd man out, but for different reasons. Instead of playing the part of the village idiot or the social eccentric, he has assumed the role of the village plutocrat, the economic outsider whose commercialism and wealth set him apart from all the other citizens of Gschaid, who still rely primarily on nature and the natural economy rather than on commerce.

One of the major changes Stifter introduces into this story when revising it for inclusion in *Bunte Steine* is an expansion of the history of the shoemaker and his family, in particular an elaboration on his commercial operations. Whereas this section supplying personal background encompasses only six pages in *Der heilige Abend* (144–50), it occupies ten pages in *Bergkristall* (193–203).[14] In the revised version, Stifter seems intent on rescuing the shoemaker from the relatively negative picture painted of him in *Der heilige Abend*. For example, whereas in the first version he is called, prior to his remarkable conversion, a *Gemsedieb*, a "chamois poacher" who is clearly involved in illicit activities (146), in *Bergkristall* he is simply referred to as a *Gemsewaldschütze*, an "expert chamois huntsman" (195). The detailed exposition of the ways he organizes and manages his business would also seem to be a redeeming factor. However, viewed from the perspective I am outlining here, the structures he introduces appear to be nothing other than measures for rationalizing his shoemaking industry, making it more efficient, increasing his customer base, and turning a better profit. Although in *Der heilige Abend* the shoemaker seems merely to be running a cottage industry, himself manager, laborer, and salesperson all rolled into one, in *Bergkristall* he occupies several workers. Moreover, he is extremely selective about those he employs: "He only employed the best workers, and he ordered them around [*trillte sie noch sehr herum*] when they were working in his workshop, so that they obeyed him and did things the way he commanded" (196). The shoemaker, in short, is a veritable taskmaster—the verb *trillen* is associated in particular with military drills—perhaps even a tyrant, who expects from his workers the very same discipline he demands of himself. Since we can assume that his pool of employees is drawn from Gschaid, his shoe business becomes the center from which the techniques of rationalization and the commercial practices of a protoindustrial economy are disseminated in the village. The rationalization of production develops to such an extent that the shoemaker creates a ledger, assigns each pair of shoes a serial number, and keeps records of each sale and the customer's level of satisfaction (197). He even installs a showroom in his house with windows to the outside, and the "shining" shoes and boots put out on display—reminiscent of the display cases Stifter describes in "Waarenauslagen und Ankündigungen"—attract the attention and awaken the *Kauflust*, the lust to buy them, in people throughout the valley, who come to stare longingly at these shoes through the glass (196–97).

The proof of the pudding is in the eating; but the proof of prosperity is in the earning. In this respect, as well, the shoemaker can take pride in his economic success. His roomy, well-kept, and comfortably furnished house stands on the main square in Gschaid, alongside all the better homes

(193). Whereas previously even the people of Gschaid had had their shoes made outside the village, not only they, but the inhabitants of the entire valley, now order their shoes from the shoemaker in Gschaid. Ultimately even some people from Millsdorf and from other valleys begin to buy his superior-quality footwear (196). Finally, because one of his economic strategies is specialization in hiking boots, his reputation even reaches well beyond the region in which he lives: "His fame even extended into the flat-lands, so that many people who wanted to travel in the mountains had their hiking boots made by him" (196). As a result, the shoemaker can afford the kind of luxury that, as he learned from his father-in-law, is the sole measure of honor and prestige, and he even accumulates some savings (193). But honor and prestige have their price. In the shoemaker's case, the price is such fanatical devotion to his work that he almost completely neglects his family. His wife suspects "that he does not love their children in the way she imagined he should" (199), and on the Christmas Eve when the children set off to trek across the pass to Millsdorf, he is so preoccupied with customers that he scarcely takes notice of their plan (203).

Stifter clearly did not see the shoemaker's exaggerated work ethic as negatively as most critics would have us believe.[15] To be sure, the shoemaker's commercial tactics are so aggressive as to eliminate most of his competition. But Stifter invests considerable effort in playing down this potentially unsavory trait by stressing, especially in the second version of the story, the kindness and generosity with which the shoemaker treats his village competitor, old Tobias.[16]

> The small exception [to the statement that there is only one shoemaker in Gschaid] mentioned above and the only person who rivals the exclusivity of the shoemaker is another shoemaker, old Tobias, who, in fact, is actually no rival at all, because now he only repairs shoes [*nur mehr flikt*], is kept very busy by this, and would not dream of entering into competition with the eminent shoemaker whose house is on the square, especially since the shoemaker on the square frequently supplies him gratis with scraps of leather, parts of soles, and other such things. (194)

This passage is significant because it bears witness to Stifter's own ambivalence with regard to the commercial success of the "shoemaker on the square." Especially interesting is the way in which Stifter first introduces Tobias as an occupational rival to the shoemaker, but then retracts this designation, since Tobias has been reduced merely to repairing, not manufacturing shoes. Implicit in the formulation *nur mehr flikt* (now only repairs) is the notion that Tobias had formerly *made* shoes, as well, and Stifter leaves open whether he has ceased this activity due to old age or because he has been forced out of business by the expansion of his more accomplished "rival" on the square. And when Stifter invokes the concept of free-market competition, he does so only to assert openly that this notion cannot be used to describe the relationship between the shoemaker and Tobias. As if the tensions created by this dialectic of assertion for the sake of retraction were not enough to suggest a deep-seated equivocation on Stifter's part, the manner in which he justifies his assertion that the relationship between these two shoemakers is not a competitive one also cuts two ways. On the one hand, the shoemaker's generosity in giving Tobias his leather scraps can be taken as an act of uncommon kindness, especially since he is thereby supporting a "rival." However, since, as Stifter emphasizes, this action motivates Tobias not to consider the shoemaker his competitor, it could also be interpreted as an especially sly, even devious business strategy: by supplying him gratis with materials sufficient for the repair, but not the manufacture of shoes, he not only encourages Tobias to engage in noncompetitive pursuits, but also wins him over as an ally by means of an ostensible act of kindness.

Revising Historical Narratives: From the Misfortune to the Fortune of Commerce

The aim of this exposition of Sebastian the shoemaker and the modern commercialism and capitalist rationalization he represents has been to indicate just how intimately the thematic of possessive individualism and economic transformation is woven into the fabric of Stifter's *Bergkristall*.[17] The next step is to show the relevance of this problematic for the primary plotline of the story, the children's traverse of the pass on Christmas Eve and the threat they face and ultimately overcome. My argument is that we must read this story line allegorically. Not, however, as an allegory of the grandiosity and mercy of nature; nor as a tale of reintegration into family and community; but rather as an allegory of successful economic exchange, of a prosperous commercialism that dares to break down traditional barriers to trade and ultimately ushers in a new prosperity. Here we should recall that the Christmas story, which provides both a temporal and an ideational backdrop for *Bergkristall*, is not a tale that confirms the past, but is instead one that affirms a changing future.[18] In the Christian West, the birth of Christ is the paradigm for the beginning of a new era, the demarcation point between the old chronology and the new. My thesis is that the children's successful crossing of the pass to Millsdorf and back, like the commercial success of their father, marks a new age in the economic development of Gschaid, an era of exchange, of profitable commerce with the outside world, of protoindustrial prosperity. Nothing could be further, of course, from the traditional reading of this text as a—to be sure, nostalgic—glorification of human harmony with nature and the aggrandizement of a community held together by interpersonal commitment and moral values. My interpretation demonstrates that this discourse of "family values" is, in fact, a mere ideological disguise for a symbolic narrative that advocates the embracing of commerce as a sophisticated strategy for mastery of nature and for economic productivity and prosperity.

Taken even on the most superficial level, the children's journeys across the pass from Gschaid to Millsdorf and back represent a rudimentary form of commerce. As a rule, they carry nothing with them to Millsdorf, but on their return home they are laden with food, gifts, and sometimes even money (fig. 11). The dyer, we recall, had strictly refused to provide his daughter and the shoemaker with any financial assistance, even in the form of a dowry; but his wife does not feel herself obliged to adhere to this rule.

> She gave the children many things, and not only for the time they spent in her house. Not infrequently the things she gave them included a coin, sometimes one of considerable value, and she always packed two bundles in which she placed things she believed would be necessary or could make the children happy. And even if these very same things were nonetheless present in abundance in the shoemaker's house in Gschaid, the grandmother still gave them out of the joy of giving, and the children carried them home as something special. (*Bergkristall* 202)

11 / The two children crossing the pass between Gschaid and Millsdorf. Illustration by Josef Scharl from Adalbert Stifter, *Rock Crystal: A Christmas Tale*, trans. Elizabeth Mayer and Marianne Moore, illus. Josef Scharl (New York: Pantheon, 1945).

It is important that coins, the symbolic mediators of commerce, are specifically mentioned here. Indeed, the children themselves, in their circulation between Millsdorf and Gschaid, function as a kind of "money," as a symbolic mediator, a medium of exchange between rural village and commercially flourishing town. A monetary economy is, of course, the cornerstone of modern commercial expansion. And the ambitions of the children's father, the shoemaker, are also directly associated with his desire to collect certain coins, as we have seen. In the passage from *Bergkristall* just cited, the ambivalence of commerce is inscribed in the differing perspectives the narrator presents concerning the items the children transport: whereas to the grandmother they appear to be necessities, they are in fact revealed to be superfluous luxuries, since they are already available in abundance in the children's home. It is only in the children's Christmas traverse that the utility of these articles—and hence the grandmother's perspective—will ultimately be affirmed, for they give the children the sustenance they need to survive the frigid night in their mountain cave. This is just one respect in which the story underwrites the usefulness of commerce, and we will examine the implications of this in more detail below.

For the moment I would like to pursue a brief biographical excursus that underscores the connection between the children and acts of exchange. In a letter to Emil Kuh from August 1871, Stifter's friend Friedrich Simony, an alpine researcher and geographer, relates an incident he experienced with Stifter in the summer of 1845 that provided the immediate impetus behind the composition of *Der heilige Abend*. Hiking together in the Alps, Stifter and Simony were surprised by a violent thunderstorm. Shortly thereafter they encountered two children, drenched to the bone, who approached them on the same trail. The children spoke to Stifter and Simony, offering to sell them strawberries they had picked along the path. Stifter agreed to the purchase, under the condition that the children themselves eat the strawberries and in exchange tell the two men about their travels and how they took shelter during the thunderstorm. Simony goes on to relate how he later showed Stifter drawings of an ice cave and how the writer remarked to him about the stark contrast between the vitality of the children they had met and the desolation of this cave.[19] The details of how Stifter transformed these associations into the plot of *Bergkristall* do not interest us here.[20] What does interest us is the centrality of commerce and exchange in the encounter with the children. The children in this incident appear, as it were, in the role of entrepreneurs: they sell the wild strawberries they have picked along their hike. Scholars who have drawn on this biographical incident for examinations of *Bergkristall* have without exception ignored this commercial transaction. Yet it is central to an understanding of the way in which Konrad and Sanna, the children in Stifter's narrative, are connected to the issues of trade and commerce, those issues raised centrally by the activities of their father and grandfather. The moment of commercial exchange in the biographical incident reinforces the idea that the children in *Bergkristall* embody the commercial exchange between the protoindustrial economy of Millsdorf and the natural economy that as yet is still dominant—if threatened—in Gschaid.

The biographical incident described by Simony has its most concrete manifestation in the central symbol of *Bergkristall*: the red *Unglüksäule* (190)—literally, "misfortune column," or the marker of misfortune— which is installed at the top of the pass between Millsdorf and Gschaid as a memorial to a baker who once died trying to make the traverse between these two towns.

> On the ridge that connects the snow-capped mountain with a range of mountains on the other side is a dense forest of fir trees. At about the highest point of this ridge, where the path gradually begins to dip down into the opposite valley, there stands a so-called misfortune column. Once a baker, who was carrying bread across the pass in a basket, was found dead at this spot. The dead baker with his basket and the surrounding fir trees were depicted in a painting, under which was written an explanation and an appeal for a prayer. The painting was placed on a wooden column, which was painted red and erected at the place of the misfortune. (189–90)

The incident Simony relates and the memorial to the baker are connected by two attributes: superficially by the red color of the memorial itself, which harks back to the red strawberries the children sold to Stifter; more substantially by the commercial connection to the baker who perishes while involved in an explicitly commercial enterprise, the transport of his wares across the pass. The relevance for the children Konrad and Sanna, who likewise carry goods over the pass, is self-evident. Indeed, among the articles the grandmother places in their packs on the day of their fateful traverse is bread (207).[21]

The importance of the *Unglüksäule* as symbol is indicated by the increased frequency of its occurrence in *Bergkristall* compared to the first version of the story. In *Der heilige Abend* it is mentioned only five times and is called, curiously, a *Martersäule*, a "martyr's column,"[22] whereas in the final version the *Unglüksäule* appears no less than fourteen times (Sinka 2). Even more significant, perhaps, is its precise geographical location: it stands at the highest point of the pass between Millsdorf and Gschaid, and as such it marks the barrier that separates the two villages as well as the threshold that joins them together. This equivocation is impor-

tant, because for the baker the pass is indeed a barrier, and he pays for his
attempt to transgress it with his life. For the children, however, it is a juncture. Not only does the *Unglüksäule* mark this geographical and thematic
seam, it functions as the symbolic nodal point in the text in general. As
we will see, most lines of signification in *Bergkristall* eventually lead back
to this object and the incident, the "misfortune," it represents.

The death of the baker is, of course, itself symbolic.[23] His misfortune
stands in for a greater, more abstract misfortune: the misfortune of commerce. It is probably no coincidence that bread is the commodity he is
transporting. It is, to cite a passage from Stifter's novella *Zwei Schwestern* (Two sisters), "the simplest of things, the most widespread . . . , the
symbol and sign of all human nourishment" (1099). Indeed, bread is the
one commodity that every village would be expected to produce on its own,
presumably in each individual household, and hence would be the very
last thing that would need to be imported and transported across a pass.
Taking bread to Gschaid would be much like taking owls to Athens.[24] Moreover, the baker's commercial enterprise fails to take account of that famous
paradox of economic value first articulated by Adam Smith: namely, that
the most abundant and requisite articles, those with the greatest use value,
have little or no exchange value.[25] The baker is, in short, a misguided
entrepreneur. But that is precisely why his action can function in the text
as a kind of symbol for the aberrations of modern commerce, for an economic strategy gauged not toward the satisfaction of existential needs, but
instead motivated solely by commercial expansion and profit taking. The
baker's action ultimately represents the division of labor, the displacement
of an activity accomplished by all, the baking of bread, by a commercial
practice that introduces specialization. In this sense the baker is directly
connected to the shoemaker of Gschaid, who also introduces division of
labor, specialization, and commerce. But the baker, unlike the shoemaker—
and unlike his children in their semicommercial traverse of the pass—pays
with his life for this attempt to inject commercialism and modern economic
practices into the self-sufficient, natural economy of Gschaid. As long as
the *Unglüksäule*, the memorial to the misfortune of commerce, with its
implicit critique of modern economic practices, remains standing, it admonishes all who see it or know about it that modern economics is unwelcome

here. For the baker and his ilk, the pass is an absolute, impenetrable barrier. But the *Unglüksäule* falls, and its fall spells the end of a shared narrative, a "mythology," that relates the inherent misfortune of commerce.[26]

The *Unglüksäule* serves a double function: it is a marker that warns against entrance into the commercial age, but it also functions as a signpost. It indicates the place where the paths that connect the two valleys join and are intersected by a third path that leads up to the lifeless desolation of the glaciers. *Bergkristall* is structured in such a way that the traverse of the children parallels that of the baker—with the significant difference, of course, that they survive their ordeal. They do so despite the fact—or perhaps precisely *because*—the memorial to the baker, which serves both as an admonition against frivolous commerce and as a signpost, has mysteriously fallen down. The absence of the post as directional sign, of course, is what causes the children to stray onto the glacier: in this sense its disappearance is prerequisite for the possibility that the children will experience the baker's unenviable fate. Yet when the *Unglüksäule* is read symbolically, as a warning against the dangers of modern commerce, its fall represents the lifting of this ban and hence portends the children's rescue. The unfortunate crossing by the baker and the more fortunate one by the children thus mark two differing perspectives on the modern commercial economy. The former view, roughly that held by Stifter prior to the revolution of 1848 and manifest in the critique of commodity aesthetics voiced in "Waarenauslagen und Ankündigungen," condemns commercialism as a transgression of the self-sufficient natural economy. The latter view, the one assumed by Stifter following the revolution and expressed in the possessive individualism of his cultural-political essays, embraces modern commerce as the source of all prosperity and political stability. While both of these perspectives are present in *Bergkristall*, the latter one has the final word: since the children are symbols and mediators of commercial exchange, their rescue is also the rescue of (monetary) mediation and commerce. Thus Stifter's text ultimately valorizes modern economic principles. What *Bergkristall* relates is a historical paradigm shift in the evaluation of the modern industrial economy and its division of labor from one of misfortune to one of fortune—in both senses of that word. The mysterious, unexpected conversion of the shoemaker from profligate, intemperate dandy to hardworking, dedicated, successful entrepreneur is emblematic of this overarching historical change. That neither of these transformations is motivated in the narrative in even the slightest way, but is marked instead by a break or a logical gap, is a fact whose significance I will discuss in a moment.

The text brings considerable evidence in support of this theory of a historical mutation. We have already examined some of it in the analysis of the economic attitudes represented by the dyer and the shoemaker. But there are at least two more levels on which the story confirms this hypothesis. The most obvious is the change that follows upon the rescue of the children. At the conclusion of the tale, Stifter's narrator explicitly addresses the role of this event as a turning point in the history of Gschaid: " This event ushered in a new phase in the history of Gschaid; for a long time it provided material for discussion, and even years from now people will speak of it when the mountain is especially visible on clear days or when they tell strangers about its peculiarities" (*Bergkristall* 239). The rescue of the children opens up a new chapter in the history of Gschaid. The story of their traverse and rescue has become a new narrative, one shared by the community, that replaces an old narrative, the story of the unfortunate baker. The mythology of the villagers, in other words, has undergone a principal shift: it is no longer structured around a tale that signifies the misfortune of commerce, but around one that tells of its miraculous, unexpected success. If the shoemaker has altered the de facto economic practices of the village, his children have reshaped its economic ideology by becoming the subjects of a new narrative, of a new "history." That this new history is one that embraces commerce and possessive individualism is signaled in the language with which the children's integration into the village is described. Whereas in *Der heilige Abend* the concluding paragraph of the text begins, "From now on, after being rescued by the people of Gschaid, the children had finally become true natives [*Eingeborne*] of the village" (175), in *Bergkristall* the parallel passage runs, "From that day on the children had become all the more the *property* [*Eigenthum*] of the village, from then on they were no longer viewed as outsiders but rather as natives [*Eingeborne*]" (239; emphasis added). While in the first version the children have merely become true natives, in the final version they must first become *possessions* in order to be recognized as natives. This explains the transformation in the feelings of the shoemaker toward his children as

well. Far from abandoning the ethics of possessive individualism and recognizing the errors of his protocapitalist economic strategies, he learns to
love his children only when he can subordinate them to this ethic, viewing them as possessions among others. Property, its accumulation, and its
protection, have—literally—the final word in *Bergkristall*.

We can arrive at this same conclusion by tracing a specific set of symbolic exchanges that occur in the text. These can be identified by following the associative connections between the red *Unglüksäule* and the red
flag that signals the rescue of the children, the flag that is planted on the
Krebsstein once they have been found (*Bergkristall* 238). This flag has a
special history: "It is the red flag that the foreign gentleman who had climbed
the Gars with the young hunter planted on the top, so that the preacher
could see it with his telescope. It served as a sign that they had reached
the top, and the foreign gentleman then gave it to the preacher as a
present" (233–34). Via the young hunter, who served as a mountain guide
for the stranger, this pennant is connected to the ecotourism that is an early
symptom of the breakdown of the natural economy in Gschaid. In this
context we should recall that even the shoemaker's success is tied to this
ecotourism; his fame extends into the valley primarily for those who have
the leisure to explore the mountains and who hence buy their hiking boots
from him (196). Moreover, it is significant that it is none other than the
young hunter who is associated with this commercial tourism. Aside from
the baker, the only other narrative of misfortune and death on the mountain that the children know is the story of the old hunter, presumably the
father of the young mountain guide. The image of this old hunter, who fell
asleep and froze to death up on the mountain, motivates Konrad and Sanna
to stay awake during their ordeal (225, 227).[27] This admonishing vision
of death, as much as the coffee extract and the wonders of nature, is what
keeps the children alive. The historical transformation that takes place
between the misfortune of the baker and the fortune of the children, then,
is paralleled by the misfortune of the elder hunter and the fortune—good
fortune and tourism-derived wealth—of the young hunter. The shift in narratives represented by this generational change is concretized in the fall of
the red *Unglüksäule* at the pass and its replacement by the red flag on the
Krebsstein. If the former marked the misfortune of commerce and warned
against the demise of the self-sufficient natural economy, the latter sym-

bolizes the embracing of exchange and modern commerce as the only road to prosperity and fortune. It marks off a geographical and symbolic terrain that is higher and more visible than the pass at which the memorial to the baker and to the misfortune of commerce stood.

Throughout Stifter's works, matters of economics tend to be banished to a vague realm of contingency and chance. Wealth is often acquired as if by magic, and it often disappears just as mysteriously. One example of this can be found in the autobiographical story related by the preacher in the novella *Kalkstein* (Limestone, 1852). His great-grandfather, he tells us, was a foundling who acquired substantial wealth simply by buying raw materials at a low price and selling them at a profit (*Kalkstein* 99–100). That is all we are ever told about his economic rise, as if profit taking entailed no risks and were as easy as buying low and selling high. Even more obscure is the way in which the preacher's brother loses this fortune: again, we are told nothing concrete about his business dealings, merely that "something terrible" happened and that he was forced to declare bankruptcy (116). In the novella *Zwei Schwestern*, written at approximately the same time as *Der heilige Abend*, this contingency of economic boom and bust is directly thematized. The narrator of the tale, Otto Falkhaus, introduces himself as a "child of coincidence" (*Zwei Schwestern* 994). But the main coincidence in his life is his acquisition of wealth, which his narrative motivates with nothing other than the vague assertion that he had come into this fortune "by means of extraordinary activity and skilled calculation" (996). His friend Rikar experiences the opposite fate: he forfeits almost his entire fortune and property as a result of an unspecified lawsuit that he loses for unknown or at least unstated reasons (1072). Moreover, precisely why Rikar is able to retain one ramshackle, infertile property remains unknown even to him. Contingency as the driving force behind the entire narrative in *Zwei Schwestern* stands in for the role of chance where economic fortune and misfortune are concerned in all of Stifter's works. In this sense, Stifter's narratives carry on the theme of economic providentialism we investigated in Johann Heinrich Jung-Stilling's *Lebensgeschichte* (discussed in chapter 5), with the significant difference that providence in Stifter has been wholly secularized. Whereas Jung-Stilling could still attribute his economic windfalls to the good grace of the Christian divinity, in Stifter's texts this ideological guise is no longer necessary: economic fortune and misfortune are hypostatized as pure contingencies that escape any possibility of human understanding. Throughout Stifter's writings, the economic structures that bring financial gain or disaster are marked only by narrative gaps, by coincidences, or by miracles. Thus economics appears on the surface to be nothing but a matter of fate.

This is true for *Bergkristall* as well. Indeed, this story thematizes the contingency of economics as a contingency in nature: the historical transformation that Gschaid is undergoing, due primarily to the change in economic principles introduced by the shoemaker (following the model of the dyer), is disguised as a wonder of nature (or of religious faith). The rescue of the children is possible, the dyer reminds his son-in-law and us, because, contrary to the norm under such weather conditions, the snowstorm that stranded the children was not accompanied by wind (238). *Bergkristall* thus manifests in paradigmatic fashion what Walter Benjamin criticizes as Stifter's inability to distinguish between nature and fate. In his essay on Stifter he writes, "Stifter knows nature well, but what he knows only haltingly and portrays with a feeble hand is the borderline between nature and fate" ("Stifter" 608).[28] But nature and fate both stand in for something else in Stifter, namely for the interventions of human beings in their own economic history. This human component, self-responsibility for one's own (economic) fate, is invariably repressed in Stifter, marked by narrative discontinuities that are papered over by appeals to coincidence, nature, or chance. But what incessantly lurks behind the laws of nature in Stifter is not the "gentle law" of human morality touted in his preface to *Bunte Steine*, but rather the iron law of modern economics.[29] What we are able to discern in our reading of *Bergkristall* is the return of this repressed element both on the narrative plane, in the story of the shoemaker's economic rise, and on the symbolic level, in the transmutation of the *Unglüksäule* from a symptom of the misfortune of commerce to a sign of the fortune modern economic practices can generate. The rescue of the children is thus actually only an epiphenomenal manifestation, or a symbolic rendering, of a deep-seated economic transformation, the shift from a natural economy of self-sufficiency to a commercial economy of rationalized labor, trade with the outside world, and the use of monetary instruments. Commerce is the modern Christ child, whose birth brings salvation.

Stifter, like so many middle-class intellectuals of his age, harbored profoundly equivocal feelings toward the market economy. The fatalism and contingency associated throughout his writing with economic success and failure is just one aspect of this. In *Bergkristall* this equivocation manifests itself as the tension between glorification of the autonomy of Gschaid as rural community and valorization of the commercialism and prosperity of the shoemaker. Stifter's ideal is probably a fusion of these two economic models: capitalism with a human face, as it were. If *Bergkristall* does indeed conclude on a utopian note, then this utopia is one of a Gschaid that has successfully fused the interpersonal trust and community values of the natural economy with the economic principles and prosperity of protoindustrial capitalism. But this reading is probably too positive. A more cynical view would see the discourse of "family values" in Stifter as nothing but a veneer that hides a narrative about economic growth and prosperity for the propertied elite. If this rings similar to the strategies pursued by political conservatives even today, then that, at least, is no coincidence. What my analysis has sought to demonstrate is that *Bergkristall* cannot simply be read as the exaltation of nature and rural community that critics have traditionally discovered in this text. On the contrary, the deep structural message of this tale is the affirmation of a capitalist economic transformation that reduces nature to an exploitable resource: the myth of commerce as misfortune is banished and replaced by a narrative that views commerce as the necessary prerequisite for all fortune and prosperity—but not necessarily for the fortune and prosperity of all.

CONCLUSION

Limitless Faith in the Limitless: Money, Modernity, and the Economics/Aesthetics of Mediation in Goethe's *Faust II*

> *Surely this is the emotional success story of that predominance of the means, of that compulsion of our complex technology of life: that we add means to means, until the actual ends they are supposed to serve recede ever farther toward the horizon of consciousness and ultimately sink below it. But no single thing has played a greater role in this process than has money; never has an object that only has value as a means developed with such energy, such completeness, and such success for the totality of life, into a—merely apparent or real—aim, toward which to strive provides satisfaction in itself.*

> —Georg Simmel ("Das Geld in der modernen Cultur" 189–90)

Endless Striving and the Mechanisms of the Modern Economy

JOHANN WOLFGANG VON GOETHE'S *FAUST II* EXEMPLIFIES WHAT the passage above from sociologist Georg Simmel (1858–1918) describes as the central trait of modernism: the displacement of ends by means, or the hypostatization of means as ends in themselves. For Simmel this tendency is paradigmatically concretized in the emergence of the capitalist economy, in which money as the means for satisfying all desires becomes the supreme object of desire. The philosopher Arthur Schopenhauer (1788–1860) expressed a similar insight into money as the medium of all mediums when he noted, in "Aphorismen zur Lebensweisheit" (Aphorisms toward worldly wisdom) from his *Parerga und Paralipomena*, "Money alone represents absolute goodness, because it does not merely satisfy *one* need concretely, but rather *all* needs in the abstract" (*Sämtliche Werke* 4: 415). Schopenhauer's language is telling here; his invocation of money as the supreme "good" has quasireligious implications that suggest that money, as absolute means, has supplanted God as the *summum bonum*.

Faust II presents one of the first critical engagements in modern German literature—indeed, in world literature in general—with this hypostatization of means as ends in themselves. It indicts the central mechanisms of the modern economy—abstract, purely symbolic forms of money; excessive accumulation; colonial expansionism; industrialization; overweening mastery over nature—as symptomatic of this tendency to focus on means, with total blindness to ultimate consequences. Moreover, Goethe's text is also one of the first to explicitly thematize the complicity of literary and intellectual culture in these general economic developments. If one aim of this book has been to demonstrate the extent to which this complicity between intellectual culture and economics expresses itself *unconsciously* in philosophical and literary documents during the period in question, then *Faust II* represents one of the first works in the German literary tradition in which this unconscious complicity ascends to the level of critical *consciousness*. But *Faust II* embodies much more than simply a critical reflection on the imbrication of economics and literary-philosophical culture *from the outside*; indeed, it enacts and concretizes this intertwining in its own aesthetic construction and thereby choreographs *from the inside* the very complicity of economics and intellectual culture that it critically adumbrates. As I will try to show, Goethe's "tragedy" operates according to a literary-aesthetic practice that emulates, on distinct levels, the problematic entanglement of aesthetics and economics that has been one of the central themes of this book. In this sense, *Faust II* does not propose simple solutions to the crises of economic modernism, but rather raises questions about whether the consequences unleashed by an obsession with means and mediation as such are ultimately escapable at all—or whether they are the inevitable result of a culture that has given itself over to economic *and* aesthetic means without ends.

With his infinite striving, Goethe's Faust becomes the exaggerated representative of this modern proclivity toward defining means as ends. If it is true, as Marshall Berman has proposed, that Goethe's *Faust* is the first and best European "tragedy of development" (40), then this is the case largely because in Faust's instance development has lost its teleological purpose and has become development for development's sake: perpetual generative motion without discernible direction. For Faust, ends justify means in the more precise sense that ends exist solely for the purpose of motivating a striving that has become an end in itself. This explains why each of Faust's accomplishments, once achieved, never brings satisfaction and must be supplanted by a new purpose that demands new means. It also explains why Faust perishes while laboring under the *deception* that his final purpose, the building of dikes and canals for his utopian colony, is being accomplished, whereas in fact only his grave is being dug (lines 11557–80).[1] It falls to the angels in the closing scene of *Faust II* to legitimize this motif of endless striving in the memorable lines that equate it with entitlement to redemption: "For him whose striving never ceases / we can provide redemption" (lines 11936–37). We witness in these lines the same kind of slippage between worldly designs and religious salvation that Schopenhauer articulates in his aphorism on money as the supreme good, and that underwrote social climbing as a dictate of divine providence in Johann Heinrich Jung-Stilling's life story, analyzed in chapter 5. Of course, redemption was never one of Faust's goals, and one of the most poignant ironies of Goethe's text is that its own "end" occurs without motivation or justification, through the introduction of a genuine *deus* (or perhaps more precisely, *angelus) ex machina.* However, the angels' message appears to be that striving as such, irrespective of aims, ends, or consequences, makes one worthy of redemption. Yet this valorization of infinite striving simply places a positive veneer on that very omnipotence of means that Simmel and Schopenhauer diagnose as the perverse reflex of economic modernism.

This autonomization of means and mediation makes itself most palpable in the figure of Mephistopheles: he is not merely the most complex, many-faceted, and—frankly—most admired character in Goethe's drama,[2] but also represents on the most visceral level this absolutization of means. As the purveyor of magic, Mephistopheles is the very incarnation of mediation; he functions much like a symbolic currency, a money that has the capacity to satisfy all needs in the abstract (Jochen Schmidt 190). Seen from this perspective, Faust's striving acquires the perverse "goodness"

Schopenhauer ascribes to money, since it exploits as its instrument a universal currency (devilish magic) that valorizes abstract means over concrete ends. Faust's striving is, in many respects, nothing other than an endless quest for acquisition: for the acquisition of Gretchen, of Helen, of colonial goods, of territory, of the brute and incessant power of the ocean, of the refuge occupied by Philemon and Baucis. Yet in all these instances the objects to be acquired become secondary to the acquisitive drive itself. Surely this is what is suggested by the very compulsion to repeat, despite constant failures, that motivates Faust's incessant striving. Moreover, much like Faust himself, Mephisto represents the eventual *failure* to accomplish any ultimate end. In this regard *Faust II* relates a series of futile attempts on Mephistopheles' part to procure for Faust supreme satisfaction and thereby to acquire for himself Faust's *Unsterbliches*, his "immortal essence" (stage direction preceding line 11934). Yet like Faust the utopian colonist, who will die before his vision is realized, Mephistopheles will also never accomplish this final goal; instead, he is doomed to repetition compulsion, to remain stuck in the mode of "striving," of devising ever-new means to arrive at an end that will never be achieved. Thus from the perspective of both of the play's "protagonists," Faust and Mephistopheles, Goethe's drama highlights a process of *striving without end* in both the temporal ("endless") and the teleological ("purposeless") senses of that phrase.

In his *Untergang des Abendlandes* (Decline of the West), published immediately following World War I, Oswald Spengler (1880–1936) became one of the first devotees of Goethe and his works to associate the infamous "striving" of Goethe's Faust figure negatively with the crippling tendencies of European modernism: overblown rationality, abstraction and alienation from rural life, an unchecked thirst for increased technology, an obsessive will to mastery over nature. Moreover, Spengler acknowledged the fundamental role economics plays in this "Faustian" transformation of the modern world, dedicating the final chapter of his monumental treatise to an attack on developments in Western economic thought. His investigation culminates in an excoriating critique of money as a cultural product symptomatic of a general tendency to reduce object relations to pure functionality.[3] According to Spengler, the very power of what he calls "Faustian money" is grounded in its constitution "as function, as energy, whose value resides in its effect, not in its mere being" (1173). Spengler's analysis—although at times tinged with the nostalgic antimodernism that helped fuel racist and fascist ideologies in the Germany of the Weimar Republic—touches on several of the themes we have followed throughout this book. Most importantly, Spengler insists that economic life cannot be disentangled from the intellectual culture and the psychological makeup of the subjects who participate in it: "*Every economic lifestyle is the expression of a psychological lifestyle,*" he emphatically contends (1147).

In his historical analysis, Spengler identifies a paradigm shift from a largely rural and agrarian to a metropolitan and commercial economy—similar to what Karl Marx, in "Die deutsche Ideologie" (378–79), classified as the difference between "natural" (*naturwüchsige*) and man-made instruments of production. We have already traced the literary manifestations of this transformation in Adalbert Stifter's *Bergkristall* and in Annette von Droste-Hülshoff's *Judenbuche* (in chapters 8 and 7, respectively). It is addressed as well in Goethe's *Faust II*. For Spengler the dividing line between these two economic models is marked above all by a difference in the money form, with the rural economy relying on landed possession and substance, the commercial economy based on moveable wealth (*Vermögen*) and functional equivalencies (1165–66). Spengler claims, moreover—and in this regard he reiterates the position of those who defended physiocratic economic principles more than a century earlier—that only farmers are productive in the genuine sense of generating products vital for human existence (1162). If the agrarian economy operates on the basis of goods that satisfy immediate needs, the commercial economy is driven by commodities whose worth is constituted exclusively by their abstract monetary value, generated in the act of exchange. Ultimately, then, it is modern money, stripped of any intrinsic substance and conceived as the motor behind accelerated circulation, infinite economic growth, and endless production, that becomes for Spengler the very symbol of the contemporary, technology-driven world. Summarizing the attributes of modern money in terms that closely associate it with the qualities represented by Goethe's Faust in part 2 of the text, Spengler writes, "Money is ultimately that form of intellectual energy in which the will to mastery, the political, social, technical, conceptual power to shape, and the longing for a life in grand style converge" (1167). Intellectual energy; will to power; a political, technical, and intellectual drive to shape; longing for a life writ large: what better way to describe the motives of Faust in the second part of Goethe's tragedy? Surely it is no coincidence that the first act of Goethe's play invokes, in the well-known paper-money episode (lines 5987–6172), precisely the introduction and dissemination of fiat currency as an instrument of purported economic and sociopolitical advancement, but one that leads ultimately to political and cultural decline.

What stands out about Spengler's version of the dichotomy between the "natural" and the "commercial" economies is the way in which he exaggerates this juxtaposition into purely positive and negative poles. This is indicated already by the names he applies to these two economic paradigms. The rural, agrarian economy he calls "productive," whereas he views the commercial economy as distinguished by an ideology of "conquest."

> Every higher form of economic life develops on the basis of and by means of an agrarian class. . . . It is . . . plantlike and without history, producing and consuming for itself alone. . . . This *productive* type of economy is then confronted by a *conquering* type, which exploits the former as an object, lets itself be nourished by it, forces it to pay tribute or dispossesses it. . . . The first wars are predatory wars, the first acts of trade intimately related to plundering and piracy. . . . Politics and trade in their advanced forms—the art of achieving material gains over one's opponents by means of intellectual superiority—are both a substitute for war by other means. (1152–53)

If this passage sounds in many ways like a summary of the fourth and fifth acts of Goethe's *Faust II*, then that is probably no coincidence. Goethe figures as the intellectual muse of Spengler's entire treatise, from its Goethe epigraph, through its constant invocation of lines from *Faust*, to its very identification of modern European cultural and economic attitudes with the Faustian principle of striving. But perhaps Spengler should have associated his theory of the modern economics of productive mediation, power, mastery, and obsessive accumulation with Mephistopheles instead of with Faust. It is the former, after all, who in an infamous monologue in act 5 provides the apparent model—down to the details of semantics—for Speng-ler's economics of violent and conscienceless conquest.

> We started out with two ships only,
> but now we're back in port with twenty.
> Our cargo clearly demonstrates
> what great success we have achieved.
> On the open sea your mind is open,
> and no one gives a fig for prudence!
> You have to grab things in a hurry [*rascher Griff*]:
> you catch a fish or catch a ship,
> and once you've three in your possession,
> you soon have caught a fourth as well;
> the fifth then hasn't got a chance,
> since it's a fact that might makes right.
> Not *how* but *what* will be the only question asked.
> Unless I'm all at sea about maritime matters,
> war, trade, and piracy together are
> a trinity not to be severed. (lines 11173–88)

Where might makes right, according to Mephistopheles' analysis, move-able wealth and its accumulation constitute the essence of power. Mephi-stopheles gives voice here to a "the rich get richer" mentality that defines the accumulation of wealth in terms of a kind of geometric progression: two ships become twenty, as if by a magic of multiplication. This addition of zeros marks, as we have seen in our analysis of Adalbert von Chamisso's *Peter Schlemihl* (chapter 6), not only the logic of acquisition, but also that of inflation,[4] and in *Faust II* ceaseless acquisition is associated with the inflationary tendencies of paper money. What underwrites this mechanism of burgeoning acquisition is the new holy trinity of modern political econ-omy: war, trade, and piracy. In Spengler's terms: trade as a continuation of war by other means. Mephistopheles is clear about the implications of this for the modern economic subject: thought is instrumentalized and reduced to a means-ends logic that privileges results over methods; the human being comes to be identified with a hand in the act of grasping (*rascher Griff*); conscientious reflection on one's actions is lambasted as counterproductive moralizing; and finally, all material objects, both natural ("fish") and man-made ("ship"), become commodities acquired in limitless quantities for the sole joy of their hoarding as sterile possessions. We have already seen in our examination of Droste-Hülshoff's *Judenbuche* how the limitlessness of monetary wealth encourages a reckless exploitation of nature that culminates in mindless ecological destruction. In his role as colonial master, Faust becomes an early representative of this dialectic between commercial production and natural destruction that characterizes the industrial economy of the nineteenth century.[5]

Faust II plays out the ecological implications of this mania for possession in its final act, not merely in the destructive appropriation of Philemon and Baucis's idyllic landscape, but also in Faust's desire to assert his mastery over the sea by setting limits to its limitlessness (see lines 10227–31 and 11539–43). We recall that the wanderer who returns to the dunes occupied by Philemon and Baucis does so explicitly in order to perceive from this vantage point the *limitlessness* of the ocean (see fig. 12 for Max Beckmann's rendering of this vantage point): "Now let me walk into the open/and survey the boundless [*grenzenlose*] sea" (lines 11075–76). Faust's desire to appropriate the estate of Philemon and Baucis is motivated explicitly by a similar wish to gaze upon the infinite, "so as to grant me a boundless view" (line 11345). In this instance, however, it is not the boundlessness of nature he seeks to visually capture, as was true for the wanderer, but rather the limitlessness of his own commercial empire. Nature has already been commodified and transformed into the object of personal possession. In order to gain an overview of his empire, Faust intends to build a platform in the linden trees on Philemon and Baucis's estate; this platform will provide him with a panorama over his own unlimited landed possessions (lines 11243–50). The logic of displacement in operation here has multiple facets: not only does Faust replace the wanderer, but artifice (the platform) replaces nature (the linden trees), just as an idyllic past in which humans live in harmony with nature is unseated by a technology-obsessed present in which the material world is divided up into commodities that can be obtained and held fast.

For the anthropologist Karl Polanyi, what distinguishes modern market societies from archaic economic communities is precisely what he terms the "commodity fiction" of land and labor. "Labor is only another word for human activity that goes with life itself," Polanyi maintains, and "land is

12 / The wanderer overlooking the sea from the property of Philemon and Baucis. Illustration by Max Beckmann from his *Illustrationen zu* Faust II: *Federzeichnungen—Bleistiftskizzen*, ed. Rike Wankmüller and Erika Zeise (Munich: Prestel, 1984). © 2007 Artists Rights Society (ARS), New York/VG Bild-Kunst, Bonn.

only another name for nature" (32). The transformation of labor and land into commodities bespeaks a double alienation, from the active nature of human beings themselves as laborers and from the earth as an immediate source of nourishment. *Faust II* documents this dual alienation of modern humanity in its closing act: the commodification of labor concretized in the proletarian hordes who build the dikes and dig the canals at Faust's behest; the commodification of nature in the surplus value of the new land Faust's project conjures out of the sea. In this sense the transformation depicted in *Faust* goes beyond, or perhaps deeper than, a simple historical-economic shift from a feudal to a capitalistic paradigm, as Georg Lukács has suggested (142);[6] it reflects instead what Polanyi calls the "great transformation," the displacement of a community in which economic principles are subordinate to, and a function of, social interaction by one in which economics has become autonomous and holds sway over the social character of human beings.[7]

In the first act Faust becomes the spokesperson for an ideology that expounds pursuit of the limitless as an end in itself. In his audience with the emperor and his court, it falls to Faust to encourage the circulation of paper money as a kind of mortgage against the wealth buried underground throughout the empire.

> The excess [*Übermaß*] of wealth that lies, unproductive [*erstarrt*],
> deep in the soil beneath your territories,
> still wants to be exploited. But no mind
> is vast enough to grasp these treasures' full extent;
> imagination in its loftiest flight may strain,
> but cannot ever do them feeble justice.
> Yet minds that can look deep will have
> limitless faith in the limitless [*Zum Grenzenlosen grenzenlos Vertrauen*].
>   (lines 6111–18; translation modified)

This passage contains historical allusions to the assignats introduced during the French Revolution, which, as Karl Marx noted, were mortgaged by the real estate the revolutionaries intended to confiscate from the church and the state (*Zur Kritik der politischen Ökonomie* 64). It also invokes the paper-money experiment of John Law, which replaced the *limited* backing of money by gold with its virtually *unlimited* backing by land (Rennie 107). Faust's speech invokes precisely the limitlessness of the emperor's putative and potential wealth; hence he refers to the *excess* (*Übermaß*) of the treasures hidden underground and the necessity of an imaginative capacity that itself must open onto excess in order even to fathom the magnitude of this wealth. This is where *Faust II* moves closest to the themes we articulated in our archaeology of the German debate over physiocracy (chapter 4) and our interpretation of Chamisso's *Peter Schlemihl* (chapter 6): the linkage between excesses of the imagination and an economy of excessive wealth and expenditure. It is certainly possible to view this scene in *Faust II* as—among other things—an intertextual allusion to Chamisso's tale. Schlemihl's magic purse, which produces a boundless supply of gold, has been replaced by paper money as a mere *sign*, or representation, of a limitless wealth that otherwise remains materially absent (that is, buried in the emperor's land). Moreover, Faust's words clearly suggest that the empire's problem is not an absence of wealth as such, but rather its *liquidity*: it lies *erstarrt*, "immobile" and "unproductive" underground and must merely be brought into circulation in order for its impact to be felt. In addition, land has become the substitute for gold as the principle article of value—a substitution that has significant consequences for the closing act of *Faust II*, where the creation of land becomes a metaphor for the decidedly unnatural production of increased "natural" wealth. But as in Chamisso's tale, the "magic" that produces infinite monetary wealth is associated with the work of the devil. Yet in Goethe's tragedy, Faust has become the ideological advocate of this economic paradigm of boundless wealth, without—yet—being its beneficiary: that will only transpire later in the action. Ultimately, however, both Chamisso and Goethe express a profound skepticism about this modern economic paradigm that places limitless faith in the limitlessness of growth, wealth, and expenditure. We can imagine Faust in this scene, where he elects to champion paper money, playing the role—quite literally—of the devil's advocate: he represents to the emperor's court the ideology of limitless wealth and introduces paper money as its functional instrument, without yet subscribing to either himself. By the end of the play, however, he will have bought into this economic model wholesale. Faust's seduction by the ideology of commercial modernism, by limitless faith in the limitless, is the ultimate tragedy of this work.

An Economics of Redemption?

Goethe was one of the first to provide, in *Faust II*, a comprehensive literary rendering of this intertwining of monetary functionalism, colonialism, technological mastery, and human self-alienation. In the preceding chapters we have been able to examine individual strands of this historically evolving economic configuration as it manifests itself in German philosophical, economic, and literary discourses from the end of the eighteenth to the middle of the nineteenth century. Goethe's *Faust II* represents a convergence of these themes in a single work, and this is what makes an interpretive investigation of this drama appropriate and illuminating as a coda and conclusion for the chapters that have gone before. One is justified on several accounts in treating *Faust II* as a kind of synopsis of the economic, political, and cultural history of the West through its modernist transformation. First of all, the text itself lays certain claims to this status as a repository of, and reflection on, Western history: from the ancient Greeks, through the Holy Roman Empire, to the French Revolution, to the industrial revolution, Faust's story parallels in rough outlines the (hi)story of Central Europe from antiquity to the time of its consolidation as postaristocratic civil society in the 1830s. Goethe himself noted the significant transformation that took place in the figure of Faust between the drama's first and second parts. In a conversation with Eckermann from 17 February 1831, he contrasted the subjective individuality of the first part, as the product of a passionate individual, with the "higher, more expansive, brighter, less passionate world" manifest in the second part (*Gedenkausgabe* 24: 453). This has led to the well-nigh universal assessment that part 1 deals with the private inclinations of Faust as individual, while part 2 treats Faust as a superpersonal representative of the world in general.[8] This shift is also inscribed in the literary aesthetics of Goethe's *Faust*, with the more abstract and universalizing purview of part 2 finding expression in the appropriate mode of allegory. Heinz Schlaffer has made a persuasive case for the aptness of allegorical form in *Faust II* for an exposition and critique of the abstraction and semblance of the monetary economy, referring to Goethe's use of allegory as an "aesthetic mimesis of social abstraction" (*Faust zweiter Teil* 175).

Regarding the prominence of economic themes in part 2, we need only recall that Goethe spent the major portion of his life as a minister in the court of Sachsen-Weimar and that issues of political economy were among his primary charges.[9] Indeed, as early as June 1782 Goethe assumed the portfolio of the minister of finance in the duchy of Sachsen-Weimar, and he carried out these duties with singular success (Bradish 70). Goethe's library contained a large number of works on political economy, and he was personally acquainted with leading economists of the day, such as his brother-in-law Johann Georg Schlosser (1739–99), Georg Sartorius (1765–1828), and Johann Georg Büsch (1728–1800).[10] If political economy was, in the words of Bernd Mahl, the "fashionable science" of Goethe's day (10), then one of the things that makes *Faust II* such a "fashionable" literary work is the manner in which it integrates into its thematic texture ideas derived from the entire panoply of economic thought of the age: from the physiocratic doctrine of the sole productivity of nature, to Schlosser's connection between economic value and the power of the imagination, to the free-market principles of Adam Smith, through ultimately to the utopian socialism of the Saint Simonists.[11] There is plenty of justification, then, for following Oswald Spengler's lead and reading *Faust II* in terms of an economic transformation from a "natural" economy to one dominated by monetary abstraction, industrialization, and colonial exploitation.[12] The question is whether Goethe the economist lent credence to the emergent view, held both by market-oriented capitalist ideology and utopian socialism, that economics could provide the vehicle for human material salvation. In my opinion, *Faust II* represents a prescient argument *against* the possibility of any such *economics* of redemption.

One of the most persistent questions for critics of *Faust II* relates precisely to the matter of Faust's ultimate salvation. Can we take seriously the conclusion of this drama, which gives a religious-theological turn to the blatantly secular and worldly events that characterize Faust's life and death? This question marks the great divide in *Faust* scholarship, with interpreters typically falling on one side or the other. In general, however, those who stress the material dimensions of the drama, playing up its economic and political motifs, tend to reject any justification for Faust's salvation. My own interpretation will prove no exception. Yet how can one explain the investment Goethe made in this closing scene, which recapitulates in significant ways the rescue of Gretchen that took place at the end of part 1? We know from testimonies by Goethe himself that the conclusion was one of the first scenes he completed for part 2, finished in all significant respects already prior to 1815[13] and thus long before his intensive push to finish the drama in the final years of his life. One can, to be sure, simply take the meanderings of Faust throughout the play, but especially in part 2, as supporting one of the Lord's pivotal statements in the "Prologue in Heaven": "[H]umans err as long as they keep striving" (line 317). According to this formula, striving and error are inextricably bound up with one another; hence Faust can strive and err and yet still deserve salvation. This, in fact, seems to be the win-win (or, if you prefer, lose-lose) position Oswald Spengler assumes; his Faustian human being, after all, is condemned by destiny to go on striving, even if it spells his own demise, since this incessant striving reflects the inherent—and necessarily tragic—course of all human cultures (*Untergang* 43). But Goethe surely was no fatalist in the pessimistic, Spenglerian sense, since Faust's ultimate salvation seems to be prepro-

grammed into his "tragedy" from the outset. From a Judeo-Christian perspective one might justifiably—and only somewhat rhetorically—ask, can
the Lord really enter into a wager with the devil and *lose*? In this regard,
the conclusion of part 2 can be seen as simply fulfilling the *formal* crite-
ria laid out already in the prelude to part 1. Viewed in this manner, Faust's
salvation serves the demands of aesthetic closure more than it does those of
thematic consistency. But perhaps Goethe's conclusion, so rife with ironies,
is supposed to send a didactic message, making clear to human beings that,
barring an eleventh-hour *deus ex machina*, the historical, cultural-economic
course they are following can only lead to worldwide ecological and human
disaster, that the "digging" they take as the symptom of their economic
and technological progress actually signals, as for Faust (see lines 11555–
58), the digging of their own graves.

If this is the case—and this is the case I will try to make—then Faust's
salvation assumes the function of a strategic irony, a kind of Mephistophelean goad that admonishes and encourages human beings to strive *differently* than Faust does. We should recall here that it is in his function as
just such a goad that the Lord valorizes Mephistopheles in the "Prologue
in Heaven":

> Of all the spirits of negation
> rogues like you bother me the least.
> Human activity slackens all too easily,
> and people soon are prone to rest on any terms;
> that's why I like to give them the companion
> who functions as a prod and does a job as devil. (lines 338–43)

One can easily see how precisely this function as a goad explains why
Mephistopheles, although constantly willing evil, ultimately produces good
(lines 1335–36). Or does he? There is a telling irony in the Lord's theod-
icy, in which the existence of the devil, as the incarnation of evil, is justified
as a prod that spurs humans on to ever-greater accomplishments. For if
human beings require the devil as a constantly biting gadfly, so as to ensure
that they will never take pleasure in repose, must we not see the incessant
striving with which Faust eventually buys salvation as—paradoxically—
the work of the devil? Faust seems to be caught up in a vicious circle—

359

what Germans like Goethe would quite appropriately call a *Teufelskreis*, a devil's circuit—since the condition of his *salvation* is precisely that he be goaded on to endless striving by the *devil's* representative. This is perhaps the ultimate irony in Goethe's version of the Faust tale, and it gives ample indication that the drama's conclusion should not be taken too seriously as a *theological* position, although it may have certain justification as an *economic, anthropological,* or *sociopolitical* statement. The condition of possibility of Faust's redemption seems to be his initial sellout to evil.

Let us approach this same question from an entirely different—a rhetorical, rather than thematic—perspective. In some of the last words he would ever write, put down in a letter to Wilhelm von Humboldt on 17 March 1832, just five days prior to his death, Goethe legitimated in the following words his decision to seal up the manuscript of *Faust II* and ordain that it not see the light of day before its author had passed on.

> It would without question give me endless pleasure to dedicate during
> my own lifetime these very serious jokes to my valuable, gratefully
> acknowledged, widely dispersed friends, share them with them, and hear
> their response. But the present day is really so absurd and confused that
> I am convinced that my honest, long-pursued efforts surrounding this
> peculiar construct [*Gebäu*] would be badly rewarded, driven aground on
> the shore, stranded like a scattered shipwreck, and initially covered over
> by the sand dunes of time. (HAB 4: 481)[14]

What strikes one initially about this statement is its overwrought pathos: Goethe bemoans the lack of comprehension with which he anticipates his contemporaries will receive *Faust II*, and the displeasure his own experience of this reception would cause warrants forgoing the pleasure he would derive from the positive reaction of his friends. Yet the metaphors Goethe chooses to designate this work are peculiar. By calling it a "construct" (*Gebäu*), he stresses nothing if not the artifice of the text. He continues along this general metaphorical register when he goes on to compare *Faust II*, in its anticipated reception, to a wrecked and stranded ship. This repeated metaphorical insistence on the artificiality of *Faust II* as aesthetic entity echoes a thematic dealt with in the drama itself; one thinks immediately of the flower girls in the opening sequence of the "Masquerade" scene whose artificial flowers, although possessing the virtue of blooming year-round, are pieced together out of stray materials and ultimately demoted to the status of commercial commodities (lines 5088–115). To be sure, when viewed as a whole, even these artificial flowers are attractive and display a coherence and symmetry (5100–04). Does this constitute a self-reflection on Goethe's part regarding the aesthetics of *Faust II* itself? The work contains, after all, a peculiar collection of disparate scenes, is written in diverse verse forms, and operates with a panoply of rhetorical devices—and in its disparity is ultimately held together by the exceedingly artificial structure of the traditional five-act tragedy.

Yet there is a further, more significant dimension of self-reflexivity in the metaphors Goethe selects to describe *Faust II* in his letter to Humboldt. The image of the ship in a landscape of sandy dunes contains clear allusions to the setting of the fifth act, the return of Faust's fleet of ships to their harbor and the dunes upon which the hut and chapel of Philemon and Baucis stand. Faust's flotilla is, of course, not shipwrecked here—on the contrary, it arrives in port and safely unloads its contraband. But the wanderer whose monologue begins act 5 did once experience shipwreck at this place, only to be rescued by the couple he has returned to visit. We know that all three, the wanderer along with Philemon and Baucis, will eventually fall victim to Faust's infinite greed and powermongering. But what interests me here is the juxtaposition of Faust's ships, which enter the harbor safely with their cache of pirated goods, and the shipwreck of *Faust II* as literary-aesthetic work that Goethe envisions in his letter to Humboldt: the ship of *Faust II* fails to enter port laden with the various treasures of Western literary and cultural history it has incorporated, but instead founders and runs aground, its treasures scattered across the sands of time. Its rich cultural-historical contraband, in short, will *not* be successfully stockpiled and put on display so that its readers can encompass it in a single glance, assess its worth, and celebrate it with many feasts, as happens with Faust's colonial booty (lines 11205–16). Rather, in Goethe's imagination it will be washed ashore, fragmented and dispersed, and eventually covered over by the ocean-driven sands. Yet Goethe suggests—*ex negativo*—that precisely such an all-encompassing retrospective on the Western literary-cultural tradition would constitute the *positive*, desirable reception of *Faust II*—the kind of reception he expects from his circle of friends. But this kind of reception would have to acknowledge this work's status as an act of literary-cultural piracy, as an excessive accumulation of the intellectual wealth and treasures of the Western world, from classical antiquity through the age of colonialism to technological modernity. In other words, in order to comprehend *Faust II* in this manner, its readers would have to assume a position analogous to that of Goethe's Faust character: they would have to attain a *Hochbesitz* (line 11156), an "elevated position" of visual-historical mastery, from which they could survey, as Faust himself wishes to do, their cultural *Weltbesitz* (line 11242), their "worldly possessions."

However, if Faust as character ultimately fails to achieve this absolute cultural-economic mastery, *Faust II* as aesthetic work, at least in terms of its projected reception, must also fail to transmit this perspective of mastery over the literary-cultural past. In this final letter to Humboldt Goethe thus acknowledges several things about the production and reception of *Faust II*. It is, first of all, an aesthetic work of extreme artifice, one whose *potential* value derives from its ability to gather together in a single text the cultural booty of European history in its entirety. Second, the drive to excess and the will to power that mark the culmination of Faust's existence also characterize the relationship between *Faust II* as literary work and the Western literary-cultural tradition. Although it might be going too far to call this drama a work of parody, perhaps it can be fittingly described as one of historical-cultural *piracy*. Maybe this is what Goethe meant when he referred, in his letter to Humboldt, to the "serious jokes" (*ernsten Scherze*) he saw as the substance of this text.[15] My point here is that for Goethe himself, *Faust II* as literary-aesthetic work is implicated in the very *critique* of the principles of economic modernism, its colonialist pretensions and its overblown drive for material acquisitions, upon which the demise of its protagonist is predicated. In other words, *Faust II* does not merely *portray* the intertwining of intellectual-cultural accomplishments and economic-technological mastery, but also *performs* this imbrication in its own literary-aesthetic practice. Just as Faust cannot find *economic* redemption, *Faust II* will fail to provide its readers with *aesthetic* redemption. Its cultural booty is destined, according to Goethe, to be scattered across the shores of history. The cataclysm he projects in terms of the reception of this work thus also hints at the cataclysm in which the exploitative economic practices of Western technological modernism will culminate. What Goethe ultimately envisions in his letter to Humboldt, then, is the shipwreck of a cultural-historical paradigm in which economics holds sway over social and human values. In this sense the final message of *Faust II* might be interpreted as an admonition to human beings *not* to pin their hopes for redemption on economic principles. Faust, after all, receives salvation not *because of* his subscription to the destructive principles of economic modernism, but rather *in spite of* it. However, as we will subsequently see, the model of reception adumbrated in this letter to Humboldt is just *one* alternative Goethe imagines for *Faust II*, the receptive mode appropriate to this text as a vessel for cultural-historical *accumulation*. It is the manner of reception Goethe projects, in other words, for *Faust II* in its guise as *classical* literary work. As we will see toward the conclusion of this chapter, the aged Goethe envisioned a completely different hermeneutical response for *Faust II* in its Romantic aspect, that dimension of the text that reflects not the drive for cultural-capital accumulation, but instead invokes the excessive squandering of its exuberant and hyperactive poetic productivity.

"Pleasant Landscape" and the Economics/Aesthetics of Mediation

The opening scene of *Faust II*, "Anmutige Gegend" ("Pleasant Landscape"), assumes the difficult task of forming a transition between parts 1 and 2 of this work, between the Gretchen tragedy, on the one hand, and the actions of Faust as colonial conqueror and man of the world, on the other (Kaiser 88). If the central theme of this scene is, as critics have often recognized, the problem of mediation, concretized in the image of the rainbow (Brown, *Goethe's* Faust 137; Dye 969–72; Jaeger 499; Mattenklott 740; Pickerodt 759; Schlaffer, *Faust zweiter Teil* 67–68; Jochen Schmidt 190), then this question redounds self-reflexively on the very function of this episode itself; the scene's task is literally to mediate between the drama's two disparate parts. But before we deal with this issue of mediation as represented in "Pleasant Landscape" and its implications for the economic and aesthetic dimensions of *Faust II*, we must address the theme of Faust's forgetting and his exculpation from the sins that led to Gretchen's demise, for this has certain consequences that relate to the redemptive conclusion of the play.

Faust II opens with its hero bedded down in a flowery meadow in the evening twilight, thirsting for sleep and its metaphorical cousins, redemption and oblivion. The graceful, diminutive spirits that swarm around him are attracted by his unsettlement and misery and motivated by the drive to soothe and pacify. As their spokesperson Ariel indicates, they do not ask, nor are they concerned with, questions of guilt or innocence, but focus solely on offering balm for the wounds of human suffering.

> Small in size, but large in sprit [*Geistergröße*],
> elves are quick to be of help,
> pitying the man of sorrow,
> whether he be saint or sinner. (lines 4617–20)

The greatness of these spirits (*Geistergröße*) is clearly figurative, not literal; they are diminutive but magnanimous, and the symptom of their magnanimity is that they care not whether the person they aid is a victim or a perpetrator, a "saint" or a "sinner." Their task is to wipe away any traces of (self-)reproach or blame, relieving Faust not so much of his responsibility for Gretchen's death, as of any awareness of, or self-reflection on, his complicity in it.

> You who are circling in the air above his head,
> now demonstrate your elfin worth—
> compose the angry strife within his heart,
> remove the burning barbs of his remorse,
> and purge him of all sense of horror! (lines 4621–25)

One is tempted to view this elfin medicine as all *too* effective, relieving Faust not merely of remorse for actions and events experienced in the *past*, but even inoculating him against any *future* feelings of guilt. The elves do not merely wipe away any pangs of conscience Faust might feel for his complicity in Gretchen's death, they eradicate his capacity to experience remorse as such, as all his subsequent actions indicate. This lack of conscience and self-reflection is what distinguishes Faust as character throughout part 2: he has become a remorseless deed-doer, a man so focused on his own "striving," on the satisfaction of his own wants and selfish desires, that he is immune to feelings of pity for those he victimizes along the way. His path to wealth and glory is strewn with corpses: not only does he join forces with the emperor, the representative of sociopolitical restoration, against the anti-emperor and the spirit of revolution, all in the name of his self-interested desire to be granted the shoreline as his fiefdom; he also sends out the death squad to eliminate Philemon and Baucis so that he may take possession of the last piece of land that has otherwise evaded his grasp. Even if, as Faust claims, he is "displeased" by this "impatient act" (lines 11340–41), he shows no genuine signs of remorse or guilt. On the contrary, he is quick to find compensation for the destruction of the linden trees that he intended as his lookout post in the projected erection of a watch-tower. This displacement of what is given in nature by the products of human artifice is symptomatic of Faust's accomplishments throughout part 2. This is the entire thrust of his final project, the building of dams to win land from the sea: it transforms a natural landscape into an artificial one and practices mastery over nature so as better to replace it by art(ifice). Even the utopian vision Faust conjures up of a society in which humans live together "active and free" (line 11564), constantly challenged to salvage the artifice of their diked-off land from the pressure of the sea to take it back (lines 11569–76), has a hollow and ideologically self-deceptive ring when seen in the context of the murders of Philemon and Baucis.

There is a certain logic that links the opening scene of *Faust II*, in which the protagonist is liberated from the pangs of conscience, and the destructive conclusion of the play. In this initial scene, Faust is transformed into an individual who—in Freudian terms—is completely "liberated" from the governing psychic mechanism of a superego. The id, we might say, is allowed to run rampant throughout part 2, in the service of the voracious ego who is assisted, no less, by the conscienceless conjurations of Mephistopheles. In this sense the Faust of part 2 has truly become the devil's disciple. Goethe himself reflected, in his *Maxime und Reflexionen,* on the idea that human action demands a slumbering conscience: "The person of action is always without conscience; only the observer has conscience" (no. 251, HA 12: 399). This reflection, which juxtaposes the person of action and the passive observer, is particularly applicable to the final act of *Faust II* because, as in this meditation, the functions of action and observation are split between two characters: Faust, on the one hand, and the watchman Lynceus, on the other. As audience and readers, we only perceive the destruction of Philemon and Baucis's estate through the eyes of Lynceus, who reports it by means of dramatic teichoscopy (lines 11304–37).[16] Lynceus's report, moreover, does not possess the quality of objective and distanced observation, rather it is tinged with a pathos of horror and loss, as emblematized scripturally by the frequent exclamation marks punctuating his speech. Faust's immediate response to Lynceus's "song," furthermore, is to comment wryly on its lamenting tone: "What is that dolorous song up there?" (line 11338). Conscience, empathy, and remorse thus seem to be reserved quite literally for Lynceus, the observer, whereas the perpetrator senses only anger that his command has not been carried out to the letter, even if it has been fulfilled in spirit.[17] For this reason, Faust's admonition to Mephistopheles that he sought a fair exchange with Philemon and Baucis and was not intent on robbery—"Were your ears deaf to what I said? / I wanted an exchange, not theft" (lines 11370–71)—once more rings like hollow self-deception. In essence, Faust is able to disavow responsibility for the evil deeds perpetrated in his name by shunting them off on his deputy and his deputy's deputies, the three mighty men. Faust's own conscience—to the extent he has one at all—can remain clear. To be sure, Faust dreams of taking the place of his watchman Lynceus: his fascination with the estate of Philemon and Baucis, after all, stems predominantly from his desire to appropriate the view overlooking his newly founded colony, whose spot is marked by the linden trees he aims to expropriate (lines 11240–50). However, whereas Lynceus's focus as watchman is directed at the suffering Other and is shrouded emotionally in compassion and pity, Faust's sole concern is with personal gain and self-aggrandizement: he seeks a vantage point from which he can overlook his own achievements with pride and a sense of accomplishment. In his own imagination, no ghosts of guilt or self-reproach haunt this perspective. In this sense he envisions himself, contrary to Goethe's maxim, as an observer without conscience. But we know that he will never enjoy this panorama over the kingdom he envisions as a "land of Eden" (line 11569): the watchtower intended to replace the linden trees will never be erected, and Faust himself is struck by blindness before his utopian colony can be completely realized. It is tempting to interpret Faust's blindness precisely as a mono-gram of his lack of conscience; for if, as Goethe asserts, only the observer has conscience, then one might surmise that the incapacity to observe bespeaks an incapacity for remorse. It is true, at any rate, that throughout part 2, Faust, assuaged by the elves in "Pleasant Landscape," shows no remorse and displays no pangs of conscience. If we understand the elfin spirits as relieving Faust not simply of his responsibility for past failings, but as making him impervious to any sense of guilt, remorse, or responsi-bility for his actions whatsoever, then we can also comprehend why one of the four gray women who seeks access to Faust in the final act, *Schuld*—understood not only economically as "debt," but also ethically as "guilt"—fails to find entrance to Faust's palace. The elves' magic is so successful that the possibility of feeling remorse is banished completely from Faust's psyche: without conscience, no guilt.[18]

"Pleasant Landscape" has justifiably been viewed as a prologue not merely for the first act, but for *Faust II* in its entirety. This is true not solely because of its "higher level of abstraction," as Jane Brown has correctly asserted (*Goethe's* Faust 153), but also because it prepares the ground for many of the themes that predominate in the acts to come. Goethe himself, in one of his earliest reflections on part 2, recorded by his secretary Friedrich Kräuter and dated December 1816, emphasized the all-important role the elfin spirits play by planting the seeds for Faust's reinvigorated drives and ambitions: "At the beginning of the second part we find Faust sleeping. He is surrounded by choruses of spirits who portray for him in palpable symbols and pleasant songs the joys of honor, fame, power, and mastery. They conceal their proposals behind wheedling words and melodies, which are actually meant ironically" (Paralipomenon 70, in *Gedenkausgabe* 5: 557–58). In their role as Faust's instigators to the action of part 2, the spirits have assumed the goading function the Lord attrib-uted to Mephistopheles in the "Prologue in Heaven." Moreover, accord-ing to this paralipomenon, their alluring words and songs are dominated by the master trope of Mephistopheles' discourse: irony. Must we then see Faust as, from the outset of part 2, a naïve dupe who fails to penetrate the mask of irony? Is Faust already someone who, like the courtiers later in act 1, confuses signifier and signified and is unable to distinguish between "paper" signs and substantive material wealth (Emrich 45; Hamacher 170;

Pickerodt 758)? Put differently, should we interpret the subsequent events of the drama as a consequence of Faust's misreading, his failure to penetrate the irony inherent in the elfin spirits' discourse?

If this is the case, then "Pleasant Landscape" would also serve to introduce the theme of a fundamental discrepancy between substance and semblance presented in concentrated form in the paper-money episode and the "Masquerade" that follow in act 1. To be sure, Faust is naturally predisposed to be enticed and persuaded by the spirits' call to action in the name of fame and distinction.

> To obtain desires' fulfillment,
> look and see the radiance [*Glanze*] there!
> . . . .
> Do not hesitate, be daring
> while the aimless crowd delays:
> all is achieved by noble minds
> that understand and quickly act [*rasch ergreift*]! (lines 4658–65)

Significant in this admonition is the urge to translate thought immediately into action; for that is precisely what Faust will attempt to do when he sets about his utopian project of winning land from the sea. Indeed, in one of his last monologues, Faust echoes the words of these sprits when he characterizes himself as a man of prowess (*Tüchtigen*) and asserts that "whatever he conceptualizes can be grasped [*ergreifen*]!" (line 11448).[19] The German verb *ergreifen*, which occurs in both passages, alludes not only to the concrete grasping by the human hand—we should remind ourselves here that the German word *Faust* means "fist"—but also to the more figural "grasping" of intellectual comprehension, and it thus hints at the instrumentalization of reason for the ends of concrete action that Faust will come to represent.[20] These lines also hauntingly invoke Faust's desperate ejaculation in the famous opening monologue of part 1: "Infinite Nature, where can I lay hold of you [*Wo fass' ich dich*]?" (line 455). In many respects this line expresses the central dilemma of Faust's striving: the paradox of trying to take hold of, and hence lend finite dimensions to, all that is infinite in nature. Faust's actions at the close of part 2 represent the veritable realization of this desire to confine and take possession of endless nature. As we have seen, the ocean is characterized throughout the play by the boundlessness of its dimensions and its power; and Faust's project of building dikes and draining the sea aims precisely at giving its boundlessness arbitrary, human-made, and hence artificial boundaries. The culminating recognition of *Faust II* might thus be seen as Faust's insight that it is the shoreline between water and land, the instantiation of a *natural* boundary, where his design to "lay hold" of nature must be realized. This emphatically liminal space is, in effect, the Archimedean point from which Faust believes he can lift the reigning sociopolitical and economic world off its axis. And indeed, the coastline, with its access to sea and its transportation routes, will displace the imperial palace as the seat of power in favor of a colonial economy based on trade and the circulation of money and commodities—just as access to a river that flows to the sea is the natural condition of possibility for the economic exploitation of the forests in Droste-Hülshoff's *Judenbuche*.

The elfin spirits in "Pleasant Landscape" direct Faust's attention to one specific place from which he can purportedly derive satisfaction for all his desires: the radiance (*Glanze*) of the sky where the sun is about to rise ("To obtain desires' fulfillment, / look and see the radiance there!") (lines 4658–59). The horizon, the place where heaven and earth meet, is one more manifestation of liminality in nature, and as such it is the macrocosmic counterpart of the shoreline Faust will acquire as his fiefdom and whose very liminal characteristics he will exploit. In this sense, when the elfin spirits draw Faust's attention to the radiance on the horizon, they also plant the seed that will grow into his final endeavor. And as if on cue, when Faust turns his attention to the horizon, the sun does indeed rise, marked not only visually by its blinding radiance, but aurally as well, by a "great clamor" (*Ungeheures Getöse*, stage direction following line 4665). This clamor of the dawn is more than an innocent synesthesia, more than a transmuted representation of the sun's glorious light into a powerful sound. Transitions are frequently marked throughout *Faust* by aural indications: one thinks most prominently of the ringing of the bells on Easter Sunday in part 1, which draws Faust back from the brink of suicide (lines 735–36), or the ringing bells of Philemon and Baucis's chapel (stage direction following line 11150), which mark their occupation of territory Faust will eventually claim as his own.[21] But as we know, Faust cannot follow the elfin spirits' admonition to gaze directly at the radiance of the sun, for when he attempts to do this he recoils with pain from its blinding brilliance (lines 4702–03). Here the theme of excess enters the drama in one of its most poignant expressions; for it is the sun's *Flammenübermass*, its "super-abundance of flames" (line 4708), that causes Faust to turn away in anguish. Surely it is no coincidence that the fate Faust willfully escapes here, being struck with blindness, is the very one Care will impose upon him at the play's conclusion. We might even go further and hypothesize that, as in this early scene, so at the drama's conclusion: the threat of blindness is associated with the motif of excess. At any rate, prior to attempting to gaze at the sun's radiance directly, Faust had perceived it indirectly in its reflection off the mountaintops (lines 4695–98). After being nearly blinded, he devises a strategy for the indirect perception of this radiance: he turns his back to the sun and takes in its iridescence indirectly, through the deflection of its light rays in the mist of a waterfall.

> I am content to have the sun behind me.
> The cataract there storming through the cliff—
> the more I watch it, the greater my delight [*wachsendem Entzücken*].
> From fall to fall [*Sturz zu Stürzen*] it swirls, gushing forth
> in streams that soon are thousand, many thousands [*abertausend*],
> into the air all loudly tossing spray and foam [*Schaum an Schäume*].
> But see how, rising from this turbulence,
> the rainbow forms its changing-unchanged arch,
> now clearly drawn, now evanescent,
> and casts cool, fragrant showers all about it.
> Of human striving it's a perfect symbol—
> ponder this well to understand more clearly
> that what we have as life is many-hued reflection [*farbigen Abglanz*].
>   (lines 4715–27)

This is undoubtedly one of the most memorable passages in all of *Faust*, and it has attracted the attention of innumerable commentators. The common denominator of most interpretations revolves around the concept of mediation, and that is clearly what the rainbow emblematizes. In his illustrations for *Faust II*, Max Beckmann emphasizes this mediating aspect by

13 / "Am farbingen Abglanz": The many-hued deflection of the scene "Pleasant Landscape" as work of art rather than work of nature. Illustration by Max Beckmann from his *Illustrationen zu* Faust II: *Federzeichnungen—Bleistiftskizzen,* ed. Rike Wankmüller and Erika Zeise (Munich: Prestel, 1984). © 2007 Artists Rights Society (ARS), New York/VG Bild-Kunst, Bonn.

depicting the landscape and rainbow not as a natural setting, but instead as a painted canvas, sitting on an easel: art, Beckmann implies, is the true mediator, and we will subsequently concern ourselves with this theme in more detail (fig. 13). The symbolic texture of *Faust II* is largely dominated, as it is in this scene, by metaphors of fire and water; and it is precisely the interplay of these two elements and their metaphorical registers that constitutes the rainbow in this passage (Brown, *Goethe's* Faust 143). The story of the homunculus, for example, is guided by the teleological necessity of merging his unembodied flame with the water of the ocean. The interactions between the philosophers of nature, Thales and Anaxagoras, similarly concretize this opposition in two largely allegorical figures. They stand for larger scientific issues, such as the debate between the Vulcanists and the Neptunists that raged in Goethe's day and that finds expression in the second act.[22] In Faust's colonial endeavor in act 5, the interaction of fire and water will assume more ominous undertones: Philemon and Baucis associate the fire and flames that rage during the night with the "magic"— the technological and industrial advancements—that allow Faust's workers to speedily construct the dams and canals that will rein in the ocean's waves. Nor should we forget the flames that destroy their hut and chapel and the linden trees on which Faust has set his designs. This dialectic of miraculous production and ceaseless destruction is already figured in the intermingling of fire and water in Faust's closing monologue in "Pleasant Landscape." This dialectic is manifest not merely in the *Wechseldauer*, the permanent change and permanence *of* change embodied in the rainbow; it is similarly reflected in Faust's ever-growing delight (*wachsendem Entzücken*), in repeated intensification of singular nouns to their plural forms (*Sturz zu Stürzen; Schaum an Schäume*), and in the way the streams of water multiply in a quasigeometric progression. Productivity and growth, in other words, are two central notions that imbue this passage: this scene is a veritable celebration of nature's productivity, of a mediated merger, a joining that gives rise to an infinite proliferation of the new.

It should come as no surprise, then, that this scene symbolically prefigures the paper-money episode that will become the centerpiece of act 1. In this episode, of course, it is not nature that is productive, but rather artifice, human ingenuity, or Mephistophelean magic. In this sense, the trajectory of act 1 moves in a direction away from nature and toward artifice. When viewed in this context, the invention of paper money assumes the guise of the quintessential aesthetic act: the transference of nature's productive energies to human imaginative ingenuity (a theme we pursued in chapter 4). The imagery of fire and water is also present; gold is regularly associated with fire throughout this act—culminating in the flames of Plutus's treasure chest, which ignite the emperor's beard when he draws his face too close (lines 5920–43). In a fundamental, if metaphorical sense, paper money symbolizes the union of fire and water: the flaming essence of gold is yoked to the newfound liquidity of the empire and the fluidity of paper money's fast-paced circulation. Hence the lord steward can refer to the paper bills as "fleeting ones" (*die Flüchtigen*), whose lightning speed prevents their capture (lines 6086–87). The motif of infinite production also links the invention of paper money to the monologue that concludes "Pleasant Landscape." The way in which the paper notes are reproduced in thousandfold imitations—"quick conjurers [*Tausendkünstler*] made copies by the thousands [*vertausendfacht*]" (line 6072)—mimics the progressive multiplication of streams in the waterfall, which increase in number by "thousand [*tausend*], many thousands [*abertausend*]" (lines 4718–19). Finally, the immediate effect of the introduction of this paper currency is to stimulate both economic production ("The drapers cut their cloth, the tailors sew"; line 6094), and overall consumption ("half the world seems obsessed with eating well"; line 6092). But the fundamental point that underwrites the analogy between the generation of the rainbow as "many-hued reflection" (*farbigen Abglanz*) and the production of paper money is the union of the immaterial (light/human imagination) and matter (water particles/buried treasures). Just as the rainbow joins the energy of the heavens (light) with the materiality of the living world (water), paper money constitutes the union of the upper world and the underworld: it marks the place "that joins together in one happy union / the upper and the nether worlds" (lines 6139–40).

It is important to note in this context that according to Goethe's *Farbenlehre*, his theory of colors, the rainbow is not a simple refraction of white light, as in Newton's theory. Instead, color is generated, according to Goethe, by the marriage of white light and matter (Brown, *Goethe's Faust* 139), manifest in "Pleasant Landscape" as the tiny water droplets that rise up from the cataract. In this sense, it is strictly speaking incorrect to translate *Abglanz* as "reflection," as Atkins does; *de*flection would be a more accurate rendering, for it is a kind of visual ricochet of light off of water that, in Goethe's understanding, generates the multiple colors of the rainbow. The rainbow, then, the *farbigen Abglanz*, is nothing other than a symbol of mediation itself, of the productive intermingling of the material and nonmaterial, of the infinite productivity and reciprocity of light/fire and water, and as such it represents the incessant transformation of what is static into the permanent stasis of transformation. The rainbow, in short, becomes a symbol of dynamic productivity generated at the margin or the intersection of opposing principles, and as such it announces and prefigures the themes of economic productivity and excess that permeate *Faust II*. In this context it is certainly not serendipitous that after the loss of Helen Faust sets his sights on claiming the shoreline, the manifestation of the liminal in nature, as his fiefdom. It is precisely here that he will invest his energies to generate a new terrain of production.

As we saw in earlier chapters, one of the principal innovations in the economic thinking that underwrote the paradigm shift from a subsistence-based to a production-oriented economy was a reconceptualization of money that ceased to view it as a substance and began instead to conceive it as a function, a pure means, as a mediator among people and things. In chapter 1 we observed how semiotic and monetary theories underwent historically parallel and analogous transformations and how this change was reflected in metaphors that aligned the linguistic and monetary domains. Chapter 2 further developed the homology between money and signs as insubstantial mediators by focusing on the monetary and semiotic theories of two prominent German Romantics, Adam Müller and Novalis. Müller was the economic theoretician who insisted most radically on the purely semiotic quality of money and its concomitant mediating function. In his *Versuche einer neuen Theorie des Geldes*, for example, he unequivocally maintained that "[t]he true essence of money is . . . infinite mediation between people and things" (177–78). As we saw in chapter 3, Johann Gottlieb Fichte developed this idea of sign-money, predicated on the "credit" and faith invested in its operation, as a mediator capable of binding together individuals in an economic-communicative community. The definition of money, especially in its increasingly abstract, signifying aspect, as an exponent of mediation itself ultimately becomes a commonplace of modern economic theory. Georg Simmel, by way of example, asserts, "Money in its most sophisticated forms [i.e., as fiduciary currency, as pure signifying function] is the absolute mediator. . . . But in money mediation attains its purest reality, . . . it is mediation as such" (*Philosophie des Geldes* 264–65). Critics of the monetary form tend, in fact, to latch onto this mediating function as the focal point of their critiques. The communist Moses Hess, for example, accuses money of being a *Mittelding*, an "intermediary" and "mediating object" that intervenes into human relations and, under the pretense of bringing people together, actually alienates humans from one another ("Über das Geldwesen" 347). For Karl Marx, money as mediator represents "the fraternization of impossibilities," so that it operates as a force that "forces contradictions to embrace each other" ("Ökonomisch-philosophische Manuskripte" 567). But for Marx money also marks the crucial productive matrix between human desire and its fulfillment by commodities: "[M]oney translates my desires from their conceptual, imagined, wishful existence into their *sensual, real* existence, from imagination into life, from an imagined being into real being. As this mechanism of mediation, money is the *truly creative* force" (565). Max Beckmann's illustration for the paper-money episode emphasizes both the mediating capacity of this

14 / The creation of paper money. Illustration by Max Beckmann from his *Illustrationen zu* Faust II: *Federzeichnungen— Bleistiftskizzen*, ed. Rike Wankmüller and Erika Zeise (Munich: Prestel, 1984). © 2007 Artists Rights Society (ARS), New York/VG Bild-Kunst, Bonn.

currency and its tendency to supplant truly human interrelations: he positions the paper notes at the union of two human figures, but also blots out their very faces by superimposing the paper bills over them (fig. 14). We witness the same kind of productive mediation that Marx associates with money in the image of the rainbow from "Pleasant Landscape." However, although mediation seems to possess positive connotations in this scene,[23] when it manifests itself in money, especially in paper currency, the negative ramifications symptomatic of Marx's critique come to the fore.

It is no secret that Goethe was generally skeptical about the device of paper currencies, with which he became acquainted largely in the guise of the notoriously inflationary French assignat.[24] In "Betrachtungen im Sinne der Wanderer" (Observations in the spirit of travelers) from *Wilhlem Meisters Wanderjahre* (Wilhelm Meisters years of travel), Goethe reflects on the central role of paper money in a modern world dominated by speed, technology, trade, and debt.

> Just as we cannot take the steam out of steam engines, so are we unable
> to accomplish this in the ethical sphere. The vitality of commerce, the

furious rush of paper money, the swelling of debt so as to pay off
debts [*Schulden*]—all of these represent the frightful elements in which
a young man today invests his energies. Good for him if nature has
endowed him with a moderate, tranquil sensibility, so that he neither
makes unreasonable demands on the world nor lets himself be determined by it. (HA 8: 289)

Goethe explicitly parallels the realms of economics and of morality, and
thus it is no coincidence that the hinge on which this passage turns is the
word *Schulden*, which in German encompasses this peculiar crossover
between ethics and economics. The monstrous productivity of the new age
is emblematized in the steam engines that cannot be shut down or muffled,
themselves the symbolic counterparts of the magic broom in Goethe's famous
poem "Der Zauberlehrling" (The sorcerer's apprentice), which the apprentice can turn on but cannot turn off and whose incessant water-carrying
culminates in a ruinous flood.[25] The excessive production made possible
by advanced technology, the speed of commerce, the dizzyingly quick-paced
circulation of paper money, and the senseless multiplication of debt in order
to pay off previous debts are the interlocking pieces that form the modern
world. Goethe invents a moniker for this world of excessive speed, production, and *Schulden* (debt/guilt): he calls it, with a curious neologism, *veloziferisch* (HA 8: 289), which can perhaps best be rendered in English as
"velociferacious." Goethe's neologism combines the Latinate terms "veloc-
ity" and "feracious" to invoke the monstrous speed of ever-increasing productivity under the modern economic paradigm. But Goethe's term also
subtly suggests the adjectival form of the German for Lucifer, *luziferisch*,
so that this word might also be translated into English as "veluciferian."
Goethe's verbal coinage, in short, conjures up not merely the speed and
excessive productivity of the modern commercial economy, but also implicitly associates this unimaginable productivity with a kind of devilish magic.
The modern world is one addicted to the drug of speed, and Lucifer figures
as its primary dealer.

The world Goethe describes in this observation is, of course, the world
of *Faust II*, and his Faust, far from resisting this world by falling back on
"moderation" and a "tranquil sensibility," buys into the speed and hyperproductivity of the modernist industrial-technological paradigm—buys in

literally, through his pact with Mephistopheles[26]—and becomes its principal representative. Thus it is Faust who is ultimately responsible for the introduction of paper money, the instrument of modern hyperproduction and hypercirculation, into the economically faltering empire in act 1. Goethe's skepticism about this solution to the empire's economic (and moral) woes is demonstrated by the fact that this proves to be only a temporary fix; during Faust's interlude with Helen, economic, political, and moral chaos return to the empire with a vengeance. As opposed to Romantic thinkers such as Müller and Fichte, then, who banked on the mediating power of fiduciary currency and its purported ability to fuse people together in an economic-communicative community, Goethe emphasizes the devilish productivity of such mediation and its debilitating economic and moral consequences.[27]

One of the primary themes we have been following throughout this book has been the varied perception among eighteenth and early nineteenth-century German intellectuals of a paradigm shift—or, in Foucauldian terms, a historical discontinuity—between a steady-state economy of wealth, knowledge, and language, based on a notion of finite substance, and one that highlights infinite production and growth. In chapter 1 we introduced this transformation using the example of the shift from specie to fiduciary currencies, tracing the ways in which this transmogrification seeped into discourses about the nature of language and human thought by means of certain metaphorological transmutations. In chapter 4 we diagnosed the debate over physiocracy that raged in German-speaking Europe toward the end of the eighteenth century as the manifestation of a larger controversy about the nature of economic and cultural values, the very definition of productivity, and the role of the imagination in production and value creation. Our analysis of Stifter's *Bergkristall* was intended to demonstrate the seductive power of this new commercialism and expose how, even in a text that on its surface seeks to valorize the rural idyll of a limited and natural economy, a prominent subtext ends up underwriting the shift toward commercialization and economic rationality that generates the prerequisites for capital accumulation. Our interpretation of Droste-Hülshoff's *Judenbuche*, finally, indicated how the negative ramifications of this economic transformation were registered in the economic and moral decline of a specific rural community, and showed the ways in which the "unnatural" character of a drive for excessive moveable wealth led to senseless crimes against nature and the ecological destruction of the natural world upon which human beings depend for their livelihood and existence. Part 2 of Goethe's *Faust* intermingles all of these themes, and it looks ahead to Droste-Hülshoff's identification of overproduction, in the service of personal wealth and glory, with environmental devastation.

Allusions to this transformation in the means of production are scattered throughout Goethe's *Faust*, culminating, of course, in act 5 of part 2. However, already in the "Hexenküche" ("Witch's Kitchen") scene of part 1, Goethe conjures up this shift from a natural to a commercial economy in a dialogue between Faust and Mephistopheles about the most direct avenue to human satisfaction. In this scene, Faust expresses his reluctance to resort to magic as a means for pleasure. He consequently asks Mephistopheles if neither nature nor human ingenuity have produced a "balm" (*Balsam*) for his seething desires (lines 2345–46). Mephistopheles responds with the quasi-Rousseauian admonition that Faust return to a simple life cultivating the soil.

> Very well! A recipe
> that takes no money, magic, or physician:
> Go out at once into the country
> and set to hoeing and to digging;
> confine yourself—and your thoughts too—
> within the narrowest spheres;
> subsist on food that's plain and simple,
> live with your cattle as their peer, and don't disdain
> to fertilize in person fields that you will reap.
> Take my word for it, there's no better way
> to remain young until you're eighty. (lines 2351–61)

What Mephistopheles gives voice to here—even if his words are seeped in irony—is the creed disseminated by the French physiocrats: he ostensibly valorizes a life of subsistence, reliant on the gifts of nature in its sole productivity, directing the investment of human energy solely into physical toil for the cultivation of arable land. Mephistopheles' discourse is calculated to paint this lifestyle in the least endearing terms: the very narrowness and confinement it implies go against Faust's driving instinct for expansion, growth, and the transgression of every and all limits. Moreover, Mephistopheles subtly suggests that this rural lifestyle offers no possibility for transcendence: Faust's corpse will in the end become mere fertilizer for the soil he has cultivated. No wonder Faust rejects this alternative out of hand.

> That's work I am not used to, nor can I bear the thought
> of having to do labor with a spade.
> A life so much confined would never do for me. (lines 2362–64)

To which Mephistopheles answers with syllogistic consistency, "Since that's the case, the witch will have to help us out" (line 2365). It is precisely by invoking the agrarian lifestyle in harmony with the "laws of nature," as championed by the physiocrats, that Mephistopheles convinces Faust to give himself over to his devilish magic. In many ways this embracing of the supernatural reiterates in different—in economic—terms Faust's resolve to sign his soul over to the devil in the first place. It is Faust's refusal to accept narrow circumscription and limitation, his paradoxical drive to lay hold of the boundless, that motivates his decision to accept magic as a last resort for achieving ultimate satisfaction. Viewed allegorically, this scene encapsulates the paradigm shift from an economy based on subsistence and natural means of production to one of excess, of surplus value, and of "limitless faith in the limitless." The "natural order" of the physiocrats is supplanted by a *supernatural* one: the infinite growth and productivity made possible by technology and the "magical" forces of industrialization.[28]

Surely it is not by chance that in one of his last monologues in part 2, Faust alludes to this earlier scene in which he embraces magic. The four gray women and their "brother" Death have just made their appearance, and Faust for the first time voices something that verges on regret about the course his life has followed.

> If I could rid my path of magic,
> could totally unlearn its incantations,
> confront you, nature, simply as a man,
> to be a human being would then be worth the effort. (lines 11404–07)

379

15 / The lemurs digging Faust's grave. Illustration by Max Beckmann from his *Illustrationen zu* Faust II: *Federzeichnungen—Bleistiftskizzen*, ed. Rike Wankmüller and Erika Zeise (Munich: Prestel, 1984). © 2007 Artists Rights Society (ARS), New York/VG Bild-Kunst, Bonn.

The physiocratic vision of the noble human being confronting nature and acting as the midwife to its productive energies, which Faust previously regarded as his bane, now suddenly appears as a boon. However, in order to embrace this vision, Faust would have to forswear magic, renounce his pact with the devil, and this is impossible if only because Faust has signed off on the devil's wager. Thus Faust's diction here necessarily assumes the form of the *irrealis*, the wish that cannot be fulfilled. To be sure, Faust has engaged with the concrete task of digging in the earth, but not by taking up the spade himself and expending manual labor in the service of agriculture, nor by digging to unearth the promised hidden treasures that lie in wait just below the surface (see lines 4893–96, 5039–42). Instead, Faust turns to the magic of technology and to inexpensive human labor, exploiting proletarian earth diggers and technologically sophisticated earthmovers so as to create valuable real estate where the mighty ocean once reigned supreme. *Production*, it is significant to note, is still his aim; however, the production he strives for is of a totally different order than the *natural* production touted by the physiocrats. Surely it is no coincidence that the spade, which throughout *Faust* has become the symbol of productive engagement with nature, will eventually be the instrument that "produces" Faust's grave. Max Beckmann recognized the poignancy of the spade as symbol by placing it in the forefront of his illustration of the digging lemurs (fig. 15).

We should recall in this context that Faust's plan to take back land from the sea is initially motivated by his observation of, and meditations on, the infinite and seemingly senseless *barrenness* of the ocean's waves. For him, the repeated and relentless crashing of the waves on shore becomes the very emblem of wasteful nonproduction, despite the expenditure of immeasurable energy.

> The surging sea creeps into every corner [*abertausend Enden*],
> barren itself and spreading barrenness,
> . . . .
> Imbued with strength, wave after wave [*Well' auf Welle*] holds power
> but then withdraws, and nothing's been accomplished—
> a sight to drive me to despair,
> this aimless strength of elemental forces!
> This inspires my mind to venture to new heights,
> to wage war here against these forces and subdue them. (lines 10212–21)

It is impossible to overlook the poignant irony of this passage, which in both its thematic and rhetorical texture imitates the closing monologue of "Pleasant Landscape" that celebrates the *farbigen Abglanz* as the ultimate product of water's brute energy.[29] In the present instance it is Faust, who categorically rejects all limitations placed upon himself and is driven by the largely wasted energy of excessive desire and infinite striving, who is inspired—through his observations of the futilely crashing waves—to tame the exuberant energy of the ocean by placing it within specific constraints. Long before he is blinded by Care, Faust demonstrates in this speech the blind side of his own personality, which prevents him from applying to himself this insight into the foolishness of wasteful exuberance. Indeed, Faust has done nothing else throughout his life than expend his energies in wasteful, ultimately barren, and frequently destructive enterprises. Faust and his unproductive striving form the paradigm of what we might term, only somewhat facetiously, kinetic and emotional masturbation. Similarly, Faust is incapable of seeing in his son Euphorion the replica of himself and of recognizing in Euphorion's senseless expenditure of energy and eventual *salto mortale* the emblem of his own fate (see lines 9695–906). Par-

adoxically, even when Faust dedicates himself to transforming the barrenness of the ocean and its wasted energy into fertility and productive power,
he ultimately fails. Although in his utopian vision of the colony to be established on this newly acquired land Faust stresses its green productivity
("green and fertile fields," line 11565), the garden that adorns his own
palace is described explicitly as a *Ziergarten*, an "ornamental garden" in
which nature is forced into the strictures of conceptual artifice (scene
description prior to line 11143). The world of nature, for Faust, must always
be constrained by the limiting forms of artifice. However, if for the physiocrats artifice was by definition unproductive, Faust relies on artifice—
the digging of channels and the building of dikes—in the name of a higher
productivity. If he were to turn this strategy upon himself, of course, it
would deserve the Freudian name of sublimation: the channeling of otherwise unproductive, wasted energy into a limited, focused, and—ideally—
productive enterprise.

Among other things, *Faust II* plays out this paradigm shift from natural production honoring the limitations of nature, as exemplified by physiocratic doctrine, to artificial and exuberant (over)production founded
upon mastery over nature. Philemon correctly diagnoses the method behind
this madness as an appropriation of nature's power in an attempt to gain
mastery over nature itself (lines 11091–94). But Faust can never escape
the *Teufelskreis*, the devilish short circuit or dialectic, that ties mastery over
nature, in the name of increased productivity, to nature's destruction. It is
no coincidence, then, that at precisely the moment in act 4 when Faust
hatches his plan to conquer the power of the ocean and create new land
from the sea, Mephistopheles reminds him of the *falschen Reichtum*, the
"counterfeit wealth" generated by the introduction of paper money in act
1 (line 10245). A further anticipatory reference to digging up the earth in
the name of production occurs in the context of resolving the empire's economic woes. In this instance, however, it is neither a matter of cultivating
the soil for agriculture, nor of the industrial productivity of Faust's technological digging machines, but rather a concern with the uncovering of
material treasures that lie buried in the earth. Mephistopheles seems to be
alluding to the scene in part 1, in which Faust embraces magic, when he
encourages the emperor, as he previously had Faust, to take up the spade
and dig on his own.

Take hoe and spade and dig yourself,
this peasant labor will augment your greatness,
and from the soil you'll liberate
a herd of golden calves. (lines 5039–42)

Mephistopheles openly parodies the physiocrats' praise of peasant labor, turning the *natural* productivity of soil cultivation into the uncovering of graven images: the natural fruits of the earth are replaced by the artificiality of golden calves, symbolizing not merely the production of artificial wealth, but also alluding to a fetishistic adoration of commodities schooled on the adoration of religious idols. In his exploration of the fetish character of commodities, Karl Marx, we remember, alluded explicitly to the need to import terminology from religious rituals to describe the irrational fascination invested in the commodity as a paradoxical "sensual supersensual thing" (*Kapital* 85). In this sense, Mephistopheles' words map out the intermediary stage between the rural economy of the physiocrats and the technologically hyperproductive economy Faust envisions for his utopian colony as an economics of commodity fetishism. If for the physiocrats humans could only enhance the productive forces of nature by serving them as a kind of midwife, Faust's utopia marks the appropriation by human beings of nature's productive capacities. This was the heart of the problematic we dealt with in chapter 4, and there we pursued the resonance of this transformation in theories of aesthetic productivity as well.

This is a step we must also take in our examination of part 2 of *Faust*. But before we do, it is important to emphasize that the hinge between the first and the final stages of this economic-historical transformation is marked in this drama by the introduction of paper money as the premier form of monetary mediation and the condition of possibility for commodity fetishism. The mediation of light and water, of imagination and matter, to return to our point of departure, is what the *farbigen Abglanz* of the rainbow in "Pleasant Landscape" allegorizes. If mediation is one of the central themes of *Faust II*, as introduced in its opening scene and concretized in this suggestive image, it is not treated as a transhistorical absolute, but rather as a specific historical intervention that marks the transition from a largely agrarian, "natural" economy to one based in the art of manufacture, from the sole productivity of nature to the enhanced hyperproductivity enabled by technological mastery over nature. When he embraces paper money and designates Faust and Mephistopheles as the custodians of his treasury, the emperor alludes to paper money's mediating capacity, designating it as the place where the upper and the netherworlds meet (lines 6139–40). Paper money thus becomes a kind of Hermes, a messenger that communicates between the earthly and the divine worlds. We should recall that Hermes is, among other things, the god of merchants, of commerce, and of economic exchange. Paper money embodies mediation in its instrumentalized form: it is the concrete representation of a world that is, to use Goethe's term, *veloziferisch*, both velociferacious—uncannily quick in its ceaseless productivity—and veluciferian—devilish in its mysterious powers and their ultimately destructive consequences.

Hey, Big Spender! The Aesthetics and Hermeneutics of Excess in Faust II

In his analysis of the psychic economy of human pleasure, Georges Bataille points to the dialectical linkage that yokes together two extremes: accumulation and hoarding, on the one hand, and exuberant expenditure, on the other. The former, Bataille asserts, is in line with rational strategies for what Sigmund Freud would call the avoidance of displeasure, while the latter, marked by the irrationality of loss, paradoxically constitutes pleasure seeking in its most intensive manifestation, which Bataille associates with eroticism.

> If we follow the dictates of reason, we try to acquire all kinds of goods, we work in order to increase the sum of our possessions . . . to get richer and to possess more. But when the fever of sex seizes us we behave in the opposite way. We recklessly draw on our strength and sometimes in the violence of passion we squander considerable resources to no real purpose. Pleasure is so close to ruinous waste that we refer to it [in French] as a "little death". . . . We always want to be sure of the uselessness or ruinousness of our extravagance. We want to feel as remote from the world where thrift is the rule as we can. (*Eroticism* 170)

The scene "Masquerade" in the first act of *Faust II* can be read as a kind of prototype for this association of the economic and the erotic as a tension between considered accumulation and mindless wastefulness. In this scene, Plutus, the allegory of wealth, rides on a chariot flanked by Avarice, the allegory of accumulation, and by the boy charioteer, the representation of wasteful expenditure. But Goethe embeds this problematic of hoarding and expending in an aesthetic context by identifying the boy charioteer not merely with waste, but with poetry.

If in its economic register *Faust II* associates mediation with the excessive productivity of technological modernity, we must now consider whether this same problematic arises when the text deals with mediation in the aesthetic domain. The *farbigen Abglanz*, the many-hued *de*flection of "Pleasant Landscape," looks ahead not merely to the economic motifs of *Faust II*, but also to its aesthetic themes. For the late eighteenth and early nineteenth centuries, the notion of art as the great mediator assumed the character of a dominant ideologeme. The *locus classicus* of this conception in German letters is surely section 9 of Immanuel Kant's introduction to his *Kritik der Urteilskraft* (Critique of judgment, 1790), in which the power of judgment, which Kant identifies with the aesthetic sensibility, is ascribed the keystone place in transcendental philosophy of mediating between *Verstand* (rationality) and *Vernunft* (reason), between the necessity of natural laws and the freedom of moral dictates (*Kritik der Urteilskraft* 106–09). Friedrich Schiller further developed this idea of the mediating power of art, enlarging it to embrace the domain of politics, in one of the foundational works of classical German aesthetic theory, *Über die ästhetische Erziehung des Menschen* (On the aesthetic education of humankind, 1795). Here aesthetics, which Schiller associates with the notion of play or game (*Spiel*), is assigned the role of mediating between human beings' material and instinctual nature, on the one hand, and their intellectual and spiritual side, on the other. In a famous formulation from the fourth letter, Schiller assigns to aesthetic mediation the task of preventing human beings either from falling back into primitivism—from becoming slaves to their instincts and emotions—or of evolving into barbarians by relying entirely on rational principles and thereby killing off their sensual aspect (579). Goethe's Faust oscillates between these two extremes, moving from the blind emotional attachment to Gretchen and Helen, on the one hand, to the cold, calculating, instrumental rationality of the warlord, the pirate, the capitalist land developer, and the colonial entrepreneur, on the other.

In an entry from *Maxime und Reflexionen*, Goethe explicitly defended the mediating power of art and even considered the role of aesthetic theory as reflection upon this mediating capacity: "The true mediatrix is art. To speak about art means to seek to mediate the mediatrix, and yet this has thereby produced for us many a delicious insight" (no. 18, HA 12: 367). Although Goethe's remark implies a certain critique of aesthetic theory as a kind of paradoxical mediation of mediation, he concedes the enticing fruits such intellectual labor has produced. At the same time, Goethe himself tended to focus more on the generation of art itself than on such second-order reflections on art—and we can imagine this maxim being directed at his friend Schiller, who devoted himself tirelessly to such theoretical deliberations on aesthetics. Yet Goethe's literary texts often contain self-reflexive ruminations on the character of literature. Nowhere is this more true than in the instance of the rainbow as the mediator between fire and water, intellect and fluid matter, in "Pleasant Landscape." Indeed, in one of his scientific treatises, "Versuch einer Witterungslehre" (Attempt at a theory of weather), written in 1825—around the period in which he was also working toward the completion of *Faust II*—Goethe employed the same metaphor of mediated deflection to describe what might be termed the epistemology of art.

> We can never immediately discern Truth, which is identical with the
> Divine; rather, we perceive it only in its mediated deflection [*Abglanz*],
> in concrete example [*Beispiel*], symbol, in distinct yet related phenomena;
> we become aware of it as incomprehensible/ungraspable [*unbegreifliches*]
> life and yet cannot deny ourselves the wish of comprehending/grasping
> [*begreifen*] it nonetheless. (HA 13: 305)

Art as mediator is assigned a principal role in human epistemological pursuits: it is the very currency by which knowledge is purchased, and in that regard it—not logic, as Karl Marx derogatorily opined—is the *genuine* "money of the mind."[30] *Abglanz*, or deflection, is aligned here explicitly with poetic example, *Beispiel*, and with poetic diction and symbol, which provides a linkage between the universal and the particular.[31] In this maxim, however, mediation is not a translucent lens, a means that disappears once it brings its object into focus, or—to allude to Ludwig Wittgenstein's famous metaphor from the *Tractatus logico-philosophicus* (proposition 6.54)—a ladder one can discard once one has climbed up over it. On the contrary, mediation becomes the very emblem of a process that both opens up the human mind to the infinite vitality and permanent transformation of life, while simultaneously indicating the impossibility of ever laying hold of it in any limiting way—the German word *begreifen* signifies both "comprehend" in the abstract sense as well as "grasp" in its more concrete meaning. Mediation is, in this sense, the very mark of the limitless and of a limitless faith in the limitless. Indeed, Goethe's statement from his "Versuch einer Witterungslehre" summarizes succinctly the catch-22 of Faust's striving, his desire to grasp and thereby limit the boundlessness of knowledge and of nature. If this paradox is played out in the domain of economics in the paper-money episode and Faust's colonial project, its parallel in the aesthetic sphere is his quest to lay hold of Helen as "singular form" (*einzige Gestalt*), the paragon of classical beauty (lines 7439, 9324).

The Helen episode is of central importance for the thematic of *Faust II* precisely because it demonstrates Faust's incapacity to acknowledge and accept the recognition, presented at the close of "Pleasant Landscape," that life can only be experienced in its many-hued deflection: in mediated, but never in *im*mediate form. In this sense, the trajectory of Faust's development from the *threatened* but circumvented blindness of the opening scene—circumvented by learning a lesson about the necessity of mediation—to Faust's *actual* blindness at the drama's conclusion holds a certain tragic logic. Faust's ultimate blindness emerges as the very emblem of failed anagnorisis, his inability to hold onto and act on the insight attained in the opening scene of part 2. Thus, far from signaling a form of higher vision, in the tradition of those blind visionaries like Tiresias or Oedipus (Brown, *Goethe's* Faust 242), in Faust's case blindness is decidedly *not* tied to insight.[32] Indeed, as he stands blinded, listening to the sound of the lemurs digging his grave, mistakenly believing that they are completing the dikes and drainage of the land recovered from the sea, he becomes the classical representative of the ideologically deceived subject as theorized by Louis Althusser: Faust invokes and succumbs to an *imaginary* relationship that diverts from and distorts the *real* conditions of his existence.[33] The tragedy of Faust is the tragedy of this—ideological—self-deception, his incapacity to translate the insights gained *without* blindness in the scene "Pleasant Landscape" into an adequate lifestyle or political-economic practice.

Faust's pursuit of Helen as the paragon of beauty is emblematic of this tragic trajectory from insight to blindness. Act 1 closes, we recall, when Faust attempts to lay hold of the image of Helen that, as Mephistopheles shrewdly notes, Faust himself has conjured up (line 6546). Faust falls victim in the realm of aesthetics to the same ruse the courtiers in this act succumb to in the sphere of economics: just as they latch onto idealized money in the form of paper currency, forgetting that it is merely a symbolic substitute for the concrete wealth still hidden in the bowels of the earth, Faust attempts to take possession of Helen in all her material beauty, ignoring the fact that she is a mere shade or an idealized archetype in the Platonic sense.[34] Mephistopheles explicitly draws this parallel when he compares Helen's "ghost" with the "paper ghost" of money: "You believe that Helen can be conjured up / as easily as the paper ghost of money" (lines 6198–99). In this respect, as well, Faust's tragedy is one of failed anagnorisis, his inability to translate the recognition at which he arrives at the close of "Pleasant Landscape" into a practice acknowledging that possession of the absolute can only be realized through its mediated deflections, in its symbolic forms. When Helen appears in act 3 as a living figure, rather than as the ghostly image of act 1, her beauty is associated with the very blinding sun that Faust can only observe in the opening scene of the play through its mediated deflections (line 8601). If this were not enough to indicate the parallel between the blinding radiance of Helen's beauty and the blinding glow of the sun in "Pleasant Landscape," Phorkyas/Mephistopheles will later make the connection quite explicit when he compares Helen's entrance to the sun as it emerges from behind the clouds: "Come! Emerge from those passing clouds, o lofty sun of this our day, / you who veiled were ravishing, and who now glows [*Glanze*] in blinding light" (lines 8909–10). The radiance (*Glanze*) of Helen's beauty, although it is just as blinding as the sun, does not seem to demand deflection, *Abglanz*. Indeed, Faust's paradoxical wish is to perceive and to acquire Helen in all her physical immediacy. Act 3 holds out the possibility that this can actually occur: Faust does, at least temporarily, take possession of Helen. Moreover, Mephistopheles' words when Helen first emerges seem to imply that the intensification of her beauty as it moves from ravishing mediation (being "veiled" by clouds) to blinding immediacy can actually be experienced. The only figure for whom this is not the case is the watchman Lynceus, whose sensitive eyes cannot gaze upon Helen without forfeiting his keen sense of sight.

> Turning eye and heart towards her [Helen],
> I imbibed the gentler light [*Glanz*];
> beauty of her blinding splendor
> blinded me completely too. (lines 9238–41)

Lynceus, to be sure, must make excuses for having neglected his duties as a watchman: so dazzled is he by the radiance of Helen's beauty that he fails to report her entrance to his master. But Mephistopheles' sorcery will permit Faust—for a time, at least—to take hold of and take in Helen's beauty in unmediated form.

To the extent that Faust in act 3 succeeds in becoming, in his own words, the "co-regent [*Mitregenten*]" of Helen's "realm that knows no bounds [*Grenzunbewußten Reichs*]" (lines 9362–63), her possession is but a prelude to the colonial endeavor of act 5, in which Faust will attempt to set limits upon and thereby appropriate the boundlessness of the ocean. In this regard Faust's development replicates that of Helen's husband, Menelaus, whose response to the loss of Helen is to become a pirate on the high seas and who sought consolation in the hoarded booty that represented a paltry substitute for Helen's glory (lines 8985–87). Both Menelaus and Faust thus respond to the loss of Helen in identical ways: by incessant accumulation and hoarding ("amassed through never ceasing increments"; line 8554) of the treasures conquered in their wars of acquisition. We might, then, view Faust's colonial conquests and his ultimate drive for mastery over nature as an economic ersatz for the *aesthetic*, and inherently *erotic*, longing to possess Helen, the absolute object of feminine beauty.

The Helen of classical mythology represents nothing if not the utter seductiveness and ravishment of a beauty that knows no bounds. In this regard, she is a "possession" that, like paper money, alludes to the potential to grasp the infinite. As the embodiment of *aesthetic* and *libidinal* wealth, she most closely parallels money as the concretization of *economic* riches. In a text that constantly circles around the concept of "treasure," of *Schatz* and its plural, *Schätze*—we think of the treasures hidden in the empire's ground or of the frequent references to stockpiled treasures—Helen represents the ultimate *Schatz* of beauty (line 6315). When in act 1 Faust is named *Schatzmeister*—literally, "treasure master"—in the emperor's court (lines 6133–37), this designation comes closest to describing his aim: to become master of a panoply of treasures, whether these riches assume the form of paper money, of Helen's beauty, of colonial bounty, or of technologically manufactured real estate. Helen, like money and all these other embodiments of wealth, has the power to drive mad those who desire to possess her, and hence to unleash untold chaos. In classical mythology, the Trojan War is the emblem of this destructive madness. In *Faust II*, it is Helen herself who bemoans, in a moment of searing self-pity, the catastrophic impact she has on men, gods, and demons alike.

> . . . Alas, what cruel fate
> I suffer, everywhere so to confound
> the hearts of men that they will neither spare
> themselves nor anything we venerate.
> Stealing, seducing, fighting, snatching back and forth,
> demigods, heroes, gods, and demons too,
> have led me, much bewildered, to and fro;
> my single self wrought great confusion, my double more,
> and now a third and fourth add woe to woe. (lines 9247–55)

Helen is associated with paper money and material wealth not merely due to the insanity and chaos she unleashes in the lust for her acquisition, but also by the reflex of her own exponential growth, the multiplication of her figure that she specifically alludes to in her speech, a reflex that connects her with the "thousandfold" printing of paper bills (line 6072) and the "thousands" of streams that merge to form the cataract in "Pleasant Landscape" (line 4719). In other words, Helen is also a representation of inflationary excess and its repercussions, but in this instance in the realm of aesthetics rather than in that of economics. The common denominator that joins her with these other entities is the excess in the economy of *desire* that she calls forth.

Although its physical embodiment, Helen is by no means the sole representative of aesthetic excess in *Faust II*. She is foreshadowed in this respect by the boy charioteer in the "Masquerade" scene of act 1, who identifies himself not only with excessive expenditure, but also as an allegory for poetry: "I am that spendthrift [*Verschwendung*], poetry" (line 5573). Of all the scenes in *Faust II*, this is the one in which aesthetic and economic wealth are most closely aligned. In his pictorial rendering of the boy charioteer, Max Beckmann captures this by depicting him as a hermaphroditic vamp who barters both money and jewelry (as the valuable ornaments of beauty) and whose presence drives the masses into Dionysian ecstasy (fig. 16). The boy charioteer guides the wagon on which Plutus, the incarnation of material wealth—and hence the economic counterpart to Helen—is borne through the carnival. But if the spendthrift poetry sits at the head of the wagon, his opposite, Avarice, sits at the back. One of Goethe's paralipomena for this scene insists explicitly on this configuration, with Plutus in the middle, the exuberant expenditure of poetry in front, and the greedy accumulation of Avarice bringing up the rear: "Plutus's triumph: expenditure in front of him throws out feathers, crickets, butterflies; Avarice behind him, iron chests with dragon locks" (*Gedenkausgabe* 5: 576). Plutus's "triumph" is the birth of two forms of excess: the excessive, unproductive expenditure of the boy charioteer as an allegory for poetry, and the exorbitant hoarding of Avarice. But if it is Faust himself who wears the mask of Plutus, and who thus manifests a superabundance of wealth, it is Mephistopheles who plays the role of Avarice. Where Faust/Plutus is the font of riches, the boy charioteer represents its wasteful expenditure, and Mephistopheles/Avarice its obsessive accumulation and retention. But the wealth Faust/Plutus emblematizes here is neither of a merely economic nor of a purely aesthetic sort: he stands as well for a surplus of *libidinal* energy, the intemperate desiring that both money and beauty evoke. In this sense we might view this trio—expenditure, wealth, and accumulation— as a kind of psychological/libidinal triumvirate: Faust/Plutus, as the font of all libidinal energy, is torn between two psychic extremes, the squandering wastefulness of the boy charioteer (giving in to the prodding of the id), on the one hand, and the repressive retention of Avarice (subjugation to the repressive mechanisms of the superego), on the other. Faust, in fact, will pendulate between these two extremes as the drama develops: in his response to Helen he will play the part of the irresponsible psychological

16 / The boy charioteer as hermaphroditic vamp. Illustration by Max Beckmann from his *Illustrationen zu* Faust II: *Federzeichnungen—Bleistiftskizzen*, ed. Rike Wankmüller and Erika Zeise (Munich: Prestel, 1984). © 2007 Artists Rights Society (ARS), New York/VG Bild-Kunst, Bonn.

and economic spendthrift, who will lay all his libidinal energy and material wealth at Helen's feet; after her loss, however, he will fall into the opposite extreme of the pathological accumulator and hoarder of libido and wealth.

If in economic terms the boy charioteer is the wasteful spendthrift, in erotic/libidinal terms he is the obsessive masturbator: "As poet, I achieve fruition [*vollendet*] / by squandering my very substance" (lines 5574–75). The paradox that the boy charioteer arrives at fruition—the German *vollendet* implies a state of completion and perfection and is commonly applied to the consummate work of art—through a gesture of exuberant wastefulness suggests a kind of poetic productivity that ends ultimately in sterility, an expenditure for the sake of expenditure itself, rather than culminating in service to some productive aim. In this sense the boy charioteer prefigures the wasted energy of the ocean waves, which will motivate Faust to rein in their power. Consistent with his lack of productivity is the fact that all the "gifts" the boy charioteer strews among the crowd first bear the semblance of valuable treasures, but in the end either transmogrify into useless or even frightful objects—butterflies or crawling insects—or dissolve into nothingness (lines 5595–603). The herald, after reporting these events, sums up the boy charioteer's actions with the appropriate commentary: "For all his promises, the rogue / bestows as gold what merely glitters" (lines 5604–05). The boy charioteer, as poetic squandering, shares with the instrument of paper money both the quality of making largely empty promises and of passing off what is essentially worthless as fundamentally valuable. Like the false value generated in the paper-money episode, the boy charioteer's gifts evaporate into thin air. Yet he is the spiritual "son" of Plutus, of wealth incarnate, so that the latter can designate him as spirit of his spirit, as wealthier even than Plutus himself and as a kind of emissary who acts out the wishes Plutus merely contemplates.

> If you need a character reference from me,
> I gladly say, you are the essence of my spirit.
> You always act the way I'd wish to act,
> your treasury contains more gold than mine. (lines 5622–25)

The boy charioteer embodies, in other words, not merely the infinite expenditure of wealth, but also its inexhaustible superabundance (Pickerodt 758), and in this regard he is the personified essence of Peter Schlemihl's magic purse: no matter how much of his "substance" he squanders, it is automatically replenished so it can be squandered ad infinitum. Poetic productivity, Goethe implies here, is always spending down its capital, and yet miraculously that capital never decreases nor is it ever spent. Like Schlemihl's purse, poetic imagination is infinitely productive and hence can give vent to as much expenditure as it likes. But in the end nothing is purchased, and limitless expenditure remains sterile.

In chapter 34 of the second volume of *Die Welt als Wille und Vorstellung* (The world as will and representation, 1844), Arthur Schopenhauer reflected on the essence of the aesthetic genius as just such a reflex of excess. "The mother of the practical arts is necessity," Schopenhauer maintains, "that of the fine arts is excess. The father of the former is intellect, the father of the latter is genius, which is itself a kind of excess: namely, an excess of conceptual power beyond what is necessary for service to the will" (2: 527). The fine arts, according to Schopenhauer's meditation, are doubly coded by the trait of excess; not only is their mother characterized as excess incarnate, but their father, genius, embodies an excessive capacity for conceptualization. We should note the economic parallel implicit in Schopenhauer's juxtaposition of necessity and excess: just as the steady-state or natural economy of the physiocrats was concerned with the satisfaction of existential necessities, the surplus economy of modern hypermoney is focused on the production of surplus value—luxury items like the fine arts themselves—and on the generation of unchecked *longing* for these existential superfluities. As an allegory for the wasteful superabundance of literature, the boy charioteer is a figure for the excesses of Romantic genius. This is confirmed by the fact that Goethe specifically associated the boy charioteer, the figurative "son" of Plutus/Faust in the "Masquerade" scene, with the character Euphorion, Faust's son by Helen and, according to Goethe, an allusion to Lord Byron as the paradigmatic representative of Romantic poetry.[35] One might go so far as to imagine the juxtaposition of the boy charioteer, the big spender, and Avarice, the anal-retentive accumulator, as a reflection on the conflict between the implicit aesthetics of Romanticism and classicism. Both, to be sure, can be characterized as forms of excess. But whereas Romanticism marks the excessive, indeed, the infinite productivity of inventive genius, classicism represents a kind of superabundant stockpiling of past and present artistic treasures. Both of these forms of excess are manifest, moreover, in the literary aesthetics of *Faust II*, so that just as on a thematic level this work portrays the clash between classical and modern/Romantic economic principles, its own character as text is structured by a conflict between the exuberant productivity of Romantic genius and an exaggerated accumulation of classical poetic forms.[36]

What we witness in "Masquerade" is above all a concentrated allegory for the imbrication of poetic and economic practices: bearing incarnations of wealth, waste, and accumulation, the chariot not only alludes to the central economic principles articulated in Goethe's text, but also suggests, especially through the figure of the boy charioteer, their relationship to parallel poetic principles. Read in this way, the squandering practiced by the boy charioteer, as an allegory for poetry, does not bespeak a *resistance* to the aesthetics and economics of modernism, as Jochen Hörisch would have it (*Heads or Tails* 155), but on the contrary suggests the complicity of this poetics of waste with a modern economics of surplus value, overproduction, and obsessive, exaggerated consumption. If the boy charioteer is the emblem for inexhaustible production and consumption, then he is the very incarnation of the modern growth economy—transferred to the sphere of aesthetics. Similarly, Mephistopheles/Avarice is the representative of accumulation and retention beyond any foreseeable need. Faust, as we have seen, alternately succumbs to both of these drives toward excess. Moreover, the text of *Faust II* itself concretizes excessive production/expenditure and excessive accumulation in its own literary-aesthetic practices: this text not only exemplifies the infinite genius of Romantic invention, but also an obsessive hoarding and overt display of traditional motifs, themes, and verse forms. *Faust II* is not merely an inexhaustible machine of poetic production, but also, in its own poetic heterogeneity, a treasury of the entire literary-historical tradition.[37]

If literature, as portrayed in "Masquerade" and allegorized by the boy charioteer, is little more than a superabundance of alluring semblance— the analogue of paper money—then one might inquire into the anticipated response it will elicit from the literary consumer: in other words, into the nature of literary-aesthetic *reception* under the conditions of excessive poetic expenditure. In this regard it is surely significant that, immediately prior to the lord steward's announcement of the dissemination and spread of paper money during the carnival, the emperor comments on Mephistopheles' incredible productivity as a storyteller, comparing him with Scheherazade.

> What happy chance has brought you straight to us
> from the Arabian Nights?
> If you can match Scheherazade's fertile mind,
> I promise you the highest favors I can grant.
> Always be ready when, as often happens,
> I find this routine world unbearable. (lines 6031–36)

Literature, in the understanding of the emperor, serves above all the function of distracting people from the cares and routine of daily life, and in this sense it plays exactly the same role as the paper money that is about to be introduced at court. In this view literature is nothing but a luxury item that serves the interests of never-ending diversion—the precursor, in short, to the modern-day television. Mephistopheles' productivity and fertility in storytelling parallel the inexhaustible and hence blithely wasted wealth of the boy charioteer. The latter also provides a kind of commentary on the manner in which his creative gifts will be received by the public at large: the flames of his inspiration will jump from head to head, pausing at some, but largely manifesting themselves as feeble sparks that are quickly extinguished.

> See how I've scattered all about,
> the greatest gifts I can bestow.
> Above the heads of some among you
> there glows a spark that I ignited;
> it skips along from head to head,
> pausing on some, but not on others,
> and only now and then, as short-lived flame,
> rapidly bursting into incandescence;
> but even before most people know of its existence,
> the feeble spark, alas, has been extinguished. (lines 5630–39)

The flaming ideas that the boy charioteer richly disseminates among the crowd resemble in every respect the paper notes that are yet to come: they circulate with amazing speed, move quickly not from hand to hand, but from head to head, flame up brightly in a few isolated instances, but ultimately burn out rapidly without leaving a trace. Just as the newly introduced paper money is unable to induce the emperor's subjects to labor for the ends of increased economic productivity, the boy charioteer's iridescent thoughts and words are incapable of sparking any long-term spiritual or mental conflagration. Once again hyperproduction appears to have its corollary in hyperconsumption, and literature, like paper money or any other commodity, is simply expended for transitory ends. The patterns of literary reception, under the conditions of squandering excess, thus seem to parallel those Goethe projected for *Faust II* in his last letter to Wilhelm von Humboldt: the ship will founder, become a wreck whose treasures will be washed up on the shores, to be covered over by the sands of time.

Or will it? Mephistopheles admonishes the emperor and his subjects, as we have seen, to respond to the crisis of economic underproductivity by taking up the hoe and spade and digging themselves (lines 5039–42).

What they stand to uncover is nothing but a "herd of golden calves"; but this, at least, has more substance than the quickly extinguished flames spun out of the boy charioteer's head. And what, we might ask, would happen if we were to dig among the dunes where the scattered treasures of *Faust II* lie buried? Goethe himself, in letters written during the composition of this drama, envisioned an alternative to the image of a shipwreck as a metaphor for the reception of *Faust II*. Already in July 1828, in a letter to Carl Friedrich Zelter, he sketched a vision of reception in which his readers are motivated to stretch their own limits and let themselves be catapulted, in their reading of this play, into a kind of hermeneutical transcendence. Referring to his own labor on and hopes for his *Faust* drama, Goethe writes,

> If this thing [*Faust II*] does not continue to be indicative of an exuberant [*übermütigen*] state of mind, if it doesn't force the reader to venture out beyond himself [*über sich selber*], then it has no value whatsoever. Up to this point, it seems to me, someone with good intellect and sensibility has his work cut out for him, if we wants to make himself master of everything that has been secreted away there. (HAB 4: 292)

Reading *Faust II*, Goethe suggests, should be like a hunt for buried treasure, with the readers taking possession and making themselves masters— *Schatzmeister*, or "treasure masters"—of the valuable commodities that lie hidden within it. If Faust follows the course of becoming a venture capitalist, the readers of *Faust II* must become, according to this deliberation, venture hermeneuticists. One is struck, moreover, by the frequent use of the prefix *über*, meaning "above" or "beyond," in this passage. It is used to describe not only the high degree of creative investment Goethe himself has made in this work, but also the high-energy investment demanded of the reader. If the author is working at the limits of his own creative capacities—and this is a demand Goethe constantly placed upon himself— then his readers must also operate at the limits of their own hermeneutic abilities. Only under such conditions will they become masters of the treasures that have been "secreted away" in this text. The only proper response, in short, to the superabundant creative outlay of the text's author is excessive interpretive labor on the part of the reader. In this case, the productive excesses of the author are not squandered, but instead placed in fertile soil and cultivated. We have come a long way from the mental masturbation of the boy charioteer; but one of the primary differences resides in the conditions of literary reception, not so much in the conditions of production. Excesses of production—so might we summarize Goethe's statement to Zelter—must find their analogue in excesses of hermeneutical investment during the act of literary reception.

Goethe makes strikingly similar claims about the production and reception of *Faust* in a letter to Sulpiz Boisserée dated 8 September 1831, in which he reports having finally completed this work. Although Goethe is circumspect about the inevitable faults he has failed to correct, he nonetheless exudes a certain confidence about its reception in certain quarters.

> Here it [*Faust II*] stands, regardless of how it has turned out. And even if it still leaves enough problems unresolved, by no means offers enlightenment for everything, it will yet still give pleasure to those who feel at home with gesture, hint, and subtle suggestion. Indeed, they will find more than I was able to give. (HAB 4: 445–46)

It is no longer just a matter of the author and his readers growing beyond their given limitations in their respective engagements with the text; instead, the readers are called upon to take the cues offered by the text and move beyond even what the author might have had in mind. *Faust II* itself, Goethe implies, is so full of suggestive stimulants to interpretation that it invites precisely this sort of hermeneutical overinvestment. If *Faust II* is, among other things, about the economic consequences of hyperproduction, and if it treats as a corollary the problems of poetic-aesthetic hypercreativity, it also programs into its own aesthetic constitution the conditions for a hermeneutics of excess. The inflationary critical reception of *Faust II* is indicative of just how successful Goethe was in this respect. Moreover, if *Faust II* demonstrates especially well the complicity of literary-intellectual culture in the paradigm shift from a natural economy geared toward subsistence to a supernatural one keyed to overproduction and surplus value, it also goes one step further: forcing its readers to enter the vicious circle of overproduction by goading them on—similar to Mephistopheles himself— to incessant hermeneutical striving. But that's a claim that might justifiably be made for all the texts under consideration throughout this study—as well as for the interpretations I have presented.

An interpretation of *Faust II* stands appropriately at the conclusion of this book because this text exemplifies in its themes and its literary-aesthetic practice the complicity of the poetic, aesthetic, and intellectual culture of the eighteenth and nineteenth centuries with ideas and motifs that emerged out of the incipient discipline of economics—and this has been one of the central themes of my investigations. Conceived and written over the course of Goethe's entire life, this play represents a complex conglomerate of literary and economic ideas, and it recapitulates in fundamental ways the diverse economic themes I have sought to trace throughout this study. It problematizes, among other things, that crucial paradigm shift from a natural economy focused on meager subsistence to a hyperproductive economy bent on the generation of surplus value. And if, as we saw in chapter 1, this economic transformation has particular consequences for modern semiotic theories of language, then Goethe's drama plays out this newly theorized linguistic productivity in the very texture of its own discourse. But *Faust II* also resonates with other themes we have pursued here: it points to the seminal role of imagination and fantasy as the driving force behind an economics and poetics of hyperproduction; it alludes, in its evocation of questions about Faust's complicity in a destructive economic practice, to the interface between the ethical and economic registers attached to the German word *Schuld*, and demonstrates once more how tempting it is to sacrifice moral responsibility for economic growth; it reiterates, finally, the warning, spelled out so distinctly in Droste-Hülshoff's *Judenbuche*, that ecological destruction is one of the inevitable consequences of transforming the natural world, part and parcel, into a collection of commodities for the accrual of surplus value. Moreover, *Faust II* performs, in its very literary-aesthetic practices, both a poetics of economic wastefulness and one of avaricious acquisition. In this sense it not only *reflects on* the complicity of intellectual-literary culture with the emergence of modern economic practices, but also *exhibits* this complicity in its own aesthetic constitution.

Faust II does not escape the critique of modern economic and aesthetic pursuits voiced throughout the text itself. Although Faust, like so many of the other characters whose fates we have followed here, ultimately seeks his redemption in the implementation of certain economic practices, he decidedly does not find economic redemption. Instead, he earns economic condemnation. Nor does *Faust II*, as literary work, provide any form of *aesthetic* redemption. Perhaps this is the most important message of Goethe's text: that neither limitless faith in the limitlessness of economic growth, of poetic ingenuity, and of capital/cultural accumulation, nor a limitless desire to exploit nature for our own selfish ends constitutes a faith that is likely to ensure human salvation. Quite the contrary: as Goethe's tragedy indicates, when we mistake those actions by which we dig our own graves for the construction of our socioeconomic and cultural utopia, only "divine" intervention is capable of saving us from ourselves. We are left to hope that as we wait for the *deus ex machina* of our own redemption, we are not merely waiting for Godot.

Notes

Introduction

1 One thinks here in particular of the work of Georges Bataille, of the representatives of the Frankfurt School, especially Theodor Adorno, but more recently of the French theoretician Jean-Joseph Goux, whose book *Symbolic Economies* seeks a conscious merger of Marxian and Freudian theoretical positions. See also the essays by Amar and Borneman.

2 Throughout this book, translations from the German are my own, unless otherwise indicated. Many of the primary works treated here have either never been translated into English, or are available only in antiquated renderings. In those instances where English translations are available, these are referenced in the bibliography and can be consulted by the reader. However, since my interpretations rely heavily on close readings of the German originals, I have found it both preferable and easier to present my own English versions of cited passages.

3 For succinct and lucid examinations of the emergence of this aesthetics of autonomy, in particular in the German philosophical and aesthetic tradition, see especially the chapter "Zum Problem der Autonomie der Kunst in der bürgerlichen Gesellschaft" in Bürger's *Theorie der Avantgarde* (49–75) and Woodmansee's *The Author, Art, and the Market*. Woodmansee in particular articulates the aporias in which this aesthetic ideology culminated given the realities of a class of artists who were increasingly dependent on the structures of the literary marketplace for their economic livelihood.

4 The phrase "New Economic Criticism" has been popularized in North America above all by the Society for Critical Exchange, which dedicated two conferences to this topic. The proceedings of the first conference have been published under the title *The New Economic Criticism*, edited by Woodmansee and Osteen, and selected papers from the second appeared in a special issue of the journal *New Literary History* (31.2) in the year 2000.

5 The interpretation of economics as a communicative system is promulgated above all by Niklas Luhmann's systems theory (see *Wirtschaft* 14), on which Hörisch largely relies.

Chapter 1 / Buying into Signs

1   On the temporal extension and cultural breadth of the metaphorical field between
     money and language, see Weinrich ("Münze und Wort" 511–14).

2   Goux argues in general that the homology between language and money is structured
     around the logic of the general equivalent. See especially the chapter "Numismatics:
     An Essay in Theoretical Numismatics" in *Symbolic Economies* (9–63).

3   Achermann (47) similarly points to the representational character of money as the
     property that underwrites its affinities with conceptions of language.

4   Voltaire gives characteristic expression to this mercantilist conception of wealth in the
     entry on "Money" in his *Philosophical Dictionary*, noting that wealth is defined as
     the capacity to "circulate the most metals representative of objects of commerce" (5).

5   The significance of the debate over physiocratic economic doctrine, which raged for
     nearly two decades in Germany toward the close of the eighteenth century, is the sub-
     ject of chapter 4.

6   Throughout this book the shift from metallic coin, or specie, to more symbolic mone-
     tary instruments will be a recurring theme. I refer to such semioticized monetary
     forms variously as paper money, fiduciary currency, ersatz money, sign-money, token
     money, credit money, or fiat currency. Although these terms are generally interchange-
     able, they often exhibit subtle shifts of emphasis. The term "fiduciary currency," for
     example, stresses the faith and trust that binds the users of this currency into a coher-
     ent social group, while "credit money" emphasizes that the bill is the placeholder for
     some more concrete and substantial form of wealth (such as stockpiled gold). "Paper
     money," of course, describes the historical reality that such symbolic currencies gener-
     ally take the form of printed paper. The other terms refer most generally to the sym-
     bolic or semiotic nature of monetary forms that contain no inherent substance value
     of their own, and hence they stress the arbitrary or purely conventional nature of such
     monetary instruments.

7   For a detailed account of the Law reforms and their consequences see Gaettens (100–
     26) and Minton.

8   For an eighteenth-century reaction to the Prussian monetary crisis, see Barkhausen
     (537, 551). Gaettens (147–72) describes in detail the nature of the Prussian manipula-
     tions of the value of the taler and their horrendous inflationary consequences.

9   Struensee (227) provides a contemporary reaction to the destabilization in the prices
     of gold and silver that resulted from the influx of metals from American mines.

10 The second volume of Lambert's *Organon* contains a major section titled "Semiotik
     oder Lehre von der Bezeichnung der Gedanken und Dinge" (Semiotics or doctrine
     of the signification of thoughts and of things, 2: 3–214).

11 In his *Fragmente zur Logik* (90–92), Leibniz gave paradigmatic expression to this
     desire to invent a scientific language that would generate new knowledge, in which
     language would move in advance of thought itself.

12 On the definition of sign-money in eighteenth-century economic theory see, for exam-
     ple, Struensee (esp. 244–47).

13 It is noteworthy that this comparison of word-signs to debt counters is not unique to

Leibniz; the same image is employed by Locke, who identifies the misuse of words with the "misplacing of counters in the casting up a debt" (278).

14 My analysis of Leibniz's use of money metaphors has focused solely on the ambivalences in his theory. For more extensive elaborations of the role of money and economics in his thought in general, see Achermann (61–149). Dascal positions Leibniz's use of the money metaphor for his linguistic theory in a broader philosophical context, comparing it to similar analogies in the work of Francis Bacon and Thomas Hobbes. He does not, however, view the changing status of the metaphor against the backdrop of larger economic and monetary developments, but instead aligns it with the general intellectual framework of a Foucauldian rupture and the shift from the Renaissance to the classical paradigm (in Foucault's sense).

15 For a more detailed analysis of Lavater's vendetta against the arbitrary nature of signs and the consequences of this program for his physiognomic theories, see Gray ("Transcendence of the Body" 138–41).

Chapter 2 / Hypersign, Hypermoney, Hypermarket

1 On Müller's dialectical approach to rhetoric, see Borman, and also Henn-Schmölders.

2 Koehler (60) outlines the extent to which Müller's subsequent works were articulations of the larger project he had formulated, but left unfinished, in *Die Lehre vom Gegensatz.*

3 Müller acknowledges this debt frequently; see, above all, his homage to Novalis in the fifth lecture of his *Vorlesungen über die deutsche Wissenschaft und Literatur* (55–59).

4 On the close intellectual relationship between Novalis and Müller, see Koehler (40, 49), Wellek (2: 291), and Krättli's "Einleitung" in *Adam Heinrich Müller: Vermittelnde Kritik* (6).

5 On Müller and Friedrich Schlegel, see Marquardt (21–39).

6 On the relationship between Müller and Kleist, see Rudolf; Ogorek; and Koehler (148–62).

7 Friedrich von Gentz's translation of Burke's *Reflections on the Revolution in France* (1790) appeared under the title *Betrachtungen über die französische Revolution,* 2 vols. (Berlin, 1793).

8 For deliberations on the proto-Marxist tendencies in Müller's critique of liberal economics, see Rudolf (124–25) and Richter (86–89).

9 For a catalog of the critical invectives directed at Müller by his contemporaries, see Jens (79–81) and Ogorek (99–101).

10 For these early, as yet undeveloped reflections on monetary instruments and symbolic money, see *Elemente der Staatskunst* (1: 351–53).

11 Müller comments on this political-economic background as the impetus behind his theory of money in the unpaginated preface to his *Versuche einer neuen Theorie des Geldes.*

12 Bourdieu calls this "the world of reciprocity relationships" and limits its reach to the domain of family and friends; see his *Outline of a Theory of Practice* (186). Müller's utopian ideal represents an extension of these "familial" ties to all the citizens of a state.

13 For readers' convenience, I cite Goethe's *Faust* throughout by line numbers. For an analysis of the paper-money episode and the connection of monetary signs with a new mode of symbolization in *Faust*, see Shell's *Money, Language, and Thought* (84–130).

14 This thesis was represented most forcefully by Schmitt in his book *Politische Romantik*; Koehler gives a much more balanced view of this issue in his *Ästhetik der Politik*, which pursues this problematic with subtlety and incisiveness.

15 This is the position on rhetoric Müller assumes in his *Zwölf Reden über die Beredsamkeit*, and it is hence no coincidence that in his theory of eloquence he assigns to language the role as reciprocal mediator in interhuman relations, which is the very same structural position he attributes to money in his economic doctrine. See Müller's preface to the *Zwölf Reden über die Beredsamkeit* (303–04).

16 On the importance of Quesnay's *tableau* as graphic representation, see Vogl (*Kalkül und Leidenschaft* 69), who argues that the economic table serves to concretize a new economic order based on the linkage and interaction of all individual economic acts.

17 See also Richter (87), who elaborates on Müller's rejection of the Kantian thing-in-itself.

18 See Helene Lieser's note on this opposition between the arithmetic and the geometric in her editorial commentary to Müller's *Versuche einer neuen Theorie des Geldes* (302).

19 On the instrumentalization of the sign in Enlightenment semiotics, see Wellbery (73).

20 For readings of Novalis's semiotic theory that stress this structuralist, or even post-structuralist, orientation, see O'Brien's chapter "From *Filosofie* to *Fiction*: Language and Semiotics in the *Fichte Studies*" in his *Novalis: Signs of Revolution* (77–118), and Menninghaus's essay "Die frühromantische Theorie von Zeichen und Metapher."

21 O'Brien (95–97) has made a persuasive case for Novalis's adaptation of the concept of the schematism from Fichte's essay on language.

22 Gadamer develops this nuance of the Schillerian term *Spiel* in *Wahrheit und Methode* (99–100).

23 See Frank, *Was ist Neostrukturalismus?* (561–63), where he argues for the necessity of a "hypothetical judgment" in every act of human sign-use.

24 There are also distinct affinities between Müller's theory of the economic state based on reciprocal relations and Polanyi's conception (9–11) of the primitive economy as one grounded in the socioeconomic principles of symmetry, redistribution, and reciprocity.

Chapter 3 / Economic Romanticism

1 For general introductions to the theory and philosophy of German Romantic political economy, see the books by Harada and Scheuner.

2 For more recent deliberations on the notion of monetary nationalism and its relevance in contemporary political theory, see White's essay, "Monetary Nationalism Reconsidered."

3 In more recent times, Simmel has made this same argument in his *Philosophie des Geldes* (85–86).

4   See Krause (232–33) and Streisand (82).

5   On the utopian socialist dimensions of *Der geschlossene Handelsstaat*, see, for exam-
    ple, Beiser (59), Bloch (642, 647), Kohn (331), and Reiss (22); for more general reflec-
    tions on Fichte's political philosophy, see Willms.

6   On this connection of money and deferred gratification, see Borneman (432). See
    also Vogl (*Kalkül und Leidenschaft* 349), who argues specifically that the notion of
    credit—which manifests itself in particular, we should add, in the phenomenon of fidu-
    ciary money—contributed to a general sense of the temporalization of semiotic instru-
    ments at this time, and their connection with the displacement and deferral of time.

7   For deliberations on the role of fiat money in Plato's ideal state, see Weatherford (41)
    and Jonathan Williams (219).

8   A similar position has been assumed recently by the economist Randall L. Wray, who
    argues for a strict state theory of money in which the value of a monetary instrument
    is grounded in its acceptance by the state for the payment of taxes (49, 58).

9   See the chapter titled "Exchanging" in Foucault's *Order of Things* (166–214, esp.
    174–81).

10 For more general reflections on Fichte's problematic definition of nationhood, see Kiss.

11 Luhmann is not the sole, just the most recent thinker to articulate this conception of
    money as a communitarian bond. Apel (98, 101) argues along similar lines for the
    historically specific situation of ancient Greece. Gerloff (14, 21) makes the case more
    generally for money as a means of social communication. Taking a systems-theoretical
    standpoint as his point of departure, Heinemann (46) develops the semiotic implica-
    tions of economic exchange as the integration of the individual into a network of
    signs—a network in which, one should add, the monetary sign functions as the central
    organizing supersign.

12 Krautkrämer has investigated the symbiosis between the notion of *Bildung* and the
    theory of the political state during the period of German Romanticism in her book
    Staat und Erziehung.

13 Radrizzani offers some relevant general reflections on the affinities between Fichte's
    transcendental system and his practical political philosophy.

14 In the *Grundzüge des gegewärtigen Zeitalters* (Primary features of the present age),
    Fichte insists most pointedly on the closure his system of science is able to achieve due
    to being founded on a purely a priori principle: "All science that is purely a priori can
    be completed and its investigation brought to perfect closure" (107).

15 Hörisch has devoted considerable attention to fleshing out this analogy between the
    validity of propositions in transcendental philosophy and the monetary system; see
    especially his essay "Herrscherwort, Geld und geltende Sätze." Goux also pursues the
    analogy between economics and idealist philosophy in the chapter "Monetary Econ-
    omy and Idealist Philosophy" of *Symbolic Economies* (88–111).

16 Significantly, Fichte makes an identical case in *Reden an die deutsche Nation* for the
    transsensual nature of the *Bildung* that will unite the Germans into a coherent cultural
    nation. This education is based on "a true knowledge, one that is beyond all experi-
    ence, transsensual, rigorously necessary and universal, and which already subsumes
    within itself from the outset every possible later experience" (288). This transcenden-

tal schema becomes the model or paradigm for all empirical knowledge; it is the monetary instrument that makes experience translatable into a knowledge commodity at all.

17 Verzar (97) suggests that *Der geschlossene Handelsstaat* represents a political manifestation of the *Wissenschaftslehre*, without, however, going into a formal or structural analysis of this interconnection.

18 To be sure, by the time of *Reden an die deutsche Nation* in 1807, the catchwords of the French Revolution—humanity, liberality, and popularity—have devolved for Fichte into examples of meaningless linguistic abstraction and alienation (270–71, 321).

19 Schmitt (27) identifies Müller as the prototype of the political Romantic, with whom he associates a selfish glorification of subjectivity, a shameless opportunism (Schmitt calls it "occasionalism") in matters of thought and knowledge, and a rootlessness that allows him to shift his thinking whenever convenient so as to let him affirm the power of the creative subject over the objective contingencies of reality. For Schmitt's critique of Müller, see especially pages 57–76.

20 The primary difference between Müller and Marx rests in their evaluation of money's role as mediator. Whereas Marx is suspicious of all forms of mediation as symptoms of alienation, Müller—and for that matter Fichte as well—glorifies mediation as the basis of a genuine interhuman bond.

21 Fichte articulated a similar critique of the alienation represented by the written word and the printing press in *Grundzüge des gegenwärtigen Zeitalters* (85–91).

22 For an analysis of this development, see Arendt's arguments in *The Origins of Totalitarianism* (158–84).

Chapter 4 / Economics and the Imagination

1 For overviews of the economic principles of physiocracy and the history of the movement, see Beer; Higgs; Keller; Meek, *Economics of Physiocracy*; Fox-Genovese; and Vaggi.

2 Marx was one of the first to point to the role of physiocracy as a theoretical program that marked the transition between the feudal and capitalist economic orders; see his *Theorien über den Mehrwert* (23).

3 Mauvillon's translation appeared in 1775 under the title *Untersuchung über die Natur und den Ursprung der Reichthümer*.

4 In volume 2 of his *Chronologen* (1779), Wekherlin published a review of Iselin's journal *Ephemeriden der Menschheit*, which included praise for the provinces of Baden that had instituted physiocratic economic reforms, calling them "among the most flourishing and exemplary provinces in Germany" (95). More significant is the essay that appeared in the fourth volume of this journal, titled "Von den Ekonomisten und dem physiokratischen System" (On the economists and the physiocratic system), which avidly defended physiocracy and outlined in thirty points what Wekherlin called the "catechism" of physiocratic economic policy (25–30). Wekherlin also printed in his journal two essays by Johann Christoph Erich von Springer that were favorable to physiocratic doctrine, "Über das physiokratische System: Ein Beytrag" (On the physio-

cratic system, a contribution) and a subsequent addendum to this initial essay, titled "Beylage zu der im vorigen Band enthaltenen Materie: Über das physiokratische System" (Supplement to the material on the physiocratic system contained in the previous volume).

5 For brief summaries of this debate and its significance in the economic discourse of the period, see Hensmann (51) and Schumpeter (294). Braunreuther gives the most extensive examination of this controversy and its significance in terms of economic theory, but his analysis is unfortunately marred by his adherence to the dogmatically Marxist position dictated by the former East German state. Tribe (119–31) gives a more balanced view of the reception of physiocratic doctrine in Germany and the challenges it presented to the tradition of German cameralism.

6 Ludwig Benjamin Schmid (1737–93), one of the founding faculty members of this economic academy, published a series of letters in the important cultural journal *Der teutsche Merkur* between August 1776 and October 1777 describing the purpose and curriculum of this academic institution. For a brief history of its emergence and development see Funk (108–23).

7 In his later economic theory, Jung-Stilling refined this catalog of human wants, distinguishing three separate categories: essential, elevating, and luxurious needs. The latter he explicitly defined as harmful to human social and economic development. See his *Grundlehre der Staatswirthschaft* of 1792 (23–25).

8 On the expansion of commodity goods in Germany dictated by fashion and the economic controversy that surrounded it, see Purdy (51–73).

9 Mirabeau helped establish the terms of this valorization of rudimentary physical needs over the desire for luxury items when he argued that the aim of society, and hence of economic policy, was to bring needs and desires into the closest possible proximity. Only this, he believed, would contribute to the development of a tightly knit community. See his "Extract from *Rural Philosophy*" (59–60). Pocock notes more generally for the economic theory of the eighteenth century that frugality, as an especially touted virtue, played the significant role of making allowances for reinvestment into production (*Machiavellian Moment* 445). This is precisely the function thrift has in physiocratic theory in general.

10 See Braunreuther (16, 61), who relates the German physiocratic movement in general with the anti-Enlightenment sensibilities of the Sturm und Drang generation. However, to my mind he overstates this case, overlooking the fact that the primary representatives of physiocracy in Germany, Iselin and Schlettwein, vehemently defended traditional Enlightenment values.

11 On the innovations represented by the economic theory of the physiocrats, see Vaggi (1–2). See also Immler (12), who views physiocracy as relevant today for an ecologically oriented economic theory.

12 German cameralism tended to identify the individual closely with the needs of the state and the community, and hence concentrated on the establishment of bureaucratic and administrative policies that could promote economic and social progress. By contrast, the modern discipline of political economy, which emerged in part out of the theories promoted by the physiocrats, stressed individual needs and their satisfaction,

as well as the economic activity of the individual (as opposed to the state) as the basis of national wealth. On this transformation in Germany, see Tribe (6–8, 92).

13 Among those who reproach physiocracy due to its French origins are Schlosser ("Über das neue französische System der Policeyfreyheit" 146) and the anonymous author of the essay "Etwas über das Steuerwesen" (265).

14 See Klippel (224–25), who stresses that the failures that followed the implementation of physiocratic programs both by Turgot in France and by Margrave Karl Friedrich of Baden led to a general belief among German economists and intellectuals that physiocracy represented a noble theory, but that its principles defied practical realization. For statements by contemporaries on the impracticality of physiocratic doctrines, see, for example, Dohm ("Über das physiokratische System" 318) and Will (ix, 59–60), the latter of whom stresses in particular the utopianist aspect of physiocracy.

15 Smith is reputed to have wanted to dedicate *The Wealth of Nations* to the founder of the physiocratic school, François Quesnay, but was prevented from doing so by Quesnay's death just prior to its publication. On the relationship between Smith's theories and those of the physiocrats, see Keller (11) and Häufle (19).

16 Smith's *Wealth of Nations* was translated into German by Johann Friedrich Schiller immediately after its English publication. Volume 1 had appeared already in 1776, and volume 2 followed in 1778. The best early translation of Smith into German was that of Christian Garve, which first appeared in 1794 and was reprinted in 1799 and 1810, making it the standard German-language edition of this text throughout the nineteenth century.

17 Tribe (119–20) goes so far as to assert that the engagement with physiocratic economic policy actually helped pave the way for the reception of Adam Smith's theories in Germany, since both propounded laissez-faire attitudes with regard to government regulation of the economic process.

18 In *Theorien über den Mehrwert* Marx stresses that physiocratic policy could only logically develop in a largely agrarian society such as France rather than, for example, in relatively industrialized England (20).

19 The list of prominent rulers who advocated physiocratic reforms also includes Grand Duke Leopold of Tuscany, who became Emperor Leopold of Austria in 1790, and King Gustav III of Sweden. See Hensmann (281).

20 The correspondence between Karl Friedrich and Mirabeau was collected by Knies. For background on their relationship see Knies's introduction to the two volumes of this correspondence (xxxi–clxii).

21 Even the first historian of physiocracy and its German reception, Georg Andreas Will, whose *Versuch über die Physiokratie* of 1782 emerged as an attempt to take stock of the controversy over this economic system, knows nothing but praise for Karl Friedrich and his treatise, which Will believes could serve as an economic handbook for all European regents of the time (xiv–xvi). In keeping with his claim about the importance of this document, Will reprints the French text as an appendix to his own book.

22 On this conflict between need-based and desire-oriented economic principles and its role in the economic transformation of Germany at the end of the eighteenth century, see Vogl (*Kalkül und Leidenschaft* 230, 348).

23 On the materialist basis of the physiocratic insistence on the priority of physical nature, see Meek ("Interpretation of Physiocracy" 376).

24 On the physiocrats as precursors of the ideology and economic reforms instituted during the French Revolution, see Hensmann (172), Keller (241), and Meißner (78).

25 In the essay "Über die wirthschaftliche Organisation der Gesellschaft," Iselin gives a paradigmatic expression of this community-building function of economics. He claims that economics forms a bond by tying individuals together into a system of mutual dependencies, and he views the reform of the domestic economy as the first stage in a worldwide economic revolution that, moving outward from the reformed domestic center, forms a system of concentric circles that will ultimately encompass all of humankind (33–34). Thus the modern phrase "think globally, act locally" adequately suits the utopian sociopolitical design of Iselin's economic program—and in this regard he can be taken as representative of the physiocrats as a whole.

26 On the physiocrats' defense of landed over moneyed interests, see Hensmann (25).

27 In "Von der öffentlichen und privat Üppigkeit" Mauvillon (23–24) presents a similar critique of money, one that culminates in its connection to the production and purchase of luxury items.

28 Hirschman pursues in *The Passions and the Interests* the intellectual-historical process by which one passion, specifically the drive for economic advantage, comes to be singled out over the course of the eighteenth century and elevated to the status of a countervailing and benign "interest" that can be employed as an instrument of control over the other passions (see esp. 32–44). The result of this process is the belief that dedication to economic self-interest ultimately serves the common good (9–10).

29 Poovey (227–30) points out the ways in which, already in the thought of David Hume, providentialism is secularized by being grounded in human cognitive capacities. A similar case for the secularization of providence could be made for Smith's invisible hand, which displaces control over economic dynamics from God to the structures of the market.

30 For examples of this in the German physiocratic tradition, see Iselin (*Versuch über die gesellige Ordnung* 4), Karl Friedrich ("Kurzer Abriß" 242, 246), and Schlettwein (*Wichtigste Angelegenheit* 8–9). In *Theorien über den Mehrwert* Marx reflects critically on the physiocrats' appeal to surplus value as a gift of nature, claiming that it represents the first instance in which the surplus value created by human labor—in this case the labor of agricultural workers—is mystified and alienated when interpreted as an eternal product of nature (21, 24). For further critical reflections on the physiocratic notion of value as natural gift, and the potential relevance of the concept of natural value for present-day ecologically oriented economists, see Immler (299–301).

31 This view is given paradigmatic expression by Tscharner, who emphatically states that production in the sense of creating something new is reserved for God alone ("Zweites Schreiben" 638).

32 This anonymous respondent is most likely relying on Adam Smith's distinction between "natural price," the total cost entailed in producing a commodity and bringing it to market, and "market price," the actual price it commands as regulated by supply and demand. See *Wealth of Nations* (1: 158).

33 See Simpson (28), who notes that the desire for inessential commodities drives the shift from an economy based on subsistence to one fueled by surplus.

34 My conception of the role of human agency in Marx's theory of the economic process, in particular in his definition of the commodity, is informed by recent attempts to rescue Marxism from the criticism that it offers no theory of the human subject. See in particular Amariglio and Callari, and Pietz, who locate the rudiments of a Marxian theory of human agency in the concept of commodity fetishism.

35 Kuczynski (42) notes that the physiocrats themselves saw in the quantification and systematization of economic interrelationships, as represented in Quesnay's *tableau économique*, the promotion of economics from a purely conjectural discipline to the status of an exact science.

36 See, for example, Immler (331), who maintains, following the economist Werner Hofmann, that economics knows only two theories of value, the natural value of the earth and the labor value of human beings.

37 Marx maintains early in *Das Kapital* that throughout this treatise he will use the word "gold," for the sake of convenience, to designate the monetary form in general (109).

38 For an elaboration of this point, see Amariglio and Callari, who write, "With the concept of commodity fetishism, Marx theorized that particular consciousness which 'objectifies' human activity and thus defines the property of the objects of trade as a property of 'things'" (207).

39 Thus physiocracy can indeed be conceived as a materialist philosophy in the Marxian sense (see Meek, "Interpretation of Physiocracy" 376), but not *dialectically* materialist, as Marxian theory claims to be. One significant reflex of this materialist bent is Quesnay's claim that morality and politics must be based on the economic order of society, not vice versa ("Miscellaneous Extracts" 69). Indeed, the utopian dimension of physiocratic doctrine resides in part in the standard claim that if one establishes the "natural" economic order their theory outlines, all other dimensions of human society will also fall into their "natural" places. This represents a rudimentary, nondialectical form of the base-superstructure model.

40 Hull (4) views this transformation as one that accompanies the founding of civil society in Germany.

41 See Siegert (52–53), who outlines the tremendous influence of this book and documents the general fascination with the person and image of the farmer that swept through the German cultural scene in the wake of its reception.

42 In my opinion, Braunreuther (15–16, 61) incorrectly identifies the German defenders of physiocracy as the political-economic expression of the Sturm und Drang movement. He confuses the physiocrats' valorization of nature with the protest of the Sturm und Drang writers against the constraints of reason and artificial norms. In fact, those opponents of physiocracy (like Schlosser and Schmohl) who defend the creativity and productivity of the unfettered imagination come closer to the spirit of the Sturm und Drang than do the physiocrats.

43 In his essay "Über die Dichtkunst," for example, which was first published in 1778, Schlosser glorified the human capacity for fantasy as an ennobling endowment capable of leading human beings down the path of righteousness (386).

44 On the reliance of the physiocrats on Aristotelian economic principles, see Immler (30) and Priddat (7).

45 Van der Zande (16) makes the more absolute claim, not restricted to the domain of economics, that for Schlosser in general the imagination was the source of everything good, true, and beautiful.

46 We are reminded here of the words of *Knabe Lenker* in part 2 of Goethe's *Faust*, who identifies poetry, the work of the imagination, with excess, with *Verschwendung*, or wastefulness. See *Faust*, lines 5573–75. I will deal more fully with this question of the relationship between excess and the imagination in chapter 6 and in the book's conclusion.

47 For a summary of Schlosser's report to Margrave Karl Friedrich and his interactions with Schlettwein, see Braunreuther (31–32).

48 It is surely no coincidence that in the sixth discussion of his "Menschenfreundlicher Catechismus," Iselin refers positively to the example of Lycurgus, the Spartan ruler (228).

49 On this opposition between imagination and mimesis, see Homann (294), who argues that when the concept of imagination enters aesthetic theory at the end of the eighteenth century, it completely displaces the notion of mimesis.

50 Since these two works of prose fiction deal with similar questions, namely, the development of creative artistry on the example of a protagonist who is a painter, but temporally mark the historical rise and decline of Romanticism in German-speaking Europe, they represent ideal objects for an analysis of shifting definitions and evaluations of aesthetic creativity.

51 Coleridge, for one, did defend this linkage of aesthetic quality with notions of excess. In his preface to the *Lyrical Ballads*, published in 1800, he defined poetry as "the spontaneous overflow of powerful feelings" (qtd. in Abrams 21).

52 In his *Philosophie des Geldes* (38–40), Simmel explicitly aligns the domain of value in the modern consumer society with the psychology—indeed, the pathology—of desire.

53 Gudeman (48–70) traces the evolution of this transformation in the development of David Ricardo from his early to his late works. If in his first economic model, Ricardo, like the physiocrats, relied on the limited resource of land and its fertility, in his later model he emphasized the unlimited potential for wealth that could be derived from the infinite resource of human labor.

Chapter 5 / Counting on God

1 Karl Friedrich and the duchy of Baden profited enormously from the consolidations of German territory effected by Napoleon in the wake of the French Revolution. The duchy of Baden became a *Kurfürstentum* (electoral principality) in 1803 and a *Großherzogtum* (grand duchy) in 1806.

2 On the tremendous influence of *Das Heimweh* in Protestant religious circles, both within Germany and abroad, see Benz (25).

3 On Jung-Stilling's role as "patriarch of the Protestant revival" see Hans Schneider (196). Schwinge has presented the most detailed examination of Jung-Stilling's reli-

gious writings and his influence as a religious proselyte. For information about the history, development, common themes, and impact of the journal *Der graue Mann*, see in particular the second chapter of his *Jung-Stilling als Erbauungsschriftsteller* (50–183).

4   Jung-Stilling met Alexander I through Karl Friedrich of Baden, whose niece, Luise, was the czar's wife. Alexander I revered Jung-Stilling as one of Europe's leading religious thinkers, and Jung-Stilling, in turn, celebrated the czar as the great Christian ruler of the "East" who would command the final battle of Christianity against the forces of darkness. For a detailed exposition of Jung-Stilling's connections to Karl Friedrich's court in Carlsruhe, see Schwarzmaier.

5   On Jung-Stilling's medical practices and his career as oculist, see Berneaud-Kötz and Wittmann and Wittmann.

6   The mission of this first academy for higher learning in the field of economics and political theory is presented in a series of reports published from August 1776 through October 1777 in the leading cultural journal of the day, *Der teutsche Merkur*, by Ludwig Benjamin Schmid (1737–93) and Georg Adolf Suckow (1751–1813), the professors responsible for establishing the curriculum of this institution.

7   For overviews of Jung-Stilling's activities as economist and a summary of his theoretical views, see Krüsselberg, Lück ("Jung-Stilling als Wirtschaftswissenschaftler"), Pott, and Maria Schwarz.

8   References to Jung-Stilling's *Lebensgeschichte* follow the text as edited by G. A. Benrath and are noted parenthetically in the running text.

9   Jung-Stilling himself acknowledged the role the publication of his autobiography played in the subsequent development of his life. In the retrospective summary he appended to the fifth volume of his *Lebensgeschichte* he noted, "Stilling's autobiography laid the first significant foundation for my true calling and the adherence to my basic religious drive" (613). In this regard, see also Günther (134), who views the autobiography as an instrument for self-legitimation and self-elevation rather than as a means of retrospective stocktaking.

10   According to one estimate, 1 reichstaler was the equivalent of between 30 and 50 D-marks in 1992, which would translate approximately into 15 to 25 dollars. Using these equivalents, the honorarium Jung-Stilling received would equal between about 2,700 and 2,900 dollars today. The two major indigenous currencies of the German lands during this period were the taler and the gulden, which traded at approximately a 2 to 1 ratio. Thus if a taler is equivalent to between 15 and 25 dollars today, a gulden represents about half that amount.

11   Günther (esp. 48, 131–34) was the first to investigate this ideological dialectic in Jung-Stilling's religious position and his belief in divine providence, analyzing it as a psychological reflex endemic to German Pietism. See also Hirzel (80), who interprets this dynamic as a theological stylization intended to dispel the idea that Jung-Stilling's life and his own character and initiative stand at the center of his autobiography. Neumann (122–24) views Jung-Stilling's discourse of self-denial and his appeal to the guidance of providence as a reflex of petit bourgeois socialization, which transfers the demand for absolute submission to the authority of the biological father over to God the spiritual Father.

12 Jung-Stilling's interpretation of this unanticipated financial boon, while accurately rendering the economic relief it brought, exaggerates its salvational significance as a manifestation of divine providence by situating it in a false historical context. On this convenient twisting of historical facts, see Lauterwasser (91) and Benrath's commentary on this event in his edition of Jung-Stilling's *Lebensgeschichte* (731).

13 Translated into one of the more common currencies of Germany in Jung-Stilling's day, 1 louis d'or was the approximate equivalent of 9 guldens. See Jung-Stilling's own conversion in *Lebensgeschichte* of the sum of 20 louis d'or into 180 guldens (595).

14 Esselborn (198) goes so far as to assert that Jung-Stilling profited even in his private life from the notoriety he received based on his autobiography, arguing that this text facilitated his marriage to his second wife Selma, as well as his professorial appointments in Kaiserslautern and Marburg.

15 Hirzel (17–18) believes that the theological motif of providential intercession is the only structure that lends Jung-Stilling's *Lebensgeschichte* coherence; as we will see, economic thematics play just as decisive a role.

16 The suffix *-burg* is equivalent to the English -borough, implying a larger, more prosperous community than a simple *Dorf*, a farming village.

17 On the nature of this shift in the very conception of economics and Jung-Stilling's role as a mediator in this change, see Pott (xl).

18 In this regard it is surely no coincidence that the mayor of Florenburg and Jung-Stilling himself share the very same given names, Johann Heinrich.

19 Jung-Stilling himself admitted this addiction to the pleasures of sensual existence (*Lebensgeschichte* 608), and he also referred to his own inability to manage his limited monetary resources in a reasonable way (298). Well-meaning critics such as Benrath ("Johann Heinrich Jung-Stilling" 134) and Panthel (582) generally attribute Jung-Stilling's persistent financial woes to his generosity and exaggerated sense of Christian charity.

20 Jung-Stilling articulated this common theme of eighteenth-century economic doctrine, namely that the aim of political economy is to guarantee the greatest happiness of the individual and hence of the community as a whole, in his own textbooks on economics. See, for example, his *Grundlehre der Staatswirthschaft* (21–23), or his *Lehrbuch der Staats-Polizey-Wissenschaft* (3–6).

21 This *Merkbuch* (notebook) containing Jung-Stilling's notes about important events in his life is reprinted as an appendix to Benrath's edition of *Lebensgeschichte* (690–97). References to money and finances can be found on virtually every page of this register.

22 In his *Gemeinnütziges Lehrbuch der Handlungswissenschaft* (10), for example, Jung-Stilling the economist stresses the importance of detailed knowledge about coins and currencies for the merchant, and he later devotes an entire section of this treatise to the science of money and value (132–83).

23 Economists in Jung-Stilling's day already recognized this role of money as pure potentiality. Johann Georg Büsch, for example, wrote in his *Abhandlung von dem Geldsumlauf* of 1780, "A human being can have any sensibility whatsoever; he can be ruled by the noblest or the basest drives; but the means to satisfy these is money" (1: 89). Money, in other words, is not only wholly democratic, serving any master whatsoever, but it is also ethically indifferent to the functions it serves and the desires it fulfills.

24 Günther (125) goes so far as to propose that the idea of God as a banker constitutes the primary theme of the entire *Lebensgeschichte*.

25 Vinke (59) also comments on Jung-Stilling's tendency to discount the input of human beings in the events he ascribes to divine intervention.

26 Jung-Stilling's tendency to view other human beings as mere instruments, whose purpose is to facilitate the realization of God's plan for his own life, reaches its culmination when he reduces the role of his second wife Selma to one of "polishing" him, giving him the refinement that will eventually allow him to enter the aristocratic courts of Europe, especially that of Karl Friedrich of Baden (462–63).

27 Two weeks later, on 25 March 1787, Jung-Stilling remarks in a letter to Franz Albert von Oberndorff that, if he had been promised an adequate salary increase in Heidelberg, he would have remained there instead of moving to Marburg (*Briefe* 131), thereby confirming that finances constituted the key factor in this decision.

28 By the time Jung-Stilling composed this segment of his autobiography, *Henrich Stillings häusliches Leben*, he had already long assumed his post as professor of political economy and written several of his economic textbooks. In his *Versuch einer Grundlehre sämmtlicher Kameralwissenschaften* of 1779, for example, Jung-Stilling laid out for the businessman the fundamental rules for the wise budgeting of one's resources (158–75).

29 Vinke (58–59) points out, without providing a detailed analysis of the issues of debt and credit, that Peter Heyder is the financial resource who underwrites Jung-Stilling's medical studies in Strasbourg.

30 Neumann (128–30) remarks on the replacement of divine providence in Jung-Stilling's *Lebensgeschichte* by the role of blind coincidence in Moritz's *Anton Reiser* as paradigmatic for the *Bildungsroman* in its psychological variant.

31 One of Jung-Stilling's most original contributions to economic theory is the division of human needs and the corresponding commodities that satisfy these needs into three distinct categories: essential, useful, and harmful. Essential needs and commodities are related to the bare facts of subsistence. Useful commodities (and the needs that provoke their production) increase the comfort and refinement of life, and hence are a positive factor in human progress. However, harmful needs and commodities are those that reflect a blind drive for luxury and useless opulence, and these are held to be sinful because they draw productive energy and resources away from the satisfaction of subsistence requirements and human refinement. On this distinction see Jung-Stilling's *Gemeinnütziges Lehrbuch der Handlungswissenschaft* (128–29, 134–35) and his *Grundlehre der Staatswirthschaft* (23–25).

32 A common theme of many so-called bourgeois tragedies of this period is precisely the motif of financial rewards that accrue to the protagonists by pure chance or purported divine providence (see Fiederer 338). Jung-Stilling's *Lebensgeschichte* could be viewed in terms of a particularly persistent application of this fictional motif to the life of its protagonist.

33 In his *Lehrbuch der Staats-Polizey-Wissenschaft* (303), Jung-Stilling explicitly identifies monetary wealth with an aura that garners its possessor the personal respect of others.

34 Throughout his life Jung-Stilling held onto a pedagogical philosophy that stressed the

importance of exterminating the individual's will, and he even argued for its universal application to the life of others. See the remarks to this effect he made in letters (*Briefe an Verwandte* 32, 85).

35 On Jung-Stilling's assumption of the position of religious advisor to Karl Friedrich, see Benrath ("Karl Friedrich von Baden und Johann Heinrich Jung-Stilling" 76–77).

36 Leiser (276) points quite correctly to the centrality of financial issues throughout the correspondence between Jung-Stilling and Karl Friedrich.

37 In one letter, dated 1 September 1803, Jung-Stilling mollifies his enthusiasm and refers only to a "sufficient" (*hinlängliche*) rather than to a "handsome" (*ansehnliche*) salary (*Briefe* 330).

38 Jung-Stilling's discomfort in the Steifmann household must be read as an explicit antithesis to the sense of belonging he experiences in the family of Peter Heyder, which, as we have seen, motivated his marriage to the latter's daughter Christine.

39 In this regard see especially the fourth letter of Jung-Stilling's *Briefe eines reisenden Schweizers über die Einrichtung der Pfälzischen Fruchtmärkte* (Letters of a traveling Swiss citizen on the establishment of fruit markets in the Palatinate, 1782), in which the founding of small factories is praised as a way of stimulating production and contributing substantially to the growth of local economies (71–85).

40 In the retrospective summary appended to his autobiography, Jung-Stilling makes a point of asserting the truthfulness of his account and claims that only the initial volumes are embroidered with literary ornaments to make them more palatable (599–600).

41 See especially Kristeva's remarks about the semiotic "chora" (29–30), or her reflections on the difference between genotext and phenotext (86–89).

42 Jauss (165–66) provides a fundamental description of the negativity or "alienation" that defines literary language as such for the Russian formalists.

43 Hirschman has written with considerable lucidity and persuasiveness about the ways in which, during the eighteenth century, economic interests came to be interpreted as positive tools that could be employed for the control of the baser passions; see his *Passions and the Interests* (esp. 7–66). On the proximity of Hegel's "cunning of reason" to Smith's "invisible hand," see Vogl (*Kalkül und Leidenschaft* 44–45). See also Courtemanche (73), who argues that the capitalist order, as theorized by Smith, mimics in the domain of economics the formal structure of divine providence as a kind of steering mechanism over which humans have no conscious control.

44 For a detailed examination of Lavater's theories, see the opening chapter of my book *About Face* (1–55).

Chapter 6 / Deep Pockets

1 On the influence of Chamisso's text, especially with regard to the motif of the lost shadow, see the section on "Schlemihliana" in Wilpert (50–74).

2 For a comparison of Chamisso's and Hoffmann's tales, in particular their treatment of the fantastic, see Berger, and also Ernst Fedor Hoffmann (176–85).

3 Unfortunately, most modern English translations do not include these prefatory letters,

thereby committing the error of viewing them as extraneous supplements. However, as my arguments will try to demonstrate, they are actually integral to the economic and poetic thematic of this text. My citations are to the German text from Chamisso's *Sämtliche Werke in zwei Bänden*.

4   Despite his aristocratic birth, Chamisso himself was not affluent, and in a letter to his friend Varnhagen von Ense dated 15 August 1810, he expressed his intense desire for "a large sum of money" and ironically admonished Varnhagen, if he should somewhere stumble upon a treasure chest, to think of his friend Chamisso and share the wealth equally with him (*Werke* 5: 294). The fantasy of receiving a magical source of wealth was hence by no means foreign to Chamisso.

5   On the structures of the potlatch, see especially Mauss (37–46). Bataille ("Notion of Expenditure" 16–18) develops more fully the connection between the potlatch and extravagant expenditure or loss.

6   On the paradoxical function of zero in the inflationary economy of the 1920s, see Widdig (27).

7   McLuhan (145) develops the idea of the potlatch as the sacrifice of a surplus that itself threatens to destroy the stable social order.

8   It is certainly no coincidence that in *Schlemihl*, as well as in part 2 of Goethe's *Faust*, the infinite replication of monetary signs, whether as gold or as paper money, is brought about by machinations of the devil.

9   I thus read *Schlemihl*, in direct opposition to the interpretation proffered by Jochen Hörisch (*Heads or Tails* 216–40), not as a celebration of senseless expenditure, but rather as a defense of a modern economy based on the principle of scarcity and the limitation of desire.

10 August Heinrich Julius Lafontaine (1758–1831) was a prolific writer of popular romantic and sentimental tales. For a brief examination of possible relationships between the works of Lafontaine and Chamisso's *Schlemihl*, see Atkins (195–98).

11 The exaggerated obsequiousness of the Gray Man is stressed throughout Chamisso's story; see especially the references to this trait in the first chapter (25–27).

12 The chapbook was written, according to Rohrmann (262), in 1480, but was not published until 1509. Brockhagen (399) suggests that the *Fortunatus* material served Chamisso as a preliminary experiment with the issues that would concern him later in *Schlemihl*. Wambach provides the most detailed reading of the connections between Chamisso's "Fortunatus" fragment and its relationship to the themes and structure of *Schlemihl*.

13 The name *Breitestraße*, to which Schlemihl directly refers (30), is presumably taken from the street of the same name in Hamburg, a city Chamisso had frequently visited. Referring to the admiring remarks Chamisso expressed about this merchant city in his letters (see *Werke* 5: 267–68, 377), Freund (*Chamisso* 14–15) develops the idea that Hamburg represented for Chamisso a world in which intellectual and economic pursuits were able to coexist.

14 "Dolland" is the trade name of an achromatic (non-color-distorting) telescope named after its inventor, John Dolland (1706–61).

15 Kuzniar (196) also stresses the emblematic nature of this episode; however, she reads

the mobile telescope not as a reference to commodity circulation, but instead, in more metaphysical terms, as a reflex of indefinite displacement and as a general commentary on the impossibility of any return to origins. On the significance of this episode, see also Lahnstein (90).

16 Pavlyshyn has also noted the degree to which in this scene Schlemihl's celebration of his wealth devolves into "an orgiastic excess" (56).

17 On the temporal discrepancy between the narrating self and the narrated self of auto-biography as genre, see, for example, Neumann (1). Schlemihl as narrator of his own story twice problematizes the act of narration and his own ability to recon-struct the past and provide an accurate and truthful account of his former life (*Schlemihl* 38, 56).

18 On the role of extravagance in the chapbook *Fortunatus* see Rohrmann (262). His essay also provides a good general introduction into the problematic of superabundant money in this early text that served as one of Chamisso's motivic sources. The quota-tion in the heading above invokes the opposite of extravagance, the theme of absten-tion that is central to Chamisso's tale. The quotation alludes to the closing lines of the poem "Das Wort" (The word) by Stefan George (1868–1933):

> So lernt ich traurig den verzicht:
> Kein ding sei wo das wort zerbricht.
> [I thereby sadly learned to renounce:
> No thing can exist where words fail.] (134)

19 Flores (580) similarly comes to Rascal's defense, claiming that it is difficult to indict someone for stealing from an infinitely replenishable resource. He fails, however, to highlight Rascal's rationalistic economic practices as a positive countermodel to Schlemihl's economics of excess and extravagant waste.

20 Block (95), in particular, has stressed Schlemihl's constitutive nature as someone con-demned to be a wanderer. However, because he highlights ethnic rather than economic issues in his interpretation of this text and its protagonist, he goes on to identify Schlemihl with Ahasverus, the Wandering Jew.

21 Schelling's first outline of the principles of the Romantic philosophy of nature, his *Erster Entwurf eines Systems der Naturphilosophie*, was published in 1799, and by the time Chamisso wrote *Schlemihl*, this direction in Romantic philosophy was well established.

22 Chamisso expresses his rejection of all "speculation" and his own preference for empirical observation in a letter dated 17 November 1812 (*Werke* 5: 371). Signif-icantly, he also aligns his aversion for speculation with what he interprets as his own lack of natural ability to be a poet.

23 See, in particular, the chapter "Monetary Economy and Idealist Philosophy" in Goux's seminal book *Symbolic Economies* (88–111).

24 On the implicit relationship between the devil's pursuit of human souls and their dia-bolical value, Alexander Kluge has remarked, "Why is the devil so wild about us poor souls? Apparently we are valuable" (7).

25 This is just one of many parallels between Chamisso's novella and Goethe's *Faust*,

where Mephistopheles is ultimately cheated out of the possession of Faust's soul—despite the signed contract.

26 To the best of my knowledge, Schwann (403) is the only critic of this work who has remarked on the philosophy of self-denial to which the Peter Schlemihl of the later chapters subscribes. However, he does not offer either an analysis of how this praise of abstention relates to the extravagance and excess of the earlier phase of Schlemihl's life, or of its connection to the prominent economic themes of this text.

27 Although a few critics have taken note of this curious insertion of the intermediary stage into the motif of the pact with the devil (see, for example, Freund, *Chamisso* 42; and Schulz 435), only the Whites have sought to analyze its strategic importance. However, for them this suspension in a middle terrain of shadowless greed simply represents the device by which the devil seeks to make Schlemihl "ripe" for the ultimate exchange of his immortal soul for the return of his shadow (220–21).

28 Martin Swales ("Mundane Magic" 261) and Wambach (182) specifically note that the slippers Schlemihl dons are an allusion to the "prosaic" lifestyle of the bourgeois philistine. See also Blamberger (113), who asserts that Chamisso himself, like his character Schlemihl, is on the one hand the personification of the Romantic artist, but suffers on the other hand from an inextinguishable longing for the simple and comfortable life of the bourgeois philistine.

29 In his report on the original manuscript of *Schlemihl*, Rogge ("Urschrift" 445, 450) notes, in fact, that the word "gold" occurs even in places in which the final version contains the more general *Geld* (money).

30 The unwieldiness of ivory as monetary instrument thus contains possible allusions to Sparta under Lycurgus, in which pieces of iron functioned as monetary tokens. The very weight of iron hampers its ability to circulate widely and quickly, as well as its capacity to represent in manageable form a high concentration of value. Iron can scarcely be exchanged for expensive luxury items. Viewed against this backdrop, Schlemihl's existence after his conversion to the doctrine of limitation is indeed "Spartan."

31 For a more detailed exposition of the critique of *Naturphilosophie* implied in the Gray Man's metaphysical house of cards and Schlemihl's turn to empirical study as a kind of antidote, see Blamberger (16), Fink (49), and Pavlyshyn (54).

32 Kuzniar (201), who stresses difference and displacement as the structuring principles of *Schlemihl*, explicitly rejects the aesthetic program Schlemihl outlines as contradicting the nature of the text itself. One could, of course, turn this argument around and claim that Schlemihl's aesthetics of mimesis overrides, or perhaps even satirizes, the structures of displacement that predominate in the first segment of Schlemihl's life, prior to his conversion to a life of conscious limitation.

33 Critics have tended to see *Schlemihl* as constituted by a dialectic between the imaginary fantasies of the Romantics and the detailed descriptive attitudes of realistic writers. See, for example, Blamberger (110), Butler (6), and Martin Swales ("Mundane Magic" 251–52). Brockhagen (417) goes somewhat further by claiming that the jettisoning of Romantic aesthetic theory and practice is the condition of possibility for the very composition of *Schlemihl*.

34 Quoted from Stuart Atkins's verse translation of Goethe's *Faust*, in volume 2 of
Goethe's Collected Works.

Chapter 7 / Red Herrings and Blue Smocks

1 Fontane is referring to two works Droste-Hülshoff composed that dealt with her
Westphalian homeland, "Bei uns zu Lande auf dem Lande" (Life with us in the Westphalian countryside), an unfinished novel written in 1841 but only published posthu-
mously, and "Westphälische Schilderungen aus einer westphälischen Feder" (Westphalian
portraits from a Westphalian pen), a milieu study about her native Westphalia published in 1845. These works helped lend her the reputation of a significant "local"
poet who depicted the natural setting, human character, lifestyle, and customs of her
native province. Droste-Hülshoff initially conceived *Die Judenbuche* as part of "Bei
uns zu Lande auf dem Lande," but published it separately when she broke off writing
this larger text.

2 See Droste-Hülshoff's letter to Wilhelm Junckmann dated 4 August 1837 (*HKA* 8.1:
228). Droste-Hülshoff's works are cited throughout this chapter from the *Historisch-
kritische Ausgabe*, produced under the general editorship of Winfried Woesler, and
identified with the abbreviation *HKA*. Citations of *Die Judenbuche* refer to the text
as printed in volume 5.1 of this edition.

3 For representative interpretations that follow this strategy, see Woesler (12) and
Ronald Schneider ("Möglichkeiten" 94).

4 Huge (*"Die Judenbuche* als Kriminalgeschichte" 67) elucidates the significance of the
red herring in this text and attributes its role to Droste-Hülshoff's reliance on the
genre of detective fiction, in which the red herring has a prominent structural function.

5 This association is codified in the 1843 essay "Zur Judenfrage" by Droste-Hülshoff's
contemporary, Karl Marx, in which Judaism is explicitly aligned with the monetary
and economic practices of bourgeois capitalism (371–77).

6 On this common identification of the Jews as the chief beneficiaries of modernist economic principles, see Landes (19).

7 For a more detailed examination of the stance of the Haxthausen family with regard
to aristocratic property rights over the forests, see Moritz (24–26) and Rölleke
(*Annette von Droste-Hülshoff* 110).

8 This connection between the illegal felling of trees and the murder of human beings
in Droste-Hülshoff's novella has previously been made by Freund ("Eine Novelle
vom Töten" 15), Huszai (488), and Kilcher (261, 263).

9 Mooser (69) stresses the ambivalent attitude the lower classes harbored toward money
and the emergent monetary economy. Although they never had enough money, at the
same time it gave rise among the common people to wasteful expenditures and extravagant consumption, as documented in the frequent critiques of such behavior during
this period.

10 If we compare the dilapidated condition of the village in this initial description to its
depiction as a *Trödelbude*, a shop for secondhand wares, on the morning of the peas-

ant wedding (*Judenbuche* 27), we can confirm the economic transformation that is taking place. The term *Trödelbude* invokes a kind of superabundance of luxury items, a pursuit of flashy semblance in which all the villagers—not merely Friedrich with his silver watch—apparently participate. See also Kreis (116), who similarly emphasizes that the new economic system valorizes the acquisition of inherently useless and superficial things.

11 Mooser (46) also asserts that the claims attached to, and energies released by, wood poaching will ultimately be identical with those that nourish the later protests of the proletarian workers' movement. Droste-Hülshoff's identification of her wood poachers with this proletarian clothing indicates that she had an inkling of this connection.

12 For deliberations on this name, Mergel, see in particular Rölleke ("Kann man" 411), Moritz (68), and Helfer (228).

13 Several critics have made arguments for the representative status of Friedrich Mergel; see, for example, Freund ("Eine Novelle vom Töten" 21) and Kreis (93). Cottrell (215) and Wells ("Annette von Droste-Hülshoff's Johannes Niemand" 113) go so far as to identify Friedrich as a *Jedermann* figure, a kind of Everyman who stands in for the entirety of the human race.

14 This generalizing tendency is consistent with Droste-Hülshoff's self-understanding of *Die Judenbuche* as a milieu depiction that accurately portrays the character and historically determined situation of the natives of Paderborn.

15 See especially chapter 2 of Diamond's unsettling book *Collapse* (79–119).

16 I thus agree with Brown's assessment that the symbols of Droste-Hülshoff's novella, above all the beech tree, fail to lend the text a coherent organization ("Real Mystery" 844–45), but I read this lack of coherence not as a manifestation of the inherent mystery of poetic language (846), but rather as a reflection of the larger problematic of socioeconomic transformation.

17 Wiese ("Porträt eines Mörders" 32) identifies the Brederholz as the "locus terribilis" (the opposite of the classical "locus amoenus") of the novella, a place of darkness, mystery, and death.

18 To my knowledge, Allerdissen (205–6) is the only critic who has commented on the symbolic counterpoint of the oak and the beech in this text.

19 Chase (139) relates other cultural-historical factors that support the association of the beech tree with the Jews. See also Immerwahr (326), who connects the beech tree with the shrine of Maria Buchen.

20 This sort of ethnographic approach to *Die Judenbuche* is taken above all by Chase, who views this novella as thematizing the problematic interaction between native Germans and Jews in Westphalian society; but a similar line is followed by most critics who discover in this novella an anti-Semitic subtext. See, for example, Donahue (57), who writes of an "atavism" of Jewish traits in the character of the negative Christian figures in the text, or Helfer (230–32), who sees Simon and Friedrich as hidden Jews and believes the text problematizes the inability of Christian society to recognize the assimilated Jews in their midst.

21 Huszai (488) similarly acknowledges the connection of the beech tree to Brandis's murder.

22 Dick (268) perceptively notes that the threefold mention of the beech tree in this brief exchange takes on the aura of an incantation.

23 On the status of the narrator's speculation in this scene as a red herring, see Moritz (80), Rölleke (*Annette von Droste-Hülshoff* 152–53), Ronald Schneider (*Realismus und Restauration* 257), and Wells ("Indeterminacy as Provocation" 480).

24 Nollendorfs (334) sees the dynamic of the novella as one structured by the conflict between (feminine) loyalty to community and the universal principles of justice, as concretized above all by Friedrich's refusal to betray his uncle and Margreth's parallel decision to stand by her brother. My analysis exposes the profit motive as the dialectical opposite of this communitarian solidarity.

25 For interpretations that pursue this angle of Simon as devilish seducer, see Godwin-Jones (232), McGlathery (232), Rölleke (*Annette von Droste-Hülshoff* 148), Rölleke ("Erzähltes Mysterium" 404–06), Wiese ("Porträt eines Mörders" 37), and Betty Weber (208).

26 See also Kilcher (254–63), who interprets the destruction of the forests in terms of a disruption of the cosmological order and connects this with the Hebrew charm via the motif of "uprooting of plants" from the kabbala. This interpretation lends further support to the idea that the murder of Aaron and the actions of the wood poachers are inherently linked.

27 Schneider (*Realismus und Restauration* 281) comes to a similar conclusion, asserting that whatever evil one does unto others will ultimately come back to plague the evildoer.

28 See Droste-Hülshoff's letters to Christian Schlüter, dated 13 December 1838 (*HKA* 8.1: 329–30), and to her sister Jenny von Laßberg from 29 January 1839 (9.1: 22–23), in which she notes the resistance and anger she could expect from her Westphalian contemporaries if she were to present an unadulterated picture of them. Droste-Hülshoff thus felt compelled to compromise the factuality of her depiction, embellishing it with fictional emendations and elaborations. See in this connection also her letter to Christian Schlüter dated 23 March 1841 (9.1: 214).

29 Toury (381) stresses the manner in which the Jews became convenient targets and scapegoats who were—falsely—held responsible for the introduction of capitalist economic practices, especially in the rural communities. Whitinger (269) identifies the introduction of the figure of Lumpenmoises, who confesses to the murder of a fellow Jew named Aaron, as the central mechanism by which Droste-Hülshoff's novella marks this shift of guilt even for Aaron's murder from Friedrich to the Jews themselves.

30 Huszai (491) is to my knowledge the only other critic who views the wood-poaching incident, culminating in the murder of the forester Brandis, as the fundamental kernel of Droste-Hülshoff's novella.

Chapter 8 / The (Mis)Fortune of Commerce

1 On this banishment of labor, occupation, and the nitty-gritty of the workaday world in general from Stifter's works, see Barbara Osterkamp (2).

2 For interpretations that stress this integrative element, see Doppler (13), Kauf (58–59), and Stopp (174–75). There are several further variations on this theme: Beil (505) interprets the text in terms of successful transcendence; Cohn (259) believes the world of Gschaid is ultimately redeemed from its moral failings by the children; Egon Schwarz (266) asserts that metaphysical intervention into the course of events reveals the divine world in its mundane semblance; and Whiton (259–60) defends the general thesis that *Bergkristall* is a story about social renewal.

3 On the critique of the capitalist lifestyle implicit in its very banishment from Stifter's works, see also Höller (42, 49) and Tielke (13).

4 See the *Lesebuch zur Förderung humaner Bildung* (Reader for the promotion of humane education) that Stifter edited and published in 1854.

5 In this sense Stifter's cultural-political essays form a countermodel to the political agitation he found so distasteful in the authors of *Junges Deutschland* (Young Germany), people like Heinrich Heine (1797–1856), Karl Gutzkow (1811–78), and Heinrich Laube (1806–84). Indeed, in a letter to his publisher Gustav Heckenast from October 1849, Stifter goes so far as to blame the "phrasemongering of the pseudoliterati" for the excesses of the revolution (*Sämmtliche Werke* 18: 15).

6 Stifter's remarks anticipate in many respects the profound critique of the city and of modern commodities voiced by Walter Benjamin in the 1935 essay "Paris, die Hauptstadt des XIX. Jahrhunderts" (Paris, the capital of the nineteenth century). See also Benjamin's notes in "Ausstellungswesen, Reklame, Grandville" (Exhibitions, advertisements, Grandville), which display many similarities in theme and rhetoric with Stifter's essay.

7 In general, my interpretive methodology is informed by more recent scholars of Stifter's work, who read the details of his descriptions not as simple atmospheric evocations or as "realistic" representations, but rather as signs that carry an inherent significance of their own. This direction in criticism is represented by Küpper (184), but especially by Begemann, who stresses that Stifter's world is a world of signs (25, 32–33), and by Geulen (30), who highlights the linguistic and semiotic character of the reality Stifter portrays.

8 On the importance of narrative in Stifter, its role of preserving the past and securing the future, see Geulen (10).

9 On this contradictory attitude of the villagers to the Gars, see Oswald (78).

10 The shoemaker, the narrator tells us, "gradually bought more and more pieces of real estate with the sums of money he had left over, until he had accumulated a considerable amount of property" (198). See Motté (117), who highlights the importance money and possessions hold for the shoemaker.

11 Oswald (75) notes that the shoemaker is constantly occupied with his customers, even on Christmas Eve when the children ask permission to cross the pass to visit their grandparents.

12 Motté (96–97) emphasizes the competitive nature of the relationship between the dyer and his son-in-law.

13 Glaser (55) makes a more general case for the dominance of possessive individualism in Stifter's works, highlighting its role in the novel *Der Nachsommer* (Indian summer, 1857).

14 Egerer and Raschner's claim (lix–lx) that Stifter introduces no significant changes into the text from the first to the second version thus cannot be upheld.

15 See especially Oswald (75), who accuses the shoemaker of "hubris." In general, the traditional interpretive line, which views the threat to the children as atonement for their father's sins against the community, is founded on the assumption that the shoemaker's zeal is a thoroughly negative trait. See, for example, Doppler (13), Kauf (59–60), and Stopp (172–75).

16 This relationship of noncompetition and gentlemanly conduct between Tobias and Sebastian confirms the view of Motté (40) that the world of commerce in Stifter's works is populated by individuals who manifest only the most noble and honorable motives.

17 Erika Swales's remarks (40) about the centrality of property in *Bergkristall* are coherent with the possessive individualism of the shoemaker and the dyer.

18 My interpretation of the Christmas backdrop and its relevance for this text thus diverges significantly from that of Cohn (259), who sees the connection in the theme of salvation through the intervention of children.

19 Simony's letter is reprinted in Hettche's commentary to *Bergkristall* in *Werke und Briefe: Historisch-kritische Gesamtausgabe*, 2.4: 65–67.

20 Hugo Schmidt (323–25) has developed the ways in which Simony's influence helped transform this common experience into the events laid out in *Der heilige Abend*.

21 The connection between the bread carried by the baker and that transported by Konrad and Sanna has been noted by at least two critics, Sinka (12) and Stopp (172), but both fail to read this as a sign of changing attitudes about the role of commerce in the village.

22 The term *Martersäule*, with its allusion to martyrdom, raises a new set of questions about the text. Since the column is erected in memory of the baker, it would seem that he—not the children—is the martyr. But a martyr to what? To commerce? If so, that would confirm the arguments pursued here, since the baker would have perished for the sake of an as yet unacknowledged and unaccepted economic endeavor. But the notion of martyrdom leads to various other associations in the text, especially to the Christmas story. It may also be significant that the shoemaker, although mentioned by name only once (236), bears the name of a Christian martyr, Sebastian. Is the implication that he, too, is a martyr for commerce? Is his martyrdom somehow connected to the mysterious head wound he is supposed to have received in his days as a chamois hunter (195)? These issues can only be raised as provocative questions, for they would lead us too far away from the primary line of argumentation pursued here.

23 The death of the baker, however, is not symbolic in the sense advocated by Egon Schwarz, who interprets his death as a "divine sign" (265), nor in the sense defended by Whiton, who sees him as a Christ figure who perishes while bringing bread—that is, presumably, redemption—to human beings (266).

24 It is significant to recall, however, that this quality of superfluity is present in the commerce of the children as well, who only "import" to Gschaid things already present there in abundance. Thus the baker's commercial enterprise is not condemned for its superfluity, but for some other reason.

25 For an elaboration of this economic paradox, see Skinner's introduction to Smith's *Wealth of Nations* (47).

26 It is thus impossible to uphold Cohn's surprising claim (259) that the story of the *Unglüksäule* is nothing but a cultural anecdote in Stifter's text and has no relation to the primary narrative.

27 Sinka (10) also remarks on the associative connections linking the baker to the old hunter.

28 A related claim is that made by Requadt (155), who maintains that Stifter fails to distinguish between nature and history.

29 On this larger claim that Stifter's "gentle law" is an ideological disguise for the hard realities of capitalist economics, see Tielke (9–13, 108–09).

Conclusion / Limitless Faith in the Limitless

1 Goethe's *Faust* is cited throughout according to line numbers. English renderings are drawn from the translation by Stuart Atkins, published as volume 2 of Goethe's *Collected Works*. This translation closely follows the text and the line numbers of the German original. When necessary, I have altered or adjusted Atkins's translation, especially with regard to mechanics such as capitalization and punctuation, but in some instances in order to highlight semantic nuances relevant for my interpretation. I rely throughout on the German text as printed in volume 3 of *Goethes Werke*, known collectively as the Hamburger Ausgabe, edited by Erich Trunz. Other citations to the Hamburger Ausgabe are noted by the abbreviation HA, followed by volume and page number.

2 Madame de Staël was among the first to designate Mephistopheles, this "civilized devil," as the true "hero" of Goethe's drama; see Weinrich ("Der zivilisierte Teufel" 61).

3 See especially the subchapter titled "Das Geld" (Money) in Spengler's *Untergang des Abendlandes* (1145–82). Spengler's insight that modern money has been reduced to mere functionality is consistent with the position of Simmel, the other great early twentieth-century German critic of the money form, whose *Philosophie des Geldes* (Philosophy of money, 1900) circles constantly around the idea of money's instrumental function. Simmel asserts, for example, that "[m]oney is not merely the absolutely fungible object, of which any given quantity can be indistinguishably replaced by any other group of coins, rather it is the fungibility of things personified" (128).

4 On the sign of zero as the paradoxical mark both of nullity and of infinite growth, and hence as the very symbol of the catastrophic inflation in Germany during the 1920s, see Widdig (97–99). See also Rotman (1–6), who discusses the importance of zero as a metasign whose introduction revolutionized mathematics and economics in the West.

5 Binswanger (*Money and Magic* 32) felicitously describes this transformation as one from *patrimonium*, a sense of one's duty to attend to nature, to *dominium*, the perceived right to mastery over it. Metscher (117) makes a similar claim, asserting that Faust shifts from enjoying a social relation with nature to demanding absolute mastery over it.

6   Lukács is followed in this by the doctrinaire Marxist critic Thomas Metscher, who
    also views the socioeconomic and political transformation documented in *Faust II* as
    the demise of feudalism and the introduction of capitalist instruments of production
    ("Faust und die bürgerliche Gesellschaft" 114–17).

7   In Polanyi's analysis, whereas in the archaic model "[t]he economic system is, in
    effect, a mere function of social organization" (12), the modern commercial economy
    reverses this relationship, with the result that human society becomes "an accessory of
    the economic system" (36).

8   For a representative statement of this distinction see, for example, Brown (*Goethe's
    Faust* 169), who contrasts the "microcosmic" world of part 1 with the "macrocosm"
    of part 2. Lukács was among the first to consider the Faust of part 2 a "type" who
    reflects a greater universality (143), an idea subsequently popularized and lent critical
    legitimacy by Emrich (34).

9   Goethe's *Amtliche Schriften* provide ample testimony to the seriousness with which
    he engaged in his economic tasks and the energy he invested in them. For a concise
    summary of Goethe's writings as a court official and his effectiveness as a bureaucrat,
    see Irmtraut and Gerhard Schmid's essays "Goethes *Amtliche Schriften*" and "Behör-
    dengeschichtliche Entwicklung," appended to the volumes of the *Amtliche Schriften*
    in the Frankfurt edition of Goethe's *Sämtliche Werke*.

10 For a useful summary of Goethe's acquaintance and engagement with the economic
    theories of his time, see Binswanger's chapter "Goethe and the Economy" (*Money and
    Magic* 99–115). See also Mahl's thorough documentation of Goethe's economic
    expertise in *Goethes ökonomisches Wissen*.

11 On Goethe's engagement with the ideas of the Saint Simonists, see especially Kahle,
    Mahl (507–18), and Sagave ("Französische Einflüsse" 126–28). Schuchard (362) reads
    Faust's utopian project in act 5 as a satire on Saint Simonism, and Jaeger (24) follows
    him in this regard. It is interesting to contrast this position with that of Baxa (381),
    who, writing just prior to the fascist seizure of power, buys wholesale into Faust's
    vision and views it as a model for an ideal future German state.

12 Given the breadth of economic themes incorporated into *Faust II*, it should come as
    no surprise that economic interpretations of this work also display a remarkable diver-
    sity. Shell's early essay on "Language and Property" initiated a semiotic orientation
    toward money and linguistic-aesthetic structure that culminated in Hamacher's essay
    titled "Faust, Geld." Binswanger's *Money and Magic* offers a more historical approach
    to this problem by connecting the "magical" properties of the modern economy with
    the alchemical design of transforming worthless matter into gold. Schlaffer (*Faust
    zweiter Teil*) presents a comprehensive interpretation that aligns the abstract quality of
    Faust II's allegorical form with the abstraction inherent in the modern economic para-
    digm, while Metscher's "Faust und die bürgerliche Gesellschaft" gives a reading based
    in a doctrinaire Marxist standpoint. More recently, Kaiser and Jaeger have concen-
    trated on the critiques of progress and technological modernism that are inherent in
    the economic dimension of Goethe's drama. For a concise summary of economic takes
    on this text, see the section "Ökonomische Lesart" of Gaier's commentary in his
    Goethe: Faust-Dichtungen.

13 Goethe's friend Sulpiz Boisserée records in his diary, on 3 August 1815, a discussion
    with Goethe in which the latter claims that the concluding scene has long been
    finished and that it has turned out especially well. Boisserée's diary entry is cited by
    Ernst Beutler in his notes to Goethe's *Faust* (*Gedenkausgabe* 5: 639).

14 Goethe's letters are cited from the four-volume collection *Goethes Briefe*, edited by
    Karl Robert Mandelkow and known among scholars as the Hamburger Ausgabe
    Briefe, the complement to the Hamburger Ausgabe of Goethe's works. Citations from
    the letters are indicated with the common abbreviation HAB, followed by volume and
    page number.

15 This phrase seems to be the one Goethe identified most intimately and persistently
    with his final drama; already in a letter to Sulpiz Boisserée dated 24 November 1831,
    Goethe expressed the hope that his friends will find enjoyment in the "jokes intended
    seriously [*ernst gemeinten Scherzen*]" contained in *Faust II* (HAB 4: 461).

16 One could make the case that Lynceus functions primarily as an allegory of, or a fig-
    ure for, the device of teichoscopy, since his role as watchman and his position on his
    watchtower make him a paradigmatic embodiment of the distanced, reporting obser-
    ver. As such, he can be seen as the very embodiment of *visual* mediation in a play that
    is centrally about the problematic of mediation. This would also explain why teicho-
    scopy is such a fundamental device in this work, and why so many of the play's cen-
    tral events—for example, the emperor's signing of the paper-money template, the
    decisive battle against the anti-emperor, and the report by Philemon and Baucis about
    the nighttime digging of the channels and construction of the dikes—occur offstage
    and are only made available by means of mediated summaries.

17 Mephistopheles' fulfillment of the spirit of Faust's wish, while ignoring the letter of
    his commandment, is thus a further manifestation of the confusion of spirit and letter
    that is introduced in the paper-money episode. On the complexity of this association
    between paper currency and the letter in Goethe's play, see especially Hamacher.

18 One could also give the concept of guilt a Freudian turn in the instance of Faust.
    In *Das Unbehagen in der Kultur* (Civilization and its discontents), Freud cautiously
    distinguishes remorse (*Reue*), as self-reprehension for the actual commitment of an
    aggressive action in the past, from guilt (*Schuld*), as the projection of some imaginary
    or future aggressive action in the form of a wish (497). For Freud, then, guilt, much
    like debt, is oriented toward the future and grounded in human desire and its psycho-
    logical satisfaction, while remorse has an orientation toward the past. The elfin spirits
    of "Pleasant Landscape," when viewed from this Freudian perspective, relieve Faust
    of *both* remorse and guilt.

19 Atkins's rendering, "the things he knows are tangible," does not adequately invoke
    the immediacy with which thought is translated into deed, as is implied by Goethe's
    original German, nor does it suggest the significant connection between the grasping
    hand and the will to take possession of knowledge and things.

20 I thus disagree with Hamacher's contention (133) that the economy of *Faust II* is
    dominated more by the *open* hand than by the grasping fist; the greedy *Faust*, or
    clutching fist, in fact, is one of the master tropes of this text.

21 Several scholars have commented on the ringing bells as markers of transition; see, for

example, Schieb (285) and Jochen Schmidt (187–88). However, the connection to the audible noise caused by the rising sun in "Pleasant Landscape" has, to the best of my knowledge, thus far escaped critical attention.

22 On Thales and Anaxagoras as allegorical representatives of the Vulcanism/Neptunism debate, see especially Laine. Williams has linked this debate with the scientific controversy between Cuvier and Geoffrey St. Hilaire, suggesting that Goethe tended to align the "revolution" in science marked by this controversy with the political revolutions of the late eighteenth and early nineteenth centuries, in particular with the July Revolution in France.

23 Adorno ("Zur Schluß-Szene des *Faust*" 376) questions the ideological motivation of this scene, since for him it demonstrates how the permanent catastrophe and violence of the waterfall comes to be misconstrued as a blessing.

24 Baxa (370–80) provides a succinct summary of Goethe's reflections on the institution of paper money. For Goethe's response to the inflationary tendency of the French assignat, see his autobiographical experiences, recorded in 1792, in his *Campagne in Frankreich* (Campaign in France) (HA 10: 287).

25 For Goethe's ballad "Der Zauberlehrling," see HA (1: 276–79). This image of unleashing forces one cannot ultimately control was immortalized for generations of children by Walt Disney's cartoon rendering of this poem in the film *Fantasia*.

26 Adorno ("Zur Schluß-Szene des *Faust*" 382) was one of the first to point out that the wager Faust enters into with Mephistopheles presents the structure of economic exchange expanded into a mythic dimension.

27 Zabka ("Reiche Narren" 271) goes so far as to read the entire paper-money episode in *Faust II* as a critical satire of Müller's theory that valorizes the community-building effects of fiduciary currency.

28 This is the theme Binswanger, in his stimulating study *Money and Magic*, investigates through the interconnections between the discourses of alchemy and modern economics in *Faust II*.

29 The very thematic of the natural energy inherent in waterpower links these scenes; rhetorically they are bound together by the language of intensification ("wave after wave [*Well' auf Welle*]") and excessive production ("at a thousand points [*abertausend Enden*]"), which imitate and reiterate the rhetoric Faust employs in the closing monologue of "Pleasant Landscape" as well as during the paper-money episode.

30 In his *Ökonomisch-philosophische Manuskripte*, Marx famously remarked, "*Logic*— the *money* of the mind" (571).

31 For Goethe's celebrated theory of the symbol as unification of idea and appearance in a single image, such that the image invokes the idea but never encompasses and limits it, see entry number 749 of his *Maxime und Reflexionen* (HA 12: 470–71). Dye (972) also makes the connection between the process of mediation and Goethe's conception of the symbol.

32 Among those critics who insist that Faust's blindness is not a symptom of inner wisdom or inordinate vision, such as Kruse (382) and Schlaffer ("Fausts Ende" 773), Kaiser (52) takes the most radical position, declaring Faust's blinding to be a *parody* of the motif of the blind seer.

33 In "Ideology and Ideological State Apparatuses," Althusser formulates his famous definition of ideology as "the imaginary relationship of individuals to their real conditions of existence" (153).

34 On the parallel between the descent to the bowels of the earth for economic wealth and Faust's descent to the mothers and the underworld to capture the aesthetic treasure of Helen's beauty, see Brown (*Goethe's* Faust 156) and Kruse (123).

35 On Goethe's identification of the boy charioteer with Euphorion, see Beutler's commentary on this figure in his notes to *Faust II* (*Gedenkausgabe* 5: 657).

36 One could thus add this conflict on the plane of textual structure to the catalog of tensions between the classical and the Romantic that Zabka investigates in his study, Faust II: *Das Klassische und das Romantische*.

37 In this regard, Esslin (221) is absolutely correct to associate Goethe's literary practice in *Faust II* with the playful exuberance of postmodern literature.

Bibliography

Aarsleff, Hans. *From Locke to Saussure: Essays on the Study of Language and Intellectual History.* Minneapolis: University of Minnesota Press, 1982.

Abrams, M[eyer]. H. *The Mirror and the Lamp: Romantic Theory and the Critical Tradition.* Oxford: Oxford University Press, 1953.

Achermann, Eric. *Worte und Werte: Geld und Sprache bei Gottfried Wilhelm Leibniz, Johann Georg Hamann und Adam Müller.* Tübingen: Niemeyer, 1997.

Adorno, Theodor W. *Ästhetische Theorie.* Ed. Gretel Adorno and Rolf Tiedemann. 9th ed. Frankfurt am Main: Suhrkamp, 1989.

———. Einleitung. *Der Positivismusstreit in der deutschen Soziologie.* Sammlung Luchterhand 72. Darmstadt: Luchterhand, 1972. 7–79.

———. "Zur Schluß-Szene des *Faust.*" *Aufsätze zu Goethes* Faust II. Ed. Werner Keller. Wege der Forschung, Bd. 445. Darmstadt: Wissenschaftliche Buchgesellschaft, 1992. 374–83.

Allerdissen, Rolf. "Judenbuche und 'Patriarch': Der Baum des Gerichts bei Annette von Droste-Hülshoff und Charles Sealsfield." *Herkommen und Erneuerung: Essays für Oskar Seidlin.* Ed. Gerald Gillespie and Edgar Lohner. Tübingen: Niemeyer, 1976. 201–24.

Althusser, Louis. "Ideology and Ideological State Apparatuses (Notes Toward an Investigation)." *Lenin and Philosophy and Other Essays.* Trans. Ben Brewster. London: New Left Books, 1971. 121–73.

Amar, André. "Psychoanalytischer Versuch über das Geld." *Psychoanalyse des Geldes: Eine kritische Untersuchung psychoanalytischer Geldtheorien.* Ed. Ernest Borneman. Frankfurt am Main: Suhrkamp, 1977. 387–402.

Amariglio, Jack, and Antonio Callari. "Marxian Value Theory and the Problem of the Subject." *Fetishism as Cultural Discourse.* Ed. Emily Apter and William Pietz. Ithaca, NY: Cornell University Press, 1993. 186–216.

"Anmerkungen zu des Herrn Prof. Dohms Abhandlung über das physiokratische System." *Deutsches Museum* 4 (May 1779): 427–52.

Apel, Hartmut. *Verwandtschaft, Gott und Geld: Zur Organisation archäischer, ägyptischer und antiker Gesellschaft.* Frankfurt am Main: Campus, 1982.

Apter, Emily. Introduction. *Fetishism as Cultural Discourse*. Ed. Emily Apter and William
Pietz. Ithaca, NY: Cornell University Press, 1993. 1–9.

Arendt, Hannah. *The Origins of Totalitarianism*. San Diego: Harcourt-Harvest, 1985.

Arhelger, Reinhard. *Jung-Stilling—Genese seines Selbstbildes*. Europäische Hochschul-
schriften, Reihe 1, Bd. 1187. Frankfurt am Main: Peter Lang, 1990.

Aristotle. *Politics: Books I and II*. Trans. and ed. Trevor J. Saunders. Oxford: Clarendon,
1995.

Atkins, Stuart. "*Peter Schlemihl* in Relation to the Popular Novel of the Romantic Period."
Germanic Review 21 (1946): 191–208.

Aurenche, Emmanuelle. "Autobiographie und Textkohärenz am Beispiel von Jung-Stillings
Lebensgeschichte." *Cahiers d'Études Germaniques* 27 (1994): 7–16.

Barkhausen, Heinrich Ludwig. "Über den 20. und 24. Geldfuß." *Deutsches Museum* 1
(1776): 535–52, 575–93.

Barnouw, Jeffrey. "Faust and the Ethos of Technology." Brown, Lee, and Saine 29–42.

Bataille, Georges. *Eroticism: Death and Sensuality*. Trans. M. Dalwood. San Francisco:
City Lights, 1986.

———. "The Notion of Expenditure." *Visions of Excess: Selected Writings, 1927–1939*.
Ed. and trans. Allan Stoekl. Minneapolis: University of Minnesota Press, 1985.
116–29.

Batscha, Zwi. *Gesellschaft und Staat in der politischen Philosophie Fichtes*. Frankfurt am
Main: Europäische Verlagsanstalt, 1970.

Bauer, Gerhard, and Heidegert Schmid Noerr. "Faust, Ökonomie, Revisionismus und
Utopie." *Das Argument* 18 (1976): 780–92.

Baxa, Jakob. "Goethes volkswirtschaftliche Anschauungen: Zum Gedächtnis seines 100.
Todestages am 22. März 1932." *Jahrbücher für Nationalökonomie und Statistik* 136
(1932): 365–82.

[Becker, W. G.] "Iselins Vermächtnis an den künftigen Herausgeber der *Ephemeriden*."
Ephemeriden der Menschheit 8 (Jan. 1783): 16–29.

Beckmann, Johann. *Physikalisch-ökonomische Bibliothek* 1–15 (1770–89).

Beckmann, Max. *Illustrationen zu* Faust II: *Federzeichnungen—Bleistiftskizzen*. Ed. Rike
Wankmüller and Erika Zeise. Munich: Prestel, 1984.

Beer, Max. *An Inquiry into Physiocracy*. London: Allen & Unwin, 1939.

Begemann, Christian. *Die Welt der Zeichen: Stifter-Lektüren*. Stuttgart: Metzler, 1995.

Beil, Ulrich Johannes. "Die Erfahrung des 'Anderen' in Adalbert Stifters *Bergkristall*." *Die
Wiederkehr des Absoluten: Studien zur Symbolik des Kristallinen und Metallischen in
der deutschen Literatur der Jahrhundertwende*. Frankfurt am Main: Peter Lang, 1988.
492–511.

Beiser, Frederick C. *Enlightenment, Revolution, and Romanticism: The Genesis of Modern
German Political Thought, 1790–1800*. Cambridge, MA: Harvard University Press,
1992.

Benjamin, Walter. "Ausstellungswesen, Reklame, Grandville." *Gesammelte Schriften*.
Ed. Rolf Tiedemann and Hermann Schweppenhäuser. 12 vols. Frankfurt am Main:
Suhrkamp, 1972–85. 5.1: 232–68.

———. "Paris, die Hauptstadt des XIX. Jahrhunderts." *Gesammelte Schriften*. Ed. Rolf

Tiedemann and Hermann Schweppenhäuser. 12 vols. Frankfurt am Main: Suhrkamp, 1972–85. 5.1: 45–59.

———. "Stifter." *Gesammelte Schriften*. Ed. Rolf Tiedemann and Hermann Schweppenhäuser. 12 vols. Frankfurt am Main: Suhrkamp, 1972–85. 2.2: 608–10.

Benrath, Gustav Adolf. "Johann Heinrich Jung-Stilling." *Genie und Geld: Vom Auskommen deutscher Schriftsteller*. Ed. Karl Corino. Nördlingen: Greno, 1987. 129–39.

———. "Karl Friedrich von Baden und Johann Heinrich Jung-Stilling." *Badische Heimat, Jahrbuch für das Badener Land* (1972): 73–82.

Benz, Ernst. *Jung-Stilling in Marburg*. Marburg: Simons Verlag, 1949.

Berger, Willy R. "Drei phantastische Erzählungen: Chamissos *Peter Schlemihl*, E. T. A. Hoffmanns *Die Abenteuer der Silvester-Nacht* und Gogols *Die Nase*." *Arcadia* Sonderheft (1978): 106–38.

Berkeley, George. *The Querist*. London: Cooper, 1750.

Berman, Marshall. *All That Is Solid Melts into Air: The Experience of Modernity*. 2nd ed. Harmondsworth: Penguin, 1988.

Berneaud-Kötz, Gerhard. "Jung-Stilling als Arztpersönlichkeit: Laienmediziner, Arzt, Augenarzt und Staroperateur." *Blicke auf Jung-Stilling: Festschrift zum 60. Geburtstag von Gerhard Merk*. Ed. Michael Frost. Kreutztal: Verlag die Wielandschmiede, 1991. 19–39.

Binswanger, Hans-Christoph. "J. G. Schlossers Theorie der imaginären Bedürfnisse: Ein Beitrag zur deutschen Nationalökonomie jenseits von Physiokratie und Klassik." *Studien zur Entwicklung der ökonomischen Theorie V*. Ed. Harald Scherf. Berlin: Duncker & Humblot, 1986. 9–28.

———. *Money and Magic: A Critique of the Modern Economy in Light of Goethe's Faust*. Trans. J. E. Harrison. Chicago: University of Chicago Press, 1994.

Blaich, Fritz. "Der Beitrag der deutschen Physiokraten für die Entwicklung der Wirtschaftswissenschaft von der Kameralistik zur Nationalökonomie." *Studien zur Entwicklung der ökonomischen Theorie III*. Ed. Harald Scherf. Berlin: Duncker & Humblot, 1983. 9–36.

Blamberger, Günter. "'Ein anderer ist nun der wirkliche Anfang': Die Weltreisenden Peter Schlemihl und Adelbert von Chamisso." *Hermenautik-Hermeneutik: Literarische und geisteswissenschaftliche Beiträge zu Ehren von Peter Horst Neumann*. Ed. Holger Helbig, Bettina Knauer, and Gunnar Och. Würzburg: Königshausen & Neumann, 1996. 109–17.

Bloch, Ernst. "Fichtes geschlossener Handelsstaat oder Produktion und Tausch nach Vernunftrecht." *Das Prinzip Hoffnung*. 1959. Frankfurt am Main: Suhrkamp, 1973. 637–47.

Block, Richard. "Queering the Jew Who Would Be German: Peter Schlemihl's Strange and Wonderful History." *Seminar* 40 (2004): 93–110.

Borman, Dennis R. "Adam Müller: On the Dialogic Nature of Rhetoric." *Quarterly Journal of Speech* 66 (1980): 169–81.

Borneman, Ernest. "Schlußwort: Der Midaskomplex." *Psychoanalyse des Geldes: Eine kritische Untersuchung psychoanalytischer Geldtheorien*. Frankfurt am Main: Suhrkamp, 1977. 421–58.

Bourdieu, Pierre. *Outline of a Theory of Practice.* Trans. R. Nice. Cambridge: Cambridge University Press, 1977.

Bradish, Joseph A. *Goethes Beamtenlaufbahn.* New York: B. Westermann, 1937.

Braudel, Fernand. *Afterthoughts on Material Civilization and Capitalism.* Trans. Patricia M. Ranum. Baltimore: Johns Hopkins University Press, 1977.

Braunreuther, K[urt]. "Die Bedeutung der physiokratischen Bewegung in Deutschland in der zweiten Hälfte des 18. Jahrhunderts." Diss., Humboldt-Universität zu Berlin, 1955.

Briefs, Goetz A. "The Economic Philosophy of Romanticism." *Journal of the History of Ideas* 2 (1941): 279–300.

Brockhagen, Dörte. "Adelbert von Chamisso." *Literatur in der sozialen Bewegung: Aufsätze und Forschungsberichte zum 19. Jahrhundert.* Ed. Alberto Martino. Tübingen: Niemeyer, 1977. 373–423.

Brown, Jane K. *Goethe's* Faust: *The German Tragedy.* Ithaca, NY: Cornell University Press, 1986.

———. "The Real Mystery in Droste-Hülshoff's *Die Judenbuche.*" *Modern Language Review* 73 (1978): 835–46.

Brown, Jane K., Meredith Lee, and Thomas P. Saine, eds. *Interpreting Goethe's* Faust *Today.* Columbia, SC: Camden House, 1994.

Bürger, Peter. *Theorie der Avantgarde.* Frankfurt am Main: Suhrkamp, 1974.

Burwick, Frederick. *Mimesis and Its Romantic Reflections.* University Park, PA: Penn State University Press, 2001.

Büsch, Johann Georg. *Abhandlung von dem Geldsumlauf in anhaltender Rücksicht auf die Staatswirthschaft und Handlung.* 2 vols. Hamburg: Carl Ernst Bohn, 1780.

Butler, Colin. "Hobson's Choice: A Note on *Peter Schlemihl.*" *Monatshefte* 69 (1977): 5–16.

Chamisso, Adelbert von. "Fortunati Glückseckel und Wunschhütlein: Ein Spiel." Chamisso, *Sämtliche Werke in zwei Bänden* 1: 603–58.

———. *Peter Schlemihl.* Trans. Sir John Bowring. Illus. George Cruickshank. 1824. 3rd ed. London: R. Hardwicke, 1861.

———. *Peter Schlemihl.* Trans. Sir John Bowring. Illus. John Gincano. Philadelphia: D. McKay, 1929.

———. *Peter Schlemihls wunderbare* [sic] *Geschichte.* Illus. Adolf von Menzel. Berlin: Deutsche Buch-Gemeinschaft, n.d.

———. *Peter Schlemihls wundersame Geschichte.* Chamisso, *Sämtliche Werke in zwei Bänden* 2: 15–79.

———. *Peter Schlemihls wundersame Geschichte: Mit Farbholzschnitten von Ernst Ludwig Kirchner.* Ed. Werner Feudel. Leipzig: Reclam, 1980.

———. *Sämtliche Werke in zwei Bänden.* Ed. Werner Feudel and Christel Laufer. 2 vols. Munich: Hanser, 1982.

———. *Werke.* Ed. Julius Eduard Hitzig. 3rd ed. 6 vols. Leipzig: Weidmann, 1852.

Chase, Jefferson S. "Part of the Story: The Significance of the Jews in Annette von Droste-Hülshoff's *Die Judenbuche.*" *Deutsche Vierteljahrsschrift für Literaturwissenschaft und Geistesgeschichte* 71 (1997): 127–45.

Cohn, Hilde D. "Symbole in Adalbert Stifters *Studien* und *Bunten Steinen*." *Monatshefte* 33 (1941): 241–64.

Cottrell, Alan P. "The Significance of the Name 'Johannes' in *Die Judenbuche*." *Seminar* 6 (1970): 207–15.

Courtemanche, Eleanor. "Invisible Hands and Visionary Narrators: Why the Free Market Is Like a Novel." *Metaphors of Economy*. Ed. Nicole Bracker and Stefan Herbrechter. Amsterdam: Rodopi, 2005. 69–78.

Dascal, Marcelo. "Language and Money." *Leibniz: Language, Signs, and Thought*. Amsterdam: J. Benjamins, 1987. 1–29.

Derrida, Jacques. "Economimesis." *Diacritics* 11.2 (1981): 3–25.

———. *Specters of Marx: The State of the Debt, the Work of Mourning, and the New International*. Trans. Peggy Kamuf. New York: Routledge, 1994.

Diamond, Jared. *Collapse: How Societies Choose to Fail or Succeed*. New York: Viking, 2005.

Dick, Ernst S. "Schlag, schlagen, erschlagen: Zur Wort- und Begriffssymbolik der *Judenbuche*." *Gedenkschrift für Jost Trier*. Ed. Hartmut Beckers and Hans Schwarz. Cologne: Böhlau, 1975. 261–85.

Doerr, Karin. "The Specter of Anti-Semitism in and around Annette von Droste-Hülshoff's *Judenbuche*." *German Studies Review* 17 (1994): 447–71.

Dohm, Christian Wilhelm von. *Kurze Darstellung des physiokratischen Systems*. Cassel, 1778.

———. "Über das physiokratische System." *Deutsches Museum* 3 (Oct. 1778): 289–324.

Donahue, William Collins. "'Ist er kein Jude, so verdiente er einer zu sein': Droste-Hülshoff's *Die Judenbuche* and Religious Anti-Semitism." *German Quarterly* 72 (1999): 44–73.

Doppler, Alfred. "Schrecklich schöne Welt? Stifters fragwürdige Analogie von Natur- und Sittengesetz." *Acta Austriaca-Belgica. Adalbert Stifters schrecklich schöne Welt: Beiträge des internationalen Kolloquiums zur Adalbert Stifter-Ausstellung (Universität Antwerpen 1993)*. Ed. Roland Duhamel, Johann Lachinger, Clemens Ruthner, and Petra Göllner. Linz: Adalbert-Stifter-Institut des Landes Oberösterreich, 1994. 9–15.

Droste-Hülshoff, Annette von. *Historisch-kritische Ausgabe: Werke, Briefwechsel*. 10 vols. Ed. Winfried Woesler. Tübingen: Niemeyer, 1978–2000.

———. *The Jews' Beech. Eight German Novellas*. Trans. Michael Fleming. Oxford: Oxford University Press, 1997. 83–127.

———. *Die Judenbuche: Ein Sittengemälde aus dem gebirgigten Westphalen. Prosa, Text*. Vol. 5.1 of the *Historisch-kritische Ausgabe*. Ed. Winfried Woesler. Tübingen: Niemeyer, 1978. 1–42.

Dye, Robert Ellis. "The Easter Cantata and the Idea of Mediation in Goethe's *Faust*." *PMLA* 92 (1977): 963–76.

Eichendorff, Joseph von. *Geschichte der poetischen Literatur Deutschlands*. Vol. 11 of *Sämtliche Werke: Historisch-kritische Ausgabe*. Ed. Wolfram Mauser. Regensburg: Habbel, 1970.

Egerer, Franz, and Adolf Raschner. Einleitung. Stifter, *Sämmtliche Werke* 5: vii–xcv.

Emminghaus, A. "Carl Friederichs von Baden physiokratische Verbindungen, Bestrebungen und Versuche: Ein Beitrag zur Geschichte des Physiokratismus." *Jahrbücher für Nationalökonomie und Statistik* 19 (1872): 1–63.

Emrich, Wilhelm. "Das Rätsel der *Faust-II*-Dichtung." *Aufsätze zu Goethes* Faust II. Ed. Werner Keller. Wege der Forschung, Bd. 445. Darmstadt: Wissenschaftliche Buchgesellschaft, 1992. 26–54.

Esselborn, Hans. "Erschriebene Individualität und Karriere in der Autobiographie des 18. Jahrhunderts." *Wirkendes Wort* 46 (1996): 193–210.

Esslin, Martin. "Goethe's *Faust*: Pre-Modern, Post-Modern, Proto-Postmodern." Brown, Lee, and Saine 219–27.

"Etwas über das Steuerwesen und die physiokratischen Grundsätze, die Einrichtung desselben betreffend." *Auserlesene Abhandlungen über Gegenstände der Policey, der Finanzen und der Ökonomie gezogen aus den Jahrgängen des* Hannoverischen Magazins. Ed. E. L. M. Rathlef. 3 vols. Hannover: Helwingsche Buchhandlung, 1786–88. 3: 216–65.

Feuerbach, Ludwig. *Das Wesen des Christentums*. Ed. Karl Löwith. Stuttgart: Reclam, 1969.

Fichte, Johann Gottlieb. *Der geschlossene Handelsstaat*. Fichte, *Sämmtliche Werke* 3: 387–513.

———. *Grundlage der gesammten Wissenschaftslehre*. Fichte, *Sämmtliche Werke* 1: 83–328.

———. *Die Grundzüge des gegenwärtigen Zeitalters*. Fichte, *Sämmtliche Werke* 7: 1–256.

———. *Reden an die deutsche Nation*. Fichte, *Sämmtliche Werke* 7: 257–499.

———. Rev. of Kant's *Zum ewigen Frieden*. Fichte, *Sämmtliche Werke* 8: 427–36.

———. *Sämmtliche Werke*. Ed. Immanuel Hermann Fichte. 11 vols. 1845–46. Berlin: De Gruyter, 1971.

———. *Über den Begriff der Wissenschaftslehre oder der sogenannten Philosophie*. Fichte, *Sämmtliche Werke* 1: 27–81.

———. "Von der Sprachfähigkeit und dem Ursprunge der Sprache." Fichte, *Sämmtliche Werke* 8: 301–41.

Fiederer, Margit. *Geld und Besitz im bürgerlichen Trauerspiel*. Würzburg: Königshausen & Neumann, 2002.

Fink, Gonthier-Louis. "*Peter Schlemihl* et la tradition du conte romantique." *Recherches Germaniques* 12 (1982): 24–54.

Flores, Ralph. "The Lost Shadow of Peter Schlemihl." *German Quarterly* 47 (1974): 567–84.

Foucault, Michel. *The Order of Things: An Archaeology of the Human Sciences*. New York: Vintage-Random House, 1970.

Fox-Genovese, Elizabeth. *The Origins of Physiocracy: Economic Revolution and Social Order in Eighteenth-Century France*. Ithaca, NY: Cornell University Press, 1976.

François Quesnay et la physiocratie. Paris: Institut National D'Études Démographiques, 1958.

Frank, Manfred. *Was ist Neostrukturalismus?* Frankfurt am Main: Suhrkamp, 1983.

Freud, Sigmund. *Das Unbehagen in der Kultur. Gesammelte Werke*. Ed. Anna Freud. 18 vols. London: Imago, 1940–87. 14: 417–506.

Freund, Winfried. *Chamisso*, Peter Schlemihl: *Geld und Geist*. Paderborn: Schöningh, 1980.

———. "Eine Novelle vom Töten." *Annette von Droste-Hülshoff: Was bleibt*. Stuttgart: Kohlhammer, 1997. 11–32.

Fricke, Hannes. "Verschleierung der Struktur und Auflösung der Person: Nochmals zu Annette von Droste-Hülshoffs *Judenbuche*." *Colloquia Germanica* 32 (1999): 309–24.

Friedrich, Karl, of Baden. "Kurzer Abriß von den Grundsätzen der politischen Ökonomie." *Archiv für den Menschen und Bürger* 4 (1782): 234–63.

Funk, Martin Joseph. "Der Kampf der merkantilischen mit der physiokratischen Doktrin in der Pfalz." *Neue Heidelberger Jahrbücher* 18 (1914): 103–200.

Fürstenau, Karl Gottfried. *Versuch einer Apologie des physiokratischen Systems*. Cassel: J. J. Cramer, 1779.

Gadamer, Hans-Georg. *Wahrheit und Methode: Grundzüge einer philosophischen Hermeneutik*. 4th ed. Tübingen: Mohr, 1975.

Gaettens, Richard. *Inflationen: Das Drama der Geldentwertungen vom Altertum bis zur Gegenwart*. Munich: Richard Pflaum, 1955.

Gaier, Ulrich. "Dialektik der Vorstellungsarten als Prinzip in Goethes *Faust*." Brown, Lee, and Saine 158–71.

———. "Ökonomische Lesart." *Goethe: Faust-Dichtungen*. 3 vols. Stuttgart: Reclam, 1999–2003. 3: 581–638.

Gearey, John. *Goethe's Other* Faust: *The Drama, Part II*. Toronto: University of Toronto Press, 1992.

"Gedanken über das physiokratische System, bey Gelegenheit der Abhandlung des Herrn Hauptmann Mauvillons von der öffentlichen und Privatüppigkeit." *Gelehrte Beyträge zu den Braunschweigischen Zeitungen* 25–29 (1779). Rpt. in Mauvillon, *Physiokratische Briefe* 380–400.

Gedike, Friedrich. "Verba valent sicut numi, oder von der Wortmünze." *Berlinische Monatsschrift* 20 (1789): 253–75.

George, Stefan. *Das neue Reich*. Vol. 9 of *Gesamt-Ausgabe der Werke: Endgültige Fassung*. Berlin: Georg Bondi, 1928.

Gerloff, Wilhelm. *Geld und Gesellschaft: Versuch einer gesellschaftlichen Theorie des Geldes*. Frankfurt am Main: Klostermann, 1952.

Geulen, Eva. *Worthörig wider Willen: Darstellungsproblematik und Sprachreflexion in der Prosa Adalbert Stifters*. Munich: Iudicum Verlag, 1992.

Gille, Klaus F. "Der Schatten des Peter Schlemihl." *Der Deutschunterricht* 39.1 (Feb. 1987): 74–83.

Glaser, Horst Albert. *Die Restauration des Schönen: Stifters* Nachsommer. Stuttgart: Metzler, 1965.

Glasner, David. "An Evolutionary Theory of the State Monopoly Over Money." *Money and the Nation State: The Financial Revolution, Government and the World Monetary System*. Ed. Kevin Dowd and Richard H. Timberlake, Jr. New Brunswick: Transaction, 1998. 21–45.

Godwin-Jones, Robert. "Where the Devil Leads: Peasant Superstition in George Sand's *Petite Fadette* and Droste-Hülshoff's *Judenbuche*." *Neohelicon* 10 (1983): 221–38.

Goethe, Johann Wolfgang von. *Amtliche Schriften I* and *Amtliche Schriften II*. Ed. Rein-
hard Kluge, Irmtraut Schmid, and Gerhard Schmid. 2 vols. Vols. 26 and 27 of
Sämtliche Werke, Briefe, Tagebücher und Gespräche [Frankfurter Ausgabe]. Ed.
Friedrich Apel et al. Frankfurt am Main: Deutscher Klassiker Verlag, 1998–99.

———. *Faust I and II*. Ed. and trans. Stuart Atkins. Vol. 2 of *Goethe's Collected Works
in Twelve Volumes*. Princeton, NJ: Princeton University Press, 1994.

———. *Faust: Der Tragödie erster und zweiter Teil*. Ed. Erich Trunz. Vol. 3 of *Goethes
Werke* [Hamburger Ausgabe]. Munich: Beck, 1978.

———. *Gedenkausgabe der Werke, Briefe und Gespräche* [Artemis Ausgabe]. Ed. Ernst
Beutler. 26 vols. Zürich: Artemis, 1948–64.

———. *Goethes Briefe* [Hamburger Ausgabe Briefe]. Ed. Karl Robert Mandelkow. 4 vols.
Hamburg: Wegner, 1967.

———. *Goethes Werke* [Hamburger Ausgabe]. 8th, rev. ed. 14 vols. Munich: Beck, 1978.

Goux, Jean-Joseph. *Symbolic Economies: After Marx and Freud*. Trans. Jennifer Curtiss
Gage. Ithaca, NY: Cornell University Press, 1990.

Graevenitz, Gerhard von. "Innerlichkeit und Öffentlichkeit: Aspekte deutscher 'bürger-
licher' Literatur im frühen 18. Jahrhundert." *18. Jahrhundert* Sonderheft. *Deutsche
Vierteljahrsschrift für Literaturwissenschaft und Geistesgeschichte* 49 (1975): 1–82.

Gray, Richard T. *About Face: German Physiognomic Thought from Lavater to Auschwitz*.
Detroit, MI: Wayne State University Press, 2004.

———. "The Transcendence of the Body in the Transparency of Its En-Signment: Johann
Caspar Lavater's Physiognomical Surface Hermeneutics." *Lessing Yearbook* 23 (1991):
127–48.

Grün, Klaus-Jürgen. *Geist und Geld: Die zweite Natur des Menschen*. Paderborn: Mentis,
2002.

Gudeman, Stephen. *Economics as Culture: Models and Metaphors of Livelihood*. London:
Routledge & Kegan Paul, 1986.

Gülich, Gustav von. *Geschichtliche Darstellung des Handels, der Gewerbe und des Acker-
baus*. 2 vols. Jena: Frommann, 1830.

Günther, Hans R. G. *Jung-Stilling: Ein Beitrag zur Psychologie des Pietismus*. 2nd ed.
Munich: Reinhardt, 1948.

Güntzberg, Benedikt. *Die Gesellschafts- und Staatslehre der Physiokraten*. Staats- und
völkerrechtliche Abhandlungen, Reihe 6, Bd. 3. Leipzig: Duncker & Humblot, 1907.

Habermas, Jürgen. *Staatsbürgerschaft und nationale Identität: Überlegungen zur europäi-
schen Zukunft*. St. Gallen: Erker, 1991.

———. "Yet Again German Identity—A Unified Nation of Angry DM-Burghers?" *New
German Critique* 52 (Winter 1991): 84–101.

Hamacher, Werner. "Faust, Geld." *Athenäum: Jahrbuch für Romantik* 4 (1994): 131–87.

Hamann, Johann Georg. *Briefwechsel*. Ed. Walther Ziesemer and Arthur Henkel. 7 vols.
Wiesbaden: Insel, 1955–79.

———. "Metakritik über den Purismum der Vernunft." *Schriften zur Sprache*. Ed. Josef
Simon. Frankfurt am Main: Suhrkamp, 1967. 219–27.

———. *Sokratische Denkwürdigkeiten. Sturm und Drang: Kritische Schriften*. Ed. Erich
Loewenthal. 3rd ed. Heidelberg: Lambert Schneider, 1972. 63–84.

―――. "Vermischte Anmerkungen über die Wortstellung in der französischen Sprache." *Schriften zur Sprache*. Ed. Josef Simon. Frankfurt am Main: Suhrkamp, 1967. 95–104.

Hamerow, Theodore S. *Restoration, Revolution, Reaction: Economics and Politics in Germany, 1815–1871*. Princeton, NJ: Princeton University Press, 1958.

Hankamer, Paul. "Adalbert Stifters *Bergkristall*." *Aus Theologie und Philosophie. Festschrift für Fritz Tillmann zu seinem 75. Geburtstag*. Ed. Theodor Steinbüchel and Theodor Müncker. Düsseldorf: Patmos, 1950. 84–99.

Harada, Tetsushi. *Politische Ökonomie des Idealismus und der Romantik: Korporatismus von Fichte, Müller und Hegel*. Berlin: Duncker & Humblot, 1989.

Häufle, Heinrich. *Aufklärung und Ökonomie: Zur Position der Physiokraten im siècle des Lumières*. Münchner Romantische Arbeiten, Heft 48. Munich: Fink, 1978.

Hayek, F. A. *Monetary Nationalism and International Stability*. 1937. New York: August M. Kelley, 1971.

Hegel, Georg Wilhelm Friedrich. *Theorie-Werkausgabe*. Ed. Eva Moldenhauer and Karl Markus Michel. 21 vols. Frankfurt am Main: Suhrkamp, 1970.

Heidegger, Martin. "Adalbert Stifters 'Eisgeschichte.'" *Wirkendes Wort: Mit Beiträgen von Elisabeth Brock-Sulzer, Martin Heidegger, Otto Walter, Martin Walser*. Zurich: Schweizerische Bibliophilen-Gesellschaft, 1964. 23–48.

―――. *Sein und Zeit*. 15th ed. Tübingen: Niemeyer, 1979.

Hein, Jürgen. "Adalbert Stifter und die 'Dorfgeschichte' des 19. Jahrhunderts." *VASILO* 21 (1972): 23–31.

Heine, Heinrich. *Ideen: Das Buch Le Grand. Sämtliche Schriften*. Ed. Klaus Briegleb. 6 vols. Munich: Hanser, 1969–75. 2: 245–308.

Heinemann, Klaus. *Grundzüge einer Soziologie des Geldes*. Stuttgart: Enke, 1969.

Helfer, Martha B. "'Wer wagt es, eitlen Blutes Drang zu messen?': Reading Blood in Annette von Droste-Hülshoff's *Die Judenbuche*." *German Quarterly* 71 (1998): 228–53.

Henn-Schmölders, Claudia. "Sprache und Geld oder 'Vom Gespräch': Über Adam Müller." *Jahrbuch der deutschen Schillergesellschaft* 21 (1977): 327–51.

Hensmann, Folkert. *Staat und Absolutismus im Denken der Physiokraten: Ein Beitrag zur physiokratischen Staatsauffassung von Quesnay bis Turgot*. Frankfurt am Main: Haag + Herchen, 1976.

Herder, Johann Gottfried. *Abhandlung über den Ursprung der Sprache. Sturm und Drang: Kritische Schriften*. Ed. Erich Loewenthal. 3rd ed. Heidelberg: Lambert Schneider, 1972. 399–506.

―――. *Journal meiner Reise im Jahr 1769. Sämtliche Werke*. Ed Bernhard Suphan. 33 vols. Berlin: Weidmann, 1877–1913. 4: 343–461.

―――. *Über die neuere deutsche Literatur: Fragmente*. Ed. Regine Otto. Berlin: Aufbau, 1985.

Hess, Moses. "Über das Geldwesen." *Philosophische und sozialistische Schriften 1837–1850*. Ed. Auguste Cornu and Wolfgang Mönke. Berlin: Akademie Verlag, 1961. 329–48.

Higgs, Henry. *The Physiocrats: Six Lectures on the French Économistes of the 18th Century*. 1897. Hamden, CT: Archon Books, 1963.

Hirschman, Albert O. *The Passions and the Interests: Political Arguments for Capitalism Before Its Triumph*. Twentieth Anniversary Edition. Princeton, NJ: Princeton University Press, 1997.

Hirst, Francis W. *The Paper Moneys of Europe: Their Moral and Economic Significance*. Boston: Houghton Mifflin, 1922.

Hirzel, Martin. *Lebensgeschichte als Verkündigung: Johann Heinrich Jung-Stilling, Ami Bost, Johann Arnold Kanne*. Göttingen: Vandenhoeck & Ruprecht, 1998.

Hoffmann, Ernst Fedor. "Spiegelbild und Schatten: Zur Behandlung ähnlicher Motive bei Hoffmann und Chamisso." *Lebendige Form: Interpretationen zur deutschen Literatur; Festschrift für Heinrich Henel*. Ed. Jeffrey L. Sammons and Ernst Schürer. Munich: Fink, 1970. 167–88.

Höller, Hans. "Die kapitalistische Gesellschaft aus der Kirchturmperspektive? Anmerkungen zu Stifters Ästhetik." *Germanica Wratistawiensia* 32 (1978): 37–51.

Homann, Karl. "Zum Begriff der Einbildungskraft nach Kant." *Archiv für Begriffsgeschichte* 14 (1970): 266–302.

Hörisch, Jochen. *Heads or Tails: The Poetics of Money*. Trans. Amy Horning Marschall. Detroit, MI: Wayne State University Press, 2000.

———. "Herrscherwort, Geld und geltende Sätze: Adornos Aktualisierung der Frühromantik und ihre Affinität zur poststrukturalistischen Kritik des Subjekts." *Materialien zur ästhetischen Theorie Theodor W. Adornos*. Ed. Burkhardt Lindner and W. Martin Lüdke. Frankfurt am Main: Suhrkamp, 1980. 397–414.

Huge, Walter. *Erläuterungen und Dokumente: Annette von Droste-Hülshoff*, Die Judenbuche. Universal-Bibliothek 8145. Stuttgart: Reclam, 1979.

———. "*Die Judenbuche* als Kriminalgeschichte: Das Problem von Erkenntnis und Urteil im Kriminalschema." *Judenbuche* Sonderheft. *Zeitschrift für deutsche Philologie* 99 (1980): 49–70.

Hull, Isabel. *Sexuality, State, and Civil Society in Germany*. Ithaca, NY: Cornell University Press, 1996.

Hume, David. "Of Money." *The Philosophical Works*. 4 vols. Boston: Little, Brown, and Co., 1854. 3: 309–23.

Huszai, Villö Dorothea. "'Denken Sie sich, der Mergel ist unschuldig an dem Morde': Zu Droste-Hülshoffs Novelle *Die Judenbuche*." *Zeitschrift für deutsche Philologie* 116 (1997): 481–99.

Immerwahr, Raymond. "The Peasant Wedding as Dramatic Climax of *Die Judenbuche*." *Momentum Dramaticum: Festschrift für Eckehard Catholy*. Ed. Linda Dietrick and David G. John. Waterloo, ON: University of Waterloo Press, 1990. 321–36.

Immler, Hans. *Natur in der ökonomischen Theorie*. Opladen: Westdeutscher Verlag, 1985.

Irwin, Douglas A. *Against the Tide: An Intellectual History of Free Trade*. Princeton, NJ: Princeton University Press, 1996.

[Iselin, Isaak]. "Entwurf der *Ephemeriden der Menschheit*." *Ephemeriden der Menschheit* 1.1 (1776): 5–15.

———. "Fortsetzung des Entwurfs der *Ephemeriden der Menschheit*." *Ephemeriden der Menschheit* 2.1 (1777): 3–14.

———. "Menschenfreundlicher Catechismus." *Ephemeriden der Menschheit* 1.1 (1776):

15–23 [Erstes Gespräch], 113–17 [Zweytes Gespräch], 221–27 [Drittes Gespräch]; 1.2 (1776): 3–12 [Viertes Gespräch], 111–21 [Fünftes Gespräch], 223–30 [Sechstes Gespräch].

———. *Träume eines Menschenfreundes.* 2 vols. Basel: Johannes Schweighauser, 1776.

———. "Über die wirthschaftliche Organisation der Gesellschaft, oder Versuch einer Erläuterung der wirthschaftlichen Tafel." *Ephemeriden der Menschheit* 5 (Jan. 1780): 3–34.

———. *Versuch über die gesellige Ordnung.* Basel: Johann Schweighauser, 1772.

Jackson, Kevin, ed. *The Oxford Book of Money.* Oxford: Oxford University Press, 1995.

Jaeger, Michael. *Fausts Kolonie: Goethes kritische Phänomenologie der Moderne.* Würzburg: Königshausen & Neumann, 2004.

Jakobson, Roman. "The Metaphoric and Metonymic Poles." *Fundamentals of Language.* The Hague: Mouton, 1956. 76–82.

Jameson, Fredric. "Third-World Literature in the Era of Multinational Capitalism." *Social Text* 15 (Autumn 1986): 65–88.

Jauss, Hans-Robert. "Literaturgeschichte als Provokation der Literaturwissenschaft." *Literaturgeschichte als Provokation.* Frankfurt am Main: Suhrkamp, 1970. 144–207.

Jens, Walter. "Reaktionäre Beredsamkeit: Adam Müller." *Von deutscher Rede.* Munich: Piper, 1983. 79–87.

Jung-Stilling, Johann Heinrich. *Aus Wirtschaft und Gesellschaft: Ausgewählte kleinere Abhandlungen.* Ed. Gerhard Merk. Siegen: Jung-Stilling-Gesellschaft, 1992.

———. *Briefe.* Ed. Gerhard Schwinge. Giessen: Brunnen Verlag, 2002.

———. *Briefe an Verwandte, Freunde und Fremde aus den Jahren 1787–1816.* Ed. Hans W. Panthel. Hildesheim: Gerstenberg, 1978.

———. *Briefe eines reisenden Schweizers über die Einrichtung der Pfälzischen Fruchtmärkte.* Ed. Anneliese Wittmann. Siegen: Jung-Stilling-Gesellschaft, 1993.

———. *Gemeinnütziges Lehrbuch der Handlungswissenschaft für alle Klassen von Kaufleuten und Handlungsstudierenden.* 2nd ed. 1799. Cologne: Bachem, 1995.

———. *Die Grundlehre der Staatswirthschaft, ein Elementarbuch für Regentensöhne.* Marburg: Akademische Buchhandlung, 1792.

———. *Jubelrede über den Geist der Staatswirtschaft.* Mannheim: Hof-Buchhandlung, 1787.

———. *Lebensgeschichte.* Ed. Gustav Adolf Benrath. 3rd ed. Darmstadt: Wissenschaftliche Buchgesellschaft, 1992.

———. *Lehrbuch der Staats-Polizey-Wissenschaft.* Leipzig: Weidmann, 1788.

———. "Leitlinien erfolgreicher Wohlstandsmehrung." *Sachgerechtes Wirtschaften: Sechs Vorlesungen.* Ed. Gerhard Merk. Berlin: Duncker & Humblot, 1988. 42–62.

———. "Öffentlicher Anschlag bei dem Antritte des Lehrstuhles der praktischen Kameralwissenschaften auf der Kameral Hohen Schule zu Lautern." *Wirtschaftslehre und Landeswohlstand: Sechs akademische Festreden.* Ed. Gerhard Merk. Berlin: Duncker & Humblot, 1988. 15–26.

———. *Sämmtliche Schriften.* 14 vols. Stuttgart: Scheible, 1835–38.

———. *Versuch einer Grundlehre sämmtlicher Kameralwissenschaften, zum Gebrauche der Vorlesungen auf der Kurpfälzischen Kameral Hohenschule zu Lautern.* Lautern: Verlag der Gesellschaft, 1779.

————. *Versuch eines Lehrbuchs der Landwirthschaft der ganzen bekannten Welt*. Leipzig: Weigand, 1783.

Kafka, Franz. *Nachgelassene Schriften und Fragmente II*. Ed. Jost Schillemeit. Frankfurt am Main: S. Fischer, 1992.

Kahle, Werner. "Goethes Verhältnis zum Saint-Simonismus im Spiegel seiner Altersbriefe." *Goethe-Jahrbuch* 89 (1972): 81–85.

Kaiser, Gerhard. *Ist der Mensch zu retten? Vision und Kritik der Moderne in Goethes Faust*. Freiburg: Rombach, 1994.

Kant, Immanuel. *Immanuel Kant: Werkausgabe*. Ed. Wilhelm Weischädel. 12 vols. Frankfurt am Main: Suhrkamp, 1968.

————. *Kritik der reinen Vernunft*. Vol. 3 of Kant, *Immanuel Kant: Werkausgabe*.

————. *Kritik der Urteilskraft*. Vol. 9 of Kant, *Immanuel Kant: Werkausgabe*.

————. *Zum ewigen Frieden: Ein politischer Entwurf*. Kant, *Immanuel Kant: Werkausgabe* 11: 193–251.

Kauf, Robert. "Interpretation und 'Relevanz': Am Beispiel von *Ritter Gluck, Bergkristall*, und *Der blonde Eckbert*." *Die Unterrichtspraxis* 5 (1972): 56–65.

Keller, G. *Zur Geschichte des Physiokratismus: Quesnay, Gournay, Turgot*. Göttingen: Dieterische Buchhandlung, 1847.

Kilcher, Andreas B. "Das magische Gesetz der hebräischen Sprache: Drostes *Judenbuche* und der spätromantische Diskurs über die jüdische Magie." *Zeitschrift für deutsche Philologie* 118 (1999): 234–65.

Kiss, Endre. "Anmerkungen zu Fichtes Begriff der Nation." *Archiv für Geschichte der Philosophie* 77 (1995): 189–96.

Klippel, Diethelm. "Der Einfluß der Physiokraten auf die Entwicklung der liberalen politischen Theorie in Deutschland." *Der Staat* 23 (1984): 205–26.

Kluge, Alexander. *Die Lücke, die der Teufel läßt: Im Umfeld des neuen Jahrhunderts*. Frankfurt am Main: Suhrkamp, 2003.

Knies, Carl, ed. *Carl Friedrichs von Baden brieflicher Verkehr mit Mirabeau und DuPont*. 2 vols. Heidelberg: Winter, 1872.

Koehler, Benedikt. *Ästhetik der Politik: Adam Müller und die politische Romantik*. Stuttgart: Klett-Cotta, 1980.

Koepnick, Lutz P. "Simulating Simulation: Art and Modernity in *Faust II*." *Seminar* 34 (1998): 1–25.

Kohn, Hans. "The Paradox of Fichte's Nationalism." *Journal of the History of Ideas* 10 (1949): 319–43.

Kontje, Todd. "Private Life in the Public Sphere: Heinrich Jung-Stilling's *Lebensgeschichte*." *Colloquia Germanica* 21 (1988): 275–87.

Kraft, Herbert. "Annette von Droste-Hülshoffs *Judenbuche*." *AUMLA* 69 (1988): 78–87.

Krättli, Anton. *Adam Heinrich Müller: Vermittelnde Kritik*. Zurich: Artemis, 1968.

Krause, Werner. "Fichtes ökonomische Anschauungen im *Geschlossenen Handelsstaat*." *Wissen und Gewissen: Beiträge zum 200. Geburtstag Johann Gottlieb Fichtes 1762–1814*. Ed. Manfred Buhr. Berlin: Akademie, 1962. 224–40.

Krautkrämer, Ursula. *Staat und Erziehung: Begründung öffentlicher Erziehung bei Humboldt, Kant, Fichte, Hegel und Schleiermacher*. Munich: Berchmann, 1979.

Kreis, Rudolf. "Annette von Droste-Hülshoffs *Judenbuche*: Versuch einer sozialkritischen Betrachtung." *Projekt Deutschunterricht 6: Kritischer Literaturunterricht—Dichtung und Politik.* Ed. Heinz Ide and Bodo Lecke. Stuttgart: Metzler, 1974. 93–126.

Kreutzer, Leo. "Fiesling Faust und sein Ghostwriter Goethe: Etwas über das Verhältnis von Natur und Ökonomie in *Faust II*." *Welfengarten* 2 (1992): 22–31.

Kristeva, Julia. *Revolution in Poetic Language.* Trans. Margaret Waller. New York: Columbia University Press, 1984.

Kruse, Jens. *Der Tanz der Zeichen: Poetische Struktur und Geschichte in Goethes* Faust II. Königstein/Taunus: Anton Hain, 1985.

Krüsselberg, Hans-Günter. "Jung-Stillings Lehre der politischen Ökonomie." *Jung-Stillings Welt: Das Lebenswerk eines Universalgelehrten in interdisziplinären Perspektiven.* Ed. Hans-Günter Krüsselberg and Wolfgang Lück. Krefeld: Marchal & Mathenbacher, 1992. 72–109.

Kuczynski, Jürgen. "Zur Theorie der Physiokraten." *Grundpositionen der französischen Aufklärung.* Ed. Werner Krauss and Hans Mayer. Neue Beiträge zur Literaturwissenschaft, Bd. 1. Berlin: Rütten & Loening, 1955. 27–54.

Küpper, Peter. "Literatur und Langeweile." *Adalbert Stifter: Studien und Interpretationen.* Ed. Lothar Stiehm. Heidelberg: Lothar Stiehm Verlag, 1968. 178–88.

Kuzniar, Alice A. "'Spurlos . . . verschwunden': *Peter Schlemihl* und sein Schatten als der verschobene Signifikant." *Aurora* 45 (1985): 189–204.

Lahnstein, Peter. *Adelbert von Chamisso: Der Preuße aus Frankreich.* Munich: List, 1984.

Laine, Barry. "By Water and by Fire: The Thales-Anaxagoras Debate in Goethe's *Faust*." *Germanic Review* 50 (1975): 99–110.

Lambert, Johann Heinrich. *Neues Organon oder Gedanken über die Erforschung und Beziehung des Wahren und dessen Unterscheidung vom Irrthum und Schein.* 2 vols. 1764. Hildesheim: Olms, 1965.

Landes, David S. "The Jewish Merchant: Typology and Stereotypology in Germany." *Leo Baeck Institute Yearbook* 19 (1974): 11–23.

Lauterwasser, Walter. "Jung-Stilling als Erzähler." *Jung-Stilling: Arzt—Kameralist—Schriftsteller zwischen Aufklärung und Erweckung.* Karlsruhe: Badische Landesbibliothek, 1990. 81–111.

Lavater, Johann Caspar. *Aussichten in die Ewigkeit.* 4 vols. Zurich: Orell and Geßner, 1768–78.

Law, John. *Money and Trade Considered with a Proposal for Supplying the Nation with Money.* 1705. New York: Augustus M. Kelley, 1966.

Leibniz, Gottfried Wilhelm. *Fragmente zur Logik.* Ed. and trans. Franz Schmidt. Berlin: Akademie-Verlag, 1960.

——. *Unvorgreifliche Gedanken, betreffend die Ausübung und Verbesserung der teutschen Sprache. Hauptschriften zur Grundlegung der Philosophie.* Ed. Ernst Cassirer. 2 vols. Hamburg: Meiner, 1966. 2: 519–55.

Leiser, Wolfgang. "Jung-Stilling und Karl Friedrich von Baden." *Alemannisches Jahrbuch* 14 (1970): 273–79.

Lessing, Gotthold Ephraim. *Nathan der Weise. Gesammelte Werke.* Ed. Paul Rilla. 10 vols. Berlin: Aufbau, 1954–58. 2: 319–481.

Locke, John. *An Essay Concerning Human Understanding*. Ed. Maurice Cranston. London: Collier Books, 1965.

Loeb, Ernst. "Symbol und Wirklichkeit des Schattens in Chamissos *Peter Schlemihl*." *Germanisch-Romanische Monatsschrift* 15 (1965): 398–408.

Lück, Wolfgang. *Johann Heinrich Jung-Stilling: Wirtschaftswissenschaftler, Arzt und Schriftsteller*. Marburg: Hitzeroth, 1990.

———. "Jung-Stilling als Wirtschaftswissenschaftler." *Jung-Stilling: Arzt—Kameralist—Schriftsteller zwischen Aufklärung und Erweckung*. Karlsruhe: Badische Landesbibliothek, 1990. 71–80.

Luhmann, Niklas. "Knappheit, Geld und die bürgerliche Gesellschaft." *Jahrbuch für Sozialwissenschaft* 23 (1972): 186–210.

———. *Soziale Systeme: Grundriß einer allgemeinen Theorie*. Frankfurt am Main: Suhrkamp, 1984.

———. *Die Wirtschaft der Gesellschaft*. Suhrkamp taschenbuch wissenschaft 1152. Frankfurt am Main: Suhrkamp, 1994.

Lukács, Georg. "*Faust*-Studien." *Goethe und seine Zeit*. Bern: Francke, 1947. 127–207.

Macpherson, C. B. *The Political Theory of Possessive Individualism: Hobbes to Locke*. Oxford: Oxford University Press, 1962.

Mahl, Bernd. *Goethes ökonomisches Wissen: Grundlagen zum Verständnis der ökonomischen Passagen im dichterischen Gesamtwerk und in den "Amtlichen Schriften."* Frankfurt am Main: Peter Lang, 1982.

Mann, Thomas. "Chamisso." *Gesammelte Werke*. 13 vols. Frankfurt am Main: Fischer, 1960. 9: 35–57.

Marquardt, Hans-Jochen. "Zur ästhetischen Theorie des deutschen Frühkonservitismus: Friedrich Schlegels und Adam Heinrich Müllers Wiener Vorlesungen von 1812." *Acta Germanica* 23 (1995): 21–39.

Marx, Karl. "Debatten über das Holzdiebstahlsgesetz." Marx and Engels 1: 109–47.

———. "Die deutsche Ideologie." *Die Frühschriften*. Ed. Siegfried Landshut. Stuttgart: Kröner, 1971. 339–485.

———. *Grundrisse der Kritik der politischen Ökonomie*. 2nd ed. Berlin: Dietz, 1974.

———. *Das Kapital: Kritik der politischen Ökonomie, vol. 1*. Vol. 23 of Marx and Engels.

———. "Ökonomisch-philosophische Manuskripte aus dem Jahr 1844." Marx and Engels, Ergänzungsband, Teil I, 465–588.

———. *Theorien über den Mehrwert: 1. Teil*. Vol. 26, pt. 1 of Marx and Engels.

———. "Zur Judenfrage." Marx and Engels 1: 347–77.

———. *Zur Kritik der politischen Ökonomie*. Marx and Engels 13: 3–160.

Marx, Karl, and Friedrich Engels. *Karl Marx/Friedrich Engels Werke*. Ed. Institut für Marxismus-Leninismus. 39 vols. Berlin: Dietz, 1956–77.

Mason, Eva. "Stifters *Bunte Steine*: Versuch einer Bestandsaufnahme." *Adalbert Stifter heute: Londoner Symposium 1983*. Ed. Johann Lachinger, Alexander Stillmark, and Martin Swales. Linz: Adalbert Stifter Institut, 1985. 75–85.

Mattenklott, Gerd. "'Auf den Füßen gehts nicht mehr, Drum gehn wir auf den Köpfen': Literarische Komplexität und der Komplex Ökonomie." *Das Argument* 99 (1976): 734–46.

Mauss, Marcel. *The Gift: The Form and Reason for Exchange in Archaic Societies.* New York: Norton, 1990.

Mauvillon, Jakob. *Physiokratische Briefe an den Herrn Professor Dohm, oder Vertheidigung und Erläuterung der wahren Staatswirthschaftlichen Gesetze die unter dem Namen des Physiokratischen Systems bekannt sind.* Braunschweig: Waisenhaus-Buchhandlung, 1780.

————, trans. *Untersuchung über die Natur und den Ursprung der Reichthümer.* By Anne Robert Jacques Turgot. Lemgo, 1775.

————. "Von der öffentlichen und privat Üppigkeit (Luxe) und den wahren Mitteln ihr zu steuern: nach den Grundsätzen der neuen französischen Physiokraten." *Sammlung von Aufsätzen über Gegenstände aus der Staatskunst, Staatswirthschaft und neuesten Staaten Geschichte.* 2 vols. Leipzig: Weygand, 1776–77. 2: 1–128.

McGlathery, James M. "Fear of Perdition in Droste-Hülshoff's *Judenbuche*." *Lebendige Form: Interpretationen zur deutschen Literatur. Festschrift für Heinrich E. K. Henel.* Ed. Jeffrey L. Sammons and Ernst Schürer. Munich: Fink, 1970. 229–44.

McLaughlin, Kevin. "The Coming of Paper: Aesthetic Value from Ruskin to Benjamin." *MLN* 114 (1999): 962–90.

————. *Writing in Parts: Imitation and Exchange in Nineteenth-Century Literature.* Stanford: Stanford University Press, 1995.

McLuhan, Marshall. *Understanding Media.* 1964. London: Routledge, 2000.

Meek, Ronald L. *The Economics of Physiocracy: Essays and Translations.* Cambridge, MA: Harvard University Press, 1963.

————. "The Interpretation of Physiocracy." Meek, *The Economics of Physiocracy* 364–98.

————. "Physiocracy and the Early Theories of Under-Consumption." Meek, *The Economics of Physiocracy* 313–44.

————. "The Physiocratic Concept of Profit." Meek, *The Economics of Physiocracy* 297–312.

————. "Problems of the *Tableau Economique*." Meek, *The Economics of Physiocracy* 265–96.

Meißner, Herbert. *Die Physiokraten als wirtschaftspolitische Wegbereiter der Französischen Revolution.* Sitzungsberichte der Akademie der Wissenschaften der DDR: Geisteswissenschaften, 1990, No. 1/G. Berlin: Akademie-Verlag, 1990.

Menninghaus, Winfried. "Die frühromantische Theorie von Zeichen und Metapher." *German Quarterly* 62 (1989): 48–58.

Merk, Gerhard. *Jung-Stilling: Ein Umriß seines Lebens.* Kreuztal: Wielandschmiede, 1989.

————, ed. *Jung-Stilling-Lexikon Wirtschaft.* Berlin: Duncker & Humblot, 1987.

Metscher, Thomas. "Faust und die bürgerliche Gesellschaft." *Weltheater und Geschichtsprozeß: Zu Goethes Faust.* Bremer Beiträge zur Literatur- und Ideengeschichte, Bd. 40. Frankfurt am Main: Peter Lang, 2003. 15–161.

Michelsen, Peter. "Der Rat des Narren: Die Staatsratszene in Goethes *Faust II*." *Jahrbuch des Freien Deutschen Hochstifts* (1996): 84–129.

Minton, Robert. *John Law: The Father of Paper Money.* New York: Association Press, 1975.

Mirabeau, Marquis de [Viktor Riqueti]. "Extract from *Rural Philosophy*." Meek, *The Economics of Physiocracy* 57–64.

Mommsen, Wolfgang. *Nation und Geschichte*. Munich: Piper, 1990.

Mooser, Josef. "'Furcht bewahrt das Holz': Holzdiebstahl und sozialer Konflikt in der ländlichen Gesellschaft 1800–1850 an westfälischen Beispielen." *Räuber, Volk und Obrigkeit: Studien zur Geschichte der Kriminalität in Deutschland seit dem 18. Jahrhundert*. Ed. Heinz Reif. Frankfurt am Main: Suhrkamp, 1984. 43–99.

Mörike, Eduard. *Maler Nolten: Novelle in zwei Teilen*. Ed. Wolfgang Vogelmann. Frankfurt am Main: Insel, 1979.

———. *Nolten the Painter*. Trans. Raleigh Whitinger. Rochester, NY: Camden House, 2005.

Moritz, Karl Phillip. *Annette von Droste-Hülshoff*, Die Judenbuche: *Sittengemälde und Kriminalnovelle*. Paderborn: Schöningh, 1980.

Motté, Magdalene. "Geld und Besitz in Stifters poetischem Werk." Diss., Technische Hochschule Aachen, 1969.

Muhlack, Ulrich. "Physiokratie und Absolutismus in Frankreich und Deutschland." *Zeitschrift für historische Forschung* 9 (1982): 15–46.

Müller, Adam. *Die Elemente der Staatskunst*. Ed. Jakob Baxa. 2 vols. Jena: Gustav Fischer, 1922.

———. *Kritische, ästhetische und philosophische Schriften*. Ed. Walter Schroeder and Werner Siebert. 2 vols. Neuwied: Luchterhand, 1967.

———. *Lebenszeugnisse*. Ed. Jakob Baxa. 2 vols. Munich: Schöningh, 1966.

———. *Die Lehre vom Gegensatz*. Müller, *Kritische, ästhetische und philosophische Schriften* 2: 193–248.

———. *Schriften zur Staatsphilosophie*. Ed. Rudolf Kohler. Munich: Theatiner, 1923.

———. "Über einen philosophischen Entwurf von Hrn Fichte, betitelt: *Der geschloßne Handelstaat* [sic]." *Neue Berlinische Monatsschrift* 6 (Dec. 1801): 436–58.

———. *Versuche einer neuen Theorie des Geldes*. Ed. Helene Lieser. 1816. Jena: Gustav Fischer, 1922.

———. "Vom Papiergelde." *Ausgewählte Abhandlungen*. Ed. Jakob Baxa. Jena: Gustav Fischer, 1921. 29–34.

———. *Vorlesungen über die deutsche Wissenschaft und Literatur*. Müller, *Kritische, ästhetische und philosophische Schriften* 1: 11–137.

———. *Zwölf Reden über die Beredsamkeit und deren Verfall in Deutschland*. Müller, *Kritische, ästhetische und philosophische Schriften* 1: 293–451.

Naumann, Ursula. *Adalbert Stifter*. Stuttgart: Metzler, 1979.

Neubauer, Wolfgang. "Zum Schatten-Problem bei Adelbert von Chamisso oder zur Nicht-Interpretierbarkeit von *Peter Schlemihls wundersame Geschichte*." *Literatur für Leser* 9 (1986): 24–34.

Neumann, Bernd. *Identität und Rollenzwang: Zur Theorie der Autobiographie*. Frankfurt am Main: Athenäum, 1970.

Neumarkt, Paul. "Chamisso's *Peter Schlemihl*: A Literary Approach in Terms of Analytical Psychology." *Literature and Psychology* 17 (1967): 120–27.

Nietzsche, Friedrich. *Kritische Studienausgabe*. Ed. Giorgio Colli and Mazzino Montinari. 2nd ed. 15 vols. Munich: Deutscher Taschenbuch Verlag, 1988.

————. "Über Wahrheit und Lüge im außermoralischen Sinn." Nietzsche, *Kritische Studienausgabe* 1: 871–90.

————. *Vom Nutzen und Nachtheil der Historie für das Leben*. Nietzsche, *Kritische Studienausgabe* 1: 243–334.

Niggl, Günter. *Geschichte der deutschen Autobiographie im 18. Jahrhundert*. Stuttgart: Metzler, 1977.

Nollendorfs, Cora Lee. "' . . . kein Zeugnis ablegen': Woman's Voice in Droste-Hülshoff's *Die Judenbuche*." *German Quarterly* 67 (1994): 325–37.

Novalis [Friedrich von Hardenberg]. "Das allgemeine Brouillon." Novalis, *Schriften* 3: 242–478.

————. *Schriften: Die Werke Friedrich von Hardenbergs*. Ed. Paul Kluckhohn and Richard Samuel. 3rd ed. 5 vols. Stuttgart: Kohlhammer, 1977–88.

O'Brien, William Arcander. *Novalis: Signs of Revolution*. Durham, NC: Duke University Press, 1995.

Ogorek, Regina. "Adam Müllers Gegensatzphilosophie und die Rechtsausschweifungen des Michael Kohlhaas." *Kleist-Jahrbuch* (1988–89): 96–125.

Osterkamp, Barbara. *Arbeit und Identität. Studien zur Erzählkunst des bürgerlichen Realismus*. Würzburg: Königshausen & Neumann, 1983.

Osterkamp, Ernst. "Gewalt in Goethes *Faust*." *Peter Stein inszeniert* Faust. Ed. Roswitha Schieb. Cologne: DuMont, 2000. 297–302.

Oswald, Marcel. *Das dritte Auge: Zur gegenständlichen Gestaltung der Wahrnehmung in Adalbert Stifters Wegerzählungen*. Bern: Peter Lang, 1988.

Ovid. *Ars Amatoria*. Ed. and trans. John Henry Mozley. 2nd ed. Cambridge, MA: Harvard University Press, 1979.

Palmieri, Aldo. "*Die Judenbuche*: Eine antisemitische Novelle?" *Gegenbilder und Vorurteil: Aspekte des Judentums im Werk deutschsprachiger Schriftstellerinnen*. Ed. Renate Heuer and Ralph-Rainer Wuthenow. Frankfurt am Main: Campus, 1995. 9–38.

Panthel, Hans W. "From the 'blutrothe' to the Blaue Blume." *Neophilologus* 72 (1988): 582–87.

Pavlyshyn, Marko. "Gold, Guilt, and Scholarship: Adelbert von Chamisso's *Peter Schlemihl*." *German Quarterly* 55 (1982): 49–63.

Pfeiffer, Johann Friedrich von. *Der Antiphysiokrat, oder umständliche Untersuchung des sogenannten physiokratischen Systems*. Frankfurt am Main: Eßlingerische Buchhandlung, 1780.

————. *Grundriss der Finanzwissenschaft, nebst einem Anhang über die Unausführbarkeit des physiokratischen Systems*. Frankfurt am Main, 1781.

Phöbus: Ein Journal für die Kunst. Ed. Heinrich von Kleist and Adam H. Müller. 1808. Stuttgart: Cotta, 1961.

Pickerodt, Gerhart. "Geschichte und literarische Erkenntnis: Zur Mummenschanz-Szene in *Faust II*." *Das Argument* 18 (1976): 747–71.

Pietz, William. "Fetishism and Materialism: The Limits of Theory." *Fetishism as Cultural Discourse*. Ed. Emily Apter and William Pietz. Ithaca, NY: Cornell University Press, 1993. 119–51.

Plato. *The Laws of Plato.* Trans. Thomas L. Pangle. New York: Basic Books, 1980.

Pocock, J. G. A. *The Machiavellian Moment: Florentine Political Thought and the Atlantic Republic Tradition.* Princeton, NJ: Princeton University Press, 1975.

Polanyi, Karl. *Primitive, Archaic, and Modern Economies.* Ed. George Dalton. Boston: Beacon, 1968.

Poovey, Mary. *A History of the Modern Fact: Problems of Knowledge in the Sciences of Wealth and Society.* Chicago: University of Chicago Press, 1998.

Pott, Klaus Friedrich. "Jung-Stilling: Werdegang eines Kameralwissenschaftlers aus dem Zeitalter der bürgerlichen Selbstfindung." *Johann Heinrich Jungs gemeinnütziges Lehrbuch der Handlungswissenschaft.* Cologne: Bachem, 1995. ix–xliv.

Priddat, Birger P. *Le concert universel: Die Physiokratie; Eine Transformationsphilosophie des 18. Jahrhunderts.* Marburg: Metropolis, 2001.

Purdy, Daniel L. *The Tyranny of Elegance: Consumer Cosmopolitanism in the Era of Goethe.* Baltimore: Johns Hopkins University Press, 1998.

Quesnay, François. "Miscellaneous Extracts." Meek, *The Economics of Physiocracy* 65–71.

———. "Natural Right." Meek, *The Economics of Physiocracy* 43–56.

Quintilian. *Institutio Oratorio.* Ed. and trans. Harold Edgeworth. 4 vols. New York: Putnam, 1921–22.

Radrizzani, Ives. "Fichte's Transcendental Philosophy and Political Praxis." *New Perspectives on Fichte.* Ed. Daniel Breazeale and Tom Rockmore. Atlantic Highlands, NJ: Humanities Press, 1966. 193–212.

Reiss, Hans. *Politisches Denken in der deutschen Romantik.* Bern: Francke, 1966.

Rennie, Nicholas. *Speculating on the Moment: The Poetics of Time and Recurrence in Goethe, Leopardi, and Nietzsche.* Göttingen: Wallstein, 2005.

Requadt, Paul. "Stifters *Bunte Steine* als Zeugnis der Revolution und als zyklisches Kunstwerk." *Adalbert Stifter: Studien und Interpretationen.* Ed. Lothar Stiehm. Heidelberg: Lothar Stiehm Verlag, 1968. 139–68.

Richarz, Monika. "Einführung." *Jüdisches Leben in Deutschland: Selbstzeugnisse zur Sozialgeschichte 1780–1871.* New York: Leo Baeck Institute, 1976. 7–69.

Richter, Karin. "Der 'böse Dämon' in der deutschen Romantik: Betrachtungen zum Werk und Wirken Adam Heinrich Müllers (1779–1829)." *Weimarer Beiträge* 25.5 (1979): 82–105.

Ricken, Ulrich. *Probleme des Zeichens und der Kommunikation in der Wissenschafts- und Ideologiegeschichte der Aufklärung.* Berlin: Akademie-Verlag, 1985.

Rogge, Hellmuth. "Peter Schlemihls Schicksale: Die Urschrift des *Peter Schlemihl.*" *Das Inselschiff* 2 (1921): 312–18.

———. "Die Urschrift von Adelbert von Chamissos *Peter Schlemihl.*" *Sitzungsberichte der Preußischen Akademie der Wissenschaften* (1919): 439–50.

Rohrmann, P. "The Central Role of Money in the Chapbook *Fortunatus.*" *Neophilologus* 59 (1975): 262–72.

Rölleke, Heinz. *Annette von Droste-Hülshoff: Die Judenbuche.* Frankfurt am Main: Athenäum, 1972.

———. "Erzähltes Mysterium: Studie zur *Judenbuche* der Annette von Droste-Hülshoff."

Deutsche Vierteljahrsschrift für Literaturwissenschaft und Geistesgeschichte 42 (1968): 399–426.

———. "Kann man das Wesen gewöhnlich aus dem Namen lesen?: Zur Bedeutung der Namen in der *Judenbuche* der Annette von Droste-Hülshoff." *Euphorion* 70 (1976): 409–14.

Roscher, Wilhelm. *Geschichte der National-Ökonomik in Deutschland.* Geschichte der Wissenschaften in Deutschland, Bd. 14. Munich: Oldenbourg, 1874.

Rotman, Brian. *Signifying Nothing: The Semiotics of Zero.* 1987. Stanford: Stanford University Press, 1993.

Rudolf, Günther. "Adam Müller und Kleist." *Weimarer Beiträge* 24.7 (1978): 121–35.

Sagave, Pierre-Paul. "Französische Einflüsse in Goethes Wirtschaftsdenken." *Festschrift für Klaus Ziegler.* Ed. Eckehard Catholy and Winfried Hellmann. Tübingen: Niemeyer, 1968. 113–31.

———. "Ideale und Erfahrungen in der politischen Praxis Goethes im ersten Weimarer Jahrzehnt." *Goethe Jahrbuch* 93 (1976): 105–15.

Sandl, Marcus. *Ökonomie des Raumes: Der kameralwissenschaftliche Entwurf der Staatswirtschaft im 18. Jahrhundert.* Cologne: Böhlau, 1999.

Saussure, Ferdinand de. *Course in General Linguistics.* Ed. Charles Bally and Albert Sechehaye. Trans. Wade Baskin. New York: McGraw-Hill, 1966.

Schelling, Friedrich Wilhelm Joseph von. "Über das Verhältnis der bildenden Künste zu der Natur." *Schellings Werke.* Ed. Manfred Schröter. Ergänzungsband 3. Munich: Beck, 1959. 389–429.

Scheuner, Ulrich. *Der Beitrag der deutschen Romantik zur politischen Theorie.* Rheinisch-Westfälische Akademie der Wissenschaften: Vorträge, Geisteswissenschaften, 248. Opladen: Westdeutscher Verlag, 1981.

Schieb, Roswitha. "Veloziferische Zeit: Faust und die Dialektik des Fortschritts." *Peter Stein inszeniert* Faust. Ed. Roswitha Schieb. Cologne: DuMont, 2000. 285–90.

Schiller, Friedrich von. *Über die ästhetische Erziehung des Menschen in einer Reihe von Briefen. Sämtliche Werke.* Ed. Gerhard Fricke and Herbert G. Göpfert. 5 vols. Munich: Hanser, 1959. 5: 570–669.

Schlaffer, Heinz. "Fausts Ende: Zur Revision von Thomas Metschers 'Teleologie der Faust-Dichtung'." *Das Argument* 18 (1976): 772–779.

———. *Faust zweiter Teil: Die Allegorie des 19. Jahrhunderts.* Stuttgart: Metzler, 1981.

Schlettwein, Johann August, ed. *Archiv für den Menschen und Bürger in allen Verhältnissen.* 4 vols. Leipzig: Weygandsche Buchhandlung, 1780–82.

Schlettwein, Johann August. *Evidente und unverletzliche aber zum Unglück der Welt meistens verkannte oder nicht geachtete Grundwahrheiten der gesellschaftlichen Ordnung für Kayser, Könige, Fürsten, Grafen, und Herren aller Nationen . . . zu Herstellung der wahren Gewerbs- und Handelsfreyheit der Staaten.* Giessen: Johann Jacob Braun, 1777.

———. *Grundfeste der Staaten oder die politische Ökonomie.* Giessen: Kriegerische Buchhandlung, 1779.

———. *Die wichtigste Angelegenheit für das ganze Publicum: Oder die natürliche Ordnung in der Politik überhaupt.* 2 vols. Carlsruhe: Macklot, 1772–73.

Schlosser, Johann Georg. *Politische Fragmente*. Leipzig: Weygand, 1777.

———. "Rede auf Isaak Iselin gehalten am 4. Juni 1783 in der Helvetischen Gesellschaft zu Olten." *Deutsches Museum* 7 (Nov. 1783): 417–49.

———. *Schreiben an einen jungen Mann, der die kritische Philosophie studiren wollte.* Lübeck: Friedrich Bohn, 1797.

———. "Über das neue französische System der Policeyfreyheit insbesondere in der Aufhebung der Zünfte." *Ephemeriden der Menschheit* 1 (Feb. 1776): 117–46.

———. "Über die Dichtkunst." *Kleine Schriften: Sechster Theil*. Frankfurt am Main: Gebhard & Körber, 1794. 381–89.

———. *Xenocrates oder Über die Abgaben: An Göthe*. Basel: J. J. Thurneysen, 1784.

Schmid, Irmtraut, and Gerhard Schmid. "Behördengeschichtliche Entwicklung." Goethe, *Amtliche Schriften II* 1025–108.

———. "Goethes amtliche Schriften." Goethe, *Amtliche Schriften I* 815–54.

Schmid, Ludwig Benjamin Martin. "Briefe über die hohe Kammeralschule zu Lautern: Erster Brief." *Der teutsche Merkur* 4 (Aug. 1776): 163–72.

———. "Dritter Brief über die hohe Kammeralschule zu Lautern." *Der teutsche Merkur* 5 (Mar. 1777): 247–64.

———. "Von der hohen Kammeralschule zu Lautern: Vierter Brief; Über die Handlungswissenschaft." *Der teutsche Merkur* 5 (Oct. 1777): 52–64.

Schmidt, Hugo. "Eishöhle und Steinhäuschen: Zur Weihnachtssymbolik in Stifters *Bergkristall*." *Monatshefte* 56 (1964): 321–35.

Schmidt, Jochen. "'Was sich sonst dem Blick empfohlen, / Mit Jahrhunderten ist hin': 'Fortschritt' als Zerstörungswerk der Moderne am Ende des *Faust II*." *Sinnlichkeit in Bild und Klang: Festschrift für Paul Hoffmann zum 70. Geburtstag*. Ed. Hansgerd Delbrück. Stuttgart: Heinz, 1982. 187–204.

Schmitt, Carl. *Politische Romantik*. 2nd ed. Munich: Duncker & Humblot, 1925.

[Schmohl, Johann Christian]. "Antiphysiokratische Briefe an Herrn Ratschreiber Iselin, über Mauvillons physiokratische Briefe an Herrn Kriegsrat Dohm." *Sammlung von Aufsätzen verschiedener Verfasser*. Ed. Johann Christian Schmohl. Leipzig, 1781.

———. "Vermischte land- und staatswissenschaftliche Ideen." *Deutsches Museum* 5 (Jan. 1781): 37–53.

Schneider, Hans. "Jung-Stilling aus der Sicht der Theologie." *Jung-Stillings Welt: Das Lebenswerk eines Universalgelehrten in interdisziplinären Perspektiven*. Ed. Hans-Günter Krüsselberg & Wolfgang Lück. Krefeld: Marchal & Mathenbacher, 1992. 196–220.

Schneider, Ronald. "Möglichkeiten und Grenzen des Frührealismus im Biedermeier: *Die Judenbuche* der Annette von Droste-Hülshoff." *Der Deutschunterricht* 31.2 (1979): 85–94.

———. *Realismus und Restauration: Untersuchungen zu Poetik und epischem Werk der Annette von Droste-Hülshoff*. Kronberg/Taunus: Scriptor, 1976.

Schopenhauer, Arthur. *Sämtliche Werke*. Ed. Wolfgang Freiherr von Löhneysen. 2nd ed. 5 vols. Stuttgart: Cotta, 1968.

———. *Die Welt als Wille und Vorstellung*. Vols. 1 and 2 of Schopenhauer, *Sämtliche Werke*.

Schuchard, Gottlieb C. L. "Julirevolution, St. Simonismus und die Faustpartien von 1831." *Zeitschrift für deutsche Philologie* 60 (1935): 240–74, 362–84.

Schulz, Franz. "Die erzählerische Funktion des Motivs vom verlorenen Schatten in Chamissos *Peter Schlemihl*." *German Quarterly* 45 (1972): 429–42.

Schumpeter, Joseph A. *Geschichte der ökonomischen Analyse*. Grundriss der Sozialwissenschaft, Bd. 6. Göttingen: Vandenhoeck & Ruprecht, 1965.

Schwann, Jürgen. *Vom* Faust *zum* Peter Schlemihl: *Kohärenz und Kontinuität im Werk Adelbert von Chamissos*. Tübingen: Narr, 1984.

Schwarz, Egon. "Zur Stilistik von Stifters *Bergkristall*." *Neophilologus* 38 (1954): 260–68.

Schwarz, Maria. "Jung-Stilling: Dem Andenken an den ersten Systematiker einer deutschen Staatswissenschaft." *Jahrbücher für Nationalökonomie und Statistik* 156 (1942): 329–79.

Schwarzmaier, Hansmartin. "Jung-Stilling und der Karlsruher Hof." *Jung-Stilling: Arzt—Kameralist—Schriftsteller zwischen Aufklärung und Erweckung*. Karlsruhe: Badische Landesbibliothek, 1990. 143–64.

Schwinge, Gerhard. *Jung-Stilling als Erbauungsschriftsteller der Erweckung*. Arbeiten zur Geschichte des Pietismus, Bd. 32. Göttingen: Vandenhoeck & Ruprecht, 1994.

Shell, Marc. "Language and Property: The Economics of Translation in Goethe's *Faust*." *Money, Language, and Thought: Literary and Philosophical Economies from the Medieval to the Modern Era*. Berkeley: University of California Press, 1982. 84–130.

Siegert, Reinhart. "Johann Georg Schlossers *Katechismus der Sittenlehre für das Landvolk* (1771): Ein Symbolbuch der deutschen Aufklärung." *Johann Georg Schlosser (1739–1799): Eine Ausstellung der Badischen Landesbibliothek und des Generallandesarchivs Karlsruhe*. Karlsruhe: Badische Landesbibliothek, 1989. 52–72.

Simmel, Georg. "Das Geld in der modernen Cultur." *Aufsätze und Abhandlungen 1894–1900*. Vol. 5 of *Georg Simmel Gesamtausgabe*. Ed. Otthein Rammstedt. Frankfurt am Main: Suhrkamp, 1992. 178–96.

———. *Philosophie des Geldes*. Ed. David P. Frisby and Klaus Christian Köhnke. Vol. 6 of *Georg Simmel Gesamtausgabe*. Ed. Otthein Rammstedt. Frankfurt am Main: Suhrkamp, 1984.

Simpson, David. *Fetishism and Imagination: Dickens, Melville, Conrad*. Baltimore: Johns Hopkins University Press, 1982.

Sinka, Margit M. "Unappreciated Symbol: The *Unglückssäule* in Stifter's *Bergkristall*." *Modern Austrian Literature* 16.2 (1983): 1–17.

Sivers, Friedrich von. "Johann Georg Schlosser und Schlettwein: Ein Beitrag zur Geschichte der Physiokratie in Deutschland." *Jahrbücher für Nationalökonomie und Statistik* 24 (1875): 1–15.

Skinner, Andrew. Introduction. *The Wealth of Nations*. By Adam Smith. Harmondsworth: Penguin, 1974. 11–97.

Small, Albion W. *The Cameralists: The Pioneers of German Social Policy*. Chicago: University of Chicago Press, 1909.

Smith, Adam. *An Inquiry into the Nature and Causes of the Wealth of Nations*. Ed. R. H. Campbell and A. S. Skinner. Textual editor W. B. Todd. 2 vols. Oxford: Oxford University Press, 1976.

Sombart, Werner. *Die Juden und das Wirtschaftsleben*. Munich: Duncker & Humblot, 1928.

Spengler, Oswald. *Der Untergang des Abendlandes: Umrisse einer Morphologie der Weltgeschichte*. Munich: Beck, 1963.

Springer, Johann Christoph Erich von. "Beylage zu der im vorigen Band enthaltenen Materie: Über das physiokratische System." *Chronologen* 8 (1780): 182–92.

———. *Öconomische und cameralische Tabellen*. Frankfurt am Main, 1772.

———. "Über das physiokratische System: Ein Beytrag." *Chronologen* 7 (1780): 37–56, 139–62.

Stifter, Adalbert. *Bergkristall. Werke und Briefe: Historisch-kritische Gesamtausgabe*. Ed. Alfred Doppler and Wolfgang Frühwald. Stuttgart: Kohlhammer, 1978ff. 2.2: 181–240.

———. *Der heilige Abend*. Stifter, *Werke und Briefe* 2.2: 135–75.

———. *Kalkstein*. Stifter, *Werke und Briefe* 2.2: 61–132.

———. *Kulturpolitische Aufsätze*. Ed. Willi Reich. Einsiedeln: Benziger, 1948.

———. *Lesebuch zur Förderung humaner Bildung*. 1854. Munich: Oldenbourg, 1938.

———. "Die oktroyierte Verfassung." Stifter, *Kulturpolitische Aufsätze* 37–42.

———. *Rock Crystal: A Christmas Tale*. Trans. Elizabeth Mayer and Marianne Moore. Illus. Josef Scharl. New York: Pantheon, 1945.

———. *Sämmtliche Werke*. Ed. August Sauer. 25 vols. Prague: Tempsky, 1901–04; Reichenberg: F. Kraus, 1908–31.

———. "Der Staat." Stifter, *Kulturpolitische Aufsätze* 23–33.

———. "Waarenauslagen und Ankündigungen." Stifter, *Sämmtliche Werke* 15: 167–80.

———. *Werke und Briefe: Historisch-kritische Gesamtausgabe*. Ed. Alfred Doppler and Wolfgang Frühwald. Stuttgart: Kohlhammer, 1978–2005.

———. "Der Zensus." Stifter, *Kulturpolitische Aufsätze* 55–57.

———. *Zwei Schwestern. Studien*. Ed. Fritz Krökel and Karl Pörnbacher. Munich: Winckler, 1950. 975–1122.

Stopp, Frederick. "Die Symbolik in Stifters *Bunten Steinen*." *Deutsche Vierteljahrsschrift für Literaturwissenschaft und Geistesgeschichte* 28 (1954): 165–93.

Streisand, Joachim. "Fichte und die Geschichte der deutschen Nation." *Wissen und Gewissen: Beiträge zum 200. Geburtstag Johann Gottlieb Fichtes 1762–1814*. Ed. Manfred Buhr. Berlin: Akademie, 1962. 62–98.

[Struensee, Karl August von]. "Über Rechnungsmünze, Geld und wirkliche Münze." *Berlinische Monatsschrift* 20 (1789): 220–52.

Suckow, Georg A. "Zweyter Brief über die hohe Kammeralschule zu Lautern." *Der teutsche Merkur* 5 (Jan. 1777): 56–67.

Swales, Erika. "The Doubly Woven Text: Reflections on Stifter's Narrative Mode." *Adalbert Stifter heute: Londoner Symposium 1983*. Ed. Johann Lachinger, Alexander Stillmark, and Martin Swales. Linz: Adalbert Stifter Institut, 1985. 37–43.

Swales, Martin. "Litanei und Leerstelle: Zur Modernität Adalbert Stifters." *VASILO* 36.3–4 (1987): 71–82.

———. "Mundane Magic: Some Observations on Chamisso's *Peter Schlemihl*." *Forum for Modern Language Studies* 12 (1976): 250–62.

Thompson, James. *Models of Value: Eighteenth-Century Political Economy and the Novel.* Durham, NC: Duke University Press, 1996.

Tieck, Ludwig. *Franz Sternbalds Wanderungen.* Ed. Alfred Anger. Stuttgart: Reclam, 1966.

Tielke, Martin. *Sanftes Gesetz und historische Notwendigkeit: Adalbert Stifter zwischen Restauration und Revolution.* Frankfurt am Main: Peter Lang, 1979.

Tietzel, M. "Goethe—ein Homo oeconomicus." *Homo Oeconomicus* 9 (1992): 303–55.

Tismar, Jens. *Gestörte Idyllen: Eine Studie zur Problematik der idyllischen Wunschvorstellungen am Beispiel von Jean Paul, Adalbert Stifter, Robert Walser und Thomas Bernhard.* Munich: Hanser, 1973.

Toury, Jacob. *Soziale und politische Geschichte der Juden in Deutschland 1847–1871.* Düsseldorf: Droste Verlag, 1977.

Trapp, Wolfgang. *Kleines Handbuch der Münzkunde und des Geldwesens in Deutschland.* Stuttgart: Reclam, 1999.

Tribe, Keith. *Governing Economy: The Reformation of German Economic Discourse 1750–1840.* Cambridge: Cambridge University Press, 1988.

Tscharner, N. E., and Isaak Iselin. "Schreiben über einige wirthschaftliche Grundbegriffe." *Ephemeriden der Menschheit* 7 (Apr. 1782): 379–403.

———. "Zweites Schreiben über wirthschaftliche Grundbegriffe." *Ephemeriden der Menschheit* 7 (June 1782): 635–77.

Turgot, A. R. J. *The Economics of A. R. J. Turgot.* Ed. and trans. P. D. Groenewegen. The Hague: Nijhoff, 1969.

———. "Letter on Paper Money." Turgot, *The Economics of A. R. J. Turgot* 1–8.

———. "Reflections on the Formation and Distribution of Wealth." Turgot, *The Economics of A. R. J. Turgot* 43–95.

———. "Value and Money." Turgot, *The Economics of A. R. J. Turgot* 133–48.

Vaggi, Gianni. *The Economics of François Quesnay.* Durham, NC: Duke University Press, 1987.

Van der Zande, Johann. *Bürger und Beamter: Johann Georg Schlosser 1739–1799.* Stuttgart: Franz Steiner, 1986.

Vaughan, C[harles] E. *From Burke to Mazzani.* Vol. 2 of *Studies in the History of Political Philosophy before and after Rousseau.* New York: Russell & Russell, 1960.

Verzar, Andreas. *Das autonome Subjekt und der Vernunftstaat: Eine systematisch-historische Untersuchung zu Fichtes Geschlossenem Handelsstaat von 1800.* Bonn: Bouvier, 1979.

Vinke, Rainer. "Jung-Stillings Auseinandersetzung mit der Aufklärung." *Jung-Stilling: Arzt—Kameralist—Schriftsteller zwischen Aufklärung und Erweckung.* Karlsruhe: Badische Landesbibliothek, 1990. 48–70.

Vogl, Joseph. *Kalkül und Leidenschaft: Poetik des ökonomischen Menschen.* 2nd ed. Zurich: Diaphenes, 2004.

———. "Nomos der Ökonomie: Steuerungen in Goethes *Wahlverwandtschaften.*" *MLN* 114 (1999): 503–27.

Voltaire. "Money." *Philosophical Dictionary.* Ed. William F. Fleming. 10 vols. London: Dominion, n.d. 8: 5–13.

Walach, Dagmar. "Adelbert von Chamisso: *Peter Schlemihls wundersame Geschichte*

(1814)." *Romane und Erzählungen der deutschen Romantik: Neue Interpretationen.* Ed. Paul Michael Lützeler. Stuttgart: Reclam, 1981. 285–301.

Wambach, Annemarie. "'Fortunati Wünschhütlein und Glückssäckel' in neuem Gewand: Adelbert von Chamissos *Peter Schlemihl.*" *German Quarterly* 67 (1994): 173–84.

Ware, Norman J. "The Physiocrats: A Study in Economic Rationalization." *American Economic Review* 21 (1931): 607–19.

Weatherford, Jack. *The History of Money: From Sandstone to Cyberspace.* New York: Three Rivers Press, 1997.

Weber, Betty Nance. "Droste's *Judenbuche*: Westphalia in International Context." *Germanic Review* 50 (1975): 203–12.

Weber, Max. "Die protestantische Ethik und der Geist des Kapitalismus." *Gesammelte Aufsätze zur Religionssoziologie.* 5th ed. Tübingen: Mohr, 1963. 17–206.

Weigand, Hermann J. "*Peter Schlemihl.*" *Surveys and Soundings in European Literature.* Ed. A. Leslie Willson. Princeton, NJ: Princeton University Press, 1966. 208–22.

Weinrich, Harald. "Münze und Wort: Untersuchungen an einem Bildfeld." *Romanica: Festschrift für Gerhard Rohlfs.* Halle: VEB Max Niemeyer Verlag, 1958. 508–21.

———. "Der zivilisierte Teufel." Brown, Lee, and Saine 61–67.

Wekherlin, Wilhelm Ludwig. Rev. of *Ephemeriden der Menschheit. Chronologen* 2 (1779): 91–95.

———. "Von den Ekonomisten und dem physiokratischen System." *Chronologen* 4 (1779): 15–30.

Wellbery, David. *Lessing's* Laokoön: *Semiotics and Aesthetics in the Age of Reason.* Cambridge: Cambridge University Press, 1984.

Wellek, René. *A History of Modern Criticism 1750–1950.* 8 vols. New Haven: Yale University Press, 1955–92.

Wells, Larry D. "Annette von Droste-Hülshoff's Johannes Niemand: Much Ado about Nobody." *Germanic Review* 52 (1977): 109–21.

———. "Indeterminacy as Provocation: The Reader's Role in Annette von Droste-Hülshoff's *Die Judenbuche.*" *Modern Language Notes* 94 (1979): 475–92.

Wenzel, Regina Angela. *Changing Notions of Money and Language in German Literature from 1509 to 1956.* Lewiston, NY: Edwin Mellen Press, 2003.

Wessely, Moses. "Geld und Zirkulazion." *Berlinische Monatsschrift* 27 (1796): 301–12.

White, Ann, and John White. "The Devil's Devices in Chamisso's *Peter Schlemihl*: An Article in Seven-League Boots." *German Life and Letters* 45 (1992): 220–25.

White, Lawrence H. "Monetary Nationalism Reconsidered." *Money and the Nation State: The Financial Revolution, Government and the World Monetary System.* Ed. Kevin Dowd and Richard H. Timberlake, Jr. New Brunswick: Transaction, 1998. 377–401.

Whitinger, Raleigh. "From Confusion to Clarity: Further Reflections on the Revelatory Function of Narrative Technique and Symbolism in Annette von Droste-Hülshoff's *Die Judenbuche.*" *Deutsche Vierteljahrsschrift für Literaturwissenschaft und Geistesgeschichte* 54 (1980): 259–83.

Whiton, John. "Symbols of Social Renewal in Stifter's *Bergkristall.*" *Germanic Review* 47 (1972): 259–80.

Wichmann, Christian August. "Vorrede des Übersetzers." *Des Herrn Le-Trosney Lehrbe-*

griff der Staatsordnung, oder Entwickelung des von D. Franz Quesnay erfundenen Physiokratischen Regierungs- und Staatswirtschafts-Systems. Trans. Christian August Wichmann. Leipzig: Jacobäer und Sohn, 1780. xxii–xlvii.

Widdig, Bernd. *Culture and Inflation in Weimar Germany.* Berkeley: University of California Press, 2001.

Wiese, Benno von. "Adelbert von Chamisso: *Peter Schlemihls wundersame Geschichte.*" *Die deutsche Novelle von Goethe bis Kafka.* 2 vols. Düsseldorf: Bagel, 1967. 1: 97–116.

———. "Porträt eines Mörders: Zur *Judenbuche* der Annette von Droste-Hülshoff." *Judenbuche* Sonderheft. *Zeitschrift für deutsche Philologie* 99 (1980): 32–48.

Wilde, Oscar. *Lady Windermere's Fan.* Ed. Ian Small. New York: Norton, 1999.

Will, Georg Andreas. *Versuch über die Physiokratie, deren Geschichte, Literatur, Inhalt und Werth.* Nuremberg: Gabriel Nicolaus Rasper, 1782.

Williams, John R. "Die Rache der Kraniche: Goethe, *Faust II* und die Julirevolution." Goethe Sonderheft. *Zeitschrift für deutsche Philologie* 103 (1984): 105–27.

Williams, Jonathan. *Money: A History.* New York: St. Martin's Press, 1997.

Willms, Bernard. *Die totale Freiheit: Fichtes politische Philosophie.* Staat und Politik, Bd. 10. Cologne: Westdeutscher Verlag, 1967.

Wilpert, Gero von. *Der verlorene Schatten: Varianten eines literarischen Motivs.* Stuttgart: Kröner, 1978.

Windelband, Wolfgang. *Die Verwaltung der Markgrafschaft Baden zur Zeit Karl Friederichs.* Leipzig: Quelle & Meyer, 1917.

Wittgenstein, Ludwig. *Tractatus logico-philosophicus.* Frankfurt am Main: Suhrkamp, 1979.

Wittkowski, Wolfgang. "*Die Judenbuche*: Das Ärgernis des Rätsels und der Auflösung." *Droste-Jahrbuch* 1 (1986–87): 107–28.

Wittmann, Anneliese, and Waldemar Wittmann. "Jung-Stilling, der 'cameralistische' Okkultist." *Medizingeschichte in unserer Zeit: Festgabe für Edith Heischkel-Artelt und Walter Artelt.* Ed. Hans-Heinz Eulner. Stuttgart: Enke, 1971. 300–40.

Woesler, Winfried. "Die Literarisierung eines Kriminalfalles." *Judenbuche* Sonderheft. *Zeitschrift für deutsche Philologie* 99 (1980): 5–21.

Woodmansee, Martha. *The Author, Art, and the Market: Rereading the History of Aesthetics.* New York: Columbia University Press, 1994.

Woodmansee, Martha, and Mark Osteen, eds. *The New Economic Criticism.* New York: Routledge, 1998.

Wray, L. Randall. "Modern Money." *What is Money?* Ed. John Smithin. Routledge International Studies in Money and Banking 6. London: Routledge, 2000. 42–66.

Young, Edward. *Conjectures on Original Composition.* Ed. Edith J. Morley. London: Longmans, Green & Co., 1918.

Zabka, Thomas. Faust II: *Das Klassische und das Romantische.* Untersuchungen zur deutschen Literaturgeschichte, Bd. 68. Tübingen: Niemeyer, 1993.

———. "Reiche Narren: Zur Bedeutung des Papiergeldes im *Faust II.*" *Peter Stein inszeniert Faust.* Ed. Roswitha Schieb. Cologne: DuMont, 2000. 270–73.

Zeldner, Max. "A Note on 'Schlemiel.'" *German Quarterly* 26 (1953): 115–17.

Zielenziger, Kurt. *Die alten deutschen Kameralisten: Ein Beitrag zur Geschichte der Nationalökonomie und zum Problem des Merkantilismus.* Beiträge zur Geschichte der Nationalökonomie, Heft 2. Jena: Gustav Fischer, 1914.

Zorn, Wolfgang. "Die Physiokratie und die Idee der individualistischen Gesellschaft." *Vierteljahrschrift für Sozial- und Wirtschaftsgeschichte* 47 (1960): 498–507.

INDEX

squire, in *Die Judenbuche,* 299–300,
306–7
"Der Staat" (Stifter), 320
Staël, Madame de, 424*n*2
Steifmann household, in *Lebensgeschichte,* 221–22, 415*n*38
Sternbald, Franz, in Tieck's novel,
160–63
Stifter, Adalbert, 314, 318–22, 337,
343–45, 422*n*5. *See also Bergkristall*
(Stifter)
Stifter, Johann, 317
Stollbein, Paster, in *Lebensgeschichte,*
210
Stopp, Frederick, 423*n*21
storage function, money, 30, 84, 87,
251. *See also* hoarding; wealth
striving, in *Faust II,* 347–49, 358–60
subsistence-based economy. *See* agrarian economy
substantivist-functionalist shift. *See*
linguistics-economics, metaphorical
relationships
Suckow, Georg Adolf, 412*n*6
sun's radiance, in *Faust II,* 369–70,
388–89
Swales, Erika, 423*n*17
Swales, Martin, 236, 322, 418*n*30
Sweden, 408*n*19
symbolic cognition, in Lavater's physiognomic theory, 37–38
symbolic money, defined, 29–30. *See
also* paper money
symbolon, Luhmann's discussion, 94

talers, 27, 85, 412*n*10
teichoscopy, in *Faust II,* 366, 426*n*16
telescope, in *Peter Schlemihl,* 246–47,
416*nn*14–15

temperance lesson, in *Peter Schlemihl,*
254–69, 418*n*26
Der teutsche Merkur, 412*n*6
Thales, in *Faust II,* 371, 427*n*22
Theningen, Germany, 120, 151
Theorien über den Mehrwert
(Marx), 122–23, 134–35, 408*n*18,
409*n*30
Tieck, Ludwig, 156, 160–63
Tillsen, in *Maler Nolten,* 164–67
Tismar, Jens, 315
tobacco pipe, in *Peter Schlemihl,*
268
Tobias, in *Bergkristall,* 333–34,
423*n*16
token money: defined, 402*n*6; in
Leibniz's language theory, 33–36
tourism, in *Bergkristall,* 324–25, 342–
43
Toury, Jacob, 275, 421*n*29
transcendental idealism, and Fichte's
national currency proposal, 96–99,
405*n*14, *n*16
treasure, in *Faust II:* boy charioteer
gifts, 392; fire imagery, 371; Helen
episode, 389–90; in Mephisto-
pholes' encouragement, 382–83,
396–97; in paper money argument, 355; rainbow symbolism,
372
treasures: classicism representation,
394; in Goethe's perceived reception
of *Faust II,* 361, 396; and reading
of *Faust II,* 397
Tribe, Keith, 408*n*17
Trinius, Karl Bernhard von, 244,
272
Trödelbude analogy, in *Die Judenbuche,* 419*n*10
Tscharner, N. E., 409*n*31
Turgot, A. R. J., 26, 29, 118, 140

Ingram Content Group UK Ltd.
Milton Keynes UK
UKHW010147310523
422593UK00001B/23

9 780295 988368